WITHDRAWN
NDSU

BRITISH CENTRAL AFRICA

AN ANGONI WARRIOR

British Central Africa

AN ATTEMPT TO GIVE SOME ACCOUNT OF A PORTION OF

THE TERRITORIES UNDER BRITISH INFLUENCE NORTH OF THE ZAMBEZI

By

SIR HARRY H. Hamilton JOHNSTON, K.C.B.

F.Z.S., F.R.G.S., F.R.S.G.S., Fellow of Anthropological Institute
Royal Colonial Institute, etc.
H.M. Commissioner and Consul-General in British Central Africa

WITH SIX MAPS AND 220 ILLUSTRATIONS
REPRODUCED FROM THE AUTHOR'S DRAWINGS OR FROM PHOTOGRAPHS

NEGRO UNIVERSITIES PRESS
NEW YORK

Originally published in 1897
by Methuen & Co., London

Reprinted 1969 by
Negro Universities Press
A DIVISION OF GREENWOOD PUBLISHING CORP.
NEW YORK

SBN 8371-1910-3

PRINTED IN UNITED STATES OF AMERICA

DEDICATION

WHATEVER MAY BE WORTHY OF PRAISE IN THIS BOOK
I DEDICATE TO MY COMRADES IN BRITISH CENTRAL AFRICA
TO THE MEMORY OF THOSE WHO DIED
IN A MANFUL STRUGGLE—
CAPTAIN CECIL MAGUIRE, DR. SORABJI BOYCE, JOHN KYDD
J. G. BAINBRIDGE
LIEUT. S. ARGYLL GILLMORE, ALFRED PEILE
L. M. FOTHERINGHAM, JOHN BUCHANAN, G. HAMPDEN
CHARLES A. GRAY, H. BRIGHTON
GILBERT STEVENSON, J. G. KING, J. L. NICOLL
EDWARD ALSTON, AND LIEUT.-COLONEL C. A. EDWARDS—
AND TO THE ACCEPTANCE OF THOSE
STILL LIVING AND WORKING
IN THE SERVICE OF QUEEN AND COMPANY
WHO HAVE WROUGHT WITH ME SINCE 1889 IN THE
BUILDING UP OF THIS CINDERELLA AMONG THE PROTECTORATES

Harry Whinstey

PREFACE

NORTH of the Zambezi and in the South Central portion of the continent of Africa, bounded on the north by Lake Tanganyika and the Congo Free State, on the north-east by German East Africa, on the east, south-east and west by Portuguese possessions, lies what is now termed British Central Africa, Protectorate and Sphere of Influence. The Sphere of Influence is much larger than the actual Protectorate, which is chiefly confined to the districts bordering on Lake Nyasa and on the river Shire. The Sphere of Influence is at present administered under the Charter of the British South Africa Company; the Protectorate has always been administered directly under the Imperial Government from the time of its inception. Circumstances were so ordered that I happened to be the chief agent in bringing all this territory, directly or indirectly, under British Influence, both on behalf of the Imperial Government and of the Chartered Company; and though I was ably seconded by Mr. Alfred Sharpe (now Her Majesty's Deputy Commissioner), the late Mr. Joseph Thomson, Mr. J. L. Nicoll, and Mr. A. J. Swann, it lay with me to propose a name, a geographical and political term for the mass of territory thus secured as a dependency of the British Empire.

On the principle that it is disastrous to a dog's interest to give him a bad name, it should be equally true that much is gained at the outset of any enterprise by bestowing on it a promising title. I therefore chose that of " British Central Africa " because I hoped the new sphere of British influence might include much of Central Africa where, at the time these deeds were done, the territories of Foreign Powers were in a state of flux, no hard and fast boundaries having been determined; therefore by fair means Great Britain's share north of the Zambezi might be made to connect her Protectorate on the Upper Nile with her Empire south of the Zambezi.

PREFACE

Treaties indeed were obtained which advanced British Territory from the south end to the north end of Lake Tanganyika, where the British flag was planted at the request of the natives by Mr. Swann in the spring of 1890; but the said Treaties arrived too late for them to be taken into consideration at the time the Anglo-German Convention was drawn up.

Consequently all our Government could do was to secure from Germany a right of way across the intervening strip of territory; and the boundaries of German East Africa and of the Congo Free State were henceforth conterminous in the district immediately north of Tanganyika.

Similarly the agents of the King of the Belgians were able to make good their claims to the country west and south-west of Tanganyika. Therefore British Central Africa did not ultimately attain the geographical limits to which I had originally aspired, and which would have amply justified its title. I write this in (perhaps needless) apology for a name, which after all is a fairly correct designation of a territory in the South Central portions of the continent separated by several hundred miles from the East or West Coasts and stretching up to the equatorial regions. An almost exact geographical parallel to the British Central Africa Protectorate is the State of Paraguay in South America; which, like British Central Africa, has only free access to the sea by the course of a navigable river under international control.

This book, however, will deal only with that Eastern portion of British Central Africa which has more or less come within my personal experience, that is to say it is principally confined to the regions bordering on Lakes Tanganyika and Nyasa and the River Shire.

Although for seven years I have been connected with these countries, and have been gathering notes all that time, it is not to be supposed for a moment that the results of my work which I now publish deal more than partially with the many aspects and problems of this small section of Central Africa. The careful reader will be conscious of gaps in my knowledge; but I think he will not find his time wasted by vague generalisations. Such information as I have to give is definite and practical. During my present leave of absence I have deemed it wise to gather together and publish the information I possess while an opportunity offered and before such information is useless or stale. Two years' more residence might have enabled me to answer to my satisfaction many questions about which I am dubious, or of which I know nothing. There will be room for specialists to take up many sections of my book, and using, perhaps, this arrangement of material as a basis, to correct and supplement the statements I have made.

MY TABLE IN THE WILDERNESS

ACKNOWLEDGMENTS

IT gives me great pleasure to acknowledge the help I have received from many friends and acquaintances in the production of this book. Sir Thomas Sanderson, K.C.B., Permanent Under-Secretary of State for Foreign Affairs, has revised the proofs for me; and Sir Clement Hill, K.C.M.G., and the African Department of the Foreign Office have enabled me to obtain information on various subjects; Mr. Alfred Sharpe, H. M. Deputy Commissioner and Consul for British Central Africa, has given me from time to time interesting notes, and has taken a number of photographs for the special purposes of the book; Mr. J. B. Yule, B.C.A.A., of the North Nyasa district, has lent me many of his photographs and has supplied me with information on native manners and customs; Dr. David Kerr Cross, M.B., has allowed me to use his valuable notes on Anthropology and the Diseases prevalent among Europeans and natives; Mr. P. L. Sclater, F.R.S., Secretary of the Zoological Society, has rendered me great help in preparing the chapters on Zoology, to which also Mr. Oldfield Thomas, Dr. A. G. Butler, Mr. W. F. Kirby and other officials of the British Museum of Natural History, and Mr. W. E. de Winton, F.Z.S., have contributed information. Mr. Thiselton Dyer, C.M.G., Director of the Royal Gardens, Kew, on this occasion (as indeed on all others when I have applied to him) has given his assistance with promptness and cordiality. Mr. Alexander Whyte, F.Z.S. (Principal scientific officer in British Central Africa), has supplied me with much interesting information during six years; Mr. J. F. Cunningham, Secretary of the British Central Africa Administration, and Mr. Wm. Wheeler, Chief accountant to the same, have obtained for me photographs and information under many heads; the Rev. D. C. Ruffele-Scott, B.D. (of the Church of Scotland Mission, Blantyre), collected five vocabularies for me: I have found his dictionary of the Ci-nyanja (Chi-mañanja) language a useful book of reference. The proprietors of the *Graphic* have been very kind in permitting the reproduction in these pages of certain drawings which originally appeared in one or other of their journals. Mr. Fred Moir, the Secretary to the African Lakes Company, placed his photographs at my disposal and helped me in various ways. The Rev. A. G. B. Glossop, M.A., Mr. R. Webb, and Miss Palmer, of the Universities Mission, have been particularly kind in obtaining and lending photographs. I have also derived much information from the notes and reports of the late Lieut.-Colonel C. A. Edwards, of Commander Percy Cullen, Captain W. H. Manning, and Messrs. J. E. McMaster, A. J. Swann, R. Codrington, H. A. Hillier, J. O. Bowhill, the late J. L. Nicoll and Gilbert Stevenson, H. C. McDonald,

ACKNOWLEDGMENTS

J. McClounie, Donald Malloch, and the late E. G. Alston, of the British Central Africa Administration; while I have also to acknowledge the loan of photographs from Messrs. E. Harrhy, the late Gilbert Stevenson, Commander Percy Cullen, and many others.

A special mention should be made of the valuable Appendix to my chapter on "The Botany of British Central Africa"—the list of all the known species of plants collected there from 1859 to the present day. This list has been prepared for inclusion in my book, under the direction of Mr. Thiselton Dyer, by Mr. I. H. Burkill, B.A., a member of the Scientific Staff at Kew.

It will be seen from this long list of persons to whom I am indebted for information that my book represents the summing-up of others' researches as well as of my own, and that if praise be awarded to the book, as to the seven years' work of which it is the record, that praise must be fairly distributed among many workers. It is pleasant to me to think that one of my collaborators in this work is a native of British Central Africa.

H. H. JOHNSTON.

ORTHOGRAPHY

THE orthography of native words and names used throughout this book (except in the Vocabularies) is that of the Royal Geographical Society. All the consonants are pronounced as in English (except "ñ," which stands for the nasal sound in "ri*nging*"), and the vowels as in Italian. Where the spelling of an African name is established in a European language it is not altered: Examples— Congo (Kongo), Moçambique (Msambiki), Quelimane (Kelimān).

TABLE OF CONTENTS

		PAGE
Chapter I.	WHAT THE COUNTRY LOOKS LIKE	1
„ II.	PHYSICAL GEOGRAPHY	35
APPENDIX I.	ANALYSIS OF NYASALAND COAL	51
Chapter III.	HISTORY	52
„ IV.	THE FOUNDING OF THE PROTECTORATE	80
APPENDIX I.	THE PRESENT METHOD OF ADMINISTRATION	152
Chapter V.	THE SLAVE TRADE	155
„ VI.	THE EUROPEAN SETTLERS	160
APPENDIX I.	BILIOUS HÆMOGLOBINURIC OR "BLACK-WATER" FEVER	184
„ 2.	HINTS ON OUTFIT	185
Chapter VII.	MISSIONARIES	189
„ VIII.	BOTANY	207
APPENDIX I.	THE USEFUL FOREST TREES OF BRITISH CENTRAL AFRICA	227
„ 2.	A LIST OF THE KNOWN PLANTS OF BRITISH CENTRAL AFRICA	233
Chapter IX.	ZOOLOGY	285
APPENDIX I.	LIST OF KNOWN MAMMALS OF BRITISH CENTRAL AFRICA	322
„ 2.	REGULATIONS FOR PRESERVING BIG GAME	326
„ 3.	LIST OF KNOWN BIRDS	347
„ 4.	LIST OF KNOWN REPTILES, BATRACHIANS, AND FISH	361
„ 5.	LIST OF KNOWN LAND SHELLS, MOLLUSCA, ETC.	363
„ 6.	LIST OF KNOWN SPIDERS, CENTIPEDES, ETC.	365
„ 7.	LIST OF KNOWN ORTHOPTERA, ETC.	380
„ 8.	LIST OF KNOWN LEPIDOPTERA	381
„ 9.	LIST OF KNOWN COLEOPTERA	385
Chapter X.	THE NATIVES OF BRITISH CENTRAL AFRICA	389
APPENDIX I.	DISEASES OF THE NATIVES OF BRITISH CENTRAL AFRICA	473
Chapter XI.	LANGUAGES	479
APPENDIX I.	VOCABULARIES	488
Index		533

LIST OF ILLUSTRATIONS

PAGE	TITLE	SOURCE
Frontispiece	An Angoni Warrior	Drawing by the Author.
Vignette on Title-page	Portrait of the Author	Photograph by Miss Kate Pragnell, "The Lady Photographers," Sloane Street, S.W.
ix	"My table in the wilderness"	Photograph by the Author.
2	Borassus Palms on the Shire	,, ,, ,,
3	Tropical Vegetation on the banks of the Shire	Drawing by the Author.
5	The Leopard's resting-place: a mountain stream in Central Africa	Painting by the Author.
7	A Tree Fern	Drawing by the Author.
8	"The Genius of the Woods" (green Turaco)	Painting by the Author.
9	A Bamboo Thicket	Photograph by the Author.
10	"Jack in the Beanstalk's" Country	,, ,, ,,
11	On the Plateau	,, ,, ,,
12	The Mlanje Cedar Forests	Photograph by Mr. Wm. Wheeler.
13	A Mlanje Mountain	Photograph by the Author.
14	A Rock Garden on Mlanje	Drawing by the Author.
15	Papyrus Marsh and Saddle-billed Storks	,, ,, ,,
22	The "Sultan's Baraza"	Photograph by the Author.
25	Mount Kapemba, Tanganyika	Photograph by Mr. J. B. Yule.
26	On Tanganyika	Photograph by Mr. Alfred Sharpe.
32	Niamkolo: South end of Tanganyika	Photograph by Mr. Fred. M. Moir.
33	"His Last Fight"	Painting by the Author.
35	Forest on Mount Cholo, British Central Africa	Photograph by the Author.
36	The Mlanje Range, seen from Zomba after rainfall	Drawing by the Author.
37	Native Clearing in Forest Country	Photograph by the Author.
38	The Shire at Chikwawa, just below the Murchison Falls	Drawing by the Author.
39	Pinda Mountain and Pinda Marsh, Lower Shire	,, ,, ,,
40	Part of the Falls of the Ruo at Zoa	Photograph by the Author.
41	A Mountain Stream in Central Africa	,, ,, ,,
42	First View of Mlanje Mountain from the Lower Shire	Drawing by the Author.
43	On the Upper Ruo	,, ,, ,,
45	The Mlanje Range from the Tuchila Plain	,, ,, ,,
46	Chambi Peak, Mlanje	Photograph by the Author.
47	The Likubula Gorge, Mlanje	Drawing by the Author.
48	On Lake Nyasa	Photograph by Mr. J. B. Yule.
49	The Lichenya River, Mlanje	Photograph by the Author.
50	The Shire Highlands	,, ,, ,,
53	Portrait of a Young Bushman	From a photograph.
57	Governor's House, Tete	,, ,,
58	The Island of Moçambique, seen from the Mainland	Drawing by the Author.

LIST OF ILLUSTRATIONS

PAGE	TITLE	SOURCE
61	The Point on the South Shore of Lake Nyasa whence the Lake was first seen by Dr. Livingstone and Sir John Kirk in 1859	Photograph by Mr. E. Harrhy.
67	Mandala House, near Blantyre.	Photograph by Mr. Fred. M. Moir.
72	L. Monteith Fotheringham	Photograph by Mr. J. B. Yule.
72	John Lowe Nicoll	,, ,, ,,
73	Group of Wankonde (North Nyasa)	Photograph by the Author.
74	John W. Moir	From a photograph.
74	Frederick Maitland Moir	,, ,,
75	Mr. Alfred Sharpe in 1890	Photograph by Mr. Fred. M. Moir.
79	On the Chinde, Mouth of the Zambezi	Photograph by Mr. J. B. Yule.
83	Sergeant-Major Ali Kiongwe	Photograph by Commander Percy Cullen.
85	Mr. John Buchanan	Photograph by Mr. J. Trotter.
87	Masea and Mwitu, two of Livingstone's Makololo	Photograph by the Author.
91	Outskirts of Kotakota	,, ,, ,,
92	The late Tawakali Sudi; Jumbe of Kotakota, etc.	,, ,, ,,
93	North Nyasa Arabs: Bwana 'Omari in the foreground	,, ,, ,,
95	Langenburg, Capital of German Nyasaland	,, ,, ,,
98	Sikh Soldiers of the Contingent now serving in British Central Africa	Photograph by Mr. Wm. Wheeler.
99	H.M.S. *Mosquito*, a Zambezi Gunboat	From a photograph.
101	Fort Johnston in 1895	Photograph by the Author.
103	Captain Cecil Montgomery Maguire	From a photograph.
107	Mr. William Wheeler	Photograph by the Author.
109	Mr. Nicoll's House at Fort Johnston	Photograph by Mr. J. B. Yule.
110	Trees planted by Mr. Nicoll at Fort Johnston (two years' growth)	Photograph by Mr. J. B. Yule.
111	The Nyasa Gunboats in Nkata Bay, West Nyasa	Photograph by the Author.
112	Lake Road, Chiromo	Photograph by Mr. R. Webb.
114	The Katunga Road in pre-Administration Days	Photograph by the Author.
115	Captain Sclater's Road to Katunga in process of making	Photograph by the Author.
116	Mr. J. F. Cunningham	Photograph by Mr. Wm. Wheeler.
118	Lieut.-Colonel C. A. Edwards	,, ,, ,,
119	A Sikh Soldier in the B.C.A. uniform	Photograph by the late Gilbert Stevenson.
119	A Sikh Soldier in fighting kit	Photograph by Mr. E. Harrhy.
120	A Sikh Soldier in fighting kit	,, ,, ,,
120	Sikh Soldier in undress	Photograph by Mr. J. B. Yule.
121	Collector's House at Fort Lister	Photograph by the late Gilbert Stevenson.
122	Captain W. H. Manning	Photograph by Mr. Wm. Wheeler.
123	The Raphia Palm Marsh behind Chiwaura's	Photograph by the Author.
125	On the Beach at Monkey Bay	Photograph by Mr. J. B. Yule.
126	One of Makanjira's Captured Daus at Monkey Bay	,, ,, ,,
127	The Hoisting of the Flag at Fort Maguire	Photograph by the Author.
129	The Beach at Makanjira's	,, ,, ,,
130	Three of Makanjira's Captured Daus (Fort Maguire)	Photograph by Rev. A. G. B. Glossop.
131	A Rural Post Office, B.C.A.	Photograph by Mr. E. Harrhy.
132	Watch Tower at Fort Johnston	Photograph by Rev. A. G. B. Glossop.
133	A Sikh Sergeant-Major of the B.C.A. Contingent	Photograph by Mr. Wm. Wheeler.
134	Native Soldiers, B.C.A.	,, ,, ,,
135	An Atonga Soldier	,, ,, ,,
136	In Zarafi's Town	Photograph by the Author.

LIST OF ILLUSTRATIONS

xvii

PAGE	TITLE	SOURCE
137	Deep Bay Station	Photograph by the Author.
138	Mlozi, Chief of the North Nyasa Arabs	Photograph by Mr. Fred Moir.
139	The Transports on their way to Karonga arriving in Likoma Bay	Photograph by Miss Palmer.
141	A corner of Mlozi's Stockade	Drawing by the Author.
142	The Nyasa-Tanganyika Road (made by the B.C.A. Administration)	Photograph by Mr. J. B. Yule.
143	The Nyasa-Tanganyika Road	,, ,, ,,
144	In Fort Hill	,, ,, ,,
145	The Stockade, Fort Hill	,, ,, ,,
146	Mr. Alfred Sharpe in 1896	Photograph by the Author.
147	The Zomba-Mlanje Road	,, ,, ,,
148	A Footbridge across the Mlungusi (Zomba)	Photograph by Mr. Wm. Wheeler
150	The Gardens of the Residency, Zomba	,, ,, ,,
151	Mr. Whyte in the Gardens at Zomba	Photograph by the Author.
153	Barracks at Fort Johnston	,, ,, ,,
156	A Swahili Slave-trader	Photograph by Mr. Wm. Wheeler.
157	Arab and Swahili Slave-traders captured by the B.C.A. Forces	,, ,, ,,
158	A "Ruga-Ruga" (Mnyamwezi, Slave-raider employed by the Arabs)	Photograph by Mr. Fred Moir.
161	The Consulate, Blantyre	Photograph by Mr. E. Harrhy.
162	A Coffee Tree in bearing	Photograph by Mr. Wm. Wheeler.
163	A Planter's temporary House	Photograph by Mr. Alfred Sharpe.
165	Morambala Mount from the River Shire	Drawing by the Author.
167	Sharrer's Store at Katunga	From a photograph.
169	A "Capitao"	Photograph by the late Gilbert Stevenson.
172	In Camp after a day's shooting	Photograph by Mr. E. Harrhy.
174	Natives making Bricks	Photograph by Mr. J. B. Yule.
175	Cyprus Avenue, Blantyre	Photograph by Mr. Fred Moir.
176	Eucalyptus Avenue	Photograph by the Author.
177	A Planter	Photograph by Mr. J. F. Cunningham.
178	An Ivory Caravan arriving at Kotakota	From a photograph.
181	Ivory at Mandala Store (African Lakes Co.)	Photograph by Mr. Fred Moir.
182	Kahn & Co.'s Trading Store at Kotakota	From a photograph.
191	(1) Bishop Hornby (formerly of Nyasaland). (2) The late Bishop Maples of Likoma	Photograph by Miss Palmer.
194	Native Church at Msumba, Lake Nyasa (Universities Mission)	Photograph by Mr. R. Webb.
199	Blantyre Church (Church of Scotland Mission)	Photograph by Mr. Fred Moir.
207	Flowers of the Gardenia Tree	Drawing by the Author.
208	*Lissochilus* Orchids	,, ,, ,,
209	An *Angræcum* Orchis	,, ,, ,,
210	The *Ansellia* or "Tiger" Orchis	,, ,, ,,
211	A Red Lily	,, ,, ,,
212	Oil Palms near the Songwe River, North Nyasa	Photograph by the Author.
212	A *Raphia* Palm	,, ,, ,,
213	Raphia Palm Fruiting	Drawing by the Author.
214	Borassus Palms	Photograph by Mr. Alfred Sharpe.
214	Wild Date Palms	Photograph by the Author.
215	A Reed Brake (*Phragmites communis*)	Drawing by the Author.
217	Plumes and Young Shoot of *Phragmites*	,, ,, ,,
218	Barbed Seeds of *Stipa*	,, ,, ,,

LIST OF ILLUSTRATIONS

PAGE	TITLE	SOURCE
218	Papyrus	Drawing by the Author.
218	A Large Duckweed (*Pistia stratiotes*)	,, ,, ,,
219	An *Albizzia* Tree	Photograph by Mr. Wm. Wheeler.
220	The *Mucuna* Bean	Drawing by the Author.
221	A Baobab Tree	Photograph by Mr. J. B. Yule.
222	The Euphorbia of the Plains	,, ,, ,,
222	Candelabra Euphorbias	Drawing by the Author.
223	A *Landolphia* Liana	,, ,, ,,
224	*Sansevieria* Fibre Plant	Photograph by Mr. Foulkes.
225	Growth of Branches; Foliage; and Cones of the Mlanje Cedar (*Widdringtonia whytei*)	Drawing by the Author.
226	Young Mlanje Cedar	,, ,, ,,
290	A Spotted Hyena	Photograph by the Author.
293	The Central African Zebra	Drawing by the Author.
297	Head of a Hippopotamus	From a photograph.
299	A Wart Hog	Drawing by the Author.
302	Head of a Buffalo	,, ,, ,,
303	Horns of Congo Buffalo	,, ,, ,,
304	Livingstone's Eland	,, ,, ,,
305	Horns of Livingstone's Eland	Engraving lent by the Zoological Society.
306	A Male Bushbuck	Drawing by the Author.
307	Head of a Male Kudu	,, ,, ,,
310	Diagram showing origin and relationships of modern groups of Horned Ruminants	,, ,, ,,
311	A Klipspringer	,, ,, ,,
312	A Male Reedbuck	,, ,, ,,
312	A Male Reedbuck's Head	,, ,, ,,
313	A Male Waterbuck	,, ,, ,,
314	A Female Waterbuck	,, ,, ,,
315	The Sable Antelope	,, ,, ,,
318	A Roan Antelope	,, ,, ,,
319	Johnston's Pallah	,, ,, ,,
320	The Nyasaland Gnu (*Connochætes taurinus johnstoni*)	,, ,, ,,
329	The Elephant Marsh	Photograph by Mr. Alfred Sharpe.
335	The Syndactylous Foot	Drawing by the Author.
338	Spur-winged Geese	,, ,, ,,
339	Crowned Cranes	,, ,, ,,
343	A Pelican of Tanganyika	,, ,, ,,
343	A Stilt Plover	,, ,, ,,
344	Head and foot of Fruit-pigeon	,, ,, ,,
345	The Warlike Crested Eagle (*Spizætus bellicosus*)	Photograph by the Author.
346	A Small Falcon (*Falco minor*)	Drawing by the Author.
357	Nyasa Crocodiles	,, ,, ,,
360	*Chromis squamipennis; Hemichromis livingstonii*: Fish of Lake Nyasa	Zoological Society's Proceedings.
361	*Engraulicypris pinguis*	,, ,, ,,
371	A Termite Ant-hill	Photograph by Miss Palmer.
372	A Stick Insect	Drawing by the Author.
373	A Locustid Insect	,, ,, ,,
378	The Tsetse Fly	,, ,, ,,
388	An Angoni Man from the West Nyasa district	,, ,, ,,
390	A Mnyanja	Photograph by Mr. Wm. Wheeler.
391	A Yao Man	,, ,, ,,

LIST OF ILLUSTRATIONS

PAGE	TITLE	SOURCE
393	An Arab of Tanganyika (Rumaliza)	Photograph by Mr. Fred Moir.
395	A Mtonga Man (to show profile)	Drawing by the Author.
397	A Yao of the Upper Shire	,, ,, ,,
398	An Angoni from Mombera's country	,, ,, ,,
399	Boy with well-developed breasts	Photograph by Mr. J. B. Yule.
400	A Young Mother (showing pendent breasts)	Drawing by the Author.
401	Wankonde Men	Photograph by the Author.
403	A Munkonde from North Nyasa	Photograph by Mr. Alfred Sharpe.
405	Sketch of Muscular Development in a Yao	Drawing by the Author.
407	A Yao Woman	Photograph by Mr. Wm. Wheeler.
411	Young Munkonde Girl	Photograph by Mr. J. B. Yule.
414	A Mtonga Man	Drawing by the Author.
416	"A Good Mother" (Sketch of a Mnyanja woman)	,, ,, ,,
420	A Yao of Zomba	,, ,, ,,
421	A "Ruga-Ruga"	,, ,, ,,
423	Specimens of Tatooing; Comb; Plugs for insertion in ear, lips, nose, etc.	....
424	Example of "Pelele" in upper lip	Photograph by Mr. Wm. Wheeler.
424	Another example of the "Pelele"	,, ,, ,,
425	Wooden Hoe; and wooden Hammer for beating out bark cloth	Drawing by the Author.
427	North Nyasa Native smoking hemp	,, ,, ,,
428	Banana Grove (Mlanje)	Photograph by the Author.
431	Wankonde Cattle	Photograph by Mr. Fred Moir.
433	The Domestic Goat of South and Central Africa	Drawing by the Author.
453	A typical Native House in South Nyasaland	Photograph by the Author.
454	A Nkonde House	Photograph by Mr. Fred Moir.
457	Natives making a prone tree trunk into a canoe	Photograph by Mr. Yule.
457	A River Pilot	Photograph by Mr. R. Webb.
458	Weaving in Angoniland	Photograph by Mr. Fred Moir.
459	Weaving on the Nyasa-Tanganyika Plateau	,, ,, ,,
460	Women making Pots	Photograph by Mr. Yule.
461	Pipes for hemp and tobacco	Drawing by the Author.
462	Central African Weapons, etc.	,, ,, ,,
464	African Dancer and Drum Players	From a photograph.
465	A Mu-lungu of South Tanganyika blowing ivory trumpet	Drawing by the Author from a photograph by Mr. Yule.
467	A "Sansi"	Drawing by the Author.
470	Angoni Warriors	Photograph by Mr. J. F. Cunningham.
470	Head stuck on a pole after a native war	Drawing by the Author.
472	"Young Africa"	Photograph by the late Gilbert Stevenson.
480	Map showing the lines of migration of the Bantu tribes in their invasion of Southern Africa	Drawing by the Author.

MAPS

1. Map of British Central Africa, showing approximate rainfall, navigability of rivers, etc.	*To face page*	41
2. —— showing Orographical features	,, ,,	46
3. —— showing Administrative divisions	,, ,,	154
4. Map of the Shire Highlands	,, ,,	188
5. Map of British Central Africa, showing density of population and distribution of native tribes	,, ,,	392
6. —— showing Mission Stations and Foreign Settlers and Settlements	,, ,,	392

BRITISH CENTRAL AFRICA

CHAPTER I.

WHAT THE COUNTRY LOOKS LIKE

BEFORE I begin to discourse on the dull facts of history and geography let me try to give my reader some idea of what the country looks like by describing certain set scenes and panoramas. Perhaps from these he may derive a clearer impression of the general appearance and the many diverse aspects of British Central Africa.

A steadily flowing river. In the middle of the stream an islet of very green grass, so lush and so thick that there are no bright lights or sharp shadows—simply a great splodge of rich green in the middle of the shining water which reflects principally the whitish-blue of the sky; though this general tint becomes opaline and lovely as mother-of-pearl, owing to the swirling of the current and the red-gold colour of the concealed sand-banks which in shallow places permeates the reflections. Near to the right side of the grass islet separated only by a narrow mauve-tinted band of water is a sand-bank that has been uncovered, and on this stands a flock of perhaps three dozen small white egrets closely packed, momentarily immoveable, and all stiffly regardant of the approaching steamer, each bird with a general similarity of outline almost Egyptian in its monotonous repetition.

The steamer approaches a little nearer, and the birds rise from the sand-bank with a loose flapping flight and strew themselves over the landscape like a shower of large white petals. On the left bank of the river looking down stream is a grove of borassus palms rising above the waterside fringe of white flowered reeds and apple-green mopheads of papyrus. The trunks of the taller palms are smooth and whitish, but those of younger growth nearer to the ground are still girt about by a fierce spiky hedge of dead black-stemmed fronds. The crowns of the palm trees are symmetrical and fan-shaped in general outline, while each individual frond has in its inner side a horse-shoe curve. The colour of the fronds is a deep bluish-green singularly effective in contrast with the grey-white column they surmount. The fruit of the palms, when they can be descried, are like huge yellow-green apples thickly clustered on pendent racemes protruding from the centre round which the fronds radiate.

Behind the palm forest is a long line of blue mountain so far away that it is just a faint blue silhouette against the paler blue sky. The afternoon is well advanced, and in the eastern sky, which is a warm pinkish blue, the full moon has already risen and hangs there a yellow-white shield with no radiance. On the opposite bank of the river to the palm trees is a clump of tropical forest of the richest green with purple shadows, lovely and seductive in its warm tints under the rays of the late afternoon sun. Here are large albizzia trees.[1] Over the water-side hang thick bushes overgrown with such a drapery of convolvulus creepers

BORASSUS PALMS ON THE SHIRE

that the foliage of the bush is almost hidden. This green lacework is beautifully lit up by large mauve flowers. Above the bushes rise the heads of the wild date palm, and amid the fronds of this wild date here and there a cluster of its small orange fruit peeps out. These palms rise over masses of foliage, and occasionally top the higher trees, growing within their canopy in almost parasitic fashion. This cluster of tropical vegetation will be here and there scooped out into fairy bowers by the irregularities of the bank. Sometimes the trees will overhang the stream where the bank has been washed away. Tiny kingfishers of purple-blue and chestnut-orange flit through the dark network of gnarled trunks, and deep in this recess of shade small night-herons and bitterns stand bolt upright, so confident in their assumed invisibility against a back-

---

[1] A genus related to the acacia with the thickest foliage of pinnate leaves looking at a distance like green velvet.

ground of brown and grey that they do not move even when the steamer passes so close by them as to brush against the tangle of convolvulus and knock down sycomore figs from the glossy-leaved, many-rooted fig trees.

It is a backwater on the Shire river, or perhaps not so much a backwater as a sluggish branch of the stream which the main current has deserted and left hidden away between bosky islands and the high wooded bank. The flow of the current is not discernible, and the reflections are glassy and mirror-like in their exactitude, except that the surface of the water in the foreground is strewn with oval lotus leaves looking in shape and even colour exactly like those copper ashtrays or cardtrays made in Indian ware with slightly turned-up crinkled edges. The scene is much framed in with overarching foliage and branches from island and opposite bank. On this shore of the mainland

TROPICAL VEGETATION ON THE BANKS OF THE SHIRE

there are tall acacia trees with smooth pale-green trunks and whitish-green branches, and a feathery light-green foliage spangled with hanging clumps of tiny golden-stamened, petalless flowers which exhale the most penetrating, absolute, and honeyed of all flower scents, a scent so strong that it may be wafted on a still, hot day across a mile of water. In the middle distance is a fine group of trees, elm-like in shape, growing on the river bank above the flood limit. In the farthest distance a few sparse-foliaged acacias stand out against the grey-blue sky above a high fence of reeds. In the nearer distance one clump of spear-like reeds rises from the waterlilies and shows some fine white flowering plumes against the dark background of the forest clump. In the foreground is a huge snag, the relic of a fine forest tree that has been washed down in the flood and stranded in the mud of this backwater. On its branches are perched darters with sheeny plumaged bodies of greenish-black and chestnut-coloured necks ending in a head and spear-like beak, so slim that it seems a mere termination of the angular weapon of the neck. Amongst the waterlily leaves rise the beautiful blue-pink flowers that are styled the lotus.

We are going to climb a mountain. First there are the low foothills to surmount. The soil is red and hard; the grass is scattered and in yellow wisps, and the many wild flowers are drooping, for it is the end of the dry season. The trees are in foliage, though the rains have not yet fallen, and the young leaves at this stage are seldom green, but the most beautiful shades of carmine pink, of pinkish yellow, of greenish mauve, and even inky purple. Here and there sprays of foliage are in a more advanced development, and are green with a bluish bloom, or of the brightest emerald. But the height of the trees is not great, and their leaves, though large, are scattered in a tufty growth that yields but a feeble patchwork of shade from the hot sun; the branches are coarse, and thick, and seldom straight, they look just like the branches of trees drawn from imagination by amateur water-colour artists. In many cases the bark is still black and sooty with the scorching of the recent bush fires. The general impression of all this vegetation, though one is forced to admire the individual tints of the newly-opened leaves, is disappointing. It is scrubby. The landscape has not the dignity of a blasted heath, or the simplicity of a sandy desert; its succession of undulations of low scattered forest of such a harlequin variation of tints is such as to produce no general effect of definite form and settled colour on the eye. But this is a good game country. As you plod along the hard red path, baked almost into brick by the blazing sun acting on the red mud of the rainy season, you will suddenly catch sight of a splendid sable antelope with ringed horns, almost in a half oval, a black and white face, a glossy black body, white stomach, fringed and tufted tail, and heavy black mane; or, it may be, his beautiful female of almost equal bulk, but with smaller horns, and with all the markings and coloration chestnut and white instead of white and black. Unless you are very quick with your rifle, the beast will soon be hid and almost undiscoverable amongst the low trees and bushes.

The path is broken here and there by seams of granite. Every now and then there is a regular scramble over wayworn rocks; granite boulders are more and more interspersed amongst the red clay. Between the boulders grow aloes with fleshy leaves of green, spotted with red, and long flower spikes of crimson which end in coral-coloured flower buds—buds which open grudgingly at the tip; the edges of the sprawling aloe leaves are dentelated, and in their tendency to redness sometimes all green is merged in a deep vinous tint.

Now there is less scrub, and the trees as we ascend become larger and more inclined to stand in clumps; their foliage is thicker. We are approaching a stream, and its course is marked by a forest of a different type, fig trees of various species, tall parinariums (a tree which bears a purple plum), huge-leaved gomphias, and velvet-foliaged albizzias. On either side of the stream, also, there is a jungle of bamboos, and the path descends from out of the weary glare of the white sunlight on the red clay into a cool, moist, green tunnel through the numberless spear-heads of bamboo leaves. There are many ferns on either side of the stream bank and beautiful carmine lilies[1] are growing by the water's edge, but as the rains are still withheld there is but a thin film of water slipping down over the grey rocks and brown pebbles, and the stream may be easily crossed from stepping stone to stepping stone. Then a clamber up the opposite bank and through the bamboo out once more into the scorching sunshine, and so on and on along a winding path through a native village

---

[1] See illustration, page 211.

THE LEOPARD'S RESTING-PLACE: A MOUNTAIN STREAM IN CENTRAL AFRICA

with its untidy haycocks of huts, its clumps of bananas, plantations of sweet potatoes and tobacco, and adjoining stubble fields where gaunt isolated stalks of sorghum still linger. The blue mountain wall towards which we are aiming rises higher into the sky, and its blue vagueness becomes resolvable into a detail of purple and yellow grey. But though the sun is hotter than ever as it approaches the zenith our continual ascent brings us to a region that enjoys more benign conditions of moisture and coolness at night time. The young green grass is more advanced than down below, the herbage is so thick that the red soil is almost hidden. The wild flowers commence to be beautiful. There are innumerable ground orchids in various shades of mauve or yellow, or with strange green blossoms, or flowers of richest orange. A beautiful white clematis grows from an upright stalk, and here and there are bushes of a kind of mallow, which bears large azalea-like clusters of the most perfect blush pink. Higher up still there are more and more flowers in many shades of blue and mauve and yellow. There is a small kind of sunflower that is a deep maroon crimson, and another coreopsis more like the cultivated sunflower with flaming yellow petals. In moist places— and the path is now constantly crossing small brooks — grows the dissotis, with large flowers of deep red-mauve. The path curves and twists and runs up above heights and then down into deep ravines, and still the flowers grow thicker and thicker and more lovely, till in the ecstasy of a colour dream, all remembrance of the sun's heat, of your great fatigue and your sweat-drenched clammy garments is forgotten. On the hill-sides there are frequent clumps of wild date palms, some of which rise to a great height with their slender stems often bowed or curved and seldom

A TREE-FERN

perpendicular. Then you come to your first tree-fern, or if you are a botanist you are delighted with a rare cycad growing majestically alone and looking very much as though it were an admirable piece of artificial foliage executed in green bronze. Still ascending, with a pause here and a rest there in the absolute shade of the great forest trees, tree-ferns become so abundant at last as to make fairy forests of themselves, excluding other arborescence. Then they give way again to densely-packed thick-foliaged forest trees of low growth through which a path winds over many a bole and through many a bamboo bower in deep green gloom. Through this gloom flit the crimson-winged turacos, the lovely genii of the African forest — birds of purple-blue, bluish-green and grass-green silky plumage with a white-tipped crest, red parrot-like beaks, and bare red cheeks, but always, no matter what their species, with the broad, rounded pinion feathers of the wing the most perfect scarlet-crimson ever seen in nature. The loud parrot cries of these birds (not unmelodious) echo and re-echo through the forest glades as they call to one another; and here is a crimson flash, and there is a long crimson streak drawn across the green background as they fly backwards and forwards before the delighted intruder.

Runnels of water will at times trickle through the black leaf mould of the scarcely discernible path, and you will come to many a fairy glen where the dark, clear, cold water lies in deep pools amongst the ferns.

"THE GENIUS OF THE WOODS" (GREEN TURACO)

The forest for a time will give place to a bamboo thicket, the bamboos perhaps of a different species to those lower down, with smaller and finer leaves of a deeper green; nothing more beautiful than these bamboo glades is to be seen in the way of vegetation. It is difficult to express in words the effect which is produced by thousands of narrow, pointed leaves of shiny surface shaped like small spear blades—a wall of green facets—moving at times with a faint tremor which sends a shimmering of green around you, accompanied by the tiniest whispering sound. No transformation scene ever shown on the stage was so beautiful as a bamboo glade on the high mountain side with, invariably, water falling down the centre of the picture in tiny cascades and the soft ground carpeted with a deposit of cast leaves like thin spear blades of pale gold.

Beyond the bamboos the path becomes terrible. You emerge from the gloom of this first forest belt on to bare rock and obtain glorious views over the flower-braided hill-slopes below, over the band of dark green velvet forest, and beyond into plains that are purple-blue with a diamond flash of water here and there till the horizon is closed up with the palest silhouettes of other mountains.

The path is now scarcely apparent. It is a hazardous progress up a steep face of smooth polished rock from grass clump to grass clump. Here and there on ledges of the rock where a little vegetable soil may have collected tussocks of grass are growing, and these afford a precarious foothold; nevertheless though there is no good path it is obvious that men often pass this way up and down the mountains since the tussocks of grass that are regularly trodden

A BAMBOO THICKET

on are grey and dead in comparison to those untouched by the human foot, which remain green. Here the difficulty of your ascent will be lightened by the joy you must feel in the lobelias, if you have any sense of colour. In the crevices of these glabrous-looking mountain ribs will grow bunches of lobelias extravagant in their thousands of blue flowerets.

At last the ascent of this mountain wall is safely accomplished, and you fling yourself panting on short wiry turf growing in clumps and know that you have reached the limits of "Jack-in-the-Beanstalk's" country.

All the great mountains of South Central Africa seem to be isolated fragments of an older plateau, and most of them present more or less precipitous wall-like sides rising above the foot hills, which latter are created by land slides and *débris*, or represent smaller remains of the plateau that in course of time have been more worn away than the larger blocks constituting the big mountains or the long mountain ranges. These wall-like sides are naturally difficult of ascent; but when one has clambered up over the edge, and on to the more level surface of the upraised tableland, it is a veritable "Jack-in-the-Beanstalk's" country, quite different in aspect to the tropical plains below. Turning your eyes away, however, from the blue gulf which yawns beneath the precipitous ascent of several thousand feet—which blue gulf after analysis by the eye resolves itself into the faint map of many leagues of surrounding countries—you find that the plateau on which you stand is a little world in itself. The general surface is rolling grass land and beautifully-shaped downs, with little streams and little lakes, and little forests; and again from out of this tableland little mountains of one to three thousand feet, chiefly of granite, rise up into the clouds and in their austere rockiness contrast charmingly with the lawns of short grass, the flowery vales, and the rich woodlands at their base. Altogether the scenery is pretty rather than grand, and if you could forget the ascent you have made and your geographical position, you might imagine

"JACK-IN-THE-BEANSTALK'S" COUNTRY

yourself in Wales, and believe that country of this sort stretched illimitably before you for miles and miles, were it not that upon walking a few steps in another direction you suddenly stop shuddering on the sharp edge of an awful gulf—a gulf which on a misty day might be the end and edge of the world.

It is a "Jack-in-the-Beanstalk" country. A little section of land upraised and quite apart from the rest of Tropical Africa with a climate and flora of its own, and as a rule without indigenous human inhabitants. The fauna of these altitudes has usually peculiar features though most of the mammals differ but little from those of the plains. Antelopes, buffalos, and even elephants will scramble to these heights, if they be in any way accessible, for the sake of the sweet herbage; therefore in your ramblings over these plateaux you may catch sight of big game, and even meet in its train the lion and leopard. The woods of Cape-oak and other evergreens—the branches of which are hung with long sprays of greenish-white lichen, "the old man's beard"[1]—are resonant with the

---

[1] *Usnea*, the "orchilla" weed of commerce.

cries of turacos, possibly a species slightly differing from that found in the warmer climate of the plains or hill-sides. Most of the other birds will be allied to South African, Abyssinian or even European species—large purple pigeons with yellow beaks or pretty doves with roseate tinge and white heads; orioles of green and yellow and grey; chats, buntings, fly-catchers, plump speckled francolin and tiny harlequin-quails; few, if any birds of prey, but many great-billed black and white ravens and an occasional black crow. The wild flowers remind one touchingly of home. There are violets, there is a rare primula, there are buttercups, forget-me-nots, St. John's wort, anemones, vivid blue hound's-tongue and heather. Unfamiliar, however, are the lovely ground orchids, the strange proteas and the "everlasting" flowers. Also there are straggling arborescent heaths, almost like small conifers in appearance, though other forms more closely resemble our own heather. Near the edges of the plateau

ON THE PLATEAU

amongst the rocks grows a big kind of tree-lily with a gouty, pachydermatous, branching stem and tufts of grass-like leaves. If it be, as I imagine, the early spring when you are ascending the mountain, these otherwise ugly shrubs will be covered with white lily-like blossoms.

The air of these lofty plateaux is cool and bracing and the sunshine harmless in the day-time. When the weather is fine the sky is a lovely pale-blue. Daylight under these conditions is one long inexhaustible joy of living. Fatigue is not felt; the sun's heat is pleasantly warm; a moderate thirst can be delightfully quenched in the innumerable ice-cold brooks; but when the sun is set—set amid indescribable splendour in what appears to be the middle of the sky, so high is the horizon—nature wears a different even an alarming aspect: unless you have a cheerful log-hut to enter or a well-pitched comfortable tent (with a roaring fire burning at a safe distance from the tent porch) you will feel singularly dismal. Perhaps a thunder-storm may have come on. Enormous masses of cloud may be bearing down on and enveloping you—thunder of the most deafening description breaks around you and re-echoes worse than any roar of artillery in battle from every ravine and hill-side. The drenching rain or the driving mist may be chilling your half-naked followers into blue numbness, and even bringing them, if they are unsheltered, dangerously near death from cold. Even if it be a fine night, and the moon shining, there will be something a little repellent and awe-striking in the world outside your tent. The forest, to the vicinity of which you have come for shelter, is very black, and the strange cries of bird and beast coming from these depths quite confirm the native belief that the trees are haunted with the spirits of the departed. The stars seem so near to you,

THE MLANJE CEDAR FORESTS

and if in the moonlight you have found your way over the tussocky grass to the edge of the plateau and looked forth on a sleeping universe you feel a little frightened—so completely are you aloof from the living world of man. It is much pleasanter, therefore, to be shut up in a good tent or log cabin, snugly ensconced in bed (for it is probably freezing hard) reading a novel.

We are on the upper plateau of Mlanje, grandest of all British Central African mountains. It is early morning, say 6.30 a.m. We have been roused by our native attendants, have had a warm bath and a cup of coffee and are now inspecting our surroundings in the glory of the early sunshine. On the short wiry grass there lies a white rime of frost as we walk down the slope to the cedar woods. Here rises up before us a magnificent forest of straight and noble trees, of conifers[1] which in appearance resemble cedars of Lebanon

[1] *Widdringtonia whytei.*

though they have also a look of the Scotch pine and are actually in their natural relationship allied to the cypress. Their trunks are straight and the outer bark is often bleached white; the wood is the tint of a cedar pencil. The foliage which on the older trees grows in scant tufts (leaving a huge white skeleton of sprawling branches) on the younger trees is abundant, bluish-green

ON MLANJE MOUNTAIN

below and the dark, sombre green of the fir tree above. The extremities of each branch have a pretty upward curl.

Much of the undergrowth of these cedar woods is a smaller species of Widdringtonia with a lighter green foliage, most gracefully pendent and starlike in each cluster of needles.

Oh! the deep satisfying peace of these cedar woods. The air is thick with the odour of their wholesome resin. The ground at our feet is a springy carpet of emerald green moss out of which peep anemones and primulas. Here indeed when the mild warmth of the day has dried up the night dews might one lie half stupefied by the rich aroma of the cedar wood, "the world forgetting, by the world forgot," while the big purple pigeons with white-streaked necks and yellow beaks resume their courtship on the branches above

A ROCK GARDEN ON MLANJE

our heads. Beyond the cedar wood is the mountain-side strewn with innumerable boulders and cubes of rock which are interspersed with huge everlasting flowers and a strange semi-Alpine vegetation. If we are trying to scramble up these to reach the summit we shall hear from time to time the musical trickle of water in caverns and holes, closed in by these strong boulders and thickly hung with mosses and ferns. Should we then have reached any of the great summits of Mlanje and looked down into its central crater we shall realise that here must have been at one time volcanic action. The

PAPYRUS MARSH AND SADDLE-BILLED STORKS

WHAT THE COUNTRY LOOKS LIKE

scene before us is an indescribable wilderness of stones and boulders which look as though they had been hurled right and left from some central eruption.[1]

On the left-hand side stretches an arid plain of loose friable soil once formed below the water, and white with the lime of decomposed shells blazing in the reverberating sunshine of noonday—the refracted heat of its surface so great that the horizon quivers in wavy lines before our half-blinded eyes; on the other side a papyrus marsh with open pools of stagnant water. Beyond the arid waste of light soil on which a few grey wisps of grass are growing, lie the deep blue waters of a lake—almost an indigo blue at noonday and seen from this angle. Behind the papyrus marsh is a line of pale blue-grey mountains—a flat wash of colour, all detail veiled by the heat haze. We are at the mouth of a great river and the marshes on one side of us represent either its abandoned channels half dried up or its back water at times of overflow. For a mile or so the eye, turning away with relief from the scorching, bleached, barren plain which lies between us and the lake, looks over many acres of apple-green papyrus. The papyrus, as you will observe, is a rush with a smooth, round, tubelike stem, sometimes as much as six feet in height. The stem terminates in a great mop-head of delicate green filaments which are often bifid at their ends. Three or four narrow leaflets surround the core from which the filaments diverge. If the papyrus be in flower small yellow-green nodules dot the web of the filaments. With the exception of this inflorescence the whole rush—stem, leaves, and mop-head—is a pure apple-green and the filaments are like shining silk.

The water in the open patches in between the islands and peninsulas of papyrus is quite stagnant and unruffled and seemingly clear. Sometimes the water is black and fœtid but its tendency to corruption is often kept in check by an immense growth of huge duck weed,—the *Pistia stratiotes*, for all the world like a pale green lettuce.

A pair of saddle-billed storks are wading through the marsh, searching for fish and frogs and snakes. Their huge beaks are crimson-scarlet, with a black band, and their bodies are boldly divided in coloration between snowy white, inky-black, and bronze-green.

On Lake Nyasa. The steamer on which you are a passenger, in imagination, has left her safe anchorage in the huge harbour of Kotakota in the early morning and rounding the long sandspit which shields the inlet from the open lake, finds herself breasting a short, choppy sea. The waves at first are a muddy green where the water is shallow but soon this colour changes to a deep, cold, unlovely indigo. A strong southern breeze is blowing in your teeth and each billow is crested with white foam. The "Mwera" or south-easter—the wind which ravages the lake at certain times—is to-day against you, and you are condemned by circumstances to steam southwards opposed by this strong gale. As you get out into the middle of the lake the situation is almost one of danger, for the vessel on which you are travelling, though dignified with the name of "steamer," is not much larger than a Thames steam launch. In such weather as this she could not possibly go far with the billows on her beam

---

[1] These isolated fragments of granitic rock are found miles away from the Mlanje mountain in the plains below bearing all the appearance of having been hurled through the air for miles into the surrounding country. Mlanje mountain is evidently a large slice left of the pre-existing tableland from which again volcanic cones have risen.

or she would be rolled over; then again if the steamer went northwards with a following sea she would be speedily swamped; her only course—and it happens on this occasion to fit in with preconcerted arrangements—is to steam southwards, facing both wind and waves. At times the vessel seems to be standing on end as she crests some huge ridge of water; and as she descends into the furrow this broad-backed roller comes up under her stern and floods the upper deck. Then again she mounts, to fall again and mount again and fall again, until the best sailor in the world would be dizzy with this hateful see-saw motion. In fact, if it were not quite so dangerous, an ordinary passenger would give way to seasickness; yet on this occasion you are too frightened that the ship may be swamped and founder to bestow much attention on the qualms of your stomach.

But the captain is hopeful, and tells you that as this is the third day the wind has been blowing it will probably cease towards the evening. Overhead, in spite of the whistling wind, the sky is clear of clouds and a pale blue. The lake is dark indigo, flecked with white foam—not the rich, creamy, thick, white froth of saltwater, but a transparent clear foam like innumerable glass drops reflecting the sunlight coldly from many facets.

The lake is perhaps forty miles broad. North and south there is a clear sea horizon. East and west there are pale greyish-blue outlines of mountain ranges; but owing to the driving wind and the slight diffusion of spray at lower levels, or some such atmospheric cause, the lower slopes of the mountains are invisible and the distant land has no direct connection with the sharp-cut line of the indigo, foam-flecked water.

But with the afternoon heat the wind gradually lessens in force—lessens to a positive calm an hour before sunset; and the waters of the lake so easily aroused are as quickly and as easily appeased. As the wind diminishes in force the waves grow less and less till they are but a gentle swell or a mere ripple. At last, half an hour before sunset, you have the following scene before you. The steamer is now travelling smoothly and on an even keel along the south-east coast of Nyasa. The eastern sky is a yellowish white, which near the horizon becomes a very pale russet pink. The distant range of mountains facing the rays of the almost setting sun has its hollows and recesses and ravines marked in faint shadows of pinkish-purple, while the parts bathed in sunlight are yellowish grey. On the left-hand side of the picture the land projects somewhat into the lake in a long spit surmounted with low wooded hills, where the ground is reddish-brown dotted with white rocks, and the trees are a warm russet green in their lights and mauve-blue in their shadows. In the middle of the view, breaking the long line of the water horizon under the distant mountains are three warm-tinted blots of brown-pink, that represent three islets.

The water of the lake, however, gives the greatest feast of colour. Its ground tint near the horizon is a lemon white, which changes insensibly to silver-blue close up to the ship's side. But this immobile sheet of lemon-white, melting into palest azure, is scratched here and smeared there (like plush which has had the nap brushed the wrong way) with streaks and patches of palest amber. The whole effect is that of a great mirror of tarnished silver. The amber-white of these disconnected areas of ripples, where the expiring breeze faintly ruffles the perfect calm of the reflected sky, resembles the pinkish brown stains on a silver surface just becoming discoloured from exposure to the light.

Presently it will be night with a sky of purple grey studded with pale gold specks of stars and planets, all of which will be reflected in the calm lake, so that the steamer will seem to be carving her way through a liquid universe.

In a native village near to a great river there are three Europeans in a hut. Although styled generically a "hut" this native dwelling is of considerable size, with a high-peaked thatched roof like a broad-mouthed funnel in shape, the straggling ends of the thatch coming down to within a couple of feet of the ground and so, to some extent, shielding from the sun the raised verandah of grey mud which runs half round the outside. But the low-hanging thatch screens the doorway into the hut, making the interior dark even though the European occupants have broken small holes in the clay walls to let in a little more light from the shaded verandah. Inside, the rafters of palm ribs, which form the structure of the roof, are all shiny cockroach-black with the smoke of many months which has ascended to the roof and found its way out through the thatch. Cobwebs, covered with soot, hang from the rafters.

Of the three white men inside this hut two are well and hearty—faces red, and arms sun-tanned—and are seated upon empty provision cases: the third is sick unto death, with dull eyes, haggard cheeks and—if there is daylight enough to see it by—a complexion of yellowish-grey. He is stretched on a low camp bed, is dressed in a dirty sleeping suit, and partially covered by two trade blankets of garish red, blue and yellow, one of which slips untidily to the dusty floor of hardened earth. The two healthy men are smoking pipes vigorously; but the smell of strong Boer tobacco is not sufficient to disguise the nauseous odours of the sick room, and the fumes of whisky, which arise both from an uncorked bottle and from the leavings of whisky and water in two enamelled-iron cups.

By the sick man's bedside on a deal box is an enamelled-iron basin containing grey gruel-like chicken broth, in which large bits of ship's biscuit are floating. The soup has been made evidently without skill or care, for it has the yellow chicken fat floating on the top and even an occasional drowned feather attached to the sodden remnants of fowl. Also, there are a cup containing strong whisky and water (untouched), a long-necked bottle of lime juice, and a phial of Quinine pills.

The sick man turns ever and anon to the further side of the bed to vomit, and after one of these attacks he groans with the agony of futile nausea. "Cheer up, old chap!" says one of his companions, "we sent yesterday morning to the doctor-man at the mission station: it is only about thirty miles away and he ought to be here this afternoon." The doorway is darkened for a moment but not with the doctor's advent. A negro girl has stooped under the thatch to enter through the low doorway and for a moment obscures the dubious light refracted from the small piece of blazing sun-lit ground visible under the eaves. "Here, *git*, you black slut," shouts one of the men (he with the sandy beard and pockmarked face), lifting up a short whip of hippopotamus hide to enforce his remark. "Hold on," says the other healthy one, a tall brawny Cornishman, with dark eyes and black beard, "it is only his girl; harmless enough too, poor thing, considering she has known him more 'n a fortnight. It's wonderful what these nigger girls 'll do for a white man."

"There are all sorts of girls, there is every kind of girl,
 There are some that are foolish, and many that are wise,
 You can trust them all, no doubt, but be careful to look out
 For the harmless little girlie with the downcast eyes,"

sings the pockmarked man, in reminiscence of a smoking concert he attended months ago at Salisbury, before he and his companions tramped northwards across the Zambezi in search of gold and any other profitable discoveries they might make in the unknown North.

The woman, who has taken little or no notice of the other men, has seated herself on the floor near the sick man's bed and is fanning away the flies from his death-like face. He scarcely notices this attention, continuing as before to roll his head languidly across the rolled-up coat which serves as pillow.

Outside the hut it is a bright world enough—a sky of pure cobalt, with white cumulus clouds moving across it before a pleasant breeze. Except where these clouds cast a momentary shadow there is a flood of sunshine, making the dry thatched roofs of the round haycock houses glitter; and as to the bare beaten ground of the village site, in this strong glare of sunshine you would hardly realise it is mere red clay: it has an effulgent blaze of flame-tinted white except where objects cast on it circumscribed shadows of a purple black.

Two or three native curs, of the usual fox-coloured, pariah type, lie sleeping or grubbing for fleas in the sunshine. A lank, wretched-looking mangy bitch, with open sores on her ears and fly-infested dugs, trails herself wearily from hut to hut, seeking food, but only to be repulsed by kicks from unseen feet, or missiles hurled by unseen hands. Little chocolate-coloured children are playing in the dust, or baking in the sun clay images they have made with dust and water. Most of the houses have attached to them a woman's compound at the back, fenced in with a high reed fence. If you entered this compound from the verandah, or peeped over the high fence, you would see cheerful garrulous women engaged in preparing food. A steady "thud, thud!" "thud, thud!" comes from one group of hearty girls with plump upstanding breasts who, glistening with perspiration, are alternately pounding corn in a wooden mortar shaped like a dice box. Each in turn, as she takes the pestle, spits on her hands and thumps the heavy piece of wood up and down on the bruised corn. Another woman is grinding meal on the surface of a large flat stone by means of a smaller stone which is smooth and round; again, another wife with the aid of other flattened stones bruises green herbs mixed with oil and salt into a savoury spinach. In all the compounds and about the streets are hens and broods of chickens. Mongrel game-cocks are sheltering themselves from the heat under shaded verandahs, which they share with plump goats of small size and diverse colours—white, black, chestnut, grey; black and white, white and chestnut, grey and white. The sun-smitten village at high noon is silent but for the low-toned talk of the women, of the "thud, thud" of the corn-mortars, the baaing and bleating of an imprisoned kid, or the sudden yelp of the half-starved bitch when a missile strikes her.

Beyond the collection of haycock huts (occupying perhaps a half square mile in area), is a fringe of bananas, and beyond the bananas from one point of view the glint of a river, and across the river a belt of black-green forest. In other directions, away from the water-side is red rising ground sprinkled with scrubby thin-foliaged trees, among which here and there grows a huge gouty baobab, showing at this season digitate leaves like a horse-chestnut's, and large tarnished white flowers that depend by a straight string-like stalk from the pink and glabrous branches.

Noon declines to afternoon. The two men who are whole still remain in the hut; the sick man is obviously sicker than before. His face is an obscure yellow, he has ceased to vomit, he is no longer restless, he lies in a stupor, breathing stertorously. The black-bearded man smokes, and reads a tattered novelette, glancing from time to time uneasily at the one who lies so ill, but trying to still his anxiety by assuring himself "that the poor beggar has got to sleep at last." The man with the red hair and pockmarked cheeks sings snatches of music-hall songs at intervals and drinks whisky and water, trying hard to keep up his courage. For he is in a cold-sweating dread of death by fever—a death which can come so quickly. A month ago there were four of them, all in riotous health, revelling in the excitements of exploring a new country, confident that they had found traces of gold, merrily slaughtering buffalo, eland, kudu and sable; sometimes after elephant with the thought of the hundreds of pounds' worth of ivory they might secure with a few lucky shots; killing "hippo" in the river and collecting their great curved tusks for subsequent sale at a far-off trading station; trafficking with the natives in the flesh of all the beasts they slew and getting in exchange the unwholesome native meal, bunches of plantains, calabashes of honey, red peppers, rice, sugar cane, fowls, eggs, and goat's milk. They had not treated the natives badly, and the natives in a kind of way liked these rough pioneers who offered no violence beyond an occasional kick, who were successful in sport and consequently generous in meat distribution, and who gave them occasional "tots" of "kachaso,"[1] and paid for the temporary allotment of native wives in pinches of gunpowder, handfuls of caps, yards of cloth, old blankets and clasp knives. Yes; a month ago they were having a very good time, they were not even hampered by the slight restraints over their natural instincts which might exist in Mashonaland. They had found obvious signs of payable gold—"an ounce to the ton if only machinery could be got up there for crushing the rock"—they would return to the south and float a company; meantime they had intended to see a little more of this bounteous land blessed with an abundant rainfall, a rich soil, a luxuriant vegetation, a friendly people, grand sport, and heaps of food; and then, all at once, one of them after a bottle of whisky overnight and a drenching in a thunderstorm next day, complains of a bad pain in his back. A few hours afterwards he commences to vomit, passes black-water, turns bright yellow, falls into a stupor, and in two days is dead. "Was it the whisky, or the wetting, or neither? It could not be the whisky: good liquor was what was wanted to counteract this deadly climate; no, it could not be the whisky; on the contrary," thought the man who turns these thoughts over musingly in his mind, "he himself must take more whisky to keep his spirits up. When old Sampson was better and could be carried in a hammock, they would all make straight for the Lake and the steamers and so pass out of the country, perhaps returning to work the gold, perhaps not."

The heat of the afternoon increases. The man on the bed still snores, the woman still fans, Blackbeard has fallen asleep over his novelette and Redhead over his whisky and water. The silence of the village is suddenly broken by a sound of voices and the tramp of feet. Blackbeard wakes up, rubs his eyes and staggers out into the sunshine to greet a thin wiry European with bright eyes and a decided manner. "Oh . . . you are the Mission doctor, aren't you? Come in—in here. He is pretty bad, poor chap, but I expect you will do him a lot of good." . . .

It is early evening. The two mining prospectors have left the hut, advised

[1] Fire-water—whisky.

by the doctor to chuck their whisky bottles into the river and go out shooting. The former piece of advice they have not followed, but the latter they have gladly adopted, frightened at the aspect of their dying comrade, and only too glad to leave the responsibility of his care to the Mission doctor, who for two hours has tried all he knows to restore the patient to consciousness, without success. The woman has helped him as far as she was able, the doctor much too anxious about his patient to concern himself about the propriety of her position in the case. Outside the hut there is a cheerful noise of the awakening village settling down to its evening meal. Flights of spurwinged geese, black storks and white egrets pass in varied flocks and phalanxes across the rosy western sky. But inside, by the light of two candles stuck in bottles, which the doctor has lit to replace the daylight, it may be seen that his patient is nearing the end; yet as the end comes there is a momentary return to consciousness. The stertorous breathing has given way to a scarcely perceptible respiration, and as the doctor applies further means of restoration a sudden brightness and light of recognition come into the dull eyes. The expiring man tries to raise his head—cannot! and to speak—but no sound comes from his whitened lips, then one long drawn bubbling sigh and the end has come.

A great, untidy, Arab town near the shores of a lake, the blue waters of which can be seen over the unequal ground of the village outskirts and through a fringe of wind-blown banana trees. On one of the little squares of blue water thus framed in by dark-green fronds may be seen part of a dau at anchor with a tall, clumsy, brown mast, thick rigging, and a hull somewhat gaudily painted in black and pink. We are sitting under the broad verandah of a large house, a house which is in reality nothing but a structure of timber and lath covered with a thick coating of black mud; but the mud has been so well laid on and is so smooth, time-worn and shiny as to have the appearance of very dark stone. The roof is of thatch, descending from some forty feet above the ground to scarcely more than five feet over the edge of the verandah. This verandah only occupies one side of the house and is large enough to be—what it is—an outer hall of audience;[1] fifteen feet broad and with a raised dais of polished mud on either side of the passage which crosses the verandah to enter the main dwelling. As the interior rooms of this house are mostly unfurnished with windows and only derive their light from the central passage (which has an open door at either end) they are quite dark inside and even in the daytime little Arab lamps (earthenware saucers filled with oil and with cotton wicks) have to be lighted to see one's way about.

THE "SULTAN'S BARAZA"

---

[1] Called by Zanzibaris "baraza."

WHAT THE COUNTRY LOOKS LIKE

In front of the house, in the open public square, is a fine cocoanut tree which has been planted from a cocoanut brought from the East Coast of Africa. Across the square a ramshackle building is pointed out as the Mosque, and Arabs of all shades—of negro blackness and of European whiteness—are walking backwards and forwards through the blazing sunshine to perform their ablutions in the court of the Mosque, or to enter the building to pray.

The Sultan of the place, in one of whose houses we are tarrying (in imagination) is about to have his noontide meal, and asks us to join. He himself is seated on a mattress placed on a mud bench against the wall under the verandah, and is clothed in a long, white garment reaching down to his heels, over which he wears a sleeveless, orange-coloured waistcoat richly embroidered with silver, a shawl-sash wound round his waist, and over one shoulder a light Indian cloth of chequered pattern brightly fringed. Through the shawl waistband peep out the hilt and part of the scabbard of one of those ornamental curved daggers which are worn at Zanzibar and in the Persian Gulf; this hilt and scabbard are of richly-chased silver.

The Sultan has a face which in some respects is prepossessing. It is certainly not cruel though he is known to have done many cruel things. The once fine eyes are somewhat clouded with premature age and the exhaustion of a polygamist; but there are a sensitiveness and refinement about the purple-lipped mouth and well-shaped chin, the outlines of which can be seen through the thin grey beard. The hands have slender, knotted fingers and the nails are short and exquisitely kept.

The taking of food is preceded by the washing of hands. Attendants—who are either black coast Arabs, gorgeously habited in embroidered garments of black, silver and gold, or else dirty, blear-eyed, negro boys, scarcely clothed at all and with grey, scurvy skins (the dirtiest and stupidest-looking of these boys is the Sultan's factotum in the household and carries his keys on a string round his lean neck) come to us with brass ewers and basins. The ewers are long-spouted, like coffee pots. Water is poured over our hands, which after rinsing we dry as best we can on our pocket handkerchiefs, while the Sultan wipes his on his Indian cloth which is slung over his shoulder and is used indifferently as napkin and handkerchief. Then a brass platter of large size, covered with a pyramid of steaming rice, is placed on the dais and alongside it an earthenware pot (very hot) containing curried chicken. The Sultan having rolled up a ball of rice between his fingers and dipped it into the curry, invites us to do the same. Our fingers are scalded by the rice; but it must be admitted that the flavour of the curry is excellent. When this course is finished a bowl of pigeons stewed with lentils is brought on, and this also is eaten by the aid of our fingers. For drink we have cold, pure water from an earthenware cooler, and the milk of unripe cocoanuts.

The meal finishes with bananas and roasted ground nuts. Then more washing of hands and we recline on some dirty cushions or on lion skins, whilst the Sultan gives audience to messengers, courtiers and new arrivals. Some of these last-named glance suspiciously at us and are not disposed to be very communicative about their recent experiences in the presence of Europeans. The Sultan sees this and enjoys the humour of the situation. He is himself indifferent to the slave trade, having secured his modest competence years ago and now caring for nothing more than the friendship of European potentates, which will enable him to finish his days in peace and tranquillity. After he is gone he knows that in all probability there will be no other Sultan in his place, but a European official. In his heart of hearts, of course, he sees no harm in the slave trade. He is well aware that he is entertaining at one and the same time European officials of high standing and five or six powerful Arab slave dealers, and that his large, rambling metropolis of several square miles in area harbours simultaneously not only the Europeans and their porters, servants, and escort, but perhaps three hundred raw slaves from the Luálaba. But he is not going to give his compatriots away unless they make fools of themselves by any attempt to molest the Europeans, in which case, and in any case if it comes to a choice of sides, he will take the part of the European. In his dull way this unlettered man, who has read little else than the Koran and a few Arab books of obscenities, or of fortune-telling, has grasped the fact that from their own inherent faults and centuries of wrong-doing, Islam and Arab civilisation must yield the first place to the religion and influence of the European. He has no prejudice against Christianity—on the contrary, perhaps a greater belief in its supernatural character than some of the Englishmen he entertains from time to time—but if his inchoate thoughts could be interpreted in one sentence it would be "Not in our time, O Lord!" The change must come but may it come after his death. Meantime he hopes that you will not drive home too far the logic of your rule. When he is gone the Christian missionary may come and build there, but while he lasts he prefers to see nothing but the ramshackle mosques of his own faith and to have his half-caste children taught in the Arab fashion. He points out some to you who are sitting in the verandah of an opposite hut, under the shade of a knot of papaw trees; a hideous old negroid Arab with a dark skin and pockmarked face is teaching them to read. Each child has a smooth wooden board with a long handle, something like a hand-mirror in shape. The surface of this board is whitened with a thin coating of porcelain clay; and Arab letters, verses of the Koran and sentences for parsing are written on it by means of a reed pen dipped in ink or by a piece of charcoal.

There is a certain pathos about this uneducated old coast Arab who has been a notable man in his day as conqueror and slave raider but who has had sufficient appreciation of the value of well-doing not to be always a slave raider, who has sought to inspire a certain amount of affection among the populations he enslaved. These in time have come to regard him as their natural sovereign, though the older generation can remember his first appearance in the country as an Arab adventurer at the head of a band of slavers. His soldiers, most of them now recruited from amongst his negro subjects, cheerfully raid the territories of other chiefs in the interior, but slave raiding within his own especial kingdom has long since ceased and a certain degree of order and security has been established. Let us set off against the crimes of his early manhood the good he has done subsequently by introducing from Zanzibar the cocoanut-palm, the lime tree, the orange, good white rice, onions, cucumbers and other useful products of the East; by sternly repressing cannibalism, abolishing witchcraft trials, improving the architecture, and teaching many simple arts and inducing the negroes to clothe their somewhat extravagant nudity in seemly, tasteful garments.

He has known Livingstone and may even have secured a good word from that Apostle of Africa for hospitality and for relative humanity, as compared to other and wickeder Arabs. This casual mention of him in the book of the great "Dottori"[1] will cause him a childish pleasure if you point it out. "Has

---

[1] The name by which Livingstone is almost universally known in Central Africa.

WHAT THE COUNTRY LOOKS LIKE

the 'Quini' read this book?" he asks. "Yes," you reply. "Then the Queen has seen my name?" and this reflection apparently causes him much satisfaction, for he repeats the observation to himself at intervals and even forces it on the attention of a sullen-looking black-browed Maskat Arab who is waiting in the *baraza* to settle with the Sultan the amount of tribute he must pay for the passage of his slave and ivory caravan across the territory and over the lake by means of the Sultan's daus.

I will transport you to the south end of Lake Tanganyika.

In the background to this scene is a fine mountain which, like most Central African mountains, presents from below the appearance of a cake that has been

MOUNT KAPEMBA, TANGANYIKA

cut and is crumbling. There is first of all the granite wall of undulating outline bearing a thin line of trees along its crest. Then half-way down its slope begins below the bare shining rock walls a ribbed slope of débris, which slope is covered with luxuriant purple-green forest: the whole *estompé* with a film of blue atmosphere, which sets it back to its proper place in the distance, so that if you half close your eyes the general effect of this mountain mass is a greyish purple.

As if in abrupt contrast to this upreared mass of rocks and trees towering at least 4000 feet into the sky is a slice of bright green swamp, separating the mountain slopes from the lake water. The foreground to this picture is the broad estuary of a river at its entrance to Tanganyika. On your right hand you have a spit of yellow sand which separates the unruffled mirror of this calm water from the boisterous waves of the open lake. These are greenish blue with brown marblings and muddy white crests where they are receiving the alluvium of the river; and fierce indigo streaked with blazing white foam where the lake is open, deep and wind-swept. On your left hand the estuary of this river (where the water is a speckless mirror of the blue sky and its cream-white grey-shadowed clouds) is studded with many green islets of papyrus and girt with hedges of tall reeds — the reeds with the white plumes and pointed dagger leaves that I have once or twice before described.

This conjunction of mountain, river, marsh, estuary, sandspit, open lake and papyrus tangle brings about such a congeries of bird life that I have thought it worth the trouble to bring you all the way to Tanganyika to gaze at this huge aviary. And although on many of these journeys you are supposed to be looking on the scene with the eye of the spirit and not of the flesh, and therefore able to see Nature undisturbed by the presence of man, still on this spot you might stand in actuality, as I have stood, and, provided you did not fire a gun, see this collection of birds as though they were enclosed in some vast Zoological Gardens. For some cause or other has brought the fish down from the upper reaches of the stream or up from the lake. The water of the estuary is of unruffled smoothness. Most waterbirds detest the rough waves of the open lake, or the current of a rapid stream; even now if you turn your eyes lakewards the only birds you will see are small grey gulls with black barred faces and black tipped wings and the large scissor-billed terns (grey and white with crimson beaks) flying with seeming aimlessness over the troubled waters. But in the estuary, what an assemblage! There are pelicans of grey, white and salmon pink, with yellow pouches, riding the water like swans, replete with fish and idly floating. Egyptian geese (fawn-coloured, white, and green-bronze); spur winged geese (bronze-green, white shouldered, white flecked, and red cheeked); African teal (coloured much like the English teal); a small jet black pochard with a black crest and yellow eyes; whistling tree duck (which are black and white, zebra-barred, and chestnut); other tree ducks (chestnut and white); that huge *Sarcidiornis* (a monstrous duck with a knobbed beak, a spurred wing, and a beautiful plumage of white and bronzed-blue with a green-blue speculum in the secondaries of the wing). All these ducks and geese hang about the fringe of the reeds and the papyrus. The ducks are diving for fish, but the geese are more inclined to browse off the water-weed. Every now and then there is a disturbance, and the reflexions of the water are broken by a thousand ripples as the ducks scutter over the surface or the geese rise with much clamour for a circling flight. Farthest away of all the birds (for they are always shy) is a long file of rosy flamingoes sifting the water for small fish and molluscs. They are so far off that their movements are scarcely perceptible; against the green background of the marsh they look like a vast fringe of pale pink azaleas in full blossom.

Small bronze-green cormorants are plunging into the water for fish, diving and swimming under water, and flying away. Fish-catching on a more modest scale and quite close to where we stand is being carried on by black and white Ceryle kingfishers, who with their bodies nearly erect and the head and beak directed downwards will poise themselves in the air with rapidly fluttering wings and then dart unerringly head foremost on some tiny fish under the surface of the water.

On the sandspit two dainty crowned cranes are pacing the sand and the scattered wiry grass looking for locusts. Even at this distance—and especially if you use a glass—you can distinguish the details of their coloration. It will be seen that they have a short, finely-shaped beak of slatey black, a large eye of bluish grey, surrounded by a black ring; and the cheeks covered with bare porcelain-like skin, pure white, which is much enhanced by an edging of crimson developing below the throat into two bright crimson wattles. The head is fitly crowned with a large aigrette of golden filaments, tipped with black. The neck with its long hackles is dove grey. The back and the breast are slate colour, the mass of the wing is snow white, and its huge broadened pinions are reddish chocolate, the white secondaries being prolonged into a beautiful golden fringe hanging gracefully over the chocolate quill feathers.

The quacking of the ducks, the loud cries of the geese and the compound sound of splashings and divings and scuttering flights across the water, are dominated from time to time by the ear-piercing screams of a fish eagle, perched on one of the taller poles of a fishing weir. The bird is as full of fish as he can hold, but yet seems annoyed at the guzzling that is going on around him, and so relieves his feelings at odd moments by piercing yells. He is a handsome bird—head and neck and breast snow white, the rest of the plumage chocolate brown.

Add to the foregoing enumeration of birds stilt plovers of black and white; spur-winged plovers with yellow wattles; curlew; sandpipers; crimson-beaked pratincoles; sacred ibis (pure white and indigo-purple); hagedash ibis (iridescent-blue, green, and red-bronze); gallinules (verditer blue with red beaks); black water-rails with lemon beaks and white pencillings; black coots; other rails that are blue and green with turned-up white tails; squacco herons (white and fawn-coloured); large grey herons; purple-slate-coloured herons; bluish-gray egrets; white egrets; large egrets with feathery plumes; small egrets with snowy bodies and yellow beaks; Goliath herons (nut-brown and pinkish-grey); small black storks, with open and serrated beaks; monstrous bare-headed marabu storks; and dainty lily-trotters[1] (black and white, golden-yellow and chocolate-brown); and you will still only have got half way through the enumeration of this extraordinary congregation of water birds at the estuary of the river Lofu, on the south coast of Tanganyika.

Civilisation.—We are going to spend a Sunday at Blantyre, a European settlement in the Shire Highlands. Except for the name, however, there is no similarity between the little manufacturing town, which was Livingstone's birthplace, and the chief focus of European interests here in South Central Africa. These are the characteristics of the African Blantyre on a bright Sunday

[1] *Parra Africana.*

morning in May:—A glorious blue sky; floods of sunshine; a cool breeze and a sparkling freshness in the atmosphere which reminds one of Capetown; clean red roads, neat brick houses, purple mountains, and much greenery.

The organ is giving forth a hymn of Mendelssohn's by way of introit as we enter the church, and as, simultaneously, the choir and clergy take their places. The Norman architecture of the interior, the stained glass windows, the embroidered altar cloths, the brass lecterns and their eagles, the carved altar rails, the oak pulpit, the well-appointed seats with scarlet cushions—even the sunlight checked in its exuberance by passing through the diamond panes of the tinted windows—produce an effect on the newcomer of absolute astonishment. He requires to fix his eyes on the black choir in their scarlet and white vestments to realise that he is in Africa and not in Edinburgh or Regent's Park. The congregation consists mainly of Europeans and the service is in English. [The natives will assemble at other hours when worship is conducted in their own language.] A short service with good music, well sung by the black choir, and a quarter of an hour's sermon: then we are out once more in the sunny square, in a temperature not hotter than a mild summer's day at home, exchanging greetings with many acquaintances, almost all of whom are habited in such clothes as they would wear on a Sunday in Scotland. Some of the men turn out in black coats, light trousers, top hats, patent leather boots, white spats and brown gloves; and the ladies are wearing silk blouses and cloth skirts, with all the furbelows and puffs and pinchings and swellings which were the height of the fashion in London not more than four months ago, for there is an almost pathetic desire on the part of the Blantyre settlers to keep in touch with civilisation.[1]

In the bare, open space which so fittingly surrounds this handsome church, groups of mission boys are standing, respectably clothed in not badly-fitting European garments and wearing black felt hats. They are conversing in low tones, a little afraid of having their remarks overheard by the critical Europeans. They have a slight tendency to giggle, of which they are conscious and somewhat ashamed. A long file of mission girls, modestly and becomingly clad in scarlet and white, crosses the square to the native quarters of the mission under the guidance of a lady in dove-grey with a black bonnet and a grass-green parasol. By way of quaint contrast to these reclaimed guardians of the flock is the aboriginal wolf in the persons of some Angoni carriers who, forgetting or ignoring that Sunday was a day of rest with the European, are bringing up loads from the Upper Shire. Stark naked, all but a tiny square of hide or a kilt of tiger-cat tails, with supple, lithe bodies of glistening chocolate (shiny with perspiration), with the hair of their heads screwed up into curious little tufts by means of straw, they glide past the church with their burdens, alternately shy and inquisitive—ready to drop the burden and dart away if a European should address them roughly; on the other hand gazing with all their eyes at the wonderfully dressed white women, and the obviously powerful "wafumo"[2] amongst the white men. A smartly-uniformed negro policeman in yellow khaki and black fez hurries them off the scene, shocked at their nudity, which was his own condition a year ago.

A good-looking Sikh soldier—over on a day's leave from the neighbouring garrison, or else accompanying some official as orderly—loiters respectfully on the fringe of the European crowd. He is in undress and wears a huge blush-rose turban, a loose snow-white shirt, a fawn-coloured waistcoat, white paijamas

---

[1] Blantyre in fact is like an Indian Hill Station.   [2] Chiefs.

(baggy over the hips but tight-fitting round the calves) and pointed Persian shoes of crimson leather. His long, black beard has been rolled up after the fashion of the Sikhs, so that it makes a tidy fringe round the jaws from ear to ear; and the black moustache is fiercely curled.

We walk away home over a smooth road that is vinous-red, as all the earth is hereabout. First there is an avenue of sombre cypresses mixed with shimmering eucalyptus; then the road will be bordered by bananas or by the gardens of Europeans' houses, with neat fences. In all directions other roads branch off, and above the greenery of Indian corn patches, of banana-groves, of plantations of conifers, acacias, and eucalyptus, or clumps of Misuko trees, can be seen the house-roofs of grey corrugated iron, or rose-pink, where that iron has been coloured with anti-corrosive paint.

Bright moonlight. In a Hyphæne palm forest. Out of the shadow of the trees it is almost as bright as day, every detail can be seen in the dry grass—even the colours of some few flowers blooming in spite of the dry weather. The effect is that of a photograph—a little too much devoid of half-tones, being sharply divided into bright lights, full of minute detail and deep grey shadows, like blots, in which no detail can be descried. It is clear that this forest lies far from the haunts of man, for all the palm stems still retain the jagged stems of withered fronds. This gives them an untidy and forbidding aspect; for these grey mid-ribs stick out at an angle of forty degrees from the main trunk. The faded leaf filaments have long since disappeared from the extremities of the dead leaf fronds which themselves are so dry and so lightly attached to the stem that a few blows from a stout pole would knock them off and the palm trunk would be left bare and smooth. This is the condition of almost all palms near a native village in Africa because the natives climb them for the fruit, or more often for the sap which they tap at the summit and make into a fermented drink. Therefore whenever in tropical Africa you find palms in a forest retaining their old fronds from the ground upwards you may know that indigenous man is nowhere near.

Each palm is surmounted by a graceful crown of fan-shaped leaves in an almost symmetrical oval mass, radiating from the summit as from a centre. The fruit which is clustered thickly on racemes is—seen by daylight—a bright chestnut brown and the size of a Jaffa orange. This brown husk covering an ivory nut is faintly sweet to the taste and is adored by elephants. It is on that account that I have brought you here to see with the eye of the spirit a herd of these survivors of past geological epochs.

Somehow or other, it seems more fitting that we should see the wild elephant by moonlight at the present day. He is like a ghost revisiting the glimpses of the moon—this huge grey bulk, wrinkled even in babyhood, with his monstrous nose, his monstrous ears and his extravagant incisor teeth.

There! I have hypnotised you, and having suggested the idea of "elephants" you declare that you really begin to see huge forms assuming definite outline and chiaro-scuro from out of the shadows of the palms. Now you hear the noise they make—an occasional reverberating rattle through the proboscis as they examine objects on the ground half seriously, half playfully; and the swishing they make as they pass through the herbage; or the rustle of branches which are being plucked to be eaten. But they are chiefly bent on the ginger-bread nuts of the palms and to attain this, where they hang out of reach, they will pause occasionally to butt the palm trees with their flattened foreheads.

The dried stems and the dead fronds crash down before this jarring blow. If the fruit does not fall and the tree is not tilted over at an angle [its crown within reach of the animal's trunk], then the great beast will either strive to drag it down with his proboscis or to kneel and uproot it with his tusks. The elephants pause every now and then in their feasting, the mothers to suckle the little ones from the two great paps between the fore-legs, a huge bull to caress a young female amorously with his twining trunk, or the childless cows to make semblance of fighting, and the half-grown young to chase each other with shrill trumpetings.

But the moon is dropping over to the west. You did not think the moonlight could be exceeded in brightness. Yet in the advent of day it is only after all a betterment of night. Before the first pale pink light of early dawn the moonlight seems an unreality. In a few minutes the moon is no more luminous than a round of dirty paper and with the yellow radiance of day the elephants cease their gambollings and feasting, form into line, and swing into one of those long marches which will carry them over sixty miles of forest, plain and mountain to the next halting place in their seeming-purposeful journey.

There has been a war. The black man trained and taught by the Arab has been fighting the black man officered and directed by the European and, not unnaturally, has got the worst of it. But the fight has been a stiff one. We have had to take that walled town in the red plain, behind which are gleams of water and stretches of green swamp interspersed with clumps of raphia palms. There has been the preliminary bombardment, the straw huts within the red walls have gone up in orange flame and mighty columns of smoke [transparent black and opaque yellow according to the material burning] into the heavens above and are now falling in a gentle rain of black wisps. Here and there a barrel of gunpowder has exploded, or the bursting of a shell has elicited a terrible cry from an otherwise stolid, silent enemy. Then there has been the first charge up to the clay walls and the inevitable casualties from the enemy's fusillade directed through the loop-holes. A white officer has fallen forward on his face, revolver in hand, biting the dust literally. He is not dead, he announces cheerfully, "Only my arm smashed, I think"; but a Sikh who is attempting to arrange for his transport to the doctor out of the range of the enemy's fire, is shot through the heart, and with the last dying instinct swerves his fall to avoid falling on the officer's shattered arm. The bulk of the small force of white men, Sikhs, and negro soldiers in khaki uniforms and black fezzes, has either scaled the clay rampart or has shattered a gateway and burst into the stronghold, and the officer can now swoon away comfortably without much risk of dying, as the doctor can be seen in the distance hurrying up his little band of native hospital assistants and a couple of hammocks for the transport of wounded men. A tremendous rattle of musketry is going on. The native guns go off seldom now, but make a loud reverberating boom from the quantity of powder with which they are charged; the Snider rifles, on the other hand, give short cracks. From some of the unburnt housetops in the more distant part of the town the enemy is still keeping up a dropping fire, and in fact as we stand in imagination over the wounded officer we can hear overhead that curious "ping," that singing sound of bullets travelling high above our heads. We are not out of but under the enemy's range. Gradually the gun fire ceases, though every now and then a few more cracking shots will be heard, until the victory is complete and absolute, and the place is wholly taken.

When there is no longer any doubt about the result the native allies, who have hung on the outskirts of the white man's camp, dash forward in skirmishing order to cut off the fugitives. They are a motley crowd, these "friendlies," armed with flint-locks, muzzle-loading guns, old pistols, or with spear and assegai, bow and arrow. It would be difficult to tell them from the opposing force—for the auxiliaries of the Arab are often own brothers to the white man's helpers—but that each "friendly" has a large piece of white cloth tied round the upper part of his left arm. The chief efforts of the Europeans and the Sikhs are now directed towards restraining these inconvenient allies who would seek to perpetrate on the flying enemy, or on his wounded, the same barbarities that the Arabs and their followers recently inflicted on the tribes allied with the European—which barbarities are the cause of the white man's presence here to-day with a country at his back to help him.

War is always horrible, even if it be waged in a righteous cause, and nowhere so horrible as in savage Africa. Let us, as a useful lesson, pick our way through this bombarded town as far as the heat of the still burning houses will permit. Here amongst the black ashes of a hut is a poor, domestic cat frizzled into a ghastly mummy and close to her are numerous broiled rats: all alike were unable to escape in time from the burning building. High above our heads—for some reason I think the saddest sight of all—are the homeless pigeons, circling round and round unable to settle on the burning roof trees, dazed and stupefied with the smoke and occasionally falling down into the flames to die. Shrieking fowls are flying in all directions and after them excited "friendlies" or porters of the expedition in pursuit, heedless of the hot ashes under foot. Our first dead body: a negro soldier of the Administration, neatly clad, spick and span in spite of his scramble over the eight-foot wall. Soon after entering the town he must have been shot dead and he has fallen on his back still grasping his rifle and, strange to say, with a faint smile of triumph and no look of pain whatever on the face. A little distance beyond him lies a wretched savage who has been killed by a shell. His stomach has been torn out and his head split in two. Here and there a black arm or leg or a dead face with wide-open eyes may be descried amongst the débris of the huts, indicating the presence of others who have fallen in the fight. The doctor will presently come and search the shattered huts in case there may be any wounded and living requiring attention.

We have now reached the centremost stronghold of the town, and it is seen that great as the conflagration appeared from the outside it has destroyed but a small portion of the town. The Sikhs are now busily engaged in isolating the burning huts and putting out the fire. The officers have been examining the large houses around the Sultan's compound and have brought to light an extraordinary number of wretched women and children most of them slaves—the adults both men and women—still weighted with the slave stick.[1]

Many of these slaves are entirely naked and utterly barbarous, and all are whimpering, not with joy at the prospect of freedom but in the imminent dread that they will be immediately killed and eaten by the white men, that being the idea implanted in their minds by the Arab. A little apart from the great mass

---

[1] The slave stick is usually a young tree of heavy wood barked and all the branches removed with the exception of a bifurcation at the end. Into this bifurcation the slave's neck is thrust and the two ends of the stick are united by an iron band at the back of his neck so that this heavy log is attached to the front of the man's body. In this condition he is quite unable to run away.

of still fettered slaves is an Arab prisoner, his hands tied behind his back, kneeling or reclining with his ankles also fastened. There is a slight wound on his forehead; his face bears the expression of a caged wolf, his pale yellow skin is livid with pain, fear, and hatred. He has lost his round, white cap or fez, or turban, and his bald head looks mean and out of keeping with his careful clothes, which though soiled in warfare are still neat and presentable. Round his neck in a dirty cloth bag hangs a copy of the Koran.

From such a scene as this I walked away once over the battlefield. The fight was ended, but we were only just starting to look for the wounded. It was early afternoon; a lovely day, bright sunshine, pale blue sky. A cool breeze had blown away the smoke; apart from the scene of the chief struggle in the captured town there was no indication that war was being waged. In a secluded part of the precincts amid the scattered vegetation of the village outskirts I suddenly came across the body of a fine-looking Angoni, not many minutes dead. He might have been fighting on our side; he might have been hired by the Arabs as one of their raiders, but someone had killed him with a bullet through the head and he had fallen in his tracks, in all his panoply of war, scarcely conscious of the object for which he fought. His right hand still grasped the stabbing spear, his left still held the ox-hide shield. His throwing spears had flown from his hand and were scattered on the ground. Grimmest sight of all—four vultures had already arrived on the scene to examine him. Two birds promenaded up and down with a watchful eye, ready on noting any sign of returning consciousness to take their departure; another bird, somewhat bolder, stood on one leg and inspected him as might a thoughtful surgeon; and the fourth whirled in circles on out-spread pinions round the body, wishing to settle but frightened, in case after all it was a swoon and not a death.

NIAMKOLO: SOUTH END OF TANGANYIKA

HIS LAST FIGHT

CHAPTER II.

PHYSICAL GEOGRAPHY

IN looking through the pictures I have tried to paint in the preceding chapter to illustrate the scenery of British Central Africa, it will be noticed that I have made no mention of any desert, of any open sandy tract or stony region devoid of vegetation. The fact is that so far as my own researches and those of other explorers go, British Central Africa, east of the Kafue river, holds no desert, no stretch of country that is not more or less covered with abundant vegetation. Here and there on the line of water parting between the river systems there may be a little harsh scenery where the trees are poor and scrubby and the plants grow in scattered tufts. But, take it as a whole, the eastern half of British Central Africa is very well clothed with vegetation, especially in the Nyasa province. There is nowhere any large continuous area of thick tropical forest such as one sees in Western Africa, but in favoured districts where the soil is permeated with many springs there may be an occasional patch of woodland quite West African in character, and not only containing oil palms, of the genus *Elæis* (which are usually thought to be peculiarly characteristic of West Africa), but also not a few birds and mammals hitherto considered to be confined in their range to the West African region. From this and other facts, I am sometimes led to believe that

FOREST ON MOUNT CHOLO, BRITISH CENTRAL AFRICA

the whole of Africa was once covered with more or less dense forest, but that the climate in the eastern half of the continent being drier than in the west, the ravages of the bush fires started by man have made greater headway than the reparatory influence of nature. Only in specially favoured tracts enjoying exceptional rainfall or else provided with underground springs could the forest remain always green and full of sap all the year round, and thus be able to choke out the fire or, in the wet season, to make sufficient growth to repair the ravages sustained by bush fires.

We have therefore a well clothed country to deal with; but our abundant vegetation is undoubtedly the cause of malarial fever. The essentially healthy

THE MLANJE RANGE, SEEN FROM ZOMBA AFTER RAINFALL

portions of tropical Africa are those like Somaliland, much of the Sudan, a good deal of East Africa and all South West Africa, where the rainfall is trifling and vegetation is mainly confined to the banks of rivers.

From observations made and records kept by various officials throughout the Protectorate proper and the adjoining regions under the sway of the British South Africa Company I should compute the average rainfall of the greater part of British Central Africa at 50 inches per annum. But this average fluctuates somewhat (according to the remembrances of white men longest in the country and the traditions of the natives); and I should say that the rainfall ranged from 35 inches in years of extreme drought to 60 inches in years of excessive rainfall. There are certainly traces of a larger rainfall having once prevailed in these countries in past ages. In travelling about British Central

Africa one is constantly encountering marshes which even in native tradition (to say nothing of the geographical evidence) were once large lakes. Again, there are fertile depressions which are no longer marshes. Dry stream valleys mark the courses of once powerful torrents. This tendency towards decreased rainfall is undoubtedly due, in my opinion, to the action of man. It is scarcely exaggeration to say that had British Central Africa been left for another couple of hundred years simply and solely to the black man and the black man had continued to exist without thought for the future as he does at present, this country would have become treeless, as many portions of it were becoming when we embarked on its administration. Livingstone describes in his *Last Journals* the process that is going on in Manyema, to the west of Tanganyika, a country once covered with the densest forest. The natives make clearings for

NATIVE CLEARING IN FOREST COUNTRY

their plantations. They cut down the trees, leave them to dry and then set fire to them and sow their crops amongst the fertilising ashes. The same type of forest never grows up again. It is replaced by grass or by a growth of scrubby trees—trees of a kind which can to a greater extent resist the annual scorching of the bush fires. Besides this wanton destruction of forest for the growing of food crops (and as a rule the native merely grows one crop of corn and then moves off to another patch of virgin soil, leaving the old plantation to be covered with grass and weeds) the annual bush fires play a considerable and (if unchecked) an increasing part in the disforesting of the country. Even where large continuous areas of dense forest remain, so evergreen and full of sap as not to burn easily, each year the raging fire will sere and dry and kill those trees which are on the forest outskirts. The next year these dead trees are consumed by the fire which again dries up and kills another rank; so year by year the forest diminishes in area to extinction, unless protected by happening to grow in a deep valley with abrupt cliffs; though this condition of course restricts its area of growth.

Still, although we must, I think, admit a certain diminution in rainfall owing to the decrease of forest or other causes, the rate at which this decrease is going on has been exaggerated, and as we come to know the country better and our records grow with years of occupation, we see that there are signs of cycles of greater and less rain dependent on atmospheric conditions which we have not yet realised. The marks on the rocks show that during some ages there has been a slight—but a very slight—fall in Lake Nyasa, varied by periods of extraordinary diminution as for instance some seventy years ago when according to the natives' traditions the north end of the lake became so shallow between Deep Bay and Amelia Bay that a chief and his men waded across where it is now many fathoms deep. The highest watermark on these polished rocks is perhaps at most six feet above the present high levels of the lake in good rainy seasons. In years of relative drought Lake Nyasa may be as much as six feet below its best rainy season average. This means, of course, that instead of there being nine feet of water on the bar of the Shire where that river quits the lake there are only three feet; consequently the navigability of the Shire in the dry season becomes much embarrassed and in these bad years it can only be navigated all the year round by vessels not drawing more than one and a half feet. Yet we know that in the later "fifties" and early "sixties" Livingstone constantly travelled up and down the Shire on a vessel drawing five feet. Even in the year 1889 the *James Stevenson* which draws about three feet of water was able to navigate the Shire through almost all the year up to the Murchison falls, while vessels of five feet draught have in like manner navigated the Upper Shire above the falls. But from 1891 till 1896 the Shire fell lower and lower until at last not even Chiromo was the limit of navigation from the sea, but the Pinda rapids near the Zambezi, while the Upper Shire was practically divided into a few navigable stretches with very shallow water in between. But after the rainy season of 1895–96 Lake Nyasa rose to a height which had not been reached for many years and is apparently still continuing to rise. The result is that the Lower Shire is now as navigable as it was in Livingstone's day, while on the Upper Shire many of our low-lying stations are threatened by the flood

THE SHIRE AT CHIKWAWA
JUST BELOW THE MURCHISON FALLS

Similar fluctuations are recorded of Tanganyika; while in the case of Bangweolo and Mweru fluctuations of level would also seem to occur in cycles. The differences between Livingstone's map of Bangweolo and the map made by Giraud, the observations of Mr. Joseph Thomson, Mr. Alfred Sharpe, and Mr. Poulett Weatherley of the same lake may all be reconciled by this theory of a few feet fluctuation in its rise and fall. A few feet, more or less, would make the vast lake of M. Giraud the "restricted open water" of Livingstone, and the wide marsh with a few open pools conjectured by Sharpe and Thomson.[1]

Of course the average rainfall I have quoted must not be taken as the rainfall of each part of British Central Africa. So far as our observations go some districts receive no more than 35 inches per annum.[2] These again, especially if they contain mountains of great height like Mlanje, may record a rainfall exceeding 100 inches. A rainfall of 60 inches is common.

PINDA MOUNTAIN AND PINDA MARSH, LOWER SHIRE

In consequence of this fairly good supply of rain the country is well watered by perennial streams and rivers. At the extreme end of the dry season there are streams which dry up though water can almost always be found a short distance below the surface. Still compared to other parts of East Central Africa the bulk of our rivers and rivulets may be described as perennial, that is to say containing running water all the year round. This is not suprising as so much of the country is mountainous and in these highlands the rain is spread a little less unequally over the area. It may safely be said that above altitudes of 4000 feet (and a large proportion of the land is above 4000 feet) no month passes without a fall of rain. Even at Zomba where the altitude is only 3000 feet it is a rare occurrence for no rain to fall in any given month.

But the year is clearly divided into seasons of rain and drought. The rainy season generally begins at the end of the month of November and heavy rains fall in December. There is often a short lull about Christmas time, but

---

[1] Since this passage was penned Mr. Poulett Weatherley, the explorer and sportsman, has thoroughly circumnavigated and mapped it. His observations concur rather with those of Livingstone than of Giraud.

[2] A small patch at the south end of Lake Nyasa in one year only received 26·62 inches of rain.

early in January the rains recommence and become torrential, continuing to fall very heavily until the end of March. April is a delightful month as it is in Europe, of alternate showers and sunshine. A little rain falls in May and an occasional shower in June. July is the height of the winter—cold, dry, sparkling—but is never without a few drops of rain. In August there will sometimes be a week's rain of a decided character, especially in the highlands. A shower

PART OF THE FALLS OF THE RUO AT ZOA

or two will follow in September. October is quite the driest month and in lowlands passes without a drop of rain, though in the highlands there may be an occasional thunder storm. Towards the close of November (the first half being terribly hot and dry) the big rains recommence.

As regards temperature there is considerable variation also dependent on altitude. In the valley of the Shire, on the south coast of Lake Nyasa, in the great Luangwa Valley and on the Central Zambezi, the heat is frightful just

MAP SHOWING APPROXIMATE ANNUAL RAINFALL IN BRITISH CENTRAL AFRICA & ADJOINING COUNTRIES

Compiled from data supplied by Sir H. H. Johnston, K.C.B.

EXPLANATION OF COLOURING
Rainfall of 35 Inches and under
35 to 45 Inches
45 to 60 "
60 to 75 "
Over 75 "

A Red Line thus ——— following the course of Rivers, or enclosing an area of Lakes, indicates the Limits of Navigability all the year round for vessels drawing 2 feet of water.
A dotted Red Line thus ····· indicates same thing during the height of the rainy season.

The Edinburgh Geographical Institute

before the rains, registering occasionally temperatures as high as 118° in the shade, though at night time falling to 85°, thus rendering it possible to live. In the height of the rainy season the range of the thermometer is not so high, but the heat is often more unbearable owing to its greater uniformity and the moistness of the temperature. In the months of January, February, and March the thermometer may be 100° in the daytime and only fall to 85° or 90° at night.

A MOUNTAIN STREAM IN CENTRAL AFRICA

But on the high plateaux and amongst the mountains—and these high districts after all represent the bulk of our territory—the temperature is at all times much more tolerable. Such a place as Zomba[1] for instance may be taken as a fair sample of the British Central Africa climate. Here during the cold season from May till September we have a day temperature not exceeding 75° and a night temperature ranging from 40° to 60°. In the months of September,

[1] Altitude 3000 feet above the sea.

October, November the day temperature may rise to 98° and fall at night to 65°. During the height of the rainy season the day temperature ranges from 75° to 95° and the night from 65° to 80°.

In the rainy season the wind usually blows from a northerly direction and is what one may call a benign wind, being warm and wet. During the dry season the cursed south-easter prevails. This hated wind comes up from the South Pole and is cold and dry. It is the equivalent of our east wind in England and produces much the same effects on health when it blows strongly. In the excessively dry months of September, October, and November this wind blowing across large areas of burnt plain—where the bush fires have destroyed the vegetation and the sun has baked the soil—has a bad effect on cultivated crops. It seres the leaves and causes many delicate plants to wither. Happily it soon loses its effect by passing over the mountains which are always attended by watery vapour. When the south wind prevails there is a curious mistiness in the atmosphere. This is partly caused by the diffused smoke of the bush fires, but it is also due to some other causes not yet explained. At this time of the year mists often prevail to a striking extent in the early morning. These are similar to the "smokes" which are so marked a feature in the dry season on the

FIRST VIEW OF MLANJE MOUNTAIN FROM LOWER SHIRE

West Coast of Africa. One understands how these dense fogs occur on any large river or lake, for instance. The temperature of the water is much higher than that of the air in the early morning, and so one may see clouds and vapour rising from the water surface, just as though it were boiling, and these gradually form low dense fogs which, minus the addition of smoke, are quite as thick as those we are accustomed to in the Thames Valley, which no doubt arise from the same cause.

One of the accompanying maps will give some idea of the distribution of the rainfall, and the names, length, and navigability of the more important streams. It might be mentioned that almost all the streams given in this map are perennial as far as our knowledge of them goes. Another map gives the relative height of the land and the names and altitudes of the principal mountain ranges. Only a few of these latter require special mention. So far as we yet know the highest mountain in British Central Africa is Mlanje, at its extreme south-eastern corner. Mlanje consists of a huge plateau from which again rise mountain peaks representing ancient volcanoes. It reaches at its highest point an altitude of 9683 feet. The summit was scaled by Mr Sharpe and Captain Manning in 1895. Much of the up-reared mass, which is about 200 square miles in area, exceeds an altitude of 6000 feet and is eminently habitable. The Shire Highlands—or the district between the Ruo, the Shire

ON THE UPPER RUO

and Lake Chilwa—are a mass of beautiful hills ranging from 3000 feet to nearly 7000 feet in height. The highest mountain in the Shire Highlands is Mount Zomba. This is a smaller mass than Mlanje but very similar to it in shape and arrangement. Like Mlanje it is a large plateau but its higher peaks are rather the up-reared edges of the plateau (like the rim of a dish) than independent cones that rise from the centre. The highest point of Zomba is computed to attain an altitude of 6900 odd feet. It may turn out on more careful investigation to actually reach 7000 feet. In Southern Angoniland, in the south-western portion of the Protectorate, Mount Dedza is computed at 7000 feet and other high mountains like Chongoni are not far off in altitude. In the mountains to the west of Lake Nyasa the higher peaks of the lofty Nyika plateau reach to over 8000 feet in height. The average altitude of the Nyika plateau is 7000 feet. One or two points on the Nyasa-Tanganyika plateau may touch 7000 feet and likewise in the northern part of the Muchinga (Lukinga) mountains west of the river Luangwa. Elsewhere

THE MLANJE RANGE FROM THE TUCHILA PLAIN

in British Central Africa, in the basin of the Kafue and Lunsefwa rivers, and to the west of Lake Bangweolo there is probably no greater altitude than 6000 feet.

Although they are not in British territory and therefore not within the scope of this book, a passing mention should be made of the Livingstone Mountains which border the north-east coast of Lake Nyasa and extend under various names to the south end of Lake Rukwa. They reach to altitudes which possibly slightly exceed that of Mlanje and come very near to 10,000 feet.

This is pre-eminently a country of great lakes. Lake Tanganyika is over 400 miles in length with a breadth varying from 60 to 30 miles. Lake Nyasa is 360 miles long with a greatest breadth of 40 miles and a least breadth of 15. Lake Bangweolo[1] is of such uncertain area that it is useless to give any guess at the

[1] The name of Bangweolo is quite unknown to the natives, and must have been given by Livingstone under some misapprehension. By the surrounding peoples it is known as "Liemba," or "Mweru," or "Nyanja": more often as "Mweru." Mr. Alfred Sharpe conjectures that the name "Bangweolo" may have arisen from the combination of "Pa-mweru" or "Pa-mwelu" ("r" and "l" are interchangeable in most African dialects) meaning "at Mweru." The natives are very much addicted to prefixing the locative prefix "Pa" to names of places. In the same way Livingstone

mileage of its open surface but it must contain at least 1500 square miles of navigable water. Lake Mweru is about 68 miles long by 24 broad. Lake Chilwa in the extreme south-east is also of varying extent according to the rainy season or dry season; but it is as a rule about 50 miles long by 15 broad. The salt lake Mweru which lies between the great Mweru Lake and Tanganyika is chiefly a marsh with a few open pools about 35 miles long by 20 broad. North of Lake Chilwa and separated from it by only a few miles of sandy ridge is Lake Chiuta, the source of the river Lujenda. Chiuta is about 40 miles long with a breadth which nowhere exceeds eight miles and sometimes shrinks to two. In the Lubisa country to the west of the

CHAMBI PEAK, MLANJE

Luangwa there is a small mountain lakelet about 40 square miles in area, which was called Lake Moir by its discoverer, Mr. Joseph Thomson. Lastly, may be mentioned Lake Malombe through which the Upper Shire flows. This lake had an area in 1893 of about 100 square miles; but in 1894 and in the succeeding years a large sand island grew up in the centre which became covered with reeds, and the lake as I last saw it was little more than a broad channel of the Shire divided by an enormous, flat, reed-covered island from a narrower channel or back-water to the west. There is every sign that in spite of the great rise in Lake Nyasa this island will hold its own. We shall then witness the remarkable

himself called the lakelet Malombe, "Pa-Malombe." The root "-*eru*," or "-*elu*," is a very old Bantu word for "open water." With a different prefix it reappears far to the North as "Rueru," one of the native names of the Albert Nyanza. It would seem to be connected with the root "white." It might be mentioned, however, that Mr. Poulett Weatherley appears to have heard the name "Bangweulu" in use.

MAP SHOWING OROGRAPHICAL FEATURES IN BRITISH CENTRAL AFRICA & ADJOINING COUNTRIES

Compiled from data supplied by Sir H. H. Johnston, K.C.B.

fact that in a little more than a year a lake which has existed beyond the memory of man has suddenly been resolved into a sandy marsh and a broad river channel.

I think I have enumerated all the known permanent lakes of the country, though I should not be surprised if travellers who read this book came forward and said, "You have forgotten such and such a lake in the Chambezi Valley, or the small lakelet between Chilwa and Mlanje, or the great sheet of open water on the Upper Tuchila, or such and such a lake in the Luangwa Basin." None of these sheets of water, however, as far as is yet known, have any permanent existence. They are only the creation of the rainy season floods. Seen at that time, of course, their existence is recorded; in the dry season they would be found either not to exist at all or to be confined to a patch of marsh. There were lakes at one time, undoubtedly, near the junction of the Ruo and the Shire (the Elephant Marsh) and at the junction of the Shire and Zambezi (Morambala Marsh); but in the course of time the alluvium of the rivers, together, even,

THE LIKUBULA GORGE, MLANJE

with a slight upheaval of the ground, or more probably still the deeper cutting of the river-channel have turned these former lakes into marshes or vast extents of dry alluvial soil. In like manner Nyasa was evidently united not many centuries ago with Lake Malombe; and it may be, also, that Lake Chilwa was joined with Lake Chiuta and was then the head waters of the great Lujenda-Ruvuma river. Much of the decrease in volume of the great lakes must be attributed to a slow and slight process of upheaval which has caused their waters to more rapidly drain away; but the disappearance of these shallow lakes along the courses of the rivers is chiefly due to the rivers having in course of time cut their channels deeper, so that the lakes which formerly represented their overflow have their bottoms now removed even above flood limit.

The geology of British Central Africa would appear to be relatively simple. The commonest formation, perhaps, is a mixture of metamorphic rocks, *grauwacke*, clay-slates, gneiss and schists. This prevails over much of the country lying between the west of Lake Nyasa and the Luapula River, on the Nyasa-Tanganyika plateau, in parts of the Shire Highlands, and north of the Zambezi. The valleys of the great and sluggish rivers, however, (the Shire, the Chambezi, the Luangwa) contain an upper stratum of alluvial deposit where the valleys are broad and the rocks do not strike through. The principal mountain ranges are mostly granite; and granite with its upper layers often rotten and even turned into red ferruginous clay constitutes the formation of much of the Shire Highlands. There is an outcrop of sandstone on the north-west and north-east coasts of Lake Nyasa (Mount Waller and the hills of Amelia Bay are examples); a little way back from the lake shore at the north end (in German territory); to the west of the River Shire near the Portuguese frontier; at the south end of Tanganyika; and all round about Lake Mweru and in the countries adjoining the River Luapula. Volcanic lavas and tuffs are present on parts of the upper plateau of Mlanje and at the north end of Lake

ON LAKE NYASA

Nyasa. There is a good deal of quartz in the mountains to the west of Lake Nyasa, especially to the south-west, and in parts of the Shire Highlands (such as Mlanje). The low flat hills in the Upper Shire district are composed of marble which yields a very good building lime. Much the same lime is also obtained from places on the west coast of Lake Nyasa, where there must be likewise a kind of limestone amongst the low hills near the lake shore. The surface of much of the low-lying country on the banks of the Upper Shire is little else than a deposit of the shells of molluscs mixed with black vegetable earth.

This black "cotton" soil, which is usually extremely rich for cultivation, and is so much valued in India, is found plentifully in many stream valleys and depressions, especially in the Nyasaland provinces, and is classed by me as alluvium.

On the east coast of Lake Nyasa, a few miles inland from Msumbo and Chisanga (Stations of the Universities Mission), a soap stone has been found by

Commander Cullen, R.N.R.,[1] who had noticed that the natives made use of this stone in building the mission church at Chisanga. This soap stone, according to Commander Cullen, is the same as that found in parts of Europe and used as a lubricant packing by engineers. When prepared for this purpose it is worth £8 a ton. It is quite easily worked, can be cut with a knife, and is not much—if at all—affected by weather.

In the sandstone formation of the West Shire district and round the northern half of Lake Nyasa, coal is found. On the surface it is a little shaley, but there

THE LICHENYA RIVER, MLANJE

is evidence that good combustible coal lies underneath. In the Marimba and Central Angoniland districts, also in the mountains of the West Nyasa coast region, and in parts of the Shire Highlands, a gold-bearing quartz exists.[2] Alluvial gold is reported to exist on the Northern Angoni plateau, in the West Nyasa district, and at the head-waters of the River Bua (Central Angoniland), just within the Protectorate. In the valleys of the rivers flowing south to the Zambezi (in Mpezeni's country) gold really does exist, and was worked at Misale by the half-caste Portuguese in the last, and in part of the present century. Although there are many reports that payable gold has been found in

[1] Senior Naval Officer in the service of the B.C.A. Administration.
[2] Between Nkata Bay and Sisya. The reef here is said to have slate walls.

the rock, which only needs the requisite machinery to crush out, at anything from 10 dwts. to 1 oz. per ton, no conclusive evidence has yet been offered to support these statements by specimens which can be submitted to analysis. In 1889, however, long before Europeans turned their eyes in this direction, the old Jumbe of Kotakota told me that the quartz in his country contained gold, and

THE SHIRE HIGHLANDS

soon afterwards he entered into an agreement with the African Lakes Company that this gold should be worked. The Lakes Company turned over their agreement to the British South Africa Company, on whose account prospectors have entered the Marimba district.

Specimens of something very like cinnabar were once submitted to Mr. Sharpe and myself for examination. They came from the country to the west of the Lower Shire. We attempted an analysis but although there seemed to be traces of mercury in the pan we could not authoritatively state that the substance was cinnabar. Since that time no further specimens have reached us. It is beyond dispute that the country of Katanga is rich in copper and also possesses gold. The copper of Katanga, however, is widely spread in a currency of ingots over South Central Africa. Malachite also comes from that region. There is no reason why this copper should not also be found in the same formation to the east of the river Luapula and Lake Mweru.

Specimens of lead and of graphite have been shown to me, but I was unable to identify the districts from which they were obtained, though I understood that some specimens of graphite came from the hills to the west of the Lower Shire.

Iron ore is nearly everywhere abundant. Excellent hæmatite iron comes from the Upper Shire district. We have actually used some of this iron—have had it smelted and worked by native blacksmiths—for making the parts of a gun and such other relatively simple things which were within the scope of native blacksmiths or Sikh artizans.

Garnets are found in the stream valleys of Mlanje. On the same mountain beautiful quartz crystals are met with and persons seeing them for the first time are often deluded into the belief that they have obtained diamonds. No trace of the blue diamond clay has ever yet been met with in Central Africa.[1]

There are no deposits of rock-salt, so far as I am aware, but salt is obtained from the brackish marsh called by the name of Mweru which lies between the great lake Mweru and Tanganyika; also from the marsh country in the West Shire district, and from the brackish Lake Chilwa.[2]

But salt is also obtained both good and abundant—though rather dark in colour—from the ashes of grasses and other plants growing on the mountain plateaux and in the vicinity of rivers and lakes. On the whole, in one way or another British Central Africa may be considered to be well supplied with salt manufactured by the natives, which is a favourite article of commerce and is even a good deal used by Europeans, who in their cooking, if not on their tables, at any rate in their kitchens, use it in preference to the imported article.

[1] Commander Cullen supplies the following note:—"In the upper waters of the Lintipe river (Central Angoniland) the formation is the same as that of the Vaal River Valley: and as garnets and crystals are found in it, if it were properly worked it seems probable it might prove diamondiferous."

[2] Mr. Sharpe describes as follows the way in which the natives extract salt from the Mweru swamp:—"The natives dwelling round the great Mweru salt swamp take the salt-impregnated earth round the lake shore and put it into funnels made of closely woven grass rope. They then pour in water and stir up the salt earth. The water takes up the salt and filtering through the grass funnel, carries the salt in solution into pots placed below. The water is then evaporated and cakes of pure salt are left."

APPENDIX

THE COAL OF NYASALAND

Report by the Director of the Scientific Department of the Imperial Institute on two samples of coal from Nyasaland, received through Mr. P. L. Sclater, F.R.S., from Mr. Alfred Sharpe, Acting Commissioner and Consul-General for British Central Africa:—

SPECIMEN A.—*Coal from North Nyasaland*—Fixed carbon, 57·63 %; ash, 15·57 %; volatile matter, 26·80 %; sulphur, 0·10 %; coke, 73·20 %; calorific value, 5520 units. This is a non-caking coal of very fine quality, which is likely to be useful for most purposes for which coal is employed. The percentage of ash is rather high, but the coal is remarkably free from sulphur.

SPECIMEN B.—*Supposed Coal from the Songwe River*—Fixed carbon, 47·46 %; ash, 8·4 %; volatile matter, 44·54; sulphur, 0·52; coke, 55·5; calorific value, 6050 units. This also is a non-caking coal of good quality, yielding very little ash, and containing but little sulphur. This coal would be serviceable either for heating or for metallurgical purposes. (Signed) WYNDHAM R. DUNSTAN.

CHAPTER III.

HISTORY

BRITISH CENTRAL AFRICA only comes within the domain of written history quite recently, Tanganyika and much of Nyasa scarcely forty years ago. It is just barely possible that the south end of Lake Nyasa, and it is certain that a portion of the river Shire which flows from it, were known to the Portuguese explorers at the latter end of the sixteenth century. The unwritten history, the history which can be deduced from researches into language, examinations of racial type, native traditions, and archæological researches, extends back into the usual remoteness connected with the movements of the human genus, though in no part of the world is it so indefinite or is there such scanty and slight material on which to construct theories.

It may be that something of this kind occurred. Until further facts come to light, the tendency of such little knowledge as we at present possess of the past history of the evolution of man is to lead us to believe that he was developed from the pithecoid type somewhere in Asia, not improbably in India.[1] It would seem, at any rate, as if the earliest known race of man, inhabiting what is now British Central Africa, was akin to the Bushman-Hottentot type of negro. Rounded stones, with a hole through the centre, similar to those which are used by the Bushmen in the south for weighting their digging sticks, have been found at the south end of Lake Tanganyika, and specimens of them were brought home thence by me and given to the British Museum. I have heard that other examples of these "Bushman" stones have been found nearer to Lake Nyasa, but I have not seen the alleged specimens. In one instance I alighted on a curious tradition, which would make it appear

---

[1] At any moment this theory, which at present holds the field, may be upset by unlooked-for discoveries in African palæontology. Quite recently a discovery of the most extraordinary importance and interest has been made by Dr. Forsyth Major in Madagascar, an island which was united to Africa in the early part of the tertiary epoch. This consists of the fossil remains of a monkey-like form called *Nesopithecus*, a form intermediate between the Cebidæ and the Old World monkeys. The Cebidæ are the American monkeys, a type which is connected with the Lemuroids by transitional forms. Mr. R. Lydekker deduces from these discoveries that the primal stock of the monkeys had its home in Africa; that from the African continent branched off the Cebidæ, which found their way to America, and there lingered, while they became extinguished in the Old World; and the Simiidæ, or Old World monkeys, which in turn gave rise to the anthropoid apes and man. So far as we yet know evidence preponderates in favour of the anthropoid apes having arisen in Southern Asia, whence they penetrated Africa; and the famous discovery by Dr. Dubois, in Java, of *Pithecanthropus erectus*, a form almost intermediate between the anthropoid ape and the human species, would lead us to imagine that man likewise originated in the Asiatic continent, which served as a distributing centre. The lowest known forms of man living at the present time, or only recently extinct, are found in Tasmania, Australia, South Eastern Asia, and Central and Southern Africa. At the same time further discoveries may equally well show that the development of the anthropoid ape into man took place in Africa, a guess once hazarded by Darwin.

that until recently the Bushman type was lingering on the upper plateau of the Mlanje mountain mass at the south-east corner of the Protectorate. The Mañanja natives of that district assert positively that there used to live on the upper part of the mountain, a dwarf race of light yellow complexion with hair growing in scattered tufts, and with that large development of the buttocks characteristic of the Bushman-Hottentot type. They gave these people a specific name, "Arungu," but I confess that this term inspired me with some distrust of the value of their tradition, as it was identical with the word for "gods."[1] The resemblance, however, may have been accidental. They declare this people to have been found on the top of Mlanje until quite recently. Similar rumours were collected by a Portuguese officer stationed at Mlanje, and by him communicated to me, quite independently of my own researches, and the same idea occurred to him as to myself, that the traditions referred to a Bushman type. I have at different times exhaustively searched, or caused to be searched, the upper parts of the Mlanje mountain; but although traces of human residence in some of the caves have been reported, no definite proof of the existence of any people differing from the modern type was discovered. That is to say, traces of human habitation in those caves and hollows consisted chiefly of fragments of pottery, which is certainly not a characteristic sign of Bushman habitation. It is probably known to my readers, however, that real undisputed Bushmen are found (I have seen them myself) in South Western Africa, in the same latitudes as the southern part of the British Protectorate under review. Bushman tribes were discovered by Serpa Pinto and other explorers as far north almost as the 14th parallel south latitude, in the countries near the Upper Kunene river.

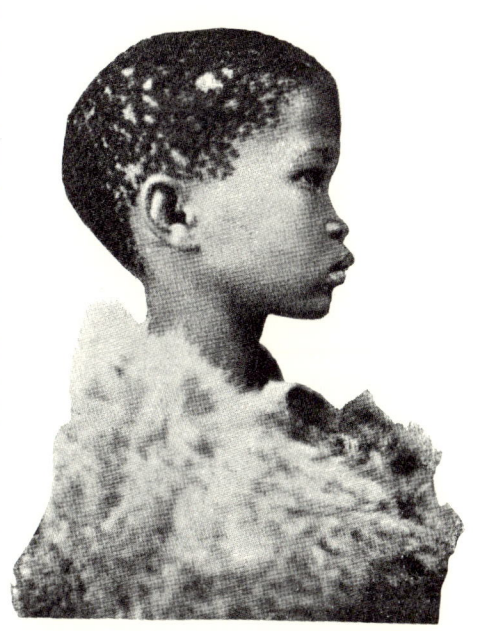

PORTRAIT OF A YOUNG BUSHMAN

Here and there, in Nyasaland, one meets with faces and forms amongst the natives which suggest a cropping out of the Hottentot type, as though the present Bantu races had, on their first invasion of these countries, absorbed their Bushman predecessors by intermarriage. This Bushman-Hottentot mixture, however, is not nearly so apparent as it is in the Basuto and certain Kafir tribes of South Africa. Indeed when South African negroes come to Nyasaland for work and one is able to contrast them with the local natives, one is struck at once by the resemblance they offer to Hottentots, in their paler skins, more prominent cheek bones, deep set eyes and flattened nose. It is evident that the Basuto-Bechuana people especially have much mingled with the Hottentots in times past. It would seem from the researches of Mr. Theodore Bent in the ruined cities of

---

[1] Murungu=a god. A-rungu=gods. Yet this is not the ordinary plural which is Mi-lungu or Mi-rungu, though it is A-rungu in the more northern dialects.

Mashonaland that those earlier settlers from Southern Arabia, who mined for gold some two thousand years ago and less, in South Central Africa, were only acquainted with native inhabitants of a Bushman-Hottentot type, to judge by the drawings, engravings and models they have left, intended to depict natives engaged in the chase.

The evidence which I have quoted at length in my book on Kilimanjaro,[1] and in the prefatory chapters to the *Life of Livingstone*, derived from a comparative study of the Bantu languages, leads me to believe that the invasion of the southern half of Africa by big black negro races, nowadays so familiar to us, was relatively recent in the history of man—perhaps not much more than 2000 years ago. Some cause, such as the dense forests of the Congo Basin, must have checked their descent of the continent from the Sudan. They may also have been held back for a long time—especially on the eastern side of the continent where the forests could never have been in recent times a serious obstacle—by the sturdy opposition of the prior inhabitants of Bushman-Hottentot type. Be that as it may, I do not think the black negroes, the present inhabitants of South Central Africa, have been in possession of those countries from time immemorial, and in their own traditions they vaguely recall a descent from the North.

It is possible that when the Sabæans and Arabs traded with South-east Africa, during the first half of the Christian era, one or another of them may have penetrated into the countries round Lake Nyasa. With this proviso, however, as to the possibility of such a journey having taken place, it must be stated that as far as we know, the Arabs did little more in regard to British Central Africa than to settle on the coast of the Indian Ocean, or to establish a trading depôt at Sena, on the Lower Zambezi.

It would seem to me as though 3000 years ago the distribution of races in Africa had stood thus. The southern half of the continent, from a little north of the Equator to the Cape of Good Hope, was very sparsely populated with a low Negroid type, of which the Bushmen and Hottentots, and possibly the pigmy tribes of the Congo forests,[2] are the descendants. The North and North-east of Africa, from Morocco to Egypt and Egypt to Somaliland, was peopled mainly by the Hamites, a race akin in origin and language to the Semitic type, which latter was certainly a higher development from a parent Hamitic stock. The Hamites themselves, however, obviously originated as a superior ascending variety of the Negritic species, from which basal stock had been derived in still earlier times the Bushman-Hottentot group, whose languages—especially that of the Hottentot—are thought by some authorities to show remote affinities in structure to the Hamitic tongues. Westward of the Hamites, and an earlier divergence from the original Negritic group, were the true black negroes, more closely allied in origin perhaps to the Bushmen-Hottentots than to the more divergent Hamites. But 3000 years ago, I am inclined to believe that the true negroes were bounded in their distribution by the northern limits of the Sahara Desert, the Atlantic Ocean, the great forests of the Congo Basin, and either the Nile Valley or the Abyssinian Highlands on the East. Here and there these different sections of the Negritic stock mingled, producing races superior to the pure negro, like the Nubians, the Somalis, and the Fulbe, which dwell more or less on the borderland between the negro and the Hamite. When the true negroes invaded the southern half

---

[1] *The Kilimanjaro Expedition*, pp. 478-483.
[2] These latter much mixed I am sure with the black negroes.

HISTORY

of the African continent, some 2000 to 3000 years ago, they carried with them such culture, domestic animals, and cultivated plants as they had derived indirectly from Egypt. I should think that in Nyasaland and along the shores of Lake Tanganyika, the history of negro culture has been retrograde, until the coming of the Arab and the European. In one or two places on the shores of Lake Nyasa old pottery has been dug up at a considerable depth below the surface, with trees of great girth and age growing over these remains. The pottery has been found imbedded in the sand of an ancient shore-line of Nyasa, now covered by about 5 feet of humus, in which baobab trees are strongly rooted. From the approximate age of the trees, and the time it should have taken to accumulate this vegetable soil, some of this pottery must have been 500 or 600 years old. One large pot thus found has been deposited by me in the British Museum. These few remains exhibit evidences of greater skill and taste than is shown by the pottery at the present time in the same districts. Researches founded on the study of languages, of religions, of traditions, and on the records of Portuguese explorers in West Africa, would also seem to show that in Western Africa many of the negro States were in a far higher state of culture 500 years ago than they are now.

The line of the migration of the Bantu negroes in British Central Africa will be treated of in Chapter XI., which describes their languages. It will be sufficient to say, as regards history, that we may presume them to have entered into possession of these countries—driving out or absorbing the antecedent Bushman race—about 1000 years ago.

With the doubtful exception of the visit of an occasional Arab slave dealer, they had no contact with the outer world until the arrival of the Portuguese on the East Coast of Africa, which is the first definite landmark in the history of this portion of the continent. Vasco da Gama, after rounding the Cape of Good Hope in 1495, stopped at the Arab settlements of Sofala (near the modern Beira) and Moçambique, and thence passed onwards to Malindi (near Mombasa) and India. On his return from India he further explored the South-east Coast of Africa, and (probably from information given by Arab pilots) entered with his little fleet the Quelimane River,[1] which was connected intermittently with the main Zambezi, and which, until the other day, was thought to be the only certain means of reaching the Zambezi above its delta. This river he called the "Rio dos Bons Signaes," or the "River of Good Indications." The name "Quelimane," which he applied to a small village 12 miles inland from the mouth of the river (the origin of the now important town of Quelimane, the capital of Portuguese Zambezia) is stated by the Portuguese to have the following etymology. This village belonged to a certain individual who acted as interpreter between the Portuguese and the natives. He appears to have been an Arab, or a half Arab. In those days Portuguese navigators seem to have been acquainted with Arabic, a language which probably still lingered in the southern part of Portugal, where Moorish kingdoms existed till the twelfth century. The name which the Portuguese applied to this individual was "Quelimane" (pronounced Kelimān). Now in the corrupt Coast Arabic "Kalimān" is the word for "Interpreter."[2] Consequently the name of the modern town Quelimane[3] is simply derived

---

[1] On Jan. 22nd, 1498.   [2] In Swahili this becomes Mkalimani.
[3] I have taken the opportunity to give this bit of etymology as there has long been a misapprehension as to the correct spelling of Quelimane, which was thought wrongly to be derived from "Kilimani," which means in Swahili "on the hill." But there is no hill within eighty miles of Quelimane. The true native name of this place is "Chuabo."

from the term "Interpreter," applied to this guide and go-between of Vasco da Gama.

For some five centuries before the Portuguese arrived the Arabs of Southern and Eastern Arabia had formed or re-formed settlements along the East Coast of Africa from Somaliland to Sofala.[1] In the direction of British Central Africa they were chiefly established at Moçambique, Ngoji (Angoche), and Sena on the Zambezi. They apparently found no direct entrance into the Zambezi River which could be easily navigated by their daus, and preferred to use the Quelimane River. This in exceptional rainy seasons at the present day becomes connected with the Zambezi river, by overflow creeks; and possibly some centuries ago was the most northern branch of the delta. The Arabs would seem, therefore, to have gone up this river past Quelimane, and then to have travelled either by water when the river was full, or overland at other seasons, to Sena, a settlement not far from the junction of the Zambezi and the Shire. From Sena again they had overland communication to their settlements at Sofala, near the modern town of Beira.[2]

At first the Portuguese were received by the Arabs in a friendly fashion, and several of the Portuguese were taken up by Arab guides from Quelimane to Sena. Before many years[3] were over the Portuguese had dispossessed the Arabs, and driven them away. From Sofala to Moçambique they replaced them so completely, with the exception of their settlements at Angoche,[4] that they disappeared entirely and never returned, even after the temporary decay of the Portuguese power which enabled the Arabs to reconquer the East Coast of Africa as far south as Kilwa.

At first Sena, on the Lower Zambezi, was the headquarters of the Portuguese Administration, and from hence various expeditions, during the sixteenth century, were sent southwards to discover the gold mines of Manika—expeditions which were mostly unsuccessful, owing to the unhealthiness of the climate and the presence of the Tsetse fly. Another obstacle in the way of Portuguese enterprise was the kingdom of Monomotapa,[5] a powerful empire of Bantu negroes, probably related in stock to the Zulus. The influence of Monomotapa must have ranged from the vicinity of the south end of Lake Nyasa to the Limpopo River. Simultaneously with the first Portuguese "Conquistadores"

---

[1] I say "re-formed" because we are now practically certain that some races of Southern Arabia had founded their ancient settlements—possibly in connection with the Phœnicians—in South-eastern Africa, not only on the East Coast but far in the interior of Mashonaland. These settlements were, it is supposed, destroyed by the advent of the Bantu tribes from the North, who were far more formidable enemies to tackle than the feeble Bushmen and Hottentots. It is possible that the natives of Arabia did not entirely give up their African trade, though they had to quit the interior and confine their settlements to the coast. But whether or no there was a gap in Arab enterprise in the early part of the Christian era, there was a great revival in the tenth century, and in the eleventh century a strong Arab kingdom was formed at Kilwa (midway between Zanzibar and Moçambique) which exercised a kind of suzerainty over the other settlements or Sultanates. Mosques were built at this period, the remains of which may be seen at the present day.

[2] Beira was the name given to this place not many years ago by the Portuguese, when it was first founded, after Col. Paiva d'Andrada's explorations of the Pungwe river. "Beira" is the name of one of the principal provinces of Portugal, and the eldest son of the heir to the throne of Portugal always bears the title of "Principe da Beira." Beira is pronounced "Bay-ra" in Portuguese. Consequently, with their usual perversity, the English people have decided to call it "By-ra," for it is one of our national peculiarities to devote all our best energy to a mispronunciation of foreign words.

[3] I believe the Arabs remained in possession of Sena until near the end of the sixteenth century.

[4] Which really remain unconquered to this day.

[5] This name was derived from the native appellation of the Makaranga chief, and is apparently a corruption of "Mwene Mutapa"="Lord Hippopotamus"; or "Mwana-Mutapa"—"Child of the Hippopotamus." The hippopotamus was much reverenced by the tribes of the Central Zambezi, and is so, to some extent, still.

HISTORY

and mining adventurers came lion-hearted Jesuit Missionaries, resolved on repeating in the Zambezi countries the successes they had obtained in Christianising the kingdom of the Congo. Several of these men were martyred by the orders of the Emperor of Monomotapa; but eventually they established themselves at Zumbo, on the Central Zambezi, at the confluence of the great Luangwa River.

The modern capital of Tete,[1] which is the most important town on the Zambezi, was not founded until the middle of the seventeenth century, and was merely a station of Jesuit Missionaries originally, though afterwards taken over by the Portuguese Government. At first, however, the principal towns were Zumbo and Sena.

GOVERNOR'S HOUSE, TETE

The Portuguese soon penetrated northward of the Zambezi, in the direction of the Maravi country and the watershed of Lake Nyasa. Here they discovered, or re-discovered, from hints given by Arabs or natives, the gold deposits of Misale,[2] and for some century or so afterwards these gold mines were extensively worked. Curiously enough, however, the chief mineral discoveries of the Portuguese at this time lay in the direction of silver, though at the present time we have no knowledge of any existing silver mines in the Zambezi countries.

In 1616 a Portuguese, named Jaspar Bocarro, offered to carry samples of Zambezi silver overland from the Central Zambezi to Malindi, a Portuguese settlement to the north of Mombasa, without going near Moçambique. The

---

[1] Tete is the name for a reed. The plural "Matete" means "a reed-bed." It is possible that this was the etymology of the name, as the shore is very reedy about that part of the Zambezi. But the native name of Tete is "Nyungwi."

[2] Nowadays Misale lies within the British sphere of influence, and a British company is attempting to work its gold.

THE ISLAND OF MOÇAMBIQUE, SEEN FROM THE MAINLAND

motive of this offer lay in the fact that considerable friction existed between the Central Government of Moçambique, which was under the Viceroys of India, and the Portuguese adventurers on the Zambezi, who strongly objected to the grinding monopolies which the Moçambique Government sought to establish. Jaspar Bocarro apparently journeyed from where the town of Tete now stands to the Upper Shire River, crossing that stream near its junction with the Ruo; and then, passing through the Anguru country in the vicinity of Lake Chilwa, he entered the Lujenda Valley, and so travelled on to the Ruvuma River, and thence to the coast at Mikindani. From Mikindani he continued his journey to Malindi by sea. So far as reliable records go, this was the first European to enter what is now styled "British Central Africa."

The Jesuit priests from Zumbo had journeyed westward into the country of the Batonga or Batoka,[1] and northwards up the Luangwa River. They

---

[1] Sir John Kirk, when travelling with Livingstone, in 1859, discovered groves of fruit trees in the Batoka country which may have been introduced by the Jesuits.

HISTORY

transmitted rumours of a great lake (Nyasa), which they styled Lake "Maravi." This really meant "a lake in the country of the Maravi," Maravi being an old name (now nearly extinct) of the Nyanja tribes in the south-west of Nyasaland. But in the middle of the eighteenth century the Jesuits were expelled from all the Portuguese Dominions by order of the Marquez de Pombal; and after their departure from the Central Zambezi there was a temporary diminution of Portuguese activity. At the very end of the last century, however, the interest of the Portuguese Government in its East African possessions was revived by the British Government having taken possession of the Cape of Good Hope at the outbreak of the war with France. In the year following the seizure of Cape Town[1] by an English force, Dr. Francisco José Maria de Lacerda e Almeida, a distinguished scientific man who was a native of Brazil, and a Doctor of Mathematics at Coimbra University (Portugal), addressed a very remarkable letter to the Portuguese Government, setting forth that the results of the English invasion of Capetown would be the creation of a great British South African Empire, which would, if not counteracted in time, spread northwards across the Zambezi, and separate the Portuguese Dominions of Angola and Moçambique. This, I think, at the period and with the limited geographical knowledge then possessed by even a Portuguese University, was one of the most remarkable instances of political foresight which can be quoted. The Portuguese Government was so struck with Dr. Lacerda's arguments that it appointed him Governor of the Rios de Sena,[2] and authorised him to conduct an expedition "á contra-costa"—across Africa from the Zambezi countries to Angola, establishing Portuguese Suzerainty along his route.

It should be stated at this juncture that not nearly so many white Portuguese had assisted in opening up the East African territories, as had settled in Angola, and on the West Coast of Africa. In those days the Portuguese East African possessions were generally knit up with their Viceroyalty of India, and the pure-blooded Portuguese in the Zambezi countries were few in number compared to the "Canarins" or Canarese. These people were half-caste natives of Goa, with more or less Indian blood in their veins, and constituted the principal element in the Portuguese Zambezi settlements. They were very enterprising men, though they relapsed into semi-savagery, and as slave-traders and robbers had a record almost more evil than that of the Arabs. Nevertheless the European blood in their veins sharply distinguished these Goanese from the unlettered black people, and of some of their journeys they kept more or less intelligent records. Two Goanese of the name of Pereira, father and son, had gone gold hunting to the north of the Zambezi, and had eventually pushed on with their armed slaves till they reached the Kazembe's country, near Lake Mweru. The reports which they gave of the Kazembe (a lieutenant or satrap of the Muata Yanvo of Lunda) decided Dr. Lacerda to proceed thither on his way across to Angola. His expedition numbered about 75 white Portuguese, and the two Pereiras accompanied it as guides. Dr. Lacerda, however, only succeeded in reaching Kazembe's capital, near the south end of Lake Mweru, and eventually died there on the 18th October, 1798. After his death the expedition became so disorganised that instead of continuing the journey to Angola it returned to Tete.

At the beginning of the present century two half-caste Portuguese, named Baptista and Amaro José, crossed from the Kwango River in the interior

[1] Which took place in 1795.   [2] The old name for the Zambezi.

of Angola to the Kazembe's country, near Lake Mweru, and thence to Tete on the Zambezi. In 1831 Major Monteiro and Captain Gamitto conducted a mission from Tete to the Kazembe, and some years subsequently Silva Porto, a Portuguese colonist, of Bihe, in the interior of Benguela, is also said to have rambled over much of South Central Africa; further, a certain Candido de Costa Cardoso claimed that he sighted the south-west corner of Lake Nyasa in 1846; but none of these explorers, with the exception of Dr. Lacerda, possessed any scientific qualifications, and their journeys led to little or no geographical information or political ascendancy. Indeed, what is remarkable about Dr. Lacerda, to say nothing of the other explorers, was the extraordinary bad luck which prevented him from sighting any important river or lake. He reached a point within a few miles of the large Lake Mweru, and yet either never saw it, or thought it not worth mention. He heard vague rumours of Tanganyika and of Nyasa, but did not direct his steps in either direction; and, stranger still, he missed the recognition of the remarkable Luapula, which we now know to be the Upper Congo, though he must have actually been within sight of it.

The real history of British Central Africa begins with the advent of Livingstone. This intrepid missionary had gradually pushed his explorations northwards from the Cape of Good Hope until he reached the Central Zambezi in 1851, accompanied by the celebrated sportsman Mr. Oswell. Impressed with the importance of his discovery Livingstone returned to Cape Town, and with the generous assistance of Mr. Oswell, was enabled not only to send his wife and children out of harm's way, but to equip himself for the tremendous exploration of South Central Africa, which he had determined to accomplish. Having perfected himself in astronomical observations, under the tuition of the Astronomer-Royal of Cape Town, Livingstone started for the North and once more reached the Zambezi, near its confluence with the Chobe. Thence he travelled up the Zambezi to its source, and across to Angola and again back from Angola and down the Zambezi to its mouth, or more correctly speaking to Quelimane, on the Indian Ocean. This epoch-making journey had important and far-reaching results. Livingstone was sent back by the British Government at the head of a well-equipped expedition, and was accompanied amongst others by Dr., now Sir John, Kirk, who, besides being medical officer, was the naturalist of the expedition.

After a journey to Tete and visits to the "Quebrabaço" Rapids for the purpose of determining the navigability of the Zambezi above Tete, Livingstone determined to search for and find the reported great lake out of which the Shire[1] flowed to join the Zambezi. At this date the Portuguese knew scarcely anything of the Shire beyond its confluence with the Zambezi. They seem to have lost all remembrance of the one or two earlier journeys in that direction of Portuguese explorers. Consequently, before Livingstone and his party had ascended the Shire very far they found themselves in a country absolutely new to the white man. After several futile attempts to reach Lake Nyasa, in the course of one of which they discovered the brackish Lake Chilwa, which lies to the south-east of the greater lake, and Lake Malombe, which

[1] The name of the "Shire" river was formerly written by the Portuguese "Cherim" (pronounce, "Shĕrĭng"); this was later still written "Chire," which if the "ch" be pronounced as in "church" fairly represents the native pronunciation. But the Portuguese pronounce "ch" like "sh," therefore Livingstone heard them speak of this river as the "Shire," and thus transcribed it in English. The correct native pronunciation is "Chiri" (Cheeree), and the word means in Chinyanja "a steep bank"—Nyanja ya chiri, "the river with the steep banks."

HISTORY 61

is a widening of the Upper Shire, Livingstone and his companions finally reached the southern extremity of Nyasa, near the site of the modern settlement of Fort Johnston, on the 16th of September, 1859, the first white men, as far as we know with any certainty, who stood on the shores of Lake Nyasa. As the district in which Livingstone discovered this third greatest of the lakes of Africa was under Yao domination, he recorded its name as pronounced by the Yao, *i.e.* Nyasa; but its most common appellation is Nyanja. This is the same word as Nyanza farther north, and Nyasa, Nyanja, and Nyanza are derived from an archaic and widespread Bantu root -anza, which means "a broad water."[1]

Livingstone and his party extended their explorations of the western coast of Lake Nyasa as far north as about 11·30 south latitude, a little more than

THE POINT ON THE SOUTH SHORE OF LAKE NYASA WHENCE THE LAKE WAS FIRST SEEN
BY DR. LIVINGSTONE AND SIR JOHN KIRK IN 1859

half-way up the lake. Subsequently Livingstone travelled inland west of Lake Nyasa till he reached the watershed of the great Luangwa River, and it was upon hearing at that point of a not far distant lake that he resolved, on his succeeding journey, to proceed along the same route, and thus discovered the south end of Lake Tanganyika, Lake Mweru, the Luapula River, and Lake Bangweolo. Whilst Livingstone and Kirk were exploring Lake Nyasa and the Shire Highlands, however, they were joined by a Christian Mission under Bishop Mackenzie, which had been sent out from the two great English Universities, and which exists to this day under the name of the "Universities Mission to Central Africa." These missionaries settled in the eastern part of the Shire Highlands, just as the invasions of the Muhammadan Yao slave raiders were beginning.

[1] This root is found even among the more corrupt Bantu tongues of Western Equatorial Africa. For instance, the broad estuary of the Cameroons River is called in the Duala tongue "Muanza," and the same name is given to the Lower Congo.

Following on the Portuguese expeditions at the end of the 18th century to Kazembe's country, a great intercourse had sprung up between the Babisa tribe, which inhabits the district to the west of the great Luangwa River and the Zanzibar coast. The Babisa had acquired guns from the Portuguese, and, armed in this way, had asserted themselves effectually against tribes still armed with the bow and spear. They became an enterprising people and resolved to trade directly with the Coast. Not liking the Portuguese, however, they preferred to journey farther north, and trafficked with the Arabs of Zanzibar. About this time the Zanzibar Sultanate was increasing gradually in power. It was an appanage of the Imamate of Maskat ('Omān), and already the Maskat Arabs (who had replaced the Portuguese in all the trading settlements of Eastern Africa, between the Ruvuma River and Somaliland) had begun to push their slave and ivory trading enterprises into the interior of Eastern Africa, especially in the direction of Tanganyika. Attracted, however, by the accounts which the Babisa caravans gave of the fertile country in which they dwelt, and struck with the docility of the slaves brought down by the Babisa from the Nyasa countries, certain Arabs accompanied the Babisa caravans back to their place of origin, which was, as I have said, the countries lying to the west of the great Luangwa River. The route they followed was from ports like Kilwa on the East Coast to Lake Nyasa thence across Nyasa and south-west or due west to the Lubisa country.

In the course of these journeys the Arabs became acquainted with that race of fine physical development and stubborn character, the Yao, who inhabit much of the high country lying between the Indian Ocean and Lake Nyasa. In the Yao they found willing confederates in the slave trade, and a people much inclined to Muhammadanism. Eventually the poor Babisa were attacked and enslaved by neighbouring tribes who had been armed by the Arabs, and their importance passed away. The Arabs and Yao between them began to dominate Nyasaland. Now the inhabitants of the bulk of Nyasaland proper, with the exception of its north-west portion, belonged in the main to what may be called the A-nyanja stock. These people who are referred to by Portuguese of an earlier date as the Amaravi, and who are of the same race as the indigenous inhabitants of the Zambezi Valley between Tete and Sena and of the whole course of the Shire, are of a singularly docile and peaceful disposition, devoted to agriculture and timid in warfare—a race consequently that is always falling under the domination of more powerful and energetic tribes. Before what may be called the Yao invasion of the Shire Highlands the Nyanja people had been oppressed by Zulu invaders coming from the south-west. The convulsions which had been taking place in Zululand in the early part of this century had resulted in a most curious recoil of the Zulu race on Central Africa. It is probably not many centuries since the forerunners of the Zulus swept down from Central Africa, from the region of the great lakes, across the Zambezi, into Southern Africa, driving themselves like a wedge through the earlier Bantu invaders, the ancestors of the Basuto-Bechuana, and further displacing and destroying the feebler Hottentot people. Now, however, with the Indian Ocean in front of them, and internal commotions and increase of population compelling them to find more space for settlement, sections of them began to turn their faces back towards the Zambezi. The foundations of the Matabele[1] kingdom were laid, and band after band of Zulus crossed the Zambezi about

---

[1] Or Amandabele, as it ought to be written but that we English love inaccuracy in pronunciation and spelling for its own sake. Matabele is the Se-chuana corruption of the Zulu "Amandabele."

1825-6, and in their raids and conquests almost penetrated as far as the southern shores of the Victoria Nyanza, whilst they were constantly heard of on the east coast of Tanganyika. In the west and south-west of Nyasaland they had founded kingdoms and enslaved the local inhabitants, when the Yao from the north-east hurled themselves on the fertile Shire districts. So that the unfortunate Nyanja people were caught between Zulu and Yao, and suffered greatly. The British missionaries and explorers, however, saw little of the Zulu raiders in those earlier days.[1] At the beginning of the "sixties" they were chiefly concerned with the Yao invasion. After in vain attempting to defend their Nyanja converts from the attacks of the Yao, the Universities Mission lost so many of its members from sickness, and was additionally so discouraged by the abandonment of Dr. Livingstone's schemes, that it withdrew from the country for a time. Livingstone and his Expedition were recalled by the British Government at the end of 1863, and quitted Zambezia in 1864.

The fact was that the British Government was at that time discouraged from any further work in the Zambezi countries by the following obstacles: the political opposition shown by the Portuguese;[2] the acknowledged sway of the Portuguese over the coast line which made it impossible to communicate with any British Possessions which might be founded in the interior; the unhealthiness of the coast lands; and the seeming absence of any easy way into the Zambezi River, all the known mouths of which were cursed with dangerous and shallow bars. The discovery of the Chinde mouth, which afterwards revolutionised the whole question, had not then been made; or, it may be, the Chinde branch of the Zambezi as an easily navigated river did not then exist, for there have evidently been great fluctuations in the Zambezi Delta with regard to the course taken by the principal body of its water.

Following on Livingstone's first journey across South Central Africa, a great interest had sprung up in France and Germany regarding the existence of the reported Central African lakes. The German Missionaries in the pay of the Church Missionary Society in East Africa, had discovered the snow mountains of Kenia and Kilimanjaro and had reported, from native information, the existence of the Victoria Nyanza, of Tanganyika and of Lake Nyasa. Foremost amongst the African explorers of that day, and, at the time, second in importance to Livingstone only, was a young lieutenant in the Indian Army—Richard Francis Burton—who, stationed at Aden, had attempted the exploration of Somaliland with a brother-officer named Speke. After some difficulty Burton had induced the Geographical Society and Her Majesty's Government to provide him with the funds for an expedition which would start from opposite Zanzibar to discover the great Central African lake or lakes. He chose Lieut. Speke as his companion, and together they discovered Lake Tanganyika, Speke afterwards being dispatched by Burton to look for the great lake of Ukerewe, which Speke declared with truth to be the main source of the Nile and which he named the Victoria Nyanza. Burton and Speke were the first Europeans to arrive on the shores of Lake Tanganyika. They explored its northern half, but not very much work was done in the way of

[1] Livingstone however came in contact with them when he explored the western shores of Lake Nyasa.
[2] But it must be distinctly stated that throughout the whole course of Livingstone's first and second Zambezi expeditions though the Portuguese Government may have viewed with distaste the interest evinced by England in the Zambezi and the interior of East Central Africa, the courtesy and kindness shown by the Portuguese authorities to Livingstone and the rest of his expedition were praiseworthy in the extreme. For particulars of this see my *Life of Livingstone*.

mapping beyond visiting the western shore and making a rough outline of the northern portion of the lake. Prior to Burton's journey, a young Frenchman started from Zanzibar for the same purpose, but had been murdered on the way to Tanganyika, and after Burton's expedition a German doctor, named Ernst Roscher, had set out for Lake Nyasa in the disguise of an Arab. He reached the eastern shore of the lake at a place called Lusewa, on the 19th November, 1859, two months after Livingstone's discovery. On his attempted return to the coast, however, he was murdered by the Yao, a murder which was to some extent avenged by the Sultan of Zanzibar, who brought influence to bear on the Yao chiefs to send the ostensible murderers to Zanzibar to be executed. Another German traveller of some celebrity, Baron von der Decken, who was the first systematic explorer of Kilimanjaro, had attempted to reach Lake Nyasa, but scarcely got half way.

Meantime Livingstone, after a year's sojourn in England, had managed to scrape together funds for another Central Africa exploration. He was very desirous of resuming his journeys in search of other lakes to the west of Lake Nyasa. Travelling by Bombay and Zanzibar he landed at Mikindani at the end of March, 1866. He was, I believe, the first explorer to attempt taking with him natives of India as guards or soldiers; but it must be confessed that although the employment of Indians in Central Africa has since proved very successful, the Muhammadan Sepoys who accompanied Livingstone turned out utter failures, and were eventually sent back from Mataka's, a town in the Yao country. Livingstone also tried to introduce the Indian buffalo, an experiment not repeated until my reintroduction of this animal from India in 1895. It is interesting to note that Livingstone's buffalos passed through the tsetse fly country, and, seemingly, were not affected by the bites of that insect, though they all subsequently died as the result of maltreatment at the hands of the Sepoys.

Livingstone again reached the shores of Lake Nyasa, at its south-eastern gulf, on the 8th of August, 1866; but being unable to cross without a dau he walked right round the southern end, and thence turned his steps northwards. At Marenga's town, near the south-west corner of Lake Nyasa, there were rumours of Angoni-Zulu raids, which greatly scared the coast-men of Livingstone's caravan, who consequently abandoned him here; and to excuse themselves at Zanzibar for their act of bad faith, they reported, with much corroborative detail, the death of Livingstone at the hands of the Angoni.

Livingstone, after the desertion of these coast-men (who were natives of the Comoro Islands) pursued his way northwards, and reached the great Luangwa river in December, 1866; on the 28th of January, 1867, he crossed the Chambezi river, which issues from the Bangweolo marshes, under the name of the Luapula, and is in reality the extreme Upper Congo. On the 1st of April he reached the south end of Lake Tanganyika, and for the time being, believed it to be a separate lake under the name of Liemba; on the 8th of November, 1867, he discovered Lake Mweru; on the 18th of July, 1868, Lake Bangweolo. Returning from Bangweolo, he journeyed with an Arab caravan from Kazembe's town near the south end of Lake Mweru, to the west shore of Tanganyika, which he crossed to Ujiji, reaching that place in March, 1869. After attempting in vain to organize a caravan for a journey round the north end of Lake Tanganyika he recrossed the lake to the opposite side in July, and having joined a large party of Arabs and Swahilis, he wandered with them in the Manyema country for many months. His object was the Lualaba river (the Upper Congo) of which he had heard much to excite his curiosity, and which river, he believed, with occasional misgivings, to be the Upper Nile. But so erratic were the wanderings of the Arabs to and fro in the Manyema country that Livingstone did not actually reach the banks of the Lualaba until March, 1871. Resolved to devote himself now to the tracing of what he believed to be the Upper Nile from its source on the Nyasa-Tanganyika plateau to its entrance into the Albert Nyanza, Livingstone decided to return to Ujiji and renew his stock of trade goods and provisions. His journey from the Lualaba to Ujiji was accompanied by indescribable hardships, which produced such an effect on his constitution that they eventually led to his death two years later. Soon after returning to Ujiji he met Henry M. Stanley, who had been sent by the *New York Herald* to "find Dr. Livingstone, living or dead."

Stanley's arrival certainly added two years more to Livingstone's life, as by a series of accidents and frauds he found himself absolutely destitute of resources after his return to Ujiji. Together the two men made an exploration of the north end of Lake Tanganyika, and then journeyed eastwards to Unyanyembe, half way to Zanzibar. Here Livingstone insisted on parting company with Stanley, though the latter earnestly entreated him to return to Europe; but with Livingstone the idea of finding the ultimate sources of the Nile had become almost a monomania, and he was resolved not to return to Europe until he had mapped the upper waters of the Chambezi and the Luapula, together with the river Lualaba, which took its rise in the Katanga Highlands to the West. So he started off once more for Lake Bangweolo in August, 1872, passing round the south end of Lake Tanganyika, and reaching the eastern shores of Lake Bangweolo in the month of April, 1873. But his race was run, and he died at a village near the south end of that marshy lake on or about the 1st of May, 1873.

Meantime Nyasaland had not long remained without English visitors. In 1867 Lieut. Young conducted an expedition to the south end of Lake Nyasa to examine into the reports as to the murder of Livingstone by the Angoni. Young (who only died a few months ago) conducted this expedition in a most remarkably successful manner. He left England in the middle of May, 1867, reached the Zambezi with three European companions and a steel boat on the 25th of July, journeyed with his baggage in the steel boat (which was named *The Search*[1]) and in a flotilla of smaller boats and canoes up the Zambezi and the Shire to the Murchison cataracts; conveyed the steel boat overland to the Upper Shire; reached Mponda's town at the south end of Lake Nyasa; collected a mass of information which conclusively proved that Livingstone was not killed but had started unmolested on his way to the West; returned to the Zambezi, and reached England at the beginning of 1868 after only eight months' absence.

Young had been greatly helped in his transit of the Shire Highlands by the Makololo whom Livingstone had left behind in that district after his withdrawal from the Zambezi in 1864. Those who have read the well-known works dealing with Dr. Livingstone's explorations will remember that on his first journey of discovery up and down the Zambezi he had been accompanied by certain faithful Makololo porters who had followed him from the Barutse country, on the Upper Zambezi. The so-called Makololo were a section of the Bechuana people who, leaving Basutoland after tribal

---
[1] And is still plying on the Shire.

disturbances, journeyed across the Kalahari Desert, and established themselves in the Barutse country.¹ When Livingstone reached Tete on his journey back to the East Coast in 1856 he left behind at that place the so-called Makololo (about 25 in number), who had followed him from the Upper Zambezi. On his return in 1858 he picked them up again and added to their numbers several others who followed him of their own free will on his second visit to the Barutse country.

These men were very useful to his expedition in exploring the River Shire, and were of a masterful nature, easily imposing themselves as superior beings on the timid Mañanja people of the Central Shire. When Dr. Livingstone had to leave the country, anxious to put a check on the depredations of the Yao coming from the east, and the Angoni coming from the west, he armed these Makololo, and left them behind to protect the Mañanja natives. The result was that they very soon constituted themselves the chiefs of that country, and they subsequently played a most important part in checking the advances of the Yao and the Angoni, and in sturdily resisting any attempts on the part of the Portuguese to conquer the Shire countries.

In 1874 Mr. Faulkner, who was one of the party accompanying Lieut. Young, R.N., returned to the Shire as a hunter of big game. He was, I believe, eventually killed by the natives. He had a son by a native wife who now bears his name, and who was the first half-caste, so far as we know, born in the Protectorate.

Livingstone's death caused a tremendous enthusiasm to spring up for the continuation of his work as a Missionary and as an Explorer. Cameron completed Burton's and Livingstone's map of Lake Tanganyika; Stanley, at the expense of the *Daily Telegraph*, continued the exploration of the Congo from Nyangwe, where Livingstone had left it, to the Atlantic Ocean; but in Nyasaland proper Livingstone's work was immediately continued by the Scotch Missionaries. The Livingstonia Free Church Mission was founded in 1874 and sent out its first party of Missionaries with a small steamer in sections, for Lake Nyasa, in 1875. They were joined, in 1876, by the Pioneers of the Church of Scotland Mission, who chose the site of the present town of Blantyre, and established themselves in the Shire Highlands, while the Free Church applied itself to the evangelisation of Lake Nyasa. It is interesting to note that the leader of the first Missionary expedition—Dr. Laws—who went out in 1875, and the engineer of the first Mission steamer placed on Lake Nyasa (the *Ilala*, which is still plying), Mr. A. C. Simpson, are still alive and well, and hard at work in Nyasaland, the one as a senior member of the Mission he has served so devotedly for twenty-one years, and the other as a prosperous planter at Mlanje.

Shortly after the Church of Scotland Mission had established itself at Blantyre, a young gardener, named John Buchanan, was sent from Scotland to assist the Mission in horticulture.²

In 1878 Captain Frederick Elton had been appointed Consul at Moçambique, and had obtained permission to conduct an expedition to Lake Nyasa to report

---

¹ Barutse is stated to be derived from "Bahurutse" the name of another of the Bechuana septs These Bechuana emigrants who sometimes called themselves the Makololo had conquered the Barutse country, from its native chiefs of Baloi race. But as a matter of fact these famous Makololo porters who have played such a part in the history of Nyasaland were very few of them of Bechuana blood. Many of them were slaves of Baloi, or kindred races of the Upper Zambezi.

² He was the means of introducing and planting the coffee shrub in Central Africa.

on the slave trade. He was accompanied by Mr. H. B. Cotterill, Mr. Herbert Rhodes,[1] and Captain Hoste.

With the aid of the little Mission steamer *Ilala* Consul Elton explored the north end of Lake Nyasa, which he was able to show extended much farther northwards than had been supposed by Livingstone and Kirk. This northward extension of the Lake was further verified a few years afterwards by numerous observations for Latitude taken by Mr. James Stewart, an engineer in the employ of the African Lakes Company. Consul Elton first made known to us the remarkable Livingstone or Ukinga Mountains, at the end of Lake Nyasa, which attain an altitude, in parts, of nearly 10,000 feet. Unhappily Consul Elton died in Wunyamwezi on his way to Zanzibar.

The Missions had not been long established when they found it impossible

MANDALA HOUSE, NEAR BLANTYRE

to conduct the necessary trade with the natives (for provisions could only be obtained by barter) and the transport service between the coast and Lake Nyasa, in addition to the ordinary Missionary work; so it was resolved, in Scotland, to found a small Company for trade and transport, subsequently styled "The African Lakes Company," which would be affiliated to the Missions (in so far that its employés should be required to do a certain amount of missionary work), but be conducted independently and on a commercial basis. Two brothers, John William Moir and Frederick Maitland Moir, were sent to Nyasaland as joint managers. They had been previously at work in the employ of the late Sir William Mackinnon, on a road to Lake Tanganyika which that philanthropist intended to construct inland from Dar-es-Salām, opposite Zanzibar. The headquarters of the Lakes Company were fixed at

---

[1] Mr. Herbert Rhodes was a brother of Mr. (now the Right Honourable) Cecil J. Rhodes, and had come to Nyasaland to shoot big game. He accompanied Consul Elton as far as the north end of Lake Nyasa, and then returned to the Upper Shire, where he established himself for some time shooting elephants. He gained a great reputation amongst the natives for bravery and fair dealing, and is still spoken of by the older men at the present day under the name of "Roza." He was burned to death in 1880 by the accidental setting on fire of his hut.

"Mandala" (now a suburb of Blantyre), about one mile from the headquarters of the Church of Scotland Mission. Mr. John Moir built a substantial house there, which still endures; and as he wore spectacles he was called by the natives "Mandala," a name meaning "glass." This nickname was soon applied to his residence, and gradually came to mean both the African Lakes Company, and the place where they settled near Blantyre. Mandala is now the official name of the headquarters of the African Lakes Company and of an important suburb of Blantyre.

The Church of Scotland Mission in those days—that is to say at the end of the seventies—was under the direction of two able men, the Rev. Alexander Duff and the late Mr. Henry Henderson, the latter being the business manager and the principal lay member; but it had attached to it also certain lay members who were either badly chosen, or who developed into bad characters when they came into contact with African savagery. It is only necessary to specify one of these—George Fenwick—whose name cannot be ignored in the history of this Protectorate. These men soon began to treat the natives with great harshness, and taking advantage of the dread in which white men were held, to bully and extort, and raise themselves almost to the position of petty chiefs. Indeed, in reviewing all that has happened since Europeans settled in this part of Africa, I have been increasingly struck with the rapidity with which such members of the white race as are not of the best class, can throw over the restraints of civilisation and develop into savages of unbridled lust and abominable cruelty. These lay members of the Mission attempted to exercise a kind of jurisdiction over the natives in the vicinity of the Mission stations, and so severe were their punishments that one native was sentenced to death and was shot, while other natives actually died from the awful floggings they received. Two English sportsmen, returning from Nyasaland, conveyed the news of these outrages to the consular authorities in Portuguese East Africa; the Foreign Office took up the matter, and eventually the Church of Scotland Mission sent out commissioners to hold an enquiry into the charges. Mr. Nunes, H. M. Vice-Consul at Quelimane, represented Her Majesty's Government on this enquiry, which resulted in the charges being in great measure proved.[1] The ordained minister who was at the head of the Mission at Blantyre resigned; though no blame was imputed to him, as he did not possess the means of controlling the actions of his subordinates. But after what had occurred he preferred to withdraw from the Mission[2] Mr. John Buchanan also at this time left the Mission, and set up for himself independently, as a coffee planter. George Fenwick and other lay members of the Mission, who were implicated in the deeds referred to, were dismissed, and the first-mentioned went to live among the natives as an elephant hunter In 1881 the Revs. D. C. Scott and Alexander Hetherwick came out to Africa and took charge of the Church of Scotland Mission, implanting on its work a very different character to the ill-fame which had temporarily clouded its earlier days owing to the misdeeds of its lay assistants. The indirect result, however, of the increasing British settlement in Nyasaland[3] was to induce Her Majesty's Government to establish a British Consul for Nyasa, and in 1883

[1] The evidence gathered by this commission makes very painful reading, and further expatiation on this subject is neither necessary nor desirable.
[2] See an excellently written book called *Africana*, by the Rev. Alexander Duff (Sampson Low & Co.) —one of the best books ever written on Africa.
[3] By this time the African Lakes Company had placed their small steamer, *The Lady Nyasa*, on the Zambezi.

HISTORY

Capt. Foot, R.N., went to Blantyre with his wife and children, taking with him Mr. D. Rankin as private secretary.

During all these years the Makololo chiefs had become increasingly powerful. At first they had seemed disposed to welcome the British, but there were times when they became arrogant and exacting in their demands. Still, on the whole, they were a valuable counterpoise to the aggressive Yao, some of whom became highway robbers and rifled the Mission and African Lakes Company's caravans. There were two of the Makololo chiefs specially prominent—Ramakukane and Chipatula. Ramakukane was seemingly of real Makololo origin, and had been the son of a chief or headman in the Barutse country, who had accompanied Livingstone back to Nyasaland, after his second visit to the Barutse country. Chipatula was one of Livingstone's old porters. Ramakukane was established at Katunga on the Central Shire, and Chipatula at or near the modern Chiromo, where the river Ruo joins the Shire, and where the present Anglo-Portuguese boundary runs. Ramakukane was, on the whole, friendly to the Europeans. Chipatula chiefly concerned himself in repelling the attempts of the black Portuguese from the Zambezi to establish themselves as slave traders on the Shire. He not only kept these half-castes at bay, but even extended his rule far down the Shire towards the Zambezi. The George Fenwick of whom I have made mention, after leaving the service of the Mission had set up for himself as a trader and elephant hunter. He was a headstrong, lawless man, who inspired fear and admiration alternately, in the minds of the natives. He had had several commercial transactions in selling ivory for Chipatula, and visited that chief at Chiromo in 1884 to settle accounts with him. Both men had been drinking spirits; Chipatula refused to accept Fenwick's version of accounts and applied opprobrious terms to him. Fenwick started up in a rage and shot Chipatula dead. Before the chief's astonished followers could take any action he rushed out of the hut towards the river shore, and shouted to them, "Your chief is dead, I am your chief now," but seeing that the natives were rather more inclined to avenge Chipatula's death than to adopt his slayer as his successor, he got into a canoe at the river side, and paddled across the river to Malo Island. Here for three days he led a wretched existence attempting to defend himself from the attacks of the natives. He was at last overcome and killed, and his head was cut off. The Makololo chiefs then became quite inimical to the white settlers. They shot at and sunk the little steamer *Lady Nyasa,* and they sent an insolent message to Blantyre, demanding that Mrs. Fenwick, the wife of the adventurer, should be delivered over to them, together with an enormous sum as compensation for the death of Chipatula. Consul Foot finally succeeded, with the help of Ramakukane, in restoring peace, and Mr. John Moir recovered the *Lady Nyasa.* Consul Foot, however, died not long afterwards from the effects of the fatigue and anxiety he had undergone. Chipatula was succeeded by a man named Mlauri, also one of Livingstone's men, but not friendly to the British; and old Ramakukane died. The demeanour of the Makololo as the years went by became increasingly insolent and hostile towards the Europeans, English as well as Portuguese.

In 1881 a fresh element of British influence had appeared on the shores of Lake Nyasa, in the arrival of the Rev. W. P. Johnson and Mr. Charles Janson, of the Universities Mission to Central Africa—that Mission whose first bishop, Mackenzie, had died near Chiromo on the Shire in 1862. It will be remembered that the Universities Mission had been founded at the instance of Livingstone, but after establishing itself in the Shire highlands in 1862 had been obliged to quit that country owing to the hostilities shown by the Yao. Since that time the Mission had concentrated itself at Zanzibar, and had founded stations on the East Coast of Africa. That really great man, Bishop Steere, the third of the Missionary bishops to Central Africa, had set his heart on reopening work in Nyasaland. He walked overland from the Indian Ocean to the east coast of the lake. Subsequently Lake Nyasa was reached by the Rev. W. P. Johnson, accompanied by Mr. Charles Janson. The latter fell ill, and died on the shores of Lake Nyasa In his will he bequeathed a sum of money for the construction of a Mission steamer to be placed on the lake. Other subscriptions were raised, and eventually the *Charles Janson* was launched on Lake Nyasa, where she still exists. The Rev. Chauncey Maples and other recruits from the Mission had meantime joined Mr. Johnson. Bishop Steere had been succeeded by Bishop Smythies,[1] who if anything took an increased interest in the establishment of his Mission on Lake Nyasa, to which lake he paid repeated visits. The Rev. Chauncey Maples was made Archdeacon of Nyasa.[2] Seeing the troublous condition of the Yao countries, and the shores of Lake Nyasa, where the unfortunate A-nyanja inhabitants were alternately raided by Magwangwara,[3] Arabs and Yao, the Universities Mission resolved to establish its headquarters on the Island of Likoma, which is distant about eight miles from the east coast of Lake Nyasa, and consequently is not so subject to the attacks of the Magwangwara or Yao.

The Livingstonia Mission under the able guidance of Dr. Robert Laws, M.D. had been for years making steady progress on the west coast of Lake Nyasa. Their first experiments at Cape Maclear,[4] a promontory which divides the southern end of the lake into two gulfs, were not very successful. The settlement of Livingstonia,—which still exists but where only native adherents of the Mission dwell at the present time,—proved to be extremely unhealthy for Europeans, and many missionaries died there. Dr. Laws decided, therefore, to transfer the headquarters of the Mission to Bandawe, about midway up the west coast of the lake, a place in the middle of the Atonga country. Here the Free Church Mission was confronted with an immediate difficulty in the shape of the Angoni-Zulu of the interior, who were gradually exterminating and enslaving the indigenous people of the lake-coast, known as the Atonga, who were related in origin to the A-nyanja stock. The Free Church Mission, therefore, set itself to work to conciliate the Angoni, and obtained such influence over them, after some years, that they stopped to a great extent their raids over the coast people. At any rate the Mission stations served as a harbour of refuge for the harried Atonga, who were eventually able to recover their position and assert themselves against the invaders.

About the end of the seventies the London Missionary Society resolved to take up Tanganyika as a sphere of work. Their journeys thither were made overland from Zanzibar; but when they decided to have a steamer placed on Tanganyika they found it easier to send its sections by the Lake Nyasa route. The explorer, Joseph Thomson, had reached the north end of Lake Nyasa in 1880, and had journeyed thence to Tanganyika. This exploration

---

[1] Died at sea on his way back to England in 1894, worn out by ten years of incessant toil and physical fatigue.
[2] Became Bishop of Likoma in 1895, and was drowned in Lake Nyasa a few months afterwards by the capsizing of his boat in a storm.
[3] A section of the Angoni-Zulu, established east of Lake Nyasa.
[4] Named by Livingstone after the Astronomer-Royal of Cape Town.

had assisted in fixing the relative position of the two lakes and showing that the land transit between them did not much exceed 200 miles. The African Lakes Company were entrusted with the contract for conveying the London Missionary Society's steamer from Nyasa to Tanganyika, an enterprise successfully accomplished in 1885. Mr. James Stevenson, a director of the Lakes Company, was struck with the idea of making a permanent road from lake to lake, and subscribed a sum of, I believe, £2000 or £3000, for the purpose of making preliminary surveys. The Stevenson road, however, was never completed, but the route it was to follow was roughly cleared for about sixty miles from Lake Nyasa. The engineers concerned in this work died of fever, and further operations were checked by the outbreak of war with the Arabs. The London Missionary Society did not, at first, think much of the Lake Nyasa route to Tanganyika, but preferred the overland journey from Zanzibar. They therefore devoted their attention more to the middle portion of the lake, especially the west coast opposite to Ujiji, and established themselves here on the island of Kavala. The unhealthiness of this place, however, and the troubles which began to arise on Tanganyika after the first Belgian expeditions, and from the subsequent uprising against the Germans, obliged the London Missionary Society's agents to alter their plans. They transferred their establishments to the south end of the lake, in order to be brought into more direct communication with the British settlements in Nyasaland.

The first serious danger which may be said to have menaced the infant settlements in Nyasaland, was the trouble with the Makololo chiefs, to which I have already referred. The next danger, and a much more serious one, arose from the conflict with the Arabs who had settled at the north end of Lake Nyasa. When Livingstone and Kirk first explored Lake Nyasa they practically only found the Arabs established in a few places—at one or other of the ports on what is now the Portuguese coast of Lake Nyasa, and at Kotakota on the western shore of the lake;[1] at which latter place Livingstone visited an Arab settlement under the control of a person called "Jumbe," who was a coast Arab, and a representative or *wali* of the Sultan of Zanzibar. Jumbe means "prince" on the mainland opposite Zanzibar, and the Sultan had no doubt chosen as his representative a man who went to Nyasa for trade purposes principally, but who was of sufficiently good standing to exercise some show of authority, in the Sultan's name, over the Arabs wandering in those regions. When I use the term "Arabs" I mean both Arabs with white skins of pure blood (and usually natives of 'Oman or of Southern Arabia) and every degree of intermixture and type between the Arab and the negro, so that some of our so-called Arabs in Nyasaland are quite black, though in the shape of their features or in their beards, they may retain traces of the intermixture of a superior race. But all these so-called Arabs are sharply distinguished from the ordinary negroes by dressing in Arab costume, using the Arabic language, and by being stricter and more intelligent in their practices of the Muhammadan religion.

The first interference of the Arabs with Nyasaland was merely to secure a passage across the lake in their caravan journeys to the countries of Senga, Lubisa, and Luwemba, which journeys were undertaken for ivory, or slaves, and had commenced, as I have already related, by their following back into South Central Africa the Babisa caravans that formerly traded with Zanzibar. The

---

[1] "Ngotangota"—as the natives call it, the Arabs having corrupted the name into the easier pronunciation of Kotakota.

Arabs, however, soon established themselves in strong stockades in the Senga country, through which the great Luangwa River flows. Then they began to adopt, as an alternative route to the journey across Lake Nyasa, the direct journey from Zanzibar overland across the Nyasa-Tanganyika plateau; and gradually the strong Arab dominion on Lake Tanganyika became connected with the settlements in the Senga country and on Lake Nyasa. The Arabs had also found a friend and ally in Merere, an intelligent and enterprising chief of the Wa-sango people, who had his capital in the high mountainous region to the north of Lake Nyasa. In their journeys to and fro between Senga and the sea coast, by way of the Nyasa-Tanganyika plateau, the Arabs became struck with the magnificent fertility and the wealth in cattle of the Nkonde country at the north end of Lake Nyasa. A certain Zanzibar Arab, named Mlozi,[1] appears to have commenced by trading in the country, and gradually proceeded to surround his trade establishments with stockades and by degrees take forcible possession of this delectable land. Mlozi had, with several other Arabs, established strong trading stations in the Senga country, and was almost a prince among slave traders. But Mlozi's schemes were not to be so easily accomplished. Prior to his settlement in the Nkonde country, or simultaneously with it at any rate, the Lakes Company had obtained a footing at Karonga for the purpose of opening up communication with Lake Tanganyika.

L. MONTEITH FOTHERINGHAM

The Lakes Company had employed amongst other Europeans two notable men to conduct the expeditions which transported the London Missionary Society's steamer in sections from Nyasa to Tanganyika. These men were Low Monteith Fotheringham and John Lowe Nicoll. Mr. Fotheringham had become finally their agent at Karonga, on the north-west coast of Lake Nyasa, while Mr. Nicoll was chiefly employed on Tanganyika and in going backwards and forwards between Nyasa and Tanganyika. Fotheringham was a man of very strong character and upright disposition, severe occasionally with the natives in maintaining the laws which he laid down for the maintenance of order, but of great bravery, and absolutely just in his dealings. No qualities ensure a man greater favour amongst the negroes than mingled firmness and justice; and the natives of the north end of Lake Nyasa, the Mambwe of the Nyasa-Tanganyika plateau, and the Atonga of West Nyasa, came by degrees to look upon Mr. Fotheringham[2] as their natural leader and champion. The Arabs under Mlozi began to press their rule on the Nkonde people. The Wankonde looked to Fotheringham for advice and protection. Fotheringham was at first disinclined to interfere in the quarrels, as he feared that the

JOHN LOWE NICOLL

---

[1] Mlozi means in Swahili "an almond tree"; but I expect the real derivation of the word is from Mulozi (= a sorcerer) in the dialects spoken in the Senga and Bisa countries.
[2] Whom they called Montisi, from an Africanising of his second name.

results of a fight with the Arabs might seriously prejudice the Lakes Company's position, and cut off communication with Lake Tanganyika; but he was not long left the choice of remaining neutral, for the Arabs appear to have come to the conclusion that the conquest of all the Nkonde country was impossible until they had first driven out the British traders and Missionaries; for two missionaries, the Rev. Mr. Bain and Dr. Kerr Cross,[1] had already settled at the north end of Lake Nyasa in the service of the Free Church Mission. Of course much of the friction that had arisen between the Arabs and the Lakes Company's agent came from the undoubted sympathy which the British traders showed for the Wankonde in their hopeless struggle against the Arab forces. One fact may be cited in particular as an example of the atrocious way in

GROUP OF WANKONDE (NORTH NYASA)

which the Arabs conducted this war of conquest. The Wankonde, who were entirely and only armed with spears, had been defeated in an engagement with the Arabs, and took refuge on the banks of the Kambwe lagoon, on the shore of Lake Nyasa. The Arabs surrounded them, set fire to the dry reeds, and compelled the wretched Wankonde to enter the water, where hundreds of them were devoured by crocodiles, and large numbers were shot, stabbed, or drowned.[2] Several refugees from this and other fights found their way into the Lakes Company's station, which was then unfortified. Mr. Fotheringham's refusal to give them up and his answering the Arab threats by commencing to fortify Karonga were no doubt the causes which decided the Arabs to make an attack on the Karonga station. Fortunately before this attack took place

[1] Dr. Kerr Cross is still serving as a medical missionary in this part of Africa, where he has done great good amongst the natives, as well as having nursed into recovery many sick Europeans.
[2] For a faithful description of these horrors see pp. 80, 81, and 82 of the late Mr. Fotheringham's book *Adventures in Nyasaland* (Sampson Low).

reinforcements were received. Mr. Nicoll arrived from Tanganyika and the little steamer *Ilala* returned from South Nyasa bringing Consul O'Neill, of Moçambique, and Mr. Alfred Sharpe and two other gentlemen who had decided to come to the rescue of the Europeans threatened by the Arabs.

Karonga was attacked and besieged for days though the Arabs were finally repulsed after desperate fighting; but eventually the British position became untenable, and after communicating the news of his dangerous situation to the Manager at Mandala, Mr. Fotheringham, Mr. Nicoll, and the others who had joined them, decided to withdraw with the Wankonde chiefs into a part of the country where they would be better sheltered from the Arab attack. They removed most of their goods in canoes, abandoned the station at Karonga, and remained in the country at the extreme north end of the lake until reinforcements arrived. Amongst the volunteers who came to their aid, were Mr. Consul Hawes and Mr. John Moir. The arrival of these slight reinforcements and the aid of five thousand natives enabled Mr. Fotheringham to attack, enter, and partially destroy Mlozi's stockade at Mpata (in which attack both Mr. Alfred Sharpe

JOHN W. MOIR

and Mr. John Moir were wounded). But the native allies abandoned the stockade after having loaded themselves with loot and the whites had to retreat without consummating their defeat of the Arabs by the destruction of all their stockades. After this all the volunteers returned to South Nyasa and Messrs. Fotheringham, Nicoll, and Kerr Cross lived for a time at Chirenje, to the north-west of Karonga, while the Arabs regained to some extent their former position, though they never were able actively to assume the offensive. Early in March, more volunteers returned to North Nyasa. With them came Mr. John Buchanan (Acting Consul) and Mr. Fred Moir, joint manager of the Lakes Co. Mr. Buchanan attempted to negotiate a peace with the Arabs, but the negotiations had no result. Hostilities were then resumed, but Mr. Fred Moir was severely wounded, and again owing to the vacillation of their native allies the British failed to score any great success.

When the news of this fighting at the north end of Lake Nyasa reached the outer world, several gentlemen volunteered to assist the Lakes Company, the principal among these being Capt. Lugard,[1] who was constituted by the Lakes Company the Commander of their forces in North Nyasa. Capt. Lugard was subsequently rejoined by Mr. Alfred Sharpe,[2] by Mr. Richard Crawshay (who had also come to the country as a hunter), by Mr. John Moir, and others.

FREDERICK MAITLAND MOIR

[1] Now Major Lugard, C.B.
[2] Now Her Majesty's Deputy Commissioner and Consul. Mr. Sharpe originally came to Nyasaland to hunt elephants and big game, but hearing of the Lakes Company's distress he came to their assistance with Consul O'Neill in the manner above related. After being wounded and proceeding to the south to recover he returned with Captain Lugard and fought out the rest of the campaign, marching up overland at the head of a large number of Atonga.

Mr. Frederick Moir, whose arm had been severely wounded, had returned to Scotland to recover his health. From thence he succeeded in sending out a 7-pounder gun, as it was felt the Arabs could only be adequately fought with artillery. But unfortunately, although this gun ultimately reached its destination, it was not provided with the right kind of ammunition. Its

MR. ALFRED SHARPE IN 1890

shells merely drilled round holes in the tough stockades which, being made of withes and mud, did not offer sufficient resistance for a real breach to be made. A good deal of damage was done to the Arabs who were shut up in their fortresses and much inconvenienced for lack of food, but the British, on the other hand, suffered severely, having one of their officers killed and several more or less severely wounded, besides the terrible ill-health which resulted from fighting during the rainy season. Amongst the wounded was Captain Lugard who returned to Blantyre, got his wound partially healed, and then once more took command at Karonga. Captain Lugard finally quitted Nyasaland in the spring of 1889, finding it impossible to bring the Arab war to a conclusion without disciplined troops and efficient artillery.

An attempt was made by Sir Charles Euan-Smith, Her Majesty's Consul-General at Zanzibar, to induce the Sultan of that place to intervene, and to bring the war to a conclusion by compelling the Arabs to come to terms with the British. The Sultan accordingly dispatched an envoy, but he commanded very little weight in the councils of the Senga Arabs, who considered themselves quite independent of the Sultan's authority.

The consequences of this war with the Arabs, which was clearly known by the natives of Nyasaland to be a war for the suppression of the slave trade, aroused a good many expressions of ill-feeling against the English on the part of the Muhammadan Yao on the east coast of Lake Nyasa. Mr. John Buchanan, who had been Acting Consul since the departure on leave of Mr. Hawes, attempted to open up friendly relations with Makanjira, the Yao chief on the south-east coast of the lake. He paid him a visit with the Rev. W. P. Johnson, in the Mission steamer, the *Charles Janson*. To their surprise, however, they had no sooner landed than they were seized, stripped of their clothes, and grossly maltreated. They were imprisoned in huts, and Makanjira announced his intention of killing them, and would probably have done so, but for the persuasion of some Zanzibar Arabs, who represented that their deaths would certainly be avenged, and that the Sultan of Zanzibar would hold them—the intercessors—responsible, after what had occurred, if English subjects were killed in their presence, and without remonstrance on their part. Makanjira accordingly held his captives up to ransom. They were obliged to write to the engineer of their steamer, which was in the offing, to send on shore an enormous supply of trade goods and ship's stores. When these things arrived Makanjira released them, though he neither restored their clothes nor the personal property of which they had been robbed. Mr. Buchanan, the Acting Consul, had even been whipped with a chikote[1] by Makanjira's orders—not severely, but just with two or three stripes to show his contempt for the British.

After a little vacillation the Arabs of Tanganyika had decided not to join with their fellow countrymen in the war against the British, and indeed after a little more deliberation, that section under the orders of Tiputipu[2] had determined to protect the British missionaries on Lake Tanganyika from violence at the hands of any other Arabs who might, in consequence of their uprising against the Germans, have resolved to assassinate all Europeans in the interior. Likewise the Arab settlement at Kotakota, which was under the third in succession of "Jumbes," who continued to be the *wali* of the Sultan of Zanzibar, resolved to remain neutral. Generally speaking, it may be said that at this crisis the influence of the Sultan of Zanzibar was exercised *strongly* in favour of the British. Had he not compelled peace and a good understanding with them, all the Arabs of Central Africa would have gladly united in a war to drive us out of Lake Nyasa, and would have doubtless succeeded in doing so, as in those days owing to difficulties with the Portuguese, it was found very difficult to import supplies of guns and ammunition.

The general situation in British Central Africa, before I was personally connected with its fortunes, was as follows.

[1] A whip of hippopotamus hide.
[2] Whom, of course, the British *will* call "Tippoo-tib."

HISTORY

In the Barutse country, a strong kingdom of large extent, existed a ruling caste of Bechuana (who had first organised the territories on the Upper Zambezi into a large kingdom, and had been subsequently dispossessed of power to some extent by revolution) and the descendants of the old rulers, who were of Baloi, or Balui, stock. These latter had replaced in sovereign power the Bechuana[1] kings. But otherwise the government of the Upper Zambezi countries in their political tendencies remained much what it was in the days when Livingstone first discovered Barutseland. Eastwards of the Barutse country, the lands of the Bashikulombwe, of the Batonga and Manika, remained in a state of utter barbarism, fiercely recalcitrant to European researches. Little was known of the country since the explorations of Kirk and Livingstone; Dr. Emil Holub, an Austrian explorer, had been repulsed; Mr. Selous, who had penetrated farthest into this part of Central Africa, was attacked and obliged to fly for his life; and Jesuit Missionaries had either been maltreated, killed, or expelled, in their attempts to penetrate these countries. On the lower part of the great Luangwa river, the country was harried by black chieftains from the Zambezi, who called themselves " Portuguese," on the strength of remote Goanese descent. In the Senga and Lubisa countries, Arabs and Swahilis were carrying on the slave trade, and gradually establishing themselves in the land by means of building stockaded towns. At the south end of Lake Tanganyika there were one or two missionaries settled and building. At the north end of Lake Nyasa a war between Arabs and Scotch traders had been going on for two years. Missionaries were peacefully at work in West Nyasaland, but on the east coast of the lake their work was paralysed by the hostility of Makanjira. The Yao, who, since Livingstone's first arrival in the country, had gradually conquered much of the Shire Highlands, and had established themselves at the south end, and along the south-east and south-west coasts of Lake Nyasa, were engaged, either in incessant civil war amongst themselves, in attacks on their weaker neighbours, or in hostilities against the British. In the Shire Highlands coffee-planting had already begun under Mr. Buchanan, who had been joined by two of his brothers, and under Mr. Sharrer, a British subject of German descent, who had established himself as a planter and trader in Nyasaland. In the Shire Highlands the missionaries of the Church of Scotland Mission had acquired a considerable influence, an influence justly due to their high character and their devotion to the interests of the natives, but an influence which at that time they were too much inclined to exercise with the view to governing the country themselves, independently of Consuls or other representatives of Her Majesty. The rival to the Scotch Missionaries, as a governing body, was the African Lakes Company, which was half hoping for a Charter, and was striving to obtain from the native chiefs a concession of governing rights. Sometimes the interests of the Lakes Company and the Mission were conflicting, and not infrequently the two or three independent planters could agree with neither. The Universities Mission was supposed to hold the opinion that the war with the Arabs was unwise, and owing to its friendly relations on the lake with the Arabs more or less attached to the Sultan of Zanzibar, that Mission did not identify itself with any movement for the expulsion of the Arabs from Nyasaland. A French Evangelical Mission had established itself in the Barutse country, and was acquiring a very great influence over the natives.[2] The seat of this Mission, however, lay in British South Africa, and so far

[1] *i.e.*, Makololo. [2] An influence always used for disinterested and proper ends.

as these French Missionaries had any political sentiments at all they were on the side of bringing the Barutse under British influence. The history of Barutseland is only artificially connected with the rest of British Central Africa, by the fact that at present it is included within the same political sphere. Otherwise its history is mainly connected in the past with that of British South Africa, and in the future it will unquestionably become an appanage of that portion of the Empire.[1]

The greatest difficulty which at that time hampered the development of the eastern part of British Central Africa, was the fact that it could only be approached from the outer world through Portuguese East African Possessions. In those days, anyone wishing to proceed to Lake Nyasa, and shirking the overland journey from Zanzibar, which was lengthy, arduous, and often full of risk, landed at Quelimane, a little to the north of the Zambezi delta, journeyed up the Kwakwa River in small boats to a point called Mopeia, then crossed overland, a distance of three or four miles, to Vicenti, a trading station on the Zambezi. At Vicenti one was met by either of the African Lakes Company's two steamers, the *James Stevenson* or the *Lady Nyasa*, and so travelled on up the Zambezi and up the Shire, as far as the season of the year, and consequent depth of the waters would permit, and thence overland to the British settlements. This route, however, compelled travellers to land at the Portuguese port of Quelimane; and even assuming the Kwakwa to be, like the Zambezi, an international waterway, a fact which could not be asserted and maintained, it was impossible to reach the waters of the Zambezi without crossing a mile or so of Portuguese territory. No arrangement existed with Portugal to secure us exemption from Customs duties or even graver hindrances that might be placed in our way by the local Portuguese authorities, and these authorities—bearing in mind that the boundaries of Portuguese and British influence in the Hinterland had not yet been settled—were naturally very jealous of this immigration of British subjects, the said British subjects being never too careful of Portuguese rights and susceptibilities. It was this difficulty with the Portuguese which had caused Her Majesty's Government in 1863 to arrive at the conclusion that the Zambezi expedition of Livingstone must be recalled. It was again this difficulty which hampered Her Majesty's Government in the "eighties," in preventing them from affording active assistance to the traders on Lake Nyasa in their war with the Arabs, and, indeed, in formulating any decisive policy in regard to Nyasaland. Had it been possible for vessels of fair size and draught to enter the river Zambezi from the sea, all these difficulties from overland transport would have disappeared. Her Majesty's Government had for some time past maintained the principle of the freedom of navigation of the Zambezi, but although ships did occasionally succeed in getting over the bar of the Kongone mouth—a bar on which at low tide there was only a depth of 5 to 6 feet of water—the enterprise was too uncertain to be often prosecuted, and the best proof of its impracticability lay in the fact that the African Lakes Company had almost abandoned this way into the Zambezi, and preferred to pay the heavy Customs duties of Quelimane and submit to all reasonable restrictions on the part of the Portuguese, rather than attempt to communicate with the Shire by means of the Kongone mouth of the Zambezi—an attempt indeed which they could only make at fitful

---

[1] Whereas, on the other hand, the history of the eastern half of British Central Africa, east of the Kafue River, has always been mixed up with that of Zanzibar and the northern half of Portuguese East Africa.

intervals, and by specially chartering ocean-going steamers, as no established Steamship Line would hear of calling in at the Kongone mouth as a matter of course.

At this juncture a discovery of the greatest importance was made, which completely altered the political aspect of the question. Mr. Daniel J. Rankin, an explorer who had originally proceeded to Nyasaland as private secretary to Consul Foot, and who had also acted in a Consular capacity at Moçambique, was enabled by the Royal Scottish Geographical Society to institute an exploration of the Zambezi delta. In the course of his journey he discovered the Chinde mouth of the Zambezi, which apparently was quite unknown to the Portuguese Government, though it had probably been first discovered by a Portuguese planter who was working a concession in the delta. This planter's information put Mr. Rankin on the track of his discovery, which he announced to the world in the spring of 1889.[1] It was briefly this, that the Chinde mouth of the Zambezi possessed a bar shorter and safer and simpler than that of any other outlet of the Zambezi, and with a minimum depth of water at high tide of 17 feet (as against, say, 10 feet at the Kongone). At the time Mr. Rankin sounded the bar, I believe he found a depth of water on it of 21 or 22 feet, a depth which has several times since been recorded, but chiefly at that season of the year when the river was visited by Mr. Rankin, namely when the Zambezi is in full flood. Ordinarily the depth of water at high spring-tides is 17 to 19 feet. Not only was the Chinde bar a far less serious obstacle than that of any other mouth of the Zambezi, but its channel from the sea into the main Zambezi was easier of navigation than the other branches of that river. In its far-reaching political importance, probably no greater discovery in the history of British Central Africa has been made than that of the navigability of the Chinde River from the Indian Ocean to the main Zambezi.

[1] In the *Times* Newspaper.

ON THE CHINDE MOUTH OF THE ZAMBEZI

CHAPTER IV.

THE FOUNDING OF THE PROTECTORATE

ANY direct personal interest which I may have taken in the affairs of Nyasaland dates from the commencement of 1884.

I had returned from a prolonged examination of the western basin of the River Congo and my opinion was invited at the Foreign Office on certain points connected with the proposed treaty with Portugal regulating the political and commercial affairs of the Lower Congo.

This treaty contained a clause providing that Portuguese political influence should cease in the direction of Nyasaland at the junction of the Ruo and Shire rivers. Had the treaty been ratified this clause would have obviated any further frontier disputes with Portugal, north of the Zambezi; but owing to unreasonable opposition in certain quarters it was not ratified, and then the Berlin Conference was called to deal generally with questions affecting the Congo and the Niger, and Zambezian affairs were postponed in their settlement. The Portuguese were now free of any obligation in regard to Nyasaland, and being an enterprising and ambitious people, determined once more to revive their scheme of a trans-continental Empire from Angola to Moçambique, including the southern part of what is now Central Africa. They were aided in these assumptions by the remarkable journeys of their explorers, Capello and Ivens.

Lord Salisbury's Ministry, however, had succeeded to power, and in several speeches in the House of Lords the Premier could not conceal the interest that he felt in the struggle going on between the Arabs and the African Lakes Company, or his resolve to maintain Nyasaland as a country open to British enterprise without the restrictions which would result from its transference to any other European Power. Owing to the difficulty about a direct water route into the heart of South Central Africa to which I have alluded in the last chapter, I believe it was not the object of Her Majesty's Ministers in 1887 to establish any actual Protectorate over Nyasaland: they merely wished that it should become neither German nor Portuguese, but be ruled by its native chiefs, under the advice, it might be, of a British Consul, but in any case that it should remain open to the British traders, planters and missionaries without let or hindrance.

In 1888 I had returned from three years of Consular work in the Niger Coast Protectorate, and in the summer of that year Lord Salisbury held a short conversation with me at Hatfield in which he developed his views about Zambezia. From this conversation I date, to a great extent, my own conception of the policy to be pursued.[1] In the autumn of 1888 I was offered and accepted the post of Consul to Portuguese East Africa. At the beginning of 1889 it was decided by the Foreign Office that I should travel in the interior, and report on the troubles which had arisen with the Arabs, and above all with the Portuguese; and that in those districts admittedly beyond Portuguese jurisdiction I should take measures to secure the country from abrupt seizure by other European Powers, by concluding treaties of friendship with the native chiefs, in which they bound themselves not to transfer their governing rights to any European Power without the consent of Her Majesty's Government. Before starting for my post, however, it was thought by Lord Salisbury that I might, by personal intercourse with the Portuguese Authorities at Lisbon, suggest some *modus vivendi* with regard to the settlement of our conflicting claims. I, accordingly, spent some six weeks in Portugal, and in conjunction with Her Majesty's Envoy, Mr., now Sir George, Petre, discussed the subject of Nyasaland at the Portuguese Foreign Office. A draft arrangement was drawn up, which after some modifications was shown to the Portuguese Minister for Foreign Affairs, and approved by him. It was then submitted to the English Foreign Office, but as it did not provide for the exclusion of the Shire Highlands from the Portuguese Sphere it was not deemed acceptable by Her Majesty's Government, as the chief object of any such arrangement at that time was to secure the work of the English missionaries and planters from interference. This arrangement might, however, have been modified in that respect without difficulty on the part of the Portuguese, but the fact was that the Government felt reluctant to push the matter to an immediate conclusion in the face of two obstacles, one being the want of direct water communication with the interior beyond the Portuguese Sphere, and the other, the difficulty which would be experienced by the Imperial Government at that time, in finding funds for incurring the great responsibility of administering the districts bordering on Lake Nyasa, a territory that did not then promise much or, indeed, any local revenue of its own. Two things now occurred to dispel Government anxieties on these accounts: Mr. Rankin announced his discovery of the Chinde mouth, and Mr. Cecil Rhodes arrived in England to obtain a Charter for his Company. I made the acquaintance of Mr. Rhodes, and found him much disposed to interest himself in the extension of British influence across the Zambezi. As the result of several conferences Mr. Rhodes was able to assure the Foreign Office that his proposed Chartered Company would find at least £10,000 a year, for several years, for the development and administration of Nyasaland. Under these new circumstances, therefore, the Government felt justified in attempting to secure for Great Britain a reasonable amount of political influence over those countries of Central Africa, not claimed by Germany, Portugal, or the Congo Free State. The form of Treaty that was drawn up was not, however, altered, as it was not intended to proclaim any Protectorate, if more indirect means of political supremacy could be attained.

It should, perhaps, be stated that the attention of Her Majesty's Government had been drawn in the spring of 1889 to the imposing expedition which was to be commanded by Major Serpa Pinto in Portuguese Zambezia.

Explanations had been asked for in Lisbon as to its eventual destination,

---

[1] What this conception was may be found in an article in the *Times* of August 22nd, 1883, which it may be interesting for some persons to re-read now as it was written at a time when such ideas as a British dominion, including an establishment on the shores of Tanganyika and through communication between the Cape and Egypt had never before been specifically enunciated.

but the Portuguese Minister for Foreign Affairs assured Her Majesty's Government that Serpa Pinto would merely proceed to the Portuguese establishments on the Upper Zambezi and on the Luangwa River, and would not enter the debatable ground of the Shire Highlands. Consequently, as the Portuguese claim to Zumbo and to the Lower Luangwa had not been contested—or indeed their claims anywhere where occupation or political supremacy could be shown—it was thought that if the Portuguese did not attempt to impose their rule on any new lands where our interests might be affected, no such direct step as the establishment of a Protectorate on our part should be undertaken until negotiations with Germany and Portugal had, more or less precisely, fixed the limits of our political influence.

I started for Moçambique in the early summer of 1889. On my arrival at that place the Foreign Office, at my request, appointed Mr. W. A. Churchill,[1] Vice-Consul, so that I might be free to start on my journey to the interior, without leaving Consular matters unattended to. Soon after I reached Moçambique there arrived H.M.S. *Stork*, a surveying vessel commanded by Lieut.-Commander Balfour, R.N. The *Stork* had just returned from Chinde, where it had been sent to verify Mr. Rankin's discoveries. The Commander informed me that in his steam-launch he had passed up into the Zambezi, and had found the channel all the way deep enough for even the *Stork* herself, and the *Stork* was a vessel drawing $13\frac{1}{2}$ feet. I felt that it would be good policy to show that I had reached these regions of the interior, without necessarily landing on Portuguese territory, so I obtained permission from the Government to use the *Stork* for the conveyance of my expedition. At the same time the authorities at Moçambique were made fully aware of the purposes I intended to fulfil, namely the negotiation of a peace with the Arabs and the conclusion of treaties of friendship with the local chiefs, who were not under Portuguese jurisdiction. The Governor asked me pointedly if I intended to proclaim a British Protectorate, and I told him I was authorised to do nothing of the kind, so long as Major Serpa Pinto or other Portuguese explorers took no political action outside Portuguese territory. No difficulty whatever was placed in my way by the Portuguese, whether or not they approved of my expedition. I think particular stress should be laid on this fact, as had Portugal been animated by really hostile intentions to Great Britain, there were a hundred pretexts by which they might have stopped my journey. So little need was there to preserve any mystery about my operations, that instead of proceeding direct to Chinde, I called in with the *Stork* at Quelimane, and there visited the Portuguese officials, and communicated with the African Lakes Company. The *Stork* crossed the bar of the Chinde mouth without difficulty, on the 28th of July, 1889, and steamed up the Chinde River into the main Zambezi, to the unbounded astonishment of such few inhabitants as were on the banks, for neither they nor any other people had seen so large a vessel enter the Zambezi before. A short distance above the confluence of the Chinde with the main Zambezi the *Stork* came to anchor, and we continued our journey in a flotilla of steam launches and boats, by which means we finally came up with the African Lakes Company's steamer, the *James Stevenson*, near Morambala, a very notable mountain which is situated some twenty miles up the Shire River. My expedition consisted of Mr. J. L. Nicoll, formerly of the Lakes Company's service,[2] whom I had engaged at Quelimane as an assistant; Ali Kiongwe, my Zanzibari headman, who had accompanied me on my journey to Kilimanjaro, and whom I

---

[1] Now Consul at Moçambique.   [2] Just returning from the Arab War.

had re-engaged at Zanzibar in 1889; and fifteen Makua, engaged with the consent of the Portuguese authorities at Moçambique. The *James Stevenson* was a river steamer of about forty tons burden, worked by a stern wheel, and with fairly comfortable cabin accommodation, and an upper deck. In this steamer we pursued our course up the river, until we reached Serpa Pinto's camp, which was a little distance below the confluence of the Ruo and the Shire. I had been startled, on reaching Quelimane, to learn from the Portuguese officials there, that Major Serpa Pinto, after journeying to Sena on the Lower Zambezi with his expedition, had suddenly, and abruptly, deflected his course northwards to the Shire, and was apparently making for the Makololo country, and the Shire Highlands. Major Serpa Pinto had been apprised of my coming, and when the *James Stevenson* drew near he dispatched an officer and a boat, so that I might land and see him. I found Serpa Pinto surrounded by a staff of white officers, and was informed that he had with him over seven hundred Zulu soldiers.[1]

SERGT.-MAJOR ALI KIONGWE

The Major received me in a little hut, and after insisting on my sharing his afternoon tea, we began to discuss the political situation. He informed me that he sought my intervention with the Makololo people, to persuade them to allow him to pass unhindered through their country, as he was on his way to Lake Nyasa in charge of a Scientific Expedition. "We go," he said, "to visit that Portuguese subject, Mponda, at the south end of Lake Nyasa."[2] I replied to Major Serpa Pinto, "If you are only in charge of a Scientific Expedition, you need, at most, an escort of fifty soldiers; but the Makololo are sure to view your journey with distrust if you attempt to bring so large an armed force into the country; moreover, your Government has distinctly assured us that the object of your mission was the Upper Zambezi, and not the Shire. Consequently, if you take any political action north of the Ruo, which we consider, provisionally, to be the Portuguese limit, you will oblige me, on my part, to go beyond my immediate instructions and effectively protect the interests of Her Majesty's Government. If you merely wish to pass through the country for scientific purposes we will travel together, and I will do my best to persuade the Makololo to offer no opposition."

Major Serpa Pinto did not give any very definite reply to these remarks of mine, merely reiterating his hope that I would prevail on the Makololo to offer no opposition to his passage; otherwise he would be obliged to fight them.

I proceeded on my way in the *James Stevenson*, and soon afterwards

---

[1] Many of these men were inhabitants of Gazaland and Inyambane, but a few of them were undoubtedly Zulus, who had been recruited in Swaziland and in the vicinity of Delagoa Bay.

[2] I was aware that the Portuguese had endeavoured by means of Senor Cardozo, the only Portuguese explorer who had at that date reached the shores of Lake Nyasa, to conclude a treaty with Mponda, but it was common knowledge that although he had received the Mission in a friendly way, he had not signed the treaty.

we passed the junction of the Ruo and the Shire, and the steamer stopped at Chiromo, on the north bank of the river Ruo. Here we found a large native village, under two young chiefs, Mbengwa and Makwira, sons of the Chipatula who had been killed by Fenwick. There was an English trading station at Chiromo, belonging to two young English elephant hunters, named Pettitt. Whilst the steamer stopped at Chiromo, I saw the two chiefs, and explained to them that they were not to take any aggressive action against the Portuguese, even if the latter crossed the Ruo in force. In such a case as this they were to inform the Acting Consul at Blantyre. From Chiromo we passed on up the River Shire, through the Elephant Marsh, but as we approached nearer to the Makololo settlements beyond the Elephant Marsh, the captain of the *James Stevenson* became greatly perturbed as to the attitude which might be observed by the powerful Makololo chief, Mlauri. Mlauri was no more friendly at that time to the English than to the Portuguese. Towards the English he had been very aggressive on account of his not having been recognised as supreme chief of the Makololo. He had several times tried to get hold of the two young chiefs of Chiromo, in order that he might kill them, and was furious with the Pettitts and with a Mr. Simpson, an engineer in the service of the Lakes Company, for having intervened to protect them. Mlauri in those days occupied a strong position at Mbewe, a place some little distance below Katunga, the termination of river navigation on the Lower Shire. The set of the current compelled all steamers to pass close under the cliff of Mbewe, and they were therefore completely at the mercy of Mlauri's guns, and Mlauri was frequently in the habit of firing at the steamers to compel them to stop, and either give him a present or await his good pleasure in other respects. He had been the leading spirit in the sinking of the *Lady Nyasa* at the time of the disturbance following the death of Chipatula, and not having been punished for this his tyrannical obstructions to river navigation were becoming unbearable.

As we neared Mbewe, we saw the banks lined with armed men. The captain of the *James Stevenson* at first determined to steam by at full speed, but the natives shouted from the banks that if we did not stop and come to an anchor they would fire on us. I therefore advised the captain to anchor his vessel at Mbewe, and determined to go on shore and interview Mlauri, with the double object of protesting against his behaviour towards the British steamers, and cautioning him about falling out with the Portuguese. The Rev. Alexander Hetherwick, of the Church of Scotland Mission, was a fellow traveller with me on board the *James Stevenson*, and when he heard of my intention to see Mlauri, he kindly volunteered his services as interpreter. In those days I could speak nothing but Swahili, and although this language might be partially understood by Mlauri, it was preferable to talk straight to him in his own language—Chi-nyanja.

We landed amongst a jeering crowd of warriors, armed with guns, who were rather inclined to hustle us, but eventually we found our way without misadventure to the presence of Mlauri, who was seated in an open space on a chair, with a gaudy blanket wrapped round his loins, and a tall white chimney-pot hat on his head. He was surrounded by a semi-circle of warriors and headmen, and directed us to be seated on some rickety-looking camp chairs placed opposite to him, evidently in readiness for our visit. On our attempting to sit on the chairs they collapsed, and we fell to the ground amid

FOUNDING THE PROTECTORATE

shouts of derisive laughter from the natives. After this I lost my temper, and so severely rated Mlauri in Swahili that whether he understood the drift of my words or not, he was convinced I was extremely angry, and being—like most of these negro chiefs—a coward as well as a bully, he became quite apologetic. When fresh and more secure seats had been brought for us I explained to him—through Mr. Hetherwick—firstly, that these attempts to obstruct the navigation of the Shire would get him into trouble with Her Majesty's Government, and, secondly, that he had better not attempt to fight the Portuguese if they forced their way through his country, but should leave this matter to be decided between the two Governments. Mlauri replied, discursively, giving as his reason for annoying the steamers that he was not allowed to seize Chipatula's two sons, and that the English would not recognise him as paramount chief of the Makololo. Also that he felt convinced that we were in league with the Portuguese, and that all white men were equally bad. He would, therefore, fight Major Serpa Pinto, unless the latter broke up his camp and retired to the Zambezi.

I reiterated my advice to him, not to pursue such a course, and then returned to the steamer, which was allowed to leave without further opposition on the part of the natives. We soon reached Katunga's, which in some sense is the port of Blantyre, that place being about twenty-five miles distant over the hills. At Katunga I was met by Mr. John Buchanan, the Acting Consul; by the Rev. D. C. Scott, of the Church of Scotland Mission; Mr. John Moir, the Manager of the Lakes Company; and by a trader whom I will call Mr. S., who was a British subject of German origin. I explained to these gentlemen the end that I had in view, namely, to secure treaties of friendship with the Makololo and Yao chiefs, but not to declare a British Protectorate if possible, unless the Portuguese forced my hand, for I considered it better to leave the ultimate decision as to a Protectorate with Her Majesty's Government, who would probably wait till they had first negotiated a settlement of boundaries with the Portuguese. Mr. Buchanan and Mr. Moir were delighted at the idea of the treaties of friendship, but a violent opposition was declared thereto by Mr. S., the trader, an opposition which, at the time, I was totally unable to understand, but which was made clear to me afterwards by the discovery

MR. JOHN BUCHANAN

that Mr. S. had, himself, attempted to conclude treaties with the native chiefs, by which they were to yield to him their sovereign rights. He had not, up to that time, succeeded in inducing them to do so, but he was counting much on exploiting the ill-humour of Mlauri. It is not very clear what were the intentions of Mr. S.—whether to start a Chartered Company of his own, or, having acquired a sovereignty over the Shire Highlands, to make terms for himself with either England or Germany, England being the country of his adoption, and Germany the land of his birth. I do not give this gentleman's name in full, because, when the British Protectorate was finally declared, he accepted it loyally. I only mention the incident here because it was one which rather precipitated our political action.

A treaty of friendship was concluded by Mr. Buchanan at Katunga with all the Makololo chiefs except Mlauri. Subsequently, when Mlauri had received his first defeat at the hands of the Portuguese, he made a treaty also with Mr. Buchanan.

Mr. Moir, the manager of the Lakes Company, had invited me to be his guest at Mandala, near Blantyre, and had brought down a horse for me to ride. In those days there were only two horses in British Central Africa; one of these was ill, and the other lent to me was rather an unmanageable beast. It had evidently been bored by the long delay in treaty-making at Katunga, and was desperately anxious to return to the pleasanter climate of Blantyre, so that when I mounted at Katunga station, it instantly bolted, nearly beheading me in the low gateway which formed the entrance to the station. Its frantic gallop was checked at the ascent to the hills, and I regained command over it; but soon afterwards the rotten leather bridle came to pieces, and before I could clutch at the two ends they had fallen to the ground, the horse had put his foot on them, snapping them off, and there I was on his back, without any means of controlling him. He realised the situation, and once more raced along the narrow path. I did not fall off, but entered Blantyre more like Mazeppa than a well-conducted British official. In passing through the various archways and tunnels covered with very thorny roses, which diversified the garden approach to Mr. Moir's house, I could only save myself from serious damage by lying as flat as possible on the horse's back, with my arms round his neck. He made straight for his stable, and at the fortunately closed door came to a dead stop. I rolled off his back, bleeding and bruised, and have always regarded that first ride from Katunga to Blantyre as the greatest risk I ever ran in British Central Africa.

At Blantyre treaties were concluded with the Yao chiefs; and I organised, with the help of Mr. John Moir, my expedition to the north end of Lake Nyasa. Before leaving for the lake, I made arrangements with Mr. John Buchanan as to the course which should be pursued if the Portuguese attempted to take forcible possession of the Shire Highlands. In such an event as this, if the Portuguese crossed the Ruo in force and gave any evidence of an intention to occupy the country politically, Mr. Buchanan was to proclaim a British Protectorate over the Shire province, between Lake Chilwa and the Kirk Mountains of Angoniland, the River Ruo and Zomba Mountain. This step, however, was not to be taken and Her Majesty's Government was not to be pledged to a Protectorate over the Shire Highlands, unless there was no option between such a proceeding and passively admitting the Portuguese conquest of the country.[1]

Subsequent to my departure the following events took place. Major Serpa Pinto advanced northwards, along the west bank of the Shire, and was attacked by the Makololo[2] under Mlauri. Mlauri excused himself for this action afterwards by complaining that the Portuguese on the east bank of the Shire had

[1] The Protectorate was proclaimed September 21, 1889, after the news of the first conflict between the Portuguese and the Makololo (at Mpatsa, just below the Ruo) had reached Mr. Buchanan, who was then trying to pacify the Makololo.
[2] November 8, 1889.

FOUNDING THE PROTECTORATE

been the aggressors, and had raided some of his villages. His attack, however, was completely repulsed by the Portuguese, who inflicted upon him a very sanguinary defeat. Up to this point Major Serpa Pinto had not crossed the hypothetical boundary of English and Portuguese interests, which had been once or twice mentioned to be the River Ruo, and a line—more or less parallel with the confluence of the Ruo—drawn westward across the Shire. So far as I am aware Major Serpa Pinto never crossed this line, but when brought face to face with the question of doing so, and thereby bringing the Portuguese Government into almost open conflict with the British, he left the expedition

MASEA AND MWITU, TWO OF LIVINGSTONE'S MAKOLOLO

under the charge of Lieut. Coutinho, and proceeded to Moçambique for further instructions.[1] In his absence, however, Lieut. Coutinho, whose attitude towards Major Serpa Pinto may be described in Lady Macbeth's lines—

"Infirm of purpose! Give *me* the dagger!"

resolved to conquer the Shire province, and meet English remonstrances with a *fait accompli*. Hitherto all the other Makololo chiefs had followed my advice, and had not joined Mlauri in attacking the Portuguese. Mlauri's action was quite isolated, but Lieut. Coutinho had established a camp on the other side of the River Ruo, facing Chiromo. The two young Chiromo chiefs were careful to give no cause of offence to Lieut. Coutinho, who suddenly crossed the Ruo and seized Chiromo. The Makololo withdrew before him, and he destroyed their village and erected very strong fortifications on the small spit of land,

[1] Arriving there December 25, 1889.

which is a peninsula, with the Shire on the one side and the Ruo on the other.[1]

The Portuguese forces then marched up both banks of the Shire, driving Mlauri before them. Prior to his first defeat at the hands of the Portuguese Mlauri had concluded a treaty with Mr. Buchanan, but as the latter had forbidden him to fight with the Portuguese, he was not encouraged, after his defeat, to take refuge at Blantyre, whither all the other Makololo chiefs proceeded. The Portuguese forces advanced as far as Katunga, and were making preparations to occupy Blantyre, when the English Ultimatum to Portugal brought matters to a standstill. I have always believed that the Portuguese Government in Lisbon neither sanctioned nor approved this forcible entry into the district in dispute between England and Portugal, and that they even transmitted instructions to Major Serpa Pinto and others not to cross the Ruo, if by so doing any conflict was likely to arise with British interests; but that their representative at Moçambique desired a bolder policy and acted far beyond his instructions, and even in defiance of them : for at the time when the Portuguese Government in Lisbon had assured Lord Salisbury that Major Serpa Pinto had left for Moçambique, and that the expedition would proceed no farther in the direction of the Shire Highlands, the Portuguese Governor-General at Moçambique issued an official gazette announcing that the Shire province had been annexed to the Portuguese dominions, and appointed Lieut. Coutinho "Governor of the Shire." These acts were annulled by the Portuguese Government after they were brought to their knowledge by the Ultimatum, and the Portuguese forces were withdrawn to the Portuguese side of the Ruo, though they continued to exercise a strict control over the Shire navigation, frequently stopping the British steamers and boats. At the same time, I think it is only right, in historical justice to Portugal, to make it clear that although this struggle for the possession of Nyasaland was a sufficiently acute question to the Portuguese, and one in which they were passionately interested, no such struggle for priority of rights was conducted with more fairness and even chivalry. For instance, had Major Serpa Pinto been an unscrupulous man he would have, on some pretext or another, stopped my small expedition, and whilst detaining me on this pretext, have marched ahead and arbitrarily seized the country, before anything could be done to preserve British interests. Again, even after the Portuguese had advanced as far as Katunga, and occupied both banks of the Shire river, between that place and Chiromo, they placed no obstacle in the way of my return. On the contrary, the following incident occurred between myself and Lieut. Coutinho, who had been appointed "Governor of the Shire." When I passed down that river on my return from Tanganyika my boat was stopped by his orders and drawn into the bank by a Portuguese sergeant. I was, at first, annoyed at what seemed to be an attempt to arrest my progress towards the coast, but fortunately, before I could give expression to my angry sentiments, Lieut. Coutinho had met me on the bank, and, raising his hat, said, " I have taken the liberty of stopping you so that you might not miss your mail-bags which are here awaiting you. As you have had

---

[1] Chiromo means "a big lip," from the word -romo, or -lomo, which in so many Bantu languages means "a lip." The chi- or ki- prefix in Chi-nyanja has the effect of an augmentative. Mromo means "a lip"; "Chiromo" means "a big lip." This chi- prefix, which becomes si- in Zulu, has in that language the effect of a diminutive, consequently " Silomo," the Zulu name given to a well-known member of Parliament by the Swazi Envoys, means "a little lip," but is otherwise identical in origin with the name of this place in British Central Africa, for a year such a bone of contention between England and Portugal.

FOUNDING THE PROTECTORATE

a long and arduous journey in the interior, and are also, I hear, short of provisions, I have taken the liberty of making up this small supply for your use on your way to Quelimane." Therewith he handed into the boat two hampers, which contained not only a supply of champagne and other wines, but all sorts of little luxuries very grateful to the jaded palate of a travel-weary man. Then, giving me a letter to ensure my not being stopped on my way to Quelimane, he bade me farewell. Upon my expressing my thanks very warmly, he said, "We are both doing our best for our respective countries, and however much our political views may differ that is no reason why one white man should quarrel with another in Central Africa." This was indeed the keynote of the Portuguese demeanour towards me, then and thenceforth, and I feel it only just to place these facts on record, for I have been often vexed at the unjust aspersions which have been cast upon the Portuguese in the British Press.

On my way up the Shire to Blantyre I had encountered Mr. Alfred Sharpe, who was travelling up the river in his own boat. Knowing that a great deal of ground would have to be covered in treaty-making, and that I should be unable to reach all parts of British Central Africa myself, I desired to engage some one who might suitably represent me in such portions of this territory as lay outside my line of route, especially in Central Zambezia and the countries between Nyasaland and the Barutse. The latter country had been placed under the British flag by Mr. Rhodes's agents acting for the Chartered Company.

I had heard much of Mr. Alfred Sharpe from persons acquainted with Nyasaland. He had taken a leading part in the war between the Arabs and the Lakes Company, in which war he had been wounded. Mr. Sharpe, who had been trained for the law, had held a Colonial appointment in Fiji for some years, but when this appointment, in common with many others, was abolished at a time when the state of Fiji finances compelled severe retrenchments, he had been offered a District Commissionership on the Gold Coast. For a time, however, he preferred to travel and hunt in Central Africa. In 1890 Mr. Sharpe accepted employment under the British South Africa Company, in whose service he remained about a year, securing for them many important concessions north of the Zambezi. Early in 1891 he was appointed H.M. Vice-Consul in British Central Africa.[1] It had been arranged between Mr. Sharpe and myself, before I quitted Blantyre for the north, that he should proceed due westward to beyond the Portuguese dominions at Zumbo, and secure to the British the Central Zambezi, and that afterwards he should make treaties along the Luangwa River and, northwards, to Lake Mweru and Lake Tanganyika. All this he successfully accomplished. After passing into the service of the British South Africa Company he made an expedition to Katunga, but did not succeed in making a treaty, as the chief, Msiri, though expressing a desire to remain on friendly terms with all white men, refused to become subservient to any particular European Nation. Subsequently Msiri similarly refused to make a treaty with Captain Stair's expedition, which represented the Congo Free State, and having assumed a hostile demeanour towards the expedition he was shot by the late Captain Bodson, who himself was killed immediately afterwards by Msiri's followers. His country was afterwards annexed to the Congo Free State.[2]

[1] Consul in 1894; Deputy Commissioner in 1896.
[2] Msiri does not deserve much pity. He was a stranger to the country of Katunga, being merely a Mnyamwezi slave trader who by the aid of an armed rabble of Wanyamwezi freebooters and coast Arabs had carved out a kingdom for himself in South Central Africa. He was a persistent slave raider and was hated by the people over whom he ruled. These latter rallied to the Belgian authorities after Msiri's death.

Mr. Joseph Thomson in 1890 came out with Mr. J. A. Grant, on behalf of the British South Africa Company, and supplemented Mr. Sharpe's work by securing further treaties and concessions in the central region of British Central Africa, but the main credit of having secured all this portion of our new dependency to the British Flag emphatically lies with Mr. Sharpe, who traversed the country with a following scarcely exceeding fifteen to twenty men, and, by the weight of his personal influence only, secured these countries to British interests, besides adding a great deal to our geographical knowledge.[1]

In my journey from Blantyre to Lake Nyasa along the Upper Shire, my progress was beset with great difficulties owing to the civil war which was raging between the Yao chiefs, Mponda and Msamara.

My assistant, Mr. Nicoll, took charge of that portion of the expedition which travelled by water, whilst I marched overland. As we neared the south end of the lake we were stopped by Msamara's forces in the belief that we were about to render assistance to Mponda. I managed, however, to pacify Msamara by making a treaty of friendship with him, and months afterwards I succeeded in patching up a peace between him and Mponda.

Mponda's reception of us was rather doubtful. He denied having concluded any treaty with the Portuguese, but was averse to concluding even a treaty of friendship with Great Britain, at any rate without the sanction of the Sultan of Zanzibar's representative on the lake—the Jumbe at Kotakota. Mponda was a very repellent type of Yao robber, alternately cringing and insolent. Had not the Universities Mission steamer arrived by good chance to give me a passage to Likoma (where I was to see Bishop Smythies) I might have been robbed and murdered by Mponda. As it was my retreat to the Mission steamer was very like a flight. However, I got away safely with all my goods and proceeded to the Island of Likoma. My object in seeing Bishop Smythies was to obtain the use of the *Charles Janson* for a period, in order to enable me to bring about peace with the Arabs. At that time the Lakes Company had only one steamer plying on the lake, the little *Ilala*—which besides being much out of repair, was too small for the conveyance of even my limited expedition. The Bishop was good enough to place his steamer at my disposal, for though the Universities Mission then and always declared its intention of remaining absolutely neutral in political matters, they were anxious to do all in their power to assist me to bring about peace between the Lakes Company and the Arabs.

We then crossed to Bandawe on the west side of the lake. From this place Mr. Nicoll proceeded direct to Karonga in the *Ilala*, bearing letters from me to the North Nyasa Arabs. I remained some days at Bandawe, concluding treaties with the Atonga chiefs. Then the *Charles Janson* called in and took me down to a point fifteen miles distant from Jumbe's capital at Kotakota, where its commander landed my expedition on the lake shore. His reasons for not proceeding to Kotakota arose from two considerations. One was that Jumbe, after all, was an Arab and might make common cause with the north-end Arabs and seize the steamer. The second was that at that time the harbour at Kotakota was unsurveyed and was not thought to be safe for steamers of considerable draught. I must admit that I landed with Ali Kiongwe, my

---

[1] The late Mr. Joseph Thomson's claims to fame and to our gratitude are so numerous that it is no loss to him to spare a few laurel leaves to Mr. Sharpe. The treaty which Mr. Thomson made with the Emperor of Sakatu on behalf of the Royal Niger Company, was alone a transcendent benefit to British interests never to be forgotten.

FOUNDING THE PROTECTORATE

headman, and my small expedition of fifteen Makua in some considerable trepidation. The Lakes Company half feared that Jumbe was going to join the Arab movement at the north end. At this time, too, all Arabs in Central Africa were much incensed against Europeans by their quarrels with the Germans and the Belgians. The way in which they would receive me, therefore, was very doubtful. Makanjira on the opposite coast had recently stripped and flogged a British Consul and held him up to ransom, and no measures had been taken to avenge this insult. After landing near the mouth of the Bua river I sent Ali Kiongwe ahead to interview Jumbe and to deliver to him the letters that I had brought from the Sultan of Zanzibar. On my journey down the east coast of Africa I had stopped at Zanzibar, and had conferred with the late Sir Gerald Portal, then Acting Consul-General at that place, on the subject

OUTSKIRTS OF KOTAKOTA

of my mission to Lake Nyasa. Mr. Portal (as he then was) had interested himself very much in this undertaking to make peace with the Arabs, and urged the Sultan Khalifa bin Said (whose own envoy previously dispatched had been unsuccessful in bringing the Arabs to reason) to provide me with the most authoritative letters to his representatives on Lake Nyasa, notably to the Jumbe of Kotakota, who was the Sultan's ostensible *wali*, or representative. The Sultan Khalifa willingly gave these letters, which were most potent in effecting the subsequent results.

Some hours after Ali Kiongwe had started for Kotakota, a Swahili soldier of Jumbe's came rushing down into our camp, dropped on one knee and seized me by the leg, as an act of homage. He then said, " Master, do not be alarmed, Jumbe sends us to greet the representative of the great Queen and of the Sayyid of Zanzibar, and he has told us to fire a salute of guns in your honour." Shortly afterwards a tremendous fusilade commenced, much to the alarm of my porters, who had not understood the purport of Jumbe's message. We then started for Kotakota, Jumbe's men insisting on carrying me in a machilla.[1] Jumbe was waiting to receive me as I entered the town. A large house and compound was set aside for my use. Oxen were killed for myself and

---

[1] Machilla is a Portuguese word (Latin *Maxilla*), which is universally applied in Eastern Africa to a hammock or chair slung on a pole and carried by porters.

my men, and quantities of provisions of all kinds were sent in for our sustenance. After a day's rest I had a long conversation with Jumbe, to whom I exposed frankly the whole political situation. As soon as I had quitted the Shire River I had felt free to take open political action, as after my stay in Lisbon there had been a tacit understanding between the Portuguese and ourselves that although the Shire province and a portion of the east coast of Lake Nyasa were territories not to be seized by either Power without arrangement, the west coast of Lake Nyasa was admittedly open to British enterprise. I therefore advised Jumbe, who was now practically recognised by the Sultan of Zanzibar as an independent Prince, to place his country under British protection, and to mobilise a sufficient number of his men to compel the North Nyasa Arabs to agree to make terms of peace; and in the event of their not so agreeing to place this force at my disposal for their coercion. Jumbe, in return for all these services, was to receive a subsidy of £200 per annum. The slave trade was to be declared at an end in his dominions. After one day's deliberation with his head men, Jumbe assented to my propositions. Treaties and agreements were signed, the British flag was hoisted, and the first portion of British Central Africa was secured. I should then have been picked up by the *Ilala* and conveyed to the north, but unfortunately the *Ilala*, unknown to me, had been wrecked in a storm, and she did not resume her voyages on the lake for several years afterwards. Meantime I waited on and on at Jumbe's, treated by that chief with unwearied hospitality, though I used up almost all his stock of candles, and consumed all his supplies of tinned fruits. The only thing I could offer him in return for all his hospitality was a bottle of yellow Chartreuse. Jumbe was a very strict Muhammadan, especially on the subject of alcohol, but he suffered much from asthma. He appealed to me repeatedly for medicine, and as I had no drugs with me I was in despair, until it occurred to me that a small glass of Chartreuse might at any rate distract his thoughts if it did not remedy the asthma. I gave him a taste of what he called "the golden water." He at once declared himself cured, and the least I could do was to hand him the entire bottle, which he spent, I believe, several months in consuming. It was the one

THE LATE TAWAKALI SUDI
JUMBE OF KOTAKOTA, WALI OF H.H. THE SULTAN OF ZANZIBAR ON LAKE NYASA

thing, he told me afterwards, that he felt obliged to deny to his head wife, "the lady Siena."[1]

At last my detention was becoming a little tedious, and I was very anxious about the missing steamer. To soothe my anxiety, Jumbe sent for his necromancer, who was to ascertain, by means of "raml" (sand), what the

NORTH NYASA ARABS: BWANA 'OMARI IN THE FOREGROUND

immediate future had in store for me as regards steamer communication. The necromancer informed us that the small steamer (the *Ilala*) had run aground on the rocks, but the "Bishop's steamer"[2] would shortly call for me. This information turned out to be perfectly correct, and no doubt the necromancer had other sources of knowledge than those which were occult.

[1] Or the "bibi mkubwa," ("great lady") as she was commonly called.
[2] The *Charles Janson* used to be always called by the Arabs, "Istima-al-Askaf," the "Bishop's steamer."

His news was true, for eventually the *Charles Janson*, with Archdeacon Maples on board, came to fetch me and convey me to Karonga.

I found on arrival here that Mr. Nicoll had concluded in my name a truce with the Arabs, and that the ground was prepared for negotiation. I may briefly relate that as the Arabs were very distrustful, I arranged to meet them in the bush midway between their nearest stockade and Karonga, stipulating that they should only be accompanied by a small escort, and that I would only bring with me the same number of men. I was accompanied by Mr. Nicoll, Mr. Monteith Fotheringham, and a few armed Atonga. Mlozi, Kopakopa, Bwana 'Omari, Msalemu, and other Arabs, duly met me at the point agreed upon. After a brief discussion I read out to them the terms of the treaty which I proposed, and told them that if they refused it we should prosecute the war to the bitter end until not one of them was left in the country. They accepted these terms almost without deliberation and the treaty was forthwith signed, and peace was declared.

A bull was killed as a sacrifice, and the flesh was distributed amongst our men and the men who had accompanied the Arabs. On the following day the British flag was run up at Karonga, and the native chiefs from the surrounding districts came in and signed treaties, accepting British protection. On the following day the Arabs paid us a return visit at Karonga, signed treaties of protection and accepted the British flag. Mr. Crawshay[1] then arrived from Deep Bay with a large number of Wahenga chiefs in canoes, who signed treaties of protection. Thus protection treaties had now been concluded between Jumbe's territory on the south-west of Lake Nyasa, and the extreme north-east corner of the lake.

I was at this time much exercised about the want of a secure harbour at the north end of Lake Nyasa. Karonga was an open roadstead, most dangerous for landing, for it must always be remembered that Lake Nyasa is as rough at times as the British Channel, with heavy breakers on unprotected shores. The existence of a secure harbour in Kambwe lagoon, $3\frac{1}{2}$ miles to the north of Karonga, had not then been made known, or it may be that owing to various circumstances it did not then exist as a harbour which vessels of considerable draught could enter. After examining carefully the north coast of Lake Nyasa, I decided to secure the harbour of Parumbira, at the extreme northernmost corner of the lake, for the African Lakes Company. I accordingly bought the land for them, and placed an agent there to build and occupy. Subsequently, however, by the Anglo-German Agreement of 1890, the boundary between the two European Powers was drawn at the River Songwe, and Parumbira fell to Germany. It is now the headquarters of the German Government, on Lake Nyasa, and has been rechristened Langenburg.

Only one week was occupied at Karonga in making peace with the Arabs; securing North Nyasa by treaty; choosing this harbour for the African Lakes Company; and arranging my caravan for Lake Tanganyika. But the reason

---

[1] Mr. Crawshay, originally a lieutenant in the Inniskilling Dragoons, had come out to British Central Africa to shoot big game, and had joined the Lakes Company's forces as a volunteer in the war against the Arabs. After Captain Lugard had captured Deep Bay, an important harbour on the north-west coast of Lake Nyasa, used by the Arabs as the end of a ferry to the east side of the Lake, Mr. Crawshay for some months garrisoned this place as a fort, and kept the Arabs out of Deep Bay. He acquired a considerable influence amongst the Wahenga, and was of much service to me in the early days of the Protectorate. Until quite recently he was Vice-Consul for the north of Lake Nyasa, but retired from this appointment on account of ill-health.

FOUNDING THE PROTECTORATE

why it was possible to dispatch such a mass of important business in seven days, was that I was most ably seconded by Mr. J. L. Nicoll. My having secured this gentleman at Quelimane as my second in command really did more than anything else to secure the complete success to my mission. We started for Tanganyika on the 10th of November, 1889. To obtain as much territory for England as possible I journeyed at first in a northerly direction, and penetrated as far to the north-east as the southern shores of Lake Rukwa, a salt lake of considerable size. Mr. Nicoll, Dr. Kerr Cross (who had joined us) and myself, were the first Europeans to discover the southern end of this lake. The country all round Rukwa, however, was so desolate and inhabited by such a reprehensible set of slave raiders, that I concluded no treaties with them, and was thankful to get my expedition out of their clutches without loss of goods or lives. Returning to the beautiful Nyasa-Tanganyika plateau, we found ourselves again among people

LANGENBURG, CAPITAL OF GERMAN NYASALAND

who were warm friends of the British, and who everywhere concluded treaties with expressions of positive enthusiasm. The A-mambwe, especially, had come to look upon the British as their champions against the Arab slave traders, and were almost frantic in their expressions of friendship. Nevertheless the A-mambwe were very quarrelsome amongst themselves, and when I reached the London Missionary Society's station at Fwambo, about thirty miles from the south end of Lake Tanganyika, I found the Missionaries were in a serious fix. In the first place they had been for more than a year cut off from supplies and letters and were much delighted to get their mails and such supplies as I could bring them, but they were still more seriously embarrassed because two chiefs were fighting one another, and their servants had left them to join the respective sides to which they belonged. A little good-humoured argument, however, secured peace between these rival chieftains, who in turn concluded treaties with us ; and I reached the south end of Tanganyika with no further difficulty except occasional scares amongst my porters caused by the dread of Awemba raiders. At the south end of Tanganyika I was greeted by Mr. A. J. Swann, who was the master of the London Missionary Society's steamer on that lake. Mr. Swann threw himself heart and soul into assisting me in my projects. Unfortunately the Mission steamer was laid up for repairs, but Mr. Swann placed their sailing boat at my disposal. By means of this boat I visited all the chiefs on the south end of Lake Tanganyika, made treaties with them, and further penetrated to the settlements of Kabunda, an Arab trader, who had almost constituted himself a native chief. It was important in those days to conciliate Kabunda, who had remained neutral in the war between the Arabs and Lakes Company, and who had a great influence over the native chiefs. He was really a Baluch in origin, not an Arab, and considered himself in some respects a British subject. He entertained Mr. Swann and myself with the greatest hospitality, and assisted us to enter into treaties with the chiefs of Itawa, in the direction of Lake Mweru. This being the limit of the journey which I had to perform (Mr. Sharpe was working for me to the west), I decided to return at once to the Shire Highlands, as rumours had reached me of war with the Portuguese. It was a great disappointment for me to turn back at this juncture, as I desired to go to the north end of Tanganyika and secure for England the north end of that lake,[1] but I felt it to be my duty to get through to the coast and send a report of the work already done; so I reluctantly postponed the completion of a scheme, which was, as I hoped, to give us continuous communication between Cape Town and Cairo, either over international waterways or along British territory. On my return journey, in which no unpleasant incident occurred, I found Mponda, the Yao chief at the south end of Lake Nyasa, in a more reasonable frame of mind, and concluded a treaty with him. I reached Moçambique at the end of January, 1890, telegraphed the result of my work to the Foreign Office, and subsequently proceeded to Zanzibar to make arrangements for the conclusion of treaties at the north end of Tanganyika. Not being able to return thither myself, as my health was failing, I entrusted the task to Mr. A. J. Swann, and sent up to him an expedition under the leadership of my invaluable Swahili headman, Ali-Kiongwe. Mr. Swann's expedition was entirely successful. Treaties were made and the British flag was planted at the extreme north end of Lake Tanganyika. Unfortunately, however, his treaties arrived too late to be taken into consideration at the conclusion of the Anglo-German Convention; but Lord Salisbury managed to secure by that Convention facilities for the crossing of German territory between Tanganyika and Uganda, which will be very important to us in future developments.

In forwarding my report to the Foreign Office I proposed the term "British Central Africa" for the territories just brought under British influence. Soon after my return to England in the early summer of 1890 the Anglo-German Convention was signed, which, among other important gains to Great Britain, set a seal on the work which the British South Africa Company, Sharpe, Nicoll, Swann, Fotheringham, Buchanan and I had done. This was followed by an abortive Convention with Portugal which, however, proved to be the basis of a definite understanding concluded with that Power in 1891. In the spring of 1891 the British Protectorate over the countries adjoining Lake Nyasa was proclaimed, and by the Conventions with Germany and Portugal, the remainder of British Central Africa was declared to be an exclusively British sphere of influence.

After the conclusion of the Anglo-German Convention Her Majesty conferred on Mr. John Buchanan a C.M.G., and on myself a C.B. Mr. W. A. Churchill, who, during my absence in the interior, had done excellent work

---

[1] With land hunger *l'appetit vient en mangeant.*

FOUNDING THE PROTECTORATE

at Moçambique, when matters had been in a most critical state with Portugal, was promoted to be Her Majesty's Vice-Consul; Mr. Alfred Sharpe and Mr. Alexander Carnegie Ross[1] (who had been British Vice-Consul at Quelimane) were equally made Commissioned Vice-Consuls; Mr. J. L. Nicoll (who had remained a year at Tanganyika to strengthen the British position at the south end of that lake) was given an important post in the Administration of the new Protectorate; Mr. John Buchanan, when he ceased to be Acting Consul, was made a Vice-Consul; Mr. Crawshay, Mr. Swann, and Mr. Belcher (the Commander of the Universities Mission steamer on Lake Nyasa)[2] all subsequently joined the Administration of the British Central Africa Protectorate. Mr. Monteith Fotheringham, the agent of the Lakes Company at Karonga, who had rendered me very great services, preferred, however, to remain in the employment of the African Lakes Company, as he was subsequently offered the important post of manager at Mandala.

In the autumn of 1890 Her Majesty's Government began to consider the administration of these new territories. It was finally decided to confine the actual Protectorate to the regions adjacent to Lake Nyasa and the River Shire, and to administer that Protectorate directly by a Commissioner under the Imperial Government, and further to place all the rest of the Sphere of Influence, north of the Zambezi, under the Charter of the British South Africa Company, subject of course to certain conditions. I was appointed to be Commissioner and Consul-General to administer the Protectorate, and was chosen by the British South Africa Company as their Administrator north of the Zambezi, an unpaid post which I held for nearly five years.[3]

By an arrangement between the Chartered Company and Her Majesty's Government, the former contributed annually for a certain number of years the sum of £10,000 per annum, for the maintenance of a police force to be used by me indifferently in the Protectorate and in the Company's Sphere. The Company also met the cost of administering its own Sphere of Influence north of the Zambezi, and further agreed to provide us, by arrangement with the African Lakes Company, with the free use of that Company's boats and steamers.[4]

On my return to British Central Africa as Commissioner and Consul-General and Administrator for the British South Africa Company's territories to the north of the Zambezi, I appointed to my staff Lieut., now Captain, B. L. Sclater, R.E. (who took with him three non-commissioned officers of the Royal Engineers); Mr. Alexander Whyte, F.Z.S. (as a practical Botanist and Natural History Collector); and, with the consent of the Indian Government, engaged

[1] Now H.M. Consul at Beira.
[2] Now H.M. Vice-Consul at Quelimane.
[3] I preferred to receive no pay from the Company, so that I might not in any way compromise my position as an Imperial Officer.
[4] Roughly speaking the Company thus pledged itself to spend about £17,500 a year on British Central Africa. For the first two years, however, the average amount spent per annum did not reach this sum, but in the third year it was deemed advisable that I should come to some definite agreement with the Company in regard to their annual contribution, which was then fixed at £17,500. In addition to this allowance Mr. Rhodes agreed to provide as much as £10,000 for the special purpose of conquering the chief Makanjira, who persistently raided the south-eastern portion of our territories. Of this sum a little over £4,000 was actually spent. In 1894 this arrangement came to an end. At the beginning of the financial year 1895, the Company ceased to provide any contribution whatever towards the administration of the Protectorate, and the Imperial Government returned to them a proportion of the amounts already contributed. The Company in 1895 undertook the administration of its own Sphere at its own expense, and the Protectorate was thenceforth assisted by contributions from Her Majesty's Government only.

Captain Cecil Montgomery Maguire[1] (of the Haiderabad Contingent Lancers) to raise a small force of Indian troops as a nucleus for our police force in Central Africa. Captain Maguire was to start from India and meet me at the mouth of the River Chinde. Captain Sclater and the rest of my staff were to leave England subsequent to myself and also meet me at Chinde. In the meantime I proceeded to Zanzibar and Moçambique, to make arrangements for the disembarkation of my expedition at the mouth of the Zambezi. In the autumn of 1890 Lord Salisbury had resolved to place two gunboats on the Zambezi, and these vessels, the *Herald* and the *Mosquito*, were very ably put together at Chinde under the superintendence of the Senior Naval Officer, Commander J. H. Keane, R.N., C.M.G., who managed to launch his gunboats without undue friction with the Portuguese. All the various sections of my

SIKH SOLDIERS OF THE CONTINGENT NOW SERVING IN BRITISH CENTRAL AFRICA

expedition arrived with delightful punctuality at Chinde, and with the aid of the two gunboats and the steamers of the African Lakes Company we conveyed men, beasts, and goods without accident to Chiromo.

By the Anglo-Portuguese Convention of 1891 we had lost a little territory to the west of the Shire basin, but had been allotted in exchange by the Portuguese a portion of the right bank of the River Shire, below the Ruo Junction. This brought the British Protectorate almost within sight of the Zambezi. On my journey up the river, therefore, in H.M.S. *Herald*, I had to fix the Anglo-Portuguese boundary according to the Convention, and take over political possession of the Lower Shire District.

We had no sooner arrived at Chiromo in the month of July, 1891, than we were greeted with the news that the Yao chief, Chikumbu,[2] had attacked the British settlers who had commenced coffee-planting in that country. The

---

[1] Captain Maguire obtained from the Indian Army seventy volunteers, of whom about forty were Mazbi Sikhs, of the 23rd and 32nd Pioneers, and the remainder Muhammadan cavalrymen from the various regiments of Haiderabad Lancers. As nearly all our first batch of horses died of horse sickness or tsetse fly, the Cavalry became useless and were eventually sent back to India. We subsequently decided to engage in future nothing but Sikhs for our Indian Contingent.

[2] A recent arrival in the Mlanje district, who had developed by degrees into a powerful African chief.

ill-feeling between Chikumbu and the British was of some years' duration. Chikumbu was a Yao who had settled amongst the peaceful Nyanja people of Mlanje, whom he had been gradually subjugating until in 1890 they appealed to Mr. John Buchanan for protection. The old Nyanja chief, Chipoka, had died in 1890, and on his death-bed had, with the consent of all his sub-chiefs and subjects, transferred the sovereign rights of his country to the Queen, in order to pledge the British Government to the protection of the indigenous Nyanja people against Yao attacks. Two or three planters had just begun to settle in the Mlanje district, and although they had paid

H.M.S. "MOSQUITO," A ZAMBEZI GUNBOAT

relatively large sums to Chikumbu he continued to extort larger and larger payments from them; and at last, upon their refusing to give any more, committed various acts of violence, and stopped the natives working for them. Chikumbu was a very great slave trader and kept up a direcct communication with the East Coast of Africa at Angoche, whither his caravans of slaves were generally forwarded. He was allied with Matipwiri and other Yao slave-trading chiefs.

Accordingly Captain Maguire was dispatched two days after our reaching Chiromo, with a force of Sikhs to bring Chikumbu to reason. The campaign was not of long duration, though there were one or two days of stiff fighting. Chikumbu fled and his brother was taken prisoner. The latter was eventually released and appointed chief in Chikumbu's stead, upon his giving promises of good behaviour which have since been kept. After a considerable banishment Chikumbu was recently allowed to return, and lives now as a private individual.

Whilst Captain Maguire was thus engaged I had to spend two months at Chiromo, settling a great many matters in connection with the Lower Shire districts. I did not reach Zomba till the month of September 1891, and here I was joined by Captain Maguire. After a brief rest we were both obliged to start with a strong expedition for the south end of Lake Nyasa, owing to troubles of a complex kind which had broken out between Mponda and other Yao chiefs, and between Mponda and Chikusi, a chief of the Southern Angoni. We took with us a force of 70 Indian soldiers and 9 Zanzibaris; also a 7-pounder mountain gun, and marched up the east bank of the Shire. Although we had come to mediate between the chiefs whose fighting was temporarily stopping communications on the Shire and were not bent on any punitive measures except in regard to Makanjira, we were obliged to take considerable precautions against Mponda, who was uncertain in his attitude towards the British, and who waged these wars chiefly with the intention of securing slaves for the Kilwa[1] caravans which visited his country. To avoid coming into collision with him unnecessarily we encamped on the uninhabited reed wilderness opposite his main town on the east bank of the Shire, about three miles distant from the south end of Lake Nyasa. Though some of these Yao chiefs had invoked our intervention at a distance, their attitude became suspiciously hostile upon our entering their country with an armed force. Accordingly Captain Maguire deemed it prudent to throw up fortifications round our camp opposite Mponda's town. These had to be erected with stealth as Mponda was continually sending to enquire what we were doing, and we were anxious to avoid any attack on his part until we were capable of defending ourselves and our stores. Accordingly the defences of what Captain Maguire called, half in fun, "Fort Johnston," were constructed during the day-time in separate sections, which apparently had no connection with one another. Mponda was informed, when he came to see what we were doing, that these pits and sections of embankment were intended as sleeping shelters for the men. We then took advantage of a moonlight night, when the moon was half full, to work almost twelve hours on end, and by the next morning our camp was completely surrounded by mud and sand breastworks behind a revêtement of bamboo. Before this point was reached, however, an engagement had taken place with one of our enemies. Makandanji, a chief who dwelt on the south-east corner of Nyasa, had tied up and imprisoned our envoys. His town was about seven miles distant from Fort Johnston. Captain Maguire resolved on the true Napoleonic policy of crushing our enemies singly, and not waiting for them to come to terms as to a combined movement against us. He suddenly fell on Makandanji and drove him out of his village, releasing our imprisoned men, and scattering Makandanji's forces, which were never again able to take the field against us. Mponda, however, instead of joining Makandanji, seized the opportunity to capture nearly all the runaways, whom he forthwith marched off to his own town and sold as slaves to the Swahili caravans waiting there. Over seventy of the captives he had the insolence to drive through our camp at Fort Johnston, at a time when Captain Maguire was absent and I was left with only ten men. As soon as Captain Maguire was back and the little fort was completed, I summoned Mponda to set all these slaves at liberty. He declined to do so, and commenced warlike proceedings against us. We had timed our ultimatum for a day which was followed by full moon, and resolved to attack

[1] Kilwa, on the east coast of Africa, was formerly the great distributing depôt of the Nyasa slaves.

at night. Accordingly at nine o'clock, on the evening of the 19th of October, 1891, one hour after the expiration of the term given for the restoration of the slaves, we fired a shell across the river into Mponda's town, perhaps a quarter of a mile distant. Mponda had no conception of the range of artillery fire, or the effects of incendiary shells. The return fire of his guns and his muzzle-loading cannon was harmless, as we were almost beyond their effective range. A few more shells soon set much of Mponda's town on fire, and he called for a truce. This was granted, but he only made use of it to withdraw with his women and ivory to a strong place he possessed in the hills. His fighting men remained and we renewed the struggle, which we kept up till the early morning, when we landed on the opposite shore and drove the remainder of the defenders out of Mponda's town, which we then destroyed. A great many slaves were found by us in the town, and brought over to our camp. Many of these wretched people had come from vast distances in the interior of South Central

FORT JOHNSTON IN 1895

Africa. The following day Mponda asked for terms of peace, and peace was eventually concluded. He then informed us as to the whereabouts of the slave-trading caravans: Captain Maguire pursued these people, capturing seven of them and releasing large numbers of slaves. The terms of peace offered to Mponda were very fair, and he probably rather gained in power by coming to an understanding with us. For four years afterwards he kept the peace; then in the belief that we were going to get the worst of it at the hands of Zarafi, he unwisely went to war once more, with the result that he is now temporarily exiled from his country.

Makandanji, the first chief with whom we had fought, acknowledged the supremacy of Zarafi, a powerful chief who dwelt on a very high mountain 20 miles to the east of Fort Johnston. We knew little about Zarafi in those days, except that he had not long succeeded his mother, a famous woman-chief called Kabutu. Zarafi, imagining that we should follow the attack on Makandanji by an advance into his country, sent envoys down to treat with us for peace. We, therefore, on one day, concluded treaties with Mponda, Zarafi, and Makandanji, and seemed to have accomplished the pacification of South Nyasa.

Encouraged by this success, we then and there resolved to undertake the chastisement of Makanjira, who had, as already related, committed various outrages on British subjects, and had recently robbed the Universities Mission of a boat and killed some of their boatmen. We hired the African Lakes Company's steamer *Domira,* and mounted our 7-pounder gun in the bows Arriving suddenly off Makanjira's in the early morning, we were saluted by volleys from his fighting men, who were drawn up on the beach, and who had evidently been expecting our arrival. A shell landed in the middle of this yelling crowd produced an impression on them which was absolutely novel, and there was soon not one of the enemy in sight. After setting fire to a portion of the town with other shells, I effected a landing with a small number of Sikhs, whilst Captain Maguire kept the enemy at bay by bombarding the town from the steamer. We managed to land with only one or two casualties, and the Sikhs carried off two of Makanjira's cannon and set fire to one of his daus.[1] The enemy, however, came on us in such strength that we had to retreat to our boat, and should probably have not escaped with our lives had not Captain Maguire arrived with reinforcements. He drove the enemy back into the town, and completed the destruction of the dau.

The next morning Captain Maguire landed in force, and after hard fighting, in which several of our Sikhs were severely wounded, he captured all Makanjira's defences. I joined him, and we then drove the enemy out of the huge town, which we completely destroyed. We also destroyed two or three of their daus.

After waiting a day in vain to see if any person would come from Makanjira to treat for a peace, we steamed over to the opposite side of the lake, where it was necessary to come to an understanding with Kazembe, who lived opposite to Makanjira and was a near relation. Lake Nyasa is at its narrowest opposite Makanjira's town. Its breadth here is probably not more than fifteen miles. The favourite ferry across Lake Nyasa, therefore, has generally been between these two points, the one on the eastern shore held by Makanjira, the other on the west by Kazembe. Kazembe was a great slave trader, but was not hostile to the British. He had concluded a treaty with me in 1890, but it was necessary to warn him that the slave trade could no longer continue. He took the warning in good part, and promised good behaviour in future. This promise was not faithfully adhered to, and the result was that Kazembe was exiled from the Protectorate for a few months, but was subsequently restored to power, and is now chief in Makanjira's place.

After leaving Kazembe's, we revisited Makanjira's coast in the *Domira.* Captain Maguire landed at a town belonging to Makanjira's headman, Saidi Mwazungu, in the southern part of Makanjira's country, for the purpose of acquiring information. The people had not evinced unfriendliness as we approached, and Captain Maguire landed under a flag of truce. He was received by an Arab (who was said to have been a native of Aden) with a show of courtesy, but no sooner had he reached the veranda of the Arab's house than he was suddenly fired on by the Arab himself, who by some marvellous accident missed him, though only two or three yards distant. Captain Maguire had landed with only six men; but, hearing the shot, I immediately dispatched reinforcements to his assistance, and the town was soon taken and destroyed. The two remaining daus of Makanjira, in search

---

[1] A "dau" is an Arab sailing vessel, sometimes of considerable size. Spelt phonetically it should be *dau,* but the British, with their extraordinary racial perversity in matters of spelling, prefer without rhyme or reason to spell it "dhow."

of which Captain Maguire had landed, were either not there or had escaped before our coming.

We now returned to Zomba, leaving a garrison behind at Fort Johnston. We had no sooner reached Zomba than we heard of trouble from Kawinga, a powerful Yao chief who lived on a hill which was at the north-eastern extremity of the Zomba range. It was deemed advisable to dispatch an expedition against Kawinga, and this was accompanied by Mr. John Buchanan, C.M.G., who had become a Vice-Consul in the service of the Protectorate. Kawinga's fortress proved however to be a much harder nut to crack than we had expected. A gallant attempt was made by Captain Maguire and Mr. Buchanan to scale the hill in face of a heavy fire. Captain Maguire was wounded in the chest, several of our men were killed or wounded, and the force was partially repulsed, though it had captured nearly all Kawinga's positions except the highest, and had so far scared him that he treated for peace and obtained it. After the conclusion of peace with Kawinga, Captain Maguire considered it necessary to return to Fort Johnston, to complete the building at that place, and relieve the garrison. He was to be back at Zomba to spend Christmas with me, but I was doomed never to see him again.

Upon reaching Fort Johnston he had received information as to the locality where Makanjira's two daus were hidden. Without waiting to consult me, therefore, he started in the *Domira*, with a small force of Indian soldiers. He found the daus—in a little cove close to where Fort Maguire is

CAPTAIN CECIL MONTGOMERY MAGUIRE
DIED DECEMBER 15, 1891

now situated, and somewhat to the north of Makanjira's main town. He landed with a small force of about 28 men, and was proceeding to destroy and incapacitate the daus, when Makanjira, with about 2,000 men, attacked him. He retreated to the beach.

Unfortunately a storm had arisen which had wrenched his boat from her moorings, and had dashed her on to the rocks. The *Domira* in endeavouring to approach as near as possible in order to come to his assistance, was blown on to a sand-bank, and stuck fast within a short distance of the shore. When he had lost three of his men Captain Maguire told the others to enter the water and make for the *Domira*. After seeing them off, and with a few faithful Sikhs repulsing with the bayonet the onslaught of the enemy, he turned to the water himself, but just as he was nearing the steamer a bullet apparently struck him in the back of the head and he sank. Just about this time the master of the *Domira*, Mr. Keiller, was wounded, and shortly after Mr. Urquhart, the second engineer, was severely wounded. All the Indian soldiers except the three who had been killed reached the steamer safely, and preparations were at once made to defend the *Domira* from the attack of Makanjira's men, who were at very close range. After two or three days' incessant fighting, Makanjira's people put up a flag of truce. His envoys were received on board and offered, in return for a certain ransom (which was paid), to cease fighting and to assist in moving the *Domira* off the sand-bank, and to give up the bodies of Captain Maguire and the dead sepoys. The negotiations were chiefly conducted by Dr. Boyce[1] and Mr. McEwan,[2] in order that the two wounded Europeans might not be shown to the enemy. After peace had, seemingly, been concluded with Makanjira's envoys, the latter said that no effect could be given to the provisions of this agreement until the white men had visited Makanjira on the shore, and as an extra inducement for them to come they promised Dr. Boyce that he should receive for burial the body of Captain Maguire. Owing to the two wounded officers being concealed in the cabin below, it appears that Makanjira's envoys imagined Dr. Boyce and Mr. McEwan were the only white men on the steamer. They therefore made a point of insisting they should both come to see Makanjira.

No idea of treachery seems to have entered the minds of the Europeans, who did not even think of insisting on Makanjira's leaving hostages on board, whilst they went on shore. They therefore started for the beach with only a few unarmed attendants. One of these was Captain Maguire's orderly, an Indian Muhammadan soldier. Soon after reaching the beach an Arab led this orderly away from the rest of the party, offering to show him Captain Maguire's body. So far as is known, after taking the orderly for a roundabout walk he urged him strongly to return to the boat, which the man did.[3] Dr. Boyce and his party were told that Makanjira was just a short distance from the shore, in the bush, awaiting them. They were thus led on to a distance of perhaps two miles from the lake shore; then they suddenly found themselves surrounded by a number of Makanjira's men, at the head of whom was Saidi Mwazungu, a man half Arab and half Yao. Saidi Mwazungu suddenly called out, "Makanjira has ordered the white men to be killed." His men then turned their guns on the party. Mr. McEwan was shot repeatedly. Dr. Boyce was shot several times, but did not die. They therefore threw him down and cut his head off. The Swahili servants who had accompanied this party were not killed, but secured and subsequently sold as slaves.[4] The Atonga steamer-boys were killed, or left for dead. One of these Atonga, however, whom the Arabs believed themselves to have killed, managed in spite of his terrible wounds to crawl by degrees to the lake shore, where he shouted for help. He was got on board the steamer, and gave them an account of what had happened. Meantime the survivors in the steamer heard the Yao shouting on the shore that all the white men were killed, and that now was the time to attack the steamer. The Sikhs behaved splendidly, but the hero at this crisis was Mr. Urquhart, the wounded engineer, who by dint of almost superhuman efforts, and by working at the dead of night, managed to get the steamer afloat. After a five days' detention—five days without sleep, in constant and incessant danger, and almost

---

[1] Dr. Boyce was a Parsi Doctor of Medicine, who had been engaged by me at Zanzibar as Surgeon to the Indian contingent.

[2] The first engineer of the *Domira*.

[3] The orderly, with the horror of what had taken place during these few days, subsequently went out of his mind, and was never able to give a coherent account of the circumstances, but it is believed that the Arab did not wish a fellow Muhammadan to be killed, and therefore induced the orderly to return to the steamer.

[4] After the most extraordinary adventures they succeeded in reaching the coast.

without food—the steamer floated off the sand-bank into deep water. The 7-pounder gun was silently got ready by the Sikhs, and before the vessel steamed away, shells were fired in rapid succession into howling crowds of Makanjira's men, who were dancing round camp fires, confident that a few more hours would see the *Domira* in their possession.

The death of Captain Maguire took place on the 15th December, 1891. No news of it reached me until Christmas Eve, just at the time when I was expecting him to arrive for Christmas day. I left at once for Blantyre, which I reached on the evening of Christmas day, and there conferred with Mr. John Buchanan and Mr. Fotheringham, the manager of the African Lakes Company. The latter at once proffered his co-operation in meeting the difficult situation on Lake Nyasa. We both started for the Upper Shire by different routes, and reached Fort Johnston at the end of December. Here we found that the chief Msamara who lived a little below Mponda on the west bank of the Shire, had turned against us and with Zarafi had sent a force of men to attack Fort Johnston, and although nothing more had come of the attack but a few wild shots, he had nevertheless been raiding all round the Fort.

The bad news had brought volunteers hurrying up from the south. Amongst them came Mr. J. G. King, from Port Herald; Dr. A. Blair Watson; the late Mr. Gilbert Stevenson; and, a little later on, Commander J. H. Keane, R.N.[1] Fortunately Mponda had remained loyal, and although for a few days the Fort and its garrison of wounded and exhausted men lay at his mercy, he had not only been neutral but had assisted to defend the place against Zarafi's attacks. My arrival soon restored the morale of the Sikhs, who were literally in tears at the death of their commander, but the Muhammadan Indian soldiers had not rallied from the feeling of discouragement caused by this disaster. Soon afterwards they had, in fact, to be sent back to India, though there were men amongst them who had strikingly distinguished themselves. It must be remembered, however, that they were all cavalry men, and not used to fighting on foot, or on board a ship, and all things considered behaved as well as might be expected. The Sikhs, however, throughout all this crisis, never showed their sterling worth more effectually.

Another attack on Makanjira was impossible until we had got gunboats on the lake. So I decided to restore our prestige by subduing those enemies who were nearer at hand and more vulnerable, to wit, Msamara and Zarafi. The chief Msamara was captured and imprisoned in the fort, together with some of his headmen, whilst an enquiry was instituted into his culpability for the recent raids. I regret to say that whilst in prison he poisoned himself but it was fortunately done with the knowledge and connivance of his followers and consequently no slur was cast on the Administration for his death, his headmen themselves asserting that their chief had committed suicide because he believed he was going to be hanged, an eventuality, however, of which there was little probability. The war against Zarafi was a more difficult matter. I was able with the help of the volunteer officers and the Sikhs to capture all Zarafi's villages in the plains with relatively little loss of men; but to attack Zarafi in the hills was another matter. While on our way thither, all Mponda's men who were acting as our porters ran away, and we were therefore compelled to retreat to Fort Johnston. Under the circumstances the flight of our porters was the best thing that could have happened to us, since we were embarked on an enterprise far beyond our strength, although we did not know it at that time;

[1] Afterwards made C.M.G.

for another march would have brought us to the base of Zarafi's hill, where we should probably have met with as serious a disaster as subsequently happened to another expedition.

During all this crisis we were much helped by the Angoni, under Chifisi, who dwelt at the back of Mponda's country. These men came down in hundreds to assist us in fighting Zarafi. Unfortunately the Angoni are not as brave as they look, and we subsequently found they were very broken reeds to depend on in hard fighting. Zarafi had, nevertheless, suffered so much at our hands by the loss of all his villages in the plains that he ceased his raids, and commenced negotiations for peace. No doubt these negotiations were only intended to gain time, but I welcomed them as a valuable respite, and did not intend to take any further steps against Zarafi until I could receive reinforcements of officers and men. By the capture of Zarafi's low-lying towns I had prevented for some time to come any attempts on his part to obstruct the navigation of the Shire; this end was still further attained by the imprisonment of the chief Msamara who subsequently committed suicide at Fort Johnston.

I again returned to Zomba, determined to apply myself now to the consideration of our financial position, for since my arrival in British Central Africa in July, 1891, I had not had a spare day in which to turn to accounts. Up till this time it must be remembered that I had to be my own secretary and accountant, and the pressure of office work was almost more than I could stand. Captain Sclater was busily employed in making roads, and this work was so necessary I did not like to call him off it for other purposes; Mr. Sharpe was not yet back from leave of absence in England.

I had just begun to settle down once more to office work at Zomba when another message arrived with disastrous news. On the 24th February, 1892, I received a note from Dr. Watson informing me that after my departure a large force of Angoni had come down and placed their services at the disposal of Mr. J. G. King, whom I had left in charge of Fort Johnston as chief of that station; and Mr. King had resolved, then and there, to attack Zarafi, who had once more become troublesome; that the expedition had resulted in a very serious repulse at the foot of Zarafi's hill, in which but for the dogged bravery of a Naval Petty Officer, Mr. Henry Inge, lent by the river gunboats, nearly the whole of the expedition must have been annihilated. He went on to relate that at the beginning of the engagement Mr. King had been shot through the lungs, and that he himself (Dr. Watson) had been wounded in the fight; that some six Indian soldiers had been killed and several Swahilis; that another fourteen Indian soldiers were missing;[1] and that the 7-pounder gun which Mr. Inge used till the ammunition was exhausted, to distract the enemy from following the defeated expedition, had had to be abandoned in the bush. Fortunately at this juncture Commander Keane, R.N., was staying with me, having only quitted Fort Johnston a short time before. On my invitation he returned there and restored the situation as well as possible.

I am glad to say that both Mr. King and Dr. Watson recovered from their wounds. The recovery of the former was quite extraordinary as he was practically shot through the lungs.[2] Our ultimate losses were found to have consisted of the 7-pounder gun, a few rifles and cases of ammunition; and six

---

[1] These subsequently reached Fort Johnston by devious routes, one after more than thirteen days in the bush with nothing but grass, leaves, and roots to eat.

[2] For years afterwards he was Vice-Consul at Chinde; but to my deep regret died at that place on November 30, 1896.

FOUNDING THE PROTECTORATE

Indian sepoys and three Zanzibari soldiers killed. This time may be taken as the nadir of our fortunes. The slave-trading chiefs at Chiradzulu began to give trouble by committing highway robberies on the roads between Zomba and Blantyre and Blantyre and Matope. The Ndirande[1] people joined them in these depredations, and Matipwiri, a very powerful Yao chief who dwelt near the Portuguese border at the back of the Mlanje Mountain, together with Kawinga, sent out raiding parties from time to time to rob our carriers and to carry off slaves. Makanjira having received an enormous accession of strength and prestige from the death of Captain Maguire, crossed the lake to the opposite peninsula of the Rifu, and with the aid of the disaffected party there drove Kazembe from power as punishment for his alliance with the English. Kazembe fled to the south. Thus both sides of this narrow ferry were in the hands of the enemies of the English. Makanjira's next attempts were directed against Jumbe, and he began a war with him, which eventually terminated in the following year by Jumbe's loss of all his territory except his capital town. Fortunately the Arabs at the north end were not ready to recommence the war; and Mponda, who held the key of the situation at the south end of Lake Nyasa, remained faithful to us. Then Mr. Sharpe returned from leave of absence in England, and the terrible pressure of the official work on my shoulders was lightened. Moreover I received my first accountant in the person of Mr. William Wheeler, who assisted me in getting our finances into order.

Captain Sclater had been of great assistance to me through this trying time, and had made a rapid journey to the coast to obtain things that were wanted, and to engage some more men. Amongst his recruits was Mr. Wheeler, who had come to us from a position of accountant in the service of the Union Steamship Company.

But in March, 1892, after the disaster at Zarafi's, the fortunes of the young Administration seemed certainly at their lowest ebb; and what distressed me much more at this period than our wars with the Yao, or any trouble that could be given by the black men, was the attitude of the white settlers and some of the missionaries. It cannot be said that the Administration in its earlier days was universally popular amongst the Europeans, especially those who dwelt in the Shire province. The proclamation of the British Protectorate had been followed by a wholesale grabbing of land; or, where it is not fair to describe the acquisition of land as "grabbing," at any rate huge tracts had been bought for disproportionate amounts from the natives, and there were

MR. WILLIAM WHEELER

---

[1] Ndirande is a mountain overlooking Blantyre.
[2] Now the chief accountant of the British Central Africa Administration.

many claims that overlapped and required adjustment. The settlers knew that I was entrusted with the task of enquiring into and settling their claims, and many of them anticipated with some accuracy that their claims would not be sanctioned, either wholly or even at all. They were therefore disposed to weaken my position as much as they could by cavilling at all my acts, and making all the capital they could out of my misfortunes. In regard to a certain Missionary Society in the Shire Highlands, its hostile attitude was of more complex origin. It had acquired, and acquired by good means, a very strong influence over the natives. Its representatives were men of great natural ability who, whether conscious of it or not, enjoyed to the full the power of governing. Still they had not been appointed to administer this country by the Government, and it was impossible to allow them to take the law into their own hands as they were in the habit of doing, by holding informal courts and administering justice. Loth as I was to come into conflict with any Missionary Society—as I have always been a sincere admirer of the results of mission work—I found myself inevitably at issue with certain men at Blantyre and elsewhere. It is not worth while describing the ways in which through misrepresentation in the Press, letters to the Foreign Office, and strong local opposition my life and the lives of my subordinates were made unbearable: for I suppose the same conflict has occurred with the commencement of all attempts to found an Administration among headstrong, sturdy pioneers. I merely refer to these foolish dead-and-forgotten quarrels because in a small way they enter into the woof of our history at this period, for I cannot too strongly assert, as a fact perhaps not sufficiently appreciated, that during my seventeen years' acquaintance with Africa the difficulties raised up against my work by Europeans have infinitely exceeded the trouble given me by negroes or Arabs.

Captain Charles Edward Johnson, of the 36th Sikhs, arrived in the month of June to take the place of the late Captain Maguire. He soon brought order into our disorganised forces, and there accompanied him a small detachment of Sikhs which proved a very useful reinforcement. Commander Keane was released by the arrival of Captain Johnson and received a C.M.G. in reward for his services. Before Captain Johnson could get an expedition ready I was obliged to dispatch a small force under Mr. Sharpe and Captain Sclater against the highway robbers of Mt. Chiradzulu.[1]

At the beginning of July, 1892, we received a visit from Admiral Nicholson, who was commanding on the Cape Station. Being absent at Fort Johnston, I dispatched Mr. Sharpe to meet the Admiral at Chiromo, whilst I journeyed to Blantyre. As regards bad news, I had one hour after I reached Blantyre which I shall always remember as a kind of Job's experience. Within that one hour arrived the following pieces of information. First came a messenger to say that a raid had been made by the Yao on the Blantyre-Zomba road, a caravan attacked and a quantity of goods stolen. Then came another message from Katunga, on the Shire, with the news that Mr. Sharpe's boat, on his way down to Chiromo, had been capsized by a hippopotamus, and that Mr. Sharpe and all his companions were drowned.[2] Lastly came the post with the news

---

[1] Chiradzulu is a very fine picturesque mountain about 5,500 ft. in height, midway between Zomba and Blantyre. The Yao settled on this mountain since the Yao raids of 1861-2 and -3 were very troublesome to the first missionaries and planters, and gave a great deal of annoyance in the early days of the Administration. They were thoroughgoing slave-raiders, and were not finally subdued until the winter of 1893.

[2] Two or three of Mr. Sharpe's men were drowned, but he fortunately succeeded in swimming ashore where he was eventually picked up by a native canoe. He lost, however, everything he had with him, including some valuable guns.

FOUNDING THE PROTECTORATE

that the New Oriental Bank, in which were invested a good proportion of our funds, had failed.[1] Following close on this tale of disasters came Admiral Nicholson, fortunately accompanied by Mr. Sharpe, the news of whose untimely death had fairly taken all the heart out of me. Probably Admiral Nicholson has never known to this day why I received him with so much emotion.

In May, 1892, Mr. John L. Nicoll had returned from leave of absence in England, and had entered the service of the British Central Africa Administration. He was appointed collector for the South Nyasa district, to reside at

MR. NICOLL'S HOUSE AT FORT JOHNSTON

Fort Johnston. In nearly three years' residence he effected a remarkable improvement in affairs on the Upper Shire and at the south end of the lake. Zarafi's raids were checked, the river was policed and rendered safe, and Mponda was kept in order. In the summer of this same year two important expeditions arrived in the country. One was the dispatch from England of three gunboats in sections for Lake Nyasa and the Upper Shire. These boats had been obtained by the initiative of Lord Salisbury, when the news first arrived of the disasters on the lake, consequent on the death of Captain Cecil Maguire. The Admiralty undertook the charge of furnishing these gunboats, and they were sent out under the charge of Lieutenant (now Commander) Hope Robertson, R.N.[2] The other expedition was that

[1] The Bank subsequently paid us in full, though not for about a year afterwards.
[2] For his services in conveying these gunboats to Lake Nyasa, bringing about their rapid and successful construction, and afterwards commanding them on Lake Nyasa in various campaigns, Lieutenant Robertson was promoted, and was made a C.M.G.

under Major von Wissmann, who at the head of a large expedition was conveying a steamer (named after himself) to Lake Nyasa, on behalf of the German Anti-Slavery Society.

In the middle of 1892 our Customs Regulations received definite form. Mr. H. A. Hillier, who had joined the Administration in 1891, was made principal Customs Officer at Chiromo, and the efficiency of our Customs service owes much to his organization. In 1896 he was made Director-General of Customs. In 1892 also the first steps were taken to institute a Hut tax. The question of the taxation of the natives was in its initial stages a

TREES PLANTED BY MR. NICOLL AT FORT JOHNSTON (TWO YEARS' GROWTH)

difficult one to settle. In taking over the Lower Shire district on the west bank of the Shire from the Portuguese in the middle of 1891, the natives who had been accustomed to pay taxes to the Portuguese had asked me to assess their taxes, if possible, at a lower rate. On enquiry I ascertained that they had paid a capitation tax of something like half-a-crown a head per annum, which tax was levied indifferently on men, women, and children. The chiefs of the Lower Shire natives, however, were of opinion that they would prefer a Hut to a Poll tax. Estimating the average number of hut occupants at three, their former Poll tax would have resulted in each household paying about 7s. 6d. per annum. I therefore proposed to compromise the matter by fixing the annual Hut tax at 6s. per annum and abolishing the Capitation Dues. The natives seemed well satisfied with

FOUNDING THE PROTECTORATE

this proposal. Gradually, however, it became obvious that if the natives of the Lower Shire district were to pay taxes, the other natives of such portions of the Protectorate as we were obliged to administer at our own cost, should do the same. For a year I talked this over with the leading chiefs of the Shire province (the only portion of the Protectorate we were then prepared to administer), and got most of them to agree to the principle that the natives of the Protectorate should contribute, to a reasonable extent, towards the revenue. The idea of taxing the natives, however, was strongly opposed by the missionaries, and also by many of the traders and planters, who believed it would cause discontent and would make native labour dearer. I still held to my view, nevertheless, that those natives of British Central Africa who

THE NYASA GUNBOATS IN NKATA BAY, WEST NYASA

were unable to protect themselves from the incursions of slave raiders, or who by their own misconduct compelled the intervention of the Administration for the maintenance of law and order, should contribute as far as their means allowed towards the revenue of the Protectorate, for it was not to be supposed that the British taxpayer, or the British South Africa Company, could continue indefinitely finding subsidies for the support of the Protectorate; that the Protectorate must justify its existence by eventually supporting itself on its locally raised revenue. At a meeting with some of the leading missionaries and planters at Blantyre, in the winter of 1892, I agreed to propose to the Secretary of State that the Hut tax should be reduced to 3s. per annum, and eventually it was fixed in the Queen's Regulations at that sum.

The only other taxation incumbent on the natives was the taking out of a gun license, for which the same sum was charged as in the case of Europeans and foreigners, namely, £1 for five years, or in the case of the natives, 4s. per annum. The payment of the Hut tax was at first confined to certain portions of the Shire province. Gradually it was enforced throughout the Shire province. At the present time it is enforced throughout all the Protectorate with the exception of that portion of the West Nyasa district which is inhabited by the northern Angoni, who at present decline to pay taxes to the Administration but on the other hand remain quiet and free from civil war, and therefore do not compel us to go to the expense of administering their country. Eventually, no doubt, by friendly arrangement the Hut tax will be enforced even here. In all other parts of the Protectorate it has never been put in force without a proper arrangement being come to with the native chiefs, except in such districts as where the chiefs—Yao or Arabs— have gone to war with us. Then as one of the conditions of peace or one of the results of conquest, the Hut tax has been eventually enforced. The

LAKE ROAD, CHIROMO

revenue derived from this source in 1893 was about £1,639. In the financial year ended March 31st, 1896, it amounted to £4,695 in value.

In the early autumn of 1892 I commenced the land settlement, and by degrees every estate or land claim between the Lower Shire district and Lakes Tanganyika and Mweru and the Upper Luapula was visited and enquired into by Mr. Alfred Sharpe, Captain Sclater or myself. Admissible claims were divided into two kinds: claims to mineral rights, and claims to land with or without mineral rights.[1] In the case of treaties conferring mining rights the investigation was relatively simple. The chief or chiefs alleged to be the grantors of such concessions were examined and if they admitted making the grant, and it could be shown that they had received fair value for the same, the mining concessions were confirmed. In regard to land, long occupation and improvements were regarded as almost the best titles. These qualifications, however, applied to very few estates in British Central Africa, as in most cases

[1] Inadmissible claims were those which conferred sovereign rights or granted any monopoly of trade inconsistent with the various treaties with Foreign Powers to which Great Britain was a party.

the settlers had only arrived after the proclamation of the Protectorate. Only in cases of very lengthy occupation and much cultivation or building were claims sanctioned which were unsupported by properly executed documents. Even when land had been purchased, and the sale on the part of the chief was not repudiated, and the deed of sale was authentic, the concessionnaire was required to show what consideration had been paid, and if the grantor was not considered to have received fair value for his land the grantee had either to supplement his first payment by another, or the area of his estate was reduced to an extent fairly compatible with the sum paid. As land was of very little value before the establishment of the Administration, and as undoubtedly the settlers had conferred great benefits on the country by clearing and planting, land was not rated at a high value in these settlements. Threepence an acre was the maximum, and this only in exceptionally favoured districts like Mlanje and Blantyre. Sometimes the value of the land was computed at as low as a halfpenny an acre. Except on very small estates the existing native villages and plantations were exempted from all these purchases, and the natives were informed that the sale of the surrounding land did not include the alienation of their homes and plantations. The fact is, that at the time the chiefs sold land to the Europeans they were very heedless of the results. All they desired was the immediate possession of the trade goods or money given in payment. The tenure of the land in reality was tribal; that is to say theoretically the chief had no right to alienate the land, but he had assumed such right and his assumption was tacitly accepted by his people. It was, however, highly necessary to secure these people from the results of their chief's heedlessness, in many cases, as they were apt to become the serfs of the white man when he began to appear as their over-landlord. One of the results of the land settlement, therefore, was to completely free the natives from any dependency on the white settler, by restoring to them the inalienable occupancy of their villages and plantations. Moreover, in sanctioning the various concessions in the name of the Government we reserved to the Crown the right to make roads, railways, or canals over anybody's property without compensation; the control of the water supply; and where mining rights were included in the concession, a royalty on the produce of the mines. In each deed (the deeds were styled "Certificates of Claim") the boundaries of the property were set forth with sedulous accuracy, and it was provided that all these deeds should be eventually supplemented by an authoritative survey made by a Government surveyor, a process which is fast being completed. On the whole the settlement was well accepted by the Europeans, while it gave distinct satisfaction to the natives, and was approved without modification by Her Majesty's Government. Throughout the whole settlement I believe I am right in saying that only one dispute regarding boundaries was brought into Court and not settled amicably and informally in my office. When all these claims had been arranged I concluded, on behalf of the Crown, treaties with all the chiefs of the Protectorate, securing Crown control over the remainder of the land, which the natives were henceforth unable to alienate without the sanction of the Commissioner. In some cases large sums of money were spent by the Government in buying up the waste land from the natives where it was deemed advisable that a complete control over its disposal should be exercised. Except over a small area of land which is absolutely Crown property, a percentage on the selling price or the rent is paid to the native chief when portions of the Crown lands are let or sold.

In the same year, 1892, the foundation of our Courts of Justice was laid. At my recommendation a number of officials were given warrants as magistrates by the Secretary of State, and were thus enabled to administer justice to Europeans and other foreigners under the "Africa Orders in Council of 1889 and 1893."[1] It was theoretically supposed that justice to natives only was administered by native chiefs, but in reality the native courts are practically held by British magistrates in the name of the local chief or as his representative; for over most of the districts the native chiefs have surrendered to us by treaty their justiciary rights. Still, in some districts, native chiefs are encouraged to settle all minor cases themselves, and the natives are not allowed to go to the European magistrate except where the native chief cannot be relied on for fairness. No native chief or British magistrate, however, is

THE KATUNGA ROAD IN PRE-ADMINISTRATION DAYS

allowed to carry out a death sentence on a native without first referring the case to the Commissioner for consideration, and obtaining his sanction to the verdict and sentence.

As far back as 1891 we had commenced road-making. Captain Sclater had begun to clear a road from Chiromo to Zoa, with the intention of ultimately carrying on this road to Mlanje in one direcion, and to Blantyre and Zomba in another. It was found, however, to be of more urgent need to the community that the road between Katunga and Blantyre should be made passable for waggons. Consequently Captain Sclater undertook the reconstruction of the Katunga road,[2] which proved to be a very lengthy and expensive business and is not yet finally completed.

In the summer of 1892 Captain Stairs' expedition returned from Katanga,

[1] That of 1889 only applied to British and British protected subjects; that of 1893 gave us, in virtue of treaties concluded, jurisdiction over all subjects of Foreign States within the limits of the Protectorate.
[2] It had been originally made by the Lakes Company, but it was little more than a rough track, without bridges, and almost impassable for waggons.

through Nyasaland ; but Captain Stairs, who had been very ill with black-water fever, died at Chinde before he could embark on the ocean steamer.

1893 dawned on us with somewhat brighter prospects. I had spent a very pleasant Christmas at Blantyre, and had been cheered by the safe return of Mr. Sharpe from an extensive journey through the Tanganyika, Mweru, and Upper Luapula districts, where he had added to our geographical discoveries, and had settled many outstanding difficulties with Arabs and native chiefs. M. Lionel Décle arrived at the beginning of 1893 on a scientific mission for the French Government. In the course of this mission he had already travelled over South Africa from the Cape to Nyasaland. He eventually continued his journey

CAPTAIN SCLATER'S ROAD TO KATUNGA IN PROCESS OF MAKING

through British Central Africa to the south end of Tanganyika, and thence to Uganda and the east coast of Africa.

In January, 1893, came Mr. J. F. Cunningham to be my private secretary.[1]

In the month of February, 1893, however, we found ourselves face to face with a serious outbreak on the Upper Shire, an outbreak of slave traders that had long been threatened. The upper portion of the Shire was ruled over by a chief named Liwonde, who was a relation of Kawinga's.[2] Liwonde had

[1] In 1894 he became Secretary to the British Central Africa Administration. Mr. Cunningham, besides organising our printing establishment and Gazette, was—among many other accomplishments—a great road-maker. He constructed the road between Blantyre and Zomba as a "holiday task" while I was absent in South Africa in the spring of 1893. To praise one's private secretary is scarcely less difficult than to praise oneself; such commendation must be private. Still I should like to acknowledge here how much I owe to this gentleman's unflagging industry and zealous co-operation during the period between 1893 and the present day.

[2] Kawinga, to whom constant allusion will be made in the pages of this History, was a powerful Yao chief of the Machinga clan, who had settled on Chikala Mountain, near the north-west end of Lake Chiloa, at the end of the fifties or beginning of the sixties. He is referred to by Livingstone in his *Last Journeys* as Kabinga. The chief Liwonde was his relation, and had, with some Yao followers, acquired the sovereignty of the Upper Shire about thirty years ago.

received me well in 1889, and had made a treaty with me; but he was incurably addicted to the slave trade. An old Arab, named Abu Bakr (a white Arab of Maskat), lived with Liwonde, and acted as go-between for the supply of slaves to the Swahili caravans. At the beginning of 1893 one of these caravans had kidnapped and carried off some boys at Zomba who worked in Mr. Buchanan's plantations. Captain C. E. Johnson, who happened to be staying at Zomba, hurried off in pursuit of the caravan, accompanied by Mr. George Hoare (formerly a N.C.O. in the Royal Engineers) and a few Makua police. They came up with the caravan in Liwonde's country, and succeeded in releasing the Zomba boys, together with a large number of other slaves, but the slave traders managed to elude them. On the return of the rescue party to the banks of the Shire, in Liwonde's country, they were attacked by Liwonde's men. One of the Makua police was killed, and others were badly wounded, while Mr. Hoare had to swim for his life down the river till he was out of the range of the enemy's guns. Fortunately the rescued slaves were not recaptured. The whole river now was up in arms wherever there were Yao. A boat of the African Lakes Company was coming down in charge of some Atonga. It was seized by Liwonde's men, and one of the Atonga had his throat cut in Liwonde's presence. Others, though wounded, managed to escape. Finally, the *Domira* unfortunately chose this moment to make one of her rare periodical trips down the Upper Shire to Matope, and stuck on a sandbank opposite to one of Liwonde's towns. When we heard the news at Zomba, we scraped together all the forces we could collect, but these only consisted of Makua police and Atonga labourers. With these men Captain Johnson and I started for the Upper Shire. At Mpimbi we were joined by Messrs. Sharpe, Gilbert Stevenson, and Crawshay. We fought our way up the river to the place where the *Domira* was stranded. Here we were over three days in a very disagreeable position. Our camp was commanded by the higher ground in the vicinity, from which the natives continually fired into us. They also kept up a steady fire on the *Domira*, and Mr. Stevenson, in going on board that steamer, was gravely, almost mortally, wounded.[1]

MR. J. F. CUNNINGHAM

[1] He was shot through the body just in front of the kidneys, but made a marvellous recovery, and subsequently did excellent service in the Protectorate in the Mlanje district. When out shooting game in September, 1896, his gun went off accidentally and killed him.

We were getting anxious as to our position, owing to the possible exhaustion of our ammunition and the fact that the enemy had reoccupied the banks of the Shire behind us, thus cutting us off from overland communication with the Shire Highlands. The boats which attempted to go up or down the Shire were fired at, and several boatmen and soldiers were wounded. Mr. Alfred Sharpe was the first to relieve the acute crisis of our position by stealing out with a few Atonga from the stockade, and lying in ambush along one of the paths which the enemy used for advancing in our direction. In this way he was able to pick off with his rifle several of Liwonde's most noted warriors and leaders, and this considerably damped the enemy's ardour.[1]

On the third day of our beleaguered state there arrived very welcome reinforcements in the shape of Herr von Eltz (who was in charge of Major von Wissmann's expedition, intended to convey a steamer to Lake Nyasa), a German non-commissioned officer, a Hotchkiss gun, and about twenty Sudanese soldiers. These really relieved us from any peril, and enabled those who had been three days in this camp without sleep or a proper meal, to get both whilst the new arrivals kept watch. On the following day Lieut. Commander Carr, who commanded H.M.S. *Mosquito* on the Zambezi, arrived with Dr. Harper and about twenty blue-jackets.

We had succeeded in getting the *Domira* off the sand-bank, she had gone to Matope, and returned with Mr. Sharpe and further reinforcements. We were now, therefore, able to advance up the river and capture Liwonde's town which was done without much serious fighting; the brunt of the struggle falling to Herr von Eltz and his Sudanese, and Mr. F. J. Whicker.[2] Liwonde's town was on an island and our forces advanced on both banks of the river. We managed to wade across one branch of the Shire to the island which the enemy had already abandoned on our near approach.

Lieut. Carr and the blue-jackets assisted us in building two forts and then returned to the lower river, one or two blue-jackets remaining behind for a few weeks to assist us in garrisoning the forts. Commander Robertson and myself passed on up the river to the limits of Liwonde's country in the *Domira*, but had no fighting of any serious character. Liwonde fled and we did not succeed in capturing him for several years, during which he occasionally gave us trouble.[3] The pacification of the country was ably effected by Mr. F. J. Whicker, under whose superintendence the Upper Shire has become one of the most prosperous districts in the Protectorate, with an abundant and contented population.

In March, 1893, Captain Sclater was obliged to return to England on account of his health and the expiration of the time for which he was seconded. In April I started for South Africa to confer with Mr. Rhodes and the secretary of the South Africa Company, in regard to the contributions to be furnished by that Company towards the adminstration of British Central Africa.

On my way down the river I met Lieut. (now Lieut.-Colonel) Edwards, who had arrived from India with a large reinforcement of Sikhs. For two years past the armed forces in the Protectorate had consisted of one English officer, sixty to seventy Indian Sepoys, and about fifty Zanzibaris and Makua (the latter being natives of Moçambique). The Indian soldiers, again, included over forty Mazbi Sikhs and about twenty Indian Muhammadan cavalrymen. The term for which these men were allowed to volunteer from the Indian Army

---
[1] An important settlement was afterwards founded here and called "Fort Sharpe."
[2] Subsequently collector for the Upper Shire district.
[3] He is however now exiled to Port Herald on the Lower Shire.

would expire in the summer of 1893, and I had therefore made arrangements with the Indian Government for their relief, but had asked on this occasion, at the suggestion of Captain Johnson, that when the second Indian contingent was sent out, all the new Indian soldiers should be Jāt Sikhs and not Mazbis.[1]

Lieut. Edwards brought with him a hundred Sikhs on this occasion. A few months after their arrival the time expired of the Mazbi Sikhs, and the few Indian cavalrymen that remained were sent back to India. Later on in the year another hundred Sikhs arrived, under the command of Lieut. (now Captain) W. H. Manning, thus bringing up the full strength of our Indian contingent to 200 men, which maximum it has not since exceeded. In regard to black troops we had first of all tried natives of Zanzibar, but these men had not proved very satisfactory. They were nearly as expensive as the Sikhs, they were not all of them very brave or reliable in warfare, and they were difficult to procure, owing to the restrictions which had been placed at that time on the expatriation of the natives of Zanzibar; restrictions rendered absolutely necessary owing to the drain on the population of that island caused by the engagement of Zanzibaris for the many expeditions engaged in African exploration. I had been much struck with the good qualities of the Makua of Moçambique. The escort I had taken with me in my journeys of 1889-90 was composed of Makua, recruited at Moçambique. I had also obtained Makua for the Thomson-Grant expedition to Bangweolo, and these men after Mr. Thomson's return had passed into our police force. We were also beginning to employ as police the Atonga natives of West Nyasa. I therefore decided to pay off and send back our few remaining Zanzibaris, and to replace them by Makua and natives of Nyasaland. Meantime, however, at a suggestion from the late Mr. Portal, I tried the experiment of forming a small corps of Zanzibar Arabs (most of them ex-soldiers of the Sultan of Zanzibar's bodyguard). These men were of poor physique, and we only kept them in our service from one to two years. They were very plucky and, contrary to some people's anticipation, perfectly loyal.[2]

LIEUT.-COL. C. A. EDWARDS

During the year 1893 arrangements which had been begun for the division of the British Central Africa Protectorate and the adjoining Sphere of the

---

[1] I need scarcely remind my readers that the Sikhs are not a *race* but merely a religious sect. They are really a section of the Panjāb people of very varied types of humanity, some being dark coloured and of almost Dravidian aspect, others having faces of Greek outline and very pale complexions. The Jāt belongs to the cultivator class and is supposed to be much more aristocratic than the Mazbi. Between the Mazbis and the Jāts, however, I could see very little difference in general appearance, and to my thinking both kinds of Sikhs were equally good; perhaps in one or two points the Mazbis had the advantage in regard to physical endurance, while on the other hand the Jāts were more cheery in disposition, and even more loyally enthusiastic than the Mazbis. In the days when the Sikhs set much store by caste, the Mazbis were the "sweepers" or lowest caste of all, and by some were hardly recognised as proper Sikhs.

[2] A detailed description of our present military force in the Protectorate will be found in the Appendix to this chapter.

FOUNDING THE PROTECTORATE

British South Africa Company into administrative divisions were completed. The Protectorate was divided into twelve districts, the names of which will be found in the accompanying map, and that portion of the South Africa Company's territory which we were able to administer was divided into the districts of Tanganyika, Chambezi, Mweru and Luapula.[1]

During my absence in South Africa Mr. Sharpe had taken an important step towards controlling the Mlanje district, and guarding our south-eastern border from the raids of a very troublesome chief, known as Matipwiri. To check these raids he had founded Fort Lister in the pass between Mounts Mlanje and Michesi. The idea of building a fort at this spot was no new one. It had first occurred to Consul Hawes in 1886, and I had taken up the idea again after my first visit to Mlanje in 1892. After that journey I decided that as soon as we could obtain reinforcements from India, we should build forts to guard the north and south ends of Mlanje Mountain. These forts I subsequently named Fort Lister and Fort Anderson to commemorate the sympathy and assistance I had received at the hands of Sir Villiers Lister and Sir Percy Anderson of the Foreign Office, in carrying out my projects for the suppression of the slave trade. Captain C. E. Johnson commenced the construction of Fort Lister, but although his advent in this country was warmly welcomed by the indigenous A-nyanja chiefs, it was anything but welcome to the Yao slave traders, prominent among whom was the chieftain named Nyaserera.[2] Nyaserera seems to have disliked the idea of making an attack in force on the fort as long as it was defended by a white man, but the idea apparently occurred to him to attempt the assassination of Captain Johnson. That, at least, was the belief of most of the native witnesses whom we subsequently examined. What took place was this: One night as Captain Johnson was sitting down to dinner in his temporary bungalow he heard a slight noise in his adjoining sleeping apartment, and on looking up saw a man with a spear concealed behind a portière. He at once attempted to seize the intruder. The latter grappled with him in the bath-room, to which he had retreated, and stabbed the Captain till he swooned. He then made off before assistance came. This news was conveyed to me by the Indian hospital assistant at Fort Lister.

A SIKH SOLDIER IN THE B.C.A. UNIFORM
(BLACK, WHITE, YELLOW, RED)

A SIKH SOLDIER IN FIGHTING KIT

I hurried over there with Mr. Whyte, and such was the panic created amongst the natives by Nyaserera's sudden evidence of hostility towards us that we had the greatest difficulty in getting any porters to carry our loads. Part of

[1] I believe to these districts the South Africa Company have now added the Mpezeni district and the Luangwa districts. The capital of the latter is Fort Jameson.
[2] Nyaserera though he ruled Yao and identified himself much with the Yao cause, was in reality a Mlolo from the countries west of Lake Chilwa. The A-lolo are closely related to the Makua and speak nearly the same language.

the way we had to travel through Nyaserera's country, and between bands of sullen-looking warriors on either side of the narrow path. They would probably have attacked us but that an escort of Sikhs had come out to meet us from Fort Lister.

At this place I held meetings with many chiefs, and endeavoured to detach from Nyaserera his relations and allies; and this diplomacy proved so far successful that when later on Lieut. Edwards arrived from Fort Johnston he had only Nyaserera to fight, and subdued him after a brief campaign.

Later in the year further troubles broke out in the Mlanje district, with the chief Mkanda, whose subjects had been concerned in recent road robberies, and who was continually kidnapping women for the slave trade. I took advantage of the arrival of the second detachment of 100 Sikhs to bring Mkanda to his senses, but I thought at first it would be sufficient for him to be made aware that the Sikhs were encamped in the plain on their way to Fort Lister, while the collector of the Mlanje district (Mr. Bell) visited Mkanda in the mountains with a small escort and delivered an ultimatum, to which I believed Mkanda would submit. Mkanda, however, was very insolent, and his men commenced attacking Mr. Bell's escort. To protect themselves in retreating the escort set fire to some houses and loose stacks of grass for thatching, and succeeded in reaching the main force encamped in the plain. They then communicated with Captain Johnson at Fort Lister, and awaited instructions as to further procedure. Mkanda took advantage of this temporary inaction to attack the Scotch Mission station on the borders of his territory. The missionaries took to flight and Mkanda's men gutted and burnt most of the houses, and succeeded in carrying off several guns and a quantity of ammunition. Fortunately the uprising spread no farther, and the other Yao chiefs did not join in, though Matipwiri sent out skirmishers to see what he could do in the way of highway robbery.

Mkanda's men also intercepted and slew several Atonga labourers on their way to a European plantation, but after several days' hard fighting among the crags and precipices of Mlanje, Captain Johnson succeeded in capturing all Mkanda's positions, and Mkanda fled.

A SIKH SOLDIER IN FIGHTING KIT

SIKH SOLDIER IN UNDRESS

His near relation Kada, who had remained on our side during this struggle, succeeded him in the chieftainship. Most of his people returned when peace was made, and were allowed to settle in the plains instead of amongst the

FOUNDING THE PROTECTORATE

mountains. Mkanda himself eventually made terms with us and returned to his country. So did Nyaserera, who, strange to say, is now one of our greatest friends.

It was perhaps just as well that this outbreak occurred when it did, as it prevented Mkanda attacking us when all our forces were subsequently engaged in the Makanjira expedition. For this expedition I had been continually preparing since the death of Captain Maguire. I had succeeded in getting the gunboats placed on Lake Nyasa and the Upper Shire. These vessels were now completed, and in the summer of 1893 Admiral Bedford,[1] Commander-in-chief on the Cape Station, had paid me a visit at Zomba, and had proceeded with me to Lake Nyasa to witness the launching of the two gunboats and to inspect the already completed vessel for the Upper Shire.

I had discussed the need for this expedition with Mr. Rhodes when

COLLECTOR'S HOUSE AT FORT LISTER

visiting Capetown, and he had agreed in addition to the ordinary subsidies of the Company to find £10,000[2] for increasing the police force in order to grapple with Makanjira and subdue him. This aid had enabled us to obtain an additional 100 Sikhs from India, who came out under the command of Lieut. W. H. Manning.[3] It was high time we moved because our faithful ally Jumbe was almost at his last gasp. A certain Yao headman of Jumbe's named Chiwaura had been encouraged by Makanjira to rebel, and with the assistance of Makanjira's men had defeated Jumbe and forced him to retire to his capital. Chiwaura had built a very strong town about five miles inland from Kotakota, with high loopholed walls of red clay, and an inner citadel surrounded by trees of great girth. Except on one side Chiwaura's town was surrounded by an impassable marsh, a swamp which it was almost impossible to cross.

Accordingly we decided first of all to relieve Jumbe before proceeding against Makanjira directly. The African Lakes Company's boats *Domira* and *Ilala* were chartered to convey the troops, while some of the officers

---

[1] Now Sir Frederick Bedford, K.C.B.
[2] Of which sum over £4,000 were spent and the balance returned to Mr. Rhodes.
[3] Now Captain Manning and second in command of the B. C. A. forces.

and myself travelled on the gunboats which were under the direction of Commander Robertson, R.N. The officers consisted of Captain Johnson, Lieut. Edwards, Dr. Watson, and a volunteer in the person of Mr. Glave, who had come out to Central Africa to study these countries on behalf of the *Century*, an American magazine.[1] Mr. Alfred Sharpe also accompanied the expedition.

CAPT. W. H. MANNING

Our terms were rejected by Chiwaura who felt illimitable confidence in his clay walls, not realising that his town was absolutely at the mercy of a bombardment. It lay in a marshy plain within 700 yards of the precipitous cliffs of a little plateau. The approach to this plateau was not defended by Chiwaura, though he might have made it very difficult for our forces to get there except with great loss of men; but without other difficulties than those attending transport on men's heads, we succeeded in planting our 7-pounder guns on the edge of the aforementioned cliffs. From this position we shelled Chiwaura, and the main town was soon in flames. The people retired to the inner citadel, which was not in the same way destructible, since the shells burst harmlessly in the adjoining forest. The enemy after a while called for a truce, but *more Africano* employed this interval in the hostilities to strengthen his defences, and when he was ready to begin again he announced the fact by firing on our soldiers when they approached the walls under cover of the truce. In fact in African warfare the hoisting of a white flag really means, "I want a breathing spell," and when both sides are rested they go on again without troubling themselves to announce the cessation of the truce.

Jumbe had put 4,000 men under arms and had accompanied us to the scene of the fight, where he remained the whole of the time with his head wives. Jumbe though old and feeble was not lacking in bravery, and would willingly have risked his life against Chiwaura had I not held him back, but Jumbe's commander was by no means a rash man. He was gaudily dressed in scarlet cloth and had innumerable charms hung about him to dispel ill-luck, but he was very much afraid of coming to close quarters with the enemy. During the truce we would watch with amusement this great mass of several thousand men surge across the quarter of a mile of plain which lay between us and Chiwaura's town, but as soon as a gun was discharged from the ramparts by the enemy, Jumbe's commander would shout "Tamanga! tamanga!" (Run! run!), and the whole four thousand would surge back to the base of the cliffs. At last the afternoon was drawing towards evening, and the enemy showed no disposition to yield. Jumbe's people were beginning to doubt whether the white man was equal to taking such a place as Chiwaura's. It was necessary to show them that not only could we set a place on fire at a distance of half a mile through our shells, but if incumbent on us we could come to close quarters and take a town by

---

[1] Mr. Glave was an Englishman who had served with Stanley on the Congo. He subsequently journeyed through British Central Africa to the Congo Free State, thence down the Congo to the vicinity of the Atlantic Ocean, where he unfortunately died of fever before he proceeded on board the ocean-going steamer.

FOUNDING THE PROTECTORATE

assault, even at the risk of losing lives in so doing. Accordingly Captain Johnson gave orders for a general assault, and with about seventy Sikhs and thirty Makua dashed across the plain through the ruined precincts of the outer town and up to the high wall of the inner citadel, over which he and the other officers and the Sikhs swarmed and scrambled. The first Sikh

THE RAPHIA PALM MARSH BEHIND CHIWAURA'S

who succeeded in climbing to the top of the wall, which was about eight feet high, and began to haul up his comrades, was shot dead. Otherwise there were no casualties on our part but severe wounds. Once the troops had got on the top of this high wall of the citadel the enemy were completely at their mercy and huddled together in a seething mass below. Appalled at the idea of the slaughter that must ensue from continual firing, Captain Johnson gave the order "cease firing." This leniency on his part was taken by the enemy for sudden fear, and a furious fusillade was opened on our men by which several more were wounded. Then with or without order our guns went off, and numbers of the enemy were shot down. The bulk of them, however, including Chiwaura, scrambled over the further wall and dropped into the marsh below, where a good many of them were drowned. Chiwaura himself was shot as he was running away, and fell dead into the marsh. The citadel was then entered by our men, and hundreds of women were found cooped up in the houses, many of them in slave sticks. They were set free and directed to proceed to Kotakota, where many of them had their homes.[1] That same night our forces returned to Kotakota. The next two days were spent in levelling the walls of Chiwaura's town.

We then decided to proceed down the south-west shore of the lake, part of us going overland and the remainder on the gunboats and steamers to the Rifu peninsula, which was strongly held by Makanjira, whose relation Kuluunda, a famous woman chief amongst the Yao, had displaced Kazembe, our ally and her nephew. Whilst attacking Kazembe's old town (Kazembe himself had joined us with a few men remaining faithful to him) we received information that a dau had just crossed from Makanjira's with seventy fighting men on board, and a large quantity of gunpowder, and would probably land in "Leopard Bay." H.M.S. *Pioneer* was dispatched thither under the command of Lieut. Villiers, R.N. Although the *Pioneer* did not succeed in preventing the dau from reaching the shore she fired into her and disabled her so that she stranded on the rocks. But Makanjira's men succeeded in escaping to the hill overlooking Leopard Bay where they were joined by the defeated enemy who had been driven out of Kazembe's town. The situation was further complicated by the arrival of a large Arab slave-trading caravan, commanded by four or five white Arabs and containing several hundred slaves. The Arabs joined their forces to those of Kuluunda and Makanjira, and for several days we besieged these people by land and water round the lofty hill which overlooks Leopard Bay. Eventually the Arabs of the slave caravan, Kuluunda, and most of her followers were captured or surrendered; but meantime a force of Jumbe's men was left to continue the siege of the hill while our Sikhs, Makua, and 300 of Jumbe's soldiers, together with Jumbe himself and all the officers, were conveyed across the lake to Makanjira's main town. We had made the journey by way of Monkey Bay so as to have a short rest before embarking on the most critical part of our programme. We had timed ourselves to arrive at Makanjira's town at dawn. The enemy were taken somewhat by surprise, and we succeeded in effecting a landing on the sandy promontory to the south of Makanjira's huge straggling metropolis of many thousand huts and houses without meeting with any serious resistance. This promontory was separated from the town by a strip of low-lying swampy country. After entrenching ourselves in a camp the bulk of our forces started with Captain Johnson, Lieut. Edwards, and Mr. Glave to try conclusions with Makanjira's forces, while the town was shelled over their heads by Mr. Sharpe from the camp and from the two gunboats which steamed along the shore. The *Pioneer* found

---

[1] Not a few of these poor women were far gone with child, and the terror of the bombardment so upset them that on the way to Kotakota woman after woman sat down by the way and gave birth to a child, which she straightway abandoned in her panic fear of Chiwaura's pursuit. It was a quaint though touching sight to see the Sikh soldiers gravely gathering up the new-born babes and carrying them with their many other burdens of rifle and kit into Kotakota, where they were afterwards impartially distributed among the various women who claimed to be recently parturient. Never in any historical tale or Gilbertian burlesque were babies so hopelessly "mixed."

one of Makanjira's daus drawn up in a narrow creek near to or at the place where Captain Maguire had been killed. In spite of a heavy fire from the enemy this dau was attached by a hawser to the gunboat,[1] and towed out into the lake.[2]

After about five hours' fighting Makanjira's forces gave up the struggle and disappeared. We then had at our mercy his many villages. Several times he asked for terms of peace, but apparently without any idea but to gain time. The place where Captain Maguire had been killed and Boyce and McEwan

ON THE BEACH AT MONKEY BAY

massacred was destroyed, with several other villages and towns in Makanjira's country. These extreme measures were only resorted to, however, after Makanjira had refused our terms of peace.

Kuluunda was sent as an exile to Port Herald on the Shire.[3]

As Makanjira would not make peace with us I had now to consider what steps should be taken to occupy his country. Some of my staff were of opinion that it would be better after destroying the towns to remove our forces, as we could always return on other occasions and prevent any attempt on the part of Makanjira to rebuild; but my own views were different. It seemed to me

[1] This deed was accomplished by Hajji Askar, a Persian, who was an interpreter on board the *Pioneer*.
[2] It now plies to and fro across the lake under the British flag conveying natives over the Government ferry.
[3] In 1896 she was allowed to return to her country on the promise of good behaviour.

that the expeditions against Makanjira would have to be annual unless we permanently occupied his country. I therefore decided to leave Major Edwards behind with a large force of Sikhs to build a strong fort near the place where Captain Maguire had been killed. This fort was then named "Fort Maguire."

Having chosen the site and seen the British flag hoisted with great ceremony I returned to Zomba and spent the winter in attending to the civil organisation of the Protectorate. At the beginning of 1894 Makanjira attacked Fort Maguire and the surrounding villages with a large force of men, but was defeated with great loss by Captain Edwards, who soon after succeeded Captain Johnson as the senior officer in command of the B.C.A. forces.

ONE OF MAKANJIRA'S CAPTURED DAUS AT MONKEY BAY

Early in this year Mr. Harrhy, who had been lent by the Postmaster-General of Cape Colony (Mr. French) for a year to organise our Postal Service, returned to Cape Town, and his place was taken by Mr. J. E. McMaster (now Vice-Consul at Chinde), who has been a most efficient Postmaster-General.

In April, 1894, I returned to England for a much-needed holiday, Mr. Sharpe conducting the administration of the country during my absence. Besides reasons of health which necessitated this return, the time had come when the development of the Protectorate required its administration to be placed on a thoroughly sound basis, and the period during which the South Africa Company had agreed to contribute towards the cost of its administration being near expiration it would be necessary for Her Majesty's Government to consider the financial provision which was needed for the future maintenance

THE HOISTING OF THE FLAG AT FORT MAGUIRE

FOUNDING THE PROTECTORATE

of the Protectorate. The summer and autumn of 1894 were spent in making these arrangements, the results of which were that the Civil Service was henceforth efficiently organised, and the South Africa Company's subsidies were devoted to the administration of the Company's own territory; the direct administration of which was taken over from me by the Company in 1895. The Imperial Government repaid to the South Africa Company and to Mr. Rhodes a proportion of the sums spent on the defence and development of the Protectorate.

The Civil Service of the Protectorate and the Postal Service were put on a satisfactory footing. A postage stamp[1] was designed and issued. Arrangements were made for taking over the lake gunboats from the Admiralty and working them henceforth by the Administration of the Protectorate.

Freed from all future anxieties concerning finance I started for India to

THE BEACH AT MAKANJIRA'S (PRESENT SITE OF FORT MAGUIRE)

settle the question of the Indian contingent on a definite basis with the Indian authorities.

A very satisfactory arrangement was come to, lasting six years, which permits of our employing as many as 200 Sikhs from the Indian Army in British Central Africa.

I left India on the 1st of April, 1895, and reached Chinde on the 19th of that month, and Zomba on the 4th of May. I found that during my absence everything had proceeded smoothly until the early spring of 1895, when the Yao chief Kawinga, whose attitude had long been threatening, had attempted a very serious attack on the British Protectorate. He had felt his way by first raiding the villages of a chief named Malemia, in whose territory the Church of

[1] The design for this was slightly altered of late and differently printed, but remains practically the same as that devised in 1894. It consists of the Coat of Arms of the Protectorate (which is on the cover of this book). This Coat of Arms was designed by me, with the assistance and advice of Sir Albert Woods It may be described as a shield sable, with a pile or, and over all a fimbriated cross argent, bearing an inescutcheon gules on which is imprinted the Royal Arms in or. The shield is poised on an outspread map of Africa; supporters, two negroes, one carrying a pick and the other a shovel; crest, a coffee-tree in full bearing; motto, "Light in darkness." Put in plain language the shield is intended to illustrate our three colours, black, yellow, and white, with a touch of the English red. Into the sable mass of Africa I have driven a pile (wedge) of Indian yellow. Over all is the white cross, representing in its best significations the all-embracing white man. The inescutcheon of English red shows the Arms of the protecting Power. The motto, "Light in darkness," was the suggestion of the late Sir Percy Anderson.

Scotland Mission was established. Mr. Sharpe sent a small force of Sikhs and Atonga under Corporal William Fletcher, and an Atonga sergeant named Bandawe, to defend Malemia's principal village where the Scotch missionaries were.

This expedition, which only consisted of six Sikhs and a few Atonga, built a "boma"[1] to protect themselves against any sudden attack from Kawinga. It was fortunate they did so, because a day or two afterwards he descended on them with 2,000 men, many of them recruited from amongst the warlike Anguru of the countries east of Lake Chilwa. It appears that Kawinga, in alliance with Zarafi and Matipwiri, had really resolved on attempting to drive the British out of the Shire Highlands. An attack was first to be made on the unarmed Mission stations at Domasi. Their men, whetted with success, would then feel the necessary courage to attack the Residency at Zomba. Having captured this and possibly succeeded in murdering the Commissioner, the forces of Zarafi and Kawinga would advance on Blantyre, whilst

THREE OF MAKANJIRA'S CAPTURED DAUS (FORT MAGUIRE)

Matipwiri sweeping through the Mlanje district, would unite his forces to theirs, and the Yao then counted on taking possession of the gunboats at Chiromo. Zarafi had sent his son and some of his fighting men to assist in the preliminary attack on Domasi.

War with Kawinga was always felt, since our abortive attack on his positions in 1891, to be a serious affair not lightly to be encountered. We had therefore put up with a great deal of robberies, outrages and slave kidnapping on the part of Kawinga without renewing the war with him till we had larger forces at our disposal. Mr. Sharpe therefore at first intended to do no more than guard the approaches to the main station at Domasi,[2] though he made preparations for assembling as large a force of Sikhs and Atonga as were available.

Kawinga's aggressive action however got no farther than "Fletcher's boma." This trumpery little fort was so splendidly defended by the Sikhs

---

[1] Boma is a Swahili word meaning "a fence," "a stockade." It is a term which has come into general use in British Central Africa, and is often applied to Government stations, most of which were at first provided with some such defence.

[2] Domasi station was defended by Mr. S. Hewitt-Fletcher, 2nd Accountant to the British Central Africa Administration. Some confusion arose between the two Fletchers in the subsequent newspaper descriptions.

and the Atonga that the Yao again and again recoiled before the well-directed rifle fire. At last the ammunition on the side of the British was giving out, and in spite of the heavy losses amounting to over a hundred men on the part of the enemy it looked as though the defence must come to an end. At this juncture a reinforcement of Atonga was seen to be arriving, brought up by two planters, Messrs. Hynde and Starke. Bandawe proposed to Fletcher that they should charge the demoralised enemy who were already aware of the approach of reinforcements. Accordingly the defenders sallied out from the fort firing their last volleys. The Yao broke and fled, and were pursued for miles by the Sikhs and Atonga. Many prisoners were captured by Malemia's men, who had hitherto decidedly "sat on the fence," apparently ready, had Kawinga prevailed, to side with the conqueror against the British.

A RURAL POST OFFICE, BRITISH CENTRAL AFRICA

Among the prisoners taken was a son of Zarafi, whom Malemia caused to be beheaded.

Kawinga retired to his mountain of Chikala. It seemed however to Mr. Sharpe that whilst the army remained demoralised was the time to definitely bring this struggle with Kawinga to a close. At this time his reinforcements of Sikhs had arrived from Fort Johnston under the command of Lieut. Hamilton and Captain W. H. Manning.

Kawinga's stronghold was approached by a new route and the enemy were taken by surprise. They defended the fords of the rivers with some pertinacity, and a few casualties took place amongst our native soldiers and allies. But while the main approach to the town was still being contested

Lieut. Hamilton had entered the place with his Sikhs from another quarter and the enemy broke and fled.[1]

With the subdual of Kawinga the road robberies, except in the Mlanje district, came to an end; a sense of security spread over the southern portion of the Protectorate which was quite pleasantly unfamiliar. It was felt that in a very trying crisis Mr. Sharpe had acted with decision and promptitude and without flurry, and many of the European settlers expressed the sense of obligation which they felt towards Mr. Sharpe.

In other respects the record of the Protectorate during my absence in England had been singularly peaceful. By negotiations which Mr. Sharpe had commissioned Major Edwards to undertake, a civil war that had long raged between the Angoni chiefs Chikusi and Chifisi was brought to a close.[2]

Mr. Sharpe returned to England on leave of absence, and Major Edwards and myself began to make steady preparations for the inevitable campaign against Zarafi, a campaign rendered absolutely necessary because this chief finding that he was not visited with war after his co-operation in the Kawinga raids, began to attack Fort Johnston. However, our plans in regard to Zarafi were temporarily postponed because Matipwiri attacked one of our hill patrols in the Mlanje district, and it was obvious that this chief would renew his raids in that direction directly our forces were engaged with Zarafi.

WATCH TOWER AT FORT JOHNSTON
ERECTED BY CAPTAIN C. E. JOHNSON TO WATCH ZARAFI

I was at Chiromo when the news came of Matipwiri's hostility. I therefore

---

[1] Kawinga has subsequently made peace with us, and though not allowed to return to Chikala he is stationed on British territory. Chikala Mountain is now guarded by a fort. As an instance of the rapid way in which the negro accepts the results of an appeal to force, and his want of rancour, I may state these facts: that when in 1896 we proceeded against Zarafi Kawinga did his very best to help us, giving as his reason for so doing "that he had been well beaten by the British; it was now time that Zarafi had a licking." Kawinga's son provided us with guides who led us along the best route to Zarafi's country, and Kawinga sent with me a special bodyguard of Yao who were charged to look after my personal safety, and who certainly did their best in this respect.

[2] In this war Chikusi, who was a very ill-conditioned young fellow, had been the aggressor, and the way in which he was almost compelled to make peace with Chifisi left a certain amount of rancour in his mind against the British, which ill-feeling finally culminated in his attacking the British Protectorate in the autumn of 1896, in his defeat, and death. In our counter attack on Chikusi we had the entire support of Chifisi and his men.

FOUNDING THE PROTECTORATE

A SIKH SERGEANT-MAJOR OF THE BRITISH CENTRAL AFRICA CONTINGENT

started for Mlanje where I arranged to rendezvous with Major Edwards. We made very careful preparations and suddenly fell on Matipwiri, travelling all night over the distance which separated his principal town from Fort Lister. His men made but a feeble stand and Matipwiri and his brother Kumtiramanja[1] fled to Tundu hill, where they made their last stand. From this position they were driven off by Captain the Hon. W. E. Cavendish and Lieut. Coape-Smith, and large supplies of war material were abandoned

[1] The more powerful chief of the two.

in their flight and captured by Captain Cavendish. Subsequently both Matipwiri and Kumtiramanja were taken prisoners by Lieut. Coape-Smith. A fort was built in their country and Matipwiri's former subjects settled down very contentedly under our rule, and the country has since been perfectly peaceful. This settlement was rendered all the easier because Matipwiri, like most of the Yao chiefs, was a usurper, and not a native of the district in which he had established himself. Many of his subjects belonged to the A-lolo stock and spoke a language akin to Makua.

From the hills in Matipwiri's country we were able to look out eastwards over a most wonderful country hitherto untraversed by any white man, but within the Portuguese Sphere of Influence. We could see splendid ranges of mountains almost as high as Mlanje—that is to say, reaching in parts to an altitude of 8,000 feet. When the interior of Portuguese East Africa is opened up this A-lolo country should become a great resort of European planters, as it is very fertile and admirably well watered.

NATIVE SOLDIERS, BRITISH CENTRAL AFRICA

In the Matipwiri expedition we had for the first time tried our new military organisation, especially in regard to the Native levies, and we were greatly encouraged by the results and proceeded with some confidence on the expedition against Zarafi. This expedition was brought to a completely successful result after a week's fighting in which we lost our best Sikh non-commissioned officer. The heights of Mangoche Mountain were successfully taken by storm, the lost 7-pounder cannon was recovered, and Zarafi fled far to the eastward into Portuguese East Africa, where of course we were unable to follow him. A fort was planned on the site of Zarafi's town, and was subsequently built by Lieut. Alston. We then proceeded to try conclusions with Mponda, who after several years of doubting had at last decided to renew his struggle with us and had retired to a strong place, Mauni, in the mountains of the Cape Maclear peninsula. Major Edwards started with a strong force for Mauni, but Mponda at the last moment deemed discretion to be the better part of valour, and, eluding the force sent against him, came down in a canoe to Fort Johnston and surrendered to me. As much bloodshed was saved by this act of Mponda's I dealt as leniently with him as possible, and secured to him his personal property, though I deemed it necessary to send him away from his country for a time as his presence was so obnoxious to the mass of the population which of late years had placed themselves under the British. Mponda, like most of the other chiefs in the southern part of the Protectorate, was of Yao origin, and the bulk of his subjects were A-nyanja.

Major Edwards now advanced against Makanjira who of late had renewed his raids into British territory and had founded a new capital in the hills, just over the British side of the border, and about ten miles from the south-east coast of Lake Nyasa. This town was taken and destroyed by Lieut. Coape-Smith. Makanjira's forces were completely routed and fled in disorder into Portuguese territory.

On my return to Fort Johnston from Zarafi's I received letters from Karonga at the north end of Lake Nyasa and from Mr. Crawshay, the Vice-Consul at Deep Bay, informing me that the situation at the north end of the lake was serious, as Mlozi and the Arabs were now raiding in all directions for slaves, and openly announced their intention of fighting the British as soon as the rainy season began. Mlozi had captured and severely flogged a lay missionary named Stevens; he had even threatened the Free Church Mission station near Fife on the Nyasa-Tanganyika plateau, and Dr. Cross, a medical missionary, had been obliged to proceed to that place to bring away the wife of the missionary through German territory.

Mlozi had amongst other things attacked the populous villages of the Awa-wandia, and besides slaughtering many of the men had carried off women and children to his stronghold. He had concluded an alliance with the powerful Awemba tribe to the west, and it was obvious that unless we moved first he would soon be attacking Karonga with an overwhelming force. I may state here parenthetically that since my return from England I had in July, 1895, made a special journey to the north end of Lake Nyasa to see Mlozi and persuade him to keep the peace according to the original treaty concluded by him in 1889; but on

AN ATONGA SOLDIER

arriving at Karonga Mlozi had flatly refused to see me, and had even written me a very threatening letter, in the course of which he remarked, "The British have closed my route to the coast: very well, I will close their road to Tanganyika."

IN ZARAFI'S TOWN

The Arabs were not able to go to war with us at that time, and also they wished first of all to gather in their crops. They knew besides that the Europeans fought at a disadvantage in the rainy season, and it was evident if we did not take steps to reduce the Arab power before the end of December they would attack us in January with many chances in their favour.

Accordingly with some reluctance I resolved to continue our campaigns on Lake Nyasa by an expedition against the Arabs. Our little force had by this time been nicknamed the "ever victorious army." We had now 400 men (100 Sikhs and 300 natives) on whom we could place absolute reliance, and the force had been strengthened by the advent of several volunteer officers. The officers on the staff consisted of Major C. A. Edwards; Captain F. T. Stewart;[1] Captain the Honble. W. E. Cavendish; Lieut. H. Coape-Smith; Lieut. G. de Herries Smith; and Lieut. Alston;[2] Dr. Wordsworth Poole and Sergeant-Major Devoy.

It was essential that the Arabs should be taken by surprise; that we should fall on them with all our available force and surround their strongholds before they could escape to the interior, for they might prefer to run away instead of fighting out the struggle, which they could renew at a more convenient season. Therefore, our most important problem was how to transport 400 men, seven officers and the necessary munitions of war in one trip. The gunboats would only carry about fifteen men each and a similar proportion of our stores; the African Lakes Company's steamer *Domira* could not take much more than

---

[1] Who with Captain Cavendish was left to watch Makanjira and Zarafi.
[2] The Volunteers were Major L. Bradshaw (of the 35th Sikhs), Major F. C. Trollope (Grenadier Guards), and last, but not least, Mr. Walter Gordon Cumming. These gentlemen served in the autumn campaign of 1895 without pay and at their own expense. Major Trollope and Mr. Gordon Cumming were visiting the country for the purposes of sport. Major Bradshaw, who was a brother officer of Major Edwards, and assisted us when in India to recruit Sikhs, was very anxious to study the question of Indian soldiers fighting in Africa, and had obtained leave of absence so that he might join our campaign.

100 men. I bethought myself of the German steamer the *Wissmann*, which was fortunately at that moment lying off Fort Johnston. I had an interview with her Commander, Captain Berndt, and relying on him as a man of honour, communicated my plans to him, and asked whether I could hire the German steamer to carry them out. He at once assented and proposed terms which were generous financially as they provided merely for the working expenses of the steamer. I may say here that my plans were kept absolutely secret by Captain Berndt, and that no hint reached the Arabs as to our intentions.

Major Edwards and I made a hasty journey to Zomba for final preparations and the expedition left Fort Johnston on the 24th of November, 1895. On the way to the north end of the lake Major Edwards fell ill, so that when we landed at Karonga I was temporarily deprived of the services of my commander-in-chief, who for a few days was obliged to lie up. But his plans had been so well

DEEP BAY STATION

laid that they were carried out without a hitch by Lieut. Coape-Smith, who succeeded him temporarily in the command. Major Bradshaw was also an invalid, but fortunately both he and Major Edwards recovered in time to take part in the final assault on Mlozi's stockade. Our plan of campaign was this:[1] Mlozi's stockaded town was situated about eleven miles inland from Karonga, the station of the African Lakes Company on the shore of Lake Nyasa. About six miles inland from Karonga were the stockades of Msalemu and Kopakopa which guarded the ford of the River Rukuru. Mlozi's town was in the plain near the south bank of the River Rukuru. It was overlooked by a ridge of hills to the south which ran transversely to the course of the river. The Arab road from Kopakopa's stockade to Mlozi's ran through a pass in these hills, and this low range on the side of the pass nearest the river terminated in a rather high house-shaped hill which it was possible to climb to the summit, and where guns could be planted. Our idea was to send out about 300 men and a number of

[1] In drawing up this plan at Zomba Major Edwards and I were greatly helped by the notes and maps of Mlozi's stockade which had been made for us by Dr. Kerr Cross and Major Trollope.

officers under the command of Lieut. Coape-Smith, who should proceed by a circuitous course northwards till they came opposite Mlozi's town, with the River Rukuru running in between. This march should be undertaken at night and the River Rukuru forded in the darkness, opposite the house-shaped hill, which eminence was to be seized and garrisoned by one division under Major Trollope. Lieut. Coape-Smith was then to place a section of his force under Lieut. Alston to guard the approach to the River Rukuru from Mlozi's town. A further division under Mr. Gordon Cumming was to pass round to the back of Mlozi's town and take up a position to the west of it. Major Trollope's force by occupying the house-shaped hill would command the pass through which the road to Kotakota passed, and thus be able to cut off Mlozi's retreat in that direction. Mr. Walter Gordon Cumming's force would be able to check his flight westward and Lieut. Alston prevent him from crossing the

MLOZI, CHIEF OF THE NORTH NYASA ARABS

River Rukuru to the Tanganyika road. Having posted these three divisions in the darkness of the night Lieut. Coape-Smith was to return along the banks of the river to Kopakopa's, and meet me there at eight o'clock in the morning; for I in the meantime should have started with the naval division and a force of Sikhs under Lieut. de Herries Smith and have attacked, and presumably mastered Kopakopa and Msalemu. Lieut. Coape-Smith accordingly left Karonga at eight o'clock at night on the 1st of December, and although it was raining cats and dogs and the night was pitch dark he carried out the whole of the operations entrusted to him without a single mistake or deviation, and punctually turned up at Kopakopa at eight o'clock next morning. I left at five o'clock in the morning of the 2nd of December with a strong force of artillery under Commander Percy Cullen, R.N.R. (the senior naval officer on Lake Nyasa), and accompanied by Lieut. Rhoades and Phillips (of the Lake Nyasa gunboats); the petty officers of the said gunboats; Sergeant-Major Devoy; Dr. Poole; and Lieut. Herries Smith who commanded the Sikhs. We reached Msalemu's stockades soon after

FOUNDING THE PROTECTORATE 139

daylight, and began to shell it. A few shots were fired by the enemy, but their resistance was soon overcome and they fled from Msalemu's and Kopakopa simultaneously, and crossed the Rukuru River. We therefore entered the stockades and took possession of them. Kopakopa however had resolved to make but little stand here and to unite his force with those of Mlozi in the defence of the latter town, where the war would really be fought out. He had therefore retreated from his stockade in the night, directly the rumour of our landing had reached him, and although he lost some of his men from the fire of Major Trollope's party he succeeded in effecting his retreat to Mlozi's.

After a short rest at Kopakopa's we marched along the Arab road to Mlozi's stockade and came up with Major Trollope's force at 1 p.m. Getting the guns into position Commander Cullen commenced a most effective fire, which would have probably burned Mlozi's town to the ground then and there but for a terribly heavy rain falling at the time. The enemy returned our fire with

THE TRANSPORTS ON THEIR WAY TO KARONGA
ARRIVING IN LIKOMA BAY, EAST NYASA

vigour but could only use against us rifles, muzzle-loading guns, and one muzzle-loading cannon. Although their firing was fairly good we kept pretty much outside their range. We sheltered ourselves in one or two outlying villages which apparently had been built for the housing of slaves. One of these settlements was within 250 yards of the main entrance of Mlozi's stockade and this we managed to occupy, with only one serious casualty. It is true we were not very well sheltered from Mlozi's fire in this position, but then the fire of his men was rather high and the bullets whistled harmlessly over our heads. We now drew the cordon tighter round Mlozi's stockade in an almost continuous ring of armed men. About 700 Wankonde people had tendered their services as carriers for our guns, and these men though unwilling to get within fire still assisted us in repelling sorties from the stockade, which, as the bombardment continued, became fiercer and more frequent.

Mlozi's town was of large extent, perhaps half a square mile in area, and it was surrounded by a rather remarkable stockade which consisted of a double fence of withes thoroughly coated with hard clay and with a flat roof of wooden beams, thatch and clay. This hollow stockade was cut up by transverse partitions into innumerable dwellings. It was loopholed in two rows and pits were dug below the level of the ground for the shelter of the defenders who fired from the upper and the lower loopholes. Here and there angles of the stockade were guarded by specially strong bastions, and in most places there was a kind of moat below the *glacis* of the stockade. At intervals small gateways had been made, their doors being of heavy hewn planks and the passages through the doorway into the town most intricate. It was an admirable stockade for the purpose as shells had no effect on it, merely making a round hole as they passed through, the resistance being too weak to cause any breach to be made by an exploding shell. Mlozi's weakness lay, however, in his not having built his stockade alongside the water from which he was separated by nearly a quarter of a mile. We had cut him off from his water supply, and although rain fell in abundance the water obtained was not sufficient for the enormous number of people cooped up in the stockade, and the cattle. Moreover within the stockade the houses were closely packed with inflammable grass roofs, and these were soon set on fire by incendiary shells. Naturally many of the people took shelter in pits below the ground; still the bombardment caused great loss of life. A *sortie en force* was made on the night of the 2nd of December, but was smartly repelled by Commander Cullen with his Nordenfelt gun.

At seven o'clock in the morning of the following day just as we had resumed our artillery fire, Mlozi hoisted a flag of truce. We ceased firing and I walked up to within a short distance of the walls to meet Mlozi who had come out of the main gateway. I was going to meet him face to face, but that one of the black sailors of the gunboats, a native of Zanzibar, warned me that he had overheard the Arabs advising Mlozi to stab me as soon as I came from under the guns of the fort and then to retreat through the open gateway. This may or may not have been Mlozi's intention. At any rate I deemed it prudent to halt him at about eight yards distance, and from this point I spoke to him. He asked what would be our terms of peace and I replied "the immediate surrender of himself and all the other Arabs and of their fighting men, and the giving up of their guns and the release of all slaves held in the fort." If he would fulfil these conditions I promised the Arabs and all their men their lives, but declined to commit myself to any other promises until I had investigated the whole case. Mlozi after some hesitation said that he would return and consult Kopakopa. Meantime two of his leading men were given to us as hostages, so that we might approach nearer to the fort and converse with the Arabs. Presently, however, an Arab—it may have been Mlozi—came out of the gateway and shouted to us that they would go on fighting; if we wanted them we must come and take them. We therefore released the hostages and allowed them to return, but before the flag of truce could be taken down Mlozi had opened fire on Lieut. Alston and on my camp. Fortunately the bullets passed through Lieut. Alston's helmet and left him uninjured, while I had just entered a hut and so escaped the fire directed at me.

I hesitated to sanction an immediate assault on the stockade as it appeared likely to result in a terrible loss of life to our men. I therefore decided it was best that we should continue the bombardment and protract the war, so as to cause Mlozi to use up much of his ammunition before we finally assaulted the stockade. But matters were precipitated by the excellence of our artillery fire. A refugee Mhenga chief, who had escaped from the stockade during the truce, pointed out to us the exact situation of Mlozi's house, the roof of which rose somewhat above the other buildings. Commander Cullen sighted a 9-pounder gun very carefully, and Sergeant-Major Devoy landed three shells in the middle of this, one passing through the doorway and killing four men. One of the shells that burst in Mlozi's house, wounded Mlozi in the head and killed one of his followers. The rumour went about that Mlozi was dead and a furious sortie took place—a sortie which elicited from us no pity because it was almost as much an impetuous attack on our own positions. The bullets simply whistled through the air, and it was marvellous that we did not meet with more casualties; but our soldiers fought splendidly, and strange to say the timid Wankonde also came to the front and between two and three hundred of Mlozi's men were shot or speared; amongst them fell four Arabs, one of them alleged to be Kopakopa, though it would afterwards seem he was Kopakopa of Tanganyika, and not the man who had built the stockade

A CORNER OF MLOZI'S STOCKADE

near Karonga. The latter is said to have been severely wounded but is still living in the Senga country. Our attempts to repulse the sortie brought the Sikhs close up to the walls, and somehow or other with or without command from their officers they scaled the ramparts and stood on the roof. Lieuts. de Herries Smith and Coape-Smith were dragged up on to the roof of the stockade by the first Sikhs who had got there, and the first man to jump down into the stockade was Lieut. de Herries Smith, who immediately fell, shot through the right arm. Lieut. Coape-Smith and Mr. Gordon Cumming followed Herries Smith, lifted him up and carried him out of the Arab fire. Majors Edwards and Bradshaw had by this time arrived from Karonga, and together with Commander Cullen, Dr. Poole and myself and the other officers made for the stockade. Lieut. Alston and Major Trollope had joined the party under Coape-Smith. Edwards and Bradshaw scrambled over the walls. Commander Cullen made a breach through the doorway with axes, and he and I passed in, having been preceded by a number of Wankonde who drove out the cattle. Night had now fallen; we had lost one Sikh and three Atonga killed, and Lieut. de Herries Smith severely wounded, besides one Sikh hospital assistant and five Sikhs and five native soldiers were more or less severely wounded.

Nothing had as yet been seen of Mlozi. Every effort had been made to protect the women, no matter whether they were the Arabs' wives or their slaves, and fortunately little or no loss of life took place amongst them. They were soon safely housed in our main camp and here they gave us valuable information as to the whereabouts of Mlozi. All search for this man in his dwelling, however, proved fruitless, and we were returning to our camp at night very disconsolate, when suddenly the rumour went up that he had been

THE NYASA-TANGANYIKA ROAD
MADE BY THE BRITISH CENTRAL AFRICA ADMINISTRATION)

captured and brought in by Sergeant-Major Bandawe of the Atonga. Bandawe soon appeared leading Mlozi captive and related the remarkable feat of his capture which was as follows :—After the Sikhs and officers had given up searching Mlozi's house Bandawe had remained behind feeling certain that there was some secret hiding place. After an interval during which he remained perfectly quiet he fancied he heard voices speaking underground. In the corner of the main room was a bedstead, and under the bedstead was an opening leading to an underground chamber. Crawling under the bed Bandawe heard Mlozi asking, "Who is there?" Mimicking the voice of a Swahili, he replied "It is I, master," and descended to the underground chamber, where he found Mlozi being guarded by a man with a spear. Bandawe had no weapon with him but threw himself on the man and wrenched his spear from him which he then ran through his body. Turning to Mlozi he threatened to kill him at once unless he followed him without resistance. Mlozi who was stupid with his wound did so, and he was safely brought into the camp by Bandawe.

We had found out from some of the runaway slaves that during the bombardment Mlozi had caused a good many of the hostages whom he had detained from the natives to be slaughtered. I therefore summoned a council of the Wankonde chiefs, and under my superintendence they tried Mlozi on this count. He was found guilty and sentenced to death. When called upon for his defence he merely said, "What is the good? These people are resolved that I shall die. My hour is come."

He was sentenced to be hanged, but it was originally intended that this sentence should be carried out at Karonga. After the trial, however, a number of Mlozi's men who were prisoners succeeded in overpowering the guard and escaping, and the rumour went about that Kapanda-nsaru's forces were at hand coming to the relief of Mlozi. As a strong flank attack on the part of the Arabs might have cut off our line of retreat to Karonga, it was resolved that Mlozi's execution should take place immediately, so that we might be released

THE NYASA-TANGANYIKA ROAD

from the responsibility of guarding him. He was accordingly hanged on the afternoon of the 4th December, in the presence of the Wankonde chiefs.

On the fourth day of the campaign we were back again at Karonga; but here we found to our great disgust that the s.s. *Domira*, contrary to my orders, had been sent away by the agent of the African Lakes Company. The departure of the officers and men was therefore delayed for some weeks. Meantime I left for the south with Major Edwards to attend to other matters that were pressing.

My three days at Mlozi's without sufficient shelter in the midst of pouring rain, without proper food and having to place my mattress on the wet ground and to drink the foul water of the early rains, had begun to make me very ill, and a few days after leaving Karonga I was down with an attack of black-water fever, in which I was most tenderly and carefully nursed by Major Edwards who conveyed me on the German steamer to Fort Johnston and thence to Liwonde, where I was joined by Dr. Poole, who eventually landed me safe and sound and recovered at Zomba. Meanwhile Lieut. Coape-Smith and Mr. Gordon

Cumming were destroying the remainder of the Arab stockades in the North Nyasa districts, and Lieut. Alston and Mr. A. J. Swann were conducting a brilliantly successful expedition in the interior of the Marimba district where the notorious Saidi Mwazungu[1] had induced the powerful chief Mwasi Kazungu to declare war against the British.

After a little fighting Saidi Mwazungu surrendered, but Mwasi declined to make peace. His capital was stormed and taken. He himself escaped, but soon afterwards committed suicide. He was of Achewa race, but was allied to the Angoni, and had under him many Angoni headmen. Originally it was intended that his attack on our positions in Jumbe's country should coincide

IN FORT HILL.

with the Arab outbreak, but the movements were not quite simultaneous and we were therefore able to deal with each in turn.

It had finally been resolved by me that the campaign should close with the driving out of two Yao robber chiefs who had settled in the Central Angoniland district—Tambala and Mpemba. Captain Stewart led an expedition into Central Angoniland which was joined by Lieut. Alston. Tambala's stronghold was captured and he himself fled. Mpemba hid in the bush but later on was made prisoner by Commander Cullen and Mr. Gordon Cumming. The latter succeeded Captain Stewart in the command of the Central Angoniland district, and did a great deal to bring it into order.

Here as elsewhere in Nyasaland we were much assisted in our campaigns by the real natives of the country who were almost always opposed to the

[1] This was the man who as before related ordered the massacre of Dr. Boyce and Mr. McEwan. After our conquest of Makanjira's country, Saidi Mwazungu fled to the west of Nyasa, and settled with Mwasi Kazungu where he was surrounded by a number of refugees from Makanjira's.

FOUNDING THE PROTECTORATE

chiefs of alien origin who ruled over them and were in conflict with the British. The bulk of the inhabitants in Central Angoniland are neither Angoni nor Yao but Achewa and A-chipeta, branches of the A-nyanja stock.

At the north end of Lake Nyasa a new Administration station was built by Mr. G. A. Taylor the collector, near Karonga, and a strong fort, called Fort Hill,[1] was erected near the British South Africa Company's boundary by Mr. Yule, for the purpose of guarding the Nyasa-Tanganyika road from the raids of the Awemba.

The Awemba are a warlike race inhabiting the regions of the Nyasa-Tanganyika plateau which are watered by the River Chambezi. They

THE STOCKADE, FORT HILL

originally came from the country of Itawa on the south-west coast of Tanganyika. In Livingstone's day they do not appear to have been a particularly warlike or aggressive race; but soon after they came under Arab influence and were supplied by the Arabs with guns and gunpowder, and thenceforth took to slave raiding with extraordinary zest. For several years past they had harried not only the Nyasa-Tanganyika plateau at the south end of Tanganyika, but even the territory that has recently come under German influence; and of late they had been taken up by Mlozi as his special allies, and were introduced by him into the North Nyasa district from which their stragglers have been expelled since the conclusion of the Arab war. As a people, however, they are by no means indisposed to come to terms with us if they see that we are a strong power.

A strong fort was built in the spring and summer of this year by Lieut.

[1] After Sir Clement Hill, the head of the African Department at the Foreign Office.

Alston on the site of Zarafi's town at Mangoche Mountain. Zarafi's former capital was situated on a neck or pass between high mountains and constituted one of the most obvious and frequented roads into British Central Africa. The boundaries of this Protectorate are so well guarded by lofty and inaccessible ranges of mountains or by broad lakes and swamps that there are not many routes by which it can be easily approached from the East Coast. The road through Zarafi's country however is so easy that it will always require to be specially guarded if the slave trade is to be stopped.

In the month of May, 1896, I had a serious relapse of bilious remittent fever which ultimately developed hæmaturic symptoms. I therefore returned to England on leave of absence, being relieved by Mr. Sharpe, who had been in England during the second half of 1895. Since my return the progress of the country has continued almost without check or interruption. Raids on the part of the southern Angoni into the south-western portion of the Protectorate occurred in the autumn of 1896, apparently as a reflex of the agitation amongst their Matabele kindred in the south. These were sharply punished by a force dispatched against the chiefs Chikusi and Odete under Captains F. T. Stewart and W. H. Manning, and Lieut. Alston. The latter had previously captured a slave-raiding chief named Katuri who lived near Fort Mangoche, and who might be described as the last unconquered adherent of the Zarafi clan. With these exceptions the tranquillity of the Protectorate has not been further disturbed. The Imperial Government has placed the British South Africa Company's forces in the adjoining Sphere of Influence under an Imperial Officer who is subordinated to the control of Lieut.-Colonel Edwards, or whoever commands the armed forces in the British Central Africa Protectorate. The efficiency of the Administration was further recognised by the Admiralty who proposed handing over to us the gunboats on the Zambezi and Lower Shire, in a way similar to the transference of the lake gunboats in 1895; but for various reasons it has been deemed preferable to retain these vessels under the White Ensign.

A brief summary of the results of the British administration of this Protectorate from 1891 to 1896 may be expressed as follows:—

At the commencement of our administration in July, 1891, there were, as far as I can calculate, fifty-seven Europeans resident in the British Central Africa Protectorate, and in the adjoining Sphere of the British South Africa Company. Of these one was French, two were Austrian Poles, and the

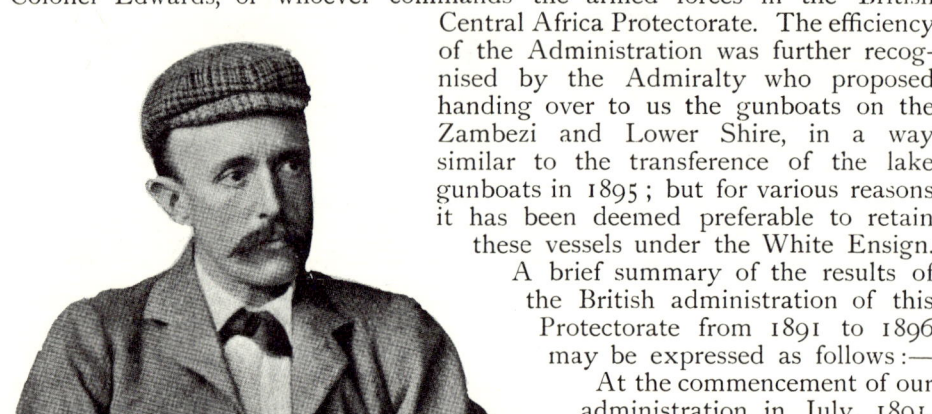

MR. ALFRED SHARPE IN 1896

remainder were British. In the summer of 1896 the European settlers in the Protectorate alone exceeded 300 in number, and probably amounted to forty-

FOUNDING THE PROTECTORATE

five in the adjoining Sphere of the British South Africa Company.[1] At the time I made this calculation as to the number of the Europeans in the Protectorate, in the summer of 1896, I ascertained that 30 were non-British subjects, and consisted of 13 Germans, 8 Dutch, 1 Frenchman, 2 Italians, 5 Austro-Hungarians, and 1 Portuguese. Amongst the British subjects in the late summer of 1896 there were 119 Scotch, 123 English and Welsh, 7 Irish, 2 Australians, 23 South Africans, 1 Anglo-Indian, and 3 Eurasians. The number of Indians has risen from *nil* to 263, of whom 56 were Indian traders. All these Indians, with the exception of 14 who were natives of Portuguese India, were British-Indian subjects.

The total amount of trade done with British Central Africa in 1891, so far as I could calculate from information supplied by the African Lakes Company,

THE ZOMBA-MLANJE ROAD

was £39,965 in value. In April, 1896, the year's trade was computed at £102,428. The export of coffee in 1891 amounted to at most a few pounds. It is computed that in 1896 320 tons were shipped home from British Central Africa, and much of this coffee attained the very high prices of 113s. 0d. and 115s. 0d. a cwt.

In 1891 there were four British steamers[2] on the Zambezi and Lower Shire (besides one steam launch owned by Mr. Sharrer), two of which were gunboats belonging to Her Majesty's Navy. There are now seventeen British steamers on the Zambezi and the Shire, and forty-six cargo boats mostly built of steel, besides innumerable small wooden boats and large cargo canoes. On Lake Nyasa and the Upper Shire the number of steamers has increased from three in 1891 to six in 1896, in addition to which there are several large sailing boats

[1] At the date of the publication of this book the number of Europeans in the *Protectorate* amounts to 315.
[2] In the twelve months from the 1st of January, 1895, to the 31st December, 1895, 109 steamers, 360 barges, 169 boats, and 178 large canoes entered and discharged at the British port at Chiromo on the Lower Shire.

and cargo barges. The captured daus it may be noted have been repaired by us and are now plying in the service of the Government.

There was of course no postal service in 1891, and letters were generally sent through the African Lakes Company to the Vice-Consul at Quelimane together with money for postage stamps, and this official stamped the letters with Portuguese stamps, and sent them home from the Portuguese Post Office. We commenced to establish a postal service in July, 1891. There are now eighteen Post Offices in the Protectorate, and five in the British South Africa Company's sphere, while our postal service extends from Chinde at the mouth of the Zambezi to Tanganyika, Mweru, and the Congo Free State.

A FOOTBRIDGE ACROSS THE MLUNGUSI (ZOMBA)

In the month of November, 1895, which was taken as an average month, the total number of articles carried by our postal service in the Protectorate, including letters, postcards, book packets, newspapers, and parcels, inwards and outwards, was 29,802 as compared with 25,592 in November, 1894, and 19,383 in November, 1893. Besides this we carry the mails of the German Government from Lake Nyasa to Chinde.[1] Our parcel-post service was started in 1893 and has been extended to the South African Colonies and England and to Zanzibar and Aden and India. A money order system has just been established.

Want of funds in 1894 compelled us to adopt a rather cheap and inferior

[1] In return for which the German subsidized steamers carry our correspondence between Chinde and Zanzibar

FOUNDING THE PROTECTORATE

issue of stamps, but by a grant from the Treasury we have now been able to have a thoroughly satisfactory issue engraved by Messrs. De La Rue. The design of the stamps is that of the Coat of Arms of the Protectorate. Their values are 1d., 2d., 4d., 6d., 1s., 2s. 6d., 3s., 4s., £1, £10. They are used alike in the collection of revenue as in the payment of postal charges.

At Chinde on the British Concession there is a Post Office of Exchange, at which mails are landed from or transferred to the ocean-going steamers. Letters or other material arriving from the outer world at Chinde are sorted at this Post Office of Exchange into bags for the various postal districts in British Central Africa, and into bags for the German territories and for the Congo Free State, and are then shipped up river by the various steamers plying between Chinde and Chiromo. At Chiromo the bags are sent overland to the different Post Offices of distribution between the Lower Shire and Lake Nyasa, being carried by native postmen who wear a special uniform of scarlet and white. These men travel at the rate of 25 miles a day, and are wonderfully faithful and careful in the delivery of their precious charges. Cases have been known where postal carriers have been drowned in the crossing of flooded rivers by their obstinacy in not parting from their mail bags, and where they have fought bravely and successfully against odds in an attack by highway robbers. The negro of Central Africa has a genuine respect for the written word. Of course the time will come when attendant on the growth of civilization, native postmen will probably commit robberies of registered letters, as is occasionally done by their European colleagues; but at the present time our mails are perfectly safe in their hands.

In 1891 there was about one mile of road—that between the Mission station at Blantyre and the African Lakes Company's store—over which a vehicle could be driven. By the end of 1896 we had constructed some 390[1] miles of roads suited for wheeled traffic, while another 80 miles of broad paths have been cleared through the bush for the passage of porters and "machillas."[2]

Attempts in great part successful have been made to improve the navigability of the Shire by removing the snags from the approaches to Chiromo, and the sharp stones from the Nsapa Rapids on the Upper Shire; and by deepening the bar at the entrance to Lake Nyasa. Last, and not least, the Slave trade, and it may almost be added the status of Slavery, have been brought absolutely to an end. Between 1891 and 1894, 861 slaves were released by various officials of the Protectorate, and between 1894 and 1896, 1700. Native labour is now organised in such a way as to protect the interests of both the white man and the negro.

1600 acres of land were under cultivation at the hands of Europeans in 1891, as against 5700 acres in 1896.

In 1891 no coin was in circulation in the country, except to a very limited extent amongst Europeans. Transactions with natives were carried on by means of the barter of trade goods. In the three following years the use of English coinage was introduced by the Administration. We imported several thousand pounds' worth of gold, silver and copper coins from the Royal Mint, and put them in circulation amongst the natives who immediately took to the

---

[1] *i.e.*, Katunga to Blantyre, Blantyre to Zomba, Zomba to Fort Liwonde (*via* Domasi), Zomba to Fort Lister, and thence round Mlanje to Fort Anderson, Fort Anderson to Chiromo, Chiromo to Chiradzulu and Ntonda, Blantyre to Cholo, Karonga to the Nyasa-Tanganyika Plateau, and short roads in the Blantyre, Zomba, South Nyasa, Central Angoniland and Marimba districts.

[2] A "machilla" it must be remembered is a hammock or wicker-work couch slung on a pole.

new system. In these efforts we were effectively seconded by the African Lakes Company which established a Banking Company, with its main office at Blantyre and branches at Chinde and Fort Johnston. Native wages are now paid in cash, and the Administration receives most of the native taxes in cash, though produce is still accepted in payment of taxes in the outlying districts. Finally, it may be stated that the local revenue raised from Customs Duties, Stamp Duties, and Native Taxes, which in the year ended March 31st, 1892, was only £1700 in value, was in the year ended March 31st, 1896, over £22,000.

THE GARDENS OF THE RESIDENCY, ZOMBA

Attempts, in some degree successful, have been made to check the indiscriminate slaughter of the elephant, rhinoceros, and gnu,[1] and this protection has now been accorded to the zebra, wild swine, buffalo, and most of the rare or more beautiful African antelopes. Two game reserves for the breeding of these animals unmolested by any attacks from man have been formed, and regulations for the protection of wild game were drawn up by the Foreign Office early in the present year (these will be found in an Appendix to Chapter IX.).

Some mention should be made of the excellent work done by Mr. Alexander Whyte, F.Z.S., the head of our scientific department. He discovered on Mount Mlanje that most interesting conifer the *Widdringtonia Whytei*—discovered

---

[1] The same restrictions also apply to the giraffe, but the giraffe is of very doubtful existence in British Central Africa.

FOUNDING THE PROTECTORATE

it just in time to save it from extinction at the hands of the natives who would every year ignite bush-fires on the upper parts of Mlanje, which were rapidly destroying this valuable tree. Successful efforts have now been made to replant other districts with the *Widdringtonia*, the seed of which has also been introduced into England, where it is now cultivated at Kew Gardens and at the establishments of one or two leading horticulturists. Mr. Whyte, with the co-operation of many officials in the B.C.A. Administration has made remarkable zoological and botanical collections which have enriched our national and provincial museums. (Some idea of the work we have done in this respect may be obtained by glancing at the Appendices to Chapters VIII. and IX.) Mr. Whyte laid the foundations of a Botanical Garden at Zomba, and has distributed amongst the planters seeds and plants which he has introduced on behalf of the Administration, or obtained from Kew. The authorities at Kew Gardens have from time to time sent out Wardian cases containing varieties and species of coffee, of bananas, of vanilla, and of a great many other useful and beautiful trees, shrubs, and plants suited to cultivation in a tropical country.

Coal has been discovered by our officials in various districts, and specimens have been sent home for analysis.

MR. WHYTE IN THE GARDENS AT ZOMBA

APPENDIX I

THE PRESENT METHOD OF ADMINISTERING BRITISH CENTRAL AFRICA

CHAPTER IV. may be usefully supplemented by a brief statement of the present methods of administration.

There are the following Civilian officials :—

H.M. Commissioner and Consul-General :

H.M. Deputy Commissioner and Consul :

A Vice-Consul and Agent of the British Central Africa Administration at Chinde :

An Assistant Agent and Head Postmaster at the same place :

A Vice-Consul at Blantyre, and another at Fort Johnston :

A Secretary to the Administration ; an Assistant Secretary and 2 clerks :

A Judicial Officer at Blantyre, who is at the head of the Judicial Establishment :

A Chief Accountant ; 3 other Accountants ; a Store-keeper and Commissariat Officer ; an Assistant ditto and a native assistant ditto ; a local Auditor :

A Postmaster General ; a head of the Scientific Department (Mr. Alexander Whyte) ; an Assistant and Forester in the same department :

A Principal Medical Officer, and 2 other medical officers :

A First Surveyor (European); 3 other Surveyors (Indian, lent by the Indian Government) ; a Superintendent of Road-making, and two Assistant Superintendents :

A Superintendent of Public Works, with a European assistant and 6 Indian artisans :

12 Collectors, 8 of whom hold Judicial Warrants :

15 Assistant Collectors.

Most of the Collectors and Assistant Collectors hold in addition the office of Postmaster. There are further, besides the Postmaster-General at Blantyre, and the Head Postmaster at Chinde, 2 special Postmasters at Blantyre and at Zomba.

The Armed Forces consist of the following officers and men :—

A Commandant (Lieut.-Colonel C A. Edwards) :

Second-in-Command and Staff Officer ; Third Officer and Quarter-Master :

Accountant, Clerk, Sergeant-Major of Artillery, and Transport Officer, and 2 Indian clerks.

(The foregoing are specially attached to the Indian Contingent, though their control extends to the rest of the armed forces.)

In the Contingent of Native troops there are :—

6 British Officers ; 2 native Sergeant-Majors ; and a number of Police Corporals and Interpreters.

The troops consist of

180 Sikhs, with 20 followers and 2 Indian hospital assistants, and about 1,000 native soldiers, armed porters and policemen.

APPENDIX

The Naval Service consists of a

Commandant (Commander Percy Cullen, R.N.R.) and
3 other Naval Officers, all of whom are chosen from the Royal Naval Reserve; and
4 Warrant Officers, who are pensioners in the Royal Navy;
A Chief Engineer, and 4 other engineers;
4 Indian Artificers;
Other European carpenters, clerks, store-keepers, &c.; and about
80 "Sidi Boys," or native seamen.

BARRACKS AT FORT JOHNSTON

There are at present in the service of the Protectorate on the Upper Shire and on Lake Nyasa, 3 gunboats, 1 barge, 5 steel boats, and 2 daus (Arab sailing vessels). The war vessels are well armed with suitable guns. A new gunboat of considerable size is being built for service on Lake Nyasa, and should be launched at the beginning of 1898.

The most important "item" in the service of the Protectorate is probably the "Collector." This official superintends the collection of Customs Duties, the assessment and levying of native taxes; he directs the Civil police in his district; administers justice to Europeans and between Europeans and natives where he holds a Warrant from the Secretary of State to act as a judicial officer; superintends the administration of native justice; and acts generally as political officer and Tribune of the people. In all Civil matters he is supreme in his District, and only subordinate to the Commissioner. In many cases he is also responsible for the conduct of the postal service. If he possesses a great deal of power he is at the same time almost invariably an overworked individual, with many cares and responsibilities on his shoulders.

Justice is administered to British subjects and other Europeans and foreigners under the Africa Orders in Council of 1891 and 1893; and to the natives by such native chiefs as are authorised to hold Courts of Justice; or more ordinarily by the judicial officers in the district, acting in the name and by the authority of the native chiefs. Capital punishment on Europeans can only be carried out after the Minutes of the Trial have been submitted to a Supreme Court[1] which revises the sentence, and if it is confirmed sanctions the execution. Capital sentences on natives of the Protectorate, imposed by the native Court, cannot be carried out until they have received the sanction of the Commissioner of Zomba, to whom Minutes of the case are submitted[2] by a provision under the Africa Orders in Council. Additional laws, governing the Protectorate and the Sphere of Influence, can be made by the issue of "Queen's Regulations," which, after receiving the assent of the Secretary of State for Foreign Affairs, are promulgated by the Commissioner for British Central Africa. Special legislation of this kind is chiefly directed to the establishment of Customs Duties and Taxation, to the protection of Big Game, to the regulation of native labour and of navigation on the rivers and lakes.

These Regulations and other announcements of a Governmental kind are published in the *British Central Africa Gazette*, which is the official organ of the Administration and appears fortnightly, issued by the Government Press at Zomba.[3]

Government land is sold by public auction, and its upset price at present varies from 2s. 6d. to 5s. 0d. an acre.

There is a central Hospital at Zomba for the treatment of the European servants of the Administration, and a native hospital.

For Administrative purposes the Protectorate is divided into the following districts:—

Lower Shire (Capital, Port Herald).   Upper Shire (Capital, Liwonde).
Ruo (Capital, Chiromo).   South Nyasa (Capital, Fort Johnston).
Mlanje (Capital, Fort Anderson).   Central Angoniland (Capital,[4] Tambala).
Zomba (Capital, Zomba).   Marimba (Capital, Kotakota).
Blantyre (Capital, Blantyre).   West Nyasa (Capital, Nkata).
West Shire (Capital, Chikwawa).   North Nyasa (Capital, Karonga).

[1] Which at present is the High Court of Cape Colony.

[2] There have only been four executions for murder amongst the natives since 1891. One was the execution of a native of Kotakota, who killed a Makua soldier; the second, the execution of Mlozi: the third, the execution of Saidi Mwazungu, who killed Dr. Boyce and Mr. McEwan; and the fourth the execution of the Angoni Chief, Chikusi.

[3] Where there are 1 European superintendent and 6 native printers.

[4] It is probable that the capital will be removed to Chiwere.

THE RESIDENCY, ZOMBA

MAP OF BRITISH CENTRAL AFRICA SHOWING ADMINISTRATIVE DIVISIONS

CHAPTER V.

THE SLAVE TRADE

IN regard to the slave trade, a few words of explanation and description may be of interest. Slavery has probably existed among mankind from time immemorial, and no doubt one race of negroes enslaved another ages before the ancient Egyptians and Phœnicians introduced the slave trade, by which is meant the deliberate expatriation of negroes to countries beyond the sea, or to parts of Africa not inhabited by the negro race. But the horrors of the slave trade are attributable, firstly to Europeans, and secondly to Arabs.

The English, Spanish, Portuguese and French had commenced trafficking in negro slaves from the West Coast of Africa when that coast became opened up to geographical knowledge in the fourteenth and fifteenth centuries. In the sixteenth century organised attempts were made to replace the disappearing aborigines of the West Indies by negro slaves; then came the introduction of negroes into the southern States of North America. At first the trade was confined to the West Coast but the Portuguese commenced to export slaves from East Africa in the seventeenth century, and thenceforward a mighty slave trade sprang up in the valley of the Zambezi which is not yet extinct, although several measures for its abolition have been taken by the Portuguese Government during the present century.

Maskat Arabs who warred with the Portuguese in East Africa and gradually supplanted them in all the settlements between Aden and the Ruvuma River, organised a brisk traffic to supply the markets of the East with black concubines, black eunuchs, and strong-armed willing workers.

Slaves thus became indispensable to Arabia, Egypt, Mesopotamia and Persia, and Abyssinian slaves were even introduced in numbers to the West Coast of India where they were turned into fighting men or into regular castes of seamen.[1]

The Moors of Northern Africa, however, had almost shown the way in the matter of the slave trade to the nations of Western Europe by developing an active intercourse with the regions of the Nigerian Sudan, so that all Northern Africa was abundantly supplied with a caste of negro workers while negro blood mingled freely in many of the Arab and Berber tribes.

The worst horrors of the slave trade were probably the miseries endured by the closely-packed negroes on slave ships, where from want of ventilation and of such treatment as would nowadays be accorded as a duty to cargoes of beasts, they endured untold miseries and developed strange maladies. Moreover, to

---

[1] Curiously enough some of these slaves revolted and formed communities of their own in Western India, now recognised by the Imperial Government as small tributary States under negroid rulers of Abyssinian descent.

supply the slave market in America incessant civil war was raging amongst the coast tribes of West Africa. But the Arabs of East-Central Africa have run us hard in the matter of wickedness. I do not need to recapitulate the horrors of slave raids and the miseries of slave caravans: they are graphically described by Livingstone.[1]

The Arabs of Maskat from the Zanzibar coast and the half-breed Portuguese from the Zambezi joined together to devastate what is now called British Central Africa.

The slaves from the Senga and Bisa countries in the Luangwa valley and from much of Southern Nyasaland found their way to Tete on the Zambezi, and thence to Quelimane and Moçambique, where they were picked up by American ships as late as the beginning of the "sixties." Some of these ships eluded the British gunboats; others were captured and taken to Sierra Leone. Here, strange to say, many inhabitants of Nyasaland and of the countries as far west as the Lualaba, were landed in the "forties" and "fifties" of this century, and were examined as to their languages by Mr. Koelle, a German missionary of great learning, who, in his *Polyglotta Africana*, produced one of the finest books ever written on the subject of African languages. Long before the existence of Lakes Nyasa and Tanganyika were known to Europe, Mr. Koelle, of Sierra Leone, was writing down the vocabularies and languages spoken on the shores of those lakes, gathered from slaves that had come from Moçambique and Quelimane.

A SWAHILI SLAVE-TRADER

In between Moçambique and Quelimane the Arabs still retain to this day a hold on certain little-known ports, such as Angoche and Moma. From these points slaves from Eastern Nyasaland were shipped to Madagascar, which until its recent conquest by the French was another profitable market for slaves. In addition, the Matabele Zulus, who had surged back into South-Central Africa from Zululand at the beginning of this century raided across the Zambezi for slaves, and slave-raiding was also carried on by the Basuto who, under the name of the Makololo, conquered the Barutse kingdom. From the middle of the 18th to near the end of the 19th century British Central Africa has been devastated by the slave trade. Whole tribes have been cut up and scattered; vast districts depopulated; arts and crafts and useful customs have been forgotten in the flight before the slave-raiders. The whole country was kept in a state of incessant turmoil by the attempt to supply the slave markets of the Zambezi, of Madagascar, of the United States, of Zanzibar, Arabia, Persia, and Turkey.

A great blow was dealt to this trade by the conclusion of the American Civil War and the abolition of slavery. This and the Emancipation of Slaves first in the West Indies and subsequently in Brazil, brought the West African

[1] I have attempted also to give descriptions based on a good deal of personal observation as well as on much reading in my book, *The History of a Slave*.

slave trade to a close and largely diminished the source of profit in the South-East African slave trade; for American ships came no longer to the Moçambique coast to take away cargoes of slaves and to evade the British cruisers. Then the Portuguese awoke to a sense of duty and a series of edicts made slavery very difficult and the slave trade practically impossible in all the settled portions of Portuguese East Africa. But the Eastern market always

ARAB AND SWAHILI SLAVE-TRADERS, CAPTURED BY THE B.C.A. FORCES

remained open and the Arabs carried their slaving enterprise farther and farther into the heart of British Central Africa. They had enlisted on their side powerful tribes like the Wa-yao, the Wa-nyamwezi, the Awemba, and the Angoni Zulus. Dr. Livingstone, however, appeared on the scene and his appeals to the British public gradually drew our attention to the slave trade in Eastern Central Africa until, as the direct result of Livingstone's work, slavery and the slave trade are now at an end within the British Central Africa Protectorate, and are fast disappearing in the regions beyond under the South Africa

Company; and the abolition of slavery at Zanzibar will shortly be decreed as a final triumph to Livingstone's appeal.

The attitude of our Administration in British Central Africa towards the status of slavery has been this: we have never recognised it, but where slavery existed without its being forced on our notice through an attempt to carry on the slave *trade*, or through unkindness to the slaves, we have not actually interfered to abolish the status. But if ever a slave has run away from a district not administered by us to a more settled portion of the Protectorate, we have always refused to surrender him. If the slave was a female and it could be shown that she was a wife or concubine of the man who owned her or that he had inflicted no unkindness she was usually given back upon a promise of immunity from punishment. When a district from various causes has come under our our immediate administration we have always informed the slaves that they were not slaves and that they were free to go and do what they pleased as long as they did not break the law. But it has rarely happened that the slaves of a chief who were well treated have chosen to quit their masters; therefore, being free to do as they liked, if they chose to remain and work as slaves nobody interfered to prevent their doing so. The slave *trade*—still more slave-raiding—has always been punished, and it may be safely stated that such a thing does not now exist in the Protectorate, though it is still carried on in such districts as are not wholly under the control of the British South Africa Company; while Mpezeni alone among the unconquered Angoni chiefs raids the countries round his settlements and apparently adds his slaves to the population of his kingdom, or sells them to the Arabs on the Luangwa.

A "RUGA-RUGA"
(MNYAMWEZI)
Slave-raider employed by Arabs

The hardships of the slave trade were these:—Homes were broken up, a large number of men, women and little children were collected together and dispatched on a many-hundred-mile journey overland to the coast, on which they often had to carry heavy burdens Their slave-sticks[1] were no light weight, and they were ill-fed and provided with no clothing to shield them from the cold or wet in mountainous regions. If they lagged by the way or lay down, worn out with exhaustion, their throats were cut or they were shot. Often before reaching the coast the Arabs would stop at some settlement and roughly castrate a number of the young boys so that they might be sold as eunuchs. Some died straightway from the operation, others lingered a little longer and

---

[1] The slave-stick in most of the languages of East-Central Africa is called gori, goli, or li-goli. It consists usually of a young tree lopped off near the ground and again cut where it divides into two branches. The ends of these two branches are left sufficiently long to enclose the neck of the slave. Their ends are then united by an iron pin which is driven through a hole drilled in the wood and hammered over on either side.

The thick end of the gori-stick is usually fastened to a tree at night time when the caravan is resting, though sometimes it is merely left on the ground as the weight of the stick would make escape nearly impossible, especially as stubborn slaves have their hands tied behind the back. When the slaves are engaged in any work the end of the gori-stick is sufficiently supported to enable them to bear its weight and yet perform the task allotted to them. Except in the case of children, on whom no stick is placed,

eventually perished from hernia induced by this operation. Those who survived usually had an extremely comfortable and prosperous after-life in the harem of some Turk, Arab or Persian. The mortality amongst the children was terrible: the Arab slave-drivers do not appear to have been actuated by motives of commercial expediency in endeavouring to land as many live and healthy slaves on the coast as possible. They seem on the contrary to have been inspired by something more like devilish cruelty at times in the reckless way in which they would expose their slaves to suffering and exhaustion, and then barbarously kill them.[1]

as they are sure to follow their mothers or friends, or of comely young women who are the temporary concubines of the slave-drivers, and who, with the facile nature of the negro, rapidly become attached to their brutal husbands—all slaves are usually loaded with this terrible weight. Nevertheless escape does sometimes take place. Most slaves must of necessity have their hands free when on the march, especially if they are to support the weight of the gori-stick. They then often manage to secrete a knife or razor, or some sharp substance with which during the night they will attempt to saw through one of the branches of the stick round the neck. They are then able to twist the iron pin round and release their necks from the burden. To escape in a strange country is impossible, and the attempt is invariably followed by a return to slavery in some shape or form. As a rule when the journey to the coast is half done the slaves are sufficiently to be depended upon for docility to be able to travel without the slave-stick.

[1] Much of my information about slavery was derived from an interesting man, several years in my service, who was originally a native of the east coast of Lake Nyasa, and had been sent as a slave to the coast with an Arab caravan when he was about twelve years old. The slaves whom he accompanied were captured by a British cruiser. This boy was taken to Zanzibar and set free, was educated at the Universities Mission, and became the servant of a succession of Admirals on the East Coast Station, ending up with Admiral Hewett; after whose death he passed into my service, and was, until his recent death, the principal servant at the Consulate at Moçambique.

CHAPTER VI.

THE EUROPEAN SETTLERS

AS mentioned in a preceding chapter, there were 345 Europeans at the end of the year 1896 settled in the eastern part of British Central Africa, of whom about thirty were non-British subjects. These Europeans are divisible into four classes—officials, missionaries, planters and traders.

The missionaries and their work will be dealt with in Chapter VII. The officials have been referred to in the Appendix to a preceding chapter; there remain therefore the planters and traders to be now considered.

The planters come from very much the same class which furnishes the coffee planters of Ceylon, India, Fiji, and Tropical America. They are most of them decent young fellows of good physique and good education, who, possessed of a small capital, desire to embark on a life which shall combine a profitable investment for their money, with no great need for elaborate technical education, and an open-air life in a wild country with plenty of good sport, and few or none of the restraints of civilisation. One of our planters can look back on something like twenty-two years' experience of British Central Africa, another on eighteen years' experience, a third ten, a fourth nine; but most of the men did not arrive in the country before 1890 or 1891. The planters now probably number nearly 100. The chief thing grown is coffee; but tea has been started on two estates (on one of which it has been growing for about six years), and on others cinchona and ceará rubber, cotton and tobacco are cultivated. Some planters go in a great deal for cattle keeping and breeding.[1]

The coffee plant was originally introduced into British Central Africa by Mr. Jonathan Duncan, a horticulturist in the service of the Church of Scotland Mission, but the idea owes its inception to the late Mr. John Buchanan, C.M.G., who was at the time also in the service of the Church of Scotland Mission,[2]

---

[1] During the past two or three years the use of cattle by the European settlers in the Protectorate has greatly increased. When I first came to British Central Africa in 1889 no one except at two or three mission stations and at the African Lakes Company's establishments at Mandala and at Karonga kept any cattle. A few native chiefs had herds of 20 or 30 beasts hidden away in the mountains, afraid to avow their existence in case they should be raided by the Angoni or the Yao. At the north end of the lake the Wankonde had enormous herds, as was the case with the Angoni in the west of the Protectorate, but no one came forward to trade in cattle and distribute oxen among the Europeans in the Shire Highlands. All this is now changed. Many Europeans have been up into the Angoni country, and certain Administration officials have interested themselves in the introduction of cattle into the Shire province. The price of milch cows now stands at a little more than two or three pounds a head, while oxen may fetch as little as 15/. each. The chief inducement in keeping cattle is to use the manure for the coffee plantations, but of course the supply of milk and butter is a valuable adjunct to health.

[2] Which he joined as a lay member specially in charge of horticultural work in 1876.

and who on his arrival at Blantyre had arranged with the curator of the Botanical Gardens at Edinburgh for the sending out of coffee plants.

Three small coffee plants of the Mocha variety *(Coffæa Arabica)* which were leading a sickly existence at Edinburgh were entrusted to Mr. Duncan to transport to Blantyre. Two of these plants died on the voyage, the third survived and was planted in the Blantyre Mission gardens, where until quite recently it was still living. Two years after it was thus replanted it bore a crop of about 1000 beans which were all planted, and from which 400 seedlings were eventually reared. In 1883, 14½ cwts. of coffee was gathered from these young trees. Mr. Henry Henderson of the Blantyre Mission brought out a small supply of Liberian coffee seed in 1887; but this variety has never met with much success in British Central Africa, as it will not grow well on the hills, though it answers well in the plains. Moreover, it does not fetch nearly such good prices as the small Mocha bean. Later on varieties of Jamaica coffee were introduced by the Moir Brothers whilst managers of the African

THE CONSULATE, BLANTYRE

Lakes Company at Mandala. The "blue mountain" variety of Jamaica has succeeded very well in the Shire Highlands, and to a less extent the "orange" coffee in the same locality has prospered. Still the bulk of the coffee trees now existing in this Protectorate owe their origin to the one surviving coffee plant introduced from the Edinburgh Botanical Gardens. It may therefore be said without much exaggeration that it is Scotch coffee which is the staple growth of British Central Africa.

Owing to the troubles which broke out in the Church of Scotland Mission (briefly referred to in a previous chapter), much of the Society's work in connection with planting was suspended, though not before it had introduced coffee into the Zomba district through Mr. Buchanan; but when Mr. Buchanan left the Mission in 1880 he determined to establish himself independently as a coffee planter. For years he and his brothers (who eventually joined him) struggled on with a very limited capital, having almost insuperable difficulties to contend with in the shape of recalcitrant chiefs, ill-health, and invasions of the Angoni, which drove away all their native labour. They remained however without any rivals in the field until Mr. Eugene Sharrer, a British subject of German origin, arrived at Blantyre in 1889, bought land and started coffee planting. The Lakes Company also commenced planting about the same time, but the shipments of the Buchanan Brothers had already established the fact that coffee of the very best quality could be grown in British Central Africa. Moreover, the labour difficulty was being gradually solved. When the natives around the infant settlements of Blantyre and Zomba were convinced that the white men would pay fairly for their labour, they began to come in increasing numbers to work in the plantations, and strangest of all, the warlike Angoni came down with their slaves, not to raid and ravage as before, but to obtain employment for three or four months in the year in the coffee plantations.

The total amount of coffee exported from this Protectorate in 1896 was 320 tons. This coffee was sold in London at prices ranging between 99s. and 115s. per cwt., much of it fetching prices over 100 shillings. The lowest price ever fetched by British Central Africa coffee was 86s. per cwt.

The coffee undoubtedly varies according to the amount of rainfall, the fertility of the soil, and the manner in which it is plucked, pulped, dried and packed. Manure and shade[1] seem to be absolutely necessary to complete success. Artificial manures are now being imported, and as already stated cattle are kept in increasing quantities so that their dung may be used for the coffee plantations, and guano has recently been discovered on the islands of Lake Nyasa, which will prove very useful. It is also necessary that the plantations shall be scrupulously weeded. When the soil is fertile, and all these conditions of manure, shade and weeding have been fulfilled, a yield of as much as 17 cwt. per acre has been taken. On the other hand, in much neglected gardens no more than 50 or 60 lbs. per acre has been realised. The average yield in the plantations is $3\frac{1}{2}$ cwt. per acre, though it is the opinion of experts that this yield would be greatly increased if more care was shown in the cultivation of the coffee.

A COFFEE TREE IN BEARING

In some years of poor rainfall or where the first rains have fallen early, and have brought coffee prematurely into blossom leaving the newly-formed seed to suffer from the subsequent drought, the berry grows diseased or the husk is found to be empty with no kernels at all inside. Some people are of opinion that this empty husk or diseased berry is caused by the presence of a small beetle. Others assert that it is the result of a plague of green

---

[1] To attain this end, I believe, in new plantations for every two coffee shrubs inserted in the ground one African fig tree is planted. These splendid wild fig trees grow to a great height and give absolute shade. They also serve to protect the coffee trees from being wind blown or seared by the hot air coming off the plains in the dry season.

bugs which suck the sap of the coffee tree. All are agreed, however, that the only preventative of the defective berry is *plenty of shade* and manure.

A system of "topping"[1] has now been almost universally adopted, though perhaps not to the same extent to which it is carried on in Ceylon and India, for it is difficult to train immediately a sufficient staff of natives who will handle and prune the coffee in a proper manner; and careless topping does more harm than good. The effect of the soil of this Protectorate on the coffee shrub is apparently to bring it into bearing at three years of age or under, and to cause it in its second crop to exhaust its vitality, if it be not previously pruned. Left to itself the coffee shrub in this main or second crop would give an enormous yield from the primary shoots and as a result of this exhaustion no secondary branches would be developed from which the next year's crop would come; consequently instead of bearing year after year for something like fourteen years the coffee shrubs would be useless when four or five years old. The coffee tree generally blossoms during the dry season in the months of September and October, especially if a few showers of rain fall, as they often do at this time of the year. The berries are usually ripe and ready for picking at the end of June.

In my report to the Foreign Office on the trade of British Central Africa during 1895 and 1896 I have estimated that a planter requires a capital of about £1000 for the upkeep and bringing into bearing of 100 acres of coffee. This sum should purchase an estate of say 500 acres and provide for the cost of clearing it, obtaining coffee seedlings and planting them, and building a fairly comfortable house, and of meeting the expense of the planter's living on a moderate scale during the three years. It would not, however, provide for the erection of a substantial brick house, nor of the pulping vats, and special machinery for pulping. With this he would have gradually to supply himself out of the profits his plantation would make after the first three years. Perhaps it may enable my readers to obtain a clear idea of the average experience of a young coffee planter; what difficulties he has to face; what are the chances of success—what in fact any reader of my book who intends to become a coffee planter in British Central Africa would have to undergo—if I give here extracts from the imaginary letters of a typical planter, so far as my imagination will enable me to enter into the mind of A, B, C, or D, and reveal their thoughts and the impressions which are made on them by what they see and feel.

A PLANTER'S TEMPORARY HOUSE

"BALBROCHAN, AYRSHIRE, SCOTLAND.

"DEAR FRED,—As I have failed in my last chance for the army, the governor has decided that I am to go coffee planting somewhere in Central Africa. He has heard all about it from old Major McClear, who it appears has gone out there with his son (he is a widower you know) and is going to supplement his pension by making money out of

[1] "Topping" means cutting about four inches off the top of the tree, so as to throw it back and cause the secondary branches to develop and come into bearing.

coffee. You see, as I have failed finally to pass my exams for the army, I must not be too particular, as there are younger brothers and sisters to be educated and put out in the world, and my father is not over well off; besides, I hear there is capital sport, and the climate is not so bad though one gets a touch of fever every now and then. The governor can only afford £1000 to start me, and I am going to do my best not to cost him another penny before I am self-supporting. . . . I think the country is called the British Central Africa Protectorate; it is close to Lake Nyasa, and is about 300 or 400 miles inland from the east coast. I am getting my equipment ready, and shall leave on the 1st of May by the *Edinburgh Castle* for Durban, where I change into the "Rennie" boat *Induna*, and so travel up the east coast to a place called Chinde which is at the mouth of the Zambezi. Here I change into the river steamer, and travel up the Zambezi and the Shire, and so on to Blantyre where I shall stay with the McClears and look about me. . . . As to equipment,[1] I am not taking very much as I am told that most things can be got fairly good and cheap out there, and it saves one the bother of a lot of luggage, and the risk of loading yourself with things that you don't want. I shall simply take along with me all my old clothes and a dress-suit in case there is any 'society.' Of course I am taking guns—a doubled-barrelled 12-bore shot gun and an express rifle. I have been strongly advised not to take a helmet, as it is said to be a ridiculous kind of headgear for Central Africa, where one requires something like a light Terai hat, and where it appears you should always carry a white cotton umbrella when the sun shines. The helmet is cumbersome and ugly and does not shield the body from the sun. It seems from what I can gather that a chap gets far sicker from the effect of the sun on his body than on his head, and that the best way to avoid sun fever and sunstroke is to carry an umbrella wherever one goes. I shall take a good saddle with me and riding gear, as most of the people in the Shire Highlands (the name of the coffee district) ride about on ponies. I think as I pass through Durban I shall invest in a Basuto pony (they are said to be the best for the purpose) and take him along with me up to Blantyre. I hear they are very cheap at Durban, about £8 will buy a good one, and it only comes altogether to about £25 or £26 to convey the little beast up river to a place called Katunga, and there you get on his back and ride up to Blantyre. I shall also take out my bicycle as some of the roads are fit for cycling. Nearly everything else can be got on the spot, but my mother insists on giving me a small medicine chest, so that I can dose myself with quinine and other things if there is no doctor handy. I shall also take out a small photographic camera and plenty of books.

"And now good-bye for a bit in case I don't see you again, but as soon as I get out there I will write and let you know what it is like."

"CHIROMO, BRITISH CENTRAL AFRICA, *June 12th*.

"DEAR FRED,—I am now in British Central Africa, and before I get any further into the country as I have a day or two to spare here I will give you an account of what my journey was like.

"I managed to get my pony all right in Durban through Messrs. —— and ——, who seem to be universal providers in that city. I had to give £9 for him but he is an extra good little beast. We changed into the *Induna* at this place. She was very crowded and therefore not very comfortable, but the journey to Chinde only occupied five days as we ran through direct.

"Chinde, you know, is one of the mouths of the Zambezi, and the only one which has a bar that can be crossed without risk by a well-navigated steamer. The *Induna* crossed the bar all right and landed us on the British Concession, a piece of land which was granted by the Portuguese Government for the use of the British Central Africa Protectorate so that goods can be transhipped here from the ocean-going steamers

---

[1] *vide* Appendix II., p. 185.—H. H. J.

into the river boats. I did not stay on the Concession, however, but on a place called the Extra Concession which has no privileges regarding exemptions from Customs dues. I put up at an hotel which is run by ———. Of course everything seems very rough to me who have never been farther away than Switzerland before, but fellows here tell me that Chinde is simply luxurious to what it was a few years ago. In 1890 it was practically unknown to Europeans, and there was not even a hut on the present sandspit, which is the site of the town—everything was covered with thick bush ; now, although the place is horribly ugly, being built almost entirely of corrugated iron, it is fairly neat and clean. Most of the houses are of one story, but ———'s hotel is not half a bad place, a sort of bungalow built of iron and wood with broad shady verandahs. The food is anything but good, however, as fresh provisions are scarce and most of the things we eat come out of tins.

"Chinde is a great peninsula of sand intersected with marshy tracts, which projects into the Indian Ocean, having the sea on one side and the Chinde mouth of the Zambezi on the other.

* * * * * * * *

"Two days after our arrival at Chinde we started in the Lakes Company's steamer, the *James Stevenson*, which conveyed us up river as far as Chiromo. After leaving Chinde we pursued a tortuous course up the Chinde River till we got into the main Zambezi. Here the country was very uninteresting. The Zambezi is extremely broad and you are never sure whether you are looking at the opposite bank or a chain of long flat islands. Islands and shore are equally covered at this season of the year by grass of tremendous height, and except an occasional fan-palm you see nothing behind the grass. Hippos are very scarce and shy now owing to the way they have been shot at. Occasionally however you see little black dots at a distance, and if you are looking through glasses you can distinguish a hippo raising his head and stretching his jaws, but they always duck when the steamer gets anywhere near. At the end of our second day we got to a place called Vicenti, a sort of Portuguese station. A little while before we got there we began to see something more interesting than the grass banks—the outline of a blue mountain called Morambala, which overlooks the Shire River. Morambala is the only hill to be seen for miles farther on beyond Vicenti. You hardly notice where you get into the River Shire, as the country seems to have become quite demoralised at the junction of the Shire with the Zambezi by the intersection of innumerable channels of water and swamps. Morambala looks a splendid mountain, however (about 4,000 feet high), as it rises up above the fœtid Morambala marsh. Beyond Morambala the banks are dotted with innumerable tall palms which I could not help thinking very picturesque with their lofty whitish-grey stems, and their crowns of elegantly-shaped blue-green fronds.

* * * *

MT. MORAMBALA, FROM THE RIVER SHIRE

"The first place we stopped at in British territory was Port Herald on the west bank of the Shire, a pretty little settlement with very rich vegetation. The steamer had to stop here for a day for some reason or other so I and two of my fellow passengers went out for a shoot. The Administration official at the station lent us a guide, and we had awfully good sport, coming back with a large male waterbuck,—a beast as big as a red deer—and two reedbuck which are somewhat the size of a roe and very good eating. The meat of the waterbuck is no good, so we gave it to the natives ; but as I had shot the beast I kept the horns which are very fine though not at all like a stag's, being quite simple without branches and with an elegant curve and ever so many rings. Jones, one of my fellow passengers, saw a lion whilst we were out shooting on this occasion, but was in too much of a funk to fire, so the beast got away. He says his cartridge jammed! but I don't believe him.

"Chiromo is an awfully pretty little place. The roads are broad and bordered with fine shady trees planted close together. Some of the buildings are quite smart, though of course at home we should think them small.

"Up to the present the climate has been lovely and I have not had a touch of fever. It is quite cool at nights and one seldom gets mosquitos, but I am told that in the rainy season they are an awful pest. In the middle of the day it is about as hot as a summer's day at home, but not too hot to walk about with or without an umbrella. This is the beginning of the cool season of the year."

"BLANTYRE, *June 30th*.

"I got up to Blantyre on June 18th. The small steamer of the Lakes Company took us on from Chiromo to Katunga, up the Shire. You cannot go beyond Katunga by water, or at least much beyond, because of the rapids and falls. The Steamer Company arranged about the transport of my baggage and I simply saddled my pony, which was in capital condition, and rode him gently up to Blantyre. The distance is about 25 miles. I had sent a telegram from Katunga to say I was coming and old McClear rode out and met me half-way. His plantation is not in Blantyre but about seven miles out. However, we slept that night at an hotel in Blantyre and went on to his plantation the next morning. The country is awfully pretty—very thickly wooded in parts and with hills and mountains of bold outline. Water seems to be most abundant; every few miles you cross a running stream or rivulet. As far as climate goes you might think yourself back in England, anywhere near Blantyre, at this season of the year. All the houses are built of brick and every room, nearly, has a fireplace.

"It is very jolly at night to sit round a huge log fire and enjoy it, with the temperature outside almost down to freezing point. In fact some mornings there is a white rime on the ground when you first go out.

* * * * * * * *

"I have almost settled on buying a piece of land adjoining McClear's plantation. It belongs to the Crown and I shall have to take these steps to buy it:—First of all I have to get one of the surveyors here to go over the land with me and make a rough plan of the boundaries so that we can get at some idea of the area and furnish the Commissioner's Office with sufficient information to enable the officials to decide where the land is and whether it can be sold. With these particulars I send a fee of £2, which includes the surveyor's fees and the cost of inserting an announcement in the *Gazette*. If the Commissioner decides to sell the land he will put a notice to that effect in the *Gazette* and an upset-price will be fixed (probably 5s. an acre) and notice will be given that the estate will be sold by public auction a fortnight after the announcement appears. The sale will take place at the Court House in Blantyre. I shall have to go there and if nobody bids against me I shall get the estate knocked down to me at the upset-price.

* * * * * * * *

"BLANTYRE, *August 1st*.

"I have bought my land—nobody bid against me—but I have had my first attack of fever. Perhaps it is just as well to get it over, as they say you have it all the worse if it is bottled up in your system. I think mine must have come on from a chill. I had played in a tremendous cricket match got up at Blantyre, "The Administration *v.* Planters," and after getting very hot went and sat about in the cool breeze, which is about the most fatal thing you can do. The next day after breakfast I began to feel a bit cheap—very shivery and a horrid pain in the back, and rather a sensation as though

I was going to have a tremendous cold. I am staying at Major McClear's and he told me at once I was in for a dose of fever, made me go to bed, gave me a purge and put hot water bottles at my feet. Then I began to get awfully hot — my temperature went up to 102 degrees — and after that came a sweat which soaked all the bed clothes, and then I felt a bit better and wanted to get up but they advised me to stay in bed. I seemed all right the next morning except that my ears were singing, but towards evening again I felt beastly bad. I went to bed and vomited ever so many times, and thought I was going to die. A doctor came to see me and found my temperature 103 degrees; he brought it down with a dose of phenacitine. Eventually I got to sleep and woke up much better, but I was down again the third day though not so bad. After that I felt

SHARRER'S STORE AT KATUNGA

very weak and looked very yellow for a day or two, and then my appetite came back and now I am just as fit as it is possible to be — a tremendous appetite and think the country is the finest in the world though I can tell you whilst I had the fever on me I made an awful ass of myself, telling them all I was going to die and sending all sorts of messages to my people! I hear everybody does that when he has fever and no one seems inclined to make fun of you on that account.

"Well: I have bought my land — 500 acres at 5s. makes £125. I shall have to pay the Stamp Duties and eventually the cost of a survey. All this will come to about another £20 — say in all £150. I have arranged to live with old McClear (it is awfully kind of him to propose it) and learn the business whilst my own estate is being got ready. He will give me a room and my board, and during all the time that I can spare off my own land I am to help him and his son on their estate; this of course will teach me something about coffee planting.

"Blantyre is not half a bad place but it seems to me a good deal of hard drinking goes on there. Smedley, the Missionary doctor, says a white man ought not to touch alcohol in Africa except when it is given to him as a medicine. That is all very well but I can't see that a little lager beer does much harm, or a glass of good claret; and as the drinking water at Blantyre is not first rate and one can't always be swilling tea the entire teetotal plan does not suit me; at the same time I am willing to admit that a deal too much whisky is consumed here. Somehow or other most of the chaps who come out here to plant seem to get into the way of it. Perhaps I shall do the same. I must say on these very cold nights before one turns in, whilst you are sitting round the pleasant log fire a glass of hot whisky and water is very tempting and surely can't be harmful? The Doctor says it is, under all circumstances, and that all spirits have a most prejudicial effect on the liver in Central Africa.

* * * * * * * *

"Pazulu, *September* 10*th.*

"This is the name of old Major McClear's plantation. I believe it means 'up above.' It is on a hill-side looking down on the River Lunzu and the bush is being burnt in all directions. I am awfully fit and have been very busy clearing my land of bush. This is how I have had to set about it. I found that a man named Carter had just come down from the Atonga country on the west coast of Lake Nyasa with a huge gang of Atonga labourers. Some of the chaps do this every now and then when they have got time on their hands — go up the west coast of Nyasa (where they get very good sport) and come back with a gang of men for work. After supplying their own plantations they pass on the others to planters and traders who want men. All these men are registered at the Government office, either in the country they come from or at some place like Blantyre. You have to engage them before a Government official and everything is written down fair and square—the time you engage them for, the amount you are going to pay them, and so on. Each man gets a copy of the contract and you have to pay a shilling for the stamp on it, that is to say a shilling for each labourer. You may not engage them for more than a year even if you want to, and if they want to stay. Ordinarily one takes them for six months and you have to give a deposit or a bond to provide for the cost of their return passage money to their homes. If a man runs away before the time of his contract is completed without any breach of the agreement on your part he can be punished and you can proceed against him for damages up to a certain amount if he refuse to complete the term for which he is engaged; of course you have a further hold over them because you do not pay them the full sum for their services till their time is up. When you pay them off you have to do so before the Government officer who sees that what you give them is that which is owing to them.

"I have got a gang of fifty men and a 'capitao.' They are all Atonga—a cheery lot though rather unruly at times and ready to knock off work if you do not keep a sharp look out. The head man of any gang is called a 'capitao' which I believe is a Portuguese word—the same as 'captain.' My 'capitao' when he is at work wears precious little clothing, but on Sundays he puts on a long coat with brass buttons and a red fez which he has bought at a store or which was part of his last year's payment. His name is Moses. Of course he has got an Atonga name of his own but the missionaries in this country will give them all Biblical names (which I think is awfully bad taste, but the Atonga do not share my views and Mosesi, as he calls himself, admires his Bible name tremendously). I am to pay these men three shillings a month each and the 'capitao' five shillings. Besides this they get their food allowance or 'posho' as it is sometimes called. This I generally give to them in white calico (which costs me $2\frac{3}{4}d.$ a yard). I give my men four yards a week each with six yards for the 'capitao.' This with occasional extras brings up the cost of their food to $2d.$ a day with a little extra for the head man. Some of the other traders here only give out food allowance at the rate of three yards a week per man, but food has become very dear, relatively speaking, round Blantyre; and if our labourers do not receive sufficient food cloth or money in lieu thereof they are bound to steal from the native gardens and so get into trouble. I wonder some of the planters and traders here do not see that it is far and away the best policy to treat one's labourers generously in the way of food. There is nothing which will attach the negro more to your service than to give him plenty to eat. A man who feeds him well may beat him as much as he pleases in moderation and the man will still remain attached and return to the same plantation year after year; besides you can get a lot more work out of the men if they are well nourished, and really I assure you no one ever did such credit to good food as a negro whose eyes are bright whose skin is clear and whose temper is sunny, when he is well fed.

"Talking about beating; of course it goes on to some extent though it is illegal in the eyes of the Administration, but a certain amount of discipline must be kept up by the head man of a gang and trifling corrections are not noticed by the authorities provided the men make no complaint; but in old days, I am told, before there was any Government here the amount of flogging that went on was a great deal too bad, and some cases were downright savage. The instrument used is a 'chicote'[1]— a long, thin, rounded strip of hippopotamus hide about the thickness of a finger .... stiff but slightly pliant. If this is applied to the bare skin it almost invariably breaks it and causes bleeding. For my part I am jolly careful not to get into trouble, and when one of my chaps was caught stealing the other day I preferred to bring him up before the Police Court and have him punished there instead of taking the law into my own hands.

A "CAPITAO"

* * * * *

"The first part of the estate we began to clear was the possible site for a house. I chose this on a little knoll overlooking the Lunzu and about fifty feet above the bank of the river which is seventy yards distant. I flattened the top of the knoll and had to cut down one or two trees. After this I selected the site of my nurseries and resolved to thoroughly clear, in addition, about 100 acres for planting. The process of clearing is now going on briskly. I get up every morning at six and walk over from McClear's house to my own plantation and turn out my Atonga who are living in *misasa* (ramshackle shelters of sticks and thatch which they make to house themselves). Then the men turn out with cutlasses and axes and set to work cutting down the terribly rampant grass and herbage, and here and there a useless, shadeless tree or shrub. I am carefully leaving all the big trees for the shade they will give to the coffee; they will grow all the finer for the clearing of the growth around them.

"All the bush which is thus cut down will be left to lie in the sun and dry. Then the Atonga will pile it into heaps a few yards distant one from the other and set fire to it, and when it is burnt to ashes they will spread the ashes over the soil and dig it in. I am advised to get native women of the district to do this for me with native hoes. The women here work exceedingly hard—much better than the men—and ask less pay. A little while later on they will be beginning to prepare their own plantations before the big rains so it is as well to get them now if I can. For chance labour like this, for any term less than a month and within their own district I shan't have to register them."

[1] A Portuguese word.—H. H. J.

"Pazulu, *November 20th.*

"I have been much too busy to write any letters for the last two months—awfully busy but wonderfully well and not the least bit dull. When I had cleared my ground for the plantation I had it lined out in regular rows from six feet to seven feet apart, and at intervals of about six feet along these rows we dug pits 18 inches wide and 18 inches deep. The pits were left open for some six weeks "to weather," then we filled them up with soil, which was mixed with a manure made of cow-dung and wood ashes. After each pit had been filled up we stuck into the middle of it a bamboo stick (bamboos grow in abundance along the stream bank and on the hill-sides and are very useful) to mark the place where the coffee plant was to be put it. I made arrangements with a neighbouring planter to buy sufficient coffee seedlings of a year's growth to plant up the 50 acres I have cleared. Every day we expect the rainy season to begin now—in fact to-day the 20th November is the date on which the big rains ordinarily begin near Blantyre (we had occasional showers in July and August and one or two in September, but no rain at all in October, only a lot of thunder and lightning and an occasional dry tornado). As soon as the rains have really broken I shall put the coffee plants in these pits. I am told that whilst the coffee grows the weeds grow even quicker, and that the hardest time I shall have with my own men will be during December, January and February, keeping the weeds down. If we are not incessantly at work hoeing in between the coffee plants they will be smothered by the growth of weeds.

"It is so very good of old McClear to put me up in his house that I have been doing my best to help him in between working on my own plantation. He gathered his first coffee crop this year, and is very pleased at the result. The berries were picked off the trees (which are three years old) at the end of June and the beginning of July, and all this was over before I arrived on the scene; but I saw the berries when they were being pulped by machinery. By this process the sweet fleshy covering of the berries is taken off and the bean is disclosed encased in its parchment skin. You know of course that this splits into two seeds when you take off the dry skin and it is merely these seeds which you see when the coffee reaches you at home. I shall not get a pulper till I have owned my plantation for about four years, as it is hardly worth while for a poor man to have a maiden crop off a small plantation pulped by machinery.

"After the beans are pulped they are passed into a brick vat where they are left to ferment for between 24 and 36 hours. Then they are removed to a second vat and thoroughly washed in water. Then they are taken out and dried on mats. After this they are further dried in a drying house and constantly turned over to prevent anything like mould. All through the end of September and the beginning of October we were busy packing the coffee in stout canvas bags, weighing about 56 lbs. each. Each bag was numbered and marked with McClear's initials by stencil plates, and handed over to one of the transport companies here to be shipped direct to London, *via* Chinde. It will of course be carried partly on men's heads and partly in waggons down to Katunga, and then they will send it down river to Chinde. It is to be hoped they will be careful not to put the bags into a leaky boat or steamer, because if they are wetted the coffee will be quite spoiled. The cost of sending this coffee from Blantyre to London is about £8 a ton.

* * * * * * * *

"Blantyre, *January 1st.*

"In spite of the rainy season which is well on us, we have spent a very jolly Christmas at Blantyre. Most of the planters from Cholo and the other districts round Blantyre have congregated here for Christmas week. We had a little mild horse-racing and a shooting competition. Like most of the other Europeans here I belong to the Shire Highlands Shooting Club, but I did not score over well on this occasion, because I was a bit off colour, having had another little touch of fever—caused by the beginning of the rainy season I expect. We had a smoking concert in the Court House which was lent to us for the occasion, and the missionaries got up a big bazaar in aid of their school-house, and afterwards a lot of us were entertained at the Manse by the senior missionary where we heard some really good music. You have no idea what a pretty place the Manse is. It is rather a rambling house with a low thatched roof, but all the rooms open on to the verandahs with glass doors and plenty of windows so that they are very light inside though shielded from the sun.

* * * * * * * *

"There is a fairly good club here with lots of newspapers. I belong to the club and get a bedroom there whenever I come into Blantyre. I cannot say I think much of the hotels. Perhaps when more Europeans come to the country it will be worth while building a good place to receive them where a check will be set on the unlimited consumption of whisky, which at present tends to a good deal of noise and brawling of a not very creditable kind. Whisky is the curse of this country as far as Europeans are concerned, and is the cause of more than half the sickness.

"One of the chief drawbacks to this place, after all, is the lack of news. Blantyre is a hot-bed of gossip and rumours simply because it has no daily newspaper. There are no Reuter's telegrams to read at the club every day because we are not in direct telegraph communication with the outer world. The mails arrive with much uncertainty; this is partly owing to the irregular way in which the ocean-going steamers call at Chinde. There are supposed to be two mails from Europe landed at Chinde in the month, but sometimes they both come together and then there is a month's interval before another mail arrives; or when the mail is landed at Chinde there may be no steamer ready to start up-river with it. Again, in the dry season the steamers may stick on a sandbank before they reach Chiromo, and then the mails have to be sent overland to Blantyre, but the mail-carriers may have to ford flooded rivers, or they may be scared by a lion, so the time they take varies from two and a half to five days. Usually our letters and papers from England are six to seven weeks old when they reach us and I suppose my letters take the same time to reach you. Yet it is wonderful how much up to date people are here in information. It is astonishing what a lot everybody reads, and what heaps of newspapers and magazines are taken in. The Administration has started a lending library with a very decent collection of books, and although this is supposed to be primarily for Administration officials outsiders may by permission be allowed to join. We have a Planters' Association and Chamber of Commerce.

* * * * * * * *

"The best fun I think is shooting. Game near Blantyre is getting scarce though there are heaps of lions and leopards, but it is so difficult to see them in the long grass and thick bush. What I enjoy, however, is going from a Saturday to Monday towards a mountain called Chiradzulu, and along the river Namasi. We always give our labourers on the plantations a Saturday half-holiday, and I can generally trust the capitaos to see that the men do a fair amount of work in the Saturday morning, so that I can sometimes get away on the Friday night with a companion or two. We take tent, beds, folding chairs and table, a few pots and pans and a basket of provisions. One of the chaps who generally comes with me brings his cook with him, a native boy trained at the Mission and not half a bad cook either. We usually ride out on our ponies as far as the Administration station on the Namasi river, as there is a good road there. Here we leave the nags under shelter and then strike off into the bush. Of course the rains are now on us and this sort of thing is not so pleasant in wet weather, but it was very jolly at the end of the dry season when the dense grass and bush were burnt, after the bush fires, and one could get about easily and see the game. We generally chose a place by the banks of a stream with plenty of shade, for our camp. The next day we would walk something like twenty miles in the course of our shooting, and although our luck varied we seldom failed to get two or three buck at least. As to the guinea fowl, they were there in swarms! It was awfully jolly sitting smoking round a huge camp fire, so perfectly safe and yet in such a wild country with lions roaring at intervals not far away, and the queer sounds of owls and tiger-cats and chirping insects coming from the thick bush. Our boys used to build rough shelters of branches to sleep in and try to keep up fires through the night, more to scare away wild beasts than for any other reason. Recently these little jaunts have been more charming on account of the gorgeousness of the wild flowers, for this is the spring of the year. I am a bit of a botanist, you know, but even if I was not I could not help admiring the gorgeous masses of colour which the different flowers produce among the young green grass, on the bushes, and on the big trees."

IN CAMP—AFTER A DAY'S SHOOTING

"PAZULU, *February* 14*th*.

"We have had an anxious time here with young McClear. He went down the Upper Shire to look at some land that his father is thinking of investing in for growing sugar (as the sugar cane grows there in tremendous luxuriance and there is a great local demand for sugar), but he is a very careless chap, you know, and what with getting wet through with rain and exposing himself too much to the sun and drinking whatever water he comes across, he has fallen ill with black-water fever since he came back to Blantyre. Nobody can quite account for this peculiar disease. Some people say it comes from turning up the new soil of a very rank kind; others—and they are generally doctors—assert that the germ is quite different from that in malarial fever, and enters the system from water, either through the pores of the skin in bathing or through the stomach, if the infected water is drunk. Therefore there should be one very simple preventative by having all one's washing and drinking water boiled. However it may be, young McClear went down with it very suddenly only two days after he got back. He seemed quite well in the morning, ate his breakfast as usual, and went out to the plantation, but at eleven o'clock I met him coming back to breakfast (we have an early breakfast at six and a big breakfast at eleven—no luncheon) an hour before the usual time. I thought he looked awfully queer. There was a grey look about his face and he was very dark about the eyes. He told me he felt a frightful pain in his back and was very cold. Instead of coming to breakfast he went to bed. Presently his boy came down to tell us that 'Master was very bad.' Old McClear went up and found that his son had got the 'black-water' fever. He vomited steadily all that day, and at night-fall was as yellow as a guinea, besides being dreadfully weak. Of course we had the doctor over as soon as possible, but in this disease doctors at present can do very little. Quinine is of no avail and all that you can aim at is keeping up the patient's strength. Young McClear was smartly purged and then given champagne and water to drink, and he went on vomiting all night and the greater part of next day. The doctor then injected morphia into his arm and this stopped the vomiting and gave him a little sleep. After that he managed to keep down some chicken broth, and the third and fourth days he mended. In six days he was seemingly all right, though a little weak, and on the seventh day he was actually up and about, and his skin had almost regained its normal colour.

"After a go of black-water fever it is always better to leave the country for a change if you can, but you ought not to hurry away too soon lest the fatigues of the journey should bring on a relapse, and therefore McClear will wait till April and then run down to Natal and back for a trip. Many men who come to this country never get black-water fever, either because they take great care of themselves or because the germs which cause the disease by attacking the red-blood corpuscles cannot get the mastery over their systems, but where a man finds himself to be subject to attacks of this disease I should advise him to quit: Central Africa is not for him."

"Pazulu, *May 2nd.*

"Our rainy season came to an end a couple of weeks ago and I want to lose no time about building my house as a large quantity of bricks will have to be made during this dry season. I have hired some native brickmakers from Blantyre. They will be able to make about 1,000 bricks a day. I shall need about 45,000 bricks for my house. I have been cutting timber on McClear's land by arrangement, for joists and beams. The doors, match-board skirting, &c., I shall buy at one of the stores in Blantyre, where I shall also get corrugated iron for the roof and the timber for the inner ceiling, without which the bare iron would be a great deal too hot in the summer and too cold in the winter. I shall take care that all the rooms have fire-places. I cannot tell you how necessary fires are here for health and comfort. Fortunately we have any quantity of fire-wood. As I am trying hard to keep within my thousand pounds I shall not build a house of more than three rooms with a nice large verandah, and a portion of the verandah will be cut off as a bath-room and communicate with the bed-room by a door.

"The other two rooms will be respectively dining-room and office in one, and private sitting-room. I shall also run up a small brick store with a strong roof and a strong door (to prevent thieving). My kitchen will be wattle and daub with a thatched roof and a brick chimney and will stand at a little distance from the house connected with it by a covered way. Another corner of the verandah beside the bath-room will be enclosed as a pantry and private store-room for provisions. In building my house I am strongly cautioned to avoid "a through draught." The principle on which the oldest planters' houses were built was a very unhealthy one. The front door opened into a kind of hall which was used as a dining-room, and immediately opposite the front door was a back door by which the food was brought in to the table. The result was that persons sitting at the table sat in a draught, and to sit in a draught in this country or to get a chill in any way is the surest cause of fever.

"My verandah will be paved with tiles which I can obtain in Blantyre from the men who make them. The foundations of the house will be brick, over which I shall put a good layer of cement to stop any nonsense on the part of white ants, though on my estate we are not troubled with these pests so far as I know, but Thomas, of Blantyre, who lives near here, after building a very nice house has been awfully troubled with the white ants, who in a few nights would build up a huge ant-hill in the middle of the drawing-room, if he was away and the house shut up. They also came up under his bed and broke out all through the walls. The result was he had to take up his carefully laid floors, and dig and dig and dig, until he rooted out at least three separate nests. In one case he was obliged to tunnel down something like ten feet before he found the queen; and until you have found and extirpated the queens your work has been for nothing, for if you fill up the hole the white ant community soon gets to rights again and recommences operations. The worst of it is, you never know whether there may not be more than one queen in the nest and whether you have destroyed them all!

NATIVES MAKING BRICKS

"In front of my house I intend to have a small terrace, which I shall plant in an orderly way with flower beds. Last month I ran over to Zomba for a visit and stayed with one of the officials of the Administration, and there I saw old W—— who is in charge of the Botanical Gardens, who has given me lots of flower seeds, and promised me any amount of plants and strawberries, as soon as my garden is ready to receive them. W—— is giving away strawberry plants to everyone and I wonder that they are not more run after as those planted at Zomba produce excellent crops year after year, the fruit season lasting about five months. They are not large strawberries like those at home, but a small Alpine kind. Yet they are very fragrant and very sweet.

"Down in the lower country near Lake Chilwa, you see a most extraordinary Euphorbia growing, which I am afraid most of the planters call "cactuses."[1] These are both quaint and ornamental, and I am going to plant some of them along the bottom of my garden. In the centre of my flower beds I shall put wild date palms, which grow in the stream-valleys, and at each corner of the terrace there shall be a raphia palm.

[1] There are no cacti in Africa, except the *Opuntia* (prickly pear) introduced from America into North and South Africa.—H. H. J.

THE EUROPEAN SETTLERS

There is one attraction in this country for people who like flowers and palms on the table and about the house. Here they cost absolutely nothing. You have only to send a boy into the bush and he will come back with a young palm which would cost at least a guinea at home, or with a handful of flowers such as you might see in a horticultural show.

"My coffee presents a most thriving appearance. I keep it studiously free from weeds. Next October I shall be ready to plant up another fifty acres.

"You asked me to give you some idea of Blantyre. It seems hardly correct to speak of it as a town as the houses are still very scattered, yet it is now constituted as a township, and rather well laid out with roads. When all the blanks between the present dwellings are filled up, it will be a very large and important city. At present its future greatness is, as the French would say, only *ébauché*. The most striking feature is the church, which is a very handsome red brick building, apparently a mixture of Norman and Byzantine styles with white domes. It is really an extraordinarily fine church for the centre of Africa, and is appropriately placed in the middle of a large open space or square, without any other buildings near at hand to dwarf its proportions. When we had the Kawinga scare two or three months ago (I forgot to tell you that Kawinga the old slave-raiding chief to the north of Zomba attempted to try conclusions with the British two months ago), it was reported by the natives that Kawinga's object in invading Blantyre would be to secure the church to himself as a residence! It is at present the mean by which all natives measure their ideas of a really fine building. On one side of the square there are gardens belonging to the mission; on the other side a very handsome school designed somewhat in the Moorish style of architecture. Along the Zomba road to the north of the church are the residences of the European missionaries. This church square is connected with the rest of Blantyre by a handsome avenue of cypresses and eucalyptus. The growth of the cypresses is astonishing, as well as their lateral bulk, and the road is completely shaded and delightful for a stroll, because of a strong wholesome perfume from these conifers. The soil about here is very red, and the neatly-made roads branching off in all directions passing through very green vegetation give a pretty effect to the eye.

CYPRESS AVENUE, BLANTYRE

There are no buildings along this road until you reach the vicinity of the Administration headquarters which are locally known as the 'Boma.'¹ Here we come to a good many buildings, and all of them red brick with corrugated iron roofs and of one storey. The corrugated iron is not as ugly as you might think as it is mostly painted red, which gives it more the appearance of tiles.

¹ "Boma" is a Swahili word for "stockade." The first settlement of the Government here was on a piece of property belonging to a native which had a stockade of thorn around it. Soon after this was purchased, however, the thorn hedge was done away with.—H. H. J.

"Continuing along the straight road, and leaving the Government buildings to the right, you cross the Mudi stream by a fine bridge,[1] built by the African Lakes Company. On the other side of the Mudi one is on the property of the African Lakes Company which is a large suburb, called Mandala, on rising ground, from which a fine view can be obtained of the Mission settlement. At Mandala there are many houses and stores and workshops and stables — all very neatly made of brick, with iron roofs. There are handsome roads and gardens and a perfect forest of eucalyptus. The company has extensive nurseries there which extend down to the banks of the Mudi, and has had the good taste to preserve a bit of the old forest which covered the site of Blantyre when the missionaries first arrived. This forest chiefly consisted of a species of acacia tree which has dense dark green foliage in flat layers giving to it at a distance almost the appearance of a cedar. Beyond Mandala one joins the main road to Katunga, and the scenery becomes absolutely beautiful as you mount up towards the shoulder of Soche mountain. Here in all directions there is a beautiful forest, and the views in the direction of the Shire river might vie with the average pretty scenery of any country. There are still numbers of coffee plantations on the outskirts of Blantyre, though the tendency of the planters would naturally be to keep their future plantations farther away from the vicinity of the town. The natives of Blantyre are a rather heterogeneous lot. The foundation of the stock is of Mang'anja race, crossed with Yao, who invaded the country some years ago; but for many years refugees from other parts of the Protectorate have been gathering round the Mission station, the Lakes Company, Sharrer's Traffic Company, and other large employers of labour, all of whom have brought men down from the lakes and up from the Zambezi, who have gradually made their permanent homes at Blantyre. Morality is very low, and although they are not strikingly dishonest still they are not above petty pilfering, and the coffee plantations which are too near the town are apt to have their berries picked by the black Blantyre citizens at night, and the coffee thus acquired is sent out and sold to native planters— for some of the educated natives and small chiefs have started coffee plantations.

EUCALYPTUS AVENUE, ZOMBA

"Unfortunately, the water supply here is very bad, though a little energy would set it all right. There is the Mudi stream, for instance, which flows perennially without much diminution, even in the dry season; but the upper waters of the Mudi flow through native villages and the settlements of the missionary scholars, and all these people wash their clothes and persons in the river, besides emptying into it all kinds of filth. The

---

[1] The Mudi is crossed higher up by another bridge which the Administration has just made.—H. H. J.

result is that its waters are quite unfit for drinking purposes. A few of the settlers have wells, but all of these except two seem to produce slightly brackish unwholesome water. Away to the north of Blantyre arises another very fine stream, the Likubula. This is rather too much below the level of Blantyre to make it easy to convey the water to the township. The simplest expedient would seem to be the purification of the Mudi.

"But if the Mudi be at present unwholesome its banks are charming for the foliage of the trees and the loveliness of the wild flowers. I would notice specially one crimson lily which gives a succession of flowers for many months of the year.

"And yet how extraordinary people are in regard to wild flowers! I remember when I had just been admiring these red lilies on the Mudi's banks I went to dinner with one of the married couples in Blantyre, and the lady of the house apologised to me for the bareness of the table, complaining that her garden as yet produced no flowers. Yet she had only got to send one of the servants out to the banks of the stream and to the adjoining fields and she could have decked her table with red lilies, mauve, orange, and white ground-orchids, and blue bean flowers in a way which would excite anyone's envy at home.

"My reference to 'married couples' reminds me to tell you that a good many of the men settled here are married and their wives seem to stand the climate as well as if not even better than their husbands, because, I imagine, they are exposed less to the sun and do not have so much outdoor work. Although it is not consistent with the duties of the planter still it is borne in on my mind that the healthiest life in Central Africa is an indoor life. People who keep very much to the house and do not go out or go far afield between 9 a.m. and 4 p.m. never seem to get fever. At the same time you should not remain out after sunset as you are apt to get a chill.

* * * * * * * *

I do not know whether in the foregoing extracts from supposititious letters I have succeeded in giving a fairly correct idea of the life that Europeans lead under present conditions in British Central Africa. More will be said on this subject in dealing with the Missionaries.

For the trader and the planter I think it may be said that the country offers sufficiently sure and rapid profits for their enterprise to compensate the risk run in the matter of health. The various trading companies in the country appear to be doing well with an ever-extending business and to be constantly increasing the number of their establishments. Even traders in a small way, if they have energy and astuteness, may reap considerable earnings with relatively small outlay. One man, for instance, went up to Kotakota on Lake Nyasa with a few hundreds of pounds at his disposal, bought a large number of cattle at a very low price in the Marimba district and purchased all the ivory the Arabs at Kotakota had to dispose of, and on his total transaction made a clear profit of £2000 by selling the cattle and ivory at Blantyre; but it appears to me that as time goes on the European trading community will be limited to the employés of two or three

A PLANTER

great trading companies commanding considerable capital, and to a number of British Indians who will not in any way conflict with the commerce of the Europeans because they will often act as the middlemen buying up small quantities of produce here and there from the natives which they will re-sell in large amounts to the European firms and agencies.

The remainder of the European settlers will be rather planters than traders, disposing likewise of their produce to the commercial companies in British Central Africa. Originally when there was very little or no cash in the country every planter had likewise to be a trader on a small scale as all labourers were paid in trade goods, and all the food that he bought from the natives was purchased in the same manner. Now the country is full of cash, and in many districts the natives refuse to accept any payment except in money, preferring to go to the principal stores and make their purchases there. To a certain extent, moreover, money payments are now compulsory between European employers and their native employés; moreover a planter often objects to taking out a trading licence and prefers instead to relinquish his small commerce in this respect.

Briefly stated, the only serious drawback to British Central Africa as a field of enterprise for trader or planter is malarial fever, either in its ordinary form, or in its severest type which is commonly known as black-water fever. I shall have a few words to say about this malady further on.

AN IVORY CARAVAN ARRIVING AT KOTAKOTA

The advantages are, at the present time, that land is cheap; the country is almost everywhere well watered by perennial streams, and by a reasonable rainfall; the scenery is beautiful in many of the upland districts; the climate is delicious—seldom too hot and often cold and pleasant; there is an abundance of cheap native labour; transport, though offering certain difficulties inherent in all undeveloped parts of Africa, is growing far easier and cheaper than in Central South Africa, as the Shire river is navigable at all times of the year, except for about 80 miles of its course, and Lake Nyasa is an inland sea with a shore line of something like 800 miles. Moreover, the cost of simple articles of food such as oxen, goats or sheep, or of antelopes and other big game, poultry, eggs, and milk is cheap, together with the prices of a few vegetables like potatoes or grain like Indian corn; and all the European goods are not so expensive as they would be in the interior of Australia, in Central South Africa, or in the interior of South America because of the relative cheapness of transport from the coast and of the very low Customs duties.

To sum up the question, I might state with truth that *but* for malarial fever this country would be an earthly paradise; the "but" however is a very big one. Whether the development of medical science will enable us to find the same antidote to malarial fever as we have found for small-pox in vaccination, or whether drugs will be discovered which will make the treatment of the disease and recovery therefrom almost certain, remains to be seen. If however here, as in other parts of tropical Africa, this demon could be conjured, beyond all question the prosperity of Western Africa, of the Congo Basin and of British Central Africa would be almost unbounded.

Ordinary malarial fever is serious but not so dangerous as that special form of it which is styled "black-water" or hæmaturic. The difference between the effects of the two diseases is this. Ordinary malarial fever is seldom immediately fatal but after continued attacks the patient is often left with some permanent weakness. Black-water fever is either fatal in a very few days or has such a weakening effect on the heart that the patient dies during convalescence from sudden syncope; but where black-water fever does not kill it never leaves (as far as I am aware) permanent effects on the system of the sufferer. One attack, however, predisposes to another and as a rule each succeeding attack is more severe than its predecessor. Consequently a man who has had, say, two attacks of black-water fever should not return to any part of Africa where that disease is endemic.[1]

The origin and history of bilious hæmoglobinuric or "black-water" fever are still obscure. No mention of this disease would appear to have been made until the middle of this century when it was described by the French naval surgeons at Nossibé in Madagascar. According to Dr. Wordsworth Poole, the principal medical officer of the British Central Africa Protectorate, true black-water fever has occurred in parts of America and in the West Indies besides those portions of Africa and Madagascar to which I have made allusion in the footnote. Dr. Poole states that he has seen a case of it in Rome and that it is said to occur in Greece. The cases occurring in tropical America which Dr. Poole cites I should be inclined to ascribe to a variation of the ordinary type of yellow fever. Now yellow fever, in my opinion, is a very near connection of black-water fever, and some writers on Africa have stated that yellow fever was actually engendered on the slave ships which proceeded from West Africa to South America, and have suggested it was simply an acute development of the ordinary African hæmoglobinuric fever.

One remarkable feature in this disease appears to be that assuming it is only endemic in certain parts of Africa, its germs would seem to be capable of lying dormant for some time in the human system and then to suddenly multiply into prodigious activity and produce an attack of black-water fever some time after the individual has left the infected district. For instance, in 1893 after having been absent nearly two months from British Central Africa in Cape Colony and in Natal, I had a most severe attack of black-water fever, which commenced at Durban on board a gunboat and finished at Delagoa Bay. Again, when travelling through the Tyrol in the autumn of 1894, I was suddenly seized with a slight but obvious attack of this fever after returning from a mountain ascent. Although only ill for about twenty-four

[1] At the present time black-water fever is endemic on the West Coast of Africa from the Gambia on the north to Benguela on the south, and inland as far as the limits of the forest country of West Africa. It extends over the whole of the Congo basin. I believe a few cases were noted on the White Nile and the western tributaries of the Nile before the Mahdi's revolt expelled the Europeans from these parts. It is endemic in the regions round the Victoria Nyanza and Tanganyika; in the eastern half of British Central Africa; along the whole course of the Zambezi between Zumbo and its mouth; in the Portuguese province of Moçambique; in German East Africa; and in British East Africa. It is said not to be endemic in the islands of Zanzibar and Pemba and that those persons who have suffered from it there brought the germs of it from some other part of Africa. I have not heard that it exists at Beira or south of the Zambezi, but should not be surprised to learn that cases of it occasionally occur there. Roughly speaking, it may be said that as far as we know the Upper Niger regions, the North Central and Eastern Sudan, Abyssinia, Somaliland, Galaland, Egypt, Northern Africa and Africa South of the Zambezi are free from it. It is said to occur in Madagascar.

hours I had every symptom of black-water fever in a marked form. A case occurred with one of the ladies of the Universities Mission at Zanzibar who had an attack of black-water fever which came on after her return to England.

The mortality in black-water fever is about 40 per cent. among those who have the disease for the first time; 50 per cent. among those who have it for the second time; 75 per cent. among those who have it for the third time; and it is very rare that anyone survives more than three attacks. Not counting the trifling little touch in the Tyrol, I have had four attacks of this disease at different periods from 1886 to 1896. I know one of the German officials in East Africa who has survived five attacks and is apparently in robust health, and Dr. Kerr Cross mentions an European in North Nyasa (in good health at the present time) who has had this fever ten times!

On the last occasion when I had black-water fever I derived very great benefit from a single injection of morphia, which checked the vomiting and gave the body time for repose and recuperation. Otherwise I know of absolutely no drug which has been proved really efficacious in treating this dangerous disease. All we can say at the present time is that good nursing and a good constitution will generally pull patients through an attack. Quinine appears to be of little use, unless during convalescence.

The symptoms of the disease are the following:—

The patient ordinarily complains of a severe pain in his back and a general sense of *malaise*. This is often succeeded by a violent shivering fit. Upon passing urine the latter is found to be a dark sepia colour, and subsequently becomes a deep black with reddish reflexions, which accounts for the popular name given to the fever. Sometimes the colour is almost the tint of burgundy or claret. Not many hours after the attack has begun the colour of the patient's skin becomes increasingly yellow. The temperature may sometimes be as high as 105 degrees following on the shivering fit, but high temperatures are not necessarily a very marked or serious symptom in black-water fever. A most distressing vomiting is perhaps the most customary symptom next to the black water.

The best way to treat this fever is to put the patient immediately to bed, placing hot-water bottles at his feet, and to give him a strong purge. At first the vomiting should not be checked, but as soon as it tends to weaken the patient it ought to be stopped, if not by some opiate drug administered through the stomach, then by an injection of morphia. When it is deemed that the patient has vomited sufficiently to get rid of the poison in the system, and the further vomiting has been to some extent checked, nourishment should then be administered at frequent intervals—strong beef-tea, milk and brandy, eggs beaten up with port wine, &c. Champagne and water, especially if this drink can be iced and made into a champagne-cup, is excellent. Champagne is often of great use in this disease in restoring the patient's strength. Once the dangerous crisis of the disease is passed and any relapse is guarded against by the most careful nursing, the patient is pretty sure to recover, unless he has naturally a very weak heart. The recovery is often pleasantly quick. In all my attacks of black-water fever there has rarely elapsed more than a week between the commencement of the disease and the power to get up and walk about, and convalescence in other ways has come rapidly.

Undoubtedly much ill-health might be avoided in tropical Africa by the adoption of very temperate habits. I have written strongly on the drink question in such Reports to the Government as have been published; I do not therefore propose to repeat my diatribes in this book. But it should be added that what I object to is not the drinking of good wine or beer, but the consumption of spirits. Whisky is the bane of Central Africa as it is of West Africa, South Africa and Australia. I dare say brandy is as bad as whisky but it has passed out of fashion as a drink, and therefore it has not incurred my animosity to the same extent as the national product of Scotland and Ireland.[1] Moreover, brandy is invaluable in sickness. If any spirits are drunk it seems to me that gin is the least harmful, as it has a good effect on the kidneys. In hot climates like that of Central Africa whisky seems to have a bad effect on the liver and on the kidneys.

I do not suppose these words will have much effect on my readers.

IVORY AT MANDALA STORE (AFRICAN LAKES COMPANY)

Alcoholic excess is our national vice, and while we are ready enough to deplore the opium-eating-or-smoking on the part of the Indians or Chinese, —a vice which is not comparable in its ill effects to the awful abuse of alcohol which is so characteristic of the northern peoples of Europe,—we still remain indifferent to the effects of spirit-drinking which has been the principal vice of the nineteenth century. The abuse of wine or beer, though bad like all abuses, is a relatively wholesome excess compared to even a moderate consumption of spirits. Though I think of the two extremes total abstinence is the better course to follow in Central Africa, I do *not* recommend total abstinence from all forms of alcohol. I think, on the contrary, the moderate use of wine is distinctly beneficial, especially for anæmic people.

Trading with the natives on a large scale is, as I have said, chiefly confined to two or three large companies—the African Lakes, Sharrer's, the Oceana Company and Kahn & Co. But a small amount of barter chiefly for provisions

[1] Which alone, I believe, among strong waters develops the poisonous Fusel Oil.

is still carried on by all Europeans residing in the less settled parts of British Central Africa. The imported trade goods consisted chiefly of cotton stuffs from Manchester and Bombay, beads from Birmingham and Venice, blankets from England, India and Austria, fezzes from Algeria and from Newcastle-under-Lyne, boots from Northampton, felt hats from various parts of England, hardware and brass wire and hoes from Birmingham, cutlery from Sheffield, and various fancy goods from India.

The trade products which British Central Africa gives us in exchange for these goods and for much English money in addition are: Ivory, coffee, hippo. teeth, rhinoceros horns, cattle, hides, wax, rubber, oil seeds, sanseviera fibre, tobacco, sugar (locally consumed), wheat (ditto), maize (ditto), sheep, goats and poultry (ditto), timber (ditto), and the *Strophanthus* drug.

KAHN AND CO'S TRADING STORE AT KOTAKOTA

It only remains to say a few words about the relations between the Europeans and the natives. I am convinced that this eastern portion of British Central Africa will never be a white man's country in the sense that all Africa south of the Zambezi, and all Africa north of the Sahara will eventually become—countries where the white race is dominant and native to the soil. Between the latitudes of the Zambezi and the Blue Nile, Africa must in the first instance be governed in the interests of the black man, and the black man will there be the race predominant in numbers, if not in influence. The future of Tropical Africa is to be another India; not another Australia. The white man cannot permanently colonise Central Africa; he can only settle on a few favoured tracts, as he would do in the North of India. Yet Central Africa possesses boundless resources in the way of commerce, as it is extremely rich in natural products,—animal, vegetable and mineral. These it will pay the European to develop and should equally profit the black man to produce. Untaught by the European he was living like an animal, miserably poor in the midst of boundless wealth. Taught by the European he will be able to develop this wealth and bring it to the market, and the European on the other hand will be enriched by this enterprise. But Central Africa is probably as remote from self government or representative institutions as is the case with India. It can only be administered under the benevolent despotism of the Imperial Government, though in the future and developed administration there is no reason to suppose that black men may not serve as officials in common with white men and with yellow men, just as there are Negro officials in the administration of the West African colonies, and Malay officials in the Government of the Straits Settlements.

It must not be supposed that the Administration of British Central Africa has always had, or will always command the unhesitating support of the white settlers now in the country. It sometimes seems to me that the bulk of these sturdy pioneers (excellent though the results of their work have been in developing the resources of the country) would, if allowed to govern this land in their own way, use their power too selfishly in the interests of the white man. This I find to be the tendency everywhere where the governing white men are not wholly disinterested, are not, that is to say, paid to see fair play. From time to time a planter rises up to object to the natives being allowed to plant coffee, in case they should come into competition with him, or urges the Administration to use its power despotically to compel a black man to work for wages whether he will or not.

The ideal of the average European trader and planter in Tropical Africa would be a country where the black millions toil unremittingly for the benefit of the white man. They would see that the negroes were well fed and not treated with harshness, but anything like free will as to whether they went to work or not, or any attempt at competing with the white man as regards education or skilled labour would not be tolerated.

As a set off against this extreme is the almost equally unreasonable opinion entertained by the missionaries of a now fast-disappearing type, that Tropical Africa was to be developed with English money and at the cost of English lives, solely and only for the benefit of the black man, who, as in many mission stations, was to lead an agreeably idle life, receiving food and clothes gratis, and not being required to do much in exchange but make a more or less hypocritical profession of Christianity. This mawkish sentiment, however, no longer holds the field, and there is scarcely a mission in Nyasaland which does not inculcate among its pupils the stern necessity of work in all sections of humanity. The great service that Christian missions have rendered to Africa has been to act as the counterpoise to the possibly selfish policy of the irresponsible white pioneer, in whose eyes the native was merely a chattel, a more or less useful animal, but with no rights and very little feeling.

It is the mission of an impartial administration to adopt a mean course between the extreme of sentiment and the extreme of selfishness. It must realise that but for the enterprise and capital of these much-criticised, rough and ready pioneers Central Africa would be of no value and the natives would receive no payment for the products of their land, would, in fact, relapse into their almost ape-like existence of fighting, feeding and breeding. Therefore due encouragement must be shown to European planters, traders and miners, whose presence in the country is the figure before the ciphers. Yet, it must be borne in mind that the negro is a man, with a man's rights; above all, that he was the owner of the country before we came, and deserves, nay, is entitled to, a share in the land, commensurate with his needs and numbers; that in numbers he will always exceed the white man, while he may some day come to rival him in intelligence; and that finally if we do not use our power to govern him with absolute justice the time will come sooner or later when he will rise against us and expel us as the Egyptian officials were expelled from the Sudan.

APPENDIX I.

BILIOUS HÆMOGLOBINURIC: OR, BLACK-WATER FEVER

BY DR. D. KERR CROSS, M.B.

THIS form of fever has been met with in the Mauritius, Senegal, Madagascar, the Gold Coast, French Guiana, Venezuela, in some parts of Central America, and the West India Islands. It is even said to have been seen in some parts of Italy and Spain. It has been carefully studied in Nosi-bé, on the north-west of Madagascar, where it is estimated that one in fourteen of the Malarial Fevers treated there were Hæmoglobinuric. Some cases observed in Rome have been carefully studied, with the result that some are associated with the *Plasmodium Malariæ*—the Bacterium in Malarial Fever—while others are not. The same has been the case on the Gold Coast. The generally accepted opinion is that Hæmoglobinuric fever may arise apart from any malarial affection. Any bacterium which destroys the Red Blood Corpuscles and sets free the red colouring matter—Hæmoglobin—will bring about this form of fever. Hæmoglobin is an irritant to the kidneys, and brings on a congested state of that organ. In this form of fever we always find the kidneys abnormal both in size and in weight, while there is a bleeding into the tissue under the capsule and in the interstitial cortical substance, or with the discoloration which we know to result from these conditions. The Epithelia lining the convoluted tubes of the kidney are larger than normal and are cloudy, while the tubes themselves contain casts that are stained yellow; this yellow staining being in a very fine state of division or, in some cases, in large granules. There is a marked obstruction of the tubules of the kidney, both in the cortical and pyramidal portion. The blood vessels and capillaries are often found to contain corpuscles that are deeply stained. This is also the case with the glomeruli of the organ. The serum of the blood contains great quantities of free hæmoglobin which gives it a yellow colour. This yellow colour is seen in the serum obtained from the application of a blister to the surface and in blood drawn for microscopic purposes.

This form of fever begins as a regular remittent. There is usually severe vomiting of bilious matter—indeed, my experience is that in a severe case there is vomiting every half-hour night and day. There are bilious stools of a frothy yellow substance. There is very marked jaundice over the whole body. There is delirium of a violent form. Sometimes there is a free discharge of black urine or, it may be, of actual blood. Towards the close of a fatal case there is suppression of the urine resulting in coma and convulsions. Everything in this affection points to the wholesale destruction of the Red Blood Corpuscles, and to a desperate effort on the part of the system to throw something off. From the suddenness with which the tissues of the whole body become yellow, we might say that every tissue takes on itself the power of secreting bile. Bile is eliminated by the bowels, by the skin, by the kidneys, and by the liver. The patient vomits, purges, sweats, and in some cases bleeds. The gums, it may be, become spongy and sore, and may even shed blood. There may be bleeding from the mouth and nose and over purple spots on the skin. As in the case of yellow fever, there may be a bleeding from the mucous membrane of the stomach and bowels, which, acted on by the digestive fluids, may lead to a Black Vomit. A marked feature, too, in some cases is that the attacks are paroxysmal. They come on with a shivering fit, with pains in the back, retention of the testes, vomiting, and lowered temperature. Two hours afterwards, when the urine is passed, it is bloody, contains albumin, and deposits a thick sediment. The dark urine may continue to be passed for three or four days, but in other cases after a few hours there is a return to the normal state. I have known of seizures to come on every morning about eight o'clock for ten or twelve days in succession. Gradually, however, they seemed to diminish in severity, and then to pass off. Between the attacks the urine seemed perfectly normal.

There is another form where we get actual blood in the urine. The blood is intimately mixed with the urine, and is like "porter."

Then we may get actual suppression of urine. The malarial poison acts on the kidneys like a poison. The result of this suppression is uræmic poisoning.

It seems to be the case that certain constitutions have a predisposition to this form of fever. There are many who have resided in British Central Africa for ten or more years who have not once suffered from its effects, while others have not been resident as many months, and have suffered from several attacks. It is not the case that quinine taken in prophylactic doses every day arms the constitution against it. For myself personally I take this drug only when I think I need it, and not as a preventative medicine; and while I have suffered from ordinary fever I have not once in eleven years had the more serious affection. This also seems to be an accepted fact: one attack of black-water fever predisposes to another, so that eventually every attack of malarial fever will take this form. I think this explains the fact of one European at the north of Lake Nyasa having had ten consecutive attacks in a period of three years.

From the suddenness of its onset and the equal suddenness of its disappearance, together with its remarkable tendency in some cases to come on in paroxysms, I think that the explanation is to be found in the study of the neurotic supply of the kidney.

It is remarkable, too, that women and weakly persons are seldom affected. It seems to be confined to young, healthy individuals, in whom there is great muscular waste. It comes on, too, after a long spell of the most robust health, and that with great suddenness. I think, too, that it is a disease of mountainous regions. It does occur in the lower parts, but my observation leads me to affirm that it is more prevalent in hilly districts in the centre of malarious regions.

APPENDIX II.

HINTS AS TO OUTFIT FOR BRITISH CENTRAL AFRICA

1. FLANNEL is a great mistake unless it is mixed with a large proportion of silk. Pure flannel is an abomination in the tropics. Either on account of some inherent property of the wool, or probably of some chemical compound with which it is prepared, the action of perspiration on the flannel in a tropical country is to at once create a most offensive smell, even in persons who are constantly changing their clothes, and who attend to personal cleanliness. Moreover, no flannel yet invented (all advertisements on the subject are to be absolutely disbelieved) ever failed to shrink into unwearableness after, at most, the third washing. Again, the feel of the flannel on the skin in a warm climate is singularly irritating and hurtful. Persons going to Africa are strongly advised to wear not flannel, but either silk and wool underclothing, or merino. Merino is excellent. It is cleanly, absolutely odourless, stands any amount of washing, and is pleasant in contact with the skin. Under almost all circumstances save those where the temperature rises above 100 degrees in the shade, a merino under-garment should always be worn

next the skin, night and day, over the chest and stomach, though for the sake of cleanliness the garment should be constantly changed. Especially is this necessary at night time, when very dangerous chills often occur by the sudden lowering of the temperature after midnight and the exposure of the naked body to this lowered temperature when covered with perspiration. The best form of underclothing of this kind is merino vests and merino drawers. Pantaloons are preferable to the short drawers which are sometimes worn, which reach no further down than the knee. The reason of this is that it is as well to protect the calf of the leg as much as possible from the attacks of insects which may succeed in piercing the trousers with their probosces, but find it difficult to get through the merino as well. Many of the ulcers from which people suffer in Central Africa have their origin in mosquito bites, or in the attacks of certain flies which deposit their eggs under the skin. While a merino vest should be worn next the skin at night, the drawers, of course, are removed, and it is only the upper part of the body (especially the stomach) which requires careful protection from chill. Night-gowns are quite obsolete. I believe these indecent inadequacies still survive in remote parts of the United Kingdom and on the benighted "Continent," but they have long since been banished from the life of Europeans in the tropics. Sleeping suits or paijamas are worn. These consist of a jacket and trousers. They can be obtained at any shop in London. The most suitable material is of silk and wool, but cotton paijamas are quite sufficient for ordinary purposes, provided a merino vest is worn. Clad in paijamas the wearer can with perfect propriety walk about on the deck of a steamer or on the verandah of his house in the early morning.

Another much praised invention which is almost useless in Central Africa is the pith helmet. Such a thing, I suppose, is scarcely ever seen there now. By far the most suitable hat is a light canvas helmet or a large thick felt hat with a huge brim, which is sufficiently stiff to turn up or down to shade the wearer's face or to allow the cool air to have free access as the case may be. The Terai hat is, on the whole, the best kind, but it does not appear to me to have a sufficiently wide brim. I believe suitable felt hats, cheap and of the kind I am inclined to recommend, can be purchased at the Army and Navy Stores. No hat should be heavy. All hats should, if possible, be ventilated by small holes at the top. Another kind of hat, which is very useful and protects the head a good deal from the sun, is the straw hat with a wide brim supplied to the blue-jackets in the Navy in tropical countries. These are called, I believe, "Sennet" hats. Besides other places, they can be obtained from Messrs. S. W. Silver and Co., of Cornhill.

A small round polo cap is very useful for wearing on the head when sitting on verandahs, or under the awning of a steamer. To go about with a bare head outside a house is often bad, as one is exposed to catching cold from the breeze, or may even feel the effect of the sun through the awning of a steamer, or by refraction from a wall or a piece of bare ground.

2. *Clothes.*—It is a good thing for a traveller to take out with him all his old English clothes, which prove to be very useful in the cool uplands of British Central Africa. A warm great-coat is *absolutely essential*. It should be remembered that people suffer much more from *cold* in British Central Africa than they do from *heat*.[1] A macintosh which will not come to pieces in warm weather is also useful for going about in the rain. A man should never be without his great coat in Central Africa. He may need it at any moment, especially if he has been perspiring freely and evening is drawing near. The evening dress, which is usually worn by employés of the British Central Africa Administration, consists of an ordinary dress coat, white shirt, white tie, dress waistcoat of yellow cloth with brass buttons, and black trousers. A short evening coat without tails is often worn. Lounge coats and smoking jackets come in very handy.

Amongst other exposed absurdities are knee-boots, that is to say, boots which are

---

[1] N.B.—The great coat should not fit tightly to the figure; it should be comfortably loose and provided with a very deep collar which can, if necessary, be turned up to shield the neck and throat, and reach almost to the back of the head.

continued up to the knee. They are soon discarded in Central Africa as uncomfortable and unwearable. Field boots should be of tanned leather, laced up and only coming to the ankle. The soles should be thick, but the boots must be light and not cumbersome. When walking or riding, cloth gaiters from the ankle to the knee, or spats from the instep to half way up the calf of the leg, are comfortable, suitable, and usually worn. Cloth or canvas gaiters are better than leather, as leather becomes so hard in this climate. Some people wear knickerbockers. This involves stockings however, and stockings are very hot for the legs, and the attempt to keep them up with garters causes a disagreeable constriction about the knee. It is much better to have trousers that can be pulled up slightly and the gaiters buttoned over them. The trousers can then be slightly folded over the top of the gaiter or the spat. A thick cloth cape to cover the shoulders and button round the throat is very convenient when riding or bicycling (and already a good deal of bicycling is done in Central Africa) or driving, when it is not convenient to take an umbrella.

3. Umbrellas.—One black silk umbrella for the rain should be taken, but several good strong light sun umbrellas *must* be taken. These should be double-lined, with a space between the linings—white outside and green within. They must be very *light* to hold. The reason why a helmet is such a mistake as a protection from the sun is that besides being cumbersome and ugly, it at most shields the top of the head, or the head and neck. Where the sun is felt even more than on the head is on the shoulders and along the spine. To shield the body from the sun in fact, the only way is to carry a white umbrella, and this should be done on almost all occasions except when to do such a thing would be positively ridiculous, as, for instance, in the middle of a battle. There is no more effectual aid to the maintenance of health than to constantly carry a white umbrella when compelled to face the strong sunshine.

4. Socks, &c.—Stockings I have already alluded to as inconvenient for various reasons. Socks should be of merino. Cotton socks though cool wear out very rapidly. The merino socks should be not too thick and *must* be well-fitting to the foot, as if they are the least bit too large the redundancy of sock makes walking uncomfortable, and often causes blisters. Plenty of handkerchiefs should be taken, cotton and silk. One or two mufflers for the neck are good when the traveller is on the cold uplands.

5. Boots.—In addition to ankle boots several pairs of light shoes should be taken, both shoes that can be blacked and that look smart, and tennis shoes. There should of course be one pair of slippers. Anyone who intends to stay any length of time at the European settlements will require at least one pair of nice-looking patent leather boots and a pair of pumps for evening wear.

Generally, I may say this about clothing, that a man should always strive to dress neatly and becomingly in Central Africa, or he will quickly lapse into a slovenly state of existence. At Blantyre and at Zomba people are almost always expected to dress for dinner at the various dinner parties, and to appear nicely dressed at church on Sundays, and if anyone imagines he is going out amongst a lot of rough pioneers who chiefly dress in red flannel shirts and buckskin breeches, he will be vastly surprised when he finds out how very carefully and becomingly as a rule the men do dress in Central Africa, whether they be officials, missionaries, planters or traders.

6. Guns.—As a rule guns, rifles and revolvers can be purchased in British Central Africa at the sales which take place from time to time of the effects of sportsmen who are returning home. Nearly every dry season a number of people come out to shoot big game, and to avoid the expense of the carriage often sell some of their guns before leaving the country. It is not as a rule wise for anyone who is not going to Central Africa specially for sport, to furnish himself with a large armament, before he gets to understand pretty clearly what kind of gun suits him best for that country. A double-barrelled 12-bore shot gun is always very useful. The right barrel should be choke bore and the

other not, so that in the left barrel bullet cartridges can, if necessary, be used, as sometimes when one is out after guinea-fowl, one might meet a lion or an antelope. The best kinds of shot are Swan shot; "A.A.A."; No. 1; No. 2; and No. 5. No. 5 is useful for pigeons and similar birds; as a rule however most African birds that the average man wants to shoot will succumb to little less in size than the No. 2 shot. It will be found that duck require either No. 2 or A.A.A., and Swan shot is useful for very big water birds or small mammals. For the average individual the best rifle is the ·450 single barrelled. Some people speak highly of the Lee-Metford, but though very deadly if the bullet comes in contact with the bone, its cartridge does not seem to have the same stopping effect where it merely pierces through the fleshy parts. A Martini-Henry is a very useful weapon. Elephant rifles are quite a special subject in themselves and the enquirer is referred to the various articles which have appeared on the subject in the *Field*, or have been written by Mr. Selous and other authorities. The revolver is not, as a rule, a very useful weapon, except for accidentally shooting oneself.

7. Plenty of *books* should be taken for reading. The traveller will miss books terribly if he is much alone in the evenings. Messrs. Mudie sell at a very cheap rate library books that have been some three months in circulation and all the great publishers nowadays issue cheap "Colonial" editions of all new and striking books. Maps of B. C. A. can be obtained from Mr. J. G. Bartholomew, Edinburgh, and Messrs. Stanford, Cockspur Street, Charing Cross.

8. Boxes.—No leather portmanteaus or wooden boxes should be taken, as they are liable to the attacks of white ants, and also suffer from the damp climate. All boxes should be of tin. The Army and Navy Stores and Messrs. Silver thoroughly understand the kind wanted. No boxes should be large and no packages should weigh more than 55 lbs. on account of the porterage on men's heads. The leather valise or dressing bag is useful and permissible. One or more rugs should certainly be taken, and a thoroughly waterproof "hold-all" is a very useful thing. Beds and tents are best obtained locally, as the right kinds are for sale at the various stores; but if it is desired to take one's own tent out then Messrs. Benjamin Edgington, of London Bridge, know exactly what is required for Central Africa, and can be thoroughly depended upon. The same firm supplies excellent camp furniture. I especially recommend their folding camp tables. A good dispatch-box is very useful, and Messrs. Silver, of Cornhill, supply very good articles of this description.

8. Sketching materials.—If the traveller intends to sketch or to photograph he should get his materials in London, as they are amongst the few things that cannot be purchased in British Central Africa. As regards sketching materials, Messrs. Kemp and Co., near Victoria Station, S.W., have for a long time past been in the habit of supplying me with what is required for Africa, and thoroughly understand the subject; and their materials have always proved to be suited to the exigencies of the climate.

9. Provisions of all kinds are much better purchased at the stores in British Central Africa; almost the same may be said for drugs, but a small private medicine chest is not a bad thing, and can be procured from Messrs. Burroughs and Wellcome, of Holborn.

I think this constitutes almost all the things which the average traveller should burden himself with before leaving England for British Central Africa. It must be remembered that the better extreme to go to of the two is to buy too little rather than too much, as many more things can be procured locally than one would generally suppose, and the prices at the stores in British Central Africa, compared to Matabeleland and the inner parts of South Africa, are very reasonable, on account of the cheapness of transport and the low Customs duties. Moreover it is not until a man is already established in Central Africa that he realises his own wants. He is then able to write home and order such things as he specially requires.

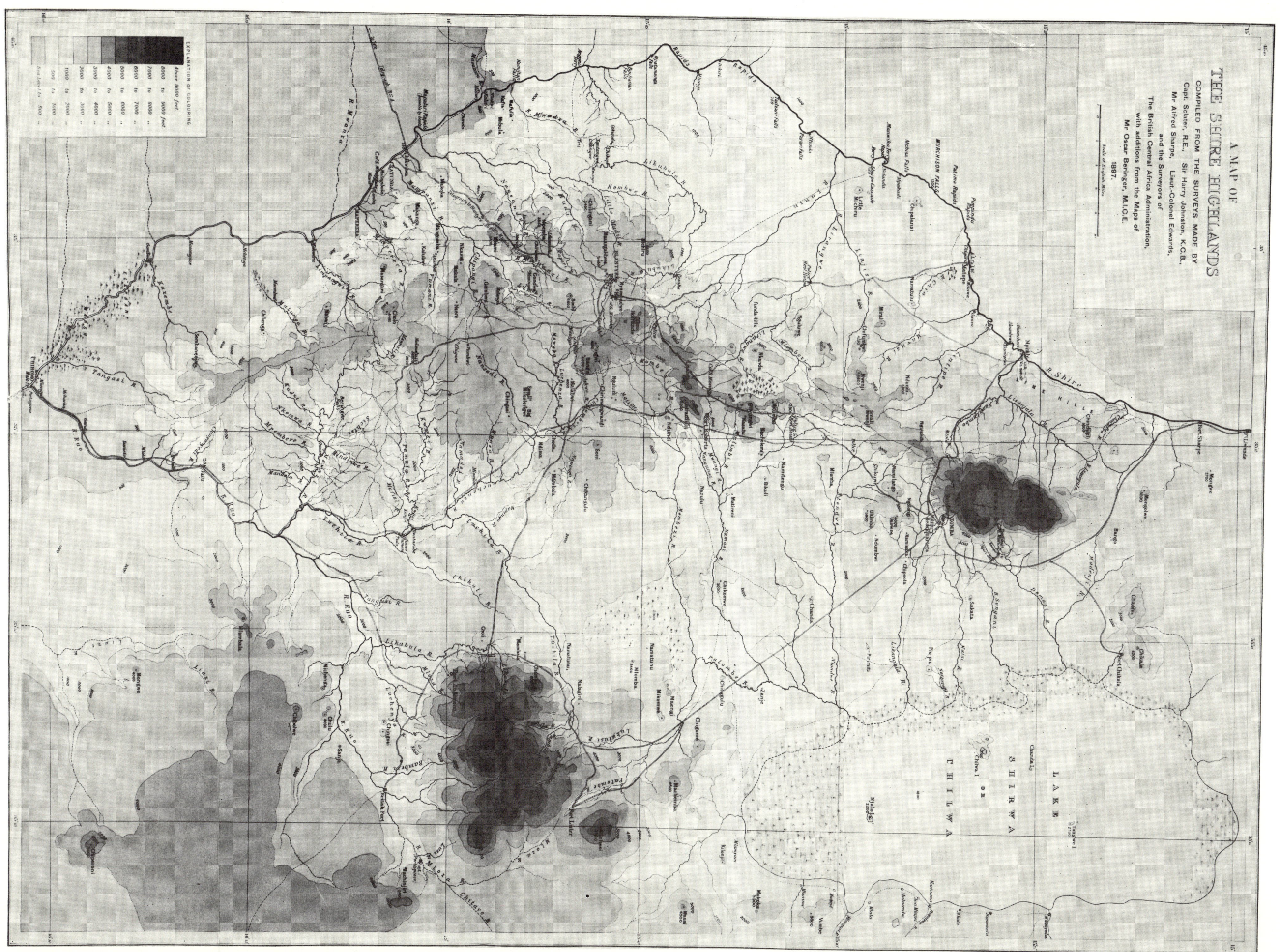

CHAPTER VII.

MISSIONARIES.

THERE are at present eight Missionary Societies at work in the eastern half of British Central Africa[1]:—

1. The Universities Mission, which is Anglican, occupies the eastern shore of Lake Nyasa, the islands of Likoma and Chisumula, and has a station at Fort Johnston at the south end of the lake. The same mission is also strongly established at Kotakota in the Marimba district on the south-west coast of Lake Nyasa. They are probably about to build a large station at or near Fort Mangoche in Zarafi's country. Outside British territory they have (besides their stations in Eastern Africa) an establishment on the plateau of Unango in Portuguese Nyasaland. This mission is presided over by Dr. Hine, Bishop of Likoma.

2. The Livingstonia Mission of the Free Church of Scotland occupies the western and north-western parts of the Protectorate.

3. The Church of Scotland East African Mission, better known perhaps as the "Blantyre Mission," has stations in the Shire Highlands.

4. The London Missionary Society (Independents or Wesleyans) has been long established on Lake Tanganyika. Its settlements are now confined to the British coast of that lake and to the Nyasa-Tanganyika plateau southwards, but I believe they will be opening shortly a station on Lake Mweru.

5. The Algerian Mission of the White Fathers (Roman Catholic), besides being represented by many stations on German or Belgian territory in the Tanganyika district, has recently established itself on the Nyasa-Tanganyika plateau and at one or two places in the Luemba country in the valley of the Chambezi.

6. The Dutch Reformed Church Mission (Dutch Calvinists), originally a branch of the Livingstonia Mission, has been established for some years in Central and Southern Angoniland.

7. The Zambezi Industrial Mission (Undenominational) works in Southern Angoniland in the Shire province.

8. The Nyasa Baptist Industrial Mission (Baptist) has stations in the Blantyre district.

In addition to this might almost be included the Jesuit Mission on the Zambezi, which was until recently established in the eastern part of the Mlanje district. Their stations were attacked and destroyed by the Yao chief, Matipwiri, who was subsequently punished for this action by the Administration, and is now exiled to Port Herald on the Lower Shire. It is therefore expected that the Jesuit Missionaries on the Zambezi will recommence their work in the south-eastern portion of the British Central Africa Protectorate.

[1] For Map showing Mission Stations see page 392.

The enumeration of the Missionary Societies at work in the whole of British Central Africa might be completed by citing the Jesuits on the Central Zambezi, and the French Evangelical Mission which has been so long and successfully at work in the Barutse country on the Upper Zambezi.

A Missionary Society originally founded by F. S. Arnot (Plymouth Brethren) has been for some years past established in Katanga, in the south part of the Congo Free State. This mission, I believe, contemplates founding stations on Lake Mweru within British territory, and I believe it has three stations on or near the River Kafue in Eastern Barutseland.

The past history of the more important and longest established Missions has been touched on in the general review of the history of British Central Africa. Further details concerning the number of their stations, the attendances at their schools and churches and other technical information is given in my report to the Foreign Office, "Africa No. 5, 1896," and it would be tedious to repeat the statistics here. I will confine myself in the present chapter to treating all missionary work in this part of Central Africa in a more generalised manner, giving my impressions as the opinions of any ordinary, fair-minded individual who wishes to arrive at true conclusions uninfluenced by sentiment or prejudice.

No person who desires to make a truthful statement would deny the great good effected by missionary enterprise in Central Africa. Yet why is it that in some quarters missionaries are heartily disliked, and the benefit of their work is denied or depreciated, even occasionally by clerics who, from a religious point of view, should be their natural supporters? If, on the one hand, the impartial observer must pronounce a verdict regarding the value of missionary work in Central Africa which is almost wholly in its favour, on the other hand he is compelled to ackowledge the existence of the prejudice and dislike with which missionaries are regarded by other white men not following the same career.

The causes of this feeling in my opinion are two—(1) The Cant which by some unaccountable fatality seems to be inseparably connected with missionary work, and (2) the arrogant demeanour often assumed by missionaries towards men who are not of their manner of thought and practice, though not necessarily men of evil life.

I think these two causes exist still, and were so prominent in past times that they are quite sufficient to account for what is really a long continued and unreasonable aspersion of the value of missionary work. It will be seen from the tenour of my remarks that I am striving to write on this difficult question from the point of view of an absolutely impartial outsider—let us say, for a moment, from the point of view of one who might be of any religion, or none at all. I take up this position because I honestly believe that much of the work done by European missionaries in Africa is of a kind which can be appreciated and praised without reserve by any fair-minded Muslim, Hindu, or Agnostic. Any thoughtful cultured man of no matter what religion, who is alive to the interests of humanity in general, must after careful examination of their work accord this meed of praise to the results which have followed the attempts to evangelise Central Africa.

Let us take into consideration the first count of the indictment against missionaries: Cant. Although matters have much improved under this heading since the "forties," when Cant reached an appalling pitch, and accounts were written of missionary work which are almost too repulsive for modern taste on that account (driving even sincere Christians into ribaldry and

MISSIONARIES

parody, as a natural relief), cant still exists, as can be seen by anyone who reads most missionary journals and hears many missionaries discourse. It exists ordinarily amongst the rawest and newest of missionaries and in the youngest of the missionary societies. In such missions as those of the Universities, the Church of Scotland and the Livingstonia Free Church, cant is extinct to a great extent locally, though it still lingers in the home compilations, in the journals which professedly give an account of the work of these establishments and which are published for home consumption. Sincere friends of mission work, such as Robert Needham Cust and Canon Isaac Taylor, have at times expressed their wonderment that missionaries should think it right or necessary to attach to descriptions of their work given verbally or in writing such expressions of mawkish piety, and so many statements which are an insidious perversion of the truth. In the latter case I can only imagine it is done on the assumption once attributed to the Jesuits, that it is right to do evil that good may come: that the missionaries are as convinced as I am of the ultimate good they effect, and that to encourage the British public to find funds for the carrying on of such work they think it excusable or even lawful to "gammon" them, if I may put it vulgarly, to repeat speeches of high-flown piety, on the part of savage and uncultured converts, which could not have been uttered with serious consciousness of their meaning, and, indeed, could never have been formulated from such poor arrested brains.

1. BISHOP HORNBY (FORMERLY OF NYASALAND)
2. THE LATE BISHOP MAPLES, OF LIKOMA

Then again—especially in the case of newly-formed missionary societies who, in the rush of unreasoning enthusiasm have embarked on African evangelisation without counting the cost or making the necessary preparations —articles too profane to be quoted are written of how God has taken to Himself "dear Sister So-and-so" or "Brother Somebody-else," to "cherish them on high" and give them a reward for their labours, as if there had been a special intervention of providence, when to the outside observer it is obvious that the sister or brother would never have died or even been ill if he or she had been properly housed or properly fed. My indictment on this score is not half strong enough. I kept by me at one time the journals and records of certain missionary societies, intending to quote them in some such book as this: a few months ago, however, I tore them up, as they were not wholesome literature, and perhaps I should have been flogging a dead horse in laying bare to the public this awful accumulation of Cant, when I knew such cant to be as strongly condemned as I can condemn it by missionaries of old standing, and when I began to see so many signs of its rapid disappearance. Missionary work in British Central Africa, believe me, has only to tell the plain truth and nothing but the truth to secure sympathy and support. Let the societies cease to humbug the people, let them tell frankly of their trials, their sorrows, their disappointments, as well as of their successes, and the sympathy created by the truthful picture which will then be rendered of the great struggle against spiritual darkness and savagery will be far stronger than the limited support which is accorded in sectarian circles, when the vulgarest and coarsest instincts of the unlettered Christian are appealed to by the aid of stupid falsehoods, lies of that worst kind which are usually founded on a substratum of truth.

The second complaint against missionaries is on the score of their arrogant demeanour. Some of the average European pioneers are not, I am sorry to say, very creditable specimens of mankind. They are aggressively ungodly, they put no check on their lusts; released from the restraints of civilisation and the terror of "what people may say," they are capable of almost any degree of wickedness; but the missionary is too apt to assume that all new Europeans with whom he comes in contact are of this class, and that because they do not belong to a mission they are necessarily wicked men; and he shows this so plainly in his manner that the result is naturally a reciprocal suspicion and dislike on the part of the stranger layman. There is an undoubted tendency on the part of missionaries to hold and set forth the opinion that no one ever did any good in Africa but themselves. That they have done more good than armies, navies, conferences and treaties have yet done, I am prepared to admit; that they have prepared the way for the direct and just rule of European Powers and for the extension of sound and honest commerce I have frequently asserted; but they are themselves to some extent only a passing phase, only the John-the-Baptists, the forerunners of organized churches and settled social politics. It is their belief that they hold an always privileged position, that they are never to fit into their proper places in an organized European community, which causes so much friction between them and the other European settlers or lay officials by whom they are gradually being far outnumbered; nor are they always ready to recognise that there is some credit due to the missionaries of commerce as well as to the missionaries of religion; that the savage man cannot live decently by faith alone; that he must have something to occupy his mind besides religion, and that unless his attention is drawn to hard work and to gaining money in an honest manner, "Satan will find some mischief still for his idle hands to do."

Now let me leave off preaching and try to give my readers some idea of what missionary life is like in Central Africa, always from the point of view of the lay traveller and dispassionate investigator.[1]

Try, reader, to imagine yourself in the position of some weary man travelling in Central Africa on Government business, or as a pioneer trader, or engaged in

[1] To do this I find myself obliged to quote to some extent from an article on Missionaries which I wrote for the *Nineteenth Century Review* of November, 1887, but which, though ten years old, still gives what I believe to be such a faithful general picture of the average missionary home in Central Africa that in some passages I find it difficult to describe the same in other language.

natural history research, or merely for the sake of exploration or sport. You have just quitted the slightly civilised coast-belt for the little known and savage interior, and you may have sickened with the first touch of fever. With all the enthusiasm for exploration which leads most white men into this unhealthy but fascinating continent, you feel temporarily depressed and saddened at the snapping of all ties which bind you to the world of culture and comfort: your new tent is leaky and lets in the rain, or it fails to mitigate the blazing heat of noontide; your untried cook cannot at once acquire the art of producing a decent meal amid the many difficulties of camp life; you have long ceased to eat bread, or the fragments of mouldy toast that may be served up to you are piteous relics of the pleasant sojourn at some relatively civilised town on the coast whence you started.

Or, it may be, the circumstances under which you are travelling are somewhat different. You are at the end of some great journey, some expedition which has had its moments of exhilarating success, of wonderful discovery, but now the excitement is over and is succeeded by a dull apathy that is almost despair: you no longer anticipate with a joy that can scarcely be outwardly repressed the pleasures which are about to reward your months of toil, privation and danger—the first night's sleep in a comfortable and spacious bed, the first well-cooked meal into which you will crowd all your favourite delicacies, the first good concert or theatre you will attend; you are weary of running over in your mind the public dinners that may be given to you or the praises of scientific societies which will reward your discoveries; you merely confine yourself to reflecting dully on the probabilities of reaching your destination alive and of doubting whether under any circumstances, and especially the present ones, life is worth living. In either case, whether your work lies behind you, finished, or before you, to be accomplished, you jog along the narrow winding path, tired, alone, heart-sick, home-sick, your sore and weary feet tripping over stocks and stones, your aching eyes fixed on the ground, seeing nothing, your face scorched with the hot wind, your hands scratched with the grass blades that have to be continually pushed aside in your dogged progress. Perhaps even you may be enduring worse discomfort, you may be drenched to the skin—macintosh notwithstanding—in some torrential downpour; and overweighted with your heavy, streaming rain-coat, you stagger along half blindly through slushy mud and soaked vegetation. Then you hear your guide saying to someone that he recognises the district, that the white man's house is near at hand. "What white man?" you ask apathetically, too weary to show an interest in anything. "People of the Mission," the guide replies, and then if you only know of this modern type of evangelist by tradition you will smile bitterly and say to yourself, "Oh, a missionary! H'm, I don't feel much in a mood to pray or sing hymns just now!" Then you continue plodding on in stupid resignation to whatever fate awaits you.

I will suppose, to make this picture more effective, that it is now late afternoon. The sun—if it is the sun that has chiefly troubled you during the day's march—is at last sinking behind an imposing clump of forest trees, and the fierce heat of noon is beginning to be tempered by the rising breeze. Or the murky rain clouds are drifting away in ragged, piled up masses to the east, leaving a large space of the western heavens clear; and this expanse of open sky has become a pale lemon-yellow through the diffused misty glory of the declining sun. The surrounding country has a more pleasing appearance. Here and there in the distance are bright green and yellow patches diversifying the grey scrub and sombre forest, and these clearly indicate the existence of plantations, while the vicinity of man is proved by occasional puffs and spirals of blue smoke where the natives are burning weeds. The path, too, is clearer, wider, and better made; the obtrusive wayside vegetation has been checked and no longer impedes your progress. Then you begin to meet occasional inhabitants of the distant unseen settlements—women with babies slung on their backs and earthen pitchers poised on their heads on their way to the spring to obtain their evening supply of water; or men returning from the chase armed with long-barrelled ancient-looking guns, spears, assegais, or clubs, and accompanied by several snarling curs, whose collars are hung with little bells. To your surprise, instead of plunging terror stricken into the bush or assuming a defiant and hostile attitude, each native greets you politely with "Morning! Goo' morning!" for they have learned from the missionaries our matutinal salutation, which they indifferently make use of at all hours of the day and night. On each side of the widened road a straggling row of young plantain trees begins to make its appearance, evidently planted with the view of its forming ultimately a shady avenue: then behind a wooden fence appear thriving plantations of vegetables and hedges of pine-apples, and at last, a turn in the road brings into view a garden of flowers and flowering shrubs—blazing with brilliant masses of colour—and a long, low-built dwelling house of one storey, with white-washed walls, green window shutters, and a wide overhanging roof of thatch forming a verandah round the building. Behind the house are other dwellings of a humbler architecture, more or less hidden with green shrubs and trees; and further in the background is a huge barn-like building, also white-washed and with a thatched roof, but having about it an indefinably ecclesiastical air, and this is certain to be a church, possibly used as a school also during the week.

NATIVE CHURCH AT MSUMBA, LAKE NYASA
(UNIVERSITIES MISSION)

As you are toiling up the red path towards the house, taking in all these details with slow and tired comprehension, there comes towards you, half striding, half running, a white man whose outward presentment is something like the building you have taken for a chapel—a sort of compromise between homely rusticity and ecclesiastical primness. Probably he wears a large soft, grey felt hat with a broad brim, a crumpled white tie, a long grey clerical coat, cut close up to the neck, grey breeches and gaiters, and heavy boots. His face has homely features, but it is pleasantly lit up with an expression of hearty kindliness.

Behind your new acquaintance—who has introduced himself to you as the agent of some well-known British Protestant mission—follow half-a-dozen loutish boys, mostly clad in gay coloured jerseys or shirts, with Manchester cottons round their lower limbs, one or two more favoured ones being hideously clothed in coats and trousers. These lads have lost the easy carriage and independent bearing of the unsophisticated native, and shuffle and slouch along in a lazy, loose-jointed manner that is a distinct irritation to a person of energetic, active temperament, and their semi-circular grin as they lounge up to you with a loud greeting produces on your part an involuntary frown rather than an answering smile. In a half-hearted manner they relieve your foremost porters of their burdens, and the straggling procession proceeds on its way up the red clay path and through the flower garden towards the house. It is probable that at the head of the steps leading to the raised verandah, the missionary's wife awaits you, clasping and unclasping her hands, and letting her smile wax and wane as your slow approach through the garden gives her a slightly nervous feeling of conscious expectancy. Involuntarily her hand goes to her throat—yes! the gold locket is there; she has not forgotten it. She glances at the little bouquet of flowers in her bosom—how quickly they are fading in the hot air! She smoothes the crumpled pale blue ribbons that give her homely dress an almost pathetic remembrance of former smartness, and pulls out the sleeve puffs; touches her hair to ascertain its smoothness; shakes out the limp folds of her skirt; clears her throat; calls up the smile again, now that you are close, and finally loses all affectation when she takes your hand and gazes into your pale, tired, spiritless face, and in a burst of womanly pity bids you welcome, and hurries away to make arrangements for your comfort.

When you have bathed and changed your clothes, a pleasant languor succeeds your crushing fatigue. The missionary's wife is busy in her household, devising additions to the evening meal; the missionary has excused himself, and is gone to wind up the school affairs, and dismiss the scholars from the chapel. You are left for a short time in not unwelcome solitude. As you sit in the porch, gazing dreamily on the glowing sunset, and inhaling the strong, sweet, mingled perfume of the nicotianas, frangipanis, mignonette, and lilies in the garden, your ears catch the shrill, clear voices of children singing five verses of an evening hymn. Were you with them in the building, the glib utterance, thin melody, and nasal twang of the performance would jar upon you; as it is, here, softened by distance, it strikes a sweet note in the unruffled harmony of your surroundings. From the native village, half hidden among the tall umbrageous trees, which stand out in velvet blackness against the western sky, comes the faint murmur of voices; and an occasional laugh of the women and girls, returning with their pitchers from the water-course, echoes pleasantly through the air. In the yellow-flowered thorn hedge at the bottom of the garden a bulbul[1] is piping and warbling his mellow notes. You feel enveloped in an atmosphere of peace, which is doubly refreshing because of its contrast to the weary tenour of your past life.

The loud clanging of the school bell disturbs your reverie. The missionary is once more at your side with many excuses for having for a brief while left you to your own devices. The evening meal is announced, and you follow your host to the dining-room, or, rather, the one large sitting-room of his house. Here his wife, seated at the table before an ample tea-tray, welcomes you to the repast, and perhaps adds a quite unnecessary apology for its character. As you unfold your clean napkin, you glance

---

[1] *Pycnonotus.* In parts of the Shire Highlands and other mountainous districts there are thrushes that sing sweetly.

over the table and are quite satisfied with your present lot. There is, for instance, to open the repast, a tureen of good chicken soup; and a cold pigeon pie, a rolled tongue, sardines, and boiled eggs are other items. There are dishes of home-grown potatoes baked in their skins, and golden slices of fried plantain. A superb pineapple imparts its fragrance to the mingled odours of the steaming tea and the savoury broth. Little glass dishes of luscious jams and sweet biscuits fill up spare gaps in between the *pièces de résistance*, and it is probable that a few bright flowers in a slender vase give a grace to the outspread meal which clearly indicates feminine supervision. When your thoughts and your gaze are wandering thus, you see your hostess suddenly pause in the tea-outpouring, and lower her head and clasp her hands, while your host, who has once or twice endeavoured to arrest your attention, rises somewhat bashfully and pronounces a brief benediction on the repast. Then, this duty over, he serves and carves and cuts with a will. If you are a man of any tact, and desire to administer a little harmless flattery to your kind hosts, you will compliment your hostess on her delicious tea. Then she will tell you of the difficulties which attend the procuring of fresh milk in Africa, and of how, in her case, these difficulties have been met and conquered. She will enumerate her nanny-goats, and describe the vagaries of her half-wild cow. And you must especially dwell on the excellence of the cold pigeon-pie. This will no doubt elicit from your hostess the avowal—with a little blushing—that she herself made it. Her husband shot the pretty green fruit-pigeons—"poor little things! it seems a shame, doesn't it?"—and she made the pie-crust. "You know the native girls can learn to cook most things, but they never can be taught to make pastry, so I always go into the kitchen and do that myself."

When the meal is over, you are doubtless made to take the easiest chair, which is drawn up to the open brick fire-place, where fragrant logs are burning. You really feel permeated with comfort, while gratitude for the kindness shown you lends, or ought to lend, a brighter look to your eyes and a more sympathetic tone to your voice. The missionary's wife has taken up some needlework to occupy her fingers. Her husband, out of politeness, is sitting idle with his hands before him, trying to make conversation; but if you question him adroitly, you will soon find out that he has some hobby that he rides, some favourite pursuit that he follows in his leisure time. Perhaps it is the study of the native language; and on your expressing an encouraging interest, he will bring out delightedly his bulky manuscript vocabularies and chatter to you of prefixes and suffixes and infixes, of clicks and nasals, guttural-labials, aspirated sibilants, and faucal sounds—all the cacophony of barbarous tongues. Or you will discover that his passion is entomology, and a very little persuasion will induce him to open his boxes and tins, redolent of camphor, and to fetch down from his study-shelves his spirit-jars, and to display before your somewhat wearied gaze a bewildering collection of insect forms — beetles big as mice, and gorgeously clad in golden-green and chestnut-brown, tiny jewel-like beetles caught in the calyces of orchids, fantastic longicorns, clumsy scarabs, lovely chafers, brilliant cantharides, all the coleopterous forms of the surrounding district. He will recall your wandering attention to a marvellous mantis, mimicking a large green leaf to perfection, or assuming the form and appearance of a dry branching twig. He will show you butterflies from the forest which, when their wings are folded, can scarcely be distinguished from a dead leaf, or other splendid *Papilionidæ* of the tropics not afraid to exhibit their beauties openly, and revelling in the display of brilliant colours, attractive markings, and eccentric shapes. Then will follow for your inspection rows of bugs, scarlet and green, yellow and black; repulsive cicadas with huge stupid heads and disgusting fat bodies, giving a nasty oily odour which even the camphor cannot suppress; dapper-looking grasshoppers, neatly and prettily coloured; and dragon-flies with gauzy wings, some purple-blue, some orange, others umber-brown or crimson.

If you are not reviewing insects or discussing languages, you may be turning over portfolios of dried plants; or it is birds that the missionary shoots and skins, or geological specimens that he collects, or he may even concentrate his interest exclusively within the narrow domain of spiders or land shells. Whatever his hobby may be, having once started him off, it is hard to arrest him, and with the best intentions you find yourself after a little while arduously acting an interest you cease to feel, and paralysing the muscles of your jaws with suppressed yawns. The missionary's wife detects your fatigue. Long use has accustomed her to regard her husband's favourite pursuit with indulgent unconcern; so rising, and gathering her needlework together, she says, "John, it is time for prayers; I am sure Mr. So-and-so must be tired." The obedient husband assents, puts away with a sigh his manuscripts, or his collections, and goes outside into the verandah, to ring the bell. Then he returns with *un visage de circonstance*, gets down his big Bible and seats himself in the armchair at the head of the table. Presently there is a whispering, giggling, and shuffling in the passage, and in come the loutish boys you have seen before. They are lugging along some wooden forms, which they place in the room near the door. Then they retreat and return again, this time bearing piles of Bibles and paper-covered hymn-books. They are followed by a small number of lollopy girls, some clad in loose garments like short nightgowns, a few bearing still an appearance of being but half reclaimed and in their savage innocence scorning to hide their virginal breasts in a frowsy gown, while the draping of the light cottons round their limbs and heads retains an element of innate good taste which the older, more civilised girls have lost. These latter, too, are oppressed with a sense of self-consciousness at the sight of a stranger, and alternately glance at you with sidelong languishing looks, and then make you the subject of sniggering whispers among themselves, until they are checked by a stern look from their mistress, which makes their eyes drop with one accord on their open Bibles. After prayers are over the youths drag out the forms again, the maidens bob and curtsey, and each with shrill monotony yelps out, "Good night, ma'am; good night, sah," to which your host and hostess reply, with wearisome punctiliousness, "Good night, Amelia, good night, Florence, good night, Susannah, good night, Rebecca," and so on to the end of the list. Then you stand for a few minutes purposeless, gazing at the prints of Bible subjects hung round the walls, staring vacantly at your hostess's sewing machine, opening the gift books on the table or softly trying the harmonium with one finger and an intermittent pressure on the pedals. The missionary's wife, who has just been with her servants to ascertain that all your requirements in your bedroom have been anticipated, returns and bids you good night with a kindly-worded wish that you may benefit by your night's rest. You chat a few minutes longer with your host, and then repair to your bedroom, where you will be sure to find a comfortable bed and a shelf of books, with one of which you beguile the moments till sleep comes to close your tired eyelids.

Perhaps in the morning you awake ill with threatened fever. Sick, dazed, and trembling, you attempt to dress, but your host, who is learned in the treatment of such maladies, insists on your returning to bed where for days to come you toss and rave, while the vulture Death approaches in ever-narrowing circles, until by patient nursing, thoughtful care, unwearying attention the missionary and his wife have conquered the disease and restored you to health. Or, more probably, the first night's quiet rest under a rain-tight roof, the good food and cheering kindness of your evening's entertainment at the mission, have successfully dispelled the incipient malady, and at the clanging of the school-bell you awake from slumber, to find yourself light-hearted and full of energy, braced by this little interlude of comfort to face with stout determination the solitude of the wilderness.

Your host and hostess are loth to part with you, and before you go, you must in very grace inspect the church or chapel and the schools; listen while the school children sing a simple English glee, and "God Save the Queen"; look over their specimens of hand-writing; and give them easy problems to solve in mental arithmetic. You may find it hard to take an interest in or suppress a repugnance for the hulking youths or plump girls, who instead of being—as they ought to be—engaged in hard wholesome manual labour, are dawdling and yawning over slate and primer, and in whose faces sensual desires struggle for expression with hypocritical sanctimoniousness; but the little children, the little, naked, bright-eyed children just captured from the village, and now demurely ranged in rows, solemnly picking out and wrongly naming cardboard A's and B's and C's—you surely can find no difficulty in loving them, and saying something to encourage the missionary's wife, whose pets they are? The school inspection over, you yield to very pressing invitations and stay to an early luncheon, after which your host starts you on the right road to your next destination, and your hostess slips some dainty package of eatables into your satchel.

The foregoing sketch illustrates perhaps the commonest type of missionary household in Central Africa, for the bulk of our missionaries are Protestants and married. Most missionary societies distinctly encourage their agents to marry and take their wives out to live with them in Africa. I only know of one Protestant mission where celibacy is approved. That is the Universities Mission which is mainly supported by the High Church party in England, and the way in which its work is carried on is very similar to that of the Roman Catholic missions. In some respect the system of the Anglicans and Roman Catholics has much to recommend it. In their establishments there are separate communities of men and women who lead a life which is monastic only in its best features, and who not being troubled by any family affairs, can devote themselves to the work of the mission as long as health permits. But then it must be remembered that these celibate missions are to some extent served by picked men and women, who are mostly volunteers and receive no salary for their services, and are merely lodged and boarded at the expense of the mission. This system of celibacy undoubtedly does not suit the British missionary as a rule. Given an average man, young and in the prime of manhood, who is sent to work in Africa unmarried, unsolaced by the company of a wife, you will find him prone to be restless and discontented, or to find a consolation which arouses scandal. Married to a wife of his own nation and rank his whole career may be different. He is happy, contented, pure-minded, and disposed—from the fact of his having made his home there—to devote himself to a life-long work in Africa: in fact, a married missionary becomes more or less a missionary colonist, a result which the parent society is desirous to attain. Moreover, it is certain that a married man has far more influence among the natives, for to the African mind celibacy is either an unnatural or dishonourable condition provoking suspicion or contempt. A man-missionary, moreover, if he is to avoid the breath of scandal must have as little to do with the native women-folk as possible. Yet in the interest of his work it is quite as—perhaps more—important that the women should be

CHURCH OF THE CHURCH OF SCOTLAND MISSION, BLANTYRE

instructed as the men. As mothers and wives they wield an influence for good and bad which it is hard to overrate. From an evangelistic point of view women are needed for missionaries as well as men. This need is met in the Roman Catholic Church and in some Anglican missions by the employment of good women as nuns or teaching sisters, and many of the Protestant missions often have attached to them unmarried women whose usefulness in teaching is quite equal to that of the men. But somehow I have noticed that few of these unmarried women helpers, if they were of British nationality, were rigid advocates of celibacy. Sooner or later most of them have found missionary husbands, or have married Europeans outside the mission. It is a subject on which I cannot dogmatise, having before my mind's eye many examples of beautiful, pure, and most useful lives led in Eastern and Central Africa by devoted women who lived a nun's life and were never married; and yet I must own these were the exceptions rather than the rule, and that personally I shrink from advocating the sending out to Africa of young unmarried women. It is far better they should go there, or live there, as wives. Even in marriage, however, it is not right to conceal the fact that there are drawbacks to the healthy happy life of the married white woman in a barbarous country, with a sickly and tropical climate. A blithe pretty girl from one of the three countries which form the United Kingdom, with the wild rose bloom on her cheek, arrives in Africa and espouses her missionary husband; or, it may be, that they are married in England, and make the voyage out their honeymoon. Everything in her new life is a shock to her mental and physical system. The unvarying, enervating heat and the enforced changes in her mode of dress; the strange tropical nature, overpowering at first sight with its luxuriance and its amazing growths; the different kind of food, and even the altered manner of passing the hours of daylight; sometimes, too, the total absence of any kindred society of her own sex—all these new experiences, united, form a complete reversal of her previous life, and must at first react on her physical organisation. Then, too, think of a modest girl who has been hitherto shielded with such jealous care from contact with anything coarse or impure, so that she has, in fact, grown up stupidly innocent: think of her suddenly thrust into a barbarous country where the natives are naked and not ashamed, and where the conventions of decency are often unknowingly transgressed by them in a way which to her English prudery must appear very indecent; where, too, the women among whom she has come to minister, will, when she understands their language, talk glibly to her of matters that the most depraved of her sex at home would hesitate to mention to a young and inexperienced woman. The effect of this ordeal even on a young wife is not without its risks of moral deterioration, and is sometimes only acquired at the cost of a certain loss of delicacy.[1] This rude contact with coarse animal natures and their unrestrained display of animal instincts tends imperceptibly to blunt a modest woman's susceptibilities, and even, in time, to tinge her own thoughts and language with an unintentional coarseness.

Every year, however, makes it easier for married women to share the lot of their husbands in countries like British Central Africa, where civilisation is rapidly increasing and numbers are multiplying. The missionary societies working here early recognised that it was their bounden duty to supply medical missionaries to attend to the health of their European agents as well as to the medical wants of the natives. In consequence of this the missionaries' wives who have children have not suffered as has been the case in earlier days in other parts of Africa. Children are frequently born to the married missionaries, and are reared in the African climate with fair success, and eventually grow up healthy boys and girls in England. Every year makes it easier for the missionary to support his wife in Africa with reasonable comfort and chance of good health. Women, indeed, seem to stand the climate better than men. Moreover, nowadays, our ideas on the subject of women are widening; we are coming to see that many burdens hitherto borne by the male can be equally supported by the female. On the whole, I think women make better missionaries than men, and are always much more lovable in that aspect. Let them, therefore, continue to go out to Africa as celibates if they are over thirty-five, but otherwise as married women.

If the supposititious traveller, whose hypothetical experiences in one type of

[1] I am writing of course of the average woman, not of exceptional characters who can walk through any amount of mire and come out unsoiled.

missionary household I have already described, should stay at a station of the Universities Mission in Central Africa or with any of the Roman Catholic Fathers, he will have very pleasant experiences, though they may be of a different nature. The good Fathers of the Roman Catholic Church, and the Anglican priests from our two great Universities, will entertain him with a whole-hearted hospitality, though he will not perhaps enter so much into their private lives as with the married Protestant missionary. In the case of the Anglican missionaries he will derive more the impression that he is staying at a college, a college where there is very plain living and high thinking. With the Roman Catholics the food is thoroughly good, well cooked and appetising, and all reproach of luxury removed from it when it is understood that it is almost all of local production and due to the energy and husbandry of the Fathers and their pupils. I repeat, there is something very suggestive of the English public-school about the Anglican missionaries. Athletics bulk largely and wholesomely in their curriculum. Their boy pupils are soon taught to play football and cricket, and to use the oar rather than the paddle; but it cannot be truthfully said that these missionaries keep a good table or care sufficiently for their creature comforts. Their houses are often of poor construction, untidy and unattractive: it is obvious that they are under no care of womankind. The missionary snatches his meals hastily, scarcely tasting what goes down his throat. On his untidy bureau there will be at one and the same time the newest philosophical treatise from England and an ugly tin teapot of over-stewed tea. But I shall not continue my criticisms in this respect, as these missionaries are now much of the same opinion as myself on the subject of the sheer necessity of comfort, if one intends to lead a healthy life in Africa, and I believe steps are now being taken to supply each University Mission Station with one or more lay brothers who will attend to household cares.

I have made many allusions to missionary hospitality. Missionaries and the Portuguese are alike in this respect. As a people the Portuguese are the most hospitable I know in any part of the globe's surface, showing their hospitality as a kind of instinct alike to friend and enemy. The missionary, in the same way, regards hospitality as a sacred duty. No matter whether his guest is disposed to cavil at his work or to sympathise with it he gives him the best he has, and often more than he himself can afford; and too frequently the return both to the Portuguese settler or official and to the missionary is thankless abuse, or ridicule, on the part of the passing traveller. I have known explorers who owed their lives and the success of their journeys and the saving of a vast amount of expenditure to Portuguese officials, planters or traders, who helped them by the way. When they returned to Europe, however, it was only to dilate on all that was defective in the Portuguese system of government, or faulty in the characteristics of the race. Likewise how many travellers and sportsmen have lived for weeks light-heartedly at the expense of a missionary or of a series of missionaries, and then have taken the earliest opportunity of sneering at them and spreading calumnious reports as to their mode of life. I remember an instance of this in one who is now dead and therefore shall be nameless. He had visited the French priests at Bagamoyo, on the East Coast of Africa. Wishing to do him honour as an explorer and an Englishman, the good Fathers concerted together, and agreed to sacrifice their last bottle of champagne (kept as an occasional medicine) in his honour. What was the result? He returned to Europe and said, "Those missionaries live like fighting-cocks, they drink champagne every day."

How few of the many hundreds who have enjoyed missionary hospitality, nursing and assistance have remembered that their entertainers were men receiving salaries from £80 to £300 a year, often with a wife and family to maintain. How many have attempted to make any subsequent return for the help afforded, not perhaps in monetary or other gifts, but in fair words.

It has been so fine a thing at first to encounter in the wilderness such disinterested goodness, such heroic attempts in the face of the greatest difficulties and dreariest discouragements to lead oneself and to teach others to adopt the higher life, that your first impressions are of unbounded admiration for the missionaries and their work. If you stay in the country, say three years, your final verdict is likely to be that of your first impression; but if you frequent the mission for merely three weeks you will find yourself beginning to criticise; the demeanour of the mission girls has lost all shyness and may even perhaps be lacking in modesty, for these young women when they get beyond childhood have lost all fear of the white man and have not been subjected to the excellent native discipline which enforces amongst the women a modest bearing and a certain amount of deference towards people of the opposite sex. You will, at first, be disagreeably impressed with the native catechists, or readers, or deacons, or whatever title the trained native adherents of the mission may bear: with their profuse display of religious phrases, their clumsily cut European clothes,[1] contrasting with an often sensual face, their off-hand manners and great conceit. But pause a moment before you too hastily condemn the results of mission teaching. These clothed negroes, whose very clothing is an offence as it often induces uncleanly personal habits, and a consequent disagreeable personal smell, and whose aping of European ways is a provocation to criticism, are nevertheless more useful members of the community than an untutored savage. They may be cheeky if you attempt, as many white men do, a bullying manner, but they are men of the world. They will not offer you physical violence nor attempt to oppose your researches into their country; on the contrary they will make common cause with you, and espouse your cause if necessary against their wild brothers. They are now British subjects, emphatically as much wedded to the British policy with all its mistakes and even with any temporary injustice it may entail, as you are. Gradually they or their descendants will find their proper place. When by education and inherited culture they are on the level of the white man, then by all means let them take their place as his equal. The British Empire is, or should be, independent of considerations of race and colour, and should take as its sole standard of citizenship, mental, moral and physical qualifications. Otherwise we have no right to interfere with these alien races, and teach them to walk in our ways, and submit to our rule.

The fact is that it takes at least three generations before any clear appreciation of the principles of morality, truth, gratitude and honour can penetrate the intellect and curb the instincts of the negro. Nor in this disadvantage is he singular amongst the backward races of mankind. The same statement applies equally to the Red Indian, the Polynesian or the Papuan. You cannot in a year or two convert a wolf into a sheep dog, or a skulking jackal into a black and tan terrier; this change cannot be effected in the one individual, as a rule, no matter how long he may live; the result can only be attained by generations of transmitted culture, induced by constant restraint and careful education.

---

[1] This item of criticism cannot be made to apply to the pupils of the Universities Mission who are very wisely made to dress in long "kanzus," or garments of Arab style.

Even then, when the bulk of your subjects are firmly established in their new mode of life, and breed true, there will be occasionally disappointing reversions. A young sheep dog will take to worrying sheep, or a black and tan terrier be detected killing fowls.[1]

I know several ordained missionaries who are pure negroes, and who are most worthy men. Close your eyes and you might be talking to a cultivated Englishman. But I only recall, at most, three instances of negro priests of this excellent description who have been, in the one individual, raised up from a condition of utter savagery to that of an educated civilised man, and who have maintained themselves on this high level; almost all others having undergone similar experiences relapse at one time or another in a manner very similar to that described in Grant Allen's striking story, *The Reverend John Creedy*. But my hope for the eventual results lies in the knowledge of what has been done amongst the negroes of the West Indies. Some of the best, hardest-working and most satisfactory, sensible missionaries I have ever known have been West Indians—in colour as dark as the Africans they go to teach, but in excellence of mind, heart, and brain-capacity, fully equal to their European colleagues. But then these men were at least three generations removed from the uncivilised negro, and were as much strangers to Africa and African habits as the average European. *Per contra*, what disappointing results on a *surface* examination would appear to him who first commenced studying the effects of mission work in Central Africa. If he has really been a student of African History, if he has read old Blue-books, old descriptions of travel, old missionary records, he will have noted that at the end of the "seventies" or the beginning of the "eighties," the missionaries of the day wrote with rapture of the remarkable progress in learning and in religion which had been made by John Makwira, Joseph Evangel, Robert Ntundulima, Simpson Chokabwino:[2] of how John Makwira and Simpson Chokabwino had been

---

[1] As an instance of the disappointing naughtiness which may occur even amongst people who have lived round the mission station for years, I would tell the following story. While cruising on Lake Nyasa in 1895 on one of our gunboats I visited the Island of —— an important station of the —— Mission. We arrived on the Saturday evening, dined with the missionaries and were invited to lunch with them the next day. Early on Sunday morning a number of youths came off from the shore in canoes bringing small tins and bottles of milk. I am exceedingly fond of milk and it is not an easy thing to get in Africa as a rule, I was therefore delighted at the enterprise shown by the natives of ——. The Commander of the gunboat accordingly bought up all the milk that was offered for sale and that morning we feasted on porridge and milk and *café-au-lait*, and put aside plenty of milk for tea in the afternoon and puddings in the evening. As it is very difficult ordinarily to obtain milk at all from the natives in this part of Africa, as the cows and goats are often allowed to run about unmilked, (the natives not caring for milk themselves) we were full of praise regarding the enterprise of these mission boys. Later on we appeared at lunch, and the ladies and gentlemen of the mission apologised to us for handing round tinned milk, than which nothing becomes more hateful to the resident in Africa, "but," said the missionaries "our boys you know are very strict sabbatarians. On Sundays they absolutely refuse to milk the goats, so we have to go without, though we get plenty of milk on the other days of the week." I was just going to exclaim "How extraordinary! why lots of your boys came off this morning with quite a large quantity of milk for sale" when an idea struck the Commander of the vessel and myself simultaneously and we held our peace. On enquiry we found these youths of sabbatarian instincts reserved the Sunday's milk for themselves, and on occasions were very willing to sell it to strangers.

[2] The names of course are fictitious but they give some idea of the want of taste too often shown by the missionaries in naming their converts. This would be very apparent to anybody who takes up one or other of the missionary journals published in Central Africa and reads the list of baptisms. I quote haphazard from *Life and Work in British Central Africa*, the organ of the Blantyre Mission for September, 1896, and on the first page amongst the baptisms I find the names of " Mungo Park Kalima and Tabitha his wife who have just had a little daughter christened ' Bonnie ' ;" and of " Marcus Aurelius Mbumju." Either let a European Christian name and surname be given straight away, or keep to the child's existing name or to any other native appellation and there is nothing to grate on the ear; but Agnes Tangalanga and Dora Chokabwino, Athanasius Ndodo and Wilfred Pujapuja are incongruous, absurd and distasteful.

sent to the Lovedale Institute in South Africa, and Robert Ntundulima and Joseph Evangel to Scotland; and of the great things which were to be expected from the raising up of a native Pastorate. Then this student will in the later "nineties" visit British Central Africa and it will gradually dawn on him that this disreputable scoundrel, living with and constantly beating four wives, and so often inebriated with native forms of alcohol that he is continually in the police courts, is Simpson Chokabwino; or that this lying "capitao" who is brought before a magistrate charged with defrauding his employer (a coffee planter) by a forged bill is Joseph Evangel. Perhaps Robert Ntundulima may be found to have settled in douce sloth, though still a church goer with one wife, but with all religious enthusiasm dead and an expensive education wasted on market gardening.

At the present moment although missionaries have been at work in British Central Africa since 1875, the numbers of real, sincere, believing, *professing* Christians amongst their native adherents are relatively small. The Universities Mission may count 300, the Church of Scotland 400, and the Free Church Mission 500, because the missionaries themselves are grown far honester than their predecessors of the "forties" and "fifties" and are very careful not to confuse converts with adherents and scholars, therefore in their returns they only give the actual number of baptised and confirmed Christians, but this in no way gauges the real results of their work.[1] Their scholars may be numbered by the thousand though those scholars may not be sufficiently advanced in their religious belief to be baptised; and their adherents—that is to say, all the surrounding natives who more or less follow their advice and are benefited by the example of the mission in striving to live peacefully and decently—number thousands more. Even if the actual religious results of so much labour and expenditure of lives and wealth *seem* inadequate it is consoling to reflect on the immense service which missionary enterprise has rendered to Africa and to the world at large. When the history of the great African states of the future comes to be written, the arrival of the first missionary will with many of these new nations be the first historical event in their annals, allowing for the matter of fact and realistic character of historical analysis in the 21st century. This pioneering propagandist will nevertheless assume somewhat of the character of a Quetzalcoatl—one of those strange half-mythical personalities which figure in the legends of old American empires; the beneficent being who introduced arts and manufactures, implements of husbandry, edible fruits, medical drugs, cereals, domestic animals. To missionaries rather than to traders or government officials many districts of tropical Africa owe the introduction of the orange, lime, and mango, of the cocoanut-palm, the cacao-bean and the pine apple. Improved breeds of poultry and pigeons, many useful vegetables, and beautiful garden flowers have been and are being taken further and further into the poorly-endowed regions of barbarous Africa by these emissaries of Christianity. It is they too who in many cases have first taught the natives carpentry, joinery, masonry, tailoring, cobbling, engineering, book-keeping, printing, and European cookery; to say nothing of reading, writing, arithmetic and a smattering of general

[1] In other parts of Africa, principally British possessions, large numbers of nominal Christians exist, but their religion is discredited by numbering amongst its adherents all the drunkards, liars, rogues, and unclean livers. Among the natives in or near European settlements in one of the oldest of our West African possessions all the unrepentant Magdalenes of the chief city are professing Christians, and I remember when visiting the place referred to in 1888 seeing a black Messalina going to church in pomp, clad in a white silk dress and followed by a train of negro admirers.

knowledge. Almost invariably it has been to missionaries that the natives of Interior Africa have owed their first acquaintance with the printing press, the turning lathe, the mangle, the flat iron, the saw mill, and the brick mould. Industrial teaching is coming more and more into favour, and its immediate results in British Central Africa have been most encouraging. Instead of importing printers, carpenters, store clerks, cooks, telegraphists, gardeners, natural history collectors from England or India, we are gradually becoming able to obtain them amongst the natives of the country, who are trained in the missionaries' schools, and who having been given simple wholesome local education have not had their heads turned, are not above their station in life, and consequently do not prove the disastrous failures I have introduced in my foregoing references to typical individuals sent for their education to South Africa or the United Kingdom. At the Government press at Zomba there is but one European superintendent—all the other printers being mission-trained natives. Most of the telegraph stations are entirely worked by negro telegraph clerks also derived from the missions. As an instance of the intelligence of some of these missionary scholars, I have given at the end of the chapter dealing with the flora of British Central Africa a list and description of the native trees which is a really remarkable essay sent to me in the native tongue by a Blantyre scholar.[1]

Who can say with these facts before them, with the present condition of the natives in South Africa to consider, with the gradual civilisation of Western Africa,[2] that missionary work has been a failure or anything but a success in the Dark Continent?

Is it of no account, do you think, is it productive of no good effect in the present state of Africa, that certain of our fellow-countrymen—or women—possessed of at least an elementary education, and impelled by no greed of gain or unworthy motive—should voluntarily locate themselves in the wild parts of this undeveloped quarter of the globe, and, by the very fact that they live in a European manner, in a house of European style, surrounded by European implements, products, and adornments, should open the eyes of the brutish savages to the existence of a higher state of culture, and prepare them for the approach of civilisation? I am sure my readers will agree with me that it is as the preparer of the white man's advent, as the mediator between the barbarian native and the invading race of rulers, colonists, or traders, that the missionary earns his chief right to our consideration and support. He constitutes himself informally the tribune of the weaker race, and though he may sometimes be open to the charges of indiscretion, exaggeration, and partiality in his support of his dusky-skinned clients' claims, yet without doubt he has rendered real services to humanity in drawing extra-colonial attention to many a cruel abuse of power, and by checking the ruthless proceedings of the unscrupulous pioneers of the white invasion.

Indirectly, and almost unintentionally, missionary enterprise has widely increased the bounds of our knowledge, and has sometimes been the means

---

[1] This essay has been kindly translated for me into English by the Rev. Alexander Hetherwick of the Church of Scotland Mission, but I understand sufficient of Chinyanja, having the original with me, to know that the translation though a smooth one imparts no sense into the text which is not to be found in the original document. To test the intelligence of these scholars of the Blantyre Mission Schools I had offered a small prize for the best essay on this subject. There were many competitors and some of the essays were very good besides that one which I now publish, and which was adjudged to be the best.

[2] Where the Basel missionaries have played much the same part as the British missionaries in Nyasaland in introducing industrial teaching.

of conferring benefits on science, the value and extent of which itself was careless to appreciate and compute. Huge is the debt which philologists owe to the labours of British Missionaries in Africa! By evangelists of our own nationality nearly two hundred African languages and dialects have been illustrated by grammars, dictionaries, vocabularies, and translations of the Bible. Many of these tongues were on the point of extinction, and have since become extinct, and we owe our knowledge of them solely to the missionaries' intervention. Zoology, botany, and anthropology, and most of the other branches of scientific investigation have been enriched by the researches of missionaries, who have enjoyed unequalled opportunites of collecting in new districts; while commerce and colonisation have been so notoriously guided in their extension by the information derived from patriotic emissaries of Christianity that the negro potentate was scarcely unjust when he complained that "first came the missionary, then the merchant, then the Consul, and then the man-of-war." For missionary enterprise in the future I see a great sphere of usefulness—work to be done in the service of civilisation which shall rise superior to the mere inculcation of dogma; work which shall have for its object the careful education and kindly guardianship of struggling, backward peoples; work which, in its lasting effects on men's minds, shall be gratefully remembered by the new races of Africa when the sectarian fervour which prompted it shall long have been forgotten.

CHAPTER VIII.

BOTANY

THAT botany plays a very important part in British Central Africa north of the Zambezi will be plain to the most unobservant traveller. It does not take the first rank in popular interest, as in West Africa, for vegetable growth is less marvellous and fantastic than in the hot rainy countries along the West Coast belt and in the Congo Basin. Zoology, perhaps, has the first claim on the attention of the naturalist in South Central Africa; still botany comes in as a good second; for all this district (as I have incidentally pointed out in a previous chapter) is a kind of secondary development of the forest region; it is

FLOWERS OF THE GARDENIA TREE

on the whole much more clothed with vegetation than is East Africa, North-Central or South Africa.

Flowering plants and trees are either much more abundant or, owing to the less dense vegetation, much more apparent than in West Africa. Perhaps there are not colour displays quite as gorgeous as the evanescent sheets of bloom to be met with in Temperate North or South Africa, but then the show of flowers is not confined to a few weeks in the year, but is pretty constant throughout all the twelve months. Of course there is a marked bursting into bloom at the beginning of yearly rains and again in the benign autumn when the violence of the rainy season is over and yet the soil is still moist.

LISSOCHILUS ORCHIDS

I have not been able to understand (as I have mentioned in a preceding chapter) why certain naturalists have spread abroad the impression that singing birds, sweet smelling flowers and gorgeous displays of bloom are practically confined to the temperate regions and are not characteristic of the Tropics. No doubt these impressions were formed from an exclusive acquaintance with the dense forests of Tropical America and Malaya, where, just as in West Africa, (owing to the preponderating gloomy forest) there is an immense display of foliage varied by no more than an occasional flower or spray of blossoms. And however wonderful the orchids of these regions may be, they rarely grow in sufficient numbers or near enough to the purview of the human eye to constitute a blaze of colour. But no one who has kept his eyes open in the drier regions of Central Africa can refuse to acknowledge that the flower displays are marked and very gorgeous, especially in that part of the country which lies a thousand feet and more above sea level. In the swamps and on the low-lying land it is possible to pass through the country seeing little sign of any flowers during certain months of the year; though here, again, the traveller, to be consistent in his declaration that he has seen no flowers, must be very careful not to look too closely into the details of the landscape or he will falsify his own statement; for in the marshes there are blue or white water-lilies; amongst the high reeds on the forested banks of the rivers trailing convolvuluses seem to be always in bloom. The white plumes of the reeds and the efflorescence of many rushes are often beautiful and form a pleasant feature of the landscape.

But if these low-lying lands are visited in the spring-time the display of flowers is quite as gorgeous as elsewhere. The acacia trees are loaded with small orange-coloured blossoms; a creeper (which sometimes grows independently as a bush) has all along the under part of the stalk a continuous mass of small crimson petalless flowers. When these are fully out and the branches are twined round some smaller tree or trailing on the ground they are like great wreaths of crimson. A strange leafless shrub which resembles a miniature baobab tree, has large blossoms that are rose-coloured and white; every moist glade teems with Crinum lilies of the purest white, or else white with a line of pink (the scent of their flowers being almost intoxicating when in close proximity); the india-rubber vines have sweet-scented, chaste white blossoms; there are shrubs

AN ANGRÆCUM ORCHIS

allied to the jasmine with flowers like those of that plant; the *Pterocarpus* trees for one fortnight in the spring are loaded with immense masses of yellow laburnum-like blossom. Other papilionaceous trees of the genus *Lonchocarpus* flower profusely and resemble the *Wistaria* in colour and appearance; the *Gardenia* tree has, as the reader will see by the illustration, large handsome white flowers which in the centre are touched with pink and orange; then there are the various species of *Erythrina*. One of these, at least, has blossoms so gorgeous that I should like to get it introduced into cultivation. The tree belongs to the bean family; the flowers which grow in large clusters are vivid crimson-scarlet. It usually has but few leaves on it when it bursts into bloom. Suddenly meeting with it in the jungle—great crimson splodges radiating from the gnarled grey trunk—you rub your eyes thinking that it must be some optical delusion. Then there is a mighty tree of the genus *Spathodea* (probably *S. campanulata*). Its flowers again are crimson-scarlet with a curious velvet hood of even deeper and richer crimson; and there is the *Bombax*, whose flowers also are vivid scarlet-crimson with a mass of dull-black anthers and a calyx of yellow-green. Both *Spathodea* and *Bombax* are trees of great height and stateliness. The *Bombax* is the more effective object because the leaves are not much out when the flowers burst forth; and the spectacle is such that if Linnæus gave way to tears before a field of gorse, one wonders what he would have done in full view of a mighty *Bombax* with its branches hung with pendant crimson flowers, like innumerable red lamps. Even the baobab's flowers, though they tarnish quickly, are beautiful for a brief space, while they retain the creamy white of their petals and the pale gold dazzle of their multitudinous stamens.

There are many beans of the genus *Tephrosia*, growing as creepers or erect shrubs with flowers usually a rich purple, but in one species (*Tephrosia Vogelii*) with the corolla snow-white and the calyx, stalks, and ovaries the deepest purple. Other bean flowers (*Crotalaria* and *Eriosema*) are yellow. There are Hibiscuses, with huge flowers of lemon-yellow crimson-centred; others of pure white, others of pale pink.

There are shrubs of the genus *Copaifera* whose flowers have large, crinkly petals of pure white streaked with rose, and a powerful aromatic scent; and straggling cucurbits with cold-white blossoms and gaudy-coloured gourds. The *Cnestis* shrub exhibits big seed-vessels, several in a clump, covered with orange or scarlet velvet, through the valves of which the black-headed beans protrude. Ground orchids, chiefly of the genus *Lissochilus*, grow amid the grass with columns of red, mauve, or sulphur-yellow flowers. Epiphytic orchids are not so common, and are only found in clumps of dense forest, where they are chiefly represented by the genera *Ansellia* and *Angræcum*.

Everywhere in moist places straggles the *Commelina* with its blooms of cobalt-blue, yellow, or white—flowers that wither before the noonday sun, but are lovely in the morning hours.

This enumeration is wearisome to the eye from the constant

THE ANSELLIA OR "TIGER" ORCHIS

citing of Latin names; but I wish to substantiate my statements regarding the beauty of the flora by enabling the reader to identify the objects of my admiration. He should derive from this list the just impression that throughout at least six months in the year even the low-lying plains of Central Africa are bright in colour with flowers and fruits; but if this is the case with the lowlands what adjectives can be employed to adequately picture the flora of the highlands? One sweeping statement must be made that during spring-time they are gorgeous with their flower displays—gorgeous with lakes of azure-blue and mauve, stretches of pinkish-white, mounds of rose-tint, columns of purple, sheets of ultramarine, circles of orange, constellations of pure white, stains of blood-red, billows of yellow. Anything more beautiful than these wild flower gardens in the country which lies between 1000 and 4000 feet in altitude I have never seen. And as I have already remarked, although in its full effulgence during the spring months (October, November, December) and in the autumn revival (April, May, June), yet the flower display in the uplands maintains itself throughout the whole year. Why should I weary the reader further by Homeric lists of scientific names? All these can be found in the Appendix; and those inclined to doubt or minimise my statements may look up the various genera and species in the Gardens and at the Herbarium at Kew, and (taking for granted the truth of my statements that the flowering plants frequently grow in masses which contribute great effects of unbroken colour) may even without a visit to British Central Africa become once for all convinced that whatever may be the case with the gloomy forests of the Amazon or Malay Archipelago, the open, reasonably-rained-on parts of Tropical Africa are as splendidly endowed with flower shows as with singing birds. Up in the high mountains this is still more marked. Here an emotional person would faint away before the rocks hung with blue lobelias, and the clumps of smalt and cobalt *Disa* Orchids.[1]

A RED LILY

GROWING IN ALL THE STREAM VALLEYS IN THE SHIRE HIGHLANDS

There is a tree lily (*Vellozia splendens*) which in the spring-time bears from its gouty stems (ordinarily finished by a tuft of grass-like leaves) sprays of creamy-white blooms, so beautiful that even the botanists of Kew were touched, and called it "splendens."[2]

[1] Perhaps the loveliest ground orchid in the world—*Disa hamatopetala*. This is well figured from our specimens in the *Transactions of the Linnæan Society* for May, 1894.

[2] Botany should be dealt with by a class of sylphs; instead of which its priests are often old and unenthusiastic men. Plod through page after page of botanical description, and where do you find any hint as a rule of the matchless beauty they should be describing? Little if any mention is made of the colour of the "corolla" (as it is correct to call the showy part of the flower), but what the botanist likes to note with so much satisfaction is that the plant is either glabrous or scabrous, that it is possibly caulescent

OIL PALMS, NEAR THE SONGWE RIVER, NORTH NYASA

Then there are the numerous *Coreopses* (relations of the Sunflower)—golden-yellow, creamy-white, and blood-red; pinkish-white anemones; purple iris (*Aristea*); rosy-tinted, salmon-tinted, apricot-tinted gladioli, or even a gladiolus with huge blossoms of a pale buff colour like *café-au-lait*. There is a great range in the colour of these gladioli. One has a flower of purplish-green. The *Hypericum* shrub, like the St. John's wort in England, has large pale yellow blossoms. In the stream valleys there are balsams of pink-mauve; by the water side at the greatest altitudes is the blue *Cynoglossum*, and there are silver and gold Helichrysums. And yet I have only signalised by name a twentieth part of the flowering plants of these high mountains in Central Africa.

A RAPHIA PALM

and that the outer whorl is covered with black emergences. He likes the perianth cup to be short and fleshy and prefers the anthers to be sessile. Not a single exclamation of praise or prayer at the flower displayed. Of course he is right: science must be unemotional. A good drawing of this *Vellozia* is given in the *Transactions of the Linnæan Society* for May, 1894.

BOTANY

So much for beauty of colour; now for the beauty of outline. There are five species of palm abundantly represented in British Central Africa: the Borassus, the Hyphæne, the Wild date, the Raphia, and the Oil palm.[1] The cocoanut palm grows at one or two places on the Shire River and on Lake Nyasa, but it is an introduction from the East Coast. The most graceful of

RAPHIA PALM FRUITING

[1] The oil palm, either the *Elais guineënsis* of West Africa or a nearly-allied species grows in North-West Nyasaland. It is found chiefly in the very fertile plain lying between the Nkonde mountains and the Lake shore; also in the well-watered hill country of the Atonga. So far as I am aware it is not found further south than the latitude of Bandawe—about the middle of Lake Nyasa—nor does it seem to reach any part of the east coast of that lake. It may be reported eventually from the Chambezi River which flows down the Nyasa-Tanganyika plateau and becomes the Upper Congo, but it has not been recorded up to the present. Therefore, after quitting Lake Nyasa and ascending to the Nyasa-Tanganyika plateau one does not encounter the oil palm again until the south shore of Tanganyika is reached. Here there are a few examples but it is not abundant. On the Upper Luapula, however, Mr. Sharpe found it growing in considerable numbers and apparently identical with the West Coast species; but this may be the result of direct introduction by the Alunda—a West African people who make considerable use of its oil for food. Mr. Whyte and myself have done our best to introduce the oil palm into South Nyasaland and the nuts planted in the Zomba Botanical Gardens have already grown to the height of a couple of feet. Even if there was no idea of exporting the palm oil and thus competing with West Africa it would be extremely useful locally for cooking purposes. The illustration I give here is done from a photograph taken of a clump of oil palms at the north end of Lake Nyasa.

these palms is the Raphia, a species as yet unnamed. The trunk or stem seldom reaches to any great height above the ground; it has enormously long fronds which rise into the air and give the idea of height. The foliage of these fronds is a glaucous green, but the midrib in the living frond is bright orange.

BORASSUS PALMS

The seeds are much like the cones of certain conifers. They are covered with glossy brown scales and are extremely hard, taking a whole year to germinate in the ground. This palm would no doubt produce a wine-like sap, as is the case with its near congener the *Raphia vinifera;* but I have not heard of the natives using it for this purpose in Central Africa. The midribs of its enormous fronds are of greatest service to man, being very light, easily straightened, somewhat uniform in girth and very strong. The Raphia midribs at once constitute a light and effective ladder 20 feet long by small rungs being inserted in the holes made on the leaf-bearing surface of the midrib. This palm also in the same manner furnishes rafters for houses. The destruction of it at the hands of the natives has been somewhat wanton, and we have taken measures in the more settled districts to protect the Raphia, besides gathering the seeds and replanting them extensively.

The *Borassus flabellifer* grows to a great height. Its fronds curl into a semicircle and make the familiar palm fan of the East. The fruit is large—as big as a child's head—and the husk is a pale yellowish-green when ripe. I believe the kernel to be of little use The trunk of the palm is very good for certain purposes in building.

The Central African Hyphæne is so similar in appearance to the Borassus that the one is often mistaken for the other by the passing traveller. They are distinguished chiefly by the difference in their fruit. The fruit of the Borassus I have already described. That of the Hyphæne is much smaller—the size of a large egg-shaped Java orange. Its covering is a rich chestnut-brown and has a sweetish taste, like gingerbread. The kernel of the nut is white and extremely hard and can be used as a sort of vegetable ivory. Innumerable things are made of the tough and lissom fronds, and the trunk of this palm can be made very useful in building as it is easily split with wedges into board-like segments. It takes a beautiful polish, having a very handsome grain.

WILD DATE PALMS

A REED BRAKE (*Phragmites communis*)

BOTANY

I have not observed in British Central Africa the curious swelling of the stem either of the Borassus or Hyphæne which is so noticeable in other parts of Africa, such as the East Coast or the Congo Basin.

A wild date grows either on high mountain slopes which are well watered or on the banks of large rivers or the shores of a lake. It is a handsome palm; though occasionally when growing to a great height the stem becomes spindly and has a tendency to curve and lean. The fronds are extremely green and never have that glaucous tint so characteristic of the date palm. The fruit when ripe is just eatable. It looks and tastes like a very poor form of date.

The cocoanut palm should do well in the vicinity of all our lakes and rivers judging by the examples already growing at Kotakota and on the Central Shire. The fruit produced at Kotakota is excellent.

Handsome Cycads grow on the lower slopes of Mount Mlanje. I have not observed them elsewhere. Wild bananas (*Musa ensete*) grow on the hillsides. They are really beautiful objects; the trunk is much thicker and the foliage more statuesque and ample than in the cultivated species. They would be familiar objects to Londoners, as allied forms are planted in the London parks during the summer.

Although it forms an abominable growth to force one's way through on account of the stiff spear-blades, the *Phragmites* reed[1] can be an object of great beauty with its enormous flower-plumes of grey-white. But the leaves though not exactly rigid are stiff and have a sharply-pointed termination, and these points pierce the skin if abruptly encountered. There are innumerable other grasses, handsome in the outline of their growth and beautiful in their flowering. One small, low grass in the height of the rainy season spreads the ground with a fleecy carpet of pale mauve, its abundant inflorescence being of

[1] *P. communis.*

PLUMES AND YOUNG SHOOT OF PHRAGMITES

that tint. Still the grass of Central Africa is one of its great plagues. Between the months of November and February there grows up a monstrous herbage under the influence of the sun and rain. The grass stems will sometimes reach eight feet in height. Not only do many of their leaves cut like razors or stab like spears but in the autumn months of April and May their seeds ripen and in some cases seek distribution by methods painful to the human animal. There is one especially—a species of *Stipa*, whose seeds I here illustrate. As you pass along a native path which is almost invisible (for grass growing on either side leaves nothing but an obscure narrow tunnel), the seeds of this *Stipa* easily detach themselves and descend with a spiral flight on to your person, the slight impetus of their fall carrying the sharp barbed point of the seed right into the clothing; here the movement of the body acting on the barbs of the seed works it farther and farther in, so that it eventually reaches and scratches the skin. There are cases reported of this *Stipa* where the seed has actually penetrated the skin of certain animals. At one time the idea was mooted that the seed germinated thus in the flesh, but this is not true. It is a mere accident that the barbed

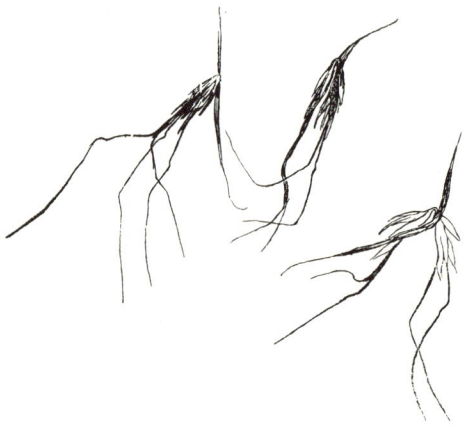

BARBED SEEDS OF STIPA

PAPYRUS

A LARGE DUCKWEED
FOUND ON ALL STAGNANT WATER IN TROPICAL AFRICA (*Pistia stratiotes*)

grain happens to alight on an animal. What it intends to do is to pitch, point first, on the ground, which is hardened by the dry weather, and pierce its way through the soil by the same means that will enable it to pass through a coat of thick texture. The feathery plume attached to the seed acts as a kind of float to carry it through the air perpendicularly towards the ground.

There is no lawn grass indigenous to Central Africa, but the Dūb grass of Ceylon has been introduced by Mr. Whyte and the late Mr. John Buchanan,

AN ALBIZZIA TREE

and has thriven wonderfully. With this we can get excellent lawns and very superior fodder for horses and cattle.

Among rushes there is the king of them, the papyrus. I have referred once or twice before in this book to its great beauty, and will not weary my readers by the repetition of my descriptions. The pith of the papyrus which was used by the Egyptians as a material on which to write, and which has given its name to "paper," appears to possess a sugary or starchy quality, so that when the flattened strips of rolled-out pith are moistened the edge of one can be laid on the edge of the other, and will adhere to it; and this, I believe, is the way sheets of paper were made. Why it should not once more be brought into use as a paper-making material I do not know.

Amongst the graceful types of vegetation mention must not be omitted of the tree ferns on the mountains and the many beautiful ferns to be found in moist places. The Osmunda grows luxuriantly in the stream valleys, and there are many varieties of maiden-hair. The dear familiar bracken appears directly an altitude of 3000 feet is reached, and flourishes thence up to 6000 feet; in company with it grows the blackberry bramble, and the two together gladden the exile's heart like emissaries from home.

There are many noble forest trees to be signalised for their beauty of outline and foliage.

There are the Parinariums, which tower up a hundred feet into the air; the velvet-foliaged *Albizzia;* the Ebony (*Diospyros*); the Khaya (*K. senegalensis*); the *Pterocarpus*, with its glorious fortnight of efflorescence, when the whole tree is a mass of large yellow flowers, and exhales an intoxicating odour of honey, attracting thereby thousands of bees; and glossy-leaved fig trees of the genus *Ficus*.[1] These handsome forest trees, however, are generally restricted to the banks of rivers or the shores of lakes, or else to moist mountain slopes. The bulk of the country is covered by a forest of thin and poor type—chiefly Trachylobiums and Copaiferas, Hymenocardias, Anonas and Misuko (*Uapaca kirkiana*), besides certain vines of large size growing in the habit of a shrub, and acacias which are of various forms and very little foliage. Some of these acacia trees are more clothed when they grow near water, and the scent of their flowers is delightful; but in the form of bushes they are intolerable. Were it not that the uniform pale green of the trunks and branches of the better developed acacias and their feathery light-green foliage and orange-coloured flowerets class them as beautiful, I should have been inclined to put them in the division of the vicious.

THE MUCUNA BEAN

There is malicious vegetation in Africa. There is a small plant—a kind of asafœtida—which gives forth the most noxious smell of bad drains when it is trampled on. There are various kinds of arums that give out a sickening odour; an euphorbia which, when broken, spurts out a poisonous milk, one

---

[1] These are especially beautiful at the north end of Lake Nyasa where they are grown by the natives for the sake of the shade they give. Their branches have long brown rootlets which gradually reach to the ground where they make independent growth, as is done by the Banyan tree in India.

drop of which in the eye will bring about severe inflammation; very thorny mimosas (sensitive plant); and a horrid little vine[1] growing on all cultivated ground, and springing up from underground tubers which are very difficult to extirpate. An atrocious pest, the "Spanish needle," has reached this country. It is found all round the world now in the cultivated regions of the Tropics. The flower is a poor irregular composite, like a lanky daisy, with white petals and yellow centre, and seeds that develop at one end a number of tiny hooks, so that passing through a field where this weed grows one's trousers bristle with innumerable brown seeds, clinging tightly to the cloth. A still greater pest is the *Mucuna*[2] bean, of which I give an illustration. It is a creeper that grows over bushes and trees. The seed pods are covered with tiny silky hairs of a reddish-brown. These, if touched by the skin, cause a most extraordinary, most extravagant irritation—a sort of nettle rash. The skin is covered with large white weals and the irritation and heat are so bad that nothing but stripping and rubbing oneself with a cooling lotion afford relief. This cow itch is of very subtle dispersal. Clothes which have been washed are laid out to dry on bushes, and attract a few of the hairs off the seed pods of the *Mucuna*. To all appearance they might have nothing on them to attract attention, but they are no sooner worn next the skin than a sensation as of innumerable fleas attacking one begins to be felt until at last the irritation is unendurable. The cow itch is a thing which particularly affects old clearings and abandoned plantations, and therefore grows frequently by the roadside in Central Africa where the path traverses districts that have been inhabited.

BAOBAB TREE

A *Smilax* yam is a noxious thing, as it twines round the shrubs and plants and throttles them; moreover the under side of the stalks are armed with sharp thorns which tear the skin when one is forcing a way through the bush. A lily, supposed to be the species which for inadequate reasons was named by Linnæus *Gloriosa superba*, is very poisonous to cattle or horses. But for this reputation (which is not absolutely proved) it is a pretty thing; the flowers develop, as they expand, from yellow-green to brownish-crimson and the terminations of the leaves are prolonged into fantastic tendrils.

The grotesque in vegetation is well represented. Look at the Baobab tree without its leaves! Is it not as though nature had perpetrated a loathsome jest? Its enormous bulk (they have been measured 80 feet in girth) which

[1] This *Vitis serpens*, as it is called, clambers over and throttles plant after plant. At the same time when it has reached a fence and spread itself out with its pretty red-currant-like grapes it is very decorative.   [2] *Chiteze* of many parts of Nyasaland.

after all is nothing but soft, fibrous, pithy wood inside the hard rind; its gouty limbs springing from the massive trunk and so inadequately fulfilling the promise of majesty; and the leprous look of the whole object with its smooth, shiny, dirty-pink bark make up a total that is wholly grotesque. The leaves only remain on this tree for about five months, and even then they are so thinly scattered as to give no shade. The flowers are handsome as they open, but soon tarnish and turn brown, as though the whole tree were permeated with a sickly taint. The seed vessels, shaped like huge bean-pods, hang perpendicularly from the branches by string-like stalks and are covered with a thin grey plush. Broken open they will be found to contain a white pith, yielding a pleasant acid taste, which can be made into a drink faintly resembling lemonade.

Another grotesque thing is the *Euphorbia*, which grows in the plains—a cube-like stem with a few flat segments branching off it; or the Candelabra Euphorbia found in the low country and on the harsher uplands. The species of this Euphorbia which grows in the hills does not reach the same size as the monster of the plains. It looks, with the blood-red aloes growing in the same locality, a fit vegetation to surround the entrance to a witches' cavern. The subsidiary branches are like innumerable scorpion tails, as though a congeries of immense scorpions were collected in a knot with their tails in the air.

THE EUPHORBIA OF THE PLAINS

There are many other Euphorbias not already instanced which are distinctly quaint, though their absurdity has a dash of the saturnine. Their determination to grow absolutely green flowers, when nearly every other plant goes in for colour, shows a trait of originality.

The Aloe when it is in blossom and throws up its spike of coral coloured tubes, can be almost pretty; otherwise without flowers it is grotesque as it sprawls over the ground and its thick-spotted red and green leaves with sharp serrated edges and long whip-like terminations writhe in ascending whorls from the crouching woody stem.

The *Kniphofia* (the "red-hot poker" of our gardens) is on the borderland between the grotesque and the beautiful. When its flower spike is in full bearing and the many

CANDELABRA EUPHORBIAS

little tube-like flowers are scarlet, lightening into yellow, it offers a fine body of colour; but without the bloom the plant with its limp attenuated leaves (green and spotted with white, having much of the aloe's fleshiness without its pompous stiffness) looks like some monstrous caricature of a lily made in a madman's world. The *Protea* has tried to be beautiful but it merely succeeds in being strange, with its immense saucer-shaped flowers like gigantic daisies. These soon wither and yet remain on the bush, hideous black objects, for many months afterwards. The Protea shrub is only fit to look at during one month in the year.

The many creepers of the forests develop huge lianas. These are chiefly characteristic of the various rubber-vines of the genus *Landolphia*.

The *Sansevieria* plants should be classed amongst the grotesque if they did not lead us by a natural transition to the useful. They are absurd things, just segments of crude vegetation which might be stalks, but which are, I suppose, leaves that come up out of the ground anyhow. One triangular leaf may be standing alone, although there may be a Stonehenge clump of four or five others growing stiffly together and yet having as little connection with each other as possible. It is very rare to see these things in flower. When they do flower the blossom comes out at the side of the leaf, which makes you think that the leaf after all is a stalk. Ordinarily they look as though they had forgotten where they came from and what they were doing, and whether they should or should not have leaves or stalks or flowers. They are fleshy, but with limp leathery edges, and they produce excellent fibre. A company has been started for the cultivation of the *Sansevieria*, which grows in dry, stony ground; but unfortunately at the present time the price of fibre is so low that the export of the *Sansevieria* will not yield large profits.

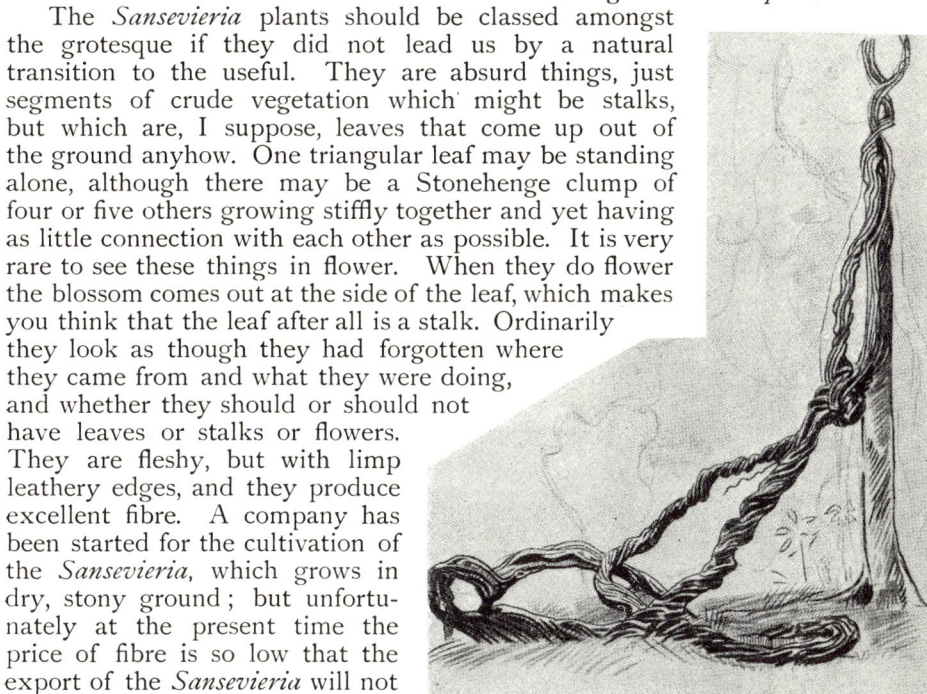

A LANDOLPHIA LIANA

Fibre is also obtained from the Aloes, Baobab and the arboreal *Hibiscus*; the extraordinary *Kigelia* tree (whose seed pods are sometimes nearly as thick as a man's thigh and like a huge pendant sausage in shape) contains in its seed pods a fibrous material like the Egyptian Lufah which can be used for rubbing the skin after a bath, and might be utilised for many other purposes. The natives take the seeds of these *Kigelia* pods and roast and eat them in times of scarcity. A species of hemp, probably introduced, grows wild all over British Central Africa. It is smoked by the natives, as I have already stated. This hemp might also be got to yield a fibre, and some of the palms would do the same.

Oils are produced by the *Sesamum* (a handsome flowering plant with large mauve-pink blossoms), by several species of *Vitex*, by the Castor oil plant (*Ricinus*) (which grows in extravagant abundance in and near to the native settlements), by the Oil palm found in North-West Nyasaland, by the ground nuts (Arachis and Voandzeia, which are almost indigenous); and by other seeds and nuts not yet identified.

For timber there are the African teak (*Oldfieldia*); the *Khaya*; the

Grewia (often twelve feet in circumference with black hard wood in the middle through which no insect can penetrate); various species of *Vitex*; the *Parinarium*; the *Afzelia* (whose bark is often made into boxes); the Ebony (*Diospyros*); the Ironwood (*Copaifera*); the Msuko (*Uapaca kirkiana*); and the Mlanje Cedar (*Widdringtonia whytei*).

SANSEVIERIA FIBRE PLANT

Drugs are obtained from the *Strophanthus* creeper[1] (used for poisoning arrows and killing fish, valuable in affections of the heart); from the *Erythrophlœum* (the bark of which produces a violent emetic or poison known as *Muavi*); from the roots of certain nettles (which furnish purgatives); from the seeds of the Crotons, the Castor oil plant, certain beans, euphorbias, and innumerable

[1] The *Strophanthus* may be recognised by the extraordinary position of its two seed pods which grow exactly at the end of the stalk and opposite to each other so that they look like one large pod placed at right angles to the end of the stalk.

roots, leaves, flowers, seeds and barks not as yet identified and named. Many of these like the *Strophanthus* may prove valuable additions to our Pharmacopœia.

The natives eat the fruit of the Amomum. The flower of this plant appears a short distance above the ground in the spring months. One species is a lovely purple-red, another a pink-mauve, a third crocus-yellow, and a fourth

GROWTH OF BRANCHES; FOLIAGE; AND CONES OF THE MLANJE CEDAR
(*Widdringtonia whytei*)

white. They look at a distance like exaggerated crocuses. Preceding the florescence of the yellow species, large flat, yellow leaves appear, and spread over the surface of the soil; but in the case of the purple Amomums the flower goes before the leaf, and the tall foliage which then follows is somewhat like a dwarf banana, to which genus the Amomums are distantly related. Their seed vessels are bright red, and are divided into sections, each with a black seed. The pulp surrounding them is pleasantly acid and is chewed by the natives. The seeds of one Amomum are very aromatic, and form the "Mala-guetta" pepper from West Africa—of which our ancestors were so fond, that it proved in the beginning of our trade with the Dark Continent, a more powerful motive for sending ships to West Africa than the obtaining of slaves or gold.

The fruits of the Msuko (*Uapaca*), the Parinarium, the Tamarind (a very common tree in the lowlands), the Sycomore fig, certain species of *Strychnos*,

YOUNG MLANJE CEDAR

the *Anona* or Custard Apple, and the various kinds of *Landolphia* are much eaten by the natives. With the exception of the Tamarind, they offer little attraction to the European.

Many trees have a sweet or an edible gum, but I have not been able to identify the species. From the fact that a *Trachylobium* is found there may be gum copal, but I cannot say that any has been brought to light as yet. Rubber is obtained from two or more species of *Landolphia*, also from *Ficus*, and from the handsome tree or shrub *Tabernæmontana*.

APPENDIX I.

The following essay on the "Useful Trees of British Central Africa" is the prize essay among several sent in from the native scholars of the Blantyre Mission Schools (Church of Scotland) to compete for a prize I offered for the best description in the Ci-nyanja language of the Useful Trees of the Protectorate.

The essay here given was written in Ci-nyanja by Harry Kambwiri, one of the native scholars of the Mission, and has been kindly translated for me into English by the Rev. Alexander Hetherwick, M.A., of the Church of Scotland Mission.—H. H. J.

AN ESSAY ON
THE USEFUL TREES OF BRITISH CENTRAL AFRICA

By HARRY KAMBWIRI

Chirama grows near marshy ground, or in the middle of the marsh itself. It is of smooth bark, in parts scaly: It bears a fruit which is used as medicine for pleuritic or neuralgic pains in the chest. The fruit is plucked, then roasted by the fire, and applied to the painful spot, for the relief of the pain.

Chandimbo[1] grows on any kind of sandy soil. It has an edible fruit, black in colour. On removing the outer rind it is found exceedingly pleasant, or on simply chewing in the mouth it resembles a sweetmeat. The wood of it is used for making pestles, spoons, pillows and drums. It is apt to crack. The tree is not a pretty one; it has a large number of branches; the wood is not hard; it is useless as a firewood; cuttings planted out grow well, and are employed as fencing poles.

Msuko[2] grows on sandy soil, and nowhere close to water. Its fruit reaches maturity in October, and is edible in November and December. When the fruit is ripe it falls of itself, and is picked up as an edible fruit exceedingly good. In famine seasons people squeeze the fruit into a dish, mash it up, and eat it.

The wood of it is used for boards, which are good for tables, chairs, desks, etc., etc. The boards are red in colour, but are apt to crack. If left, however, till thoroughly dry it does not crack.

It is used by women as firewood for burning pots, plates, etc., but it leaves a very abundant ash.

It is employed in medicine. Pieces are chipped off and steeped. The water is then drunk. It has an astringent taste.

It is not a deep rooter—only the tap root goes down any distance.

It is good for charcoal making; also is used for couples, etc., in house-building, as it cannot be bored by wood insects. If the seeds are planted they grow into a tree, but very slowly.

Mpindimbi[3] grows on sandy soil near water. The fruit is edible, but bad smelling, and is usually only eaten by animals. The timber is white, and is easily made into boards. If cut green the wood cracks, but not if cut dry. It is made into spoons, mortars, pillows, etc. One species, called *chipindimbi*, is used in medicine. If a child is feverish its leaves are taken and pounded and mixed with water, in which the child is then bathed.

---

[1] *Erythrina tomentosa* (?).—H. H. J.   [2] *Uapaca kirkiana.*—H. H. J.   [3] *Vitex* sp.—H. H. J.

Mnyonyeve[1] grows in flat, open, damp soil, or near water. Its fruit, when ripe, is black, and is edible. I think the Europeans might employ it after pounding in the manufacture of ink. Its wood is used in furniture-making.

Mpingo[2] is a good wood, used in making the masts of dhows. With the inner wood natives make canes, knife-handles, etc. It grows near streams, and is always seen on the banks of big rivers. Long ago people employed this wood in making arrow-heads, as it is exceedingly hard.

Mkundanguluwe grows on sandy soil. Is used in making knobkerries, tobacco pipes. It takes on a good polish.

Mpinjipinji is a choice fruit tree. It is propagated from cuttings, and takes five years before reaching maturity.

Masau grows anywhere on high ground. The surface of the tree is covered with small prickles. It has short, small leaves and a small fruit. When ripe the fruit is red. It is then plucked or picked off the ground where it may have fallen. It is boiled in a pot into which a gun-barrel has been inserted. The pot is covered up, and a fire is kindled beneath it. Water is poured on the gun-barrel, and the distilled liquid is caught in a bottle as *Kachaso* (spirits).

Mkakatuku grows on sandy soil. It is a very hard wood, hence its name. The wood is good at the heart of the stem. People scrape off the bark, steep it, and drink the liquid.

Mkwesu grows near the river or lake on small ant hills. The wood is very hard. The fruit is long and finger-like. The wood is good for making boards for furniture, etc.

Mtundula grows near a stream. Its fruit is edible and sweet. The bark is used for dyeing cloth of a red colour, like Turkey-red calico. The wood can be made into boards.

Muungutwa—a large tree growing in the long grass near a stream. It produces a red fruit inedible save by elephants. The wood is used for making mortars, and also for canoes.

Chitasya is a hard wood that does not, however, grow to any size. It grows on sandy soil. The wood is used in making head-rests (pillows) and lip ornaments for women.

Mkuyu[3] grows either near a stream or on high ground. If the stem is cut it exudes a white sap which is used in smearing arrows, so as to harden them. The fruit is called *nguyu*, and is edible. In seasons of famine the fruit is plucked when still green, and pounded and eaten as a porridge with fowl as relish. If picked up hard and dry the fruit is mashed up and cooked. The bark of the tree gives good bark-rope. It affords good shade. The fruit is eaten by the birds. There is another species of fig called *mpumbe*, with a larger fruit. If many of the fruit are eaten they are apt to cause sore throat.

Mbawa[4] grows near a stream or in dense clumps of forest. It is a large tree. The fruit is not edible, but the seeds of it are roasted, pounded, and used in dyeing or softening bark-cloth. The bark of the tree is thick. The wood is used in canoe-making. The Europeans make excellent boards of it, as it does not crack, which they make into articles of furniture. The natives use it as a medicine for the stomach. They chip off pieces of bark and steep them in a dish, and drink the water.

Mngwenye is a special large-sized tree, which grows near streams. Chips of the bark are used as medicine for the stomach. They are steeped in water, and the water is drunk. The leaves are long and narrow. The fruit is small and inedible. The wood makes excellent boards, of a light colour, which crack only to a small extent. The wood is very hard, and is used for making furniture. It is also used in canoe-making.

---

[1] *Nuxia congesta.*—H. H. J.   [2] Ebony—*Diospyros* sp.—H. H. J.
[3] *Ficus sycomorus.*—H. H. J.   [4] *Khaya senegalensis.*—H. H. J.

Msumbuti grows anywhere on sandy soil. Its bark is used in making bark-cloth, and also bark-rope. When dry the timber makes good firewood.

Napiri[1] grows on flat, open, wet plains, also on higher ground. The natives use the wood in making pestles for pounding grain, as it is hard and heavy. It makes good firewood.

Mlombwa grows anywhere on sandy soil or on the hills. By partially burning it makes good charcoal. The sap is red and is sticky to the touch. The natives make mortars, drums, spoons, pestles, etc. It makes beautiful boards. The bark is used as medicine for nettlerash. The fruit is used in pleuritic pains of the chest. It is roasted, and the ash is punctured into the painful spot.

Nkomwa grows near a stream. It is used in making drums, pestles, spoons, pillows. It is a very light wood, and makes good boards. The leaves are small, and the bark is thin.

Mjombo[2] grows near streams or on sandy soil. The fruit is eaten by baboons. Natives make bark-cloth and strong bark-rope.

Mkalate grows on sandy soil, especially near the foot of hills. It is used in making wall posts for houses, and roofing.

Balisa grows on high ground. It makes into good boards. The wood of it is very hard. The natives here make good pestles of it.

Nkako grows near streams or in clumps of forest trees. Natives make head-rests of it, and wooden arrow-heads for shooting small birds. The wood is good and hard.

Mlendimilo grows on high ground or on hills. It blossoms into flowers on the approach of the rainy season. Natives use the wood for making drums, which are strong and give out plenty of sound. Chips of the bark are used in medicine.

Mbanga grows on high ground. It is an exceedingly hard wood. The leaves are used as medicine in headache. They are pounded or steeped in a pot or basin, and the face is washed with the water. Sometimes simply the smell of the leaves is sufficient. It makes an excellent medicine, and effects a cure after repeated applications. When dry the wood makes good firewood which leaves no ash.

Mlambe,[3] the largest tree in this country, grows near water. It produces a fruit called malambe, the inside of which is white and is eaten thus:—the inside is scooped out, mixed with water, and eaten. Large strips of the wood are taken and beaten, so as to form a fibre from which cord is made. The tree produces very few leaves.

Mkongomwa is a good tree for shade. It grows near the River Shire, and also in the Mangoni country.

Ngosa grows on flat plains near rivers. The wood on being cut is very soft. The bark is used in making cord for weaving nets or sewing sleeping mats. The fruit is roasted and mixed with tobacco snuff as a flavouring.

Mlundo grows anywhere on sandy soil. The leaves are small; the wood is hard: the fruit is inedible. It is used as medicine for the stomach by steeping the bark and drinking the water, or by twisting it into a cord and wearing the cord tied round the waist.

Chikujumbu grows on sandy soil or near a stream. The bark is covered with small scales. One is growing in the Square at Blantyre Mission. The wood is used for making mortars, pestles, spoons and pillows.

Chumbu is used as stomach medicine. The bark is chipped off and steeped, and the water is drunk. It is also used in treating boils. The boil is opened with a sharp point made of this wood which prevents it recurring again. The tree grows on sandy soil near ant-hills. It is a very soft wood.

---

[1] *Copaifera* sp., allied to the Mopane or "ironwood" tree of Livingstone.—H. H. J.
[2] *Brachystegia longifolia.*—H. H. J.   [3] The Baobab—*Adansonia digitata.*—H. H. J.

Mtawa grows on any kind of soil. The wood is not hard. When dry it is not heavy, but when green, natives make good bark-cloth of it, and rope.

Msopa is used in medicine, and also to make bows. It makes good boards. Chips of it are steeped in the water where bark-cloth is steeped, so as to dye it black. The wood is hard to cut and cracks. It grows close to streams or in damp, marshy spots.

Mkwale grows on plains, as on the bank of the Tuchila. It is used for making spoons, pestles, and lip-rings worn by native women. It is very white, and does not crack.

Msolo grows on sandy soil, and makes good boards. Natives cut it into pestles, pipes, and spoons. It will not make mortars because it is too hard. The fruit is eaten by game such as bushbuck, etc.

Msechela grows on sandy soil near a hill. It is very like the *msuku* tree, but has smaller leaves. It makes as good boards as the msuku tree. The fruit is small and edible.

Mchenje grows on plains near ant-hills. The bark is rough and the leaves are small. It is used in medicine by steeping chips of it in water, and drinking the water. It is used as medicine for game-traps. The fruit is pounded and placed in the traps. In seasons of famine it is eaten as a food.

Nkungunyanjila grows anywhere near the river. Its fruit is not eatable. The wood makes good boards. It is used as medicine for sores, by steeping chips of the wood in water, and washing over the wound by means of a feather.

Chiwimbi grows near streams. The stem is light in colour. The leaves are long and narrow. The natives make the wood into pestles, spoons, mortars, etc. It makes good boards of a white colour. It is also used in making drums, and as stomach medicine in fever.

Mkwakwa produces a nice fruit. It grows on hills in dense clumps of trees. The fruit is sweet and tastes like pineapple.

Mguwanguwo is used in medicine by steeping the bark. It has a very bitter taste like quinine. It makes into good boards.

Mseje cuts into good boards. It is not hard to saw up. The wood is red in colour. It grows on sandy soil. When the tree is small its branches make good pestles.

Mjole[1] is a good wood used in canoe-making. It is a very tall tree, with the leaves all at the top. It makes into very strong canoes. It grows on the river and at Linjisi.

Sanya is a tree that grows at the river, and is used in making wall-posts of houses, and in twisting into ropes. It is a very common tree.

Mtomoni grows on sandy soil and hilly country. It is used in medicine. It makes a good tree for fence-posts, as it takes root and grows. The sap is used in smearing the tops of drums, that the india-rubber may adhere to the skin. The fruit is inedible.

Mbewe grows on sandy soil. Long ago the wood was used for arrow-heads. It is used also in smelting and working iron, that the metal may be made readily malleable.

Mpelele grows on plains near the river. The tree is one used in canoe-making, as it does not crack.

Mtondo is found at the river, and is used in canoe-making, and in making mortars, pestles, etc. The fruit, which is called *Matondo*, is edible.

Msichisi[2] grows near streams. The wood is used in making stocks of guns, pestles, pillows.

Msangu, a canoe tree. The bark is rough, the leaves are small. It grows at the river.

Msumwa grows at the river; somewhat rough in the bark. The tree is useful in canoe-making.

---

[1] *Parinarium* sp.—H. H. J.   [2] Wild date palm, *Phœnix* sp.—H. H. J.

BOTANICAL APPENDICES

Mkunde[1] grows near streams. Is useful in canoe-making. The fruit is edible, but is apt to discolour the teeth.

Dululu grows on sandy soil. It is used in making drums, mortars, spoons, etc. It makes good boards. The root also is used in drum-making. It is a light wood.

Mtondewoko is used in canoe-making. Elephants are fond of the fruit. The wood is hard and very heavy. It is used in making the big drums used by the river people.

Mtundu grows in clumps of trees or on the sites of deserted villages. Cuttings are planted at the chief's courtyard, and grow very quickly into a big tree which can be readily recognised.

Mkoloñonjo grows on plains. The wood of the stem is very full of knots. It is used in canoe-making. It is found at the river and at the Tuchila.

Ntepa makes excellent bark-rope. It grows on flat grassy plains.

Ngachi,[2] a leafless tree. If the sap drops into the eye it causes inflammation of the cornea. It is used as a fish poison. It grows on the sites of old villages.

Mdogodea cuts easily into boards. It is a smooth-barked tree with small leaves, and grows near a stream. The fruit is named Mandogodia.

Mvumo,[3] or *Ngwalangwa*, is a river tree of great height. The fruit is edible. The leaves are long like those of the date palm. It is propagated from the seed. The root also is used as food in a similar manner to the carsana plant.

Mwaja—a large tree growing on the banks of streams. It is red in colour, and produces a fruit as large as a pumpkin. When ripe the fruit falls to the ground. People pick it up, take out the seeds, roast them, and eat them. The tree is found on Mounts Mangoche and Nangu.

Nangwesu is a good tree for bark-cloth. It grows on sandy soil. Its bark is also used for bark-rope.

Mtalawanda is used for bows and sticks. The bark is smooth, and the leaves are small. It grows at the river.

Tenza is used for bows and sticks. It grows in sandy soil near streams. It is not of much use. In appearance it is very similar to the *Mtalawanda* tree.

Mtewelewe grows an edible fruit. It is used for wall-posts of houses.

Nkope is used for making bows. The wood is hard, the leaves are large, and the bark smooth. It grows near streams in clumps of trees.

Nkulakula is used in making lids of covered baskets. The wood is adzed down thin, and bent into a circular form. It is also used in making beer cups.

Nabukwi is used for mortars, drums, etc. It is also made into boards.

Chinyenye is used to make mallets for hammering out bark-cloth. Europeans may use it for wooden hammers. It grows near the river.

Mpawoni is a large tree like Mbawa. It grows near streams on the banks of the Tuchila and Nkwakwasa. In appearance it is like the Mbawa, but has not the red colour.

Mchile, or *Kalisache*, grows anywhere even as a parasite. It makes very strong bark-cloth. It is red in colour, and is used also in making bark-cloth. Its fruit is called *Ngile*.

Chisije.—The Chikunda people at Michiru take chips of the wood, mix the water in which they are steeped with *Likwanya* plant, and use it in dyeing cloth of a black colour. It grows anywhere on sandy soil.

---

[1] *Parkia filicoidea.*—H. H. J.   [2] *Euphorbia* sp.—H. H. J.
[3] Apparently these are two different palms. Mvumo is the *Borassus flabellifer*, and Ngwalangwa *Hyphæne* sp. inc.—H. H. J.

Lungwe makes a medicine for sores. Chips are taken off, placed in a pot, and heated over the fire. The infusion is applied to the sore by means of a feather.

Mkakomtela makes lip-rings, and is carved into gun-stocks.

Mkemgusa (Mlanje Cedar) is a noteable tree in British Central Africa. It is used in making tables, chairs, etc. It is easily cut and planed, and has a sweet smell. It also makes good walking-sticks.

Nkolopochi—a tree which grows on the hills, and has a fruit of the same name, which is bright red when ripe.

Mchenjilema is a tree that grows on hilly ground. It is a tree of great use. It is large in size, and grows in forest clumps. It has very large roots that grow down deep into the ground.

Msilanyama—a fruit tree, but small. People take the bark (or husks) and pound it in a mortar, and make an oil used in smearing their bodies. It grows on sandy soil. The fruit is small like a *chitalaka* bead.

Nkulukututu grows on sandy soil or near a stream. The fruit is very edible. The wood is used for making wooden spoons.

Chipisawago, like the *chinyenye* tree, is used for making wooden mallets. After adzing, they are marked with a hot iron, and are used for hammering bark-cloth. It is an exceedingly hard wood, hence its name—*chipisawago*, "the blunter of the axe." If Europeans make mallets of this tree they will find it very useful.

Mpandabwalo is easily cut into boards. It does not crack. The seeds are used by women for lip-rings.

Nakalima grows on hilly country, and makes into good boards.

Chandafu grows on hilly country; is a very large tree, and makes good boards. The tree is dark in colour, and the bark is very rough.

Nkangasa—a canoe-tree growing at the river or on the hills. It is found here, and makes good boards.

Mchelechela grows near streams or in clumps of forest trees. It is a very large tree, and is used in making, spoons, mortars, and canoes.

Nkalala grows in forest clumps. It is used in canoe-making.

Mchenga is used in making handles for hoes and axes. The leaves are small, and the bark is rough.

BOTANICAL APPENDICES

APPENDIX II.

LIST OF THE KNOWN PLANTS OCCURRING IN BRITISH CENTRAL AFRICA,

NYASALAND, AND THE BRITISH TERRITORY NORTH OF THE ZAMBEZI

COMPILED, BY PERMISSION OF THE DIRECTOR, FROM MATERIALS IN THE
HERBARIUM OF THE ROYAL GARDENS, KEW

By I. H. BURKILL, M.A.

THE following list, compiled for the most part from the plants and manuscript records in the Herbarium of the Royal Gardens, Kew, must be regarded as provisional. The knowledge of the flora of the British territory north of the Zambezi has been so rapidly extended during recent years, and is yet so imperfectly known, that any account approaching completeness is at present impossible. Little has been published hitherto, and the facts now collected together will serve to bring into one view nearly all we know of the Botany of British Central Africa.

The first collections were made by two members of the Livingstone Expedition in the years 1861, 1862. Dr. (afterwards Sir) John Kirk and Mr. J. C. Meller, while exploring the course of the Shire River and wandering in the Mañanja hills, made considerable collections, which were transmitted to Kew, some of them in time for description in the *Flora of Tropical Africa*. Subsequently Dr. Kirk journeyed up the Zambezi into the Batoka country, from the highlands of which and from the region of the Victoria Falls other plants were sent home. The new species gathered by him were described in a variety of different publications. In the following years Mr. Horace Waller, residing in the Mañanja hills, continued to transmit plants to Dr. Kirk, who was at that time H.M.'s Consul in Zanzibar. After this comes a gap of some years in which nothing was added to our knowledge, until Dr. Emil Holub, in 1879, returned from a journey during which he had made considerable collections. Of these, a few of the plants had been gathered about Sesheke, almost the most northern point which he reached, and within the territory under consideration. At the same time (1878) Major Serpa Pinto made, in his journey across the continent, a small collection on the table-land over the river Ninda, and the plants of this were, in 1881, described in the *Transactions of the Linnæan Society*. Again in this year, 1878, the late Mr. John Buchanan sent to Kew his first collection of Nyasaland plants, and Mr. L. Scott travelled collecting through the Shire Highlands to the head of Lake Nyasa.

From this date our knowledge has steadily grown. Under the influence and with the help of Sir Harry Johnston, the region of the Shire Highlands has been energetically explored. The frequent mention below of the names of J. Buchanan, G. F. Scott-Elliot, J. McClounie, J. Last, A. Whyte, and K. C. Cameron shows how much has been done in this region. Further north, in 1879, Mr. Joseph Thomson had gathered plants on the Nyasa-Tanganyika plateau, and these reached Kew in 1880. Messrs. Carson, Nutt, Scott-Elliot and Sir Harry Johnston have also collected on the plateau, and the first-named on a journey along the Kalungwizi River to Lake Mweru.

The collection made at Boroma, on the north of the Zambezi, by the Rev. L. Menyharth, is only in part known.

As a guide to the distribution, the region has been divided into four sections, as follows:—

1. Shire Highlands.
2. Nyasa-Tanganyika plateau; some of the plants probably collected on the German side of the boundary line.
3. Extreme west, where Major Serpa Pinto alone has collected.
4. Upper Zambezi.

It must be understood that all the plants collected by Buchanan were obtained in the Shire Highlands; all by Carson and Nutt, unless otherwise stated, from the region near the south end of Lake Tanganyika; all from Serpa Pinto from the one plateau near the river Ninda; and all from Menyharth from Boroma. It was not thought necessary to repeat these localities with the collectors' names.

PHANEROGAMS.

RANUNCULACEAE.

Clematis Kirkii, Oliv. (1) Mañanja hills, Kirk; Buchanan; (2) Carson; Nutt.
C. grata, Oliv. (1) Buchanan.
C. simensis, Fresen. (1) Chiradzulu, Whyte; Buchanan.
C. Thunbergii, Steud. (2) Lower plateau, north of Lake Nyasa, J. Thomson.
Clematis sp. (2) Carson.
Thalictrum rhynchocarpum, Dill. et Rich. (1) Mlanje, Whyte; Buchanan.
T. longipedunculatum, Harv. et Sond. (1) Buchanan.
Anemone whyteana, Baker fil. (1) Mlanje, Whyte; Buchanan.
Ranunculus pinnatus, Poir. (1) Buchanan.
Ranunculus sp. (2) Carson.
Delphinium dasycaulon, Fresen. (2) Nutt.

ANONACEAE.

Anona senegalensis, Pers. (1) Shire Valley, Kirk; (2) Nyasa-Tanganyika plateau, Scott-Elliot.
Anona sp. (2) Nyasa-Tanganyika plateau, Scott-Elliot.
Uvaria spp. (1) Buchanan; (4) Menyharth.
Xylopia sp.? (1) Buchanan.
Unona spp. (1) Buchanan.
Monodora stenopetala, Oliv. (1) Rapids of Shire River and west of Lake Nyasa, Kirk.

MENISPERMACEAE.

Jateorhiza Columba, Miers. (1) Buchanan.
Tiliacora (?) *funifera*, Oliv. (1) Mañanja hills, Meller; (4) Victoria Falls, Kirk.
Tiliacora sp. (1) Buchanan.
Cocculus villosus, DC. (1) Rapids of Shire River, Kirk.
Cissampelos Pareira, L. (1) Buchanan; Shire Highlands and Lake Nyasa, Scott-Elliot; Zomba, Whyte.
C. nephrophylla, Bojer. (1) Buchanan.
Stephania abyssinica, Rich. (?) (1) Buchanan.

NYMPHAEACEAE.
Nymphaea stellata, Willd. (1) Lake Nyasa and Shire River, Kirk; Buchanan; (2) Carson.

CRUCIFERAE.
Nasturtium indicum, L. (4) Menyharth.
Brassica juncea, DC. (1) Murchison Falls, Shire River, Meller; Buchanan.

CAPPARIDACEAE.
Cleome monophylla, L. (1) Zomba and Mlanje, Whyte; Buchanan.
C. chilocalyx, Oliv. (1) Shire River, Meller.
C. hirta, Oliv. (1) Maravi country, Kirk; (2) Carson; Lower plateau, north of Lake Nyasa, J. Thomson.
C. ciliata, Schum. et Thonn. (2) Carson.
Cleome sp. (1) Buchanan; (2) Carson; Nutt.
Gynandropsis pentaphylla, DC. (1) Buchanan; Shire River, Meller.
Thylacium africanum, Lour. (1) Shire River, Kirk; Buchanan.
Maerua nervosa, Oliv. (2) Lower plateau, north of Lake Nyasa, J. Thomson.
Maerua sp. (1) Zomba, Whyte; Buchanan.
Boscia salicifolia, Oliv. (1) Shire River, Kirk.
B. Carsoni, Baker. (2) Mweru, Carson.
Capparis rosea, L. (1) Shire Highlands, Scott-Elliot; by Lake Nyasa and Upper Shire, Kirk.
C. tomentosa, Lam. (1) Buchanan.
C. Kirkii, Oliv. (1) By Lake Nyasa and Upper Shire, Kirk.
Capparis sp. (1) Buchanan.
Ritchiea sp. (2) Carson.

RESEDACEAE.
Caylusea abyssinica, Fisch. et Mey. (2) Lower plateau, north of Lake Nyasa, J. Thomson.

VIOLACEAE.
Ionidium enneaspermum, Vent. (1) Blantyre, Last; (4) Menyharth.
I. nyassense, Engl. (1) Buchanan.
Viola abyssinica, Steud. (1) Mlanje, Whyte.

MORINGEAE.
Moringa pterygosperma, DC. (1) Lake Nyasa and Shire Highlands, Scott-Elliot.

BIXINEAE.
Oncoba spinosa, Forsk. (1) Shire River, Kirk; Shire Highlands, Scott-Elliot; Buchanan.
O. lasiocalyx, Oliv. (1) Lake Chilwa, Kirk.
O. petersiana, Oliv. (1) Shire Highlands, Scott-Elliot.
Flacourtia Ramontchi, L'Hérit. (1) Buchanan.
Aphloia theaeformis, Benn. (1) Mlanje, McClounie and Whyte; Zomba, Whyte; Buchanan.
Kiggelaria grandifolia, Warb. (1) Buchanan.

PITTOSPORACEAE.
Pittosporum sp. (1) Zomba, Whyte.

POLYGALACEAE.
Polygala gomesiana, Welw. (1) Lake Nyasa, Kirk; Zomba, Whyte; Blantyre, Last; (2) Nutt; lower plateau, north of Lake Nyasa, J. Thomson.
P. amboinensis, Gürke. (1) Shire Highlands, Scott-Elliot.

POLYGALACEAE.
    Polygala tenuicaulis, Hook. fil. (2) Carson.
    P. rarifolia, DC. (2) Nutt.
    P. triflora, L. (1) Buchanan.
    P. polygonifolia, Chodat. (1) Shire Highlands, Scott-Elliot.
    P. britteniana, Chodat. (2) Nyasa-Tanganyika plateau, Scott-Elliot.
    P. persicariaefolia, DC. (1) Blantyre, Last; Zomba and Mlanje, Whyte; Buchanan; Mañanja hills, Kirk and Waller.
    P. petitiana, Rich. (1) Blantyre, Last; Buchanan; Mañanja hills, Waller.
    P. virgata, Thunb. (1) Mlanje, Whyte and McClounie; Buchanan.
    P. krumanina, Burchell. (3) Serpa Pinto.
    P. micrantha, G. et P. (2) Carson.
    Polygala spp. (1) Buchanan; Blantyre, Last.
    Securidaca longepedunculata, Fresen. (1) Mañanja hills, Meller; Zomba, Whyte; Buchanan.
    Securidaca sp. (1) Nyasa-Tanganyika plateau, Scott-Elliot.
    Muraltia mixta, L. (1) Mlanje, Whyte and McClounie; Zomba, Whyte.

CARYOPHYLLACEAE.
    Dianthus Serpae, Ficalho et Hiern. (3) Serpa Pinto.
    Silene Burchellii, Otth. (1) Mlanje, Whyte and McClounie; Shire Highlands, Scott-Elliot; Buchanan; (2) Upper Nyasa-Tanganyika plateau, J. Thomson.
    Silene sp. (1) Buchanan; (2) Nyasa-Tanganyika plateau, J. Thomson.
    Cerastium africanum, Oliv. (1) Mlanje, Whyte.
    Cerastium sp. (2) Lower Nyasa-Tanganyika plateau, J. Thomson.
    Stellaria media, Cyr. (1) Mlanje, Whyte.
    Drymaria cordata, Willd. (1) Chiradzulu, Whyte; Buchanan.
    Polycarpaea corymbosa, L. (4) Menyharth; var. *effusa*, Oliv. (1) Buchanan.
    Polycarpaea sp. (4) Menyharth.

PORTULACEAE.
    Portulaca quadrifida, L. (1) Buchanan; (2) Mweru, Carson.

HYPERICINEAE.
    Hypericum peplidifolium, Rich. (1) Mlanje and Zomba, Whyte; Shire Highlands, Scott-Elliot; Buchanan; (2) Nutt.
    H. lanceolatum, Lam. (1) Buchanan; Mañanja hills, Meller; Blantyre, Last; Mlanje and Zomba, Whyte.
    H. quartinianum, Rich. (1) Upper plateau, north of Lake Nyasa, J. Thomson.
    Hypericum sp. (1) Shire Highlands, Scott-Elliot.
    Psorospermum febrifugum, Spach. (1) Mañanja hills, Meller and Kirk; Zomba, Whyte; Buchanan; (2) Nyasa-Tanganyika plateau, Scott-Elliot and J. Thomson.
    Psorospermum sp. (1) Shire Highlands, Scott-Elliot.
    Haronga madagascariensis, Choisy. (1) Zomba, Whyte; Buchanan.

GUTTIFERAE.
    Garcinia Buchanani, Baker. (1) Buchanan.

DIPTEROCARPEAE.
    Vatica africana, Welw., var. *glomerata*, Oliv. (1) Buchanan; (4) Batoka country, Kirk.

MALVACEAE.
Sida humilis, Cav. (1) Lake Nyasa, Kirk.
S. rhombifolia, L. (1) Buchanan.
S. spinosa, L. (1) Buchanan.
S. cordifolia, L. (1) Lower Shire Valley, Meller; Buchanan.
Sida sp. (4) Menyharth; Holub.
Abutilon angulatum, Mast. (1) Katunga, Meller; Chiradzulu, Whyte; Buchanan.
A. zanzibaricum, Bojer. (1) Buchanan.
A. longicuspe, Hochst. (1) Chiradzulu, Meller.
A. indicum, Don. (1) Mañanja hills, Meller; Mlanje, Whyte; (4) Sesheke, Kirk.
A. graveolens, W. et A. (1) Buchanan.
Abutilon sp. (1) Chiradzulu, Whyte.
Urena lobata, L. (2) Carson.
Pavonia Meyeri, Mast. (1) Mañanja hills, Meller; Buchanan.
P. schimperiana, Hochst. (1) Buchanan; Chiradzulu, Meller and Whyte; (2) Lower plateau, north of Lake Nyasa, J. Thomson.
P. urens, Cav. (1) Buchanan.
Pavonia spp. (1) Chiradzulu, Whyte; Buchanan; (2) Carson.
Kosteletzkya adoensis, Hochst. (1) Buchanan.
Hibiscus vitifolius, L. (1) Shire Highlands, Scott-Elliot; Buchanan.
H. diversifolius, Jacq. (1) Mañanja hills, Meller; Lower Shire Valley, Kirk; Buchanan.
H. surattensis, L. (1) Buchanan.
H. Sabdariffa, L. (1) Lower Shire Valley, Kirk.
H. cannabinus, L. (1) Zomba, Whyte; Chiradzulu, Meller.
H. gossypinus, Thunb. (1) Mañanja hills, Kirk and Meller; Chiradzulu, Whyte; Buchanan; (2) Lower plateau, north of Lake Nyasa, J. Thomson.
H. micranthus, L. (1) Katunga, Meller; Buchanan; (2) Carson; Nyasa-Tanganyika plateau, Scott-Elliot.
H. Solandra, L'Hérit. (1) Shire River, Kirk.
H. physaloides, G. et P. (1) Zomba and Mlanje, Whyte; (2) Carson.
Hibiscus spp. (1) Buchanan; Shire Highlands, K. C. Cameron; (2) Carson; Nyasa-Tanganyika plateau, J. Thomson; (4) Holub.
Gossypium barbadense, L. (1) Lake Nyasa, Kirk.
Adansonia digitata, L. (1) Lake Chilwa, McClounie.

STERCULIACEAE.
Sterculia melissifolia, Benth. (2) Carson.
S. triphaca, R. Br. (1) Buchanan.
Sterculia sp. (1) Buchanan; (2) Carson.
Dombeya multiflora, Planch. (1) Mañanja hills, Meller; Buchanan; Zomba, Whyte.
D. spectabilis, Bojer. (1) Mañanja hills, Meller; Buchanan.
D. Kirkii, Mast. (1) Katunga, Meller.
D. Burgessiae, Gerr. (1) Mañanja hills, Meller; Blantyre, Last; Chiradzulu, Whyte; Buchanan; (2) Lower plateau, north of Lake Nyasa, J. Thomson.
Dombeya sp. (2) Carson; Upper and Lower plateau, north of Lake Nyasa, Thomson.
Melhania Forbesii, Planch. (1) Buchanan.
M. acuminata, Mast. (1) Buchanan.
Waltheria americana, L. (1) Buchanan.
Melochia corchorifolia. L. (1) Buchanan; Shire Valley, Kirk.
Hermannia inamoena, K. Schum. (1) Buchanan.
H. Kirkii, Mast. (1) Buchanan.

TILIACEAE
  Grewia asiatica, L. (1) Buchanan.
  G. inaequilatera, Garcke. (1) Lower Shire, Kirk and Meller.
  Grewia spp. (1) Buchanan; Shire Highlands, Scott-Elliot.
  Triumfetta rhomboidea, Jacq. (1) Buchanan; (2) Carson.
  T. Welwitschii, Mast. (1) Near Lake Nyasa, Kirk; Buchanan; (2) Carson.
  T. Mastersii, Baker fil. (1) Mlanje, Whyte; Buchanan.
  T. Sonderii, Ficalho et Hiern. (3) Serpa Pinto.
  T. pilosa, Roth. (1) Chiradzulu, Whyte.
  T. trichocarpa, Hochst. (1) Buchanan.
  T. tomentosa, Bojer. (1) Buchanan.
  Triumfetta spp. (1) Buchanan; Blantyre, Last; (2) Lower plateau, north of Nyasa, J. Thomson; Nyasa-Tanganyika plateau, Scott-Elliot; (4) Menyharth.
  Sparmannia abyssinica, E. Mey. (1) Buchanan; Mlanje, McClounie; (2) Lower plateau, north of Lake Nyasa, J. Thomson.
  S. palmata, E. Mey. (1) Buchanan.
  Corchorus tridens, L. (1) Blantyre, Last.
  C. olitorius, L. (1) Buchanan.
  Ceratosepalum digitatum, Oliv. (2) Carson.

LINEAE.
  Erythroxylon emarginatum, Schum et Thonn. (1) Buchanan; Shire Highlands, Scott-Elliot.

MALPIGHIACEAE.
  Acridocarpus chloropterus, Oliv. (1) Shire Valley, Meller and Kirk.
  Acridocarpus sp. (1) Buchanan.
  Triaspis sp. (1) Buchanan.

ZYGOPHYLLEAE.
  Tribulus terrestris, L. (1) Buchanan.

GERANIACEAE.
  Geranium aculeolatum, Oliv. (1) Buchanan.
  G. simense, Hochst. (1) Zomba, Kirk; Mlanje, Whyte; (2) Lower plateau, north of Lake Nyasa, J. Thomson.
  G. favosum, Hochst. (2) Lower plateau, north of Lake Nyasa, J. Thomson.
  Geranium spp. (1) Zomba, Cunningham; Buchanan; (2) Lower plateau, north of Lake Nyasa, J. Thomson.
  Pelargonium sp. (2) Nyasa-Tanganyika plateau, J. Thomson and Scott-Elliot; Carson.
  Oxalis semiloba, Sond. (1) Mañanja hills, Kirk; Blantyre, Last.
  O. oligotricha, Baker. (2) Carson.
  O. sensitiva, L. (1) Buchanan; Zomba, Whyte; Blantyre, Last.
  O. trichophylla, Baker. (2) Carson.
  O. corniculata, L. (1) Buchanan; (2) Nutt.
  Oxalis spp. (1) Buchanan; Shire Highlands, Scott-Elliot; (2) Nutt.
  Impatiens capensis, Thunb. (1) Chiradzulu and Mañanja hills, Meller.
  I. Kirkii, Hook. fil. (1) Western side of Lake Nyasa, Kirk.
  I. assurgens, Baker. (2) Nutt; Carson.
  I. shirensis, Baker fil. (1) Mlanje, Whyte and McClounie.
  I. gomphophylla, Baker. (4) Carson.
  I. micrantha, Hochst. (?) (1) Mlanje, Whyte.
  Impatiens spp. (1) Buchanan; Blantyre, Last; (2) Carson.

BOTANICAL APPENDICES

Rutaceae.
: *Toddalia aculeata*, Pers. (1) Buchanan.
: *Toddalia* spp. (1) Buchanan.
: *Clausena inaequalis*, Benth. (1) Mlanje and Zomba, Whyte.
: *Citrus Aurantium*, L. (1) Buchanan.

Simarubeae.
: *Brucea* sp. (?) (4) Menyharth.
: *Kirkia acuminata*, Oliv. (1) Buchanan.

Ochnaceae.
: *Ochna leptoclada*, Oliv. (1) Mañanja hills, Meller; Maravi country, Kirk; Buchanan.
: *O. macrocalyx*, Oliv. (1) Sochi, Kirk; Mañanja hills, Meller; Zomba, Whyte; Mlanje, McClounie; Shire Highlands, Scott-Elliot.
: *O. floribunda*, Baker. (2) Mweru, Carson.
: *Ochna* spp. (1) Buchanan; (2) Lower plateau, north of Lake Nyasa, J. Thomson; Carson

Burseraceae.
: *Canarium* sp. (1) Lake Nyasa, Scott-Elliot.
: *Commiphora pilosa*, Engl. (4) Menyharth.
: *C. mozambicensis*, Engl. (1) Lower Shire River, Kirk.
: *Commiphora* spp. (4) Menyharth; Boroma and Batoka country, Kirk.

Meliaceae.
: *Turraea nilotica*, Kotschy. (1) Shire River, Kirk.
: *T. capitata*, Klotzsch. (1) Chiradzulu, Whyte.
: *Turraea* sp. (1) Chiradzulu, Whyte; (4) Menyharth.
: *Trichilia emetica*, Vahl. (1) Shire River, Kirk; Buchanan; Shire Highlands, Scott-Elliot.
: *T. capitata*, Klotzsch. (1) Shire River, Kirk; Chiradzulu, Whyte; (4) Menyharth.
: *T. Buchanani*, C. DC. (1) Buchanan; Chiradzulu, Whyte.
: *Trichilia* spp. (1) Shire Highlands, Scott-Elliot.
: *Khaya senegalensis*, A. Juss. (?) (1) Mañanja hills, Meller; Buchanan.
: *Ekebergia Buchananii*, Harms. (1) Buchanan.

Olacineae.
: *Olax dissitiflora*, Oliv. (1) Lake Nyasa, Kirk; (4) Menyharth.
: *Olax* sp. (1) Buchanan; (2) Nyasa-Tanganyika plateau, Scott-Elliot.
: *Ximenia americana*, L. (1) Buchanan.
: *Apodytes dimidiata*, E. Mey. (1) Buchanan.
: *Chlamydocarya* sp. (4) Menyharth.

Ilicineae.
: *Ilex capensis*, Sond. et Harv. (1) Mlanje, McClounie; Buchanan.

Celastraceae.
: *Celastrus laurifolius*, Rich. (1) Lake Nyasa, Kirk.
: *C. senegalensis*, Lam. (1) Chiradzulu, Whyte; Buchanan; (2)? Lower plateau, north of Lake Nyasa, J. Thomson.
: *C. serratus*, Hochst. (2) Lower plateau, north of Lake Nyasa, J. Thomson.
: *Gymnosporia laurina*, Szyszyl. (1) Mlanje, Whyte.
: *G. undata*, Szyszyl. (1) Buchanan.
: *G. buxifolia*, Szyszyl., var. *venenata*, Sand. (1) Buchanan.

CELASTRACEAE.
 Gymnosporia sp. (1) Buchanan.
 Cassine Buchananii, Loesn. (1) Buchanan.
 C. aethiopica, Thunb. (1) Buchanan.
 Hippocratea obtusifolia, Roxb. (4) Menyharth.
 Hippocratea Buchananii, Loesn. (1) Buchanan.
 Hippocratea sp. (4) Menyharth.
 Salacia spp. (1) Buchanan.
 Pleurostylia Wightii, Wight et Arnott. (1) Buchanan.

RHAMNEAE.
 Zizyphus Jujuba, Lam. (1) Buchanan; Shire Highlands, Scott-Elliot.
 Z. mucronata, Willd. (1) Shire River, Kirk and Meller.
 Gouania sp. (1) Chiradzulu, Whyte.
 Helinus ovatus, E. Mey. (1) Lower valley of the Shire River, Meller; Buchanan.
 Phylica spicata, L.? (1) Mlanje, Whyte.

AMPELIDEAE.
 Vitis erythrodes, Fresen. (1) Buchanan.
 V. congesta, Baker. (1) Katunga, Meller.
 V. abyssinica, Hochst. (1) Buchanan.
 V. rubiginosa, Welw. (1) Buchanan.
 V. serpens, Baker. (1) Zomba, Whyte.
 V. grisea, Baker. (1) Shire River, Kirk.
 V. jatrophoides, Welw. (1) Mbami, near Blantyre, Kirk; Buchanan.
 V. integrifolia, Baker. (1) Shire Highlands, Scott-Elliot; (4) Menyharth.
 V. subciliata, Baker. (1) Shire Highlands, Scott-Elliot; Katunga, L. Scott.
 V. ibuensis, Baker. (1) Buchanan.
 Vitis spp. (1) Buchanan; Shire Highlands, Scott-Elliot; Mañanja hills, Meller; (2) Nyasa-Tanganyika plateau, J. Thomson.
 Cissus aristolochiaefolia, Planch. (1) Buchanan.
 C. subglaucescens, Planch. (1) Buchanan.
 C. kirkiana, Planch., var. *Livingstonii*, Planch. (1) Buchanan.
 C. Buchananii, Planch. (1) Buchanan; (4) Menyharth.
 C. cucumerifolia, Planch. (1) Katunga, Kirk.
 C. crotalarioides, Planch. (1) Buchanan.
 Leea sp. (1) Shire Highlands, Scott-Elliot.

SAPINDACEAE.
 Cardiospermum microcarpum, H. B. K. (1) Buchanan.
 Paullinia pinnata, L. (1) Buchanan; Zomba, Whyte.
 Paullinia sp. (1) Mlanje, McClounie.
 Schmidelia repanda, Baker. (1) Shire River, Kirk.
 S. africana, DC. (1) Buchanan.
 Schmidelia spp. (1) Buchanan.
 Cupania spp. (1) Buchanan; Shire Highlands, Scott-Elliot.
 Blighia zambesiaca, Baker. (1) Lake Nyasa, Kirk.
 Lecaniodiscus fraxinifolia, Baker. (1) Shire River, Kirk; (4) Menyharth.
 Sapindus xanthocarpus, Kl. (1) Buchanan; Shire River to Lake Nyasa, Kirk.
 Dodonaea viscosa, L. (1) Buchanan; Zomba, Whyte; (2) Lower plateau, north of Lake Nyasa, J. Thomson.
 Bersama sp. (1) Buchanan; Zomba, Whyte; Shire Highlands, Scott-Elliot.

ANACARDIACEAE.
    Rhus viminalis, Vahl. (4) Batoka country, Kirk.
    R. villosa, Linn. fil. (1) Mañanja hills, Meller; Buchanan; Zomba, Whyte; var. *grandifolia*, Oliv. (1) Mbami, near Blantyre, Kirk.
    R. Kirkii, Oliv. (4) Victoria Falls, Kirk.
    R. pulcherrima, Oliv. (1) Buchanan.
    R. glaucescens, Rich. (1) Lake Nyasa, Scott-Elliot; Buchanan; (2) Lower plateau, north of Lake Nyasa, J. Thomson.
    R. mucronifolia, Sond. (1) Shire Highlands, Scott-Elliot.
    R. insignis, Del. (1) Zomba, Whyte.
    R. retinorrhoea, Steud. (4) Batoka country, Kirk.
    Rhus sp. (1) Buchanan.
    Spondias sp. (1) Shire Highlands, Scott-Elliot; (4) Menyharth.
    Sclerocarya caffra, Sond. (1) Lake Nyasa, Kirk.

CONNARACEAE.
    Rourea ovalifolia, Gilg. (1) Mlanje, McClounie.

LEGUMINOSAE.
    Crotalaria anthyllopsis, Welw. (1) Buchanan.
    C. laxiflora, Baker. (2) Carson.
    C. glauca, Willd. (1) Mañanja hills, Kirk.
    C. Vogelii, Benth. (1) Buchanan.
    C. cephalotes, Steud. (1) Buchanan; Blantyre, Last.
    C. lotifolia, L. (1) Buchanan.
    C. cleomifolia, Welw. (1) Buchanan.
    C. erisemoides, Ficalho et Hiern. (3) Serpa Pinto.
    C. lanceolata, E. Mey. (1) Buchanan.
    C. intermedia, Kotschy. (2) Lower plateau, north of Lake Nyasa, J. Thomson.
    C. natalitia, Meisn. (1) Zomba, Whyte.
    C. hyssopifolia, Kl. (1) Buchanan.
    C. recta, Steud. (1) Mlanje, Whyte; Buchanan; Mañanja hills, Waller; (2) Carson.
    C. spinosa, Hochst. (1) Buchanan.
    Crotalaria spp. (1) Buchanan; Blantyre, Last; Chiradzulu, Whyte; (2) Nutt; Carson.
    Argyrolobium shirense, Taub. (1) Buchanan.
    Adenocarpus Mannii, Hook. fil. (1) Mlanje and Zomba, Whyte; Buchanan.
    Parochetus communis, Hamilt. (1) Mañanja hills, Meller.
    Medicago lupulina, L. (1) Buchanan.
    Lotus arabicus, L. (1) Mlanje, Whyte.
    L. tigrensis, Baker. (1) Buchanan.
    Lotus sp. (2) Lower plateau, north of Lake Nyasa, J. Thomson.
    Psoralea sp. (2) Lower plateau, north of Lake Nyasa, J. Thomson.
    Indigofera vicioides, Jaub. et Spach. (4) Batoka country, Kirk.
    I. trachyphylla, Benth. (1) Buchanan.
    I. polysphaera, Baker. (2) Carson.
    I. Lyallii, Baker. (1) Mlanje, Whyte.
    I. heterotricha, DC. (3) Serpa Pinto.
    I. dodecaphylla, Ficalho et Hiern. (3) Serpa Pinto.
    I. secundiflora, Poir. (1) Upper Shire Valley, Scott-Elliot; (2) Lower plateau, north of Lake Nyasa, J. Thomson; Carson.
    I. splendens, Ficalho et Hiern. (3) Serpa Pinto.

LEGUMINOSAE.
>   *Indigofera multijuga*, Baker. (1) Buchanan.
>   *I. demissa*, Taub. (1) Buchanan.
>   *I. tinctoria*, L. (1) Buchanan.
>   *I. hirsuta*, L. (1) Buchanan.
>   *I. torulosa*, Baker. (1) Buchanan.
>   *I. emarginella*, Steud. (1) Buchanan.
>   *I. arrecta*, Hochst. (2) Karonga, L. Scott.
>   *I. endecaphylla*, Baker. (1) Zomba, Meller.
>   *I. procera*, S. et T. (1) Buchanan.
>   *Indigofera* spp. (1) Buchanan; Blantyre, Last; Shire Highlands, Scott-Elliot; (2) Nyasa-Tanganyika plateau, J. Thomson and Scott-Elliot; Nutt; Carson.
>   *Tephrosia sericea*, Baker. (1) Mañanja hills, Waller; Zomba, Whyte.
>   *T. Vogelii*, Hook. fil. (1) Buchanan; (2) Nutt.
>   *T. longipes*, Meisn. (3) Serpa Pinto.
>   *T. purpurea*, Pers. (1) Buchanan; (3) Serpa Pinto.
>   *T. linearis*, Pers. (1) Mlanje, Whyte.
>   *T. whyteana*, Baker fil. (1) Mlanje, Whyte.
>   *T. Nyasae*, Baker fil. (1) Buchanan.
>   *T. lupinifolia*, DC. (1) Buchanan.
>   *T. dichroocarpa*, Steud. (1) Buchanan.
>   *T. schizocalyx*, Taub. (1) Buchanan.
>   *T. sambesiaca*, Taub. (1) Buchanan.
>   *Tephrosia* spp. (1) Buchanan; (2) Carson; Upper plateau, north of Lake Nyasa, J. Thomson.
>   *Mundulea suberosa*, Benth. (1) Buchanan.
>   *Sesbania* sp. (1) Buchanan.
>   *Astragalus abyssinicus*, Steud. (1) Buchanan.
>   *Ormocarpum mimosoides*, S. Moore. (1) Buchanan.
>   *Herminiera elaphroxylon*, Guill. et Perr. (1) Buchanan.
>   *Aeschynomene aspera*, L. (1) Elephant Marsh on Shire River, Kirk.
>   *A. shirensis*, Taub. (1) Buchanan.
>   *A. indica*, L. (1) Buchanan.
>   *A. Schimperi*, Hochst. (1) Buchanan.
>   *A. siifolia*, Welw. (1) Zomba and Mlanje, Whyte.
>   *A. glutinosa*, Taub. (1) Buchanan.
>   *Aeschynomene* spp. (1) Buchanan; Mlanje, Whyte; Blantyre, Last; Chiradzulu, Whyte; (2) Nyasa-Tanganyika plateau, Scott-Elliot; Carson.
>   *Smithia nodulosa*, Baker. (1) Chiradzulu, Meller.
>   *S. strobilantha*, Welw. (4) Batoka country, Kirk.
>   *S. strigosa*, Benth. (1) Buchanan; (2) Nyasa-Tanganyika plateau, Scott-Elliot.
>   *S. scaberrima*, Taub. (1) Buchanan.
>   *S. sensitiva*, Ait. (1) Buchanan.
>   *S. Carsoni*, Baker. (1) Carson.
>   *Smithia* spp. (1) Zomba, Whyte; Buchanan; (2) Lower plateau, north of Lake Nyasa, J. Thomson; Carson.
>   *Geissaspis humuloides*, Hiern. (2) Nyasa-Tanganyika plateau, Scott-Elliot; Lower plateau, north of Lake Nyasa, J. Thomson.
>   *Arachis hypogaea*, L. (2) Nutt.
>   *Desmodium dimorphum*, Welw. (1) Mañanja hills, Kirk; Buchanan.
>   *D. Scalpe*, DC. (1) Buchanan.
>   *D. barbatum*, Benth. (1) Buchanan.

BOTANICAL APPENDICES

LEGUMINOSAE.
Desmodium lasiocarpum, DC. (1) Buchanan.
D. gangeticum, DC. (1) Buchanan ; Mañanja hills, Meller.
D. hirtum, Guill. et Perr. (1) Buchanan ; Zomba, Whyte.
D. ascendens, DC. (1) Zomba, Whyte.
D. latifolium, DC. (1) Buchanan ; Mañanja hills, Waller.
D. tanganyikense, Baker. (2) Carson.
D. paleaceum, Guill. et Perr. (1) Buchanan.
Desmodium spp. (1) Buchanan ; (2) Carson ; Nutt.
Pseudarthria Hookeri, W. et A. (2) Nutt.
Pseudarthria sp. (1) Buchanan ; (2) Carson.
Alysicarpus rugosus, DC. (1) Buchanan ; Shire Highlands and Lake Nyasa, Scott-Elliot.
Alysicarpus sp. (1) Buchanan.
Lathyrus sp. (1) Buchanan.
Abrus precatorius, L. (1) Buchanan.
Clitorea ternatea, H. B. K. (1) Buchanan.
Dumasia villosa, DC. (1) Buchanan.
Glycine javanica, L. (1) Lower Shire Valley, Meller ; Chiradzulu, Whyte ; Buchanan.
Glycine sp. (2) Carson.
Teramnus sp. (1) Buchanan.
Erythrina tomentosa, Benth. (1) Buchanan ; Mañanja hills, Meller.
E. Humei, E. Mey. (1) Mañanja hills, Meller ; Shire River, Kirk.
Erythrina sp. (1) Buchanan.
Mucuna coriacea, Baker. (1) Mañanja hills, Meller ; Mlanje and Chiradzulu, Whyte.
M. erecta, Baker. (2) Carson.
Mucuna sp. (1) Buchanan ; (2) Carson.
Canavalia obtusifolia, DC. (1) Mlanje, Whyte ; Buchanan.
C. ensiformis, DC. (1) Buchanan.
Phaseolus lunatus, L. (1) Lake Nyasa, Kirk.
P. Kirkii, Baker. (1) West shore of Lake Nyasa, Kirk.
Phaseolus spp. (1) Shire Highlands, Scott-Elliot ; Buchanan.
Vigna vexillata, Benth. (1) Buchanan ; Zomba and Mlanje, Whyte ; (2) Carson ; Nutt.
V. luteola, Benth. (1) Zomba and Mlanje, Whyte ; Fort Johnston, Scott-Elliot.
V. Catjang, Walp. (1) Buchanan.
Vigna sp. (1) Buchanan.
Voandzeia subterranea, Thouars. (2) Nutt.
Psophocarpus longepedunculatus, Hassk. (1) Buchanan.
Dolichos biflorus, L. (2) Carson.
D. erectus, Baker fil. (1) Shire Highlands, Scott-Elliot ; Zomba and Mlanje, Whyte.
D. platypus, Baker. (2) Mweru, Carson.
D. axillaris, E. Mey. (1) Mbami, L. Scott.
D. pteropus, Baker. (2) Nyasa-Tanganyika plateau, Scott-Elliot ; Carson.
D. simplicifolius, Hook. fil. (1) Buchanan.
D. xiphophyllus, Baker. (2) Nyasa-Tanganyika plateau, Scott-Elliot ; Carson.
D. lupinoides, Baker. (2) Carson.
Dolichos spp. (1) Chiradzulu, Whyte ; Buchanan ; (2) Nutt ; Carson.
Cajanus indicus, Spreng. (1) Mlanje, Whyte ; Buchanan.
Rhynchosia cyanosperma, Benth. (1) Mañanja hills, Meller; Chiradzulu, Whyte; Buchanan.
R. densiflora, DC. (1) Shire River, Kirk.
R. antennulifera, Baker. (1) Buchanan ; Shire Highlands, Meller.
R. caribaea, DC. (1) Buchanan.

LEGUMINOSAE.
Rhynchosia minima, DC. (1) Buchanan; Upper Shire River, Scott-Elliot.
R. comosa, Baker. (1) Buchanan.
Rhynchosia spp. (1) Buchanan.
Eriosema cajanoides, Hook. fil. (1) Mlanje, Whyte; Buchanan; (2) Carson; (3) Serpa Pinto.
E. parviflorum, E. Mey. (1) Mlanje, Whyte; Buchanan.
E. flemingioides, Baker. (1) Buchanan.
E. shirensis, Baker fil. (1) Zomba, Whyte; Shire Highlands, Scott-Elliot.
E. montanum, Baker fil. (1) Shire Highlands, Scott-Elliot.
E. polystachyum, Baker. (2) Carson.
Eriosema spp. (1) Buchanan; (2) Carson; Nutt; Lower plateau, north of Lake Nyasa, J. Thomson.
Flemingia rhodocarpa, Baker. (1) Mañanja hills, Meller; Buchanan; Chiradzulu, Whyte.
F. macrocalyx, Baker fil. (1) Mlanje, Whyte.
Dalbergia Melanoxylon, Guill. et Perr. (1) Buchanan.
Dalbergia spp. (1) Buchanan.
Pterocarpus melliferus, Welw. (1) Zomba, Whyte.
Pterocarpus sp. (1) Buchanan.
Lonchocarpus laxiflorus, Guill. et Perr., var. *sericeus*, Baker. (1) Zomba and east end of Lake Chilwa, Meller; Buchanan.
Lonchocarpus spp. (1) Buchanan.
Deguelia Stuhlmanni, Taub. (1) Buchanan.
Baphia racemosa, Hochst. (4) Batoka country, Kirk.
Baphia sp. (1) Chiradzulu, Whyte.
Osmosia sp. (1) Buchanan.
Swartzia madagascariensis, Desv. (1) Maravi country Kirk; Buchanan.
Cordyla africana, Lour. (1) Mañanja hills, Meller.
Cassia abbreviata, Oliv. (1) Mañanja hills, Meller; west shore of Lake Nyasa, Kirk; Buchanan.
C. petersiana, C. Bolle. (1) Lower Shire Valley, Meller; Blantyre, Last; Buchanan; Zomba and Chiradzulu, Whyte.
C. didymobotrya, Fresen. (1) Mañanja hills, Meller; (2) Carson.
C. Grantii, Oliv. (1) Maravi country, Kirk.
C. Tora, L. (1) Buchanan; (2) Carson.
C. Kirkii, Oliv. (1) Mañanja hills, Kirk and Meller; Buchanan.
C. mimosoides, L. (1) Buchanan; Mlanje, Whyte; (2) Carson.
C. occidentalis, L. (1) Buchanan.
C. Absus, L. (1) Buchanan.
C. goratensis, Fresen. (2) Carson.
Cassia sp. (1) Buchanan.
Bauhinia fassoglensis, Kotschy. (1) Mañanja hills, Waller; Buchanan.
B. Kirkii, Oliv. (4) Batoka country, Kirk.
B. Serpae, Ficalho et Hiern. (3) Serpa Pinto.
B. petersiana, Bolle. (1) Mañanja hills, Waller; Buchanan; Mlanje, McClounie; (2) Nyasa-Tanganyika plateau, Scott-Elliot.
B. reticulata, DC. (1) Shire River, Meller; Buchanan.
Bauhinia sp. (1) Buchanan.
Afzelia cuanzensis, Welw. (1) West shore of Lake Nyasa, Kirk; Buchanan.
Afzelia sp. (2) Carson.
Cryptosepalum maraviense, Oliv. (1) Maravi country, Kirk; (2) Nutt; Carson.
Cryptosepalum sp. (1) Lower plateau, north of Lake Nyasa, J. Thomson.

BOTANICAL APPENDICES

LEGUMINOSAE.
   Brachystegia appendiculata, Benth. (1) Zomba and east end of Lake Chilwa, Kirk; (2) Nyasa-Tanganyika plateau, Scott-Elliot; (4) Batoka country, Kirk.
   B. globiflora, Benth. (1) Shire Highlands, Whyte.
   B. longifolia, Benth. (1) Buchanan.
   B. floribunda, Benth. (1) Buchanan.
   Tamarindus indica, L. (1) Shire River, Kirk; Shire Highlands, Scott-Elliot; Buchanan; (4) up the Zambezi to the Batoka country, Kirk.
   Copaifera coleosperma, Benth. (4) Batoka country, Kirk.
   Burkea africana, Hook. (1) Buchanan.
   Trachylobium sp. Shire Highlands, Johnston.
   Erythrophleum guineense, Don. (1) Buchanan.
   Parkia filicoidea, Welw. (1) Shire Valley, Kirk; Buchanan.
   Entada abyssinica, Steud. (1) Zomba, Whyte.
   Entada spp. (1) Zomba and east end of Lake Chilwa, Meller; Buchanan.
   Piptadenia Buchanani, Baker. (1) Buchanan.
   Piptadenia sp. (1) Zomba, Whyte.
   Tetrapleura andongensis, Welw. (3) Serpa Pinto.
   Neptunia oleracea, Lour. (1) Shire River, Kirk.
   Dichrostachys nutans, Benth. (1) Zomba, Whyte.
   D. nyassana, Taub. (1) Buchanan.
   Acacia nigrescens, Oliv. (1) Shire River, Kirk.
   A. pennata, Willd. (1) Shire Valley, Kirk.
   A. lasiopetala, Oliv. (1) M'pemba hill, Kirk.
   A. albida, Del. (1) Shire River, Kirk.
   A. Kirkii, Oliv. (4) Batoka country, Kirk.
   A. Seyal, Del. (1) Mañanja hills, Meller.
   A. fastigiata, Oliv. (1) Buchanan.
   Acacia spp. (1) Buchanan.
   Calliandra sp. (1) Mlanje, McClounie.
   Albizzia anthelmintica, A. Brongn. (1) Shire River, Meller.
   A. Lebbek, Benth. (1) Buchanan.
   A. versicolor, Welw. (1) Maravi country, Kirk.
   A. fastigiata, E. Mey. (1) Buchanan; Mlanje, Whyte.

ROSACEAE.
   Parinarium Mobola, Oliv. (1) Buchanan; (4) Batoka country; Kirk.
   P. capense, Harv. (4) Sesheke, Kirk.
   Pygeum africanum, Hook. fil. (1) Foot of Chiradzulu, Kirk; Buchanan.
   Rubus apetalus, Poir. (1) Foot of Chiradzulu, Kirk; Mlanje, Whyte; Buchanan.
   R. huillensis, Welw. (1) Mlanje, Whyte.
   Rubus sp. (1) Buchanan.
   Alchemilla sp. (1) Mlanje, Whyte.
   Cliffortia linearifolia, Eck. et Zeyh. (1) Mlanje, Whyte.
   Cliffortia sp. (1) Mlanje, McClounie.

SAXIFRAGACEAE.
   Choristylis shirensis, Baker fil. (1) Mlanje, Whyte.

CRASSULACEAE.
   Tillaea pentandra, Royle. (1) Chiradzulu, Whyte; Blantyre, Last; Buchanan.
   T. aquatica, L. (1) Mlanje, Whyte.

CRASSULACEAE.
   Crassula globularioides, Britten. (1) Chiradzulu, Meller ; Mlanje, Whyte.
   C. abyssinica, A. Rich. (1) Zomba, Whyte ; Buchanan.
   Crassula spp. (1) Blantyre, Last ; Buchanan.
   Kalanchoe platysepala, Welw. (1) Shire Valley, Kirk.
   K. pilosa, Baker. (2) Mweru, Carson.
   K. coccinea, Welw. (1) Mañanja hills, Meller.
   Kalanchoe spp. (1) Chiradzulu, Whyte ; (2) Nutt ; Carson.
   Cotyledon sp. (1) Chiradzulu, Whyte.

DROSERACEAE.
   Drosera ramentacea, Burch. (1) Mlanje, McClounie.
   D. affinis, Welw. (2) Lower plateau, north of Lake Nyasa, J. Thomson.

HAMAMELIDEAE.
   Myrothamnus flabellifolia, Welw. (1) Mlanje, Whyte ; Buchanan.

COMBRETACEAE.
   Terminalia nyassensis, Engl. (1) Buchanan.
   Terminalia sp. (1) Buchanan.
   Combretum holosericeum, Sond. (1) Chiradzulu, Kirk.
   C. laurifolium, Engl. (1) Buchanan.
   C. tomentosum, Don. (4) Batoka country, Kirk.
   C. oatesii, Rolfe. (2) Nyasa-Tanganyika plateau, J. Thomson.
   C. mweroense, Baker. (2) Mweru, Carson.
   C. splendens, Engl. (1) Buchanan.
   Combretum spp. (1) Buchanan ; (2) Carson ; Nyasa-Tanganyika plateau, J. Thomson.

MYRTACEAE.
   Eugenia cordata, Laws. (1) Mañanja hills, Meller ; Buchanan.
   E. owariensis, P. Beauv. (1) Buchanan.
   Eugenia spp. (1) Buchanan ; (2) Lower plateau, north of Lake Nyasa, J. Thomson.

MELASTOMACEAE.
   Antherotoma Naudini, Hook. fil. (1) Zomba, Whyte ; (2) Nutt.
   Dissotis phaeotricha, Hook. fil. (1) Mpatamanga, Kirk ; Buchanan ; (2) Nutt ; Carson.
   D. Melleri, Hook. fil. (1) Chiradzulu and Mañanja hills, Meller ; Zomba, Kirk.
   D. princeps, Triana. (1) Mañanja hills, Meller and Kirk ; Mlanje, Chiradzulu, and Zomba, Whyte ; Buchanan.
   D. incana, Triana. (1) Mlanje, Whyte ; Buchanan.
   D. johnstoniana, Baker fil. (1) Mlanje, Whyte.
   D. cryptantha, Baker. (1) Buchanan.
   Dissotis spp. (1) Buchanan ; (2) Carson.
   Tristemma sp. (2) Carson.
   Osbeckia Antherotoma, Naud. (1) Shire Highlands, K. C. Cameron.
   Osbeckia spp. (1) Buchanan ; (2) Lower plateau, north of Lake Nyasa, J. Thomson.

LYTHRACEAE.
   Rotala filiformis, Hiern. (4) Victoria Falls, Kirk.
   Nesaea heptamera, Hiern. (1) Zomba and east end of Lake Chilwa, Meller.
   N. floribunda, Sond. (1) Buchanan ; (4) Victoria Falls, Kirk.
   Ammannia salicifolia, Monti. (2) Carson.
   A. senegalensis, Lam. (1) Buchanan.
   Ammannia sp. (2) Carson ; (4) Menyharth.
   Heteropyxis natalensis, Haw. (1) Buchanan.

BOTANICAL APPENDICES

ONAGRACEAE.
Epilobium sp. (2) Carson.
Jussiaea pilosa, H. B. K. (1) Shire Valley, Kirk; Upper Shire, Scott-Elliot.
J. villosa, Lam. (1) Lower Shire Valley, Meller.
J linifolia, Vahl. (1) Upper Shire, Scott-Elliot; Buchanan.
Ludwigia prostrata, Roxb. (1) Buchanan.
L. parvifolia, Roxb. (1) Buchanan.
L. jussiaeoides, Lam. (1) Buchanan.
Trapa bispinosa, Roxb. (1) Shire River, Kirk; Blantyre, Last; Lake Nyasa, Laws(?).

HALORAGEAE.
Myriophyllum sp. (1) Lake Nyasa, Laws.

SAMYDACEAE.
Homalium africanum, Benth. (1) Mlanje, Whyte; Buchanan.

TURNERACEAE.
Wormskioldia longepedunculata, Mast. (1) Mañanja hills, Meller and Waller; Buchanan; Mlanje, Whyte; Shire Highlands, Scott-Elliot; (2) North Nyasa, L. Scott; Carson; var. *integrifolia*, Urb., Blantyre, Last.
W. lobata, Urb. (1) Buchanan.

PASSIFLOREAE.
Tryphostemma apetalum, Baker fil. (1) Zomba, Whyte.
Tryphostemma sp. (1) Mlanje, Scott-Elliot.
Modecca stricta, Mast. (1) Murchison Falls, Meller.
Modecca sp. (1) Buchanan.

CUCURBITACEAE.
Trochomeria macrocarpa, Hook. fil. (1) North of Chiradzulu, Kirk.
Adenopus breviflorus, Benth. (1) Elephant Marsh on Shire River, Kirk; Buchanan.
Luffa aegyptiaca, Miller. (1) Buchanan.
Luffa sp. (2) Carson.
Lagenaria sp. (1) Buchanan.
Momordica Charantia, L. (1) Shire Valley, Kirk; Buchanan.
M. Morkorra, A. Rich. (2) Nyasa-Tanganyika plateau, J. Thomson.
M. foetida, Schum. et Thonn. (1) Zomba, Whyte.
Momordica spp. (1) Shire Highlands, Scott-Elliot.
Raphanocarpus Kirkii, Hook. fil. (1) Shire River, Kirk; (4) Menyharth.
Cucumis metuliferus, E. Mey. (1) Shire River, Kirk.
C. Melo, L. (1) Buchanan.
Cucumis spp. (1) Buchanan; Shire Highlands, Scott-Elliot; (2) Carson.
Zehneria microsperma, Hook. fil. (1) Katunga, Meller.
Zehneria sp. (1) Chiradzulu, Whyte; Buchanan.
Mukia scabrella, Arn. (1) Shire River, Kirk.
Cephalandra sp.? (1) Mlanje, Scott-Elliot.
Ctenolepis sp.? (1) Shire Highlands, Scott-Elliot.

BEGONIACEAE.
Begonia sp. (1) Nyasa-Tanganyika plateau, J. Thomson; Carson.

FICOIDEAE.
> *Mollugo nudicaulis*, Lam. (1) Buchanan.
> *M. Glinus*, A. Rich. (1) Lake Nyasa, Scott-Elliot.
> *M. Spergula*, L. (1) Buchanan ; (2) Carson.
> *M. verticillata*, L. (1) Buchanan.
> *Mollugo* sp. (1) Buchanan.

UMBELLIFERAE.
> *Hydrocotyle moschata*, Forst. (1) Chiradzulu, Kirk.
> *H. asiatica*, L. (1) Ruangwa, near Lake Nyasa, Kirk ; Buchanan ; Mlanje, Whyte.
> *Alepidea anatymbica*, Eck. et Zeyh. (1) Sochi, Kirk ; Zomba, Whyte ; Buchanan ; (2) Upper plateau, north of Lake Nyasa, J. Thomson ; Carson.
> *Sanicula europaea*, L. (1) Buchanan.
> *Heteromorpha arborescens*, Cham. et Schlecht. (1) Mañanja hills, Meller ; Chiradzulu, Whyte ; Buchanan ; Blantyre, Last.
> *Pimpinella* sp. (1) Buchanan ; (2) Nutt.
> *Diplolophium zambeziacum*, Hiern. (4) Batoka country, Kirk.
> *Physotrichia Buchanani*, Benth. (1) Buchanan ; Mlanje, Whyte ; Zomba, Kirk.
> *Physotrichia* sp. (1) Buchanan.
> *Peucedanum fraxinifolium*, Hiern. (1) Mañanja hills, Meller ; Chiradzulu, Whyte ; Buchanan.
> *Peucedanum* sp. (1) Buchanan ; Mlanje, Whyte ; (2) Carson.
> *Lefeburia* spp. (1) Shire Highlands, Scott-Elliot ; Buchanan.
> *Caucalis infesta*, Curt. (1) Chiradzulu, Whyte.
> *C. melanantha*, Benth. et Hook. fil. (1) Mlanje, Whyte ; (2) Lower plateau, north of Lake Nyasa, J. Thomson.
> *C. pedunculata*, Baker fil. (1) Mlanje, Whyte.
> *Caucalis* sp. (1) Buchanan.

ARALIACEAE.
> *Cussonia spicata*, Thunb. (1) Chiradzulu, Kirk ; Buchanan.
> *C. Kirkii*, Seem. (1) Shire Highlands, Scott-Elliot.
> *Cussonia* sp. (1) Mlanje, Whyte ; Buchanan.

RUBIACEAE.
> *Adina microcephala*, Hiern? (1) Buchanan.
> *Hymenodictyon Kurria*, Hochst. (1) Buchanan.
> *H. parvifolium*, Oliv. (1) Buchanan.
> *Crossopteryx kotschyana*, Fenzl. (1) Buchanan.
> *Pentas purpurea*, Oliv. (1) Mañanja hills, Sochi and Mbami, Kirk ; Buchanan ; Mlanje and Chiradzulu, Whyte.
> *P. carnea*, Benth., var. *Klotzschii*, Scott-Elliot. (1) Buchanan.
> *P. longiflora*, Oliv., var. *nyassana*, Scott-Elliot. (1) Buchanan ; Mlanje, McClounie ; Chiradzulu, Whyte ; (2) Lower plateau, north of Lake Nyasa, J. Thomson ; Carson.
> *P. confertifolia*, Baker. (2) Carson.
> *P. modesta*, Baker. (2) Mweru, Carson.
> *Pentas* spp. Buchanan ; (2) Carson ; Nutt.
> *Otomeria dilata*, Hiern. (1) Zomba and Mlanje, Whyte.
> *Otomeria* sp. (*Pentas speciosa*, Baker). (1) Mlanje, Whyte ; Buchanan ; Blantyre, Last.
> *Otomeria* sp. (2) Carson.
> *Hedyotis* spp. (1) Buchanan ; (2) Carson.

BOTANICAL APPENDICES

RUBIACEAE.
Pentodon decumbens, Hochst. (1) Zomba, Whyte.
Oldenlandia trinervia, Retz. (1) Buchanan.
O. echinulosa, K. Schum. (1) Buchanan.
O. globosa, Hiern. (1) Buchanan.
O. corymbosa, L. (1) Buchanan; (2) Nutt.
O. macrophylla, DC. (1) Buchanan.
O. macrodonta, Baker. (2) Carson.
O. effusa, Oliv. (1) Buchanan; Shire Highlands, K. C. Cameron.
O. Heynei, Oliv. (1) Buchanan; Blantyre, Last; (2) Carson.
O. Bojeri, Hiern. (1) Buchanan; (3) Serpa Pinto.
O. tenuissima, Hiern. (4) Victoria Falls, Kirk.
O. oliveriana, K. Schum. (1) Mlanje, Whyte and McClounie.
O. hedyotoides, Boiss. (1) Mlanje, Scott-Elliot.
O. lancifolia, Schweinf. (1) Shire Highlands, Scott-Elliot.
O. virgata, DC. (2) Carson.
Oldenlandia spp. (1) Buchanan; Mlanje and Zomba, Whyte; Blantyre, Last; (2) Carson.
Mussaenda arcuata, Poir. Mañanja hills, Waller; Kanjanje, Kirk; Buchanan; Shire Highlands, Scott-Elliot; (2) Nutt.
Mussaenda sp. (1) Mlanje, McClounie.
Sabicea sp.? (1) Buchanan.
Heinsia jasminiflora, DC. (1) Shire River, Kirk; Blantyre, Last.
H. benguelensis, Welw. (2) Lower plateau, north of Lake Nyasa, J. Thomson.
Heinsia sp. (1) Mlanje, McClounie.
Bertiera sp.? (4) Menyharth.
Leptactina sp. (1) Mlanje, McClounie.
Chomelia Buchananii, K. Schum. (1) Buchanan.
Randia Buchananii, Oliv. (1) Zomba, Whyte.
Randia spp. (1) Buchanan; Chiradzulu, Kirk; (2) Nutt.
Gardenia Thunbergia, L. fil. (1) Lake Chilwa, Meller; Mañanja hills, Waller; Buchanan.
G. resiniflua, Hiern. (1) Lake Nyasa, Kirk.
G. Manganjae, Hiern. (1) Mañanja, Meller; Chiradzulu, Kirk; Buchanan.
Gardenia sp. (1) Near Lake Chilwa, Kirk; Buchanan.
Oxyanthus sp.? (1) Buchanan.
Zygoon graveolens, Hiern. (1) Shire rapids, Kirk.
Empogona Kirkii, Hook. fil. (1) Lake Nyasa, Kirk; (4) Menyharth.
Tricalysia Nyassae, Hiern. (1) West shore of Lake Nyasa, Kirk.
T. jasminiflora, Benth. et Hook. fil. (1) Lower Shire, Kirk; Mañanja hills, Meller; Buchanan.
T. Kirkii, Hiern. (1) River Shire, Kirk.
Tricalysia spp. (1) Buchanan.
Pentanisia Schweinfurthii, Hiern. (2) Nutt; Lower plateau, north of Lake Nyasa, Thomson.
Pentanisia spp. (1) Buchanan; (2) Lower plateau, north of Lake Nyasa, J. Thomson.
Cremaspora africana, Benth. (1) Buchanan.
C. coffeoides, Hemsl. (1) Ruo River, Johnston.
C. heterophylla, K. Schum. (1) Buchanan.
Polysphaeria lanceolata, Hiern. (2) Karonga and Nyasa-Tanganyika plateau, Scott-Elliot.
Polysphaeria spp. (1) Buchanan; (4) Menyharth.
Canthium foetidum, Hiern. (1) Mpatamanga, Kirk.

RUBIACEAE.
    Canthium zanquebaricum, Klotzsch. (1) West shore of Lake Nyasa, Kirk.
    C. lanciflorum, Hiern. (1) Buchanan ; (4) Victoria Falls, Kirk.
    C. Guenzii, Sond. (1) Zomba, Whyte ; Buchanan ; (2) Upper plateau, north of Lake Nyasa, J. Thomson.
    Canthium spp. (1) Buchanan ; Shire Highlands, Scott-Elliot ; (4) Menyharth.
    Plectronia sp. (2) Carson.
    Vangueria velutina, Hiern. (1) Shire Highlands, Scott-Elliot ; Buchanan ; (4) Batoka country, Kirk.
    V. edulis, Vahl. (1) Buchanan.
    V. infausta, Burch. (1) Buchanan.
    Vangueria sp. (1) Shire Highlands, Scott-Elliot.
    Fadogia ancylantha, Schweinf. (1) Buchanan.
    F. triphylla, Baker. (2) Carson.
    Fadogia spp. (1) Buchanan ; (2) Nyasa-Tanganyika plateau, Scott-Elliot and J. Thomson ; Carson.
    Craterispermum laurinum, Benth. (2) Nyasa-Tanganyika plateau, Scott-Elliot.
    Ixora laxiflora, Sm. (1) Shire Highlands, Scott-Elliot.
    Ixora sp. (1) Buchanan.
    Coffea arabica, L. (1) Chiradzulu, Whyte.
    Pavetta gracilis, Klotzsch. (1) Mañanja hills, Kirk ; Shire Highlands, Scott-Elliot ; (4) Menyharth.
    P. Baconia, Hiern. (2) Nyasa-Tanganyika plateau, Scott-Elliot.
    P. schumanniana, Ferd. Hoffm. (1) Buchanan.
    P. canescens, DC. (1) Zomba, Whyte.
    Pavetta sp. (1) Mlanje, McClounie ; Zomba and Chiradzulu, Whyte ; Buchanan.
    Psychotria hirtella, Oliv. (1) Mlanje, Whyte.
    Psychotria sp. (1) Mlanje, McClounie ; Zomba, Whyte ; Buchanan.
    Grumilea Kirkii, Hiern. (1) Zomba, Kirk.
    Siphomeris foetens, Hiern. (1) Shire Rapids, Kirk ; (4) Menyharth.
    Otiophora sp. (2) Lower plateau, north of Lake Nyasa, J. Thomson.
    Anthospermum whyteanum, Britten. (1) Mlanje, Whyte.
    A. lanceolatum, Thunb. (1) Mlanje, Whyte ; Buchanan.
    Anthospermum sp. (1) Buchanan ; Mlanje, McClounie ; (2) Lower plateau, north of Lake Nyasa, J. Thomson.
    Paederia foetida, L. (1) Buchanan.
    Spermacoce senensis, Hiern. (1) Near Sochi, Kirk.
    S. dibrachiata, Oliv. (1) Mañanja hills, Kirk and Meller ; Buchanan ; Mlanje, Whyte ; Blantyre, Last.
    S. stricta, L. (1) Blantyre, Last ; Buchanan ; (2) Carson.
    Spermacoce spp. (1) Buchanan ; (2) Lower plateau, north of Lake Nyasa, J. Thomson ; Nutt.
    Richardia sp. (1) Shire Highlands, K. C. Cameron.
    Rubia cordifolia, L. (1) Shire Highlands, K. C. Cameron ; Buchanan ; Chiradzulu, Whyte.
    Galium Aparine, L. (1) Mlanje, Whyte.
    G. erectum, Huds. (1) Shire Highlands, Scott-Elliot.
    G. stenophyllum, Baker. (1) Buchanan ; (2) Nutt ; Carson.
    G. Mollugo, L. (1) Shire Highlands, Scott-Elliot.
    Galium spp. (1) Buchanan ; (2) Nyasa-Tanganyika plateau, Scott-Elliot ; Carson.

VALERIANACEAE.
    Valeriana capensis, Thunb. (1) Mlanje, Whyte.

BOTANICAL APPENDICES 251

DIPSACEAE.
   Cephalaria centauroides, Roem. et Schult. (1) Between Mbami and Sochi, Kirk; Buchanan; (2) Nutt; Carson; Nyasa-Tanganyika plateau, Scott-Elliot.
   Cephalaria sp. (2) Upper plateau, north of Lake Nyasa, J. Thomson.
   Scabiosa Columbaria, L. (1) Blantyre, Last; Shire Highlands, Scott-Elliot; Buchanan; (2) Upper and Lower plateaux, north of Lake Nyasa, J. Thomson.

COMPOSITAE.
   Gutenbergia polycephala, O. et H. (1) Lake Chilwa, Kirk.
   Bothriocline Schimperi, O. et H. (1) Blantyre, Last; Mlanje and Chiradzulu, Whyte; Buchanan.
   B. laxa, N. E. Br. (1) Blantyre, Last.
   Vernonia marginata, O. et H. (1) Shire River, Stewart; Buchanan; Zomba and Chiradzulu, Whyte; (2) Lower plateau, north of Lake Nyasa, J. Thomson.
   V. purpurea, Sch. Bip. (1) Chiradzulu, Meller.
   V. cistifolia, O. Hoffm., var. *rosea*, O. Hoffm. (1) Buchanan.
   V. Melleri, O. et H. (1) Mañanja hills, Meller.
   V. oxyura, O. Hoffm. (1) Buchanan.
   V. pteropoda, O. et H. (1) Chiradzulu, Meller and Whyte; Mlanje, Whyte; Buchanan.
   V. senegalensis, Less. (1) Near Katunga, Meller; (2) Nutt.
   V. glabra, Vatke. (1) Shire River, Meller; Buchanan; Mlanje, Whyte; (2) Lower plateau, north of Lake Nyasa, J. Thomson.
   V. shirensis, O. et H. (1) Shire Valley, Meller.
   V. oocephala, Baker. (1) Carson.
   V. livingstoniana, O. et H. (1) Mañanja hills, Meller; Shire, Stewart; Buchanan.
   V. podocoma, Sch. Bip. (1) Mañanja hills, Meller; Buchanan.
   V. aemulans, Vatke. (1) Mlanje, McClounie.
   V. cinerascens, Sch. Bip. (1) Lake Nyasa, Scott-Elliot.
   V. decumbens, Vatke. (1) Buchanan.
   V. cinerea, Less. (1) Chiradzulu, Whyte; Buchanan; Blantyre, Last; (2) Carson.
   V. natalensis, Sch. Bip. (1) Shire Highlands, Scott-Elliot; Zomba and Mlanje, Whyte.
   V. Perottetii, Sch. Bip. (2) Carson.
   V. poskeana, Vatke et Hildebr. (1) Buchanan; Upper Shire, Scott-Elliot; Blantyre, Last; Mlanje, Whyte; (2) Carson.
   V. subaphylla, Baker. (2) Mweru, Carson.
   V. whyteana, Britten. (1) Zomba, Whyte.
   Vernonia spp. (1 and 2.) There are many unnamed specimens in the Herbarium at Kew from all the botanists who have collected in these two regions.
   Elephantopus scaber, L. (1) Buchanan.
   Elephantopus sp. (2) Carson.
   Adenostemma viscosum, Forst. (1) Buchanan.
   Aster sp. (1) Mlanje, McClounie.
   Ageratum conyzoides, L. (1) Mlanje and Chiradzulu, Whyte; Buchanan.
   Eupatorium africanum, O. et H. (1) Buchanan; Mlanje and Zomba, Whyte.
   Mikania scandens, Willd. (1) Murchison Falls, Meller; Buchanan; Chiradzulu and Zomba, Whyte; (2) Carson.
   Dicrocephala latifolia, DC. (1) Mlanje, Whyte; Buchanan.
   Felicia abyssinica, Sch. Bip. (2) Lower plateau, north of Lake Nyasa, J. Thomson.
   Felicia sp. (2) Upper plateau, north of Lake Nyasa, J. Thomson.
   Erigeron sp. (2) Nutt.
   Microglossa volubilis, DC. (1) Mañanja hills, Meller; Buchanan.
   Nidorella microcephala, Steetz. (1) Shire Valley, Meller; Mlanje and Zomba, Whyte; Lake Nyasa, Scott-Elliot; Buchanan.

COMPOSITAE.
Nidorella sp. (1) Chiradzulu, Whyte; Buchanan.
Conyza persicifolia, O. et H. (1) Mlanje, McClounie; Chiradzulu, Whyte; Buchanan.
C. variegata, Sch. Bip. (1) Mlanje, Whyte.
C. Hochstetteri, Sch. Bip. (1) Buchanan.
C. aegyptiaca, Ait. (1) Mlanje, Whyte.
Conyza spp. (1) Buchanan; Shire Highlands, Scott-Elliot; (2) Nyasa-Tanganyika plateau, Scott-Elliot.
Psiadia sp. (1) Buchanan; (2) Upper plateau, north of Lake Nyasa, J. Thomson.
Blumea lacera, DC. (1) Zomba, Whyte; Buchanan; (2) Nyasa-Tanganyika plateau, Scott-Elliot.
Blumea sp. (1) Buchanan.
Laggera brevipes, O. et H. (1) Sochi, Kirk.
L. alata, Sch. Bip. (1) Buchanan; (2) Lower plateau, north of Lake Nyasa, J. Thomson.
Denekia capensis, Thunb. (4) Batoka country, Kirk.
Sphaeranthus hirtus, Willd. (1) Buchanan.
Sphaeranthus sp. (1) Shire Highlands, K. C. Cameron; (2) Carson; Lower plateau, north of Lake Nyasa, J. Thomson; (4) Menyharth.
Amphidoxa filaginea, Ficalho et Hiern. (3) Serpa Pinto.
Achyrocline batocana, O. et H. (4) Batoka country, Kirk.
A. Hochstetteri, Sch. Bip. (1) Blantyre, Last; Mlanje, Whyte.
A. Schimperi, Sch. Bip. (1) Mañanja hills, Meller; Mlanje, Whyte.
Gnaphalium Steudelii, Sch. Bip. (1) Mañanja hills, Meller; Buchanan.
G. luteo-album, L. (1) Shire Highlands, Scott-Elliot; Mlanje, Whyte; Buchanan.
Gnaphalium sp. (1) Buchanan.
Helichrysum pachyrhizum, Harv. (4) Batoka country, Kirk.
H. auriculatum, Less. (1) Mañanja hills, Meller; Shire, Stewart; Zomba, Whyte; Buchanan; Katunga, Kirk.
H. Kirkii, O. et H. (1) Mañanja hills, Meller; Sochi, Kirk; Shire, Stewart; Maravi country (?) Kirk; Buchanan; Blantyre, Last; (2) Carson; Nutt.
H. nitens, O. et H. (1) Chiradzulu, Meller; Mlanje, Whyte and McClounie; Blantyre, Last; Buchanan.
H. argyrosphaerum, DC. (1) Maravi country. Livingstone and Kirk.
H. globosum, Sch. Bip. (1) Buchanan.
H. gerberaefolium, Sch. Bip. (1) Sochi, Kirk; Shire River, Stewart; Mlanje, Whyte.
H. Petersii, O. et H. (1) Mpatamanga, Kirk.
H. oxyphyllum, DC. (1) Mañanja hills, Meller.
H. cymosum, D. Don. (1) Mlanje, Whyte; Blantyre, Last; Buchanan.
H. Buchananii, Engl. (1) Mlanje and Zomba, Whyte; Mlanje, McClounie; Blantyre, Last; Buchanan.
H. nudiflorum, Less. (1) Mlanje, Whyte; (3) Serpa Pinto.
H. whyteanum, Britten. (1) Mlanje, Whyte and McClounie; Buchanan.
H. milanjiense, Britten. (1) Mlanje, Whyte and McClounie.
H. densiflorum, Oliv. (1) Mlanje and Zomba, Whyte; Buchanan.
H. latifolium, Less. (1) Mlanje, Whyte and McClounie.
H. undatum, Less. (1) Zomba, Whyte; Buchanan; Blantyre, L. Scott.
H. Lastii, Engl. (1) Zomba, Whyte.
H. foetidum, Cass. (2) Lower plateau, north of Lake Nyasa, J. Thomson.
Helichrysum spp. (1) Buchanan; Shire Highlands, Scott-Elliot; Mlanje, McClounie; Blantyre, Last and L. Scott; (2) Upper and Lower plateaux, north of Lake Nyasa, J. Thomson.
Athrixia rosmarinifolia, O. et H. (1) Chiradzulu, Meller; Zomba, Mlanje, and Chiradzulu, Whyte; Buchanan; (2) Lower plateau, north of Lake Nyasa, J. Thomson.

BOTANICAL APPENDICES

COMPOSITAE.
Inula glomerata, O. et H. (1) Sochi, Kirk; Buchanan.
I. shirensis, Oliv. (1) Buchanan.
Inula spp. (1) Buchanan.
Bojeria vestita, Baker. (2) Carson.
Geigeria Zeyheri, Harv. (3) Serpa Pinto.
Sphacophyllum Lastii, O. Hoffm. (1) Blantyre, Last.
S. Kirkii, Oliv. (1) Zomba, Kirk.
Anisopappus africanus, O. et H. (1) Buchanan.
Anisopappus sp. (2) Carson.
Ambrosia sp. (2) Carson.
Eclipta erecta, L. (1) Buchanan.
Epallage dentata, DC. (1) Mlanje, Whyte.
Blainvillea gayana, Cass. (1) Mlanje, Whyte.
Blainvillea sp. (1) Buchanan.
Aspilia Kotschyi, Benth. et Hook. fil. (1) Buchanan.
Aspilia spp. (1) Shire Highlands and Lake Nyasa, Scott-Elliot; Buchanan; Chiradzulu, Whyte; (2) Carson; Nyasa-Tanganyika plateau, J. Thomson; Nutt.
Melanthera abyssinica, O. et H. (1) Zomba, Whyte.
M. Brownei, Sch. Bip. (1) Zomba, Whyte; (2) Carson.
Spilanthes Acmella, L. (1) Shire River, Kirk; Mlanje, Whyte; Buchanan.
Spilanthes sp. (2) Nutt.
Siegesbeckia abyssinica, O. et H. (1) Buchanan.
Guizotia bidentoides, O. et H. (1) Mañanja hills, Kirk.
Guizotia sp. (1) Buchanan.
Coreopsis Steppia, Steetz. (1) Mañanja hills, Kirk; Chiradzulu, Whyte; Buchanan; (2) Carson.
C. Grantii, Oliv. (2) Carson.
Coreopsis spp. (1) Shire Highlands, Scott-Elliot; Buchanan; (2) Nutt.
Bidens lineariloba, O. et H. (2) Carson.
B. pilosa, L. (1) Mlanje and Chiradzulu, Whyte; Buchanan; (2) Lower plateau, north of Lake Nyasa, J. Thomson.
Bidens sp. (2) Carson.
Chrysanthellum procumbens, Pers. (1) Buchanan.
Jaumea sp. (1) Buchanan; (2) Carson.
Gynura cernua, Benth. (1) Zomba and Chiradzulu, Whyte; Mañanja hills, Meller; Blantyre, Last; Buchanan; (2) Nyasa-Tanganyika plateau, Scott-Elliot; Lower plateau, north of Lake Nyasa, J. Thomson; Carson.
G. amplexicaulis, O. et H. (1) Mlanje, Whyte.
G. crepidioides, Benth. (1) Mlanje, Whyte; (2) Carson.
G. vitellina, Benth. (2) Carson.
Gynura spp. (1) Buchanan; (2) Nutt; Carson.
Gongrothamnus divaricatus, Steetz. (1) Lower Shire Valley, Kirk and Meller.
Cineraria kilimanscharica, Engl. (1) Mlanje, Whyte.
Cineraria spp. (1) Buchanan.
Emilia sagittata, DC. (1) Mañanja hills, Meller; Shire Valley, Kirk; Blantyre, Last; (2) Carson.
E. integrifolia, Baker. (2) Nutt; Carson; Lower plateau north of Lake Nyasa, J. Thomson.
Emilia sp. (1) Buchanan.
Senecio bupleuroides, DC. (1) Mañanja hills, Meller; Sochi, Kirk; Buchanan.
S. cyaneus, O. Hoffm. (1) Buchanan.

COMPOSITAE.
Senecio deltoideus, Less. (1) ? Mpatamanja, Kirk ; Buchanan.
S. subscandens, Hochst. (1) Murchison Falls, Meller.
S. mweroensis, Baker. (2) Mweru, Carson.
S. lasiorhizus, DC. (1) Mlanje, McClounie and ? Whyte.
S. latifolius, DC. (1) Shire Highlands, Scott-Elliot ; Mlanje and Zomba, Whyte.
S. auriculatissimus, Britten. (1) Zomba and Mlanje, Whyte ; Buchanan.
S. whyteanus, Britten. (1) Mlanje, Whyte.
Senecio spp. (1) Buchanan ; Shire Highlands, Scott-Elliot ; Chiradzulu, Whyte ; (2) Nutt ; Carson.
Othonna whyteana, Britten. (1) Mlanje, Whyte and McClounie.
Tripteris monocephala, O. et H. (1) Mañanja hills, Meller.
Osteospermum moniliferum, L. (1) Buchanan ; (2) Lower plateau, north of Lake Nyasa, J. Thomson.
Haplocarpha scaposa, Harv. (1) Sochi, Kirk ; (2) Carson.
Gazania serrulata, DC. (1) Sochi, Kirk.
Gazania sp. (1) Zomba, Whyte.
Berkheya Zeyheri, Sond. et Harv. (1) Kanjanje, Kirk ; Buchanan ; (2) Upper plateau, north of Lake Nyasa, J. Thomson.
B. johnstoniana, Britten. (1) Mlanje, Whyte.
B. subulata, Harv. (1) Zomba, Kirk ; Shire Highlands, Scott-Elliot ; Buchanan.
Berkheya sp. (2) Carson.
Carduus leptacanthus, Nees. (1) Buchanan.
Pleiotaxis pulcherrima, Steetz. (2) Carson.
Pleiotaxis sp. (2) Carson.
Erythrocephalum zambesiacum, O. et H. (1) Shire Valley, Waller ; Mañanja country, Kirk ; Blantyre, Last ; Buchanan ; Shire Highlands, Scott-Elliot ; Mlanje and Zomba, Whyte.
Erythrocephalum spp. (2) Carson ; Lower plateau, north of Lake Nyasa, J. Thomson.
Phyllactinia Grantii, Benth. (2) Carson.
Dicoma Kirkii, Harv. (4) Batoka country, Kirk.
D. sessiliflora, Harv. (1) Lake Chilwa, Kirk ; Buchanan ; (2) Carson.
D. anomala, Sond. (1) Buchanan ; (2) Carson ; (3) Serpa Pinto.
D. tomentosa, Cass. (4) Menyharth.
D. quinquevulnera, Baker. (2) Mweru, Carson.
Gerbera abyssinica, Sch. Bip. (1) Mlanje, Whyte and McClounie ; Zomba, Whyte ; Buchanan.
G. piloselloides, Cass. (1) Shire Highlands, Scott-Elliot ; Buchanan ; (2) Lower plateau, north of Lake Nyasa, J. Thomson.
Gerbera spp. (1) Shire Highlands, Scott-Elliot ; Buchanan ; (2) Nyasa-Tanganyika plateau, Scott-Elliot ; Upper plateau, north of Lake Nyasa, J. Thomson.
Tolpis abyssinica, Sch. Bip. (1) Mlanje and Zomba, Whyte.
Crepis sp. (1) Mlanje, Whyte and McClounie ; Buchanan.
Lactuca abyssinica, Fresen. (1) Buchanan.
L. capensis, Thunb. (1) Buchanan ; Mlanje and Zomba, Whyte ; (2) Carson.
Lactuca sp. (1) Mlanje, McClounie ; (2) Carson.
Sonchus Bipontini, Aschers. (1) Lower Shire Valley, Meller.
S. Schweinfurthii, O. et H. (1) Buchanan.
S. rarifolius, O. et H. (1) Zomba and east end of Lake Chilwa, Meller.
S. oleraceus, L. (1) Buchanan.
Sonchus spp. (1) Buchanan ; Mlanje, McClounie.
Lobelia trullifolia, Hemsl. (1) Chiradzulu, Meller.

BOTANICAL APPENDICES

CAMPANULACEAE.
    Lobelia Melleri, Hemsl. (1) Chiradzulu, Whyte; Buchanan.
    L. Nyassae, Engl. (1) Buchanan.
    L. nuda, Hemsl. (4) Batoka country, Kirk.
    L. fervens, Thunb. (1) Mlanje, Whyte.
    L. natalensis, A. DC. (1) Zomba, Whyte; (4) Victoria Falls, Kirk.
    L. coronopifolia, L. (1) Mlanje, McClounie; Zomba, Whyte.
    Lobelia spp. (1) Buchanan; Mlanje, Whyte; Blantyre, Last; (2) Carson; Nutt; Upper and Lower plateaux, north of Lake Nyasa, J. Thomson.
    Cephalostigma hirsutum, Edgw. (1) Near Katunga, Meller.
    Sphenoclea zeylanica, Gaertn. (4) Menyharth.
    Lightfootia abyssinica, Hochst. (1) Mañanja hills, Meller; Mlanje and Zomba, Whyte; Buchanan; Shire Highlands, Scott-Elliot; (2) Nutt.
    L. arenaria, A. DC. (1) Blantyre, Last.
    Lightfootia, spp. (1) Buchanan; (2) Upper and Lower plateaux, north of Lake Nyasa, J. Thomson.
    Wahlenbergia oppositifolia, A. DC. (1) Mlanje, Whyte.
    W. virgata, Engl. (1) Mlanje, Whyte and McClounie; Buchanan.
    Wahlenbergia spp. (1) McClounie; Buchanan; (2) Nutt; Lower plateau, north of Lake Nyasa, J. Thomson.

VACCINIACEAE.
    Vaccinium africanum, Britten. (1) Mlanje, Whyte and McClounie.

ERICACEAE.
    Agauria salicifolia, Hook. fil. (1) Buchanan; (2) Lower plateau, north of Lake Nyasa, J. Thomson.
    Erica johnstoniana, Britten. (1) Mlanje, Whyte.
    E. whyteana, Britten. (1) Mlanje, Whyte.
    Erica sp. (1) Zomba, Whyte; Mlanje, McClounie; Buchanan.
    Blaeria setulosa, Welw. (1) Mlanje, Whyte.
    B. microdonta, Wright. (1) Mlanje, McClounie.
    Blaeria sp. (1) Blantyre, Last.
    Philippia milanjiensis, Britten et Rendle. (1) Mlanje, Whyte.
    P. benguellensis, Welw. (1) Mlanje, Whyte.
    Philippia spp. (1) Buchanan; Shire Highlands, Scott-Elliot.
    Ericinella Mannii, Hook. fil. (1) Buchanan.

PLUMBAGINACEAE.
    Plumbago zeylanica, L. (1) Buchanan; (2) Carson.

PRIMULACEAE.
    Anagallis quartiniana, Engl. (1) Mlanje, McClounie.
    Anagallis sp. (2) Carson.

MYRSINEAE.
    Maesa lanceolata, Forsk. (1) Chiradzulu, Whyte; Buchanan.
    Maesa sp. (1) Buchanan.
    Myrsine africana, L. (1) Mlanje, McClounie; Buchanan.
    Ardisia sp. (1) Buchanan.

SAPOTACEAE.
    Chrysophyllum magalismontanum, Sond. (4) Batoka country, Kirk.
    C. Stuhlmannii, Engl. (1) Buchanan.
    Chrysophyllum spp. (1) Buchanan.
    Sideroxylon brevipes, Baker. (2) North end of Lake Nyasa, Kirk.
    Mimusops Mochisia, Baker. (4) Batoka country, Kirk.
    M. Kirkii, Baker. (1) Lower Shire Valley, Kirk.
    M. Buchananii, Engl. (1) Buchanan.

EBENACEAE.
    Royena pallens, Thunb. (1) Mañanja hills, Meller; (4) Sesheke, Kirk.
    R. whyteana, Hiern. (1) Mlanje, Whyte.
    Royena sp. (1) Buchanan.
    Euclea Divinorum, Hiern. (4) Victoria Falls, Kirk.
    E. multiflora, Hiern. (4) Menyharth.
    Euclea sp. (1) Buchanan.
    Maba spp. (1) Buchanan.
    Diospyros shirensis, Hiern. (1) Fort Johnston and River Ruo, Scott-Elliot.
    D. batokana, Hiern. (4) Batoka country, Kirk.
    Diospyros sp. (1) Shire Highlands, Scott-Elliot.

OLEACEAE.
    Jasminium stenolobum, Harv. (1) Mañanja hills, Meller; Shire Highlands, Scott-Elliot; Buchanan; (4) Batoka country, Kirk.
    J. brachyscyphum, Baker. (1) Buchanan; Mlanje, McClounie.
    J. Walleri, Baker. (1) Mañanja hills, Waller.
    J. mauritianum, Bojer. (1) Buchanan; (2) Nyasa-Tanganyika plateau, J. Thomson; (4) Sesheke, Holub.
    J. microphyllum, Baker. (1) Mlanje, McClounie.
    J. Kirkii, Baker. (1) Shire Highlands, Scott-Elliot.
    Jasminium spp. (1) Buchanan.
    Schrebera Buchanani, Baker. (1) Buchanan.
    S. alata, Welw. (1) Buchanan.
    S. golungensis, Welw. (4) Menyharth.
    Schrebera sp. (1) Buchanan.

SALVADORACEAE.
    Salvadora persica, L. (1) Buchanan; (4) Menyharth.
    Azima spp. (1) Shire Highlands, Scott-Elliot; (4) Menyharth.

APOCYNACEAE.
    Landolphia Kirkii, Dyer. (1) Zomba, Whyte.
    Landolphia sp. (1) Buchanan.
    Carissa Arduina, Lam. (1) Buchanan.
    C. edulis, Vahl. (1) Buchanan; Mañanja hills, Meller; Chiradzulu, Whyte and Kirk; (4) Victoria Falls, Kirk.
    Diplorrhynchus mossambicensis, Benth. (1) Buchanan; (4) Menyharth.
    D. psilopus, Welw. (3) Serpa Pinto.
    Rauwolfia caffra, Sond. (1) Buchanan; Mañanja and Katunga, Kirk.
    Holarrhena febrifuga, Klotzsch. (1) Buchanan; Mañanja hills, Meller; west side of Lake Nyasa, Kirk; Zomba, Whyte; Lake Chilwa, McClounie; (2) Nyasa-Tanganyika plateau, Scott-Elliot.

BOTANICAL APPENDICES

APOCYNACEAE.
Tabernaemontana stapfiana, Britten. (1) Mlanje, Whyte.
T. ventricosa, Hochst. (1) Mlanje, Whyte.
T. elegans. (1) River Ruo, Johnston.
Voacanga africana, Stapf. (1) Shire Valley, Kirk; Shire Highlands, Scott-Elliot; Buchanan.
Strophanthus Kombe, Oliv. (1) Mañanja hills, Meller; Buchanan; (4) Victoria Falls, Kirk.
S. ecaudatus, Rolfe. (1) Buchanan; (4) Batoka country, Kirk.
Strophanthus sp. (2) Carson; Nyasa-Tanganyika plateau, Scott-Elliot.
Mascarenhasia variegata, Britten et Rendle. (1) Mlanje, Whyte.
Adenium multiflorum, Klotzsch. (1) Near Metope, L. Scott.

ASCLEPIADACEAE.
Cryptolepis obtusa, N. E. Br. (1) Lower Shire Valley, Meller; (4) Menyharth.
C. Welwitschii, Schlechter. (1) Buchanan; Mlanje, Whyte; (2) Nyasa-Tanganyika plateau, Scott-Elliot.
Cryptolepis sp. (1) Mañanja hills and west shore of Lake Nyasa, Kirk; Shire Highlands, Scott-Elliot.
Raphionacme grandiflora, N. E. Br. (1) Blantyre, Last.
R. longifolia, N. E. Br. (1) Mañanja hills, Kirk.
Secamone zambesiaca, Schlechter. (1) Shire River, Kirk; Chiromo, Scott-Elliot.
Taccazia Kirkii, N. E. Br. (4) Menyharth.
Chlorocodon Whytei, Hook. fil. (1) Buchanan.
Daemia extensa, R. Br. (1) Shire Valley, Meller; Buchanan.
D. barbata, Klotzsch. (4) Menyharth.
Xysmalobium spurium, N. E. Br. (1) Buchanan.
X. Carsoni, N. E. Br. (2) Carson.
X. bellum, N. E. Br. (1) Buchanan; Mañanja hills, Kirk; Shire Highlands, K. C. Cameron; (2) Carson.
X. reticulatum, N. E. Br. (1) Buchanan.
X. fraternum, N. E. Br. (1) Blantyre, Last.
Xysmalobium sp. (2) Carson.
Schizoglossum connatum, N. E. Br. (2) Carson.
. *elatum*, K. Schum. (1) Buchanan.
S. shirense, N. E. Br. (1) Shire Valley, Kirk and Waller.
S. Nyasae, Britten et Rendle. (1) Mlanje, Whyte; Buchanan.
S. barbatum, Britten et Rendle. (1) Mlanje, Whyte and McClounie.
S. erubescens, Schlechter. (1) Mlanje, Scott-Elliot.
Schizoglossum sp. (1) Mlanje, Scott-Elliot; (4) Menyharth.
Asclepias spectabilis, N. E. Br. (1) Buchanan; Blantyre, Last; Magomera, Waller.
A. conspicua, N. E. Br. (2) Carson.
A. fruticosa, L. (1) Lower Shire Valley, Meller.
A. amabilis, N. E. Br. (2) Carson.
A. pygmaea, N. E. Br. (2) Lower plateau, north of Lake Nyasa, J. Thomson.
A. reflexa, Britten et Rendle. (1) Mañanja hills, Meller and Waller; Zomba, Meller; Mlanje, Whyte; Shire Highlands, Scott-Elliot; Buchanan; (2) North Nyasa, L. Scott.
A. lineolata, Schlechter. (1) Mlanje, Scott-Elliot; Shire Valley, Kirk and Waller; (2) Carson.
A. palustris, Schlechter. (1) Zomba, Whyte; Mlanje, Scott-Elliot and McClounie.
Asclepias sp. (2) Nutt.

ASCLEPIADACEAE.
  Gomphocarpus foliosus, K. Schum. (1) Mañanja hills, Waller; Blantyre, Last; (2) Higher plateau, north of Lake Nyasa, J. Thomson.
  Brachystelma Buchanani, N. E. Br. (1) Sochi, Chiromo and Mañanja, Scott-Elliot; Buchanan.
  Cynanchum mossambicense, K. Schum. (1) Shire Rapids, Kirk.
  Margaretta distincta, N. E. Br. (2) Lower plateau, north of Lake Nyasa, J. Thomson.
  M. orbicularis, N. E. Br. (1) Maravi country, Kirk; (2) North Nyasa, L. Scott.
  M. Whytei, K. Schum. (1) Chiradzulu, Meller; Zomba and east end of Lake Chilwa, Meller; Blantyre, L. Scott; Buchanan; Mlanje, Whyte; near Metope, Scott-Elliot.
  Dregea macrantha, Kl. (1) Chiromo, Scott-Elliot; (4) Menyharth.
  Gymnema sylvestre, R. Br. (1) Buchanan.
  Pergularia africana, N. E. Br. (1) Zomba, Whyte.
  Sphaerocodon obtusifolium, Benth. (1) Buchanan.
  Ceropegia constricta, N. E. Br. (2) Carson.
  C. debilis, N. E. Br. (1) Zomba, Buchanan.
  Riocreuxia profusa, N. E. Br. (1) Buchanan.

LOGANIACEAE.
  Mostuaea Brunonis, F. Didrichs. (1) Mlanje, Whyte.
  Buddleia salviaefolia, Lam. (1) Zomba, Kirk and Whyte; Buchanan.
  Buddleia sp. (1) Mlanje, Whyte.
  Nuxia congesta, R. Br. (1) Buchanan; Zomba, Whyte; var. *N. tomentosa*, Sond. (1) Buchanan; var. *N. dentata*, R. Br. (1) Mañanja hills, Meller.
  N. sambesina, Gilg. (1) Zomba, Kirk.
  Strychnos dysophylla, Benth. (1) Buchanan.
  S. spinosa, Lam. (1) Mañanja hills, Kirk; Buchanan.
  Strychnos sp. (1) Buchanan; (4) Menyharth.
  Anthocleista zambesiaca, Baker. (1) Buchanan; Shire Highlands, Scott-Elliot.
  A. nobilis, Don. (1) Zomba, Whyte.
  Anthocleista sp. (1) Buchanan.

GENTIANACEAE.
  Exacum sp. (1) Buchanan.
  Sebaea brachyphylla, Griseb. (1) Buchanan; Blantyre, Last.
  S. crassulaefolia, Cham. et Schlecht. (1) Mlanje and Zomba, Whyte; Buchanan.
  Sebaea sp. (4) Victoria Falls, Kirk.
  Tachiadenus continentalis, Baker. (2) Carson.
  Chironia purpurascens, Benth. (1) Buchanan; (2) Nutt.
  C. laxiflora, Baker. (1) Mañanja hills, Meller and Kirk.
  C. densiflora, Scott-Elliot. (1) Shire Highlands, Scott-Elliot.
  Chironia sp. (2) Nutt.
  Faroa salutaris, Welw. (1) West shore of Lake Nyasa, Kirk.
  F. Buchanani, Baker. (1) Buchanan.
  Swertia Mannii, Hook. fil. (1) Buchanan; (2) Carson; Nutt.
  Swertia spp. (1) Buchanan.

BORAGINEAE.
  Cordia abyssinica, R. Br. (1) Buchanan.
  C. Myxa, L. (1) Buchanan.
  C. Kirkii, Baker. (4) Menyharth.
  C. Rothii, Roem. et Schult. (4) Menyharth.

BORAGINEAE.
  Ehretia divaricata, Baker. (1) Chiradzulu, Kirk.
  Ehretia sp. (4) Menyharth.
  Trichodesma zeylanicum, R. Br. (1) Blantyre, Descamps.
  T. physaloides, A. DC. (1) Zomba and east end of Lake Chilwa, Meller; Mañanja hills, Meller; Zomba, Whyte; Buchanan; Shire Highlands, Scott-Elliot; (2) Carson; Nyasa-Tanganyika plateau, J. Thomson.
  Heliotropium ovalifolium, Forsk. (1) Shire Valley, L. Scott; Fort Johnston, Scott-Elliot.
  H. strigosum, Willd. (1) Buchanan.
  H. bracteatum, R. Br. (2) North Nyasa, L. Scott.
  H. zeylanicum, Lam. (1) Buchanan; North Nyasa, L. Scott and J. Thomson.
  H. indicum, L. (1) Shire River, L. Scott; Buchanan; Shire Highlands, Scott-Elliot.
  Cynoglossum lanceolatum, Forsk. (1) Mlanje, McClounie; Chiradzulu, Whyte; Buchanan; (2) Nyasa-Tanganyika plateau, Scott-Elliot.
  Lithospermum erythrocephalum, Baker. (2) Carson.
  Lobostemon cryptocephalum, Baker. (2) Carson.

CONVOLVULACEAE.
  Argyreia laxiflora, Baker. (1) Buchanan.
  Lepistemon africanum, Oliv. (1) Shire Highlands, Kirk; Lake Nyasa, Simons.
  Hewittia bicolor, Wight. (1) Chiradzulu, Whyte; Mañanja hills, Meller; Shire Valley, L. Scott; Mlanje, Whyte; Buchanan.
  Jacquemontia capitata, Don. (1) Shire Valley, L. Scott.
  Convolvulus hyoscyamoides, Vatke. (2) Lower plateau, north of Lake Nyasa, J. Thomson.
  C. malvaceus, Oliv. (1) Shire Highlands, Scott-Elliot; Mlanje, Whyte; Buchanan; (2) Lower plateau, north of Lake Nyasa, J. Thomson.
  C. sagittatus, Thunb. (2) Lower plateau, north of Lake Nyasa, J. Thomson.
  C. Thomsoni, Baker. (2) Lower plateau, north of Lake Nyasa, J. Thomson.
  Evolvulus alsinoides, L. (1) Buchanan; (3) Serpa Pinto.
  Ipomoea simplex, Thunb. (1) Shire Highlands, Scott-Elliot; Buchanan.
  I. Pes-tigridis, L. (4) Menyharth.
  I. tanganyikensis, Baker. (2) Carson.
  I. discolor, Baker. (2) Carson.
  I. operosa, Wright. (1) Shire Highlands, Whyte.
  I. involucrata, P. Beauv. (1) Lower plateau, north of Lake Nyasa, J. Thomson.
  I. pileata, Roxb. (2) Carson; Nutt.
  I. crassipes, Hook. (1) Shire Highlands, Scott-Elliot; Buchanan.
  I. chryseides, Ker. (4) Menyharth.
  I. Hanningtoni, Baker. (2) Carson.
  I. Welwitschii, Vatke. (1) Buchanan.
  I. angustfolia, Jacq. (1) Buchanan; (2) Lower plateau, north of Lake Nyasa, J. Thomson; (3) Serpa Pinto; (4) Menyharth.
  I. vagans, Baker. (1) Buchanan.
  I. Carsoni, Baker. (2) Carson.
  I. inconspicua, Baker. (1) Buchanan.
  I. eriocarpa, R. Br. (1) Shire Highlands, V. Scott; Buchanan; (2) Nyasa-Tanganyika plateau, J. Thomson; (4) Menyharth.
  I. mweroensis, Baker. (2) Mweru, Carson.
  I. pharbitiformis, Baker. (2) Mweru, Carson.
  I. simonsiana, Rendle. (1) Nyasa, Simons.
  I. shirensis, Oliv. (1) Shire Highlands, Kirk; Buchanan.
  I. halleriana, Britten. (1) Buchanan; Chiradzulu, Whyte; near Katunga, Kirk.

CONVOLVULACEAE.
 Ipomoea tambelensis, Baker. (1) Upper Shire Valley, Kirk.
 I. obscura, Koen. (1) Zomba, Whyte; Buchanan; (2) Nyasa-Tanganyika plateau, J. Thomson.
 I. Buchanani, Baker. (1) Buchanan.
 I. Lindleyi, Choisy. (1) Shire Valley, Kirk; Buchanan; (4)? Menyharth.
 I. aquatica, Forsk. (1) Lake Nyasa, Kirk.
 I. pilosa, Sweet. (1) Buchanan; (4) Menyharth.
 I. Wightii, Choisy. (4) Menyharth.
 I. afra, Choisy. (1) Buchanan.
 I. pterygocaulis, Choisy. (1) Shire Valley, Kirk; Buchanan; (4) Menyharth.
 I. pinnata, Hochst. (1) Buchanan; (4) Menyharth.
 I. palmata, Forsk. (1) Shire Valley, Kirk; Buchanan; (4) Menyharth.
 I. dissecta, Willd. (1) Buchanan; (4) Menyharth.
 I. kirkiana, Britten. (1) Shire Highlands, Kirk; Buchanan.
 I. fulvicaulis, Boiss. (1) Mlanje, Whyte.

SOLANACEAE.
 Solanum nodiflorum, Jacq. (1) Shire Valley, Kirk.
 S. nigrum, L. (1) Blantyre, Descamps.
 S. schimperianum, Hochst. (1) Chiradzulu, Whyte.
 S. Naumannii, Engl. (1) Buchanan.
 S. anomalum, Thonn. (1) Chiradzulu, Whyte.
 S. aculeastrum, Dun. (1) Blantyre, L. Scott; Buchanan; Mañanja hills, Meller.
 S. Rohrii, Wright. (1) Mpatamanga, Kirk.
 S. chrysotrichum, Wright. (1) Buchanan.
 S. acanthocalyx, Klotzsch. (1) Buchanan; Mlanje, Whyte.
 S. trepidans, Wright. (1) Shire Valley, L. Scott.
 Physalis pubescens, L. (1) Blantyre, Descamps.
 P. peruviana, L. (1) Blantyre, L. Scott.
 Capsicum conoides, Mill. (4) Sesheke, Kirk.
 Datura alba, Nees. (1) Shire Highlands, Kirk; Buchanan; Mañanja hills, Meller.

SCROPHULARIACEAE.
 Diclis ovata, Benth. (1) Mandala, Scott-Elliot.
 D. tenella, Hemsl. (1) Chiradzulu, Whyte.
 Halleria lucida, L. (1) Zomba, Whyte.
 H. elliptica, Thunb. (1) Mlanje, Whyte.
 Chaenostoma sp. (2) Nyasa-Tanganyika plateau, Scott-Elliot.
 Mimulus gracilis, R. Br. (1) Zomba and east end of Lake Chilwa, Meller; Buchanan.
 Craterostigma plantagineum, Hochst. (1) Buchanan.
 Torenia parviflora, Hamilt. (2) North of Lake Nyasa, L. Scott.
 Vandellia lobelioides, Oliv. (2) Nyasa-Tanganyika plateau, J. Thomson.
 Ilysanthes sp. (1) Buchanan; Shire Valley, L. Scott; (2) Nutt.
 Alectra melampyroides, Benth. (1) Mbami, near Blantyre and Mañanja hills, Kirk; Buchanan; (2) Lower plateau, north of Lake Nyasa, J. Thomson.
 Alectra, sp. (1) Buchanan.
 Aulaya obtusifolia, Benth. (1) Shire Highlands, K. C. Cameron.
 Buchnera quadrifaria, Baker. (2) Lower plateau, north of Lake Nyasa, J. Thomson; Carson; Nutt.
 B. Lastii, Engl. (1) Blantyre, Last.

BOTANICAL APPENDICES

SCROPHULARIACEAE.
Buchnera spp. (1) Mañanja hills, Meller; Buchanan; Mlanje and Chiradzulu, Whyte; (2) Upper plateau, north of Lake Nyasa, J. Thomson.
Striga elegans, Benth. (1) Blantyre, Last.
S. coccinea, Benth. (1) Shire Highlands, Kirk; Buchanan.
S. Forbesii, Benth. (1) Shire Highlands, Meller.
S. orobanchoides, Benth. (2) North of Lake Nyasa, L. Scott; Carson.
Striga spp. (1) Buchanan; (2) North of Lake Nyasa, L. Scott; Carson.
Rhamphicarpa fistulosa, Benth. (2) North of Lake Nyasa, L. Scott.
R. serrata, Klotzsch. (1) Zomba and east end of Lake Chilwa, Meller; Buchanan.
R. tubulosa, Benth. (1) Mandala, Scott-Elliot.
Rhamphicarpa spp. (1) Mañanja hills, Kirk; Buchanan; (2) Carson.
Cycnium adonense, E. Mey. (1) Mlanje and Zomba, Whyte; Buchanan; (2) Carson; Nyasa-Tanganyika plateau, Scott-Elliot.
C. longiflorum, Eck. et Zeyh. (1) Shire Valley, Kirk; Buchanan; (2) North of Lake Nyasa, J. Thomson and L. Scott.
Cycnium spp. (1) Buchanan; (2) Carson.
Sopubia lanata, Engl. (2) Carson; Nutt.
S. ramosa, Hochst. (1) Mañanja hills, Meller and Kirk; Blantyre, Last; Buchanan; (2) Carson; Nutt.
S. dregeana, Benth. (1) Zomba, Whyte; Shire Highlands, Scott-Elliot.
S. Hildebrandtii, Vatke. (1) Chiradzulu, Whyte.
Sopubia spp. (1) Mañanja hills, Meller; (2) Lower plateau, north of Lake Nyasa, J. Thomson; Carson.

OROBANCHACEAE.
Orobanche cernua, Loefl. (1) Shire Highlands, L. Scott.

LENTIBULARIACEAE.
Utricularia capensis, Spreng. (1) Buchanan; Blantyre, Last.
Utricularia spp. (1) Buchanan; Lake Nyasa, Laws; (2) Nutt; Carson; Lower plateau, north of Lake Nyasa, J. Thomson; (4) Victoria Falls and Batoka country, Kirk.

GESNERACEAE.
Streptocarpus caulescens, Vatke. (1) Buchanan.
S. Cooperi, C. B. Clarke. (1) Buchanan.

BIGNONIACEAE.
Tecoma shirensis, Baker. (1) Buchanan.
T. nyassae, Oliv. (2) Lower plateau, north of Lake Nyasa, J. Thomson.
Dolichandrone obtusifolia, Baker. (1) Shire Highlands, Buchanan and Scott-Elliot.
D. tomentosa, Benth. (2) Carson.
Stereospermum kunthianum, Cham. (1) Shire Highlands, Waller; Buchanan; Chiradzulu, Meller; West shore of Lake Nyasa, Kirk; (2) Mweru, Carson; (4) Batoka country, Kirk.
Kigelia pinnata, DC. (1) Buchanan.

PEDALINEAE.
Sesamum angolense, Welw. (1) Buchanan; West shore of Lake Nyasa, Kirk; Blantyre; Last; (2) Carson; Nutt.
S. indicum, L. (2) Karonga, L. Scott.
S. calycinum, Welw. (4) Holub.
Ceratotheca sesamoides, Endl. Buchanan; (1) Shire Valley, L. Scott; West shore of Lake Nyasa, Kirk and Simons; (2) Carson; Karonga, L. Scott; (4) Holub.
Ceratotheca sp. (2) Karonga, L. Scott.
Pretrea zanquebarica, J. Gay. (1) Zomba and east end of Lake Chilwa, Meller; (4) Holub.

SELAGINEAE.
> *Hebenstreitia* sp. (4) Holub.
> *Selago milanjiensis*, Rolfe. (1) Mlanje, Whyte.
> *S. whyteana*, Rolfe. (1) Mlanje, Whyte and McClounie.
> *Selago* spp. (1) Chiradzulu, Meller and Whyte; Mlanje, McClounie; Buchanan; (2) Lower and Upper plateaux, north of Lake Nyasa, J. Thomson; (4) Menyharth.

ACANTHACEAE.
> *Thunbergia kirkiana*, T. Anders. (1) Buchanan; Mlanje, Whyte; Buchanan.
> *T. alata*, Bojer. (1) Buchanan; Mlanje, Whyte; Mañanja hills, Kirk and Meller; (2) Carson.
> *T. lancifolia*, T. Anders. (1) Blantyre, L. Scott; Mañanja hills and Chiradzulu, Meller; Buchanan; Zomba, Whyte; (2) Carson; Nyasa-Tanganyika plateau, J. Thomson.
> *T. obtusifolia*, Oliv. (2) Upper plateau, north of Lake Nyasa, J. Thomson.
> *T. erecta*, Benth. (1) Buchanan; Blantyre, Last; Mañanja hills, Waller.
> *T. oblongifolia*, Oliv. (1) Mañanja hills, Waller; Buchanan; (2) Nyasa-Tanganyika plateau, Scott-Elliot.
> *T. subulata*, Lindau. (1) Buchanan.
> *T. mollis*, Lindau. (1) Buchanan.
> *T. manganjensis*, Lindau. (1) Mañanja hills, Kirk.
> *Thunbergia* spp. (1) Buchanan; Zomba, Whyte; Shire Highlands, Scott-Elliot; (2) Nutt; Carson; Nyasa-Tanganyika plateau, Scott-Elliot.
> *Nelsonia campestris*, R. Br. (1) Mañanja hills, Meller; Buchanan.
> *Hygrophila spinosa*, T. Anders. (1) Buchanan; Shire River, Kirk.
> *H. parviflora*, Lindau. (1) Buchanan.
> *Mellera lobulata*, S. Moore. (1) Buchanan; Mañanja hills, Meller.
> *Calophanes* spp. (1) Buchanan; Chiradzulu, Whyte.
> *Ruellia prostrata*, T. Anders. (1) Buchanan; Shire Highlands, Scott-Elliot; Lower Shire Valley, Kirk; (2) Carson.
> *Paulo-wilhelmia* sp. (1) Buchanan; Chiradzulu, Whyte; Mañanja hills, Meller.
> *Mimulopsis sesamoides*, S. Moore. (1) Mlanje, Whyte.
> *Mimulopsis* sp. (2) Lower plateau, north of Lake Nyasa, J. Thomson.
> *Eranthemum senense*, Klotzsch. (1) Buchanan; Mlanje, McClounie; Mañanja hills, Kirk.
> *Acanthopale* sp. (*Dischistocalyx confertiflora*, Lindau). (1) Buchanan.
> *Whitfieldia* sp. (2) Carson.
> *Dyschoriste*, sp. (*Calophanes verticillaris*, Oliv.) (1) Mañanja hills, Meller; Buchanan; Chiradzulu, Whyte; (2) Higher plateau, north of Lake Nyasa, J. Thomson.
> *Dyschoriste* spp. (2) Carson; (4) Batoka country, Kirk.
> *Strobilanthes* sp. (1) Buchanan.
> *Phaylopsis parviflora*, Willd. (1) Buchanan; Chiradzulu, Whyte.
> *Phaylopsis* sp. (*Micranthus Poggei*, Lindau). (1) Chiradzulu, Whyte.
> *Blepharis serrulata*, Ficalho et Hiern. (3) Serpa Pinto.
> *B. longifolia*, Lindau. (1) Buchanan.
> *Blepharis* spp. (1) Buchanan; (2) Nutt.
> *Crossandra Greenstockii*, S. Moore. (1) Mañanja hills, Meller; Mlanje, Whyte and McClounie; Shire Highlands, Scott-Elliot; Buchanan.
> *C. nilotica*, Oliv. (2) Tanganyika and Mweru, Carson.
> *C. puberula*, Klotzsch. (1) Lower Shire Valley, Meller and Kirk; Mañanja hills, Meller; Buchanan.
> *Crossandra* sp. (1) Buchanan.
> *Barleria Kirkii*, T. Anders. (1) Buchanan.
> *B. calophylloides*, Lindau. (1) Nutt.
> *B. Prionitis*, L. (1) Shire Highlands, Meller.

BOTANICAL APPENDICES

ACANTHACEAE.
    Barleria spinulosa, Klotzsch. (1) River Shire, Meller and Kirk ; Buchanan.
    B. eranthemoides, R. Br. (1) Buchanan.
    Barleria sp. (2) Carson ; Nutt.
    Crabbeanana, Nees (*C. aovalifolia*, Ficalho et Hiern.) (3) Serpa Pinto.
    Crabbea sp. (1) Buchanan.
    Lepidagathis spp. (1) Buchanan ; (2) Nutt.
    Asystasia coromandeliana, Nees. (1) Zomba, Whyte ; Buchanan ; (2) Carson.
    Asystasia sp. (2) Carson.
    Brachystephanus africanus, S. Moore. (1) Mlanje, Whyte.
    Justicia Whytei, S. Moore. (1) Mlanje, Whyte.
    J. heterocarpa, T. Anders. (2) Nutt.
    J. anselliana, T. Anders. (1) Mlanje, Whyte.
    J. melampyrum, S. Moore. (1) Mlanje, Whyte.
    Justicia spp. (1) Buchanan ; Chiradzulu, Whyte ; Blantyre, Last ; Shire Highlands and Lake Nyasa, Scott-Elliot ; (2) Nutt ; Carson ; Nyasa-Tanganyika plateau, Scott-Elliot.
    Isoglossa milanjiensis, S. Moore. (1) Mlanje, Whyte.
    Isoglossa sp. (1) Buchanan.
    Rhinacanthus communis, Nees. (1) Shire Highlands, Scott-Elliot.
    Rhinacanthus sp. (1) Buchanan ; Blantyre, Last ; Chiradzulu, Whyte.
    Himantochilus marginatus, Lindau. (1) Chiradzulu, Whyte.
    Dicliptera sp. (1) Buchanan.
    Peristrophe bicalyculata, Nees. (2) Nyasa-Tanganyika plateau, Scott-Elliot.
    Hypoestes verticillaris, R. Br. (1) Mlanje, Whyte ; (2) Carson ; Nutt.
    H. phaylopsoides, S. Moore. (1) Mlanje, Whyte.
    H. Rothii, T. Anders. (1) Chiradzulu, Whyte.
    H. latifolia, H. (1) Buchanan.
    Hypoestes spp. (1) Buchanan ; (2) Carson.

VERBENACEAE.
    Lantana salviaefolia, Jacq. (1) Buchanan ; Mlanje and Chiradzulu, Whyte ; Shire Highlands, Scott-Elliot ; (2) Lower plateau, north of Lake Nyasa, J. Thomson ; Carson ; Nutt ; (3) Serpa Pinto.
    Lippia nodiflora, A. Rich. (1) Buchanan.
    L. asperifolia, Rich. (1) Lower Shire Valley, Meller ; Chiradzulu, Whyte ; (2) Plateau, north of Lake Nyasa, J. Thomson.
    Lippia sp. (2) Carson.
    Priva leptostachya, Juss. (1) Buchanan.
    Premna senensis, Klotzsch. (1) Buchanan.
    Premna sp. (1) Buchanan.
    Holmskioldia tettensis, Vatke. (1) Banks of Shire River, Kirk.
    Vitex milanjiensis, Britten. (1) Shire Highlands, Scott-Elliot ; Mlanje and Zomba, Whyte ; (2) Nyasa-Tanganyika plateau, Scott-Elliot.
    V. Mombassae, Vatke. (1) Buchanan.
    V. paludosa, Vatke. (1) River Shire, Kirk ; Buchanan ; Mañanja hills, Meller ; (2) Karonga, L. Scott.
    V. Buchananii, Baker. (1) Buchanan.
    Vitex spp. (1) Buchanan ; Lake Chilwa, Kirk ; (4) Menyharth.
    Clerodendron tanganyikense, Baker. (2) Carson.
    C. capitatum, Schum. (1) Buchanan ; (2) Upper plateau, north of Lake Nyasa, J. Thomson ; Carson.
    C. discolor, Vatke. (1) Mlanje and Zomba, Whyte.

VERBENACEAE.
   Clerodendron lanceolatum, Gürke. (4) Menyharth.
   C. myricoides, R. Br. (1) Buchanan; Mlanje and Zomba, Whyte; Shire Highlands, Scott-Elliot; Mañanja hills, Meller.
   C. spinescens, Gürke. (1) Maravi country, Kirk; (2) Carson; Nutt.
   Clerodendron spp. (1) Mañanja hills, Meller; Lower Shire Valley, Waller; Buchanan.

LABIATAE.
   Ocimum suave, Willd. (1) Shire Highlands, Last; Chiradzulu, Whyte; (2) Nutt.
   O. affine, Hochst. (1) Blantyre, L. Scott; Mlanje, McClounie; (2) Carson.
   O. filamentosum, Forsk. (1) Mlanje, Whyte.
   O. cornigerum, Hochst. (2) Lower plateau, north of Lake Nyasa, J. Thomson.
   O. hians, Benth. (1) Mlanje, Whyte.
   O. bracteosum, Benth. (1) Buchanan.
   Ocimum spp. (1) Buchanan; Shire Highlands, Scott-Elliot, L. Scott and K. C. Cameron; (2) Upper and Lower plateaux, north of Lake Nyasa.
   Acrocephalus callianthus, Briquet. (1) Buchanan; Chiradzulu, Whyte; Blantyre, Last; Mañanja hills, Meller.
   A. zambesiacus, Baker. (1) Buchanan.
   A. caeruleus, Oliv. (2) Nutt.
   Acrocephalus spp. (1) Buchanan; Mañanja hills, Kirk; (2) Lower plateau, north of Lake Nyasa, J. Thomson; Carson; Nutt.
   Orthosiphon coloratus, Vatke. (1) Zomba, Whyte.
   O. trichodon, Baker. (1) Buchanan.
   O. Kirkii, Baker, ined. ex. Britten, in Trans. Linn. Soc. 2nd Ser. iv., p. 37. (1) Mlanje, Whyte.
   O. Cameroni, Baker. (2) Carson.
   Orthosiphon spp. (1) Shire Highlands, Scott-Elliot; (2) Carson; Nutt.
   Geniosporum affine, Gürke. (1) Buchanan.
   Moschosma polystachyum, Benth. (1) Chiradzulu, Whyte.
   M. riparium, Hochst. (1) Murchison Falls, Meller; Chiradzulu, Whyte; Last; Buchanan; Shire Highlands, L. Scott; (2) Lower plateau, north of Lake Nyasa, J. Thomson.
   Moschosma sp. (1) Buchanan; Blantyre, Last.
   Coleus umbrosus, Vatke. (1) Blantyre, Descamps.
   C. leucophyllus, Baker. (2) Mweru, Carson.
   C. punctatus, Baker. (2) Mweru, Carson.
   C. shirensis, Gürke (*Plectranthus glandulosus*, Britten, non Hook. fil.). (1) Buchanan; Zomba, Whyte.
   Coleus spp. (1) Buchanan; Chiradzulu, Whyte; (2) Carson.
   Solenostemon sp. (1) Blantyre, Last; Chiradzulu, Whyte.
   Aeolanthus Nyassae, Gürke. (1) Buchanan.
   A. ukambensis, Gürke. (1) Buchanan.
   Aeolanthus spp. (1) Buchanan.
   Pycnostachys parvifolia, Baker. (2) Carson.
   P. verticillata, Baker. (2) Carson.
   P. cyanea, Gürke. (1) Buchanan.
   P. pubescens, Gürke. (1) Buchanan.
   P. reticulata, Benth. (2) Carson.
   P. urticifolia, Hook. (1) Mañanja hills, Meller; Buchanan; Chiradzulu, Whyte.
   Pycnostachys spp. (2) Nutt; Carson.
   Plectranthus subacaulis, Baker. (2) Mweru, Carson.

LABIATAE.
Plectranthus modestus, Baker. (2) Carson.
Pl. floribundus, N. E. Br.; var. *longipes*, N. E. Br. (1) Mañanja hills, Meller; Maravi country, Kirk; Buchanan; Shire Highlands, L. Scott; (2) Lower plateau, north of Lake Nyasa, J. Thomson.
Pl. elegans, Britten. (1) Mlanje, Whyte.
Pl. primulinus, Baker. (2) Mweru, Carson.
Pl. sanguineus, Britten. (1) Mlanje, Whyte.
Pl. betonicaefolius, Baker. (2) Carson; Nutt.
Pl. densus, N. E. Br. (2) Higher plateau, north of Lake Nyasa, J. Thomson.
Pl. manganjensis, Baker, ined. ex. Britten, in Trans. Linn. Soc. 2nd Ser. iv., p. 37. (1) Zomba, Whyte.
Plectranthus sp. (*Pl. Melleri*, Britten, non Baker). (1) Mlanje, Whyte; Chiradzulu, Meller.
Plectranthus spp. (1) Shire Valley and Mañanja hills, Kirk; Buchanan; Last; Shire Highlands, Scott-Elliot; (2) Lower plateau, north of Lake Nyasa, J. Thomson; Carson.
Hoslundia opposita, Vahl. (1) Mlanje and Zomba, Whyte; Mañanja hills, Zomba and east end of Lake Chilwa, Meller.
Hyptis pectinata, Poit. (1) Zomba and Chiradzulu, Whyte; Blantyre, Descamps.
Calamintha simensis, Benth. (2) Lower plateau, north of Lake Nyasa, J. Thomson.
Micromeria biflora, Benth. (1) Mlanje, Whyte; (2) Lower plateau, north of Lake Nyasa, J. Thomson.
Micromeria sp. (1) Zomba, Whyte.
Elsholtzia sp. (2) Carson.
Achyrospermum sp. (1) Ndirande Mountain, Buchanan.
Lasiocorys sp. (2) Carson.
Leonitis pallida, R. Br. (1) Blantyre, Descamps.
L. nepetaefolia, R. Br. (2) Carson.
L. Leonurus, R. Br. (2) Carson.
L. velutina, Fenzl. (1) Buchanan; Descamps; Mañanja hills, Meller.
Leonitis spp. (1) Mañanja hills, Meller; Chiradzulu, Whyte.
Tinnea sp. (1) Mañanja hills, Kirk; Buchanan; (4) Batoka country, Kirk.
Scutellaria paucifolia, Baker. (2) Carson; Lower plateau, north of Lake Nyasa, J. Thomson; Mweru, Carson.
S. Livingstonei, Baker, ined. ex. Britten, in Trans. Linn. Soc. 2nd ser. iv. p. 37. (1) Mañanja hills, Kirk; Buchanan; Blantyre, L. Scott; Zomba, Whyte; Livingstone; (2) Mweru, Carson.
Scutellaria sp. (2) Carson.
Stachys aethiopica, L. (1) Mlanje, Whyte.
Stachys sp. (1) Buchanan.
Leucas martinicensis, R. Br. (1) Buchanan; (4) Menyharth.
L. Nyassae, Gürke. (1) Buchanan.
L. milanjiana, Gürke (*L. glabrata*, Britten, non R. Br.) (1) Mlanje, Whyte; Buchanan.
L. decadonta, Gürke. (1) Buchanan.
Leucas spp. (1) Mañanja hills, Meller; Buchanan; (2) Nutt; Carson; Lower plateau, north of Lake Nyasa, J. Thomson; (4) Batoka country, Kirk.

NYCTAGINEAE.
Mirabilis Jalapa, L. (1) Shire Valley, Meller; Mañanja hills, Kirk.
Boerhaavia repens, L., var. *ascendens*, Willd. (1) Buchanan.
B. plumbaginea, Cav. (1) Shire Highlands, Scott-Elliot.
B. Burchellii, Choisy. (1) Shire Valley, Waller.

ILLECEBRACEAE.
    1 sp.   (3) Serpa Pinto.

AMARANTACEAE.
    Celosia argentea, L.   (2) Carson.
    C. Schweinfurthii, Schinz.   (1) Shire Valley, L. Scott.
    C. trigyna, L.   (1) Buchanan ; Mañanja hills, Meller ; Mlanje and Chiradzulu, Whyte ; Blantyre, Last.
    Celosia spp.   (1) Shire Valley, Kirk ; Buchanan.
    Amarantus Blitum, L.   (1) Shire Highlands, Scott-Elliot ; Buchanan.
    A. Thunbergii, Moq.   (1) Shire Valley, L. Scott.
    A. caudatus, L.   (1) Mañanja hills, Meller ; Mpatamanga, Shire River, Kirk ; (2) North Nyasaland, L. Scott.
    Centema Kirkii, Hook. fil.   (1) Lake Nyasa, Kirk ; Elephant Marsh, Shire River, L. Scott ; Buchanan.
    Cyathula cylindrica, Moq.   (1) Chiradzulu, Whyte ; Buchanan.
    C. globulifera, Moq.   (1) Mañanja hills, Meller ; Buchanan ; Chiradzulu, Whyte ; Mpatamanga, on Shire River, Kirk.
    Pupalia lappacea, Moq.   (1) Buchanan.
    Aerua lanata, Juss.   (1) Buchanan.
    A. javanica, Juss.   (1) Shire Highlands, and throughout the Mañanja and Shire hills, Buchanan, Meller and L. Scott.
    Psilotrichum spp.   (1) Blantyre, Buchanan and Last ; Chiradzulu, Whyte.
    Achyranthes aspera, L.   (1) Blantyre, Descamps ; Chiradzulu, Whyte ; (2) Carson ; var. *argentea*, Lam.   (2) Chiradzulu, Whyte.
    Achyranthes sp.   (2) Carson.
    Alternanthera sessilis, R. Br.   (1) Shire Highlands, Scott-Elliot ; (2) North Nyasa, L. Scott.
    A. nodiflora, R. Br.   (1) Buchanan.

CHENOPODIACEAE.
    Chenopodium Botrys, L.   (1) Buchanan ; var. *C. procerum*, Hochst.   (1) Buchanan.

PHYTOLACCACEAE.
    Phytolacca abyssinica, Hoffm.   (1) Chiradzulu, Whyte ; Buchanan.

POLYGONACEAE.
    Oxygonum atriplicifolium, Baker (*Centogonum atriplicifolium*, Meisn.), var. *O. sinuatum*, Engl.   (1) Lake Chilwa, Kirk.
    Polygonum Poiretii, Meisn.   (1) Chiradzulu, Whyte.
    P. plebeium, R. Br.   (1) Buchanan.
    P. senegalense, Meisn.   (1) Banks of Shire River, Kirk ; (2) North Nyasa, L. Scott.
    P. tomentosum, Willd.   (1) Buchanan.
    P. serrulatum, Lag.   (1) Zomba, Whyte ; (2) Lake Nyasa, L. Scott.
    P. barbatum, L.   (1) Buchanan ; Lake Nyasa, Scott-Elliot.
    P. tristachyum, Baker.   (1) Buchanan.
    P. glabrum, Willd.   (1) Upper Shire, Scott-Elliot.
    P. lanigerum, R. Br.   (1) Upper Shire, Scott-Elliot ; Lower Shire Valley, Meller ; Lake Chilwa, Buchanan ; Shire Highlands, K. C. Cameron.
    P. lapathifolium, L.   (1) Lower Shire Valley, Meller.
    P. alatum, Hamilt.   (1) Buchanan.
    P. strigosum, R. Br.   (1) Buchanan.
    Rumex nepalensis, Spreng.   (1) Buchanan.
    R. abyssinicus, Jacq.   (1) Shire Highlands, K. C. Cameron ; Buchanan.
    R. maderensis, Lowe.   (2) Carson ; Higher plateau, north of Lake Nyasa, J. Thomson.

BOTANICAL APPENDICES

PODOSTEMACEAE.
Hydrostachys polymorpha, Klotzsch. (1) Tributary of Shire to north-east of Katunga, Kirk; Blantyre, Last; Buchanan.
Sphaerothylax sp. (1) Blantyre, Last.

PIPERACEAE.
Piper capense, L. fil. (1) Chiradzulu and Zomba, Whyte; Buchanan.
Peperomia reflexa, Dietr. (1) Mlanje, McClounie and Whyte; Zomba, Whyte; Buchanan.

LAURACEAE.
Cassytha guineensis, S. et T. (1) Buchanan.

PROTEACEAE.
Protea Nyasae, Rendle. (1) Mlanje, Whyte.
P. abyssinica, Willd. (1) Blantyre, L. Scott; Buchanan; (2) Nutt; (4) Batoka country, Kirk.
Protea spp. (1) Mañanja hills, Meller; Buchanan; Katunga, Kirk; (2) Higher plateau, north of Lake Nyasa, J. Thomson.
Faurea speciosa, Welw. (1) Buchanan; Zomba, Whyte.
Faurea sp. (1) Chiradzulu, Meller; near Chiradzulu, Kirk; Buchanan; (4) Batoka country, Kirk.

THYMELAEACEAE.
Arthrosolen flavus, Rendle. (1) Mlanje, Whyte; Blantyre, L. Scott; (2) Nutt.
A. glaucescens, Oliv. (2) Carson.
Arthrosolen spp. (1) Mañanja hills, Kirk and Meller; Last; Buchanan; (2) Nutt.
Gnidia Buchananii, Gilg. (1) Buchanan; Chiradzulu and Mañanja hills, Meller.
G. microcephala, Meisn. (1) Mlanje and Zomba, Whyte; Zomba and east end of Lake Chilwa, Meller.
G. apiculata, Gilg. (1) Buchanan.
G. fastigiata, Rendle. (1) Mlanje, Whyte.
Gnidia spp. (1) Foot of Chiradzulu, Kirk; Blantyre, L. Scott; Sochi, Kirk; Buchanan; (2) Carson; Upper and Lower plateaux, north of Lake Nyasa, J. Thomson; Nutt.
Lasiosiphon spp. (1) Buchanan; (2) Lower plateau, north of Lake Nyasa, J. Thomson; (4) Batoka country, Kirk.
Peddiea longipedicellata, Gilg. (1) Buchanan.

LORANTHACEAE.
Loranthus mweruensis, Baker. (2) Mweru, Carson.
Loranthus spp. (1) Lower Shire, Meller; Zomba, Kirk; Buchanan; (2) Lower plateau, north of Lake Nyasa, J. Thomson; Carson.

SANTALACEAE.
Thesium nigricans, Rendle. (1) Mlanje and Zomba, Whyte.
T. whyteanum, Rendle. (1) Mlanje, Whyte.
Thesium spp. (1) Foot of Chiradzulu, Kirk; Blantyre and Matope, L. Scott; Buchanan; Mlanje, McClounie; (4) Batoka country, Kirk.
Colpoon sp. (1) Buchanan.
Osyridocarpus scandens, Engl. (1) Katunga, Kirk.

EUPHORBIACEAE.
Euphorbia scordifolia, Jacq. (1) Buchanan.
E. zambesiaca, Benth. (1) Mlanje, McClounie; Buchanan; Zomba and east end of Lake Chilwa, Meller; (2) Mweru, Carson.
E. Grantii, Oliv. (2) Lower plateau, north of Lake Nyasa, J. Thomson.

EUPHORBIACEAE.
    Euphorbia whyteana, Baker fil. (1) Mlanje, Whyte.
    E. shirensis, Baker fil. (1) Mlanje, Whyte.
    E. indica, Lam. (4) Menyharth.
    Euphorbia spp. (1) Above Elephant Marsh and Murchison Falls, Shire River, and Mañanja hills, Meller; Katunga, Kirk; west shore of Lake Nyasa, Kirk; Buchanan; (2) Karonga, L. Scott; Carson.
    Synadenium Grantii, Hook. fil. (4) Menyharth.
    Synadenium sp. (2) Carson.
    Bridelia micrantha, Baill. (1) Buchanan.
    Bridelia sp. (1) Zomba, Kirk; Buchanan; (4) Menyharth.
    Phyllanthus nummulariaefolius, Poir. (1) Blantyre, Last.
    P. leucanthus, Pax. (1) Buchanan.
    P. maderaspatensis, L. (1) Above Elephant Marsh, on River Shire, L. Scott.
    P. hysteracanthus, Muell.-Arg. (1) West shore of Lake Nyasa, Kirk.
    P. rotundifolius, Willd. (1) Mlanje, Whyte; var. *leucocalyx*, Muell.-Arg. (1) Mlanje, Whyte.
    Phyllanthus spp. (1) Buchanan; Blantyre, L. Scott; Mlanje, Whyte; (2) Karonga, L. Scott; Carson; Nutt; (4) Menyharth.
    Securinega obovata, Muell.-Arg. (4) Menyharth.
    Uapaca nitida, Muell.-Arg. (4) Batoka country, Kirk.
    U. kirkiana, Muell.-Arg. (1) Mañanja hills, Kirk; Buchanan.
    Uapaca spp. (1) Buchanan.
    Antidesma spp. (1) Shire River, Kirk; Mlanje, Whyte; Buchanan.
    Jatropha Curcas, L. (1) Buchanan; Mlanje, McClounie; (4) Menyharth.
    Jatropha sp. (2) Carson.
    Croton macrostachyus, Hochst. (1) Buchanan.
    Croton spp. (1) Buchanan; (4) Menyharth.
    Cluytia richardiana, Muell.-Arg. (1) Buchanan; Chiradzulu, Whyte.
    Cluytia sp. (2) Lower plateau, north of Lake Nyasa, J. Thomson.
    Caperonia spp. (1) Blantyre, Last; Buchanan.
    Cephalocroton sp. (1) Buchanan.
    Micrococca Mercurialis, Benth. (1) Elephant Marsh, on Shire River, L. Scott.
    Acalypha benguelensis, Muell.-Arg. (1) Mlanje and Zomba, Whyte.
    A. villicaulis, A. Rich. (1) Mañanja hills, Meller; Mlanje and Zomba, Whyte; Buchanan; (2) Carson.
    A. pilostachya, Hochst. (1) Mpatamanga, on Shire River, Kirk; Buchanan; Chiradzulu, Whyte; (2) Lower plateau, north of Lake Nyasa, J. Thomson.
    Acalypha spp. (1) Buchanan.
    Alchornea sp. (1) Buchanan.
    Neoboutinia africana, Muell.-Arg. (1) Zomba, Whyte.
    Mallotus Melleri, Muell.-Arg. (1) Mañanja hills, Meller; Buchanan.
    Macaranga spp. (1) Buchanan.
    Ricinus communis, L. (1) Lower Valley of Shire, Meller.
    Tragia mitis, Hochst. (4) Menyharth.
    Tragia sp. (1) Shire River above Elephant Marsh, L. Scott.
    Dalechampia sp. (1) Lower Shire River, Kirk; (4) Menyharth.
    Maprounea sp. (4) Batoka country, Kirk.
    Excoecaria sp. (1) Buchanan.

URTICACEAE.
    Trema spp. (1) Buchanan; Mañanja hills, Meller and Kirk.
    Dorstenia Buchananii, Engler. (1) Buchanan.

URTICACEAE.
    Dorstenia Walleri, Hemsl. (1) Mañanja hills, Meller ; Buchanan.
    Dorstenia spp. (1) Buchanan.
    Ficus capreaefolia, Del. (1) Island in River Shire, near Mbenje, L. Scott.
    Ficus spp. (1) Katunga, Shire Valley, L. Scott; Buchanan; Kankanje, Kirk; (2) Karonga, L. Scott.
    Treculia sp. (1) West shore of Lake Nyasa, Kirk.
    Myrianthus sp. (1) Buchanan.
    Urtica sp. (1) Chiradzulu, Whyte.
    Fleurya aestuans, Gaudich. (1) Buchanan.
    Fleurya sp. (1) Shire Valley, L. Scott ; (4) Menyharth.
    Urera sp. (1) Buchanan.
    Girardinia heterophylla, Dcne. (1) Buchanan ; Mañanja hills, Waller ; Chiradzulu, Kirk.
    Girardinia sp. (1) Buchanan.
    Pilea sp. (1) Buchanan.
    Boehmeria platyphylla, Don. (1) Chiradzulu, Whyte ; Buchanan.
    Boehmeria sp. (1) Buchanan.
    Pouzolzia sp. (1) Buchanan.
    Pipturus sp. (1) Buchanan.

MYRICACEAE.
    Myrica pilulifera, Rendle. (1) Mlanje, Whyte.
    Myrica spp. (1) Buchanan.

CERATOPHYLLEAE.
    Ceratophyllum sp. (1) Blantyre, Last ; Lake Nyasa, Laws.

HYDROCHARIDACEAE.
    Lagarosiphon Nyassae, Ridley. (1) Lake Nyasa, Laws.
    Vallisneria spiralis, L. (1) Lake Nyasa, Laws.
    Ottelia spp. (1) Luangwa, west shore of Lake Nyasa, Kirk ; Blantyre, Last.

BURMANNIACEAE.
    Burmannia bicolor, Mast., var. *africana*, Ridley. (2) Lower plateau, north of Lake Nyasa, J. Thomson.

ORCHIDACEAE.
    Liparis Bowkeri, Harv. (1) Buchanan.
    Megaclinium Melleri, Hook. fil. (1) Chiradzulu, Meller ; Mlanje, McClounie.
    Eulophia callichroma, Rchb. fil. (1) Mañanja hills, Meller and Kirk ; Zomba, Meller.
    E. Nyasae, Rendle. (1) Mlanje, Whyte.
    E. aristata, Rendle. (1) Shire Highlands, Scott-Elliot.
    E. praestans, Rendle. (1) Shire Highlands, Scott-Elliot.
    E. milanjiana, Rendle. (1) Mlanje, Whyte ; Mañanja hills, Meller ; Buchanan.
    E. missionis, Rendle. (1) Mlanje, Scott-Elliot.
    E. Shupangae, Kränz. (1) Mañanja hills, Kirk and Waller ; Blantyre, L. Scott ; Zomba, Buchanan.
    E. longesepala, Rendle. (1) Mlanje, Whyte.
    E. venulosa, Rchb. fil. (*E. humilis*, Rendle). (1) Mañanja hills, Meller ; Shire Highlands, Scott-Elliot.
    Eulophia spp. (1) Mañanja hills, Kirk, Meller and Waller ; Mlanje, McClounie ; Buchanan ; (2) Nyasa-Tanganyika plateau, J. Thomson and H. H. Johnston : Carson ; Nutt ; (4) Sesheke, Holub.
    Cyrtopera Walleri, Rchb. fil. (1) Mañanja hills, Waller ; Buchanan.

ORCHIDACEAE.
Lissochilus microceras, Rchb. fil. (1) Sochi, Kirk ; Mañanja hills, Meller.
L. heteroglossus, Rchb. fil. (1) Upper Shire Valley, Kirk.
L. gracilior, Rendle. (1) Shire Highlands, Scott-Elliot.
L. livingstonianus, Rchb. fil. (1) Mañanja hills, Waller and Meller ; Mlanje, Whyte and McClounie ; between Matope and Blantyre, L. Scott.
L. arenarius, Lindl. (1) Mañanja hills, Kirk and Meller ; Shire Highlands, Scott-Elliot ; Mlanje, Whyte ; Buchanan ; (2) North of Lake Nyasa, L. Scott ; Carson.
L. Sandersoni, Rchb. fil. (1) Buchanan.
L. papilionaceus, Rendle. (2) Nyasa-Tanganyika plateau, Scott-Elliot.
L. Krebsii, Rchb. fil. (1) Mlanje, McClounie.
L. shirensis, Rendle. (1) Sochi, Shire Highlands, Scott-Elliot.
L. calopterus, Rchb. fil. (1) Lower Shire Valley, L. Scott.
L. Wakefieldii, Rchb. fil. (1) Mlanje, Whyte.
L. dispersus, Rolfe. (1) Livingstonia (Collector not known).
L. brevisepalus, Rendle. (1) Sochi and Ndirande, Scott-Elliot.
L. milanjianus, Rendle. (1) Mlanje, Whyte ; Mañanja hills, Meller ; Buchanan.
Lissochilus spp. (1) Buchanan ; Mañanja hills, Waller ; (2) Nyasa-Tanganyika plateau, Carson and J. Thomson ; Mweru, Carson.
Polystachya imbricata, Rolfe. (1) Buchanan.
P. Buchanani, Rolfe. (1) Buchanan.
P. shirensis, Rchb. fil. (1) Shire River, Meller.
P. zambesiaca, Rolfe. (1) Buchanan.
P. lawrenceana, Kränz. (1) Buchanan.
P. villosa, Rolfe. (1) Buchanan.
P. minima, Rendle. (1) Sochi, Shire Highlands, Scott-Elliot.
Polystachya spp. (1) Mlanje, Whyte and McClounie, Zomba, Kirk.
Angraecum alcicorne, Rchb. fil. (1) Mlanje ; McClounie ; Shire River, Kirk.
A. chiloschistae, Rchb. fil. (1) Shire Valley, Kirk ; Blantyre, Last.
A. megalorrhizum, Rchb. fil. (1) Shire Valley, Kirk and Waller ; Buchanan.
A. verrucosum, Rendle. (1) Mlanje, Whyte.
Angraecum sp. (1) Buchanan.
Pogonia spp. (1) Buchanan.
Stenoglottis sp. (1) Buchanan.
Holothrix Johnstonii, Rolfe. (1) Mlanje, McClounie ; Zomba, Whyte.
Holothrix sp. (1) Blantyre, Last ; (2) Upper plateau, north of Lake Nyasa, J. Thomson.
Peristylis hispidula, Rendle. (1) Buchanan.
Habenaria zambesina, Rchb. fil. (1) Buchanan.
H. subarmata, Rchb. fil. (1) Katunga, Kirk.
H. sochensis, Rchb. fil. (1) Sochi hill, Kirk.
H. Walleri, Rchb. fil. (1) Mañanja hills and foot of Mlanje, Kirk ; Blantyre, Last.
H. praestans, Rendle. (1) Buchanan ; Blantyre, Last.
H. buchananiana, Kränz. (1) Buchanan ; Mañanja hills, Waller ; Mlanje, Scott-Elliot ; (2) Nutt.
Habenaria spp. (1) Carson.
Brachycorythis pleistophylla, Rchb. fil. (1) Buchanan ; Mlanje, McClounie and Whyte ; Sochi, Shire Highlands, Scott-Elliot ; Blantyre, Last.
B. pubescens, Harv. (1) Mlanje, Scott-Elliot ; Blantyre, Last ; Buchanan.
Brachycorythis tenuior, Rchb. fil. (1) Blantyre, Last ; (2) Nutt ; Carson.
Satyrium cheirophorum, Rchb. fil. (1) Blantyre, Last.
S. minax, Rchb. fil. (1) Blantyre, Last.
S. Buchanani, Rchb. fil. (1) Blantyre, Last.

BOTANICAL APPENDICES

ORCHIDACEAE.
    Satyrium spp. (1) Mpatamanga and Mañanja hills, Kirk; Buchanan; (2) Carson; Nutt.
    Disa hircicornis, Rchb. fil. (1) Mañanja hills, Kirk.
    D. Walleri, Rchb. fil. (1) Mañanja hills, Waller.
    D. zombaensis, Rendle. (1) Zomba, Whyte.
    D. hamatopetala, Rendle. (1) Mlanje, McClounie and Whyte.
    Disa spp. (1) Buchanan; Zomba, Kirk; Blantyre, Last; (2) Higher plateau, north of Lake Nyasa, J. Thomson; Carson; Nutt; Nyasa-Tanganyika plateau, Johnston.

SCITAMINEAE.
    Kaempferia aethiopica, Benth. (1) Buchanan; Mandala, Scott-Elliot; Mañanja hills, Meller; near Blantyre, L. Scott; (2) Karonga, Carson; Nyasa-Tanganyika plateau, H. H. Johnston.
    K. rosea, Schweinf. (1) Shire Highlands, Scott-Elliot; Lake Nyasa, L. Scott; Buchanan; Lower Shire Valley, Kirk; Shire Valley, Meller.
    Kaempferia sp. (2) Karonga, Carson.
    Cadalvenia spectabilis, Fenzl. (1) Shire Highlands, Scott-Elliot; Buchanan; Blantyre, Last; (2) Nyasa-Tanganyika plateau, H. H. Johnston.
    Amomum sp. (1) Zomba, Kirk.
    Canna indica, L., subsp. *C. orientalis*, Roscoe. (1) Lower valley of Shire River, Meller.
    Musa Buchanani, Baker. (1) Shire Highlands, Kirk; Buchanan.
    M. sapientum, L., var. *M. paradisiaca*, L. (1, 2, and 4) abundant.
    M. livingstoniana, Kirk. (1) Lake Nyasa, Kirk.

HAEMODORACEAE.
    Sansevieria Kirkii, Baker. (1) Buchanan.
    Cyanastrum sp. (2) Nyasa-Tanganyika plateau, H. H. Johnston; Nutt.

IRIDACEAE.
    Moraea zambesiaca, Baker. (1) Mañanja hills, Meller; Sochi and Katunga, Kirk; Zomba, Buchanan; Mlanje, McClounie; (2) Higher plateau, north of Lake Nyasa, and between Nyasa and Tanganyika, J. Thomson.
    M. angusta, Ker. (2) Carson; Nutt.
    M. ventricosa, Baker. (2) Carson.
    M. Thomsoni, Baker. (2) Higher plateau, north of Lake Nyasa, J. Thomson.
    M. Carsoni, Baker. (2) Carson.
    M. iridoides, L. (1) Mpatamanga, Kirk.
    Aristea johnstoniana, Rendle. (1) Mlanje, Whyte and McClounie.
    Dierama pendula, Baker. (1) Mlanje, Whyte and McClounie; (2) Nyasa-Tanganyika plateau, J. Thomson.
    Lapeyrousia erythrantha, Baker. Mañanja hills, Waller.
    L. Sandersoni, Baker. (1) Buchanan; (4) Menyharth.
    L. grandiflora, Baker. (1) Mañanja hills, Meller; Buchanan.
    L. holostachya, Baker. (2) Carson.
    Crocosma aurea, Planch. (1) Buchanan; Shire Highlands, Scott-Elliot.
    Acidanthera bicolor, Hochst. (1) Buchanan.
    Gladiolus unguiculatus, Baker. (2) Nyasa-Tanganyika plateau, J. Thomson; Carson.
    G. Oatesii, Rolfe. (1) Mlanje, Whyte; Buchanan.
    G. Thomsoni, Baker. (2) Higher plateau, north of Lake Nyasa, J. Thomson.
    G. flexuosus, Baker. (2) Carson.
    G. atropurpureus, Baker. (1) Mañanja hills, Waller; Shire Highlands, Scott-Elliot.
    G. Melleri, Baker. (1) Mañanja hills, Meller and Waller; Katunga and Mpimbi, Kirk; Buchanan; Mlanje, Whyte.

IRIDACEAE.
    Gladiolus Buchanani, Baker. (1) Ndirande, Buchanan.
    G. gracillimus, Baker. (2) Carson.
    G. tritonioides, Baker. (2) Carson.
    G. Hanningtoni, Baker. (2) Carson ; Nutt.
    G. zambesiacus, Baker. (1) Blantyre, Last.
    G. oligophlebius, Baker. (2) Carson ; Nutt.
    G. erectiflorus, Baker. (2) Carson.
    G. caudatus, Baker. (2) Carson.
    G. brachyandrus, Baker. (2) Buchanan.
    G. quartinianus, A. Rich. (1) Buchanan ; (2) Carson ; Nutt.
    Gladiolus spp. (1) Shire Highlands, Scott-Elliot ; (2) Carson.

AMARYLLIDACEAE.
    Hypoxis villosa, L. (1) Buchanan ; Shire Highlands, L. Scott and Scott-Elliot ; Mañanja hills, Meller ; (2) Lower plateau, north of Lake Nyasa, J. Thomson.
    H. obtusa, Burch. (1) Shire Highlands, Scott-Elliot ; (2) Lower plateau, north of Lake Nyasa, J. Thomson.
    H. angustifolia, Lam. (1) Mlanje, Whyte.
    Curculigo gallabatensis, Schweinf. (2) R. Nsessi, L. Scott.
    Curculigo sp. (1) Buchanan.
    Crinum subcernuum, Baker. (1) Shire River, Kirk.
    Crinum sp. (4) Menyharth.
    Buphane disticha, Herb. (1) Mañanja hills, Meller ; Shire Highlands, Buchanan and Scott-Elliot ; (2) between Nyasa and Tanganyika, and upper plateau, north of Lake Nyasa, J. Thomson.
    Brunsvigia Kirkii, Baker. (2) Nyasa-Tanganyika plateau, Scott-Elliot.
    Cyrtanthus Welwitschii, Hiern. (1) Mlanje, Whyte and McClounie ; Buchanan.
    Haemanthus multiflorus, Martyn. (1) Mañanja hills, Meller ; Buchanan.
    Haemanthus sp. (4) Menyharth.
    Pancratium trianthum, Herb. (1) Shire cataracts, Kirk.
    Vellozia splendens, Rendle. (1) Mlanje, Whyte and McClounie.
    Vellozia sp. (1) Mañanja hills, Meller ; Zomba and east end of Lake Chilwa, Kirk ; Shire Highlands, Scott-Elliot and Buchanan.

TACCACEAE.
    Tacca pinnatifida, L. (1) Shire Highlands, Buchanan and Scott-Elliot.

DIOSCOREACEAE.
    Dioscorea Buchanani, Benth. (1) Buchanan.
    D. prehensilis, Benth. (1) Buchanan.
    D. schimperiana, Hochst. (1) Mpatamanga, Kirk ; Buchanan.
    D. dumetorum, Pax. (1) Mañanja hills, Meller ; Buchanan.
    D. beccariana, Martelli, var. *vestita*, Pax. (1) Shire Highlands, Buchanan and Scott-Elliot.

LILIACEAE.
    Dracaena fragrans, Ker.-Gawl. (1) Chiradzulu, Meller ; Buchanan ; Zomba, Whyte.
    D. elliptica, Thunb. et Dallm. (1) Buchanan.
    Smilax kraussiana, Meisn. (1) Mañanja hills, Kirk ; Mlanje, Whyte ; Buchanan ; Shire Highlands, Scott-Elliot.
    Asparagus virgatus, Baker. (1) Buchanan ; Mlanje, Whyte.
    A. plumosus, Baker. (1) Buchanan ; Mlanje, Whyte.

LILIACEAE.
Asparagus Paulo-gulielmi, Solms. (1) Shire Highlands, L. Scott.
A. puberulus, Baker. (1) Mañanja hills, Meller.
A. irregularis, Baker. (1) Foot of Chiradzulu, Kirk.
A. africanus, Lam. (2) Carson; Nutt; (4) Menyharth.
A. asiaticus, L. (4) Menyharth.
A. racemosus, Willd. (1) Chiradzulu, Whyte; Buchanan; (2) Carson.
A. Buchanani, Baker. (1) Buchanan.
Asparagus sp. (1) Buchanan; Blantyre, Last.
Hylonome reticulata, Webb. (1) Mlanje, Whyte.
Kniphofia longistyla, Baker. (1) Zomba, Kirk; Buchanan.
K. zombensis, Baker. (1) Zomba, Buchanan.
Aloe Buchanani, Baker. (1) Buchanan.
A. Nuttii, Baker. (2) Nutt; Carson.
A. cryptopoda, Baker. (4) Menyharth.
Eriospermum abyssinicum, Baker. (1) Buchanan; Shire Highlands, Scott-Elliot.
E. Kirkii, Baker. (1) Shire Highlands, Buchanan and L. Scott.
Eriospermum sp. (2) Carson.
Bulbine alooides, Willd. (1) Chiradzulu, Kirk and Meller.
B. asphodeloides, Schult. fil. (1) Shire Highlands, K. C. Cameron, Scott-Elliot and Buchanan; Mlanje, McClounie.
Anthericum subpetiolatum, Baker. (1) Buchanan; Shire Highlands, Scott-Elliot.
A. Nyasae, Rendle. (1) Mlanje, Whyte.
A. milanjianum, Rendle. (1) Mlanje, Whyte.
A. Cameroni, Baker. (2) Carson.
A. nidulans, Baker. (1) Chiradzulu, Meller.
A. jacquinianum, Schult. fil. (2) Carson.
Anthericum sp. (1) Buchanan; Mlanje, Whyte; (2) Nutt; Carson.
Chlorophytum blepharophyllum, Schweinf. (1) Zomba, Whyte; Fort Johnston, Scott-Elliot; Buchanan.
C. stenopetalum, Baker. (1) Buchanan.
C. brachystachyum, Baker. (1) Buchanan.
C. gallabatense, Schweinf. (1) Buchanan.
C. andongense, Baker. (1) Buchanan.
C. pubiflorum, Baker. (1) Buchanan.
Chlorophytum spp. (2) Carson; (4) Menyharth.
Dasystachys drimiopsis, Baker. (1) Buchanan; (4) Menyharth.
Dasystachys spp. (2) Carson; Nutt.
Tulbaghia alliacea, Thunb. (1) Shire Highlands, Buchanan and Scott-Elliot.
Drimia robusta, Baker. (1) Mlanje, Whyte and McClounie.
Drimia sp. (1) Zomba, Kirk.
Dipcadi longifolium, Baker. (1) Lower Shire River, Meller.
Hyacinthus ledebourioides, Baker. (1) Zomba and east end of Lake Chilwa, Meller; Shire Highlands, L. Scott.
Eucomis zambesiaca, Baker. (1) Mbami, Kirk; Buchanan.
Albuca caudata, Jacq. (1) Mlanje, McClounie; Shire Highlands, Buchanan, L. Scott and Scott-Elliot.
A. Buchanani, Baker. (1) Buchanan.
A. Wakefieldii, Baker. (? 1) Lake Nyasa.
Albuca sp. (1) Mañanja hills, Meller; (4) Menyharth.
Urginea altissima, Baker (*U. maritima*, Rendle, non Baker). (1) Mañanja hills, Meller; Mlanje, Whyte; Shire Highlands, L. Scott and Buchanan; Mpimbi, Kirk; Zomba, Whyte; (2) Carson.

LILIACEAE.

Urginea Nyasae, Rendle. (1) Mlanje, Whyte and McClounie; Buchanan.
Urginea spp. (1) Mandala, Scott-Elliot; (2) Nutt.
Scilla rigidifolia, Kunth. (2) Upper plateau, north of Lake Nyasa, and between Nyasa and Tanganyika, J. Thomson.
S. indica, Baker. (1) Shire Highlands, L. Scott.
S. maesta, Baker. (4) Menyharth.
S. Buchanani, Baker. (1) Buchanan.
S. zambesiaca, Baker. (1) Buchanan; (4) Menyharth.
Scilla sp. (1) Buchanan; Zomba, Whyte; Mlanje, McClounie.
Ornithogalum Eckloni, Schlecht. (1) Shire Highlands, Buchanan and Scott-Elliot; Mlanje, Whyte.
Ornithogalum sp. (1) Buchanan.
Androcymbium melanthioides, Willd. (1) Shire Highlands, Buchanan and Scott-Elliot.
Ornithoglossum glaucum, Salisb. (1) Blantyre, Last.
Gloriosa superba, L. (1) Mañanja hills, Waller.
G. virescens, Lindl. (1) Shire Highlands, Scott-Elliot; (4) Menyharth.
G. Carsoni, Baker. (2) Carson.
Walleria Mackenzii, Kirk. (1) Mañanja hills, Waller; Buchanan.
W. nutans, Kirk. (1) Mañanja hills, Waller.

XYRIDACEAE.

Xyris pauciflora, Willd. (1) Mlanje, McClounie.
Xyris spp. (1) Buchanan; (2) Carson; Nutt.

COMMELYNACEAE.

Commelyna benghalensis, L. (1) Buchanan; (4) Holub.
C. zambesiaca, C. B. Clarke. (2) Carson.
C. latifolia, Hochst. (1) Buchanan; (2) Carson.
C. africana, L. (1) Shire Highlands, Scott-Elliot; Zomba and east end of Lake Chilwa, Meller; Zomba, Whyte; Buchanan; (2) Carson; Nutt.
C. involucrata, A. Rich. (1) Blantyre, L. Scott; Buchanan.
C. Kirkii, C. B. Clarke. (1) Shire Highlands, Scott-Elliot; (2) Nyasa-Tanganyika plateau, J. Thomson.
C. Forskalaei, Vahl. (4) Holub.
C. Bainesii, C. B. Clarke, var. *glabrata*, Rendle. (1) Zomba, Whyte.
C. Vogelii, C. B. Clarke. (1) Buchanan.
C. Welwitschii, C. B. Clarke. (1) Shire Highlands, Scott-Elliot.
C. nudiflora, L. (1) Shire Highlands, Scott-Elliot.
C. subulata, Roth. (1) Buchanan.
C. albescens, Hassk. (1) Mlanje, Whyte.
Commelyna sp. (2) Carson; Nutt.
Aneilema sinicum, Lindl. (1) Buchanan; Mlanje, Whyte; (2) Nutt; Carson.
A. aequinoctiale, Kunth. (1) Buchanan; Chiradzulu, Meller; Shire Highlands, Scott-Elliot; Mlanje and Zomba, Whyte; var. *Kirkii*, C. B. Clarke. (1) Buchanan; var. *adhaerens*, C. B. Clarke. (1) Mañanja hills, H. Waller.
A. pedunculosum, C. B. Clarke. (4) Menyharth.
A. lanceolatum, Benth. (1) Buchanan.
A. dregeanum, Kunth. (1) Buchanan.
Cyanotis lanata, Benth. (2) Carson; var. *Schweinfurthii*, C. B. Clarke. (1) Buchanan.
Cyanotis sp. (2) Nutt.
Floscopa rivularis, C. B. Clarke. (2) Nutt.
F. glomerata, Hassk. (1) Buchanan; Zomba, Whyte; (2) Carson; (4) Victoria Falls, Kirk.

BOTANICAL APPENDICES

PALMAE.
    Elaeis guineensis, L. (1) West shore of Lake Nyasa, Kirk.
    Borassus flabellifer, L., var. *Aethiopum*, Mart. (1) Lower Shire and Lake Nyasa, Kirk.
    Raphia vinifera, P. de Beauv. (1) Shire Highlands, Kirk.
    Hyphaene crinita, Gaertn. (1) Along the Shire River and at south end of Lake Nyasa, Kirk.
    H. ventricosa, Kirk. (4) Victoria Falls, Kirk.
    Phœnix sp. (1) Matope, Scott-Elliot; (4) Central regions, Kirk.

TYPHACEAE.
    Typha angustifolia, L. (1) Shire River, below Katunga, L. Scott.
    Typha sp. (1) Mañanja hills, Meller.

AROIDEAE.
    Stylochiton spp. (4) Menyharth.
    Amorphophallus spp. (2) Nsese River, North Nyasa, L. Scott; (4) Menyharth.
    Gonatopus Boivinii, Hook. fil. (1) Lower Shire Valley, Kirk; Mlanje, McClounie; Buchanan.
    Gonatopus sp. (4) Menyharth.

ALISMACEAE.
    Limnophyton obtusifolium, Miq. (2) Mweru, Carson.

NAIADACEAE.
    Potamogeton pectinatus, L. (1) South-western bay of Lake Nyasa, Kirk; Livingstonia, Laws.
    P. obtusifolius, Mert. et Koch. (1) Zomba, Whyte.
    P. longifolius, Gay. (1) South-western bay of Lake Nyasa, Kirk.
    P. crispus, L. (1) Ruangwa, Lake Nyasa, Kirk.

ERIOCAULACEAE.
    Eriocaulon sonderianum, Körn. (1) Mlanje, Whyte.
    Eriocaulon spp. (1) Mañanja country and Katunga, Kirk; Buchanan; (2) Lower plateau, north of Lake Nyasa, J. Thomson; Nutt.

RESTIACEAE.
    1 sp. (1) Mlanje, McClounie.

CYPERACEAE.
    Pycreus flavescens, Nees. (2) Nsese River, North Nyasa, L. Scott.
    P. nigricans, C. B. Clarke. (1) Mlanje, Whyte; Buchanan.
    P. macranthus, C. B. Clarke. (1) Buchanan; (2) Nutt.
    P. Mundtii, C. B. Clarke. (1) Buchanan.
    P. sulcinux, C. B. Clarke. (2) Umbaka River, North Nyasa, L. Scott.
    P. capillaris, Nees. (1) Buchanan.
    P. umbrosus, Nees. (2) Carson.
    P. spissiflorus, C. B. Clarke. (2) Mlanje, Whyte.
    P. albomarginatus, Nees. (1) Buchanan.
    Juncellus alopecuroides, C. B. Clarke. (1) Buchanan.
    J. laevigatus, C. B. Clarke. (1) Mañanja hills, Meller.
    Cyperus nudicaulis, Poir. (1) Lower Shire River, Kirk.
    C. compactus, Lam. (1) Buchanan; (2) Nutt.
    C. angolensis, Boeck. (*Rhynchospora ochrocephala*, Boeck.) (1) Mlanje, Whyte; Zomba, Kirk; (2) Nutt.
    C. margaritaceus, Vahl. (1) Buchanan; (2) Carson; (3) Serpa Pinto.

CYPERACEAE.
    Cyperus amabilis, Vahl. (1) Buchanan; (3) Serpa Pinto.
    C. tenax, Boeck. (1) Buchanan.
    C. Haspan, L. (2) Karonga, L. Scott.
    C. sphaerospermus, Schrad. (4) Victoria Falls, Kirk.
    C. flabelliformis, Rottb. (1) Mañanja hills, Meller; Great Elephant Marsh, Shire River, L. Scott; Buchanan.
    C. sexangularis, Nees. (4) Menyharth.
    C. Deckenii, Boeck. (1) Shire Highlands, Scott-Elliot.
    C. fischerianus, Hochst. (1) Chiradzulu, Meller; Buchanan.
    C. glaucophyllus, Boeck. (1) Buchanan.
    C. longifolius, Poir. (1) Buchanan.
    C. aristatus, Rottb. (1) Buchanan; (3) Serpa Pinto; (4) Menyharth.
    C. distans, L. fil. (1) Shire Highlands, Scott-Elliot; (2) Carson.
    C. articulatus, L. (1) Elephant Marsh, Shire River, L. Scott.
    C. schweinfurthianus, Boeck. (2) Carson.
    C. maculatus, Boeck. (1) Buchanan; (2) Umbaka and Nsese Rivers, North Nyasa, L. Scott.
    C. rotundus, L. (1) Lower Shire Valley, Kirk; (3) Serpa Pinto.
    C. esculentus, L. (1) Buchanan.
    C. radiatus, Vahl. (1) Great Elephant Marsh, Shire River, L. Scott; (2) Umbaka River, North Nyasa, L. Scott.
    C. zambesiensis, C. B. Clarke, ined. in Trans. Linn. Soc. 2nd Ser. iv., p. 53. (1) Mlanje, Whyte; Buchanan.
    C. exaltatus, Retz, var. *C. dives*, Del. (1) Buchanan; Lower Shire Valley, Meller; Elephant Marsh, Shire River, Kirk and L. Scott.
    Cyperus spp. (1) Mañanja hills, Meller; Shire Highlands, Scott-Elliot; (2) Umbaka River, North Nyasa, L. Scott; (3) Serpa Pinto.
    Mariscus coloratus, Nees. (1) Buchanan.
    M. vestitus, C. B. Clarke. (1) Shire Highlands, Scott-Elliot.
    M. sieberianus, Nees. (1) Buchanan; Blantyre, Last; Mlanje, Whyte.
    M. hemisphaericus, C. B. Clarke. (1) Buchanan; Mandala, Scott-Elliot; Blantyre, Scott; Mlanje, Whyte; Lower Shire Valley, Meller.
    M. squarrosus, C. B. Clarke. (1) Buchanan.
    Mariscus sp. (1) Mlanje, Whyte.
    Kyllinga pungens, Link. (2) Karonga, L. Scott.
    K. elatior, Kunth. (1) Buchanan.
    K. alba, Nees. (3) Serpa Pinto.
    K. aurata, Nees. (2) Nsese River, North Nyasa, L. Scott.
    Kyllinga sp. (*Cyperus albiceps*, Ridley). (2) Nsese River, North Nyasa, L. Scott.
    Kyllinga sp. (1) Buchanan.
    Eleocharis sp. (4) Victoria Falls, Kirk.
    Fimbristylis dichotoma, Vahl. (2) Karonga and River Nsese, North Nyasa, L. Scott.
    F. diphylla, Vahl. (1) Buchanan.
    F. exilis, Roem. et Sch. (1) Buchanan.
    F. africana, C. B. Clarke. (1) Mañanja hills, Meller; Buchanan; Shire Highlands, Scott-Elliot.
    F. zambesiaca, Dur. et Schinz. (1) Sochi, Kirk; Blantyre, L. Scott; Kampala, Shire Highlands, Scott-Elliot.
    Bulbostylis schoenoides, C. B. Clarke. (1) Mlanje, Whyte.
    B. cinnamomea, Dur. et Schinz. (1) Buchanan.
    B. sphaerocarpus, C. B. Clarke. (3) Serpa Pinto.
    B. capillaris, Kunth. (1) Blantyre, Last.

BOTANICAL APPENDICES

CYPERACEAE.
Bulbostylis pusilla, Dur. et Schinz. (2) Nutt.
B. Burchellii, Dur. et Schinz. (1) Blantyre, Last; (3) Serpa Pinto.
B. abortiva, Dur. et Schinz. (1) Buchanan.
B. oritrephes, C. B. Clarke. (1) Mlanje, Whyte.
Bulbostylis spp. (1) Buchanan.
Scirpus articulatus, L. (1) Buchanan.
S. littoralis, Schrad. (1) West shore of Lake Nyasa, Kirk; Zomba and east end of Lake Chilwa, Meller.
S. maritimus, L. (1) Lower Shire River, Kirk and Meller.
S. costatus, Boeck. (1) Mlanje, Whyte.
Fuirena pubescens, Kunth, var. *Buchanani*, C. B. Clarke. (1) Buchanan; (3) Serpa Pin o.
F. Welwitschii, Ridley. (1) Mlanje, Whyte; (2) Nutt.
F. umbellata, Rottb. (1) Buchanan; Mbami, near Blantyre, Kirk.
Fuirena sp. (3) Serpa Pinto.
Lipocarpha argentea, R. Br. (2) Nkonde country, North Nyasa, L. Scott.
L. albiceps, Ridley. (1) Mandala, Scott-Elliot; Buchanan.
L. pulcherrima, Ridley. (1) Buchanan.
Ascolepis protea, Welw., var. *bellidiflora*, Welw. (1) Mandala, Scott-Elliot; Buchanan; (2) Nutt.
A. anthemiflora, Welw. (2) Carson; Nutt.
A. speciosa, Welw. (2) Carson.
A. elata, Welw. (2) Carson; Nutt.
A. capensis, Benth. (1) Buchanan; Mlanje, Whyte; (2) Lower plateau, north of Lake Nyasa, J. Thomson.
A. brasiliensis, Benth. (1) Buchanan; (2) Nutt; Carson.
Rynchospora candida, Boeck. (*R. adscendens*, C. B. Clarke). (1) Buchanan; (2) Nutt.
Eriospora Oliveri, C. B. Clarke. (1) Buchanan.
E. villosula, C. B. Clarke. (1) Mlanje, Whyte; Ndirande, near Blantyre, Scott-Elliot.
Scleria pulchella, Ridley. (1) Buchanan.
S. remota, Ridley. (1) Buchanan.
S. glabra, Boeck. (1) Buchanan; Mandala, Scott-Elliot.
S. hirtella, Swartz. (2) Nkonde country, North Nyasa, L. Scott.
S. catophylla Dur. et Schinz. (1) Buchanan.
S. Buchanani, Boeck. (1) Buchanan; Shire Valley, Waller.
S. dregeana, Kunth. (1) Mañanja hills, Kirk; Buchanan.
S. bulbifera, A. Rich. (1) Ndirande, near Blantyre, Scott-Elliot.
S. multispiculata, Boeck. (1) Buchanan.
S. melanomphala, Kunth. (1) Buchanan.
Scleria spp. (1) Mañanja hills, Kirk; Buchanan.
Carex boryana, Schk. (1) Mlanje, Whyte.
Carex spp. (1) Mlanje, Whyte; Buchanan.

GRAMINEAE.
Paspalum scrobiculatum, L. (3) Serpa Pinto.
Panicum sanguinale, L. (1) Buchanan; (2) Karonga and Umbaka River, North Nyasa, L. Scott; (3) Serpa Pinto.
P. brizanthum, Hochst. (1) Buchanan.
P. Crus-galli, L. (1) Shire Valley, Meller; Buchanan; (2) Umbaka River, North Nyasa, L. Scott; Carson.
P. colonum, L. (1) Lower Shire Valley, L. Scott; (2) Karonga, L. Scott.
P. indicum, L. (1) Mañanja hills, Kirk.

GRAMINEAE.
- *Panicum nudiglume*, Hochst. (1) Lower Shire, L. Scott.
- *P. paludosum*, Roxb. (1) Shire River, Kirk.
- *P. pectinatum*, Rendle. (1) Mlanje, Whyte; (2) Buchanan.
- *P. unguiculatum*, Trin. (1) Buchanan.
- *P. insigne*, Steud. (1) Mañanja hills, Meller; Buchanan; Mlanje, Whyte; (2) Nutt; Carson; (3) Serpa Pinto.
- *P. plicatum*, Lam. (2) Carson.
- *P. milanjianum*, Rendle. (1) Mlanje, Whyte.
- *P. serratum*, R. Br. (3) Serpa Pinto.
- *P. maximum*, Jacq. (3) Serpa Pinto.
- *P. nigropedatum*, Munro. (3) Serpa Pinto.
- *Panicum* spp. (1) Shire River and Mañanja hills, Kirk; Shire River, Meiler; Mandala and Shire River, L. Scott; Buchanan; (2) Carson; (4) Batoka country, Kirk.
- *Setaria* spp. (1) Mañanja hills, Waller; Elephant Marsh, Shire River, Kirk and L. Scott; Buchanan; Blantyre, L. Scott; (2) Umbaka and Nsese Rivers, North Nyasa, L. Scott.
- *Pennisetum Benthamii*, Steud. (1) Lower Shire Valley, Meller.
- *P. unisetum*, Benth. (1) Buchanan.
- *Pennisetum* sp. (1) Mañanja hills, Kirk.
- *Cleistachne* sp. (1) Buchanan.
- *Perotis latifolia*, Ait. (1) Buchanan.
- *Imperata arundinacea*, Cyr. (1) Buchanan; (3) Serpa Pinto.
- *Saccharum purpuratum*, Rendle. (1) Buchanan; Mlanje, Whyte.
- *Saccharum* sp. (1) West shore of Lake Nyasa, Kirk.
- *Hemarthria compressa*, R. Br. (1) Lower Shire, L. Scott.
- *Hemarthria* sp. (1) Elephant Marsh, Shire River, Kirk; Buchanan; (2) Nsese River, North Nyasa, L. Scott.
- *Elionurus argenteus*, Nees. (3) Serpa Pinto.
- *Rottboellia exaltata*, L. (1) Lower Shire Valley, L. Scott.
- *Manisuris granularis*, Sm. (1) Mañanja hills, Waller; near Sochi, Kirk; Buchanan.
- *Vossia procera*, Griff. (1) Elephant Marsh, on Shire River, Kirk.
- *Ischaemum* sp. (4) Victoria Falls, Kirk.
- *Andropogon ceresiaeformis*, Nees. (1) Buchanan.
- *A. squamulatus*, Hochst. (1) Buchanan.
- *A. schirensis*, Hochst. (1) Buchanan.
- *A. Sorghum*, Brot. (1) Mañanja hills, Meller; (2) Nutt.
- *A. annularis*, Forsk. (1) Lower Shire Valley, Kirk.
- *A. hirtus*, L. (1) Mlanje, Whyte; (3) Serpa Pinto.
- *A. anthistirioides*, Hochst. (3) Serpa Pinto.
- *A. pertusus*, Willd., var. *insculptus*, Hackel. (3) Serpa Pinto.
- *A. Schoenanthus*, L. (3) Serpa Pinto.
- *A. eucomus*, Nees. (3) Serpa Pinto.
- *A. intermedius*, R. Br., var. *punctatus*, Hackel. (3) Serpa Pinto.
- *A. Nyasae*, Rendle. (1) Buchanan.
- *A. cymbarius*, L. (1) Buchanan; (2) Nutt.
- *Andropogon* spp. (1) Buchanan; Mbami, near Blantyre, Kirk.
- *Anthistiria ciliata*, Retz. (1) Buchanan.
- *Anthistiria* sp. (1) Mañanja hills, Kirk.
- *Aristida barbicollis*, Trin. et Rupr. (3) Serpa Pinto.
- *A. vestita*, Thunb. (3) Serpa Pinto.
- *Aristida* spp. (1) Upper Shire Valley, Kirk; Buchanan; (4) Batoka country, Kirk.

BOTANICAL APPENDICES

GRAMINEAE.
   Sporobolus minutiflorus, Link. (1) Buchanan; (4) Holub.
   S. leptostachys, Ficalho et Hiern. (3) Serpa Pinto.
   S. indicus, R. Br. (1) Mañanja hills, Meller.
   Sporobolus spp. (1) Upper and Lower Valley of the Shire River, Kirk; Buchanan; (2) Umbaka River, North Nyasa, L. Scott.
   Agrostis sp. (1) Buchanan.
   Tristachya decora, Stapf. (2) Carson.
   T. inamoena, K. Schum. (1) Buchanan.
   Tristachya spp. (1) Blantyre, L. Scott; (2) Carson.
   Trichopteryx leucothrix, Trin. (2) Carson.
   Trichopteryx sp. (1) Buchanan.
   Microchloa abyssinica, Hochst. (1) Buchanan.
   Triraphis sp. (3) Serpa Pinto.
   Chloris gayana, Kunth. (1) Chiromo, L. Scott.
   C. radiata, Sw. (1) Buchanan.
   C. petraea, Thunb. (3) Serpa Pinto.
   C. breviseta, Benth. (2) Umbaka River, North Nyasa, L. Scott.
   Chloris spp. (1) Lower Shire Valley, Kirk and Meller.
   Harpechloa altera, Rendle. (1) Buchanan; Mlanje, Whyte and McClounie.
   Eleusine indica, L. (1) Elephant Marsh, on Shire River, Kirk; Buchanan; Katunga, L. Scott; (2) Umbaka River, North Nyasa, L. Scott.
   Leptochloa uniflora, Hochst. (1) Buchanan.
   L. chinensis, Nees. (1) Elephant Marsh, on Shire River, Kirk.
   Leptochloa sp. (1) Lower Shire Valley, L. Scott.
   Schmidtia quinqueseta, Benth. (3) Serpa Pinto.
   Triodia sp. (1) Buchanan.
   Phragmites communis, Trin. (1) Lower Shire Valley, Meller; near Blantyre, L. Scott.
   Phragmites sp. (1) Buchanan.
   Koeleria cristata, Pers. (1) Mlanje, Whyte and McClounie; Buchanan.
   Eragrostis namaquensis, Nees. (2) Umbaka River, North Nyasa, L. Scott.
   E. nindensis, Ficalho et Hiern. (3) Serpa Pinto.
   E. major, Host. (1) Buchanan.
   E. elata, Munro. (3) Serpa Pinto.
   E. aspera, Nees. (1) Buchanan.
   E. gummiflua, Nees. (3) Serpa Pinto.
   E. Lappula, Nees. (3) Serpa Pinto.
   E. obtusa, Munro. (3) Serpa Pinto.
   Eragrostis spp. (1) Mañanja hills, Meller; Buchanan; Mlanje, Whyte; (2) Umbaka and Quaqua Rivers, North Nyasa, L. Scott.
   Festuca milanjiana, Rendle. (1) Mlanje, Whyte; Buchanan.
   F. costata, Nees. (1) Mlanje, Whyte.
   Bromus milanjianus, Rendle. (1) Mlanje, Whyte.
   Oxytenanthera sp. (1) Mbami and Blantyre, Lake Chilwa, and Katunga, Kirk.

CONIFERAE.
   Podocarpus milanjiana, Rendle. (1) Mlanje, Whyte.
   Widdringtonia Whytei, Rendle. (1) Mlanje, Whyte and McClounie; Zomba, Whyte.

GNETACEAE.
   Gnetum africanum, Welw. (1) Buchanan.

CRYPTOGAMS.

LYCOPODIACEAE.
Lycopodium dacrydioides, Baker. (1) Buchanan.
L. cernuum, L. (1) Buchanan.

SELAGINELLACEAE.
Selaginella versicolor, Spring. (1) Buchanan; (2) Carson.
S. molliceps, Spring. (1) Shire Highlands, Buchanan.
S. Vogelii, Spring. (2) Carson.

EQUISETACEAE.
Equisetum elongatum, Willd. (1) Shire Highlands, Buchanan.

SALVINIACEAE.
Azolla pinnata, R. Br. (1) Lake Nyasa, Laws.

FILICES.
Gleichenia polypodioides, Sm. (1) Mlanje, McClounie.
G. dichotoma, Hook. (2) Nutt.
Cyathea Dregei, Kze. (1) Buchanan; (2) Nutt.
C. Thomsoni, Baker. (2) Lower plateau, north of Lake Nyasa, J. Thomson.
C. zambesiaca, Baker. (1) Buchanan.
Hymenophyllum australe, Willd. (1) Buchanan.
Davallia thecifera, H. B. K. (1) Buchanan.
D. Speluncae, Baker. (2) Carson.
Cheilanthes Schimperi, Kze. (1) Buchanan.
C. multifida, Sw. (1) Mlanje, McClounie.
Pellaea hastata, Link. (1) Buchanan.
P. dura, Willd. (1) Shire Highlands, Scott-Elliot.
P. Calomelanos, Link. (3) Serpa Pinto.
P. doniana, Hook. (1) Buchanan; (2) Carson.
P. pectiniformis, Baker; (2) Nutt.
Pteris quadriaurita, Retz. (1) Shire Highlands, Scott-Elliot and Buchanan; (2) Carson.
Pt. biaurita, L. (2) Carson.
Pt. flabellata, Thunb. (2) Carson.
Pt. cretica, L. (1) Buchanan.
Pt. atrovirens, Willd. (2) Carson.
Adiantum aethiopicum, L. (1) Buchanan.
A. Capillus-Veneris, L. (1) Buchanan.
A. caudatum, L. (1) Buchanan.
A. hispidulum, Sw. (1) Buchanan.
A. lunulatum, Burm. (1) Buchanan; (2) Carson.
Lonchitis pubescens, Willd. (2) Nutt.
Lomaria boryana, Willd. (1) Buchanan.
Actiniopteris radiata, Link. (1) Buchanan.
Asplenium Sandersoni, Hook. (1) Shire Highlands, Buchanan and Scott-Elliot.
A. Mannii, Hook. (1) Shire Highlands, Scott-Elliot.
A. anisophyllum, Kze. (1) Chiradzulu, Whyte; Shire Highlands, Scott-Elliot.
A. lunulatum, Sw. (1) Buchanan; Chiradzulu, Whyte; Shire Highlands, Scott-Elliot.
A. formosum, Willd. (1) Buchanan; Mlanje, McClounie.
A. brachypteron, Kze. (1) Shire Highlands, Scott-Elliot.
A. protensum, Schrad. (1) Buchanan.

BOTANICAL APPENDICES 281

FILICES.
Asplenium furcatum, Thunb. (1) Shire Highlands, Buchanan and Scott-Elliot; (2) Carson.
A. rutaefolium, Kze. (1) Chiradzulu, Whyte.
A. cicutarium, Sw. (1) Buchanan; Shire Highlands, Scott-Elliot.
A. Thunbergii, Kze. (1) Buchanan.
A. nigripes, Blume. (1) Buchanan.
A. patens, Desv. (1) Shire Highlands, Scott-Elliot.
A. cordatum, Forst. (1) Mlanje, McClounie.
Nephrodium Filix-mas, Rich., var. *elongatum*, H. et A. (1) Shire Highlands, Scott-Elliot and Buchanan.
N. patens, Desv. (1) Buchanan.
N. unitum, R. Br. (1) Buchanan.
N. molle, Desv. (1) Buchanan; (2) Carson.
N. pennigerum, Hook. (1) Buchanan.
N. cicutarium, Baker. (1) Shire Highlands, Buchanan and Scott-Elliot; Chiradzulu, Whyte.
N. albo-punctatum, Desv. (1) Buchanan; (2) Nutt; Carson.
N. athamanticum, Hook. (2) Nutt.
N. Thelypteris, Desv. (2) Carson.
Nephrolepis cordifolia, Presl. (1) Buchanan; (2) Carson.
Polypodium fissum, Baker. (1) Shire Highlands, Scott-Elliot.
P. lanceolatum, L. (1) Shire Highlands, Scott-Elliot.
Acrostichum conforme, Sw. (1) Buchanan.
A. hybridum, Bory. (1) Buchanan.
A. virens, Wall. (2) Carson.
Osmunda regalis, L. (2) Nutt.
Anemia tomentosa, Sw. (1) Buchanan.
Mohria vestita, Baker. (1) Buchanan.
Marattia fraxinea, Sm. (1) Buchanan; Mlanje, McClounie.
Ophioglossum reticulatum, L. (1) Buchanan.

MUSCI.
Polytrichum commune, L. (1) Mlanje, Whyte.
Bryum sp. (1) Mlanje, Whyte.
Holomitrium acutum, Wright. (1) Zomba, Kirk.
Dicranum sp. (1) Mlanje, Whyte.
Leucoloma sp. (1) Mlanje, Whyte.
Leptodontium radicosum, Mitt. (1) Buchanan.
Erpodium grossirete, K. Muell. (4) Menyharth.
E. Menyharthii, K. Muell. (4) Menyharth.
Pterogonium abruptum, Wright. (1) Shire Highlands, Buchanan; Chiradzulu, Whyte.
P. decipiens, Wright. (1) Shire Highlands, Buchanan.
Pilotrichella imbricata, Jaeg. (1) Mlanje, Whyte.
Aerobryum capense, K. Muell. (1) Mlanje, Whyte.
Porotrichum dentatum, Gepp. (1) Mlanje, Whyte.
Thuidium sp. (1) Mlanje, Whyte.

HEPATICAE.
Marchantia polymorpha, L. (1) Shire Highlands, Buchanan.
Metzgeria furcata, Dum. (1) Mlanje, Whyte.
M. myriapoda, Lindb. (1) Mlanje, Whyte.
Frullania brunnea, Gottsche, Lindb. et Nees. (1) Mlanje, Whyte.

HEPATICAE.
   Lejeunea gracillima, Mitt. (1) Mlanje, Whyte.
   L. decursiva, v. d. Sande-Lacoste. (1) Mlanje, Whyte.
   L. flava, Gottsche. (1) Mlanje, Whyte.
   Phragmicoma pappeana, Nees. (1) Mlanje, Whyte.
   Radula sp. (1) Mlanje, Whyte.
   Lophocolea sp. (1) Mlanje, Whyte.
   Plagiochila Rutenbergii, Gottsche. (1) Mlanje, Whyte.
   P. dichotoma, Dum. (1) Chiradzulu, Meller.

FUNGI.
   Flammula penetrans, Fr. (1) Lower Shire, Scott-Elliot.
   Schizophyllum commune, Fr. (1) Shire Highlands, K. C. Cameron; Chiromo, Lower Shire, Scott-Elliot.
   Crepidotus mollis, Schaeff. (1) Shire Highlands, Scott-Elliot.
   Hexagonia polygramma, Mont. (1) Buchanan.
   Favolus Rhipidium, Berk. (1) Shire Highlands, Scott-Elliot.
   Trametes fibrosus, Nees. (1) Shire Highlands, Last.
   T. rigidus, Fr. (1) Buchanan.
   T. pictus, Berk. (1) Chiromo, Scott-Elliot.
   Lenzites applanata, Fr. (1) Buchanan.
   L. aspera, Klotzsch. (1) Buchanan.
   Polyporus scruposus, Fr. (1) Buchanan.
   P. sanguineus, Fr. (1) Buchanan.
   P. rudis, Berk.? (1) Buchanan.
   Polystictus occidentalis, Klotzsch. (1) Chiromo, Scott-Elliot.
   Parodiella Pentanisiae, Sacc. (2) Lake Nyasa, J. Thomson.
   Physalospora Bambusae, Sacc. (1) Chiradzulu, Whyte.
   Phyllachora Hieronymi, P. Henn. (1) Buchanan.

LICHENS. [All from (4) Boroma (Menyharth), except the last two.]
   Leptogiopsis Brebissonii, Muell.-Arg.
   Collema furvum, Ach.
   Pyrenopsis robustula, Muell.-Arg.
   Ramalina complanata, Ach.
   Parmelia Hildenbrandtii, Keplh., forma *nuda*, Muell.-Arg., forma *sorediosa*, Muell.-Arg.
   P. praetervisa, Muell.-Arg.
   P. zambesica, Muell.-Arg.
   P. Zollingeri, Hepp.
   P. tiliacea, Ach., var. *scortea*, Nyl., var. *rimulosa*, Muell.-Arg.
   Candelaria stellata, Muell.-Arg.
   Physcia adglutinata, Nyl., var. *pyrethrocardia*, Muell.-Arg.
   P. stellaris, Fr., var. *acrita*, Nyl.
   P. ochroleuca, Muell.-Arg.
   P. picta, Nyl., var. *sorediata*, Muell.-Arg.
   P. aegialita, Nyl.
   Endocarpiscum Guepini, Nyl.
   Pyxine Meissneri, Tuck., var. *endoleuca*, Muell.-Arg., var. *sorediosa*, Muell.-Arg.
   Placodium perexiguum, Muell. Arg.
   Lecanora subfusca, Ach., var. *allophana*, Ach., var. *glabrata*, Ach., var. *cinereo-carnea*, Tuck.

BOTANICAL APPENDICES

LICHENS.
    Lecanora hypocrocina, Nyl.
    L. caesio-rubella, Ach.
    L. pallescens, Fr.
    Lecania punicea, Muell.-Arg.
    Callopisma cinnabarinum, Muell.-Arg., var. *opacum*, Muell.-Arg.
    C. zambesicum, Muell.-Arg.
    C. flavum, Muell.-Arg.
    Rinodina conspersa, Muell.-Arg.
    Pertusaria velata, Nyl.
    P. xanthothelia, Muell.-Arg.
    P. mamillana, Muell.-Arg.
    Lecidea russula, Ach.
    L. mutabilis, Fée.
    L. impressa, Keplh.
    Patellaria leptolytra, Muell.-Arg.
    Blastenia poliotera, Muell.-Arg.
    Buellia parasema, Körb., var. *disciformis*, Th. M. Fries, var. *vulgata*, Th. M. Fries.
    B. africana, Muell.-Arg.
    B. olivacea, Muell.-Arg.
    B. inquilina, Tuck.
    Opegrapha Menyharthii, Muell.-Arg.
    Arthonia dispersa, Nyl.
    Mycoporum pycnocarpum, Nyl.
    Placothelium staurothelioides, Muell.-Arg.
    Trypethelium Eluteriae, Sprgl.
    Lepra citrina, Schaer.
    Usnea barbata, Ach., var. *ceratina*, Schaer. (2) Carson.
    Physcia speciosa, Ach., var. *hypoleuca*, Nyl. (2) Carson.

ALGAE. [All from (1 ?) Lake Nyasa (Laws), except the first.]
    Chara sp. (2) Carson.
    Conferva sp.?
    Bulbochaete parvula, Ktz.
    Spirogyra pallida, Dickie.
    Cosmarium margaritiferum, Turp.
    Cylindrospermum Nyassae, Dickie.
    Lyngbya martensiana, Menegh.?
    Oscillaria sp.?
    Cyclotella rotula, Ktz.
    C. operculata, Ktz.
    Epithemia ventricosa, Ktz.
    E. Zebra, Ehb.
    E. alpestris, Sm.
    E. Sorex, Ktz.
    E. turgida, Ktz.
    E. clavata, Dickie.
    Eunotia tridentula, Ehb.
    Himantidium pectinale, Ktz.
    Cocconema cymbiforme, Ehb.
    C. Cistula, Hemp.

ALGAE.
>   *Amphora ovalis*, Ktz.
>   *Eucyonema prostratum*, Berk.
>   *Cocconeis placentula*, Ehb.
>   *Fragilaria undata*, Sm.
>   *Synedra Ulnæ*, Ehb.
>   *S. Acus*, Ktz.
>   *S. biceps*, Ktz.
>   *Navicula acrosphaeria*, Rabh., var. *sandvicensis*, Schmidt.
>   *N. gibberula*, Sm.
>   *N. Gastrum*, Ehb.
>   *N. elliptica*, Ktz.
>   *N. rhomboides*, Ehb.
>   *N. gracillima*, Pritch.
>   *Stauroneis Phoenicenteron*, Ehb.
>   *Diadesmis confervacea*, Ktz.
>   *Gomphonema dichotomum*, Ktz.
>   *G. intricatum*, Ktz.
>   *G. naviculoides*, Sm.
>   *G. Turris*, Ehb.

CHAPTER IX.

ZOOLOGY

ALTHOUGH British Central Africa would appear to be a purely political and artificial division of the continent it is, as a matter of fact, coincident with a clearly marked zoological sub-region as far as its mammalian fauna is concerned, though these special peculiarities in the distribution of species are not quite so marked in the birds and reptiles, and still less so in fishes and invertebrates.[1] These distinctive zoographical features of British Central Africa, however, are rather negative than positive, and relate more to what the country does not possess than to its monopoly of peculiar forms. As a matter of fact all British Central Africa as far west as the Upper Zambezi, together with the province of Moçambique, the southern part of German East Africa, and the southernmost districts of the Congo Free State, forms a remarkable break between South and East Africa in the range of well known types of mammals and birds. The British Central Africa sub-region differs from that of West Africa in not possessing any form of anthropoid ape, and in the absence of a good many monkeys, of several small antelopes, and of the interesting *Dorcatherium*. On the other hand it agrees with West Africa in possessing a peculiar Civet (*Nandinia*), one or more genera of bats, and a Colobus monkey closely allied to or identical with the common West African form. Amongst the birds which it shares alone with West Africa is the remarkable black and white vulturine fishing eagle, *Gypohierax*.[2]

Although this sub-region possesses much closer relationships (as might be supposed owing to its geographical position) with the South African sub-region south of the Zambezi, and the East African sub-region (north of the Rufiji river and to the east of Tanganyika), still it differs from these two sub-regions (which are more closely allied the one to the other than each is to British Central Africa) in not possessing the following forms, in whose distribution the interposition of this sub-region under review causes a complete break: the Caracal lynx, the Aard-wolf (*Proteles*), found in South and South West Africa and in Somaliland; the long-eared foxes, the mountain zebras, the wild asses, (to which group I consider the South African quagga to belong); the *Oryx* antelopes, the gazelles, the true jerboas, the *Orycteropus* or antbear, the secretary vulture, the typical vultures of the genera *Gyps* and *Pseudogyps*, and the ostrich.

[1] Though if a portion of Tanganyika be included—as it is intended to be—within the term "British Central Africa" this lake still more markedly than Nyasa differs in its marine fauna from the other great lakes of Africa farther to the north.

[2] I have seen it asserted by some naturalists that *Gypohierax* reappears on Pemba Island near Zanzibar but this statement is unsupported by conclusive evidence.

To this list might almost be added the giraffe, and the *Damaliscus* genus of antelopes, were it not that according to native report the giraffe is found in the southern part of the Senga country along the Lower Luangwa river above its confluence with the Zambezi, and that Mr. Sharpe believes he has seen tsessébe (*Damaliscus*) antelopes a little to the north of the same region. Still here, again, the zoological boundaries of this sub-region rather coincide with the political because it is well known that certain South African forms do cross the Central Zambezi and extend a little distance to the north of its banks, and this may, therefore, account for the existence of the giraffe and the tsessébe in the Luangwa valley. It is quite certain, however, that the giraffe is found nowhere in East Africa south of the Rufiji river and between the Moçambique coast on the east and the Angola coast on the west.[1] Neither are the ostrich nor the other antelopes and carnivora mentioned above. Yet all these forms, either the same or other species closely allied thereto, reappear north of the Rufiji river, or at any rate in Somaliland and the Egyptian Sudan; some of them even in the Western Sudan and in Senegambia. It is very curious that this break should occur right across the continent as it cannot be sufficiently explained by any reasons of climate or soil. The country is not one dense impenetrable forest like parts of the Congo Basin, nor is it a waterless desert. It is dry enough for ostriches and yet not too dry for water-loving antelopes. It must be admitted, however, that it is probably too moist for the absent animals which are rather desert-loving types.

Taken by itself the British Central Africa sub-region may be divided into two districts, at any rate as regards its mammalian fauna—Nyasaland and the adjoining countries to the east; and all which lies between the watershed of Nyasa and the northern, western, and southern frontiers of the sphere of British influence. There is not much difference between the two, but Nyasaland probably lacks a few mammalian types such as the Situtunga (*Tragelaphus spekei*); the Puku and Lechwe antelopes (*Cobus vardoni* and *Cobus lechwe*), and the Cheetah; on the other hand the western division does not possess the grey baboon (*Papio pruinosus*); the long-nosed Shrew (*Rhynchocyon*); a number of rodents; the sable antelope, and several birds which are peculiar to the mountains of the Shire districts.[2]

[1] It reaches to the Ubena country, N.E. of Lake Nyasa.
[2] I should be disposed to divide the African region into two sub-regions and these again into certain provinces. They would stand thus :
 (1) The West African sub-region (the forest country of West Africa from the Gambia on the north to the Kwanza river on the south, including the coast belt of West Africa and the whole Congo basin as far as the west coast of Tanganyika);
  (1 *a*) The Guinea province (Gambia to the Volta river);
  (1 *b*) The Lower Niger Province (Volta river to the Cameroons and the Upper Benue);
  (1 *c*) The Gaboon province (Cameroons to the Congo mouth and inland to the Congo watershed);
  (1 *d*) The Congo province (all the Congo basin except in the extreme south);
  (1 *e*) The Angola province (on the coast, the river Loge to Benguela and inland to the Congo watershed, but including the extreme Upper Zambezi).
 (2) The Ethiopian sub-region (Tropical Arabia, and all Tropical Africa not included in the West African sub-region):
  (2 *a*) The Sudan province (from the Senegambian coast on the west to the frontiers of Abyssinia on the east, with the Sahara on the north and the Congo Basin and West African Coast belt on the south);
  (2 *b*) The Abyssinian province;
  (2 *c*) The Arabian province;
  (2 *d*) The Somaliland province (bounded by Abyssinia, the Egyptian Sudan, the east coast of Tanganyika, and the Rufiji river);
  (2 *e*) The British Central African province; and
  (2 *f*) The South African province (bounded more or less on the north by the Zambezi, and up the south-west coast of Africa to the Angola province).

Monkeys are not abundant in British Central Africa, nor are they numerous in species. The most remarkable among them is the grey baboon (*Papio pruinosus*) recently discovered on the south coast of Lake Nyasa. The first specimen of this animal was shot by Dr. Percy Rendall, a medical officer in the service of the Administration. He was not at first much struck with the novelty of the creature's appearance, however, and had I not been passing at the time and observed the body of the beast as it lay dead on his verandah, it might have been thrown away, but it struck me as being very remarkable in the colouring of its fur, and I induced him to let me forward it to the British Museum, where it turned out to belong to a new species. Its fur is a pale bluish-grey above and a dirty white below and is well illustrated by the plate which appears in the Proceedings for April 1st, 1897, of the Zoological Society. The common yellow baboon is the other cynocephaline species which is found in the Protectorate. It is extremely common everywhere,[1] very bold and very cunning. It is constantly robbing the natives' plantations, and the women profess to go in terror of the large male baboons (which grow to the size of a big mastiff dog) as they say that these latter will attempt to outrage them if they see no man accompanying the party. I do not myself believe there is any truth in this idea; I think all the baboons want to ravish are the contents of the baskets of food the women are carrying; it is quite certain that they will come down and endeavour to rob women and children if they see them unaccompanied by persons armed with weapons.

When the baboons descend to raid the plantations one or more of their number (a half-grown baboon generally) invariably stands sentry to warn the rest of the troop when danger is approaching. The baboons are not very shy of approach unless one is armed with a gun. Not infrequently when I have been riding alone between Blantyre and Katunga a number of baboons have come down to the road to look at me as I went by and have even trotted along on the road in front of my horse. On one occasion their demeanour was distinctly threatening. Several of them were waiting for me on either side of the road making hideous grimaces and grunts. They dispersed, however, when I rode straight at them and showed that I had a switch. The young baboons become quite tame after a few days' captivity and are most amusing though very impudent pets.

The two commonest Cercopithecus monkeys are the white-throated and the red-rumped (*C. albigularis* and *C. pygerythrus*). The Colobus monkey (*Colobus palliatus*) is the white-thighed species. This animal is rare in British Central Africa, and is so far as I know only found in the high mountains west and north of Lake Nyasa. Its skins are much valued by the natives who use the long black and white hair to make capes and mantles and anklets for their war dresses.

The Lemuroids are represented by the great Galago[1] and the small Moholi Galago. The big species is a beautiful animal about the size of a cat. The colour of the fur (at any rate in the Nyasa variety) is quite a light whitish-grey and the tail is exceedingly bushy. This creature when captured full grown is rather intractable and difficult to tame. It can and will bite savagely. When brought to bay it stands up on its hind legs and boxes with the fore paws, partly to repel an assault and partly to seize and bite the assaulter.

---

[1] The yellow baboon (*Papio babuin*) is found nearly all over tropical Africa south of the Equator. It is in some respects the most generalised of the baboons.
[2] *Otogale Kirkii*.

The young of the great Galago are exquisite little creatures like Chinchillas. It would appear to be an animal of rather slow growth, and the young are therefore taken by Europeans to be a different species to the full grown animal.[1]

There is not much remarkable about the bats of British Central Africa so far as I am aware. They have been chiefly collected by Dr. Percy Rendall who was for a time our medical officer on Lake Nyasa. Prior to this Dr. Rendall was Colonial Surgeon at the Gambia. Whilst in that West African Colony he shot one day a curious white-winged bat which was named " *Vesperugo rendalli.*" The specimen he sent home from the Gambia was the only one known. Years afterwards, however, Dr. Rendall caught a bat on the Upper Shire, and to his surprise found it was identical with the white-winged bat of the Gambia. As Mr. Oldfield Thomas observes in his paper on the mammals of Nyasaland, " It is a curious coincidence that the second known capture of this bat should take place in a country so far distant from the Gambia as Nyasa, and that it should be due to the very same naturalist who originally discovered it and after whom it was named. There appear to be no differences of the least importance between the Gambian and Nyasan examples."

Two species of fruit-eating bats are found in Nyasaland.[2]

Among the insectivores which are few in Central Africa, are the long-nosed, jumping shrews. One genus (*Petrodromus*) (about the size of a large rat) has the nose merely prolonged into a long snout; but the more specialised genus (*Rhynchocyon*) has a positive proboscis. In spite of the development of the snout these are pretty little animals. They soon die when captured, which is the more to be regretted as with their large eyes and soft fur they would make admirable pets.

The carnivora are well represented in this country. Firstly, we have the lion —almost too abundant—and the leopard, still more common. The handsome serval-cat is also found everywhere throughout the whole of British Central Africa. Their kittens are easily reared and stand confinement well; one which I kept for three years in captivity is now in the Zoological Gardens. These serval-cats become tame to a certain extent, but never as absolutely friendly as a pet leopard. The serval resents caresses and is ready to strike out with its sharp claws. Still upon such occasions as when those that I kept escaped they submitted in a somewhat docile manner to be laid hold of and hauled about, and their cage could always be entered by the negro attendant without any aggressive action on their part.

The serval appears to me to be an interesting form for the reason that I think it represents a more generalised type of true cat, something akin to the primal feline stock from which the cheetah branched off a little lower down. The serval suggests the cheetah in many ways while it also has a marked

---

[1] The leaping powers of all the Galagos are remarkable, but reach their highest development perhaps, in the great Galago. In West Africa I used to be much struck with the bat-like movements of the smaller Galagos. A tame one would suddenly leap from my hand—I had almost said "fly"—two yards away to the window-pane and there kill a moth or fly that was buzzing against the glass. The swift movements of the great Galago still more resemble flight, and it has a habit of slightly spreading out the limbs, especially the arms, as it noiselessly jumps through the air. It can jump horizontally or upwardly; its leaps are not necessarily downwards. The large pads on the under surface of almost all the fingers except one (for a faithful feature throughout all the Lemuroids is that one finger remains thin and provided with a sharp claw, whereas the other fingers and toes are padded and provided with square nails) seem to assist this lemur in breaking the shock of its jumps, and enabling it to cling to almost any surface.

I cannot help thinking that the flight of the bats began in some such way as this, especially if the bats arose rather through a Lemuroid type than as a section of the Insectivora.

[2] *Xantharpyia* and *Epomophorus*.

relationship to the lynxes. The spots are simple like those in the cheetah and the lynxes, and although he is a true cat (in that the claws are fully retractile), still the paw is much smaller in relative size than it is with other members of the genus *Felis*, and much more like the paw of the cheetah. Also the claws are not proportionally so large. The ears have a slight approach to a tuft at the apex suggesting the lynx; the tail though much longer than that of an average lynx is still rather short but very thick; and in this particular the animal has diverged from the ancestral cat rather in the direction of the lynxes. The legs are very long which is also a characteristic of the cheetah and the lynx but may have been acquired by the serval from its hunting habits; for from all accounts it often pursues its prey instead of lying in wait and securing it by sudden leaps. Nevertheless, it is a good climber and owing to the small size of its feet and thin body can find a foothold on a ledge not more than two inches broad.

The serval is most destructive to the smaller game, but it is a beautiful animal and often attains a length of nearly four feet and a height at the shoulder of three feet. The other wild cat of British Central Africa is the *Felis caffra*, very like the form which gave rise to the Egyptian domestic cat, and which, mingled with the true wild cat of Europe and Asia, was the joint parent of the European domestic cat.

The cats kept by the natives are scarcely distinguishable sometimes from the wild *Felis caffra*, though undoubtedly the main origin of their domesticated animal (remotely derived from the cat of Egypt and Syria—*Felis maniculata*) is from a foreign source—from Europe and India, *via* the East Coast of Africa. But unquestionably the wild cat of British Central Africa mingles freely with the domestic and semi-domestic animal, and the natives often bring in its kittens from the woods and rear them as domestic cats. These animals are charming when in the kitten stage, but when they grow up they become lanky, with small heads and thin tails. The domestic cats which are too directly derived from the wild species are not very tame or tractable.

The cheetah is very rare but is found on the Nyasa-Tanganyika plateau, near Lake Mweru, probably in the Luangwa Valley, and possibly in the countries to the north-east of Lake Nyasa. I have no positive record of this hunting cat having been actually killed in the Nyasaland province. The animal has been shot by Mr. J. B. Yule (who showed me the skins, one of which I sent home) on the Nyasa-Tanganyika plateau. The cheetah in question was the common variety with black spots. I have never heard of the red spotted cheetah of South Africa having been found north of the Zambezi.

The hyena of British Central Africa is the ordinary spotted species whose range extends from South Africa to the Egyptian Sudan up the eastern side of the continent; the spotted hyena is probably found in the Central Sudan and may enter the Niger territories outside the forest region.[1]

The civet cat is extremely common. Strange to say the natives seem to make no use of its remarkable scent gland. A lovely little genet cat, whose large spots are a rich umber brown instead of black is very common, and makes a charming house pet.

[1] The remarkable brown hyena has a somewhat similar range but less continuous. I believe I met with it on Kilimanjaro; it is commonest in south-east Africa and is said to extend along the south-west coast as far as the district of Mossamedes. Up to the present it has not been recorded from British Central Africa. The range of the striped hyena is altogether far to the north. It probably nearly meets the range of the spotted hyena in the Sudan and elsewhere extends over the Mediterranean basin, Persia, and Western India.

A remarkable animal from the point of view of distribution is the palm civet (*Nandinia*) which as far as is yet known extends right across from West Africa into Nyasaland, but is not found in East or South Africa. Ichneumons of three genera are found in this country.

The only species of Jackal which is recorded from our collection is the side-striped jackal (*Canis lateralis* or *C. adustus*). It is entirely unlike the handsome black-backed jackal of South Africa, which has a black back and a silvery band of fur below the black; the centre of the back of the Nyasaland jackal is a rich chestnut brown and the silvery streak below is only faintly marked.

The Cape hunting-dog[1] has been killed on Mount Zomba and is reported from West Nyasaland. Other specimens were obtained by Mr. Crawshay in the Lake Mweru district and sent home by me. From all accounts it is not a common animal in British Central Africa unless it be in the Luangwa valley.

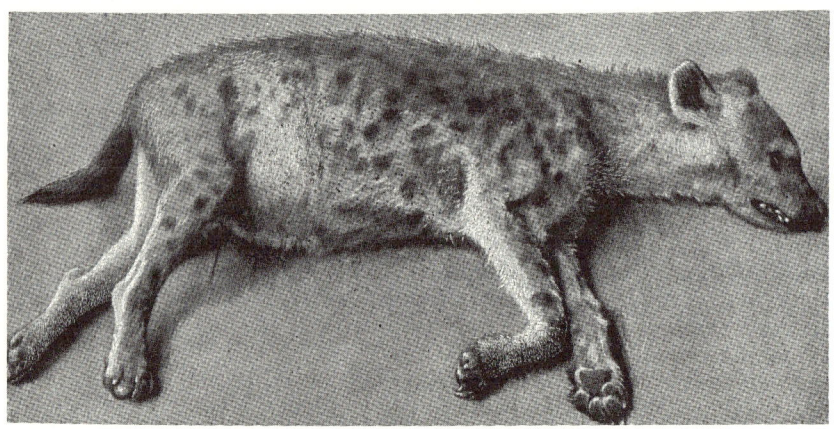

A SPOTTED HYENA

M. Foa, a French sportsman, reports these animals as frequently met with in the Makanga country to the south-west of Nyasaland.

A pretty little white-necked weasel[2] has been obtained in the Shire Highlands. I have also met with the ratel or honey badger in the same district, but we have not yet found the small black and white "Cape polecat" (*Ictonyx*), which inhabits South and East Africa, and whose range may—like that of so many other species—be interrupted by British Central Africa.

An otter is very common on the Shire, in Lake Chilwa, Lake Nyasa, and in other large waters of British Central Africa. The only species recorded by complete specimens is *Lutra maculicollis*, or the "spotted-necked otter"; but I am inclined to think that *Lutra capensis* is also found in parts of British Central Africa. I can only base my impression on dressed skins seen in the possession of natives, which I believe to have been of this animal.

Except to naturalists there is nothing very interesting in the rodents of British Central Africa. A hare is present in Nyasaland of the big species, *Lepus whytei*. One or other types of hare are also found in the western part of British Central Africa but may possibly belong to species common to South

---

[1] *Lycaon*. [2] *Pœcilogale*.

or East Africa. I should like to make a special mention of the large Octodont—one of the few Octodont rodents found outside America—the "ground-pig," *Aulacodus swinderenianus*. This creature which is especially fond of sugar-cane plantations is such a delicious article of diet that it ought to be domesticated for the table. Its flesh tastes something like that of a rabbit but has a savour quite its own.

As regards rats, I should mention that they are numerous and a great pest. The natives eat them with gusto. The common rat of the native villages and European settlements is a brown variety of the Black rat (*Mus rattus*). There is one rat which is an appalling creature to look at. It is apparently allied to the Bandicoot-rat of India—about the size of a rabbit, with pale grey fur, a long tail and hideously long snout. In captivity it is ferocious to the last degree and looks a thoroughly evil animal.

A porcupine has been found in British Central Africa but I have not been able to obtain specimens for identification and only know it from native report and from having seen its quills in use for native ornaments. The natives state that there are two species, one large and one small, for which they have slightly different names, *Nungu* and *Kanungu*.

The Hyraxes are represented by at least two species—*Procavia johnstoni* and *P. brucei*. They are chiefly confined in their distribution to the high mountains and plateaux.

The Ungulates, as elsewhere in Tropical Africa, are well represented.

There is the African elephant of course, and among the *Perissodactyla* we have the ordinary two-horned rhinoceros and the zebra. The *Artiodactyla* are represented by the hippopotamus, two genera of swine, and numerous examples of the *Bovidæ* or hollow-horned ruminants.

The elephant was formerly most abundant throughout the whole of British Central Africa, and in the years following on Livingstone's first expedition many sportsmen from England made large sums of money by the ivory which they obtained in the Shire district and at the north end of Lake Nyasa. Subsequently this great beast has become very scarce within the limits of the Protectorate though he is still found in large numbers in the rest of British Central Africa, especially in the Mweru districts, the Luangwa Valley and the country between the Luangwa and the Luapula. They are also occasionally met with in the Ruo, Zomba, West Shire, South Nyasa, Central Angoniland, Marimba, and West Nyasa districts of the Protectorate, being most abundant in Central Angoniland and in Marimba. They feed chiefly on leaves and such fruits as are in season. They also eat the top shoots of the *Phragmites* reeds and the roots of certain trees, which they are fond of chewing. These trees they uproot with their trunks and also by butting. Mr. Sharpe, who has studied elephants closely, denies that they use their tusks for prizing-up the trees or for exhuming roots. Although I respect him as a great authority on the subject I cannot agree with him in this particular. I have seen something of elephants on the Congo and at the back of the Cameroons, and there the natives have told me spontaneously that the elephant used one of his tusks for digging in the ground and for uprooting the small trees. Moreover, it often happens that one of the elephant's tusks—the "ground tusk"—is more worn and blunted than the other, probably from being put to this use.[1] At the same time

[1] The term "ground tusk" may bear two interpretations. According to old custom, when a native in Central Africa kills an elephant he gives the "ground tusk" to the Chief of the Country. This may either mean the inferior tusk worn with digging, but more probably the undermost of the two tusks—that which is touching the ground, in reference to the proprietary rights of the "Lord of the Manor."

although I have seen elephants at work in Hyphæne palm forests on the Congo actually being able to watch them from a boat working their will on these trees for the sake of the "ginger-bread" covering of the nuts, I cannot say I have seen them kneel down and uproot a tree with the tusk. One is a little puzzled sometimes to account for the enormous development of the two remaining upper incisor teeth, unless they were used for some such purpose as digging up roots. They are not so useful as defensive or offensive weapons that they should be worth development for this purpose alone. In killing animals much less in size than himself the elephant generally uses his trunk and feet, though I admit many cases occur—including one which took place a few months ago in England—where an elephant does deliberately slay his victim with his tusk. On the whole I am inclined to believe that where the elephant retains these huge teeth he uses them occasionally for digging in the ground. This belief is supported by the very distinct statements of such authorities as (the late) Sir Samuel Baker and Mr. F. C. Selous. The former writes "They (the acacia trees) are easily overturned by the tusks of the elephants which are driven like crowbars beneath the roots and used as levers, in which rough labour they are frequently broken .... It is nearly always the right tusk which is selected for this duty." Mr. Selous states that he has seen large areas of sandy soil ploughed up by the tusks of these animals in their search for roots.

Although nowhere very abundant, the ordinary two-horned rhinoceros is probably found pretty generally over all British Central Africa except on the high plateaux. But from all accounts it is absent from the south shore of Tanganyika and from the Nyasa-Tanganyika plateau. Unless, therefore, it can be proved to exist in the interior of the Moçambique district the rhinoceros will be another of those animals whose range is completely broken by the interposition of British Central Africa.[1] Is the so-called "white rhinoceros" (*Rhinoceros simus*) found north of the Zambezi? This is a question rather hard to answer in the negative or affirmative. I should not be surprised to hear that it was, though not within British territory but in the adjoining districts of Portuguese Zambezia. In 1892 an English trader, Mr. Harry Pettitt, gave me an extraordinary pair of horns which he had obtained in Portuguese territory to the south of the river Ruo. These horns were very similar in appearance to those of the "white rhinoceros," that is to say, both horns were of good length but the front one was extremely long, slender and directed forwards. There are specimens extant of the white rhinoceros in which the front horn is not directed forwards but is exactly vertical, or turned slightly backwards. Still I never remember to have seen a specimen of the ordinary two-horned rhinoceros which has the front horn directed forwards. The pair of horns to which I allude I sent to Mr. Sclater and I believe they are now in the British Museum.[2]

The zebra of British Central Africa is a singularly beautiful beast and should, if right were done, be made a type species under the name of *Equus tigrinus*[3] with three sub-species or varieties—*E. tigrinus burchelli, E. tigrinus chapmani*, and *E. tigrinus granti,* to indicate in addition to the clear and perfectly striped Central African form the three other varieties which are marred in their beauty by intermediate faint stripes, and one of which

---

[1] Abundant evidence, however, of the existence of the Rhinoceros in the vicinity of Lake Rukwa was obtained by the Rev. Harwood Nutt of the London Missionary Society.

[2] Mr. Sclater suggests they may belong to a sub-species of Rhinoceros proposed by Dr. Gray, "Gray's Rhinoceros."

[3] Namely *the* striped horse, *par excellence*.

THE CENTRAL AFRICAN ZEBRA

(Burchell's zebra) has the legs below the "knee" and hock almost without stripes.

The question with regard to the striped horses stands thus:—There is the true or mountain zebra (*Equus zebra*), a smaller animal than the zebra of the plains and with the pattern and breadth of the stripes differing from the three types of (so-called) Burchell's zebra. The true zebra is perhaps the most perfectly striped of all the Tigrine horses. This creature is nearly extinct but has always been for the last hundred years or so confined to the mountains of South Africa.

Then there is the closely allied *Equus grevyi* which inhabits the mountains of southern Abyssinia and Somaliland. From the resemblance between these two types of mountain zebra one might imagine that there had been a regular race of mountain zebras inhabiting all the highlands from the north-east to the south-west of Africa, but that all the links between Shoa and Cape Colony had died out in the course of time. It is curious that the natives of Mlanje assert that there is a small mountain zebra dwelling on Michesi Mountain which is an outlying spur of the Mlanje range. Up to the present, however, we have been unable to secure a specimen.

Then comes the race of big zebras of the plains. These are characterised by much broader stripes, by the ground colour of the skin being darker and yellower in tint than that of the mountain zebra and, in one variety, by the imperfect striping of the legs. What I object to is that this imperfect type should be taken as the type of the species merely because it was the first one to be discovered (it was named after the South African traveller Burchell).[1] Subsequently as explorers and sportsmen penetrated more and more into South Central Africa they found that the zebra of the plains was striped right down to the hoof. A specimen was sent home by a Mr. Chapman and naturalists then called it *Equus burchelli*, variety *chapmani*. But both Burchell's and Chapman's zebras have this point in common, that in between the broad black stripes there are thin hazy dun-coloured streaks, much as though one took a photograph of a striped zebra, he moved, and so the stripes were faintly duplicated. This intervening brown zigzag marking has, in my opinion, a very ugly effect. Now the zebra of Nyasaland and, as far as I know, of all British Central Africa, is without this duplication of the stripe, and is one of the most beautiful animals in existence. Its ground colour is very pale fawn, melting into white, and the stripes are broad and jet black. It is striped down to its very hoofs. But on the other hand, the common zebra of East Africa and Uganda also has these duplications of the stripes, though not in such a marked degree as the South African zebra of the plains. It would seem, therefore, that the zebra found in South Central Africa is a distinct variety, if not species. I consider it should be the type of the large zebras and that the others should be classified as inferior varieties, tending more towards the Quagga. This point, however, was first raised by Mr. Richard Crawshay, and up to the present zoologists are not agreed as to the validity it possesses.[2]

Last in the list of zebras is the Quagga which is dun coloured, with stripes only on the neck, shoulders, and forelegs. The Quagga is nearly if not quite

---

[1] The story goes that Dr. Gray, of the British Museum, and the explorer Burchell—both peppery men—had quarrelled. Dr. Gray having a new zebra to name, called it, half in fun, half in malice, "Asinus burchelli." Burchell, so far from appreciating the honour, challenged Dr. Gray to fight a duel!

[2] Since writing the above I have read the article on the subject by Mr. W. E. de Winton in the *Magazine of Natural History*, but I think it best to let my views stand as they are.

extinct and, so far as we know, is confined in its range to Africa south of the Zambezi. It is very asinine in its affinities.[1]

The zebra is still extremely common almost all over the Protectorate, and measures have now been taken to preserve it from undue diminution at the hands of sportsmen and natives. I have several times tried to tame the young but have had great difficulty in rearing them away from their mothers, and all experimented on have died within a few days of their capture.

When our system of Game Reserves is perfected we shall be able from time to time to make drives and possibly catch some of the young zebras sufficiently old to be independent of a milk diet and yet not so old as to be quite intractable. They might then be broken in and tamed as is now being done increasingly in South Africa.

The zebra of British Central Africa is slightly larger than his South African congener and is, perhaps, the largest representative of the zebra group.

When I first came to this country I found the hippopotamus so numerous on the Shire as to be a serious danger to navigation in vessels smaller than a steamer. They were very vicious and fond of pursuing and upsetting canoes. Mr. Sharpe in travelling down the Shire in 1892 was, as I have already related, upset by a hippopotamus and nearly drowned. I have been in a boat myself on the Upper Shire which was so far tilted over by a hippopotamus that most of the men fell into the water and I only saved myself by clinging to the doorway of the house. This being the case, we have never attempted to check the slaughter of these animals and they are now so far reduced in numbers on the Shire as no longer to be a source of danger. They are still abundant on parts of the coasts of Lakes Nyasa, Tanganyika, and all the other big lakes, and are found in every river with a sufficient amount of water to immerse their bodies.[2] They are said to visit Lake Chilwa at certain times of the year, travelling overland from the Shire. When we have reduced the numbers of the hippopotamus to something more compatible with the safety of canoe travelling we shall probably add him to the list of protected animals, as we have no desire to bring about the absolute extinction of one of the few great survivors of the Tertiary Epoch.

Pigs are represented in British Central Africa by the bush pigs (*Potamochœrus Africanus* and *P. johnstoni*) and the wart hog (*Phacochœrus œthiopicus*).

The bush pigs chiefly frequent the hills and mountains, though they are also found in the plains near rivers. They are weird looking creatures with long wiry hair which is yellow and grey with a few white marks. Along the back

---

[1] Summarized the revised classification of the horses might stand thus:
    A. True horses— *Equus caballus.*
                        Equus prjevalski.
    B. Asses—   *Equus kiang.*
                        Equus hemionus.
                        Equus asinus.
                        Equus somalicus.
    C. Striped horses—*Equus quagga.*
                        Equus tigrinus.
                           E.t., burchelli.
                           E.t., chapmani.
                           E.t., granti.
                      Equus grevyi.
                      Equus zebra.

[2] Though the hippopotamus will go into the Indian Ocean off the mouths of big rivers and though it can if need be swim across any African lake, still one never meets with them as a rule much out of their depth. They do not care for swimming but prefer walking along the bed of rivers or shallow lakes below the surface or resting thereon, rising every now and then to the surface to breathe and float.

HEAD OF A HIPPOPOTAMUS

there is a considerable whitish mane. The bush pigs are closely allied to the Red river hog of West Africa.[1]

The young of the bush pig are spotted and striped with white as are the young of almost all members of the genus *Sus*. This is not the case with the

[1] When this chapter had been written I learnt through Mr. W. E. de Winton that Dr. Forsyth Major, after examining the pigs' skulls in the British Museum sent home by me in 1889, had determined a new species which he had named *Potamochœrus johnstoni*, and which is remarkable as being an intermediate form between the Bush pigs and the True pigs.

young wart hogs, which are born without these white markings. The wart hog is chiefly distinguished from the true pigs by the reduction in number of its upper incisor teeth. In young animals one pair of perfectly useless incisor teeth —the outermost pair—is retained, but these fall out in the old males. In old animals it sometimes happens that there are few teeth left in the head except the molars and the canine tusks. There are also peculiarities in the number and shape of the molar teeth which separate these animals from the typical pigs. In the male there is very little hair on the body except along the line of the back where a thin mane of very long coarse bristles extends from the top of the head to the tail. This mane is not erect but falls over on either side. Around the chest there is also a frill of whitish bristles. The rest of the body is nearly bare but is sprinkled with a bristly growth. My illustration, which was drawn from life, will give some idea of this extraordinary creature. I kept a wart hog for over a year at Zomba as a pet. He was brought down from the Lake Mweru district by Mr. Crawshay and is now in the Zoological Gardens. The animal derives its name from the huge excrescences or warts on the face, four in number—the large ones seemingly serving as defences to the eyes and two small ones on either side of the nasal bones not sufficiently developed as yet to be of any particular use.

The wart hog prefers a dry country and likes a loose sandy soil in which it burrows, or at least is thought to burrow. In the opinion of some observers it does not make these holes itself but occupies the lair of some other animal, or a natural crevice in any mound. The natives state that the female wart hog seldom has more than two young ones at a time. Certainly the number of teats is much reduced, being only four, which are inguinal in position. The female is a good deal smaller than the male and has not quite such a preposterous development of head, nor are her tusks nearly as large.

As it exists, the mature male wart hog looks like a beast of another epoch. I doubt if there is any other mammal whose head is so disproportionately large.

The existence of the giraffe in British Central Africa is still a moot question. The natives report its presence in the Luangwa Valley with very circumstantial details and they are probably telling the truth; but up to the present time no European has sighted the animal in that country, nor have any tangible proofs, such as skulls, or tails, or skins, been sent back as evidence of its existence.[1]

We have seen so few specimens of the giraffe living or dead in England, and those specimens commonly exhibited have not been very good ones that perhaps we do not realise the remarkable fact that one species or sub-species of the giraffe is really a three-horned animal. I saw recently at the British Museum a head from Somaliland in which the central horn between the eyes was nearly six inches in length. As a matter of fact the giraffe is an animal which has lost its horns and retained little more than the basal portion, the bony cores from which the horns (probably in the form of antlers) once grew. An analogy may be found in the prong buck of North America, an animal which appears to be very distantly related to the stock from which the giraffe sprang. Imagine the horn cores of the prong buck increased in growth till they resemble those of the muntjac deer and you have something answering the present condition of the giraffe's so-called "horns."

[1] It is a point so interesting as to be worth a special expedition on the part of some enterprising sportsman-naturalist, as it would be desirable to know whether it differed in any way from the giraffe of South Africa and is more akin to the giraffe of East Africa and the Northern Sudan. This subject has lately been discussed by Mr. W. E. de Winton.

A WART HOG

HEAD OF A BUFFALO (*Bos Caffer*)

The buffalo of British Central Africa is the type known as the Cape Buffalo (*Bos caffer*). The range of this species probably extends from South Africa up the eastern half of the continent to the Victoria Nyanza, the White Nile, and Somaliland. Its place in Abyssinia and the Egyptian and Central Sudan is taken by another variety or species known as the Central African Buffalo.[1] It extends into West Africa as far as the southern boundaries of the district of Angola proper and thence over the whole Zambezi region into the south and east of the Congo Free State, reaching more than half-way up the coast of Tanganyika and being found on the upper waters of the Lualaba and Kasai. Thenceforward to the north and west its place is taken by the curious short-horned red buffalo of West Africa, which is the only species found in the forest part of the Congo Basin and along the west coast and in Nigeria.

It may be interesting to give here a drawing of the horns of this forest buffalo of the Congo, which I did at Bolobo on the Upper Congo some years ago. On the whole I am disposed to regard the forest buffalo of West Africa as rather a degenerate than a primitive type of buffalo. It is evidently a deteriorated race of the *Bos caffer*.[2]

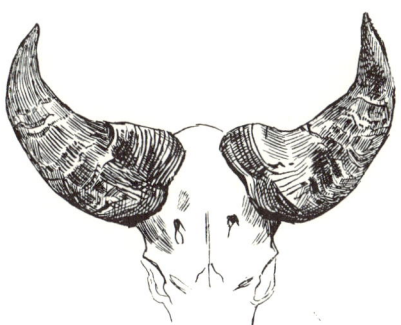

HORNS OF CONGO BUFFALO

Buffaloes are very abundant all over British Central Africa, but of course are retiring from the vicinity of European settlements. They are also frequenters of the plain rather than the mountains, though they will ascend high plateaux in the dry season for the sake of the green herbage. The favourite places of their resort are wide marshy districts like the Elephant Marsh near Chiromo, where even after the most wanton and indiscriminate slaughter at the hands of Europeans[3] they exist in large numbers—thousands, it is said. Like the Indian buffalo they are fond of wallowing in mud and water, though perhaps not as aquatic in their habits as the last-named animal. They are dangerous beasts to tackle under certain conditions though less dangerous than the elephant and lion. It is seldom that they will take aggressive action against the sportsman when not wounded.[4]

---

[1] *Bos æquinoctialis*. This variety of buffalo is much more interesting than appears from the meagre accounts given of it by all naturalists. It is to some degree a connecting link between the African and Indian buffaloes. The horns are much longer, and are directed farther backwards than in the Cape buffalo. There is not such an exaggerated boss on the forehead.

[2] The most primitive known buffalo or ox is the Anoa of the island of Celebes. This creature shows signs of affinities with the *Tragelaphs* (a group of [so called] bovine antelopes, to which the Nilgai, the Kudu, Eland, and Bushbuck belong). Even at the present day with the aid of the Philippine Islands buffalo, there are existing a series of gradations leading up to the long-horned buffalo of India, and thence through the Central African buffalo to the Cape species which may be regarded as the culmination of Bubaline development at the present day. But fossil remains from both North and South Africa show us that there existed buffalo in this continent in past ages the development of whose horns was gigantic though perhaps not as extravagant even as some extinct Indian species. Mr. Lydekker states that a fossil buffalo skull from South Africa showed horn cores which were 14 feet long, and to this length must, of course, be added that of the horn covering—a foot or so longer. One weeps to think of the degenerate days in which *we* live. The big game we pursue are but small deer compared with the glorious beasts which surrounded our pithecoid ancestors.

[3] Now checked by this stretch of country having been declared a Government Game Reserve.

[4] Occasionally out of stupid curiosity or because the traveller is standing in the way of a newly born buffalo calf, buffaloes will advance unprovoked to the attack. I remember visiting the Songwe plains at the north end of Lake Nyasa in 1889 for the purpose of sport, accompanied by the late Mr. Kydd.

"LIVINGSTONE'S ELAND"

Even when wounded it is doubtful whether they charge in the open. The danger in connection with shooting buffaloes is this, that the wounded beast retires into long grass or thickets. If the sportsman follows him up then the buffalo puts no bounds to his rage and is also very cunning. He will charge from out of his hiding place and pursue his enemy with a great deal of intelligence, that is to say not altogether in blind rage, and if he succeeds

Soon after we had landed at the mouth of the Songwe we found ourselves in the midst of an enormous herd of buffalo. So far from their retreating before us these animals began to toss their heads and paw up the ground. It seemed as though an imprudent shot would provoke a charge of buffaloes which would drive us into the crocodile-haunted reeds of the marshy lake margin, so that at first we refrained from firing until one bull buffalo advanced in front of the herd and came so near that we had no option but to shoot. The beast fell, then rose to his feet, but instead of charging made for the river, and was dropped by two more shots from our rifles. The rest of the buffaloes turned and fled.

in catching him up will gore him and kneel on him. But I can obtain no authentic record of a buffalo when wounded in open country immediately charging his assailant.

Buffalo calves are born about the end of the rainy season (March, April). Although quickly tamed they are very difficult to rear. They easily catch cold and do not much appreciate cows' milk. I have been so anxious to start the domestication of these fine animals that I brought a number of tame Indian buffaloes from Bombay in 1895, and induced one of them to suckle a young African buffalo. The little beast throve until he was almost ready for weaning, but suddenly caught a chill and died of pneumonia. The Indian buffaloes I introduced are still in the country, not one of them having died, and I am still hoping that they may be used as foster mothers to rear up the newly caught young of the African buffalo until we have established a tame breed of this animal, which should be as useful in a domesticated state as is the long-horned buffalo of India.

The Tragelaphs are well represented in this part of Africa by Livingstone's Eland, the Kudu, the beautiful *Tragelaphus angasi*, or Inyala,[1] by the remarkable Situtunga (*Tragelaphus spekei*) and the South African variety of the bushbuck (*Tragelaphus scriptus roualeyni*).

The Eland of Central Africa differs from the variety found in South and East Africa by its yellower colour, and by its retention of the Tragelaphine white stripes. Also I have never seen a specimen shot in British Central Africa which possessed that great development of "brush" on the nose so characteristic of the South African Eland. The Derbian Eland of West Africa is however quite a separate species from the Eland of Central Africa (Livingstone's Eland), which latter is after all little but a sub-species of the common form. The Central African Eland has in the male larger and longer horns than the South African species. I give an illustration here of what I believe is an exceptionally fine male eland head. It was shot not far from my house at Zomba by one of my native hunters and was presented by me to the Zoological Society. The length of these horns is $29\frac{1}{2}$ inches, and they are $16\frac{1}{2}$ inches apart from tip to tip.

The eland is seldom met with in the low-lying plains, frequenting mostly wooded hills and high-lying open grass-covered districts on the plateaux. This also is the favourite habitat of the kudu, the glory of the Tragelaphs, an animal to which shrines should be erected and worship tendered on account of its beauty. The Central African kudu is almost the finest development of the genus. Mr. Sharpe measured one pair of horns shot in Nyasaland which gave 62 inches as the length of the horn following the curve. I have myself a pair of horns which measure 48 inches along the curve.

HORNS OF LIVINGSTONE'S ELAND

I am inclined to think that the Inyala antelope of British Central Africa is limited in its range as far as we yet know to the Western and Upper Shire

[1] Locally called *Bōō*.

districts and the Lake Mweru district and may be a different variety to the Inyala of South East Africa, inasmuch as the males retain white spots and stripes on the skin to a greater extent, and do not assume such a grey fur at maturity. The Inyala, locally called Bōō, is a very rare animal frequenting dense thickets. Its horns somewhat resemble those of the bushbuck, but are much larger proportionately, much wider apart and slenderer. They may measure as much as 22½ inches in length along the curve. (I have a pair of horns giving this measurement.) I have only twice seen skins of the adult

A MALE BUSHBUCK (*Tragelaphus scriptus*)

animal. They were extraordinarily beautiful in colour—the females a deep chestnut with narrow stripes and spots in pure white and a black line along the middle of the back from the neck to the base of the tail; the male purplish-grey with white markings. The Situtunga (*Tragelaphus spekei*) is not found in Nyasaland but is met with abundantly in the swamps of Lakes Mweru and Bangweolo, in the Luangwa Valley and in other parts of British Central Africa. This Tragelaph has taken to an entirely aquatic residence and the hoofs are enormously developed.[1] The horns of the Situtunga, unlike those of the rest of the animals of the genus *Tragelaphus*, have two turns instead of a turn and

[1] Another instance of great development of the hoof for the purpose of traversing marshy ground exists in *Tragelaphus gratus* of West Africa.

HEAD OF A MALE KUDU

a half.[1] This aquatic Tragelaph further differs from the other members of the genus in having long, coarse, uniformly grey-coloured hair without white spots or stripes in the adult. The young are said to be faintly striped and spotted with white.

There remains to be considered the Bushbuck of Central Africa. I am inclined to think that the naturalists are wrong in the classification of the Bushbucks. They should restore to them that designation *Tragelaphus silvaticus* which was formerly applied to the Bushbuck of South-Central and East Africa, making it a separate species from *Tragelaphus scriptus*, the "Harnessed Antelope" of West Africa. The coloration of the Bushbuck is usually uniform between South and East Africa and so different to that of the Harnessed Antelope that it is scarcely logical to class it as merely a variety of the latter. Besides which the horns of the Bushbuck are usually long[2] and more slender than those of the Harnessed antelope and offer a more distinct beginning of a second curve. The Bushbuck is extremely common throughout British Central Africa and is without exception the most delicious eating of any mammal in the world. In tenderness and flavour its flesh surpasses the best Welsh mutton, or any venison. Here, emphatically, is an animal which should be domesticated and saved from extinction. The young and the females of the Bushbuck are a bright yellow chestnut in colour, with well marked white spots and stripes, but the adult males become bluish grey, sepia and black, with the inner side of the legs white, a few white spots and one or two white stripes on the hind quarters, two white bars on the front of the throat and neck, and the usual tragelaphine white spots and stripe on the face. There is also a scattered white stripe down the line of the back.

There now remains to be considered the great group of true antelopes, or ring-horned *Bovidæ*, found in British Central Africa.[3] These are represented by the following antelopes:—One or more species of Duyker (*Cephalophus*), the Oribi, Steinbok (*Raphicerus*), Klipspringer, Reedbuck, five species of *Cobus*, the Roan antelope, Sable antelope, Pallah, Lichtenstein's Hartebeest, possibly the Tsessébe (*Damaliscus*), and the Blue Gnu. There should be one or more representatives of the little Livingstone's Antelopes (*Nesotragus*), but no specimens have yet been obtained.

The Duyker antelopes are neither so numerous in species nor in actual numbers as they are in South and West Africa. They frequent chiefly the low-lying plains in the vicinity of water courses. The Cephalophines are an interesting antelopine group to which is related the four-horned antelope of India. Although in regard to the modification of their toes by which all

---

[1] The kudu and the lesser kudu have three turns, the eland two turns and a half, the situtunga two turns, and the remainder of the African Tragelaphs one turn and a half, and the Nilgai of India only the beginning of a turn.

[2] A pair in my possession measures $17\frac{3}{4}$ inches along the curve.

[3] There are certain families of mammals and of birds in the classification of which most naturalists, with the exception of the late Professor Garrod, seem to miss the meaning of a conjunction of characteristics and to fail to grasp true relationships, mistaking parallel developments for evidence of direct inter-connection. In no mammalian group has this persistence in error been more remarkable than in the arrangement of the *Bovidæ*. That vague and facile term "antelope" has been made to include at least two groups of hollow-horned ruminants which are only akin one to the other in that they can prove descent from a common ancestral type of hollow-horned ruminant. The term "antelope" should be reserved to the ring-horned ruminants and should include gazelles and all the African and Indian antelopes which have annulated horns. The goats and sheep and capricorns are nearly-allied sub-families. Another group of equal value is the Oxen, or *Bovinæ*, and a third similarly distinct, is the *Tragelaphinæ*, or Tragelaphs. The diagram on next page will show my idea of the right classification, arrangement and development of the *Bovidæ*. It is based on ideas expressed many years ago by the late Professor Alfred Garrod.

vestiges of the second and fifth metacarpal and metatarsal bones are lost, and even the false hoofs representing these missing toes are often flattened and reduced in size (so that some Duykers are almost completely two-toed), yet in other respects they may be regarded as a low type of antelope not far removed from the central stem from which the ring-horned ruminants branched out. The nose is quite naked and irresistibly suggests a resemblance to that feature in the pig-like *Dorcatherium* of West Africa, which is the nearest living representative of the type from which all existing ruminating Artiodactyles sprang. I believe some anatomists have discovered minute traces of an upper canine which does not pierce the gum in the young of *Cephalophus*. The species of

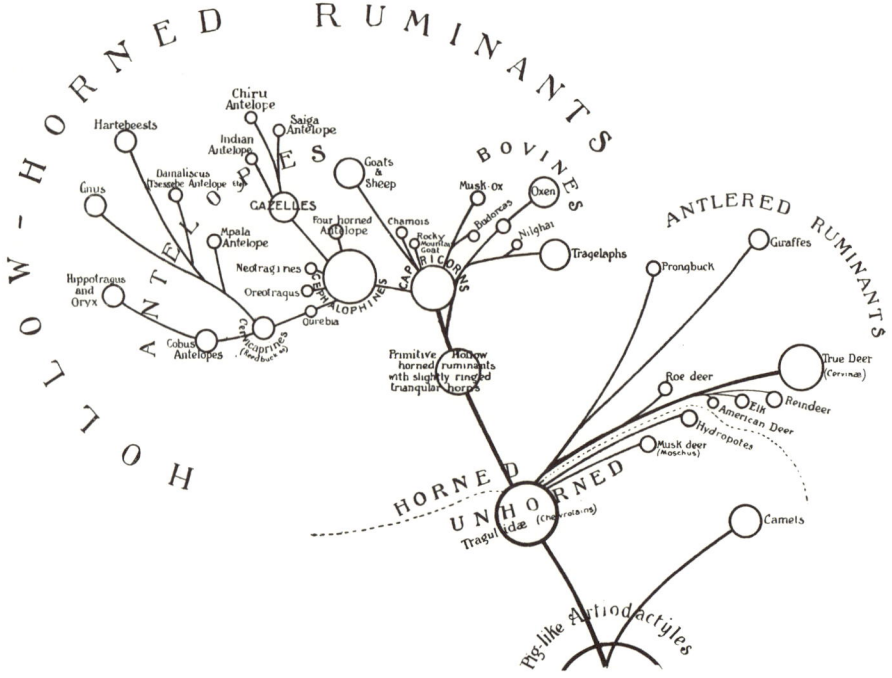

DIAGRAM SHOWING ORIGIN AND RELATIONSHIPS OF MODERN GROUPS OF HORNED RUMINANTS

this genus which is found in Nyasaland is the common Duyker, *Cephalophus grimmi*.

A remarkable little antelope of the genus *Raphicerus* was recently discovered by Mr. Sharpe at the south end of Lake Nyasa and sent home. It proved to be a new species of Steinbok and was named *R. sharpei* after its discoverer. It is illustrated in the Zoological Society's Proceedings of April 1st, 1897, and is closely allied to the Steinboks of South Africa.

The little Klipspringer is found in all rocky places and upon high mountains like Mlanje. The stories told of its jumps are almost as marvellous as those of the Ibex and Chamois. I have not myself witnessed any of these wonderful leaps but it is quite conceivable that they occur. Exaggerated stories are told of its being able to place all four feet together on a space not larger than a crown piece. Of course this is impossible, but it can stand with all of its four feet together on an area which might be covered by a very small saucer. The fur has a curious brittle, shiny appearance, as though the hairs were thickening into spines. The Oribi of British Central Africa is *Ourebia hastata* and also comes from the Portuguese province of Moçambique.

The Reedbuck of British Central Africa is a large animal of the genus *Cervicapra*. The variety found in the Mweru district has a well marked black

A KLIPSPRINGER

patch on the crown between the horns.[1] I have sometimes thought that the Reedbucks (which I illustrate on next page) found at the north end of Nyasa were exceptionally large. The drawings made are from specimens shot by myself in 1889. At the time the beasts were killed I almost thought that they were a small species of *Cobus* antelope, a genus into which *Cervicapra* insensibly melts. The Reedbuck is good eating and ranks next to the Bushbuck as

---

[1] So states Mr. Oldfield Thomas in his paper on the mammals of British Central Africa; he further says that similar patches have been noticed in South African specimens.

A MALE REEDBUCK

palatable meat. I do not think the Reedbuck is met with on high mountains or that it even cares much for hilly country, but it is very abundant on elevated plateaux of gentle undulating surface. Ordinarily it frequents the grassy plains and answers to its name by affecting beds of high reeds. On the Nyasa-Tanganyika plateau one used to see it with its head just appearing out of the high grass and tall yellow ground orchids of the genus *Lissochilus*.[1]

There are, as I have said, five species of *Cobus*, or waterbuck, to wit:—(1) the well-known South African waterbuck (*Cobus ellipsiprymnus*); (2) the nearly allied *Cobus crawshayi*; (3) the Lechwe (*Cobus lechwe*); (4) the Puku (*Cobus vardoni*); and (5) the Senga Cobus (*Cobus senganus*) also discovered by Mr. Crawshay. The common waterbuck is almost the largest member of the genus. The female, as is the case throughout all the Cervicaprines, is without horns. Crawshay's waterbuck, which is found in the Mweru district and probably thence

A MALE REEDBUCK'S HEAD

[1] See illustration, page 208 in Chapter VIII.

westward to the vicinity of Angola (where a closely allied form, *Cobus penricei* has been found), is slightly smaller than the common waterbuck. The waterbucks of Crawshay and Penrice differ from the common species in the following points:—The horns are smaller and less incurved, the rump is yellow white instead of being a mere white streak sandwiched between two patches of dun colour. Penrice's waterbuck differs from Crawshay's very slightly if at all. The known specimens, however, are slightly larger and rather blacker in colour and the horns are proportionately shorter. The common waterbuck is extremely hairy especially about the neck, the female being in my opinion even hairier than the male. She bears an extraordinarily superficial resemblance to the hind of a large species of deer. These animals have such a

MALE WATERBUCK (*Cobus ellipsiprymnus*)

strong coarse smell (something like that of a goat) that the natives say they can often smell them before they see them. In going through the Elephant Marsh with natives they have suddenly commenced sniffing the air and declared that waterbuck were near, and they have been usually right. From this cause and also because it is coarse and tough in grain, the meat of the waterbuck is not at all liked by Europeans, though I have found the flesh of the female and of the young ones just tolerable when well cooked. The Puku is not found in Nyasaland proper, but it is fairly abundant in the country west of the Nyasa watershed from Lake Mweru southwards, and at the south end of Lake Tanganyika. This animal is considerably smaller than the common waterbuck. It is a bright chestnut yellow in colour and does not assume the grey tint so characteristic of the larger waterbucks. Mr. Sharpe states that it is still found in enormous herds about the river Luapula and in the vicinity of Lake Mweru. As regards its habits, it is fond of entering the water, but not so much as the closely related *Cobus lechwe*. A smaller Cobus closely allied to the Puku has recently been discovered in the Senga country (Luangwa Valley) by Mr. Crawshay and has been described by Mr. Oldfield Thomas under the designation of *Cobus senganus*. In colour it is said to be rather darker than the Puku. The Lechwe waterbuck is one of the most water-loving antelopes known, though it must be admitted that it is some degrees less aquatic than Speke's Tragelaph which has been longer at this mode of life and has therefore developed very remarkably extended hoofs. The Lechwe though having slightly longer hoofs than in the other forms of *Cobus*, does not present any very striking development of the foot for life in the water, except that at the

FEMALE WATERBUCK

back of the toes, between the false and the big hoofs, there is a naked place not covered with hair. Mr. Sharpe and other observers relate that the Puku and Lechwe constantly associate together in large herds. Up to the presen time the range of the Lechwe does not seem to extend farther north than Lake Mweru, nor farther east than the watershed of Lake Nyasa

Amongst other heterodox opinions I hold that the Hippotragine section of antelopes, including the Oryxes, was developed from a form of waterbuck. This would appear to be absurd to anyone who merely looked at the commoner forms of Cobus; but that remarkable and most beautiful antelope, Mrs. Gray's Waterbuck (*Cobus maria*) of the White Nile irresistibly suggests in the shape of its horns and the coloration of the face an approach to the Equine antelopes which again have given rise to the Addax and to the four species of Oryx.

The *Hippotragine* or Equine antelopes are represented in British Central

THE SABLE ANTELOPE

Africa by the Sable and the Roan. Curiously enough there is no representative of the Oryx genus throughout all British Central Africa. This type at the present day is confined in its distribution to South Africa, East, North-East and North Africa, and Southern Arabia. As in the case of the zebra, of the giraffe, and of other animals quoted there is a complete break in the distribution of this genus between Moçambique and the West Coast of Africa. The Sable antelope is extremely common. Next to the Kudu, perhaps, or Mrs. Gray's Waterbuck, it is the most beautiful antelope that exists. As large as a small ox with the graceful shape of a beautiful stag, the colours of the male being jet black and snow-white (and of the female bright chestnut-brown and white), the head surmounted by a magnificent pair of horns symmetrically ringed and describing almost the curve of a half circle, the long neck clothed abundantly with a black mane, the large, long-lashed eye, and the tufted tail, make up a beast of grand proportions, striking coloration and beautiful detail, whose extermination would be one of the worst crimes that humanity has ever perpetrated.

Fortunately the Sable antelope is still extremely common in Nyasaland though it is not certain that its range extends east over the Moçambique province, or westward over British Central Africa. It is found, I believe, on the Saïsi river (on the eastern portion of the Nyasa-Tanganyika plateau). I think it is met with in parts of East Africa, and I believe that I saw one specimen of it near Taveita and another near the river Ruvu, as far north as the Kilimanjaro district. [It is sometimes difficult to tell at a distance the young male or female Sable from a Roan antelope, therefore as I did not secure the beast I cannot speak positively on this latter point though in my diary I wrote most positively on this occasion that I had seen a sable and was struck by the vivid contrast between its black and white coloration.] In any case it is not confined to South Africa, a legend still appearing in circles which should be well informed. At the present time it is one of the commonest antelopes in the Shire Highlands and throughout Nyasaland, where it frequents the wooded hills rather than the low-lying plains. I have myself only seen it in what might be called scrub country—rough land of red clay and rocks on which grow trees of sparse foliage and of no great height. In spite of their very marked colours both the male and female sable become singularly invisible in this low forest, their bodies getting mixed up with the glooms of tree trunks in black shadow or brown light. There would appear to be these differences between the sable of Nyasaland and that of South Africa. The Nyasaland variety is rather larger, the neck is somewhat thicker but the mane a little shorter and the ears are slightly longer and have a black tip at the end which I believe is missing in the South African sable.

It would seem to be a general rule that where the sable is found there the roan antelope, its near congener, is not to be met with. This animal is coloured somewhat like the immature male and female of the sable—chestnut with a tendency to black, and with bold white markings. Its horns are not so handsome as those of the sable. The ears are even longer than in the sable and the tips more recurved and ending in a tuft of black hair.[1] In all the Hippotragine antelopes (including the Oryxes) the female is horned as well as the male, a sign, of course, of great specialisation. The range of the roan antelope apparently lies mainly outside British Nyasaland though both Mr. Sharpe and myself have sometimes thought that it existed in the Ruo district and across that river in Portuguese territory, and it has been shot

---

[1] The culmination of this development of the ear is seen in the fringe-eared Oryx (*Oryx callotis*).

in the North Nyasa district by Mr. G. A. Taylor. It undoubtedly occurs on the east coast of Lake Nyasa for it has been shot there by Major Frank Trollope. To the west of Nyasaland it is the common Hippotragine species and its range probably extends north and east to the Egyptian Sudan and thence westward across Nigeria to Senegambia. A third species of Hippotragus —the Blaubok—was a bluish-grey in colour and more uniform in tint with longer hair and in some respects more suggestive of the *Cobus* antelopes. Like many other remarkable creatures in South Africa it was promptly exterminated by the European settlers.

Probably evolving from some *Cervicaprine* form we have the beautiful pallah, or mpala antelope (*Æpyceros melampus*), the shape of whose horns will be shown in the accompanying drawing which however illustrates the small Nyasaland variety.[1] The coloration of the pallah is a rich dark chestnut with a white stomach and a black longitudinal mark in the front of the feet. It also is

A ROAN ANTELOPE (*Hippotragus equinus*)

marked by a black tuft of hair on the inner side of the hind legs below the tarsus. The lesser pallah, a variety named after myself because I happened to send home the first specimens, is the one usually met with in Nyasaland, the larger pallah being found in the regions to the west and east. The accompanying illustration is the head of Johnston's pallah which differs from the more typical animal in the smaller size of the horns and body. Mr. Sharpe states that in his opinion the pallah all over Central Africa affects a special kind of country —forested plains with open glades of short grass not far removed from water.

The Nyasaland Gnu or Wildebeest would appear to be a new species. Hitherto it has been treated as a new variety of the Blue Wildebeest (*Connochætes taurinus*). The first specimen sent home was killed by Mr. H. C. McDonald of the British Central Africa Administration in the vicinity of Lake Chilwa. This example was figured in the Zoological Society's Proceedings for 1896.[2] Subsequently a fine specimen of this gnu was killed by Mr. James Harrison, an English sportsman, who was travelling in the Portuguese territories between Quelimane and the Protectorate. Mr. Harrison also saw a small herd of this gnu about sixty miles to the south of Lake Chilwa. The one

---

[1] A good drawing of the head of the larger pallah will be seen in my book on the Kilimanjaro Expedition, page 219.   [2] p. 616.

ZOOLOGY

JOHNSTON'S PALLAH

which he shot he obtained about thirty miles to the south-east of Mount Chiperone.[1] I should say that the Nyasa gnu (the range of which in Nyasaland

[1] A small photograph was taken of the head, and this was subsequently sent to Mr. W. E. de Winton, an English naturalist, who is making a special study of African mammals. To the courtesy of Mr. de Winton I owe the loan of Mr. Harrison's photograph from which together with other data I possessed I have made the accompanying drawing of the head of the Nyasa gnu. Mr. Harrison's photograph is particularly valuable for this reason. It confirms the presence on the head of this gnu of a white chevron

THE NYASALAND GNU (*Connochœtes taurinus johnstoni*)

appears to be confined to the vicinity of Lake Chilwa and to the Elephant Marsh [1] is the least differentiated of all the gnus and bears more signs of relationship to certain forms of hartebeest.

The position and origin of the gnu in the classification of the antelopes has always been a difficult one for naturalists to settle. It is obviously a very specialised animal and yet in some respects it retains more primitive characteristics than the hartebeest. For instance, the female has four *mammæ*, whereas in the hartebeests there are only two. Also the length of the head is not so disproportionately great as in the hartebeest though it possesses a peculiar

across the ridge of the nose just below the line of the eyes. This white mark had become somewhat effaced in the dry skin which we sent home, and its extent and direction were not sufficiently realised by the artist who drew the picture for the Zoological Society's Proceedings. Mr. Harrison's photograph is important, therefore, as showing the proper direction taken by the white marking of the face and the clearness of this marking which has a definite outline, and is not hazy as represented in the Zoological Society's plate. The presence of this white mark across the face, together with other peculiarities, almost constitutes the gnu of Nyasaland a different species to the Blue Wildebeests of South and East Africa. If this is the case it will be another curious instance of the closer relationship in mammalian types which subsists between North-East and South Africa as compared to South-Central Africa. It will be a parallel to the eland and the zebra.

[1] Though the existence of a gnu is reported from the Luangwa Valley, west of the Protectorate.

development of its own in the great breadth across the nose. On the whole, I should think it likely that the gnu developed from an early type of hartebeest somewhat similar to *Bubalis swaynei*.

One point about the gnu used to puzzle naturalists like Dr. Gray, who founded their classification too much on external characters, and that was that the gnu had no rings on its horns. They were apt therefore to dissociate it from its nearest congeners among the antelopes and to class it with an extraordinarily far-removed animal—the *Budorcas* of Tibet. Yet the gnu really belongs to the group of antelopes and is derived from a form which once had rings on its horns. Traces of these rings may not only be seen on the horns of the most northern species of gnu, the white bearded gnu of East Africa (*Connochœtes albojubatus*) but are present on the under side and in the inner bend of the horns in female gnus when they have not had time to wear the marks away by rubbing the horns on the ground or against trees. The male gnu, however, has completely lost any trace of annulation, and in this resembles (as a parallel case) the *Budorcas* of Tibet, and the musk-sheep (*Ovibos*) of North America, both of which animals are aberrant types of Capricorns, a central group having annulated horns (though the annulation on the horns of the Capricorns is less marked than in the antelopes, goats and sheep). On the whole I think the Nyasaland gnu from the shape of the horns and the fact that the face is almost entirely without the great black brush which grows on it in the other gnus, is the least differentiated of all the species of this remarkable genus and comes nearest to a generalised type of hartebeest.

We are now left with no order to discuss amongst the mammals but the Edentates, the River Shire and the great lakes being without any cetaceous animals such as the peculiar river dolphins which are found in the Amazon and the Ganges. The Edentates, as far as I know, are only represented by one type —the Manis or scaly Ant-eater. The Manis of British Central Africa is the short-tailed species[1] which extends in its range right across Africa from the west coast to Natal and to Somaliland. It is very common in Nyasaland, but only in the well-wooded country. Its food consists of white ants and other insects. This animal has an extraordinary power of escaping from almost any prison. Its powerful claws and the extraordinary leverage which it can exert by means of its limbs and the tripod they form with the tail, the smallness of its head and its remarkable "squeezability" and power of burrowing enable the Manis to obtain egress from almost any place of confinement. It can on occasions dig up cement with its claws by scratching it away from the edge of the wall. When shy and annoyed the Scaly Ant-eater rolls itself up into a ball. It is then an awkward animal to lift and carry away as the fingers may get between the interstices of the sharp-edged scales and be severely pinched. The animal seems to know this and promptly contracts so as to catch the fingers between the sharp edges.

The *Orycteropus*, or Aard Vark, of South and East Africa is so far as I know entirely absent from British Central Africa—another animal whose range is interrupted by this section of the continent. It may yet be found (and if so it will probably be met with in the Luangwa Valley or about Lake Mweru) but no report of its existence has as yet come to hand.[2]

[1] *Manis temmincki*.
[2] It is a curious point that such southern or eastern forms as are absent from Nyasaland but are still found in British Central Africa are usually met with in the Mweru district. The country between Mweru and Tanganyika would appear to be rather dry and desert-like, and more resembling the harsh steppes of Equatorial East Africa and of South Africa.

APPENDIX I.

LIST OF MAMMALS RECORDED IN BRITISH CENTRAL AFRICA

NOTE.—This list is principally based on the work of Mr. Oldfield Thomas, of the Mammalian Department at the British Museum of Natural History. This work is summed up in Mr. Thomas's paper in the Zoological Society's Proceedings for April, 1897. The arrangement of the species, however, is my own. In order to make the list complete I have also inserted between brackets species known to be present in British Central Africa, though not represented by specimens sent to the British Museum or Zoological Gardens. Where the species was new to science and made known through our collections, *sp. nov.* is placed after the name.

Order, PRIMATES.

[*Homo sapiens*, sub-species *æthiops* ; Bantu negroes.]

Papio babuin ; the Yellow Baboon.
Represented by live animal in Zoological Gardens.

Papio pruinosus (*sp. nov.*) ; the Grey Baboon.
Discovered by Dr. Percy Rendall at the south end of Lake Nyasa. A remarkable new species with fur of a hoary grey and dirty white colour, nearly allied to *Papio thoth* of North-East Africa.

Cercocebus aterrimus ; the Black Mangabey.
Living specimen obtained by me from Lake Tanganyika and presented to Zoological Gardens. Its actual habitat on the shores of Lake Tanganyika was uncertain. It was given to me by an Arab of Ujiji—said to come from N. Tanganyika ; scarcely to be included in a list of British Central African mammals except that natives state the animal is also found in South Tanganyika and on the Luapula River : a regular West African type.

Cercopithecus opisthostictus (*sp. nov*).
Discovered by Mr. Richard Crawshay in the Lake Mweru district : allied to *C. samango* of South Africa (*vide* P.Z.S. of November 21, 1893).

Cercopithecus albigularis ; the white-throated grivet Monkey from the Shire province, but probably spread throughout British Central Africa.

Cercopithecus moloneyi ; Moloney's monkey.

[*Cercopithecus pygerythrus*] ; the russet-rumped grivet Monkey.
Probably this is the common species of grivet so often seen as pets in European settlements.

Cercopithecus stairsi ; Stairs's monkey (P.Z.S. 1892, p. 580).

Colobus palliatus ; the white-thighed Colobus Monkey.
Found abundantly in the forested mountain regions to the west and north-west of Lake Nyasa and thence westward to the Congo Free State. This species is also, I believe, found on high mountains in East Africa ; otherwise its affinities are mainly West African.

Otogale kirki ; the Great Galago.
This lemuroid has hitherto only been met with in the Shire province.

Galago moholi.

ZOOLOGY

Order, CHIROPTERA.

Epomophorus crypturus; the Hidden-tailed Fruit Bat.
Xantharpyia straminea; the Yellow Fox-Bat.
Rhinolophus hildebranti
Rhinolophus landeri } Horseshoe-nosed Bats.
Rhinolophus capensis
Hipposiderus caffer.
Nycteris hispida.
Vesperugo megalurus.
Vesperugo rendalli (sp. nov.); Rendall's Bat.
    Discovered by Dr. Rendall; a remarkable white-winged Bat.
Vesperugo nanus.
Scotophilus nigrita.

Order, INSECTIVORA.

Rhynchocyon cirnei; long-nosed jumping Shrew.
Petrodromus tetradactylus; rock-jumping Shrew.
Crocidura (species undetermined); small musk Shrew.

Order, CARNIVORA.

Felis leo; the Lion.
Felis pardus; the Leopard,
Felis serval; the Serval.
Felis caffra; the Kaffir Cat.
[*Cynælurus jubatus*]; the Cheetah, found on Nyasa-Tanganyika Plateau.
Hyæna crocuta; the spotted Hyæna.
Viverra civetta; the Civet.
[*Genetta tigrina*]; the blotched Genet.
Nandinia gerrardi; Gerrard's Paradoxure; the "Palm Civet," found in N. Nyasaland.
    Related to West African forms.
Herpestes galera
Herpestes gracilis } Ichneumons or "Mongooses."
Rhyncogale melleri; the fruit-eating Mongoose.
Crossarchus fasciatus; the banded Mongoose.
    Allied to a West African form, and also found in South Africa.
Canis lateralis or *Canis adustus;* the side-striped Jackal.
Lycaon pictus; the Hunting Dog.
    Shot by Mr. Crawshay in the Lake Mweru district, and by Mr. Sharpe at Zomba, and reported from the Luangwa Valley and North Zambezia (M. Edouard Foa).
Pœcilogale albinucha; a white-necked weasel.
[*Mellivora ratel*]; the Honey-Badger.
    I have had the young of this animal in my possession.
Lutra maculicollis; spotted-necked Otter.
[*Lutra capensis* (?)]; the Cape Otter.
    It is thought that dried skins of this animal have been seen in the natives' possession.

Order, RODENTIA.

Sciurus mutabilis; the changeable Squirrel.

Sciurus palliatus; the pale Squirrel.

Anomalurus cinereus; the grey flying Squirrel.

Mr. Oldfield Thomas adds this flying Squirrel to his list of Nyasaland mammals as it was procured by another collection, not of our sending, from "Upper Ruvuma River, towards Lake Nyasa." It would therefore come within the British Central African province as defined by me. No specimen of a Flying Squirrel has yet been sent home from within the actual limits of the British Central Africa Protectorate.

Otomys irroratus.

Gerbillus afer; the Jerboa Rat.

Cricetomys gambianus; the Gambian Bush Rat.

Golunda fallax.

Arvicanthis dorsalis.

Arvicanthis pumilio.

Mus rattus; the common Black Rat.

Mus dolichurus; the long-tailed Tree Rat.

Mus natalensis.

Mus modestus.

Mus minutoides.

Mus incomtus.

Saccostomus campestris.

Acomys spinosissimus; the Spiny Mouse.

Obtained by Dr. Percy Rendall in the South Nyasa district.

Dendromys mesomelas.

Steatomys protensis.

Lophuromys aquilus.

Myoscalops argento-cinereus.

Aulacodus swinderenianus; the Ground Rat.

"Excellent eating."—H. H. J.

[*Hystrix, sp. inc.*]; Porcupine.

From the quills in the natives' possession there must be a porcupine in the country, but the species is not yet determined. Native name: *nungu*. A smaller species called "kanungu" is stated to exist also.

Lepus whytei (sp. nov.); Whyte's Hare.

Order, UNGULATA.

Sub-order, *Hyracoidea*.

Procavia johnstoni (sp. nov.); Johnston's Hyrax.

Procavia brucei; Bruce's Hyrax.

Sub-order, *Proboscidea*.

Elephas africanus; the African Elephant.

ZOOLOGY

Sub-order, *Perissodactyla*.

Rhinoceros bicornis ; the common African Rhinoceros.

[*Rhinoceros simus ?*]; the square-lipped (white) Rhinoceros.

    A pair of horns from the River Ruo was sent home in 1893 which strongly resembled those of the " white " rhinoceros.

Equus tigrinus ; the Central African Zebra.

    This I take as the type of the species of large Zebra of the plains, of which *Equus tigrinus burchelli, E. t. chapmani,* and *E. t. granti* are sub-species.

Sub-order, *Artiodactyla*.

Potamochœrus johnstoni ; Johnston's Bush pig.

    A connecting link between the True pigs (*Sus*) and the Bush pigs (*Potamochœrus*).

Potamochœrus africanus ; the Bush Pig.

    Allied to the Red River hog of West Africa.

Phacochœrus æthiopicus ; the Wart Hog.

[*Giraffa camelopardalis*] ; the Giraffe.

    Reported to exist in the Luangwa Valley and in Ubena, N.E. of Lake Nyasa.

Tragelaphus scriptus, var. roualeyni ; Gordon Cumming's Bushbuck.

    The common bushbuck of South and East Africa.

Tragelaphus angasi ; the Inyala. (P.Z.S. 1892, p. 98 ; 1893, p. 507 and p. 729.)

    Occurs along the west side of the River Shire and also in the Lake Mweru district. This handsome Tragelaph is probably found in other parts of British Central Africa as well as in Natal and South-East Africa.

Tragelaphus spekei ; Speke's Tragelaph.

    Lives almost entirely in the water. Frequents the swamps of Bangweolo, Mweru and the River Luapula.

Strepsiceros kudu ; the Kudu.

Oreas canna livingstonii ; Livingstone's Eland. The white-striped Eland.

Bos caffer ; the Cape Buffalo.

Cephalophus grimmi ; the common Duyker Antelope.

Oreotragus saltator ; the Klipspringer.

Ourebia hastata ; Peters' Oribi.

[*Ourebia scoparia ?*]; the Cape Oribi.

    This animal is briefly recorded in our collections from Lake Chilwa by Mr. Oldfield Thomas under the name of *Nanotragus scoparius* (P.Z.S. 1894, p. 146). As he has not repeated the name in his recent list of British Central Africa mammals it may be that the specimens have since been referred to Peters' Oribi.

Raphicerus sharpei (sp. nov.) ; Sharpe's Steinbok.

Cervicapra arundinum ; the Reedbuck.

Cobus vardoni ; the Puku.

    This waterbuck, of which I have horns in my collection, has been killed by Mr. Sharpe in the Luangwa Valley and in the Mweru district.

Cobus senganus ; the Senga Puku.

    A smaller species of Puku discovered by Mr. R. Crawshay in Northern Senga.

Cobus lechwe; the Lechwe Waterbuck.

Found by Mr. Sharpe in the Mweru district, its farthest (known) northward range.

Cobus crawshayi (sp. nov.); Crawshay's Waterbuck.

Discovered by Mr. R. Crawshay in the Lake Mweru district; remarkably similar to Penrice's waterbuck in South-West Africa.

Cobus ellipsiprymnus; the common Waterbuck.

Æpyceros melampus; the Pallah or Impala Antelope.

The larger pallah—the common type—is apparently found all over British Central Africa to the west of the Nyasaland province (*vide* P.Z.S. 1893, p. 728): but in Nyasaland and the adjoining territory of Portuguese East Africa the small Johnston's Pallah (*Æ. melampus johnstoni, sub-species nov.*) is the prevailing or exclusively represented type (*vide* P.Z.S.).

[*Damaliscus sp. inc.*]; the Tsessébe?

Mr. Sharpe believes he has seen in the Luangwa Valley an antelope allied to or identical with the Tsessébe—or "Sassaby"—of South Africa. Mr. Poulett Weatherley reports the same animal to exist in the Lake Bangweolo district.

Bubalis lichtensteini; Lichtenstein's Hartebeest.

Connochœtes taurinus johnstoni (sub-species nov.); the Nyasaland Gnu.

Found in south-east Nyasaland. A gnu is reported by the natives to exist in south-west Nyasaland and in the Luangwa Valley and on parts of the Tanganyika plateau. This may be the ordinary *C. taurinus* (Blue Wildebeest) or the *johnstoni* variety. The sub-species is determined by specimens shot by Mr. H. C. McDonald of the B.C.A.A., and by Messrs. James Harrison and Kirby.

Hippotragus equinus; the Roan Antelope. (P.Z.S. 1893, p. 728.)

This animal is not usually found concurrently with its near ally, the sable antelope. It is consequently rare in or absent from Nyasaland proper (except in the N. Nyasa and the Ruo districts), but is common to the west in the Luangwa Valley, Mweru, and Tanganyika districts.

Hippotragus niger; the Sable Antelope.

Common in Nyasaland, and said to be present in German and Portuguese East Africa.

Order, EDENTATA.
Sub-order, MANES.

Manis temminckii; the Scaly Ant-eater.

APPENDIX II.

GAME REGULATIONS OF BRITISH CENTRAL AFRICA

1. THESE Regulations shall apply to the killing, hunting, and capturing of all wild beasts within the Protectorate.

2. For the purposes of these Regulations—

"Game reserve" means all the territories within the boundaries of the Elephant Marsh Reserve and the Lake Chilwa Reserve respectively, as the same are described in the first schedule; and

"Kill, hunt, or capture" includes killing, hunting, or capturing by any methods, also all attempts to kill, hunt, or capture, and "hunt" includes molesting in any manner.

3. The Commissioner may from time to time, with the approval of the Secretary of State, proclaim any other territory as a game reserve, or may, by Proclamation, extend or restrict the limits of any game reserve; and thereupon these Regulations shall apply to the territories affected by any such Proclamation as if they had been constituted game reserves by these Regulations.

4. The Commissioner may in his discretion grant licences in such form as he thinks fit in accordance with the following scale as regards the animals authorized to be killed, hunted, or captured, the local limits to which the licence extends, and the payments to be made for the respective licences, that is to say:—

Licence.	Wild Beast.	Local Limits.	Payment.
Licence (A)	Any wild beast mentioned in Schedule II.	Any part of the Protectorate	£25
Licence (B)	Any wild beast mentioned in Schedule II., Part II.	Ditto	3
Licence (C)	Ditto	Except within a game reserve.	1

Licence (A) includes the right to kill, hunt, or capture any wild beast whether mentioned in Schedule II. or not.

Licences (B) and (C) include the right to kill, hunt, or capture any wild beast except those mentioned in Schedule II., Part I.

None of these licences entitles the holder to kill, hunt, or capture any wild beast upon, or to trespass upon, private property without the consent of the owner or occupier.

5. A person may without any licence kill, hunt, or capture any wild beast not mentioned in Schedule II. in any part of the Protectorate, except within a game reserve or on private property.

6. The Commissioner may in his discretion grant any licence for which a higher rate is payable in substitution for a licence for which a lower rate is payable, on payment of the difference, or he may on such payment make the existing licence available, by indorsement, as if it had been originally granted at the higher rate.

7. Every licence shall be in force for one year from its date, and shall then expire, and every substituted or indorsed licence shall be in force for the residue of the year for which the original licence was granted.

8. Any person who kills, hunts, or captures any wild beast in contravention of these Regulations shall, on conviction, be liable to the following penalties, that is to say:—

(*a.*) If without the proper licence he kills, hunts, or captures any wild beast mentioned in Schedule II., Part I., he shall be liable to a fine not exceeding 50*l.*, and, in default, to imprisonment for three months.

(*b.*) If without the proper licence he kills, hunts, or captures any wild beast mentioned in Schedule II., Part II., he shall be liable to a fine not exceeding 20*l.*, or, in default, to imprisonment for two months.

(c.) If without holding any licence under these Regulations he kills, hunts, or captures any animal whatever within a game reserve, or is found within a game reserve under such circumstances as to show that he was in pursuit of animals, and was not lawfully employed there, he shall be liable to a fine not exceeding 5*l.*, or, in default, to imprisonment for one month, without prejudice to his liability to any other penalty under this Regulation.

9. Nothing in these Regulations shall be deemed to relieve any person from the obligation of taking out any licence which for the time being is required to be taken out for possessing or using a gun.

10. The Regulations of the 9th September, 1896, for the preservation of wild game in certain parts of the Protectorate are hereby repealed.

11. These Regulations may be cited as "The Game Regulations, 1897."

SCHEDULE I.

GAME RESERVES.

1. *The Elephant Marsh Reserve.*

Commencing at the junction of the Ruo and Shire Rivers, the boundary of the Elephant Marsh Reserve shall follow the right bank of the River Ruo as far as the Zoa Falls, and shall thence be carried along in a straight line in a north-westerly direction until it strikes the left bank of the River Shire opposite the junction of the Mwanza with the Shire; the boundary shall then cross the River Shire and follow the right bank of the Mwanza River up stream to a point distant from the Shire 12 miles in a straight line; thence the boundary shall run in a southerly direction, keeping always at a distance of 12 miles from the right bank of the Shire River until it reaches the boundary-line dividing the Lower Shire district from the Ruo. It shall then follow that boundary-line in an easterly direction until it strikes the right bank of the Shire River; the boundary shall then follow the right bank of the Shire River up stream to a point opposite the point of commencement, namely, the junction of the Shire and the Ruo Rivers.

2. *The Lake Chilwa Reserve.*

Commencing at the source of the River Palombe in the Mlanje district, the boundary of the Lake Chilwa Reserve shall be carried in an easterly direction to the source of the most southern affluent of the River Sombani, and from this point shall be carried along a straight line in an easterly direction to the Anglo-Portuguese frontier, which it shall follow to the shores of Lake Chilwa. The boundary shall continue along the shore of the lake southward, westward, and northward, as far as the confluence of the Likangala River. It shall then follow the course of the Likangala River up stream as far as the eastern boundary of Messrs. Buchanan Brothers' Mlungusi estate, thence along the said eastern boundary of the said estate southwards to a point on the left bank of the Ntondwe River. It shall then follow the northern boundary of Mr. Bruce's Namasi estate eastwards until the said boundary reaches the Palombe River, thence along the right bank of the Palombe River up stream to its source.

SCHEDULE II.

PART I.

Wild beasts in respect of which licence (A) is required:—

Elephant.	Giraffe.
Rhinoceros.	Gnu (Wildebeest).

ZOOLOGY

Part II.

Wild beasts in respect of which licence (B) or licence (C) is required:—

- Zebra.
- Wart hog (*Phacochœrus*).
- Bush pig (*Potamochœrus*).
- Buffalo.
- Eland.
- Kudu.
- Situtunga (*Tragelaphus spekei*).
- Inyala (*T. angasii*).
- Bushbuck (*T. scriptus.*)
- Duyker (*Cephalophus*).
- Oribi (*Ourebia*).
- Sharpe's antelope (*Raphicerus sharpei*).
- Klipspringer.
- Reedbuck.
- Puku (*Cobus vardoni*).
- Senga Puku (*C. senganus*).
- Lechwe (*C. lechwe*).
- Crawshay's Cobus (*C. crawshayi*).
- Waterbuck (*C. ellipsiprymnus*).
- Impala (*Æpyceros melampus*).
- Hartebeest (*Bubalis*).
- Tsessébe (*Damaliscus*).
- Sable antelope.
- Roan antelope.

THE ELEPHANT MARSH

As to the Avi-fauna: it is a country singularly rich in bird life. Amongst the birds, however, occur the same curious gaps in the distribution of species and genera which are found to the south of the Zambezi and in East Africa but are wanting in this south-central part of the continent. The ostrich, and the secretary-vulture, three genera of true vultures, nearly all the genera and species of African larks and of bustards are represented in Africa south of the Zambezi, skip British Central Africa, and reappear again north of the Rufiji River extending thence northwards and westwards through East Africa, across the Sudan to Senegambia. There is a great paucity of species or genera amongst the guinea fowl; practically the only guinea fowl ordinarily found in British Central Africa is the common species, the origin of the domestic bird, though *Guttera edouardi*, the crested guinea fowl is met with near the Zambezi and on the Moçambique Coast. The sand grouse is only found in one part of British Central Africa, in the Mweru district.[1] There may be other examples to be quoted; but no doubt the break in distribution is less marked amongst the birds (which have easier means of distribution and are less subject to the attacks of man) than among the mammals. It will also be found that this breach in continuous distribution is less and less apparent amongst reptiles and Batrachians, fishes and invertebrates. It is practically confined to birds and mammals.

And now to notice some of the more remarkable birds which meet the traveller's eye or deserve his attention in British Central Africa. Amongst the Passerines there are two crows—possibly three—the great white-necked raven (*Corvultur albicollis*) the common black and white crow (*Corvus scapulatus*) and, I think, the black rook or crow, of South Africa (*Corvus capensis*). Of this last named no specimen has been sent home, but I have seen it—or a bird singularly like it, entirely black in plumage—on the upper part of Mount Mlanje and on the higher plateaux of Zomba mountain. Of the two first named crows the white-necked raven is extremely common in all the hill country, while the black and white crow (though also visiting the hills) replaces the larger bird in the plains. The white-necked raven has an enormous beak from which feature the bird is named *Corvultur*. It is even larger than the common raven and very handsome, its body being shiny, almost bluish black and deep dull sepia black, with a large white patch on the back of the neck, extending downwards till it nearly forms a white collar.[2] The common black and white crow is found throughout Africa from the verge of the Sahara to Natal; but I have sometimes thought that it was less prevalent in the interior, especially in the forest regions than on or near the sea coast, where it is always the bird most commonly met with. It is very useful as a scavenger and is not such a robber as the white-necked raven, which, in spite of its beauty, one is obliged to destroy, as it carries off all small ducks and chickens within its reach. There is no form of magpie or jay ever met with in Tropical Africa. Amongst the starlings we have the red-billed oxpecker.[3] It is the mission of the red-billed oxpecker to cling by its sharp claws to the bodies of buffaloes and other large herbivora and remove from their skins the blood-sucking ticks. The beautiful glossy starlings are represented by the genera *Lamprotornis* and *Lamprocolius*. One stammers in admiration before these lovely birds whose plumage is iridescent purple, emerald-green, bronze-red, and vivid ultramarine-blue. Their eyes are golden-yellow. Their plumage is literally *glossy*, and although they seldom live long in captivity, they become delightfully tame. It is only the mature birds that assume these gorgeous colours; the young begin by being brown with dull mottlings—they look very like the young of the common starling—but by degrees the gem-like feathers appear amongst the brown and gradually the whole plumage is covered with this iridescent gloss. Another very beautiful member of the starling group is the *Amydrus morio*.

Amongst the Orioles we have three, two of which are widespread species and yellow, grey, and black in colour, but one has proved to be entirely new to science and was discovered by Mr. Whyte on Mount Chiradzulu in the Shire Highlands and sent home by me in 1895 (*Oriolus chlorocephalus*). It has

---

[1] Represented by one species only.
[2] This bird is illustrated in my Kilimanjaro book.
[3] Another curious instance of interrupted distribution is that of the common African oxpecker (*Buphaga Africana*), which is found in north-east and north-west Africa, and in the Transvaal, but not in the intervening districts of South-Central Africa.

a grass-green head and throat, a golden yellow collar round the neck and the same bright tint over the breast, stomach, and edges of the tail feathers; it is olive green on the back and middle of the tail; the wings are blue-grey and the same tint is on the outer tail feathers mixed with the yellow; the eye is crimson and the beak reddish-brown.

Weaver birds are well represented. There is an elegant Widow bird (*Vidua paradisea*) the male of which in the breeding season develops enormous black plumes as an addition to his tail feathers—plumes more than three times as long as his body. The rest of the plumage is black, cream-yellow and chestnut red. It is charming to see this bird flying with an undulatory motion through the air. So far from being impeded by its tail feathers in a high wind it is as it were buoyed up by the widespread plumes to which so disproportionately small a body is attached. The Widow bird with its long black feathers may bear some resemblance (especially the upper plumes which are crimped like crape) to a widow's weeds, but is far from widow-like in disposition. The male is one of the most uxorious of birds, each cock having a harem of ten to fifteen hens devoted to him and on whom he lavishes great attention. He has an innate conviction of his own beauty and is perpetually strutting about to show off his plumes. Then there is the exquisite Bishop bird—flame-coloured and black, the flame-coloured portion of the body being like plush in appearance. This lovely creature is present in enormous numbers in the grasslands, and to see these little soft balls of flame-coloured plush hanging to the grass stems and fluttering about almost within reach of one's hands is one of the few alleviations of the unspeakable misery of travelling through long grass in Africa, the barbed seeds of which work their way through one's clothing until they penetrate the skin.

Closely allied to the Weavers are the tiny Waxbills or Weaverfinches, some of which for their minute size are only surpassed by humming birds. One of these which is spread almost all over Tropical Africa is especially noticeable. It is called by the French "Cordon bleu" and is an exquisite mixture of smalt-blue and grey. Others of these little Waxbills are rosy red, and when they come with confident tameness to a clear patch of ground to feed on the grass seeds they are so small and so exquisitely coloured that they seem like the pets of a Lilliputian race. Of course there is a sparrow in Africa (*Passer diffusus*) —common also to South Africa. The African buntings (*Emberiza* and *Fringillaria*) are pretty little birds of black, grey and yellow which have a pleasing song. The Makua are very fond of catching and taming this bird and keeping it in neatly made cages round their houses. When these men were stationed at Zomba as soldiers they would speedily catch the buntings in small traps, put them in tiny cages made of reeds, hang them up outside the hut or barrack and in a week the bird would be perfectly tame and singing away shrilly. Another favourite singing bird of the Makua, and one commonly met with, is a close ally of the wild canary, the "Serin finch" (*Serinus*, the same genus as the canary). These birds very much resemble the wild canary in appearance. There are no less than three species in Nyasaland. Wagtails of two or more species visit British Central Africa during the dry season, presumably migrating thither from the winter of South Africa. They are liked and protected by everyone—white and black—and flit about the native villages, European settlements and Arab towns with charming familiarity and freedom from fear. Their song is very pleasant.

There are two Pipits of the genus *Anthus*, three species of Thrush (which sing most sweetly), there are Bulbuls of the genus *Pycnonotus*, numerous chats (Saxicola), and twenty-five genera of Warblers, including actually a nightingale!—the nightingale of South Europe (*Daulias philomela*) which comes as a winter visitor; so there is no lack of singing birds. Indeed both Mr. Whyte and myself have remarked with emphasis at different times on the beauty of the birds' songs in the hilly regions of British Central Africa. The chorus of singing birds is quite as beautiful as anything one hears in Europe, thus quite disposing of one of the numerous fictions circulated by early travellers about the tropics, to the effect that the birds, though beautiful, had no melodious songs, and the flowers, though gorgeous, no sweet and penetrating scents.[1] The song of the Mlanje thrush (*Turdus milanjensis*) is scarcely to be told from that of the English bird. Another warbler with a sweet song is the *Pycnonotus* bulbul.

Three species of Swallow have been sent home in our collections, one of which was new to science and came from the Mlanje plateau. It is interesting to note that one of these birds is the common swallow which in its annual migrations visits England. Apparently there are five species of Woodpeckers, one a South African form, not before found north of the Zambezi, and two which have never hitherto been obtained from farther south than Zanzibar.[2]

Three species of Honey-guides (*Indicator* and *Prodotiscus*) are found pretty generally over British Central Africa, though one does not always hear the same tales there about the persistence of these birds in conducting men to the nests of the wild-bee, as is the case in Southern and South-Western Africa, where to meet the honey-guide is to be almost certain of obtaining a provision of delicious honey.[3] We have found one new species of barbet (*Smilorhis whytei*) not particularly remarkable for beauty, seeing how gorgeous some barbets can be.

Amongst Cuckoos there is the southern species of *Centropus*, with black head, chestnut wings and tail, and cream-coloured belly, which is exceedingly common and not a nice pet to keep in the aviary because of its cruelty to smaller birds. The Centropus cuckoo is remarkable for its musical call, which might be expressed in the following notation:—

Tu! Tu! tu tu tu tu tu tu Tu!

This call sounds through all the hot hours of the day in the thick clumps of grass or reeds. There are also among the cuckoos two allied to the common species found in England, several golden cuckoos and a lovely creature of the genus *Coccystes* which is a beautiful iridescent purple with a white stomach.

Among our collections there are two species of the Coly or mouse bird (*Colius*). These little creatures have rather doubtful affinities but are related to the cuckoos, the turacos, and other Picarian birds; they have their four toes so arranged that they can be turned almost any way, that is to say that the hind toe can often be placed in a line with the three others in front, or two of the toes can turn backwards. The Colies have a long graduated tail, nearly twice

---

[1] Captain Shelley, the chief authority on African birds, writes in the preface to his *Birds of Africa*—"Africa may fairly claim to be the metropolis of the song birds, for the bush resounds with their melody."
[2] *Campothera smithii* of South Africa and *C. malherbii* and *Dendropicus zanzibari* of East Africa.
[3] Still the natives do attribute this faculty to the Indicators whose native name is "nsasu" or "nsadzu." The honey-guide, they say, does not care about the honey but hopes to obtain the young bees in the comb.

the length of the body. The head is surmounted by a crest, generally abased, there is a whitish cere over the beak and the beak itself is generally red with rather a wide gape, the upper mandible turned down something like the beak of a falcon or of a turaco. The Colies frequent the low trees or bushes of the forest. They creep and run about the branches like mice which accounts for their common name in South Africa. Their plumage is greyish-brown, with a faint striation.

In an earlier chapter of this book I have dwelt on the beautiful green turacos with their crimson pinions. These lovely birds are represented by three species in British Central Africa—*Turacus livingstoni*, *Gallirex chlorochlamys*, and *Schizorhis concolor*. The first named is grass-green with dark blue wing coverts and tail, a white tip to the graceful crest and the usual crimson pinions. The second, *Gallirex*, is a dark indigo blue, shot with emerald green, with grey breast and crimson pinions. The third, however, is without the crimson pinions. Its wing feathers are black, the rest of its body is usually grey with the exception of the breast where there is a curious patch of dull green, showing the beginning of that green tint which has become so characteristic of the turacos. It would be more correct perhaps to describe the wing pinions as purple rather than black.

The green turaco is altogether a graceful and lovely creature but the Gallirex though gaudily coloured is a coarse bird of ugly outline. It has a tremendous gape and a great red throat. When it opens its beak to gulp down pieces of banana it looks singularly ugly. It seems to be a less highly developed type of plantain eater. I have reared the young of both species from the nest (they are generally two or three in number[1]). The young birds when born appear to be covered with a dark bluish grey down. Though rather sprawling they can crawl about on their legs from the first and have more activity in the nest than the young of pigeons. In this early stage the bare-looking head is rather parrot-like. The way these young birds clamber about in an almost quadrupedal fashion helping themselves sometimes with their unfeathered wings reminded me of what I had read concerning the young of *Opisthocomus*, though of course the habits were not so strongly marked, and so far as I know the young of the turacos have not the fingers of the *manus* so much developed as in *Opisthocomus*.

The ashy-coloured *Schizorhis* is not at all common in Nyasaland but is met with more frequently in the low-lying parts to the west. It is a bird which frequents the great plains of Tropical Africa rather than the forested uplands. These *Schizorhinæ* attain their greatest development, however, in the forests of West Africa, where they produce that magnificent bird the giant Plantain eater (*Schizorhis gigantea*).[2]

Parrots are poorly represented, as indeed is the case throughout Africa. The only two genera which are really indigenous to British Central Africa are *Agapornis* and *Pæocephalus*. *Agapornis* (the love-bird) is represented by a new

---

[1] It is said by the natives that four are often hatched at a time.

[2] The small family of the turacos is purely African at the present day. It should be very interesting to ornithologists as it is one of those indeterminate groups which serve as important links in the chain of development. The *Musophagidæ* (Turacos and Plantain eaters) are related to the cuckoos, more distantly to the parrots, to the colies, to *Opisthocomus*—that extraordinary South American bird which retains so many primitive characters—and to the *Gallinaceæ*. The turacos in my opinion (which, if I remember rightly, is based on that of the late Professor Garrod) appear to be the descendants of some central group of birds from which the parrots and most of Picarians branched off in one direction, while there was a connection with *Opisthocomus* and the Gallinaceous birds in another, this connection probably passing through forms like the South American Curassows (*Cracidæ*).

species discovered by us on the Upper Shire (*A. lilianæ*). This bird has not been met with anywhere else in the territory. *Pæocephali* parrots are found all over the country. The large *Pæocephalus robustus*, which is green with a little yellow and blue, is nearly as large as a grey parrot and resembles very much in appearance the green Amazon parrots. It is a sulky and untamable bird although of handsome plumage, and has an extremely harsh cry. The smaller grey-headed *Pæocephalus* likewise is not easily tamed though it lives longer in confinement than *P. robustus*.

The Grey Parrot is said to be found on the Luapula near Lake Mweru. Possibly it reaches the west coast of Tanganyika. In the former case, however, if the fact be true that the bird is found wild it is probably accounted for by its introduction from the west at the hands of native traders. The grey parrot is much prized as a pet by the Arabs and Wa-Swahili, and there is a steady flow of birds as articles of commerce from the Congo territories eastward across Tanganyika and southwards across Lake Mweru. They are not infrequently brought overland from Tanganyika to Nyasa to be sold to the Europeans. The grey parrot from the southern part of the Congo Free State is the normal variety. I have not seen any specimens like those on the Lower Congo and in Angola, where the plumage tends to become pink. So far as my own observation goes there are the following species of grey parrot—*Psittacus erithacus* and *P. timneh*. *Psittacus timneh* of Western Africa is a brownish-grey with a tail which is black or brown. This bird again offers great resemblance to some of the larger parrots of the genus *Pæocephalus* which tend to assume a brownish-grey plumage in West Africa. Then there is the ordinary grey parrot which makes its appearance on the West Coast in the form in which it is generally known about the Gold Coast and extends across the Lower Niger into the Congo Basin and Angola. The race of grey parrot, however, found on the Gold Coast and in Dahome is rather a dark neutral grey, but has a distinctly scarlet tail. In the Niger Delta the grey of the parrot becomes lighter. On Princes Island in the Gulf of Guinea there is an extraordinary variety of grey parrot, in which the plumage of the body has become a deep purple grey, while the scarlet tail is a purplish crimson. Seen hurriedly at a distance these birds appear almost black (I have been on Princes Island and so can speak with some decision). On the Lower Congo and in Angola the grey of the parrot's plumage has a beautiful silvery tint, and in this district there is a tendency in certain individuals for pink feathers to crop out amongst the grey plumage until in the variety known as the King parrot the entire plumage is almost pink and white with a large scarlet tail. It is the more normal form of ordinary grey parrot however, of the average ash-grey plumage and scarlet tail, which spreads eastward from the Niger Delta and the Cameroons right across the basin of the Upper Congo to the Albert and Victoria Nyanzas, to the West Coast of Tanganyika, and to the southern limits of the Congo Free State.

It is not true as is stated by some authorities that the grey parrot in the wild state reaches the east coast of Lake Nyasa, or any part of Nyasaland. This mistake has probably arisen by Arab or Swahili traders bringing the bird to Nyasaland from Tanganyika. The nearest allies of the grey parrot outside Africa are the Vasa Paroquets of Madagascar. The parrots are a very isolated order of birds but their nearest living relations are the Turacos.

So far only one swift has been recorded by us—*Cypselus toulsoni*—a bird hitherto supposed to be limited to West Africa but apparently extending across to Nyasaland.

The only recorded representative of the Goatsuckers is the remarkable *Cosmetornis vexillarius* which has the ninth pinion of the wing prolonged into a narrow white plume of great length. The sixth, seventh and eighth pinion feathers which are black are also lengthened beyond what is usual. The female is without these appendages.

We are actually privileged to possess two out of three species of African Trogon—*Hapaloderma narina* and *H. vittatum*. Both these birds are very rarely met with and up to the present have only been recorded from the Shire Highlands. Their plumage is a combination of blue-green, golden-green, and bronze, with crimson-scarlet stomach, a purple tail with white edges, and zebra marks of black and white on the wing.

We now come to the consideration of a group that amongst all the puzzling affinities of the heterogeneous cohorts of Picarian birds stands out as a distinct assemblage closely inter-related—the *Syndactyla*, which includes the bee-eaters, hoopoes, hornbills, kingfishers, and rollers, besides other families not represented in Africa.[1] They are well represented in British Central Africa. Notable amongst the bee-eaters is the lovely *Merops natalensis*, which is abundant on the river Shire and probably in other low-lying parts of British Central Africa. At Chiromo this bird is present in large numbers as it nests in holes in the high clay bank on the spot which divides the River Ruo from the Shire. When I arrived at Chiromo in 1891 to commence the administration of this country I found that these beautiful birds were being shot down in numbers to be skinned and sent home for the decoration of hats. I took them under Government protection, however, and since that time their numbers have greatly increased and they have become wonderfully tame. It is objected, however, to this favour shown to them that, burrowing into the bank to make holes for the reception of their eggs, they assist the water in flood time to eat away the clay and so gradually diminish the site of Chiromo. I do not think there is any fear that the bee-eaters may cause more than the loss of a few feet of clay cliffs,

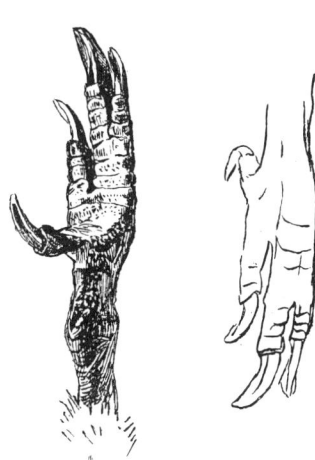

THE "SYNDACTYLOUS FOOT"
(FOOT OF THE GREAT KINGFISHER)

and the ground they are thus destroying is a piece of Government land, which is retained as a kind of a park. When these bee-eaters settle on the branches of a bare leafless bush, which they are very fond of doing, the first impression on the passing traveller is that this shrub is covered with gorgeous blue and crimson flowers, till, when he is advancing to gather them, the flowers change into birds which fly away and leave the bareness of the bush singularly apparent. They are almost the most gorgeously coloured of any living bird. The predominating colour is rose-red, deepening in places into scarlet; the other tints of their silky plumage are azure-blue, verditer-blue and black.

The Hoopoes are represented by one species and the Tree-hoopoes by two. The most remarkable form of Hornbill is the very large ground hornbill, a

---

[1] I give here a drawing of the foot of the great kingfisher (*Ceryle maxima*) to show its syndactylous character. It will be seen that the third and fourth toes are nearly joined together. This I think arose from the Syndactylous picarians originating from a Zygodactylous ancestor (toes placed two and two) and afterwards directing one of the back toes forward.

bird which amongst the Picarians is as remarkable as the large Australian Lyrebird is as a huge terrestrial development of Passerine type. It still retains in some measure the syndactylous foot though it is obvious that the toes are gradually becoming more separated. The species of ground hornbill in British Central Africa is *Bucorvus caffer*. It has black plumage with white pinions to the wings. The enormous beak and the small casque above are both black; the bare parts of the face are red but round the eye and on the wattle-protuberance of the throat the colour changes to blue in the male and to a purplish red in the female. The ground hornbills are great scavengers, devouring snakes, offal of all kinds and any reptile of convenient size they can get hold of, rats, small birds, and mammals. In spite of their ferocious aspect they make the most charming pets, using their huge bills very gently and never to my knowledge as a weapon of offence against their human friends. Anybody wishing to test this statement of mine should visit the ground hornbill presented by me to the Zoological Gardens which has been for some time living in the Eastern Aviary. I have had others of these birds and have become really attached to them. We always delighted in their quaint ways and strong originality. They are, as a rule, well able to take care of themselves, but one of these birds which almost ranked next to a human being in the opinion of the natives, so much was it a member of our family, preferred to sleep at night, no matter what was the weather, on the chimney of the Secretary's house. Unfortunately the roof leading up to the chimney sloped gradually and came near to the ground. One night a tiger cat must have ascended the roof and seized the bird while asleep, to judge from the traces which were left. They are very affectionate to persons whom they know, but they will sometimes take a sudden fancy to a stranger and insist on feeding him or her with a dreadful piece of offal, the more malodorous the choicer in the hornbill's opinion. They will hardly refuse any form of food and swallow most things on trust—a rash confidence which often leads to their death when they are the pets of a European. The natives have a superstitious reverence for this bird which they never kill. It usually lives in small flocks or companies.

In some of the more forested parts of British Central Africa the Trumpeter[1] hornbills are represented by two species, the well-known *Bycanistes cristatus* (illustrated in my Kilimanjaro book) and *B. buccinator*, a rather smaller bird with a less prominent white casque. The noise made by these hornbills I have compared in other books to the braying of an ass or the hoarse raving of a grief-stricken woman. It is at times a terribly distressing sound re-echoing through the forest. The more savage natives of British Central Africa are very fond of using the head of the white casqued hornbill (*B. cristatus*) as a terror-striking object fixed to their headdress.

Amongst the kingfishers there are four species of *Halcyon* all beautifully coloured and rather large (these Halcyons are not necessarily found near water and subsist on insects, not fish), two of *Ceryle* (one, *C. rudis* is a very common African kingfisher and is black and white, the other, *C. maxima* is the largest kingfisher known—it is black and white, blue-grey and chestnut), and beautiful little birds of the genera *Alcedo* and *Corythornis*.

The rollers are not represented by many species. There are two forms of *Eurystomus* and two of *Coracias*. The *Eurystomus* is another gorgeous bird for colouring—a combination of chestnut shot with mauve, rose colour, azure-blue and purple.

[1] Bycanistes.

Amongst Owls may be noted the fine eagle owl (*Bubo maculosus*[1]) and a remarkable fishing owl (*Scotopelia*). The ubiquitous barn owl, scarcely differing in plumage from the English bird, is found in British Central Africa as it is almost all over the world.

The Rails are another group of birds similar to the Turacos, representing a generalised type from which many other orders of birds branch off. They would appear on the one hand to have affinities with the Geese (*Anseres*) through the Screamers; with the Grebes and Divers through the Finfoots; with the Plovers (and the Plover group again gives rise to bustards, to gulls and to pigeons; from the bustards branch off the flamingoes and in another direction the Raptorial birds through forms like *Seriama* and *Serpentarius*); with the cranes; with the Gallinaceous birds through the Hemipodes; with the herons (and thence the storks), the cormorants and pelicans, and so on.

The Rails and their distant connection the still more remarkable Finfoot, are well represented in British Central Africa. In regard to the former we have a large blue Porphyrio with crimson-red beak and red feet; a black coot; pretty little rails which are often blue or dark purple, other rails scarcely distinguishable from the English water hen; and the common corncrake. The blue Porphyrios are very easily tamed but they are awkward pets to keep in the aviary, as they are most carnivorous in their tastes and will kill and eat the smaller birds. Some notice should be taken of the remarkable prehensile character of their coral-red feet which are furnished with very long toes. They are in the habit of standing on one leg while the other foot holds tightly the object they are eating which, in addition to birds, small mammals or fish, may be snails or large insects. It is interesting to see one of these birds tightly hold a large snail shell and pick out by degrees the reluctant snail. They are very clever also in moving about the branches of a tree, and their feet though so clumsy in appearance are very well adapted for climbing, and this aberrant rail *does* climb. It will go up a nearly vertical tree trunk "hand over hand" as it were, creeping about more like a mammal than a bird. The remarkable finfoot (*Podica*) is met with in Nyasaland more frequently than in the other parts of Africa over which its range extends. It is an almost untamable bird, very difficult to keep in confinement, where it soon dies from refusing food. It is awkward in its movements. The snake-like action of the head and the shape of the beak recall the darters. The finfoot dives readily and keeps under water as long as a duck. It swims with its body extremely low in the water and the bobbing head and neck often appear to be a snake swimming across the stream.

The most prominent representative of the *Anseres* is the spur-winged goose —a fine large bird with a stately walk and a handsome plumage of dark blackish-brown shot with iridescent tints of bronze-green, with white wing coverts, a white patch on the throat and on the stomach, and a dark crimson knobbed beak and bare skin round the eye. In the adult male the wing is armed at the wrist with a powerful spur sometimes over an inch long. As this spur is situated just on that joint of the wing whence so powerful a blow is so often struck by swans and geese it must be a considerable weapon of offence though it never seems to use it against man. This spur-winged goose is readily domesticated but does not appear to breed easily in captivity.

---

[1] The *Manchichi* of the A-nyanja who regard it as a peculiarly weird bird on account of its cry at night which is like the wailing of a person in agony. The manchichi is with the jackal and the leopard the associate of the *Mfiti* or witch-ghouls who dig up and devour corpses.

Unfortunately though such a fine looking bird it is very poor eating. The flesh is dark, coarse and strong in flavour.

A more eatable bird is the very pretty Egyptian goose which is a connecting link between the geese and ducks. The handsome *Sarcidiornis* (sometimes called the knob-nosed goose) is a remarkable bird, by some thought to be a duck by others an intermediate link between the geese and ducks. It has a blunt spur on the wrist of the wing, a plumage in the male of white and iridescent black with a brilliant speculum in the wing of blue green. It is fairly abundant on large sheets of water in British Central Africa.

The tree ducks are represented by at least three species. I cannot find any confirmation either by observation or native report of the idea that these birds build their nests in holes of trees though I should not like to aver the contrary. They are, however, ordinarily met with in large numbers in marshy districts where trees are altogether absent and my own impression is they nest amongst

SPUR-WINGED GEESE

the reeds. They make a curious whistling noise as a call or as a signal of danger. The genus Anas is actually represented by two specimens, the *Anas sparsa* and *A. xanthorhyncha*. There is also a true teal. The other ducks belong to several African genera. The red-beaked *Pœcilonetta* is one of the most delicious ducks for eating I have ever met with. It might well rival the canvas-back duck of America. *Nyroca*, a quaint and pretty little black duck with yellow eyes and a slight crest, is allied to our English pochard.

The cranes are well represented though by two species at most. Throughout all the low-lying parts of the country the beautiful crowned crane is present and so far as recorded specimens go it is the only crane of which the existence in Central Africa is absolutely established, but I have heard on certain plateaux and mountains of the existence of a second kind of crane, and have actually seen specimens of this at a distance of perhaps eighty yards on the swamp at the top of Zomba mountain where the river Mlungusi takes its rise. So far as I could judge this bird resembled the Stanley crane of South Africa (*Grus paradisea*).

The crowned crane is easily domesticated and a more admirable guest it would be impossible to entertain in one's garden. Apart from its extraordinary beauty and grace it spends its time searching for insects and grubs of all kinds

CROWNED CRANES

of which, with a little corn added, its diet usually consists. This crane may actually be described as a gardener, as although it is a large bird it walks so delicately amongst the flower beds as not to crush any blossom and keeps its large grey eyes vigilantly on the watch for any grub or locust.

The crowned crane is found very abundantly in the Transvaal where also it is semi-domesticated. I have not heard whether these birds will breed in confinement. If they would then it is marvellous they have not already made their way into Europe as a rival to the peacock, for the crowned crane has not only all the peacock's beauty, but it has a much pleasanter voice, and is of positive benefit to the garden, whereas we all know the one drawback to the peacock is that it eats the flowers. Once a crowned crane has become attached to a place it will never leave it and may be safely trusted with its liberty. It will take to flight occasionally round the premises but never travels far away from its home. These birds appear to consort in pairs of male and female and become very much attached to one another, apparently pairing for life. Their dancing and bowing of the head are very quaint. They are fond of promenading about at times with the wings wide spread and taking long strides in the manner depicted in my illustration. When searching the lawn for locusts they stamp every now and then with their feet on the grass to cause those insects to leap or fly and so discover themselves. They are not very fond of dogs, in whose presence they will perform the most extraordinary antics, presumably in order to terrify the beasts, but to most other creatures they exhibit a friendly and considerate demeanour. They can be trusted in the farm yard or chicken run with the certainty that they will not harm even the tiny chickens. It is evident that their intelligence is very great and that they have a natural affinity for the society of human beings, though even here they discriminate between negroes and white people, and would often display much more politeness to Europeans at Zomba than to the negroes. A pair of these birds was the solace of my exile for some three years. One of them is still living at Zomba, the other was unfortunately killed by a snake. On my journey over the Nyasa-Tanganyika plateau in 1889-90, I was accompanied by a tame crane given to me by an Arab. This bird during the march was carried in a box on a man's shoulders. Whenever we stopped to rest or to camp the crane was let out and would follow me about everywhere like a dog. When it was necessary to resume the march the door of the cage had only to be opened and the bird to be called for it to quietly step in. As the peacock from Tropical India can now stand an English winter so in like manner this charming crane which endures unharmed the sharp frosts of South Africa might very well be domesticated in England. The young as in all cranes are able to run on leaving the egg and give very little trouble in their rearing. If it were not sacrilege to mention the fact in connection with so lovely a creature I might add that this crane is excellent eating.

This country offers so few arid tracts that it is not surprising that bustards, which are birds of the desert or steppe, are poorly represented. The only species obtained and sent home up to the present time is the handsome black-bellied bustard (*Otis melanogaster*).

Flamingoes are seen occasionally on Lake Chilwa, on Lake Malombe and the Upper Shire, on parts of Lake Nyasa and above all on the south end of Lake Tanganyika. A specimen of a flamingo with immature plumage from the north end of Lake Nyasa was sent home by me in 1895, but either did not come to hand or was too bad a specimen for identification. The flamingo is probably a South African species, *Phœnicopterus minor;* though I think on Lake Tanganyika the larger *P. roseus* (common flamingo) is present. Herons and storks are well represented. The father of them all—or at any rate the bird which amongst existing forms comes nearest to the common ancestor of storks and herons—the *Scopus umbretta* or Tufted Umbre, is exceedingly common and is a great scavenger. This bird is a rich umber-brown almost without variation except that the tail is dirty white barred with dark brown and the pinions are nearly black. But on the mature bird, especially on the male, a fine purplish gloss lights up the dull brown and gives it rather a handsome colour. These Umbres are great scavengers; they are utterly uneatable and consequently are not much molested, becoming therefore far from shy. They are easily tamed and make rather amusing pets except for their harsh cry. The extraordinary Goliath heron—perhaps the biggest of all the true herons and a bird of very beautiful coloration (red-fawn, blue-grey, white, black, with green skin round the eyes and a beak which is mottled black and green) is present on every big river and lake. In the breeding season the male develops two sets of whitish plumes hanging down perpendicularly from the stomach and looking somewhat like the long muslin appendages of shirt fronts or cravats of the last century. The common heron of Europe is also met with. There are further the purple heron, the small cream-coloured squacco heron, the large, middle sized, and small egrets, the tiny buff-backed egret, several night herons and at least two bitterns. The egrets are common and beautiful sights on the rivers. The large species is seen singly or in pairs, but the little egrets and the still smaller *bulbulcus* are met with in large flocks. The last named bird is so little molested by the natives that it allows of a very near approach. These snow-white herons with their lace-like plumes over the wing are objects which never fail to excite my admiration. Towards the evening a low tree by the river bank will be a snow-white mass where these birds are roosting in a flock, and a flight of them against a background of dark forest and grey water makes a telling spectacle.

As regards storks: there is of course that huge scavenger the bold-headed Adjutant or Marabu (*Leptoptilus*). We have also the exceedingly handsome African Jabiru or Saddle-bill (*Mycteria senegalensis*) which I have illustrated in Chapter I.[1] and which is a rare bird only met with occasionally and generally in pairs, whereas the Adjutant is usually seen in large flocks especially if there is carrion about. It is probable that we also have the white-bellied stork (*Ciconia abdimia*) though I have not procured specimens. The little black *Anastomus* (*A. lamelligerus*) is very common along the rivers. It is an ugly bird with a beak the mandibles of which are bowed like the jaws of a whalebone whale, and except at the tip have a gap between the upper and lower mandibles, the edges of which are serrated. The general colour of this bird is black. On the stomach and thighs the ends of the feathers become horny and curled, somewhat in appearance like the crest of a Curassow.

Of Ibises we have the handsome Sacred ibis and the gorgeous Hagedash; also the Glossy ibis. The Hagedash ibis when immature is a dull brown but the adult bird is one mass of iridescent green, sea-blue and bronze-red. Unlike the egret the ibis is remarkably good eating.

Probably two species of cormorant are found, one a rather large bird, dark slate-colour with a white throat; the other the small African cormorant which is present in enormous numbers on the larger rivers and on the lakes—a bird uninteresting in appearance and coloration and quite useless for food, besides

[1] Page 15.

being a consumer of enormous quantities of fish. The remarkable darter with its long snake-like neck is not uncommon and is a characteristic object on quiet reaches of the river, where, perched on the limb of a naked snag, it rests from its labours. When in the water, like the finfoot, little more than the head and neck are seen above the surface. The smaller pelican is found and, I think, the larger species also, especially on Lake Tanganyika.

A PELICAN OF TANGANYIKA

There are many representatives of the Plovers. The Thick-knee, that bustard-like bird which also has a suggestion of affinity to the flamingoes, lurks on the river banks, confiding in its almost-invisibility against the bare soil. The spur-winged plover, also uneatable and, in consequence, very bold, flits in front of the boats or steamers and warns the crocodiles of their approach with its shrill wailing cry. I remarked in my Congo book on the real friendship which appears to exist between the crocodile and the spur-winged plover. I have actually seen through a glass the plovers picking at the interstices of the crocodiles' teeth whilst the latter lay half asleep, and these birds never fail to warn the sleeping reptile of the approach of an enemy. There are four species of Lapwing, and a pretty Stilt plover, which I have met with both on the Palombe river and on Lake Tanganyika. Curiously enough the common Ruff is present during certain months of the year. There is a Woodcock and there is a handsome Painted snipe. The pretty little *Parra* or lily-trotter has already been alluded to. Its feet appear enormous; in reality the actual size of the toes is not so great as the extravagant prolongation of the claws in a line with the toes which at a distance makes the total length of the foot appear nearly as long as that of the bird's body. By means of these extraordinary feet the bird can run rapidly over the floating vegetation. Even should it fall into the water it uses the feet for paddling. The male *Parra* is a pretty bird—golden-yellow, cream-white, chocolate and black.

A STILT PLOVER

On the lakes there are two species of Tern, one of them being a red-beaked scissor bill in which the upper mandible is shorter than the lower. A small Gull (*Larus cirrhocephalus*) is also commonly met with on all the lakes.

A Sand grouse (*Pterocles gutturalis*) is found in the Lake Mweru district, but has not been recorded from any other part of British Central Africa. There are many Pigeons—none of much interest except the large woodpigeon of the high mountains, which is apparently a Cape species (*Columba arquatrix*). This bird is larger even than the big English stock dove. Its plumage is a greyish-purple with white checks, and the bill is lemon-yellow. The fruit pigeons of the genus *Vinago* are very common wherever there is any forest. In coloration they are extremely pleasant—grass-green, mauve, yellow, with red skin round the eyes.

HEAD AND FOOT OF FRUIT-PIGEON (*Vinago*)

I give here a drawing of the foot of the fruit pigeon showing that it is actually assuming zygodactyle form, like that which obtains in so many climbing birds.

There is more and more tendency in these pigeons for the toes to be used two and two in grasping the branches. No doubt the zygodactyle character has been assumed independently in many groups of birds and is not necessarily a sign of common origin. Before long we shall have a zygodactyle fruit pigeon which in earlier years, when naturalists depended solely on external characteristics for classification, would have greatly puzzled them as to its position.

The Raptorial birds in this land of an abundant fauna are naturally well represented except in one group, the vultures. It is very strange that over the greater part of British Central Africa these birds should be relatively uncommon. According to Thomson they are exceedingly abundant on the high treeless plateau of Uhehe, to the north-east of Lake Nyasa. They are certainly abundant in numbers and varied in species in South Africa, and in East and North Africa. In this particular British Central Africa rather resembles the western forest region of the continent, in which vultures are uncommon and are usually limited to a species of the genus *Neophron*. Until recently I should have said there was but one vulture in British Central Africa—a *Neophron*; but I recently obtained specimens on the Upper Shire and from the vicinity of Lake Chilwa which belong to the genus *Otogyps* (the eared vulture) with a bare red head and large beak. The *Neophron* may turn out to be a new species, slightly different from the *Neophron pileatus*—differing in that the bare parts of the head and neck are rosy-pink and blue, instead of being a dull purple, and that the down which grows at the back of the bird's head and neck is a pale buff-white instead of being brownish-grey. On the bare skin of the throat there are curious ribbed excrescences white in colour. I have sent specimens of this bird home but they have either not reached or for some reason have not been described. A faithful representation of this vulture may be seen in the picture of the dead Angoni warrior, page 33. These birds will devour carrion, but they are also general scavengers and occasionally visit the vicinity of large towns or camps where they consume the ordure and offal.

Central Africa has almost the grandest of raptorial birds—the warlike Spizaetus Eagle. I give an illustration here of a fine specimen of the *Spizaetus* which was for a long time in my possession. It became fairly tame, and would allow itself to be caressed, but was deadly to any small animal which approached it. I once saw it kill a cat instantaneously. Seeing me play with the eagle the cat sidled up to me. In a second the eagle had darted out a foot and driven its claws through the cat's skull, killing it in a moment. The claws of this Spizaetus are probably proportionately longer than in other eagles.

The very handsome crested eagle (*Lophoaetus*) is a much smaller bird, but is rather richly coloured in dark black-brown with white feathered legs, a few white spots on the back and a white patch on the under wing coverts. Its crest is long and the tips of the feathers droop forward. The fishing eagles are well represented by that very handsome bird the screaming fish eagle (*Haliaetus vocifer*), the mature plumage of which is rich chocolate-brown and snowy-white; and by the aberrant Bateleur eagle (*Helotarsus*); and the remarkable *Gypohierax*.

THE WARLIKE CRESTED EAGLE (*Spizaetus bellicosus*)

The screaming fish eagle is one of the commonest African birds, and its cheerful yells occur at intervals all through the day-time on an African river, recalling one in imagination to the vicinity of the eagles' aviary in the Zoological Gardens, where while waiting to mount the elephant's back as children we have been deafened by the same not unmusical clangour. The Bateleur eagle is rather spoilt as regards shape by having a tail so short that it is scarcely visible, but the bird appears to full advantage when soaring with outspread pinions, as with the exception of the head its shape is then almost that of a crescent moon. It is perhaps the most brightly coloured of all raptorial birds, being a combination of reddish-brown, black and dove-grey with a sheen of bronze over part of the plumage. The naked skin about the cheeks and the beak is crimson-scarlet which is also the colour of the legs. The tip of the beak is black and the glossy black feathers of the head can be raised into a casque-like crest. This bird is not nearly as common in British Central Africa as it is to the east or to the south. It prefers an open country of thin vegetation where it can easily sight its prey. The *Gypohierax* which for many years was classed as a vulture but which is now known to be an aberrant fishing eagle, is found on the northern half of Lake Nyasa but not any distance to the east of that lake. It has been stated, I believe, that it is met with on the Island of Pemba, near Zanzibar, but I fancy this is a mistake. *Gypohierax* is found throughout the forest region of West Africa and its extension to Lake Nyasa I have already cited as one of the instances of western forms penetrating into British Central Africa. The Osprey is common, so is the Egyptian Kite ; and most of the genera of hawks, buzzards, and falcons are represented by various species.

A SMALL FALCON
(*Falco minor*)

A remarkable bird from its affinities is the Naked-Cheeked Serpent Hawk (*Polyboroides typicus*). This bird is very closely allied to the parent form from which the Old World vultures originated, and is also connected with a still more primitive Accipitrine, the Secretary bird of South and East Africa. Strange to say the Secretary Vulture which is so common in South Africa, and which I have myself seen in East Africa,[1] has not yet been recorded from the south-central portion of the continent,[2] being another of those forms (apparently) whose distribution is interrupted by British Central Africa. Its place is to some extent taken by its relative, *Polyboroides*, which greatly resembles it in its habits, especially as regards the killing of snakes and other reptiles. The toes of *Polyboroides* are short, though not so disproportionately short as in the more bustard-like Secretary Vulture. The leg has extraordinary mobility ; it can to some extent be bent backwards as well as forwards at the *tarsus*. The legs are long, though not as long as in the secretary bird. *Polyboroides* has the feathers on the back of the head and down the neck prolonged into a kind of crest.

The Gallinaceous birds are represented by two species of guinea fowl, several species of francolin, and a couple of quails. One guinea fowl is far from common and is probably confined to the southern and eastern parts of this natural sub-region—the crested guinea fowl (*Guttera edouardi*). The other guinea fowl found in enormous numbers throughout all British Central Africa except on the higher mountains is one of the commoner species—the horned guinea fowl.[3] Although this bird is a rapid runner and frequents the ground a good deal in search of its food, it is not perhaps sufficiently realised how fond it is of trees. It is never found far away from a forest and often roosts high

---

[1] It is also found in Senegambia and the Nigerian Sudan.
[2] Though it is found as far north as the Zambezi Valley where the natives call it Ñoma.
[3] Almost exactly like the domestic bird.

up on the branches during the hot hours of the day as well as at night. The young poults are caught by the natives and brought for sale to the European in whose fowl yards they become quickly domesticated. Yet, strange to say, the native in this case as in that of all other birds and beasts of Africa, has no idea of keeping them about his own home. His only domestic animals and birds are those which he has had introduced to him either from the north, through Egypt, or by the Portuguese. The young guinea fowl not only take very rapidly to domestication, but with a little personal attention will become extremely attached to their owners—ridiculously attached I might say—in such a manner as is never exhibited by the domestic fowl. One of these birds at Zomba used to be called the "Sergeant." It was the most extraordinarily tame creature that I have ever known amongst Gallinaceous birds, who as a rule though easily domesticated evince very little affection. But this guinea fowl would not only go for long walks with us but would every now and then run in front of us and perform strange love antics. It disliked the negroes and often chased them away by pecking at their heels unless, that is, they were obviously engaged in work with us. For instance if a squad of native police were being put through their drill then the guinea fowl in a pompous manner would march alongside the officer and not annoy the men, but if an idle native came up to beg the bird was at him in a moment and would drive him away for some distance. This was not an isolated case as several other guinea fowl have made nearly equally affectionate pets. There are two species of francolins and one of *Pternistes*. This latter is a type of francolin which has the skin of the head and a portion of the neck and face bare and brightly coloured. The francolins are remarkably good birds for the table, in size and flavour something between a pheasant and a partridge. Unfortunately they are not readily domesticated, being in this respect quite different from the guinea fowl. In captivity they sulk and generally die after a few months from deprivation of their liberty.

That curious low type of Gallinaceous bird—the Hemipode—is represented by two species—*Turnix nana* and *T. lepurana*.

Finally, I may again draw the reader's attention to the fact that the Ostrich is not present in British Central Africa.

APPENDIX III.

LIST OF BIRDS RECORDED FROM BRITISH CENTRAL AFRICA

NOTE.—This list is mainly based on the papers published in the Proceedings of the Zoological Society by Captain G. E. Shelley, to which I add a few notes of my own. I have also inserted the names of species known to be present in this country, though not represented by skins sent home. These additional names are placed between brackets. The order in which the species are arranged is slightly different to the classification adopted by Captain Shelley. The abbreviation *sp. nov.* indicates that the species was first made known by our collections.

Order, PASSERIFORMES.

SUNBIRDS.

Cinnyris falkensteini; Falkenstein's Sunbird.
Cinnyris cupreus; the Copper-tinted Sunbird.
Chalcomitra gutturalis.
Cyanomitra olivacea.
Anthothreptes longuemarii.
Anthothreptes hypodilus.

Zosterops anderssoni; white-eyed Honey-bird.

TITS.

Parus xanthostomus. | *Parus pallidiventris.*

CREEPERS.

Salpornis salvadorii.

WAGTAILS AND PIPITS.

Motacilla longicauda. | *Anthus lineiventris.*
Motacilla vidua. | *Macronyx croceus.*
Anthus rufulus.

LARKS.

Mirafra fischeri; Fischer's Lark.

BUNTINGS AND FINCHES.

Emberiza flaviventris. | *Passer diffusus.*
Emberiza orientalis. | *Serinus icterus*
Fringillaria tahapisi. | *Serinus imberbis* } African Canaries.
Petronia petronella. | *Serinus scotops*

WEAVER BIRDS AND WAXBILLS.

Hypochera funerea. | *Lagonosticta rhodoparia.*
Hypochera nigerrima. | *Lagonosticta niveiguttata.*
Vidua principalis. | *Pytelia afra.*
Vidua paradisea. | *Pytelia melba.*
Coliipasser ardens. | *Amblyospiza albifrons.*
Urobrachya axillaris. | *Ploceipasser pectoralis.*
Pyromelana flammiceps. | *Anaplectes rubriceps.*
Pyromelana nigrifrous. | *Pycobrotus stictifrons.*
Pyromelana xanthomelæna. | *Pitagra ocularia.*
Pyromelana taha. | *Xanthophilus xanthops.*
Pyrenestes minor (sp. nov.). | *Hyphantornis nigriceps.*
Cryptospiza australis (sp. nov.). | *Hyphantornis bertrandi (sp. nov.).*
Cryptospiza reichenowi. | *Hyphantornis cabonisi.*
Coccopygia dufresnii. | *Hyphantornis xanthopterus.*
Spermestes scutatus. | *Hyphantornis velatus.*
Estrilda minor. | *Hyphantornis nyasæ (sp. nov.).*
Estrilda angolensis.

ORIOLES.

Oriolus larvatus. | *Oriolus chlorocephalus (sp. nov.);* the green-headed Oriole.
Oriolus notatus.

STARLINGS.

[*Buphaga erythrorhyncha*]; the red-billed Ox-pecker. | *Lamprotornis mevesi.*
Pholidauges verreauxi. | *Lamprocolius sycobius;* the glossy Starling.
| *Amydrus morio.*

CROWS.

Corvultur albicollis; the white-necked great billed Raven.

Corvus scapulatus; the black and white Crow.
[*Corvus capensis.*]

CROW-SHRIKES.

Prionops talacoma.
Sigmodus tricolor.

Buchanga assimilis.

CUCKOO-SHRIKES.

Campophaga nigra.
Campophaga hartlaubi.

Graucalus pectoralis.

SHRIKES.

Fiscus collaris.
Enneoctonus collurio.
Nilaus capensis.
Nilaus nigritemporalis.
Laniarius mosambicus.
Dryoscopus cubla.

Telephonus senegalus.
Telephonus anchietæ.
Pelicinius bertrandi (sp. nov.).
Malaconotus poliocephalus.
Malaconotus sulphureipectus.
Nicator gularis.

BABBLERS.

Crateropus kirki; Kirk's "Babbler."

BULBULS.

Pycnonotus layardi; Layard's Bulbul.
Criniger fusciceps (sp. nov.).
Criniger placida.
Criniger flavostriatus.

Criniger olivaceiceps (sp. nov.).
Andropadus zombensis (sp. nov.).
Andropadus oleaginus.
Phyllostrophus cerviniventris (sp. nov.).

WARBLERS AND THRUSHES.

Eremomela scotops.
Camaroptera olivacea.
Sylviella whytei (sp. nov.).
Apalis flavigularis (sp. nov.).
Prinia mystacea.
Cisticola cinerascens.
Cisticola subruficapilla.
Cisticola strangii.
Melocichla orientalis.
Schœnicola apicalis.
Bradypterus brachypterus.
Bradypterus nyassæ (sp. nov.).
Acrocephalus turdoides.
Sylvia hortensis.
Erythropygia zambeziana.

Cichladusa arcuata.
Cossypha natalensis.
Cossypha heuglini.
Cossypha caffra.
Cossypha quadrivirgata.
Callene anomala (sp. nov.).
Pratincola torquata.
Tarsiger johnstoni (sp. nov.).
Daulias philomela; the Eastern Nightingale.
Turdus milanjensis (sp. nov.); the Mlanje Thrush.
Turdus libonianus.
Turdis gurneyi.
Monticola angolensis.

WHEATEARS.

Saxicola galtoni.
Thamnolæa sabrufipennis.

Saxicola pileata.

FLY CATCHERS.

Bradyornis pallidus.
Bradyornis murinus.
Bradyornis ater.
Muscicapa grisola.
Muscicapa cærulescens.
Alseonax adusta.
Smithornis capensis.

Platystira peltata.
Pachyprora molitor.
Pachyprora dimorpha (sp. nov.).
Terpsiphone perspicillata.
Trochocercus albonotatus.
Trochocercus cyanomelas.

SWALLOWS.

Hirundo rustica; the common Swallow.
Hirundo astigma (sp. nov.).

Hirundo puella.

Order, PICIFORMES.

BARBETS.

Melanobucco zombæ (sp. nov.).
Smilorhis leucotis.
Smilorhis whytei (sp. nov.).

Barbatula extoni.
Barbatula bilineata.

WOODPECKERS.

Campothera abingdoni.
Campothera cailliaudi.
Campothera smithii.

Campothera malherbii.
Dendropicus zanzibari.

HONEY-GUIDES.

Indicator indicator.
Indicator variegatus.

Prodotiscus zambeziæ (sp. nov.).

CUCKOOS.

Pachycoccyx validus.
Cuculus clamosus.
Cuculus solitarius.
Chrysococcyx cupreus.

Chrysococcyx klaasi.
Coccystes hypopinarius.
Coccystes caffer.
Centropus natalensis.

COLIES OR MOUSE-BIRDS.

Colius erythromelon.

Colius striatus.

TURACOS OR PLANTAIN EATERS.

Schizorhis concolor.
Gallirex chlorochlamys.

Turacus livingstonii.

TROGONS.

Hapaloderma narina.

Hapaloderma vittatum.

GOATSUCKERS.

Cosmetornis vexillarius; the long-winged Goatsucker.

SWIFTS.

Cypselus toulsoni; Toulson's Swift.

ZOOLOGY

OWLS.

Glaucidium capense.
Glaucidium perlatum.
Syrnium woodfordi.
Bubo maculosus.

Scotopelia peli.
Asio capensis.
Strix flammea.
Strix capensis.

ROLLERS.

Coracias garrulus.
Coracias caudatus.

Eurystomus afer.
Eurystomus glancurus.

BEE-EATERS.

Merops apiaster.
Merops superciliosus.
Merops natalensis.

Dicrocercus hirundinaceus.
Melittophagus meridionalis.
Melittophagus albifrons.

KINGFISHERS.

Alcedo semitorquata.
Halcyon orientalis.
Halcyon chelicutensis.
Halcyon cyanoleucus.
Halcyon semicæruleus.

Corythornis cyanostigma.
Ispidina natalensis.
Ceryle rudis.
Ceryle maxima.

HORNBILLS.

Lophoceros melanoleucus.
Bycanistes buccinator.

Bycanistes cristatus.
Bucorvus caffer; the ground Hornbill.

HOOPOES AND TREE-HOOPOES.

Rhinopomastus cyanomelas.
Irrisor viridis.

Upupa africana; the African Hoopoe.

Order, PSITTACIFORMES.

PARROTS.

Pœocephalus robustus.
Pœocephalus fuscicapillus.

Agapornis lilianæ (sp. nov.).

Order, GALLIFORMES.

GALLINACEOUS BIRDS.

FRANCOLINS, GUINEA-FOWLS.

Guttera edouardi; the crested Guinea-fowl.
Numida cornuta; the common Guinea-fowl.

Pternistes humboldti.
Francolinus shelleyi.
Francolinus johnstoni (sp. nov.)

QUAILS.

[*Excalfactoria adansoni*].

[*Coturnix capensis*].

HEMIPODES.

Turnix nana.

Turnix lepurana.

SAND GROUSE.

Pterocles gutteralis; the Mweru Sand Grouse.

RAILS.

Crex crex.
Porzana bailloni.
Rallus cærulescens.

Limnocorax niger.
Gallinula chloropus.
Porphyrio smaragdonotus.

FINFOOTS.

Podica petersi; the Finfoot.

CRANES.

[*Grus paradisea?*]

Balearica chrysopelargus.

BUSTARDS.

Otis melanogaster; the black-bellied Bustard.

Order, PHŒNICOPTERIFORMES.
FLAMINGOES.

[*Phœnicopterus roseus*].

[*Phœnicopterus minor*].

Order, ACCIPITRIFORMES.
SERPENT HAWKS.

Polyboroides typicus; the naked-cheeked Vulturine Hawk.

VULTURES.

Neophron pileatus.

[*Otogyps auricularis?*]

SPARROW-HAWKS.

Melierax gabar.
Astur polizonoides.

Accipiter melanoleucus.
Accipiter minullus.

BUZZARDS.

Asturinula monogrammica.

Buteo desertorum.

EAGLES.

Lophoaetus occipitalis; the black Crested Eagle.
Spizaetus bellicosus; the Warlike crested Eagle.

Helotarsus ecaudatus; the Tailless Eagle.
Haliaetus vocifer; the Screaming fish Eagle.
Gypohierax angolensis; the Vulturine fish Eagle.

KITES.

Elanus cæruleus; the bluish Swallow-tailed Kite.

Milvus egyptius.
Baza sp. inc. (probably *verreauxi*).

FALCONS.

Falco minor.

Erythropus dickinsoni.

OSPREYS.

Pandion haliætus; the Osprey.

ZOOLOGY

Order, ARDEIFORMES.
IBISES.

Ibis æthiopica; the sacred Ibis.
Plegadis falcinellus; the glossy Ibis.
[*Hagedashia hagedash*]; the iridescent Hagedash Ibis.

HERONS.

Herodias ralloides; the Squacco Heron.
Herodias alba; the Great Egret.
Herodias garzetta; the Lesser Egret.
Herodias bubulcus; the ox-frequenting Egret.
Ardea cinerea; the common Heron.
Ardea purpurea; the purple Heron.
Ardea goliath; the Goliath Heron.
Ardea melanocephala.
Ardea ardesiaca
Butorides atricapilla.
Nycticorax nycticorax; the night Heron.
Botaurus pusillus; the little Bittern.
Ardetta sturmi.

Scopus umbretta; the tufted Umbre.

STORKS.

[*Ciconia abdimii*]; the White-bellied Stork.
[*Mycteria senegalensis*]; the Saddle-billed Stork.
Leptoptilus argala; the Marabu Stork.
Anastomus lamelligerus; the shell-eating Stork.
[? *Tantalus ibis*]; the Tantalus Stork.

Order, PELECANIFORMES.
PELICANS AND CORMORANTS

Phalacrocorax africanus; the small Cormorant.
[? *Phalacrocorax gutturalis*]; the white-necked Cormorant.
Plotus levaillanti; the Darter or Snake-bird.
Pelecanus minor; the small Pelican.
[? *Pelecanus onocrotalus*]; the large Pelican (on Lake Tanganyika).

Order, PODICIPEDIDIFORMES.

Podiceps capensis; the South African Grebe.

Order, ANSERIFORMES.
GEESE AND DUCKS.

Plectropterus gambensis; spur-winged Goose.
Sarcidiornis melanonota; knob-nosed Goose.
Chenalopex ægyptiacus; Egyptian Goose.
Dendrocycna viduata
Dendrocycna fulva } Tree Ducks.
Dendrocycna arcuata
Anas sparsa
Anas xanthorhynca } True Ducks.
Querquedula punctata; the African Teal.
Pœcilonetta erythrorhyncha; the red-billed Duck.
Nyroca brunnea; the brownish Pochard.
Thalassiornis leuconota; the stiff-tailed Duck.

Order, CHARADRIIFORMES.

Parra africana; the "Lily-trotter" or Jaçaná.
Œdicnemus capensis; the Thick-knee.
Cursorius (Rhinoptilus) chalcopteros; a Courser.
Glareola pratincola; the collared Pratincole.

PLOVERS.

Lobivanellus albiceps } Spur-winged Plovers.
Lobivanellus senegalus }

Vanellus inornatus
Vanellus speciosus
Vanellus crassirostris } Lapwings.
Vanellus leucopterus

Charadrius pecuarius } Shore Plovers.
Oxyechus tricollaris }

SNIPE AND STILT PLOVERS.

Tringa subarquata; a Knot.
Tringa minuta.
Machetes pugnax; the common Ruff.
Totanus hypoleucus
Totanus glareola } Greenshanks.
Totanus nebularius

Gallinago nigripennis; the South African Woodcock.
Rhynchæa capensis; the painted Snipe.
Himantopus himantopus; the Stilt Plover.

Order, LARIFORMES.

GULLS.

Larus cirrhocephalus; the striped-headed Gull.
Hydrochelidon leucoptera; the white-winged Tern.
Rhynchops flavirostris; the orange-beaked Scissorbill.

Order, COLUMBIFORMES.

PIGEONS.

Vinago delalandii; Delalande's Fruit-pigeon.
Columba arquatrix; the Great purple Wood-pigeon.
Haplopelia johnstoni (sp. nov.); Johnston's Dove.
Turtur semitorquatus } Turtle Doves.
Turtur capicola
Chalcopelia afra; the bronze-spotted ground Dove.
Tympanistria tympanistria; the white-breasted Wood-dove.

The Crocodile is the most striking reptile in British Central Africa on account of its abundance and the enormous size to which some specimens attain. As far as we know there is but one species represented in this part of the continent, and that is the common African crocodile (*Crocodilus niloticus*). At the same time I would point out a fact which I have noticed here as in West Africa, that there are crocodiles apparently possessing the feature deemed peculiar to the alligators—that of two of the lower tusks at the extremity of the muzzle fitting into pits in the upper jaw on either side of the nostrils. I have frequently made efforts to send home a skull showing this, but some fatality always seemed to attend these specimens and either none came to hand or else the point I am now describing was already known to naturalists and was dismissed as of no particular interest.

The River Shire is a favourite haunt of these monsters which in that river are of exceptionally large size and great boldness. The power of their jaw is enormous. A crocodile which used to frequent the landing-place at Chikwawa on the Lower Shire (where it carried off many victims amongst the natives), one day rushed at an iron pail which was being let down into the river to draw up water. It seized the pail, crumpled it up in its mouth and drove great holes through the iron with its long teeth. The pail was withdrawn and for some time exhibited as an example of what a crocodile could bite through. At Fort Johnston, on the Upper Shire, near Lake Nyasa, the crocodiles would rush up to the very bank and seize people heedlessly standing near the water's edge. Several of our Indian soldiers were killed in this way until the river bank was guarded by a palisade. The crocodile seldom eats its victim immediately it has been killed by drowning. It prefers to stow it away in some crevice or hiding-place under the water until it is partially decomposed. The normal diet of these reptiles is fish without which, of course, they would scarcely exist, as it is only a rare incident for them to capture a mammal of any size; an incident which, given a number of crocodiles in any stream or lake, can only occur to each one at most once a year on an average. Curiously enough they do not appear to eat water birds. Some sportsmen have told me that when they shot ducks or geese and the birds fell into the water, the crocodiles have snapped them up, but such an incident has never been witnessed by myself. In lagoons and on sluggish rivers where the water is covered with floating pelicans, spur-winged geese, ducks of all kinds, cormorants and gulls, and in the shallower parts with innumerable wading birds, crocodiles are also present, their heads appearing just above the surface of the water, amongst the birds, or their bodies laid out in the sun on sand banks or propped against stranded trees. On the sand they may be seen lying fast asleep while water birds of all descriptions are standing about them. I confess except in the case of the spur-winged plover which warns the crocodile of danger, I cannot understand why this pact should exist between the graceful and the grotesque, and why birds should enjoy an immunity denied to mammals. Yet it is true that mammals can co-exist with crocodiles in the water, for otters are very plentiful on the Upper Shire and the crocodile and hippopotamus do not appear to fall foul of one another. Yet men, baboons, lions, leopards, antelopes of all kinds approaching the water's edge are liable to be seized and dragged under by the crocodile.

Although so many natives lose their lives every year as victims of the crocodile the negroes of Central Africa are singularly careless of danger in this respect. As a rule the crocodile never attacks human beings when there are a number of them together in the water. It is only when a man or woman is alone that the crocodile makes his rush.

As regards the crocodile's movements it does not appear to be realised by most people how he gets over the ground. I find there is a general idea that in some way the crocodile slithers along on its stomach till it reaches the water. As a matter of fact the great reptile walks or runs over the ground on its feet with the body carried horizontally and raised some inches above the surface of the soil. In this way it trots along on its short legs in a manner which is neither imposing nor picturesque, but which seems consistent with rapid movement. I have never seen this represented in pictures which are either done from dead crocodiles or represent the animal at rest on its stomach.

The Tortoise order is represented by the *Cinyxis*, or Hinged tortoise (*C. belliana*), by various species of *Testudo*, by the *Sternothærus*, and in the lakes and rivers by soft leathery-skinned tortoises of the genus *Cycloderma*. The last-named are carnivorous. Their shells are leathery and are not outwardly divided into segments. The upper jaw is prolonged into a short proboscis. These river tortoises which spend the greater part of their lives in the water and mud are very fierce and with their horny jaws can give a severe bite.

Varanus lizards are common and sometimes attain six feet in length, measured from the tip of the very long tail. They are altogether carnivorous and subsist chiefly on small mammals and birds, but their favourite article of diet is eggs. As the skin of this lizard under the name of "Iguana" is much used nowadays for making bags and purses it might be worth while to export Varanus skins from this part of Africa, as it would encourage the natives to keep down these mischievous reptiles which cause much damage in poultry yards by eating the eggs and killing the fowls.

Among other lizards may be mentioned the handsome Agama (*A. colonorum* or a closely allied species) which appears to extend its range from West Africa where it is extremely common. This Agama is almost the prettiest coloured of all lizards, the male having an orange-scarlet head and throat, a steel-blue body which in parts becomes cobalt, while the upper half of the tail is deep blue and the remainder bright red (the female is olive, spotted with brown). The most vivid development of these colours is certainly seen in West Africa; indeed the species I have observed in Nyasaland is apt to have the scarlet tints replaced by orange while the blue is a little less vivid. Three other species of Agama not so remarkable for beauty have been sent home by us. Unfortunately the Agama with the gorgeous colours loses them rapidly after death. We have discovered five species of chameleon, belonging to the genera *Chamæleon* and *Rampholeon*. All these were new to science. One of these chameleons attains a very considerable size in the male—about eighteen inches from the tip of the snout to the tip of the tail. This animal can give a severe bite owing to the strength of its jaws and the sharpness of the ridges of serrated bone which constitute its teeth. It is very savage and will occasionally dart at the hand, open-mouthed. The male has a great scaly horn projecting from his head.

Although venomous snakes are so well represented—for we have at least one cobra, a tree cobra (*Dendraspis*), a horned viper, the puff-adder, and the Cape viper (*Causus*)—it is wonderful how seldom one hears of natives dying from the bite of a snake. The cobras are chiefly dangerous to live-stock. They kill and carry off ducks and fowls, and sometimes out

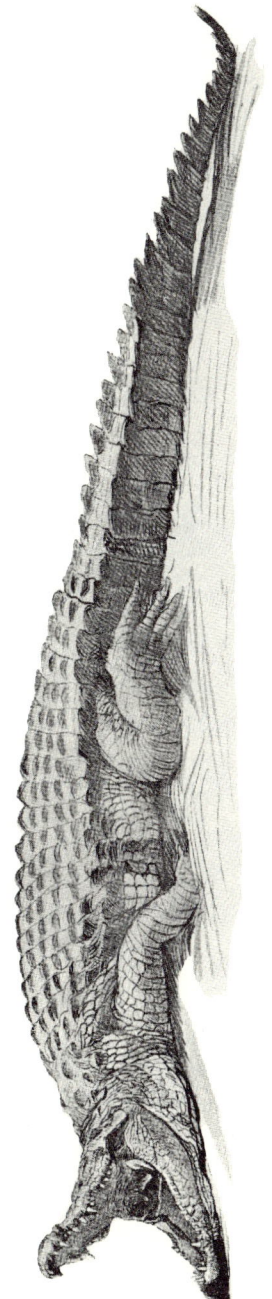

NYASA CROCODILES

of sheer ill temper have struck at and killed a tame crane or a young antelope. The cobra or one of the cobras which inhabit this part of Africa has the extraordinary faculty of ejecting its venom by a spasmodic movement of the muscles pressing on the poison gland in such a way as to spurt the venom through the air for a considerable distance from the perforated tooth. The snake is said to aim at the eyes and if the poison enters the eye it apparently sets up a severe inflammation, though it is only fatal if it manages to enter the blood. On the Congo, as in South Africa, the same peculiarity is noticed in this snake, which for this reason is called by the Boers "the spitting snake."

In all my seven years' experience of British Central Africa I cannot recall a single instance occurring within my knowledge of a native, European or Indian having been killed by a poisonous snake. Of course I would not allege that such cases do not occur amongst the natives (who have a great dread of snakes); I only say that although continually enquiring I have never had an instance brought to my notice. On two occasions, at least, my servants were struck by puff-adders, but the wound having been cauterized and the men dosed with enormous quantities of whisky a complete recovery ensued. Of course it is possible for the puff-adder to bite without causing death even if no remedies are taken, as the poison gland is sometimes exhausted or even at some seasons of the year less well supplied than at others. When we first set to work to clear the site of a town at Chiromo in 1891-92 snakes were all over the place. They chiefly inhabited the huge ant hills of the termites, but wherever they came from they swarmed over the newly-cleared ground, especially in the cool evening. On one occasion walking up the main street in the dusk I heard a low hissing sound under my feet, stopped short, and a long cobra glided out from between my feet, making no gesture of menace but quietly retiring to a neighbouring dust heap. I am almost ashamed to say I killed it here, crippling it with clods of earth, but considering its magnanimity when crawling between my legs it deserved to live. Yet, during all this period I never once heard of a native or European being bitten at Chiromo, and certainly no one died from any such cause. The natives, however, speak with great dread of certain snakes, above all of the Mamba, or tree cobra (*Dendraspis*) which in the breeding season is very savage and will dart out from the grass or bush and attack passers-by.

Pythons are sometimes met with of a very large size; one that was measured was 18 feet 2 inches long. Of course they are not poisonous and are only dangerous if anybody deliberately placed himself in contact with the snake and allowed it to coil round and crush him. As a matter of fact the python is a rather defenceless creature, inasmuch as its bulk is large and it is easily wounded, while not being as agile as smaller snakes in escaping or having any powers of defence but actual contact. Yet pythons will, if suddenly disturbed, be ready to stand at bay. Once near the north end of Lake Nyasa I suddenly disturbed a python in a thicket through which I was groping along a native path. The snake barred my way and was so menacing that I had to return to the camp and get a gun to shoot it.

There is nothing specially remarkable about the Batrachians so far as they are yet known. A list of those that have been identified will be found among the appendices to this chapter.

That remarkable connecting link, the mud fish (*Protopterus*) should be found in most parts of British Central Africa, but hitherto it has only been reported from the Tanganyika district. The French missionaries on that lake assert that the female carries the ova in a kind of sac attached to her abdomen, until they are hatched.

Dr. Günther is of opinion that barely a third of the fish in the rivers and lakes of British Central Africa have as yet been made known in spite of our recent collections. He is probably right, and remarkable discoveries may yet await us, especially on Tanganyika, where numerous travellers have reported the existence of an exceedingly large fish which occasionally rushes at boats in a

Chromis squamipennis

Hemichromis livingstonii

FISH OF LAKE NYASA

threatening manner. Similar rumours of a very large fish in Nyasa are prevalent. Both Commander Cullen and Lieutenant-Commander Rhoades (of the Lake Nyasa gunboats) have reported curious circumstances tending to show that some very large fish or marine animal lives in Lake Nyasa, which amongst other things can bite off and carry away as a bait the brass log which is towed behind the vessels. It may not be more than a huge species of *Bagrus*, a Siluroid fish. Specimens of this creature have been already obtained which reached nearly six feet in length.

The fish of Lake Nyasa, of Lake Chilwa and of the Upper Shiré offer many examples which are excellent for eating,[1] with firm white flesh and few bones.

---

[1] A new genus of fish was obtained from Lake Nyasa—*Engraulicypris pinguis*. Dr. Günther says of this fish: "It might be preserved in a way similar to anchovies and would form a useful addition to the food of the European community." By the courtesy of the Zoological Society I am enabled to give an illustration of it here.

This is also characteristic of the fish of Tanganyika and almost all the other big lakes and rivers, though except where the river is sluggish and somewhat lacustrine, the fish appear to be small and singularly full of bones. Most of the ordinary streams contain fish of cyprinoid type, more or less like the barbel.

Engraulicypris pinguis

APPENDIX IV.

LIST OF THE REPTILES, BATRACHIANS, AND FISHES RECORDED FROM BRITISH CENTRAL AFRICA

NOTE.—This list is mainly based on the papers published by Dr. A. Günther and Mr. G. A. Boulenger, in the Proceedings of the Zoological Society. I have also inserted the names of species known to be present in the country, though not represented by specimens sent home. These additions are placed between brackets.

Class, REPTILIA.

Order, CROCODILIA.

[*Crocodilus niloticus*]; the common Crocodile.

Order, CHELONIA.

[*Testudo calcarata*]
[*Testudo pardalis*]
[*Testudo geometrica*] } True Tortoises.
[*Testudo angulata*]
[*Homopus femoralis*] } Areolated
[*Homopus areolatus ?*] } Tortoises.

Cinyxis belliana;[1] the Hinged Tortoise.
Sternothærus sinuatus.
Cycloderma frenatum; the Soft Tortoise. Aquatic: ordinarily known as the Lake Nyasa Turtle. Carnivorous.

Order, SQUAMATA.

LIZARDS.

Hemidactylus mabouia; a Gecko.
Mabouia varia
Mabouia quinquetæniata } Skinks.
Sepsina tetradactyla
Lygosoma sundevalli
Gerrhosaurus flavigularis.
Lygodactylus capensis.

Lygodactylus angularis (sp. nov.).
[*Agama colonorum.*]
Agama atricollis.
Agama mossambica.
Agama kirkii.
Varanus albigularis } Monitor Lizards.
Varanus occellatus

CHAMELEONS.

Chamæleon dilepis; Flap-necked Chameleon.
Chamæleon isabellinus (sp. nov.).

Chamæleon melleri.
Rhampholeon platyceps (sp. nov.).
Rhampholeon brachyurus (sp. nov.).

[1] Sent alive to the Zoological Gardens.

Sub-Order, *Ophidia*.
NON-VENOMOUS SNAKES.

Typhlops obtusus; the Burrowing Snake.
[*Python sebæ*] ; the common African Python.
Uriechis capensis.
Coronella olivacea, var. *dumerilii.*
Homalosoma lutrix.
Dasypeltis scabra.
Psammophylax variabilis (*sp. nov.*); the Rat Snake.

Boodon lineatus.
Leptodira rufescens.
Lycophidium horstockii.
Ahætulla irregularis.
Ahætulla neglecta.
Dryiophis oatesii.
Psammophis sibilans ⎫ Hissing Sand
Ditto, var. *intermedia* ⎭ Snakes.

VENOMOUS SNAKES.

Naja nigricollis; the Black-necked Cobra.
[*Naja flava?*]; the South African Cobra : ? the Spitting Cobra.
[*Dendraspis angusticeps?*]; the Tree-Cobra; the dreaded "Mamba."

Causus rostratus.
Causus rhombeatus; the Cape Viper.
Bitis arietans; the Puff Adder.
Bitis gabonica; the "River Jack" Viper of West Africa.

Class, AMPHIBIA.
Order, ECAUDATA.

Rana johnstoni (*sp. nov.*).
Rana nyassæ (*sp. nov.*).
Rana fasciata.
Breviceps mossambicus.
Scolecomorphus kirkii.

Cassina senegalensis.
Bufo regularis.
Arthroleptis macrodactyla.
Rappia cinctiventris.
Rappia vasata.

Class, PISCES.
Sub-Class, DIPNOI.

[*Protopterus annectens*]; the African Mud Fish. Reported from Lake Tanganyika, but not elsewhere in B.C.A.

Sub-Class, TELEOSTOMI.
[Order, ACTINOPTERYGII.]

Chromis squamipennis.
Chromis subocularis.
Chromis mossambicus.
Chromis johnstoni (*sp. nov.*).
Chromis lethrinus (*sp. nov.*).
Chromis rendalli (*sp. nov.*).
Chromis tetrastigma (*sp. nov.*).
Chromis callipterus (*sp. nov.*).
Chromis kirkii (*sp. nov.*).
Chromis williamsi (*sp. nov.*).
Hemichromis modestus (*sp. nov.*).
Hemichromis livingstonii (*sp. nov.*).
Hemichromis robustus.
Hemichromis dimidiatus.
Hemichromis longiceps.

Hemichromis afer (*sp. nov.*).
Oreochromis shiranus (*sp. nov.*).
Docimodus johnstoni (*sp. nov.*).
Corematodus shiranus (*sp. nov.*).
Bagrus meridionalis (*sp. nov.*); the great Cat Fish.
[*Malapterurus, sp. inc.*]; the Electric Cat Fish.
Labeo coubie.
Barilius guentheri (*sp. nov.*).
Engraulicypris pinguis; new genus.
Haplochilus johnstoni (*sp. nov.*)
[*Pristis, sp. inc.*]; the Saw-fish.
     This creature comes up the River Shire from the sea as far as Chiromo.

ZOOLOGY

On most of the well forested hills the Land Crabs of the genus *Thelphusa* are common.

It is well known that the water mollusca of Tanganyika exhibit some resemblance to marine forms; it is also stated that shrimps and sponges are found in this lake and *Medusæ*. Mr. J. Moore, who was dispatched to Tanganyika by the Royal Society to thoroughly examine its marine fauna will probably, ere this book is published, have described his discoveries and enunciated his theories in this respect.[1]

APPENDIX V.

LIST OF LAND AND FRESH WATER MOLLUSCS RECORDED IN BRITISH CENTRAL AFRICA

NOTE.—This list is founded on that published by Mr. Edgar A. Smith in the Zoological Society's Proceedings for 1893, in his paper on the collections sent home by Mr. Richard Crawshay and myself.

[*Arion sp. inc.*]; the large Black Slug.
Ennea hamiltoni (*sp. nov.*).
Ennea karongana (*sp. nov.*).
Helix whytei (*sp. nov.*).
Livinhacia nilotica.
Buliminus stictus.
Limicolaria martensiana.
Achatina; of various uncertain species.
  (The *Achatinæ* are huge snails which attain the largest size of any terrestrial gasteropods.)
Ampullaria ovata.
Lanistes solidus.
Lanistes affinis.
Lanistes nyassanus.
Lanistes ovum.
Viviparus tanganyicensis.
Viviparus mweruensis (*sp. nov.*).
Viviparus crawshayi (*sp. nov.*).
Viviparus capillaceus.
Cleopatra johnstoni (*sp. nov.*).
Cleopatra mweruensis (*sp. nov.*).
Melania tubercalata.
Melania nodicincta.
Melania turritospira.
Melania woodwardi (*sp. nov.*).
Melania mweruensis (*sp. nov.*).
Melania imitatrix (*sp. nov.*).
Melania crawshayi (*sp. nov.*).
Physa nyasana.
Physa karongensis (*sp. nov.*).
Planorbis alexandrina.
Unio nyassensis (*sp. nov.*).
Unio johnstoni (*sp. nov.*).
Pliodon spekei.
Mutela (*Spatha*) *nyassensis*.

NOTES ON A COLLECTION OF LAND AND FRESH WATER SHELLS FROM ZOMBA

BY EDGAR A. SMITH.

This collection was made by Mr. A. Whyte on the Zomba plateau at an elevation of 500 feet and upon Chiradzulu Mountain and its slopes during July and August, 1895. It was presented to the British Museum by Sir Harry Johnston. The species are not very numerous, about thirty altogether, but probably half of them

[1] There would seem to be, however, from the collections of shells we have sent home from Lakes Mweru, Tanganyika, and Nyasa, a certain similarity in the types, so that Lake Tanganyika does not stand quite alone in the possession of a peculiar fauna. In the Appendices I give a list of the land and water Mollusca collected by us.

are new to science. Many of them are represented by large series of specimens. The large number of new forms is not altogether surprising, as this particular region has not previously been worked for land shells, and we know that in most cases the African land shells are not widely distributed, each having its special locality. Of course there are exceptions, and a very interesting one is worth referring to, namely *Kaliella barrakporensis* of Pfeiffer. This little snail was originally described from specimens from Bengal and it is also recorded from other parts of India. I have noted its occurrence in the heart of Madagascar. Messrs. Melvill and Ponsonby described it as a new species from the Transvaal, under the name of *Helix (Trochonanina) pretoriensis*, and in the British Museum collection there is a single specimen collected in Ashanti by Mr. R. A. Freeman.

The following list is a summary of the contents of the collection:

Helicarion	4 species.	*Hapalus*	1 species.
Pella	1 ,,	*Achatina*	3 ,,
Macrochlamys	2 ,,	*Subulina*	1 ,,
Martensia	2 ,,	*Opeas*	3 ,,
Kaliella	1 ,,	*Ennea*	4 ,,
Phasis	1 ,,	*Streptaxis*	1 ,,
Natalina?	1 ,,	*Physopsis*	1 ,,
Rhachis	2 ,,	*Pomatias*	1 ,,
Buliminus	3 ,,	*Lanistes*	1 ,,

It is hoped that during the year opportunity will occur of preparing a detailed account of this very interesting collection. In the Proceedings of the Zoological Society for 1893 I described a species of *Ennea* under the name of *E. johnstoni*, after the administrator of British Central Africa. As this name had already been employed for a West African form, the opportunity is now taken of substituting that of *hamiltoni* for the Nyasa shell, the name having reference to Sir H. H. Johnston's second name.

In regard to Spiders, I append a list of the scorpions, spiders and ticks we have collected.

There are large hairy Mygale spiders, and a handsome *Nephila*—usually purple-blue and yellow—builds webs of great denseness and strength from branch to branch of the trees and bushes across disused paths. There is a spider resembling a species of *Gastracantha* which I have found in the mangrove marshes in West Africa. This creature has two extraordinarily long spines projecting from the sides of the abdomen.

Scorpions are fairly abundant and of several species, two entirely new ones having been discovered on the island of Likoma. There is a terrible tick named by the Portuguese "Carapato,"[1] which inflicts a poisonous bite causing swelling, great irritation, and occasionally a little fever. This tick is found in the Arab houses occasionally, and people bitten by it imagine that they have been attacked by a more than usually venomous bed-bug.

Centipedes and millipedes are most abundant. Occasionally a very large centipede of greenish-blue colour with yellow legs is met with. This creature like others of its class is to some extent phosphorescent. It inhabits the moist soil of the forests, is sometimes as much as six inches long, and its bite is very poisonous. The large, harmless millipedes live on decaying vegetation. They

---

[1] Probably of the genus *Argas*.

are usually a glossy black with innumerable orange legs and roll into a ball if touched. Many of these centipedes in a young, half-grown stage, seem to swarm together. At the beginning of the rains one meets with them in writhing masses on the roads.

Earthworms[1] are present in the soil of the hill regions—sometimes of considerable size. Nematoid worms, similar to that described by Mr. F. Jeffrey Bell in my book on Kilimanjaro, occasionally occur in the intestines of certain mammals and in all the larger forms of *Mantis* insects. The Mantis appears to be peculiarly subject to their attack and yet to be able to continue alive until it has lost the greater part of its "inside," the worm finally occupying the whole area of the abdomen. The "Guinea" worm, or tape-worm, is said to afflict the natives but certainly not to the same extent as in West Africa. No case of guinea worm has come within my personal cognizance. Leeches are found in many localities.

APPENDIX VI.

LIST OF ARACHNIDA, CHILOPODA, AND DIPLOPODA

[NOTE.—This list has been made out from our collections by Mr. R. I. Pocock, of the British Museum.]

SCORPIONS.

Archisometrus burdoi.
**Scorpio viatoris.*
**Opisthacanthus rugulosus* (sp. nov.).

SOLIFUGÆ.

**Solpuga paludicola.*

SPIDERS.

Nephila malabarensis.
„ *hymenæa.*
Gastracantha formosa.
Lycosa ⎫
Heteropoda ⎭ Species not yet determined.

TICKS.

Argas sp.? (closely allied to *A. moubata*).
Trombidium tinctorium; small specimens.

CENTIPEDES AND MILLIPEDES.

Dacetum torigonopoda.
Trematoptychus afer.
Scolopendra morsitans.
**Alipes appendiculatus* (sp. nov.).
Archispirostreptus ⎫
Odontopyge ⎭ Not yet determined.
Orodesmus ⎫
Sphærotherium ⎭ New, but not yet described.

* Indicates species described and named by Mr. Pocock.

[1] Called by the natives "Nyongolozi."

And now we come to the consideration of the last class of animated beings of which it is necessary to treat in this brief description of the Natural History of British Central Africa—the insects: that class which seems to have been created for an almost wholly evil purpose. If the old idea still prevailed that the Evil principle was personified by a fallen deity one might well imagine that the class of insects was his contribution to the life of this planet. This idea certainly prevailed amongst the Semitic people of antiquity who called Beelzebub "the King of the Flies." From the point of view of man and most other mammals insects are the one class among their fellow creatures which are uniformly hostile and noxious. And this feeling that they were to be combated as the enemies of creation seems to have perpetually actuated the development of group after group of new creatures to prey on insects. Fish crawled out of the water to pursue primeval insects and became amphibians. Amphibians developed into reptiles and into mammals in the same pursuit, reptiles gave birth to Pterodactyls and to birds so that this hated Arthropod might be followed through the air; and mammals for the same end took to flight in the form of bats. Birds almost more than any other class have nobly devoted themselves to keeping down insects, and for this reason among many others deserve the gratitude and support of humanity to whom the insect tribe is almost more repellent and more hurtful than it is to less sensitive beings. Mr. H. G. Wells, in his interesting book of imaginative foresight, *The Time Machine*, has hinted at the awful development of insects which might ensue when these checks to their expansion were removed. When one reads of the many windmills at which philanthropy wastes its time in tilting one longs for some Peter the Hermit of Science to arise and preach a crusade against insects. With the doubtful exception of the bee (and honey nowadays can be made artificially—is made artificially whether we like it or no) and the Cochineal Aphis (now supplanted by aniline dyes), I cannot call to mind one insect that is of any benefit to man. Even when the perfect insect exhibits bright colours or pleasing patterns, as in butterflies or beetles, it is on so small a scale that the effect almost requires to be looked at through a magnifying glass, and even then is paltry compared to the effulgence of birds or the beauty of certain mollusca, and at any rate is more than balanced on the debtor side by the mischief wrought in the larval stages: while in the bugs the contemplation of a certain garish brightness of colour or quaintness of pattern is turned into loathing by the fœtid smell. There are, it is true, traitors in the camp—insects that try to be on our side by devouring other insects, but if with the disappearance of the rest of the class those too became extinct we could dismiss them with perfunctory thanks, remembering how in the Secondary epoch dragon-flies from over encouragement grew to the inconvenient length of two feet and probably presumed on their size and strength to attack the small mammals of the period.

To those of my readers who are not acquainted with Tropical countries and their insect fauna this declamation may appear strained in its tenour, but a prolonged residence in any part of Africa produces in one's mind a sweeping hatred of the insect race, a hatred not unmixed with apprehension, a dread lest by some unforeseen turn in the world's affairs the existing checks might fail to keep these creatures under, and that some awful development of insects might threaten man's very existence by direct or indirect attack—warfare with his body or the attempted destruction of his food supplies. Is this hatred ill-founded when we think of the ravages wrought by the *Phylloxera* on our vines; by the tsetse-fly on the horses and cattle with which we are attempting to open up Africa; by the jigger, or burrowing flea, which may make whole nations lame; by the mosquitoes which introduce all manner of diseases into the skin and render existence intolerable at all times in the low-lying parts of Africa, and, during the summer, in the northern regions of the globe; by the blue-bottle fly which spreads blood-poisoning; the "fish" insects which destroy our books and pictures; the maddening sand-flies; the gad-flies; the bed-bugs; the fleas; the lice; the termites which mine our houses; the warrior ants which drive us out of them; the tiny ants which get into our sugar and jam; the ephemerides that rise from the river at night, extinguish an uncovered lamp, fall into our soup and permeate it with a filthy taste; the kungu fly of Lake Nyasa which rises in choking clouds and simulates a fog; locusts that ravage continents and produce widespread famine; beetles that bore into timber, that destroy hides, whose grubs eat away the roots of flowers and food plants; innumerable moths and butterflies whose caterpillars rival the locusts in their destruction of crops; bugs which suck the juices of valuable shrubs; hornets which inflict an almost deadly sting on no provocation; the thousand unnamed insect pests with which the gardener and agriculturist have to deal under the name of "blight"; and last in the enumeration but not least in its horror, the cockroach, that foulest of all insects, the very sight of which in its mad malicious lustful flight on some hot breathless night in Africa or India round one's room fills one with more abject terror and shuddering revulsion than the entry of any wild beast of our own class or human enemy or visitor from the other world? Even in well-ordered England what precautions one has to take against the encroachments of insects! But in Africa beside this conflict the differences of opinion with slave traders and cannibals, the contention with lions and leopards as to the possession of domestic animals are incidents of a cheery rivalry with other forms of flesh and blood compared to this nightmare struggle with a class that knows no pity, that shares with us no feelings, and owns with us a community of origin so remote in its independent development that it might be the creation of another planet. It is surprising to my thinking that our asylums are not mainly filled with entomologists driven to *dementia* by the study of this horrible class; on the contrary, however, by some surprising reversal of effect following cause, the study of insects appears to produce mild spectacled men of regular habits, dull sobriety and calm optimism, just as clergymen are usually the authorities on spiders, and men of thin-lipped virtue affect the study of that most disproportionate development of generative energy, the earthworm.

This exordium is intended to explain why in my brief allusions to the insects of British Central Africa I should speak in terms of almost unmitigated blame.

Butterflies are not perhaps so striking in beauty of colouring as in West Africa, Madagascar, Tropical Asia, and South America. But as I have already said the beauty even of the most gorgeous butterflies is, in my opinion, trivial compared to that of an ordinary bird.

The most interesting feature in some of them is mimicry of their surroundings. One butterfly frequently met with on the slopes of Zomba mountain offers the most perfect resemblance to a large green leaf when its wings are closed. The two pairs of folded wings meet together almost without a break in the line of contour, and the end of the slightly prolonged "tail" to the lower wings is apposed to the branch, thus imitating the stalk of the leaf. The insect's legs are long and it has a way of tucking them up close to the body and contour of the wings. The colour of the outer side of the wings is dull green, and a dark green stripe runs right down the middle to represent the midrib of the leaf. I am fairly inured to surprises in Nature but I have been repeatedly taken in by these leaf butterflies, and to my amazement have seen what appeared to be the unmistakable leaves of a tree or bush taking to flight and then settling again, so that in a minute the eye failed to distinguish between the real and the false leaf. Some of the butterflies of the genus *Papilio* are handsome but they are widespread throughout Africa from the west and the north to Natal. There are also large smalt-blue "skippers" which are very rich in colouring. It is remarkable that the clouded yellow and other species of butterflies more associated in their distribution with Europe should be met with on our high mountains. The names of these will be found in the appendix.

The larvæ of a small moth named *Tinea vastella* burrow into the horns of dead animals, horns, for instance, that are being collected as specimens. Soon a number of grey cocoons begin to protrude from the horn as though it were budding in all directions. When these are knocked off a round hole remains so that the horn is soon quite spoiled in appearance.

It might be mentioned that the caterpillars of certain large moths are very striking objects. They are nearly if not quite six inches long and covered with a flame-coloured plush of long pile. If touched, however, the extremely fine silky hairs will sting the hand and cause a rash. The caterpillars of other moths are vicious creatures that eject a stinging liquid from their mouths.

A large carnivorous beetle with powerful nippers of the genus *Tefflus* is remarkable for its beautiful iridescent-violet tint, but it can take a piece out of the finger if incautiously handled. Such other beetles as do not attempt to get into one's eyes or drill holes in one's specimens of horns, or bore through one's rafters and drop the sawdust on the furniture below, or destroy the European flowers in one's garden, or put out the lamp at night, or creep into one's hair or rustle between one's papers, or eat and befoul one's supplies of grain, or crawl into one's ear, ought I suppose to be mentioned for their minute beauties or extravagant development of horns or wing-cases, but I have not the heart to do so.

The common flea is fortunately not truly indigenous, that is to say, it is not found in the bush or in many unsophisticated native villages; it is chiefly confined to the European settlements and to the dwellings of Arabs or semi-civilised natives: though I cannot say if it is wholly absent from any native village.

The burrowing flea (*Sarcopsyllus penetrans*) is quite a new arrival in this country. It is a native of South America and the West Indies where it is usually known as the "chigo" or "jigger," and as such is supposed to be the origin of the sailors' oath—"Well, I'm jiggered!" In the earlier "fifties" a ship from Brazil landed sand ballast at Ambriz on the West Coast of Africa and thus introduced the jigger into the soil. The animal slowly spread through the sandier regions of Angola and along the West African Coast towards the Congo and Sierra Leone. At first it made its way up the Congo slowly, but Stanley's expedition and the spread of civilisation over the Congo Free State carried the jigger far and wide. When I first visited the Congo the burrowing flea had scarcely got further up the river than Bolobo. Soon afterwards it reached the Stanley Falls and thence made its way to Tanganyika in the Arab caravans. From Tanganyika it gradually spread southwards to Lake Nyasa and was first heard of at Karonga about 1891. It reached South Nyasa the following year and in 1894 became a great pest at Zomba and throughout the Shire Highlands, finally reaching Chinde on the sea coast in 1895. Fortunately it is an insect which apparently only thrives on sandy soils and therefore in moist parts of British Central Africa it is already commencing to disappear. At first it caused terrible sufferings amongst our naked-footed soldiers, policemen and postmen, many of whom became lame by its bites. It caused the Administration to go to great expense in providing boots for all these people. Gradually, however, the natives are getting used to its attacks as they are in West Africa and in the West Indies, and by care and constant attention to the feet are able to keep it at bay. The jigger is a very minute flea only just visible. The female creeps under the skin, preferring if possible those parts where there is a slight pressure, such as between the toes or fingers. The foot, however, is that portion of the human frame which it most usually attacks. Having burrowed under the surface of the skin the insect proceeds to lay a large number of eggs which, together with itself, are enveloped in a white sac. After laying the eggs the mother dies, the young ones hatch out and proceed to devour all the surrounding tissue, burrowing in all directions until at last the neglected toe or other portion of the foot becomes honeycombed. In extreme cases mortification may set in and the whole foot be lost even if the mischief spread no farther. But such a case as this could only occur when the insect first makes its appearance in a new country and its advances are quite uninterrupted and neglected. If the jigger be removed within a few days after entry the removal is very easy and relatively painless, and the evil consequences are nil. Still Europeans who are obliged to live in jigger-haunted localities should be careful to have their feet examined once a day by a native servant. The natives are very sharp eyed and on a white skin it is easy to see the jigger burrowing like a little blue point under the surface. A little carbolic oil dropped into the hole from which the burrowing flea has been extracted will allay the irritation which is caused by some liquid the animal exudes, and will effectively kill any eggs that may have escaped from the sac. Fortunately the skin surrounding the sac is tough and a skilful operator easily removes it unbroken. The jigger attacks not only human beings but monkeys, dogs, fowls and turkeys.

In like manner the bed-bug, which is a hideous pest in any village that has been occupied by Arabs or coastmen, is usually absent from those native dwellings inhabited by naked people whose habits are cleanly and whose scanty clothing affords no harbourage for this pest. The indigenous bugs are many but confine their attacks to plants, the juices of which they suck. Many of these bugs are brightly, even handsomely coloured, but all of them possess the same faculty of emitting (as a means of protection) the same horrible smell— a smell none the less disgusting from its near approach to being aromatic.

The locust which so much afflicted British Central Africa during the years 1893, 1894 and 1895 was apparently the red locust of North Africa,[1] and not any indigenous or South African variety.[2] This locust plague from all accounts began in the Egyptian Sudan almost simultaneously with the rinderpest, and, spreading southwards, gradually reached British Central Africa, passing on from there to South Africa, where it caused very serious losses. It would seem

[1] *Pachytylus migratorioides?*
[2] Though of course there are several species of *Pachytylus* in South Africa; but in the case of the locust plague of 1893-95, the locusts came down in swarms from the far north, from Galaland and the Egyptian Sudan, whence they also spread westward to Sierra Leone. The locusts passed on steadily in a southerly direction, and have recently ravaged Bechuanaland and Natal.

as though these locust plagues were not wholly unknown in the south-central part of the continent, though fortunately they are only occasional occurrences, and locusts of the rapidly-multiplying rapacious kind do not seem to have a permanent home north of the Zambezi, as they do in North and South Africa, no doubt because the climate as a rule is too moist for their constitutions. The terrific downpour of rain during the wet season kills the mature insect and washes its eggs away. Undoubtedly much of the damage which the locusts did on their first arrival was due to laziness on the part of Europeans and natives who either could not, or would not, bother themselves with adopting extraordinary means for scaring the insects from the crops. Locusts strongly dislike noise and tremors of the atmosphere. We found at Zomba that an almost unfailing way to get rid of them when they descended in countless thousands on our gardens was to turn out large numbers of men beating drums and tin pans, clapping hands and shouting. The locusts then refrained from settling and passed on to less energetic neighbours.

In extreme cases we fired off, with much effect, charges of dynamite. This never failed to clear us of locusts. Birds, of course, were our chief allies in combating this enemy. Not only ordinary insect-eating birds but kites, hawks, and ravens; and this fact might be borne in mind by the European planter who is a little too apt to shoot these predatory birds which are in fact most useful in keeping down the locust tribe. The most effective locust killers are the crowned cranes already described, and for this purpose alone they ought to be domesticated and bred in large numbers both here and in South Africa.

Another great pest is the white ant, or termite, which is not an ant at all but a Neuropterous insect distantly related to the cockroach group. The large, more or less conically shaped ant-hills of these termites are familiar features all over the country.[1] The white ant here is probably represented by the species *Termes mossambicus* and *T. bellicosus* and by the genus *Hodotermes*. No termites as a rule are found above an altitude of 4000 feet; consequently on the colder plateaux of British Central Africa these and many other pests disappear. It is also not very fond of a sandy soil and is absent in rocky country, preferring the red or whitish kaolin clay. In spite of its persistency it is possible to drive this insect away as I have repeatedly proved.[2] All ant-hills should be demolished and the ground below them dug up to about six feet in order to discover and destroy all the queens, as if one queen is left the community will simply rebuild, whereas if all the queens are destroyed they appear to wander aimlessly to their destruction. The white ants die if exposed to the light of the sun. They are very sensitive to light and only work in the daytime in earth tunnels which they build. It is these tunnels of red clay, which are sometimes made for many feet along the trunk of a tree until a dead branch is attained, which the ants are bent on devouring, that caused Professor Drummond in his work on Tropical Africa

[1] Other Termites, however, build nests shaped exactly like a mushroom, and not more than two feet high, mounted on a tube-like stem.

[2] Where the white ant is already well established in the foundation of a house, after every effort has been made to get rid of its nests from under the foundation without success, it can sometimes be induced to quit the building by the constant application of petroleum to the walls, as, like so many other insects, it detests the smell or taste of mineral oil. The first appearance of white ants in the plaster will be long clay tunnels appearing on the surface of the wall. These should be gently knocked off and there will then remain a number of round holes out of which the white ants have come. These should be closed with a mixture of lime and petroleum and if this is done repeatedly the white ants will leave the place, especially if all the approaches to the wall from the floor of the room are further smeared with petroleum. White ants are not fond of sharing a building with human beings, or of the society of man, as they dislike the jarring sounds and the tremor caused by much traffic. There is no doubt they can be got rid of to a great extent in human settlements.

to compare the white ant to the earthworm in the creation of vegetable soil. Undoubtedly timber which falls to the ground is more rapidly reduced to soil by the thick covering of red clay with which it is coated by the termites. An interesting and lucid description of the termite economy will be found in the newly published volume on insects of the *Cambridge Natural History*. I need only remind my readers that there is a parallel resemblance between the social workings of the termites and that of bees and ants in that the community is divided into classes of breeding males and females, workers and soldiers. The two latter sections appear to be females with the sexual organs undeveloped. The mature males and females assume wings and issue forth from the nest at the beginning of the rainy season in immense numbers, mostly meeting with a well-deserved fate from such mammals and birds as devote themselves to the destruction of these insects.[1]

A TERMITE ANT-HILL.

They are usually largely eaten by the natives who collect them as follows: They build grass sheds over the ant-hills just before the rainy season, and as the winged ants issue in enormous swarms from the small holes at the base of the ant-hill they fly straight up till they come against the grass roof, and fall down into pots set into the ground with opening mouths on a level with the surface. As the pots are filled they are covered with leaves. The ants are afterwards roasted, wings and all, dried in the sun and then pounded in a mortar and eaten as a kind of relish. If the winged ant is left to itself it soon jerks off the wings, of which it apparently only avails itself to fly for a short distance from the mother nest. At this season of the year the escaped termites generally ascertain where a dinner party is being given and fly to that house, entering it by any crevice, and making straight for the lighted table, where they proceed to cast off their wings into the soup and on all the other viands, adding one more to these many grievances, the total sum of which will no doubt lead me to devote the remainder of my existence to the extirpation of the hated class of insects.

The *Orthoptera* are represented by the cockroaches, the earwigs, the mantises, the stick-insects, the locusts and crickets.

I have already touched briefly on the subject of cockroaches. There are several native species which frequent the village dirt-heaps, or are found in the forest, and one or two of these exhibit a certain amount of comeliness. The ubiquitous cockroach of Tropical civilisation is present in all large settlements, but it is not a true native of the country and is never found in the wilderness.

[1] So important a factor is the termite in the economy of tropical nature that it has probably caused the evolution of certain special types of birds and mammals. Amongst the former may be mentioned the *Orycteropus*, or Ant-bear of South Africa and the *Manis* or Pangolin of Africa and India. These two types of mammals live almost exclusively on white ants.

Scrupulous cleanliness and the absence of dark holes and corners in which these creatures may breed generally lead to its being kept under in houses and on steamers. A cockroachy steamer is without excuse and indicates a careless and dirty captain.

The mantises, or praying insects, offer a number of species, some of them very fantastic, others almost beautiful in their green colouring with large black and pink ocelli on the hinder pair of wings showing very plainly when the wings are folded. It is curious how the female mantis has taken to the conifers recently introduced into the country, as a tree in which to weave her egg-case.

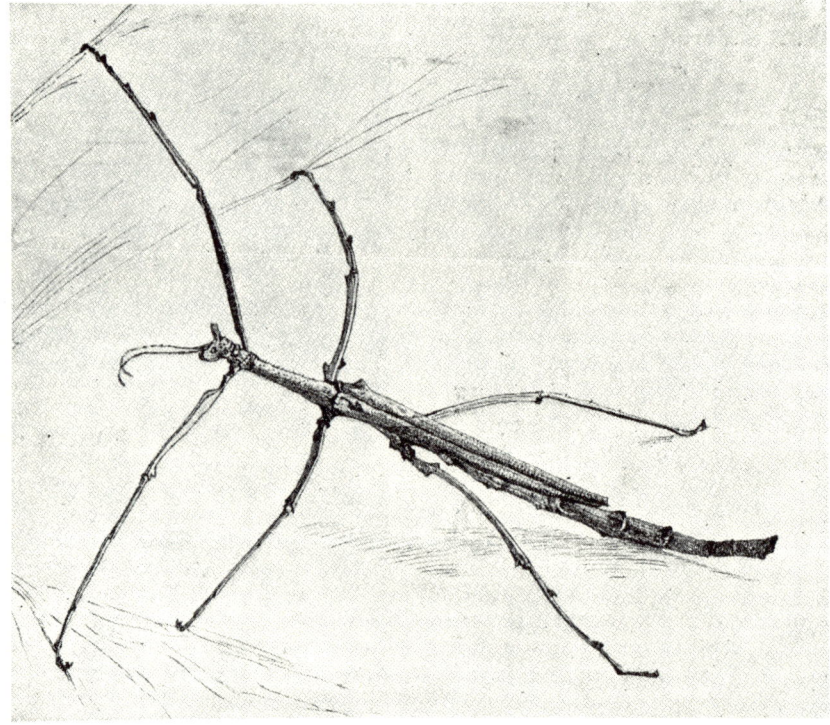

A STICK INSECT

This is a heart-shaped, grey papery structure from which the young escape when hatched.

An excellent idea of the weapons with which this horrible insect is endowed may be obtained from an article on the mantises in the *Cambridge Natural History*.[1] As will be seen the front pair of legs is greatly developed and the last two segments of the limb are furnished with teeth on the inner side. The last joint, or tibia, closes on the penultimate segment or femur, much as the blade of a penknife springs back on its hinge into the case, thus catching between the sharp teeth of tibia and femur any object which the mantis may wish to grasp. The insect always stands on the other four legs with these front

[1] Insects, part i.

legs folded up alongside its immensely elongated pro-thorax, the body gently swaying to and fro. When an insect approaches and is within reach, the mantis darts its fore limbs forwards and catches the creature between tibia and femur. It then advances the prey to the mandibles of its mouth and tears it away again, thus biting off portions. It is a nasty insect to lay hold of as it can give one's fingers a very sharp prick with the teeth of its huge fore limbs. No one ordinarily would have a desire to meddle with the mantis, but the mantis unfortunately will not leave you alone at night. Attracted by the light of your lamp it flies in circles around it and you, generally ending by settling on your hair or hand, looking at you with its huge green eyes and ready at any offensive movement on your part to tweak your ear or your finger. Fortunately the

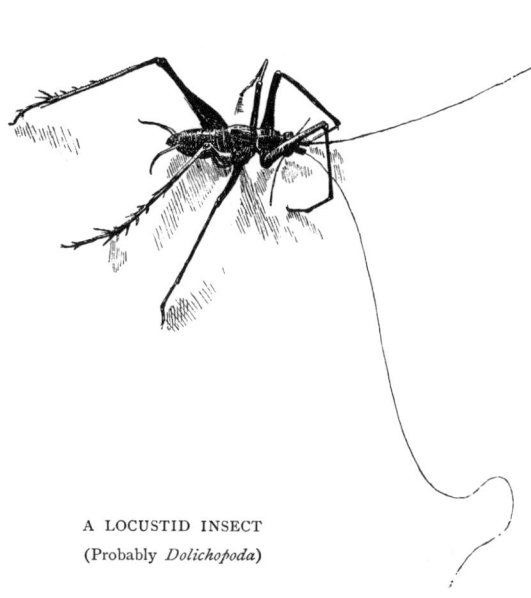

A LOCUSTID INSECT
(Probably *Dolichopoda*)

ferocity of the mantis (though it is said by some naturalists to be able to kill small birds) is mainly directed against its own hateful class, and it kills enormous numbers of insects, many more than it can eat; being in this respect the leopard of the insect race, killing for love of slaughter.

The stick-insects (*Phasmidæ*) are very abundant in the long grass, and some of them imitate the yellow stems and grey leaflets of the sun-dried herbage with the most marvellous accuracy. Others simulate small dead branches with off-shoots and thorns, the main branch being mottled with spots like lichen. This tribe produces the largest insects of the present day, some of the *Phasmidæ* attaining to a length of eighteen inches. It is not uncommon to meet with them in British Central Africa a foot long. I give an illustration (page 372) of one obtained at Zomba. This is probably a species of *Palophus*, and measured nine inches in length.

Locusts are represented by many species some of which are brightly coloured red—black and yellow, or blue and yellow. Others are a beautiful grass-green.[1] The indigenous grasshopper does not do an extravagant amount of harm. It is as I have already stated a red species of locust (probably *Pachytylus migratorioides*) from the north which has recently committed such ravages and has passed on in swarms to the south.

[1] *Locustidæ*. Some of the *Locustidæ* have enormously long antennæ. I give an illustration of one drawn from life in Central Africa. Others of these *Locustidæ* imitate leaves in a wonderful manner; others again with long green bodies have large wings of vivid rose-pink, the wing cases, however, being green so that the creature is only visible to the eye amongst the grass when it takes to flight.

The crickets are represented by several most repulsive forms. What can be more frightful than the mole cricket? Such an animal as this is a blot on creation. Some of the *Gryllidæ* are extremely predaceous and carnivorous. I have noticed one, especially, which seems to frequent the native huts, lodging generally in the thatched roof. When I have been writing at my table by the light of a lamp and some fat, fluffy, stupid moth singed and stupefied with the oil is gyrating on the table, the predatory *Gryllus* will pounce on it from the roof and literally tear it to pieces before one's eyes.

Large carpenter bees with black bodies and violet wings, and apparently the ordinary honey bee (*Apis*) are common. I imagine the honey bee of Central Africa to belong to the genus *Apis* because it is possessed of a sting which is not the case, I believe, amongst some of the honey bees of other genera found usually in tropical climates. These wild bees are present in almost all the forested regions and make delicious honey and excellent wax. Wax indeed is one of the articles of export from British Central Africa, though the natives do not pay as much heed to collecting it as they might. These honey bees can be a great nuisance, sometimes, as they are very ill-tempered. In my house at Zomba they were continually trying to build hives in the chimneys and at times would swarm there in numbers, becoming so angry at being smoked out that they would attack and sting all who came near them. On one occasion when travelling along the Upper Shire a few of my porters and myself stopped to rest under a shady tree. We were at once attacked by a swarm of bees who stung us violently and whom we could only get rid of after running for nearly a quarter of a mile through the dense grass. I received thirteen stings on the head and neck. These being at once extracted and the places rubbed with extract of witch-hazel, I felt no after ill effects.

The female of an ugly creature possibly belonging to the genus *Scolia* makes its appearance during the rainy season in houses, attracted by the light. It has an extremely long flexible body, the end of which is armed with a formidable sting. The mason wasp is a familiar sight. It has dark indigo-blue wings, yellow abdomen and black and orange legs. This wasp stings and benumbs caterpillars and spiders, then packs them into a mud cell which it has previously built on the wall of a house or in some such appropriate shelter. Having deposited an egg in the cell together with the grub it seals it up with more mud and continues to build other cells until quite a large excrescence of red mud is gathered together. As the young grubs hatch so they gradually consume the stupefied but not dead victim. They then push their way out through the top of the cell and emerge as the perfect insect. It is said that the male of this species is very much smaller than the female and there is some doubt as to its identity.

The mason wasp is rather a nuisance, however much good it may do by destroying caterpillars, as it invades all one's premises whenever a door or window is open and is perpetually building a nest on the back of books or on nicely-coloured walls, on picture frames, or even inside the piano if it can get there. It is also a great fidget, buzzing round and round one's head in circling flights; in fact when a mason wasp has got into the room I have to call servants to catch it or drive it out before I can resume my work. Nevertheless they are good-tempered insects not readily induced to sting, whereas the pale green-grey *Belonogaster* wasps, which build their papery nests of very long tubes on the roof of one's dwelling, are easily roused to hostility and sting fearfully. These are the insects which are mentioned by so many European travellers as "hornets." I question whether any hornet is found in Central Africa, but the hornet is, after all, only one amongst many wasps.

Regarding ants: there are the tiny ones which in the more low-lying districts infest the larder and crawl into the sugar; there are the red tree ants that bite venomously; and there is a black species living in marshy localities which has formidable mandibles and whose puncture of the skin is like a nip of red-hot iron. This black ant is said to sally out at times to attack the termites. It is often met marching in armies of thousands which make a perceptible rustling as they cross a road by a track which they have actually worn through the soil. The workers pass along in the middle whilst the large-jawed soldiers are thickly clustered on either side. If the progress of this army should be arrested the soldiers scour the soil seeking for the enemy, and if the human observer remained long in the vicinity these dauntless insects would have climbed up his legs and have fixed their jaws into his flesh with such tenacity that the head is often left in the wound when the body is pulled off. At times these warrior ants will enter a dwelling and force the human inhabitants to evacuate. In their passage through the house they destroy all cockroaches and other insects and even rats, so that sometimes their visit is not an unmixed curse. I believe this is the same species of ant (or a nearly allied one) as that in West Africa whose savage propensities are utilised by negroes for a hideous torture. When it is wished that a person—generally a woman—should die by inches, he or she is tied down on the ground by the home of these warrior ants. The ants are then thoroughly disturbed and enraged and left to wreak their vengeance on the unhappy human being at their mercy, whom in time they will not only kill, but whose flesh they will devour, leaving the bones picked clean.[1]

Another ant remarkable for disagreeable qualities is the *Ponera*, a rather large-sized insect for this family, perhaps three-quarters of an inch long with the abdomen striped in black and white. The *Ponera* exudes the most offensive odour, something like the smell of the little European ant known as the Pismire, only ten times stronger. This stench becomes infinitely worse if an insect is killed when it will sometimes pervade the whole house. Persons who have not actually witnessed this are not able to conceive that such a terrible fœtor can proceed from the body of so small an insect. I remember Mr. Sharpe complaining to me once that there was a bad smell like drains in the newly built Vice-consulate at Blantyre, though we both agreed that such was impossible because there were no drains. As soon as I sniffed the scent, however, I felt sure it was the Ponera ant and on taking up the matting of the ground floor one of these insects was discovered crushed underneath, and once it was removed the smell completely disappeared.

The Order *Diptera* shall conclude my survey of the insects. Amongst other pests it produces at least three species of gnats (mosquitoes); midges—otherwise called "sand-flies"; enormous horse-flies nearly an inch in length; bluebottles; house-flies; gad-flies; and the celebrated tsetse. There is also a fly not as yet identified which with its ovipositor probes the skin of human beings even through clothing, especially on the legs or back, and inserts an egg. This egg develops into a small grub which is the cause of a very painful boil from which it eventually emerges.

Of the mosquitoes there are, as I have said, apparently three kinds—one

[1] There was a case on the Niger in the early "eighties" tried by Consul Hewett, wherein a negro missionary and his wife were convicted of thus doing to death a native girl who had offended them.

large and brown in colour found in the thick grass near to rivers or lakes in a low-lying country. This creature is called by the Portuguese "Mosquito manso," or "the tame mosquito," it being too sluggish to elude capture, especially when gorged with blood. This, in my opinion, almost adds to the original injury of its puncture because the disagreeable insect allows itself to be smashed, leaving a smear of blood. Then there is the ordinary grey mosquito (whose bite is the most venomous), a tiny little black mosquito, and a species of gnat found close to rivers, which is barred grey and white, and has plume-like antennæ. Fortunately in the Shire Highlands and on all lands well above 3000 feet—and most of the superfices of British Central Africa lies above this altitude—the mosquito is almost entirely absent. This is of itself an enormous gain to comfort in living. On the River Shire, on some (but not all) parts of the coast lands of Lake Nyasa and around the south end of Tanganyika, mosquitoes are bad, though here again their presence depends a good deal on the condition of the adjacent country. If this is one mass of unkempt vegetation, especially lush grass, then mosquitoes will swarm; but as soon as the land is cleared and cultivated and the rank bush is kept under the mosquitoes lessen in numbers and even in some cases disappear. When we first occupied the ground on which Fort Johnston stands at the south end of Lake Nyasa, mosquitoes made life almost impossible, especially in the evening. At this time if anyone walked out in a few minutes his neck was covered with blood and black with mosquitoes. Dinner was only possible in the midst of thick smoke from burning weeds. Yet nowadays mosquitoes in this same place are a negligeable quantity. At some seasons of the year they disappear altogether and at other times are met with in such small numbers that their presence is not much remarked. Undoubtedly the mosquito is a source of ill-health in Africa. Apart from the maddening irritation caused by its bites it would appear to introduce some unwholesome substance, and when the person bitten is in a poor state of health the mosquito-bites turn to ulcers which are difficult to heal until the sufferer is removed to a healthy locality. As a rule one receives fewer mosquito-bites in a native hut than in a tent because they strongly dislike the smoke of the wood fires, which are burned in every native dwelling.

Midges are very troublesome in certain places, especially localities near the river. They are even found high up on the hillsides. During the rainy season at Zomba it is difficult to sit out of doors and paint or read without having an attendant present with a fan to keep the midges away or without burning incense (as I used to do), the fumes of which drive them away.[1]

Although the sand-fly is so minute as to be not much larger than a flea its bite raises a large white weal and is more painful than that of the mosquito.

The horse or "hippo" fly is a handsome insect of bronze-green and chestnut-brown and is of large size. It is not much of a pest in the highlands but swarms along the banks of all large rivers. It is easily killed by a smart blow when it settles and is about to probe with its sharp proboscis. If it succeeds in piercing the skin it raises a large red lump which is irritable and sore for some days.

The gad-flies are more annoying to beasts than to men; a horse will come in dripping with blood from their attacks after a ride through the grass during the rainy season.

[1] Incense as a pleasant protection from noxious insects is well worth carrying to Central Africa. It is much used by the Arabs and consequently can be bought readily at Zanzibar. Its fumes, thrown on hot embers, are not only very agreeable to one's sense of smell but drive away mosquitoes, midges and most other insects.

House-flies, except in some of the Arab towns and large European settlements or in places where much cattle are kept, are not nearly so severe a pest as in South Africa or the Mediterranean countries. Indeed, in cool places like Zomba the domestic fly does not give as much trouble as in many country houses in England.

And now we come to the tsetse, perhaps the most serious of all the many insect pests of Africa in its check to European enterprise. It is difficult to overestimate the importance of the part played by this noxious little insect in preventing the opening up of Central Africa.

This was first experienced by the earlier Portuguese Expeditions of five hundred or six hundred mounted men which would set out from Sena on the Lower Zambezi in the 16th and 17th centuries to secure the gold mines to the north and south. We read in Portuguese records how their horses soon succumbed to the attacks of a fly. The riders were left without steeds and the expeditions came to an abortive termination, many of the Europeans dying of fever or succumbing to the attacks of the natives through having to make their way on foot. But for the tsetse-fly the whole history of South-Central Africa would be different. It would have been rapidly traversed by mounted men, not nearly so much ill-health would have pursued explorers and pioneers forced to travel on foot, and the whole question of transport would be rendered infinitely more easy as coaches and waggons could run and huge numbers of pack animals—horses, mules and oxen—might convey goods which at present are carried on men's heads. Undoubtedly the tsetse-fly has checked the southward range of Muhammadan raiders from the north. But for the presence of this insect in the Congo Basin and in Equatorial East Africa, the Muhammadanised negroes and Arabs of the Sudan would have spread much farther south than they have done already on their sturdy little ponies.

The tsetse is a most insignificant fly in appearance. I give here drawings of it that I have done from specimens sent to the British Museum. I have purposely drawn these myself because the conscientious entomologist will persist in presenting to the public in illustrated natural history works and books of travel a tsetse-fly which the average traveller finds it quite impossible to recognise in Africa, about three times the size of the largest bluebottle and with wings spread at right angles to the body.[1]

When I first went to Tropical Africa I looked in vain for a gigantic bluebottle with vivid black and white striping, and a proboscis half an inch long: it was a long time before it occurred to me that a small brownish fly with a faintly barred brown and white abdomen (which again was generally concealed by the closely-folded wings) could be the tsetse, though I knew it was a fly capable of inflicting a disagreeable prick on my skin and not infrequently drawing from me a drop of blood. This, however, is the appearance of the true tsetse (*Glossina morsitans*), and the drawing which I give here very fairly represents its ordinary appearance with the wings closely folded over the back. The actual fly is a little smaller than the size represented in the drawing.

Fortunately the tsetse-fly is not present in all parts of British Central Africa. Roughly speaking, it may be said that it is absent from any district that is above 3000 feet in altitude and is not found in many of the low-lying lands for some hitherto unexplained reason, no doubt connected with human settlement. It is present throughout the whole valley of the great

---

[1] This figure is familiar to most persons in Livingstone's first book of travels. It has been repeated and repeated in succeeding books.

Luangwa River from the Zambezi to the verge of the Nyasa-Tanganyika plateau. It is found on part of the upper course of the River Luapula and on the shores of Lake Mweru, but is absent from the greater part of the country round Bangweolo. It is most abundant on the south coast of Tanganyika, disappearing, however, as soon as the slopes of the Nyasa-Tanganyika plateau are reached. On Lake Nyasa it is absent from almost the entirety of the east coast. On the west coast it is met with between Deep Bay on the north and the River Bua on the south, some patches in between, however, being free from it. From about Kotakota and the Marimba district it is absent. It re-appears again south of the Marimba in the northern part of the coast lands of the Central Angoniland district. From the south coast of Lake Nyasa it is almost entirely absent, but it is found again on a small portion of the Upper Shire.

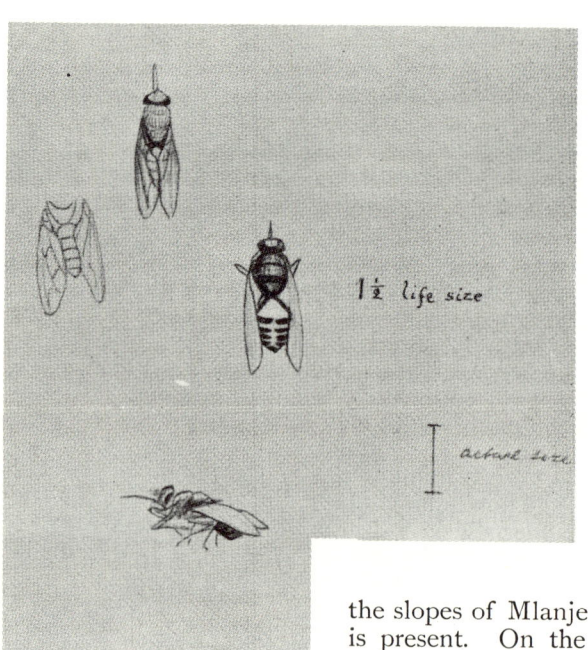

THE TSETSE FLY

In the low-lying country round Lake Chilwa up to the slopes of Mlanje and the hills near Zomba it is present. On the Central Shire at Chikwawa and Katunga there is no tsetse, but in the Elephant Marsh below it abounds, as also in much of the Ruo district and in the district of the Lower Shire. Always, however, when the land rises to 3000 feet and beyond the tsetse disappears. This insect has a great dislike to water and a still stronger dislike to a congeries of human habitations. In consequence it is possible to convey horses and cattle up the rivers without the least danger of their being bitten, as long as they remain on the boat anchored in mid-stream. They are also quite safe in the middle of any collection of huts or in any town. It is a fortunate thing that there is no tsetse at Katunga or Chikwawa on the Central Shire, as live-stock can be brought the whole way by water to this place from the mouth of the Zambezi,[1] landed there and sent up to Blantyre, and can thence be conveyed by various routes which are free from tsetse-fly to the Upper Shire and so on to Lake Nyasa. Another important fact to be borne in mind is that the tsetse-fly does not bite at night, therefore if a tsetse-haunted district must be crossed it should be done at night time—by moonlight if possible. It is said also that smearing the bodies of the animals with cow-dung will repel the insect. One bite of a tsetse-fly is not necessarily of much account, or even two ; it is where the animal is bitten three or more times that the issue is certainly fatal, though

---

[1] The tsetse is apparently absent from Chinde and Quelimane and much of the Zambezi Delta.

death is sometimes long deferred and may not occur till several weeks after the infection. The victim gradually falls off in condition, suffers from extreme depression and loss of appetite, and ultimately dies from apparent blood-poisoning.

Donkeys are far less subject to the poisonous character of its bite than horses or mules; indeed it is said that the domestic donkey of East Africa which is only one degree removed from the Abyssinian wild ass, is impervious to its attacks, and certainly none of those animals have died from tsetse bite in British Central Africa. Major Lugard, I believe, has found on his expedition to Lake Ngami, that his donkeys were the only animals which survived the attacks of the tsetse. Dogs are killed by it and even cats will not resist its attacks when too frequent. On the Mwanza river, an affluent of the Shire nearly opposite to Katunga, the tsetse are so numerous that the only domestic animals which can be kept by the natives are fowls. Its bite on man produces absolutely no effect beyond the pain of the sharp puncture. It is hardly necessary to point out that the wild game of Africa—the buffalo, the antelope and the zebra —are quite unaffected by the tsetse bite,[1] though their nearest congeners among domestic animals—the ox, goat and horse—are killed by this fly. So far as we can judge from specimens classified in the British Museum the range of the true tsetse (*Glossina morsitans*) extends from South Africa up to the Congo Basin, Lakes Mweru, Tanganyika and the borders of Somaliland. A closely allied species comes from the Congo Basin, the Niger Delta, and other parts of West Africa, a fly which, so far as we know, is equally poisonous. I am not sure that the actual tsetse is not found in the Niger Delta and in parts of the Congo Basin. Other species of *Glossina* inhabit other parts of Africa but do not appear to be poisonous. In the greater part of the Nigerian, the Central and the Egyptian Sudan the tsetse is absent, thus permitting a far more rapid and healthy development and conquest of these countries, as horses are abundant and can be employed to mount cavalry and transport travellers while for trade purposes mules and oxen can be employed; and an unlimited number of cattle might be reared.

The nature of the tsetse poison is not yet determined. It is not known that it injects any venom, it simply appears to insert the prong of the proboscis and suck the blood. Some have advanced the theory that there is no inherent poison in the tsetse itself, but that it inserts the germs of malaria. The argument sustained is that the wild animals of Africa have in the course of ages of adaptation become inured to malarial poisoning, but that they harbour in their blood the micro-organisms of malaria. These, passed on by the tsetse-fly, passing with infected proboscis from wild to tame animal, increase and multiply in the latter, which is not inoculated, and the beast dies not from a specific "tsetse" poison, but from malaria introduced into the blood by the tsetse. I confess, however, this theory, though ingenious, does not strike me as adequately accounting for all the facts. I cannot help thinking myself that the tsetse must secrete and introduce into the animal's system a peculiar venom which in the human being causes the bite to itch; but if so the poison would be of a similar nature to that of the flea, the gnat and the midge, all of which produce different effects on different people. In my own case the bites of fleas and still more of bed-bugs (especially in tropical countries) produce positively feverish symptoms whereas many other of my fellow-countrymen make little or nothing of these attacks.

[1] For simplicity of diction I speak of the tsetse "bite." It is of course a *puncture* of the proboscis.

Certainly the tsetse tends to disappear before the presence of man and the one certain cure for it would seem to be the placing of all the low-lying parts of British Central Africa under cultivation and the settlement of innumerable negroes. Fortunately the fly does not much trouble our political economy for the further reasons that so much of the country lies above its habitat. In those districts where it is healthy for Europeans to settle the altitude is already too great to permit of the existence of the tsetse-fly.

APPENDIX VII.

LIST OF ORTHOPTERA, HYMENOPTERA, AND HEMIPTERA

COLLECTED BY SIR HARRY JOHNSTON AND OTHER OFFICIALS OF THE B.C.A. ADMINISTRATION IN BRITISH CENTRAL AFRICA

By W. F. KIRBY, F.L.S., F.C.S.

ORTHOPTERA.

BLATTIDÆ.

Leucophlæa maderæ.
Gynopeltis cryptospila.
　　 „ 　*discoidalis.*

GRYLLIDÆ.

Curtilla africana.
Brachytrypes membranacea.
Acheta bimaculata.

PHASGONURIDÆ.

Libanasa fusca.
Clonia wahlbergi.
Engaliopsis petersii.
Pseudorhynchus pungens.
Mecopoda latipennis.
Tegra spilophora.
Arantia spinulosa.

LOCUSTIDÆ.

Acrida pharaonis.
　　 „ 　*pellucida.*

Mesops abbreviatus.
　　 „ 　*gracilis.*
Parga spatulata.
Xiphocera loboscelis.
　　 „ 　*haploscelis.*
　　 „ 　*atrox.*
Phymateus hildebrandti.
Petasia anchietæ.
Zonocerus sanguinolentus.
　　 „ 　*elegans.*
Taphronota porosa.
Cyrtacanthacris rubella.
　　 „ 　*ruficornis.*
Schistocerca peregrina.
　　 „ 　(?) *adusta.*
　　 „ 　(?) *genuale.*
Œdipoda flavum.
Chrotogonus hemipterus.
Phyllochoreia hippiscus.

HYMENOPTERA.

FORMICIDÆ.

Camponotus maculatus.
Hoplomyrmus gagates.
Dorylus diadema.
Paltothyreus pestilentius.
Carebara colossus.

MUTILLIDÆ.

Mutilla ignava.
　　 „ 　*astarte.*

SCOLIIDÆ.

Dielis sulcata.

BEMBICIDÆ.
Bembex undulata.

POMPILIDÆ.
Pompilus bracatus.

SPHEGIDÆ.
Pelopæus eckloni.
Pronæus maxillaris.
Sphex bohemani.

VESPIDÆ.
Polistes marginalis.

EUMENIDÆ.
Eumenes tinctor.
Rhynchium synagrioides.

APIDÆ.
Megachile rufiventris.
„   *terminata.*
Apis ligustica.
Xylocopa africana.
„   *nigrita.*
„   *flavorufa.*

HEMIPTERA.

SCUTELLERIDÆ.
Sphærocoris argus.
Libyssa duodecimpunctata.

PENTATOMIDÆ.
Atelocera foveata.
„   *viridesecens.*
Piezosternum mucronatum.
Aspongopus nubilis.
Pentatoma cincticollis.
Rhaphigaster viridulus.
Phyllocephala costalis.

COREIDÆ.
Mictis heteropus.
Petascelis remipes.

PYRRHOCORIDÆ.
Dysdercus fasciatus.

REDVVIIDÆ.
Petalochirus umbrosus.
„   *variegatus.*
Harpactor segmentarius.

NEPIDÆ.
Hydrocyrius columbiæ.
Laccotrephes ruber.

APPENDIX VIII.

LIST OF LEPIDOPTERA RECORDED FROM BRITISH CENTRAL AFRICA

NOTE.—This list is founded on the papers published by Dr. A. G. Butler, F.L.S., in the Proceedings of the Zoological Society for 1893 and 1895. The term *sp. nov.* indicates that the new species was first made known by our collections.

RHOPALOCERA (Butterflies).

Amauris ochlea.
Amauris lobengula.
Amauris whytei (sp. nov.).
Amauris dominicanus.
Limnas chrysippus.
Limnas klugii.
Limnas dorippus.
Tirumala petiverana.
Melanitis solandra.

Melanitis libya.
Gnophodes diversa.
Mycalesis (Monotrichtis) rhacotis.
Mycalesis (Monotrichtis) eusirus.
Mycalesis (Monotrichtis) miriam.
Mycalesis ena.
Samanta perspicua.
Physcœnura pione, and do var. *lucida,* n. var.

Neocœnyra ypthimoides (*sp. nov.*).
Ypthima itonia.
Ypthima granulosa.
Ypthima simplicia.
Charaxes saturnus.
    „   „ var. *laticinctus.*
Charaxes jocaste.
Charaxes guderiana.
Charaxes whytei (*sp. nov.*).
Charaxes bohemani.
Charaxes castor, var. *flavifasciatus.*
Charaxes achæmenes.
Charaxes phæus.
Charaxes pithodoris.
Charaxes cithæron.
Charaxes tiridates.
Charaxes neanthes.
Charaxes brutus.
Charaxes druceanus.
Charaxes pollux.
Charaxes candiope.
Charaxes ethalion.
Charaxes lasti.
Charaxes leoninus.
Charaxes violetta.
Charaxes eupale.
Charaxes varanes.
Hypolimnas misippus.
Hypolimnas alcippoides.
Hypolimnas inaria.
Euralia wahlbergi.
Euralia mima.
Panopea expansa.
Junonia artaxia.
Junonia nachtigalii.
Junonia tugela.
Junonia natalica.
Junonia chapunga.
Junonia ceryne.
Junonia galami.
Junonia aurorina (*sp. nov.*).
Junonia trimenii (*sp. nov.*).
Junonia calescens (*sp. nov.*).
Junonia elgiva.
Junonia cuama.
Junonia simia.
Junonia cloantha.

Junonia actia.
Junonia sesamus.
Junonia boöpis.
Junonia clelia.
Junonia cebrene.
Pyrameis cardui.
Protogoniomorpha definita.
Protogoniomorpha anacardii.
Cymothoe theobene.
Hamanumida dœdalus.
Neptis agatha.
Atella columbina.
Euphædra neophron.
Euphædra coralia.
Pseudargynnis hegemone.
Crenis natalensis.
Crenis crawshayi (*sp. nov.*).
Crenis boisduvalii.
Metacrenis rosa.
Metacrenis crawshayi.
Hamanumida dœdalus.
Catuna crithea.
Neptis agatha.
Atella columbina.
Byblia vulgaris.
Eurytela dryope.
Hypanis acheloia.
Acræa vinidia.
Acræa cabira.
Acræa excelsior.
Acræa ventura.
Acræa terpsichore.
Acræa perrupta.
Acræa lycia.
Acræa doubledayi.
Acræa empusa (*sp. nov.*).
Acræa periphanes.
Acræa caldarena.
Acræa acrita.
Acræa guillemei.
Acræa natalica.
Acræa serena var. *perrupta.*
Acræa arcticincta.
Acræa areca.
Acræa acara.
Acræa oncœa.
Acræa buxtoni.

Acræa sganzini.
Planema johnstoni.
Alæna nyassæ.
Alæna nyassæ, var. *ochracea.*
Alæna amazula.
Polyommatus bœticus.
Azanus occidentalis.
Tarucus plinius.
Nacaduba sichela.
Tingra amenaida.
Lachnocnema bibulus.
Hyreus lingeus.
Zizera knysna.
Zizera lucida.
Zizera gaika.
Lycænesthes bubastus.
Lycænesthes adherbal?
Lycænesthes liodes.
Catochrysops osiris.
Catochrysops asopus.
Castalius hypoleucus (sp. nov.).
Castalius calice.
Azanus natalensis.
Iolaus buxtoni.
Iolaus cœculus.
Myrina ficedula.
Tarucus pulcher.
Tatura philippus.
Tatura cœculus.
Virachola anta.
Spindasis nyassæ.
Spindasis homeyeri.
Axiocerses amanga.
Axiocerses harpax.
Axiocerses perion.
Mylothris agathina.
Mylothris rüppelli.
Mylothris yulei.
Nychitona aucesta.
Colias edusa.
Terias zoe.
Terias leonis.
Terias regularis.
Terias orientis.
Teracolus rhodesinus (sp. nov.).
Teracolus phlegyas.
Teracolus anax.
Teracolus opalescens.
Teracolus hildebrandtii.
Teracolus subfasciatus.
Teracolus sipylus.
Teracolus emini.
Teracolus theogone.
Teracolus subvenosus.
Teracolus omphale.
Catopsilia florella.
Catopsilia pyrene.
Belenois severina.
Belenois agrippina.
Belenois gidica.
Belenois crawshayi (sp. nov.)
Belenois thysa.
Belenois calypso.
Belenois mesentina.
Belenois diminuta (sp. nov.).
Phrissura nyassana.
Herpœnia eriphia.
Glutophrissa saba.
Nepheronia thalassina.
Eronia leda.
Eronia cleodora.
Papilio lurlinus.
Papilio policenes.
Papilio porthaon.
Papilio pylades.
Papilio similis.
Papilio leonidas.
Papilio corinneus.
Papilio nivinox (sp. nov.).
Papilio demoleus.
Papilio ophidicephalus.
Papilio constantinus.
Papilio merope.
Papilio erinus.

HESPERIDÆ (Skippers).

Tagiades flesus.
Proteides erinnys.
Sarangesa motozi.
Sarangesa motozoides?
Sarangesa astrigera (sp. nov.).
Nephile funebris.

Caprona pillaana.
Caprona jamesoni.
Hesperia dromus.
Acleros philander.
Acleros placidus.
Oxypalpus ruso.
Osmodes ranoha.
Heteropterus formosus (sp. nov.).
Cyclopides quadrisignatus (sp. nov.).
Cyclopides midas (sp. nov.).
Cyclopides willemi.

Padraona watsoni (sp. nov.).
Gegenes letterstedti.
Baoris fatuellus.
Baoris inconspicua.
Baoris amadhu?
Halpe nigerrima (sp. nov.).
Halpe lugens.
Baracus fenestratus (sp. nov.).
Ceratrichia stellata.
Acromachus? johnstoni (sp. nov.).

HETEROCERA (Moths).

Cephonodes hylas.
Ællopus hirundo.
Chærocampa osiris.
Daphnis nerii.
Nephele accentifera.
Nephele funebris.
Ægocera menete.
Ægocera fervida.
Charilina amabilis.
Xanthospilopteryx superba.
Antiphella atrinotata.
Syntomis ceres.
Diospage scintillans (sp. nov.).
Neurosymploca procrioides (sp. nov.).
Anomœotes nigrivenosus (sp. nov.).
Staphylinochrous whytei (sp. nov.).
Pleretes thelwalli.
Lepista trimenii.
Deiopeia pulchella.
Argina leonina.
Argina amanda.
Egybolia paillantina.
Hibrildes norax.
Rhanidophora phedonia.
Canopus rubripes.
Lacipa bizonoides (sp. nov.).
Artaxa ochraceata.
Olapa fulvinotata (sp. nov.)
Aroa discalis.
Leptosoma leuconoe.
Antheua simplex.
Phiala costipuncta?
Pseudaphelia apollinaris.

Bunœa epithyrena.
Gynanisa maia.
Ædia dulcistriga.
Polydesma umbricola.
Calliodes rivuligera (sp. nov.).
Calliodes glaucescens (sp. nov.).
Phægorista zebra.
Acontia graellsii.
Patula walkeri.
Cyligramma rudilinea.
Cyligramma latona.
Cyligramma limacina.
Maxula capensis.
Entomogramma pardus.
Entomogramma nigriceps.
Dysgonia algira.
Dysgonia derogans.
Grammodes geometrica.
Fodina johnstoni.
Trigonodes hyppasia.
Drasteria judicans.
Plecoptera (sp. inc.).
Azazia rubricans.
Remigia mutuaria.
Remigia archesia.
Remigia repanda.
Lacera capella.
Ophiodes croceipennis.
Deva commoda.
Plusia eriosoma.
Hypena abyssinialis.
Glyphodes sinuata.
Gonodela brongusaria.

Gonodela kilimanjarensis.
Gonodela zombina (sp. nov.).
Tephrina johnstoni (sp. nov.).
Stemorrhages sericea.

Haritalodes multilinealis.
Lygropia muscerdalis.
Cadorena sinuata.

APPENDIX IX

LIST OF COLEOPTERA RECORDED FROM BRITISH CENTRAL AFRICA

NOTE.—This list is founded on the paper published by Mr. C. J. Gahan, M.A., in the Zoological Society's Proceedings for 1893.

Cicindela clathrata.

Anthia fornasini.
Graphipterus salinæ.
Scarites superciliosus.
Tefflus violaceus.
Tefflus delegorguei.
Cyclosomus (sp. inc.).
Rhathymus melanarius.

Staphylinus procerus (sp. nov.)

Orectochilus bicostatus.

Trox melancholicus.
Anachalcos convexus.
Catharsius platycerus.
Heliocopris japetus.
Onthophagus bicallosus.
Lepidiota lepidota.
Adoretus (sp. inc.).
Cyphonistes vallatus.
Trochalus (sp. inc.).
Anomala (sp. inc.).
Popillia serena.
Popillia distinguenda.
Goliathus kirkianus.
Ranzania petersiana.
Neptunides polychrous.
Ceratorhina princeps.
Heterorhina elongata.
Genyodonta quadricornis.
Cetonia impressa.

Rhabdotis aulica.
Diplognatha hebræa.
Diplognatha silicea.
Pseudoclinteria infuscata.
Oxythyrea vitticollis.

Sternocera funebris.
Psiloptera proxima.
Psiloptera amicta.
Psiloptera (sp. inc.).
Psiloptera (sp. inc.).
Agrilus grandis.

Lycus (sp. inc.).

Trachynotus sordidus.
Anchophthalmus silphoides.
Catamerus rugosus (sp. nov.)
Zophosis agaboides.
Rhytidonota gracilis.
Psammodes dimidiatus.

Mylabris dicincta.
Mylabris bihumerosa.
Mylabris tristigma.
Epicauta nyassensis.
Epicauta cœlestina.
Coryna apicipustulata.
Lixus (sp. inc.).
Sphadasmus camelus.
Attelabus (Pleurolabus), (sp. inc.).
Blosyrus carinatus.

Mecaspis whytei (sp. nov.).
Philematium nitidipenne.
Anubis frontalis (sp. nov.).
Lophoptera asperula.
Tragocephala variegate.
Ceroplesis caffer.
Cymatura bifasciata, var. nigripennis.
Nitocris similis (sp. nov.).
Phrissoma giganteum.
Phryneta spinator.
Apomecyna latefasciata.

Sagra johnstoni (sp. nov.).
Corynodes dejeani.
Corynodes zombæ (sp. nov.).
Colasposoma cyaneocupreum.

Colasposoma (sp. inc.).
Ceralces ferrugineus.
Ceralces natalensis.
Ceralces ornata.
Atechna clarki.
Oides collaris.
Diacantha distincta (sp. nov.).
Diacantha conifera.
Ootheca (sp. inc.).
Pachytoma gigantea.
Cassida hybrida.
Cassida parummaculata.
Cydonia lunata.
Epilachna paykulli.
Epilachna hirta.
Epilachna dregei.

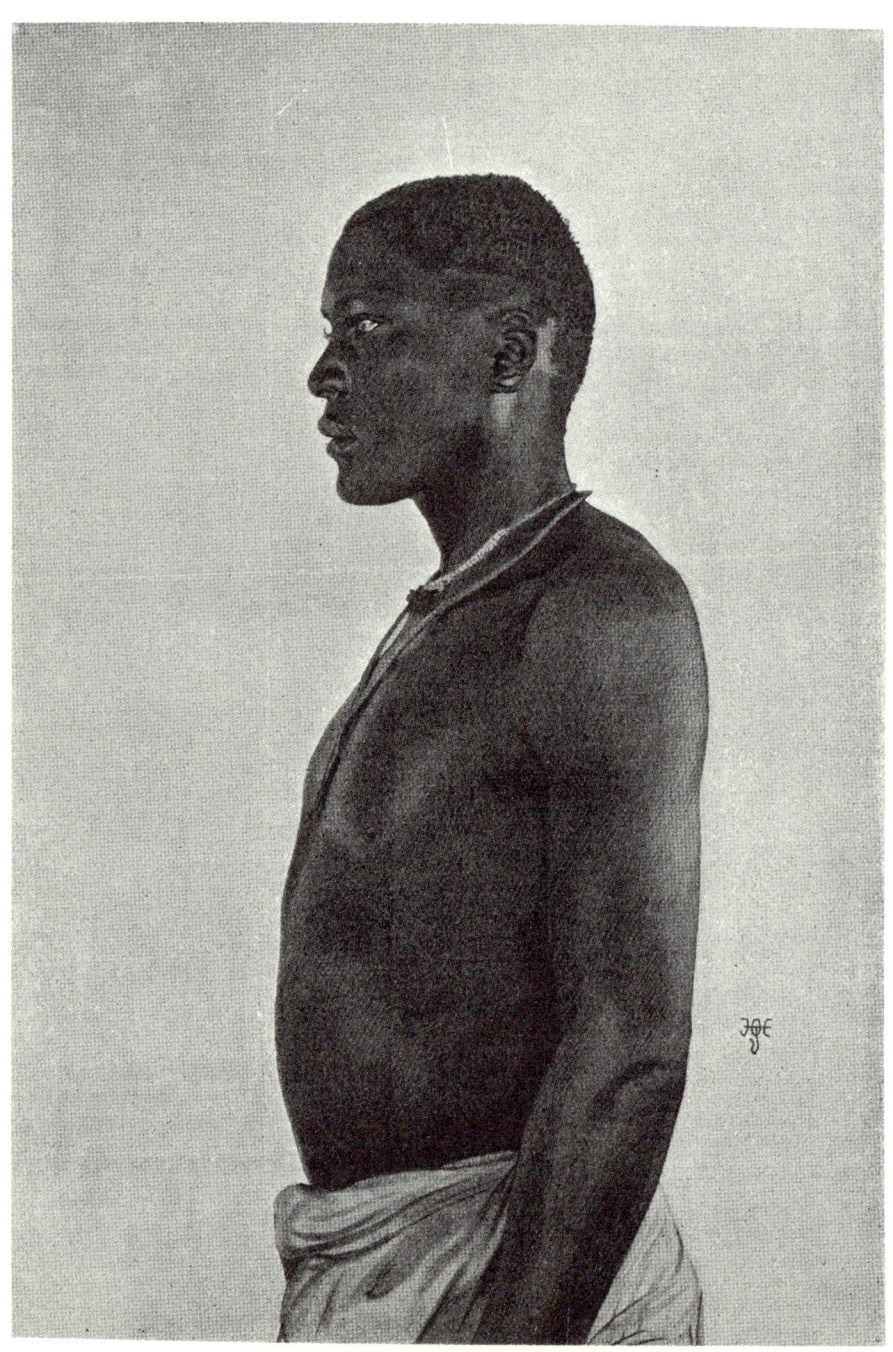

AN ANGONI MAN FROM THE WEST NYASA DISTRICT

CHAPTER X.

THE NATIVES OF BRITISH CENTRAL AFRICA

A GENERAL DESCRIPTION OF THE INDIGENOUS HUMAN RACES CONSIDERED ANTHROPOLOGICALLY AND ETHNOLOGICALLY

AS already stated in my review of the History of British Central Africa, the Native Races of this part of Africa belong at the present day to the Bantu Negro stock—entirely so, linguistically, and mainly so physically, though in certain tribes there are traces of a former Bushman-Hottentot intermixture.

Considered from the point of view of language-relationships, customs and traditions, the Bantu negroes of the Eastern half of British Central Africa fall naturally into ten groups, which, commencing in the north-west and proceeding southwards and eastwards, may be enumerated as follows :—

1. The Awemba[1] stock,—to which apparently belong also the Awa-wisa or Aba-bisa,[2] Ba-bozwa, Ba-usi[3] and the Ba-lunga. The Awemba and kindred peoples inhabit the western portion of the Nyasa-Tanganyika plateau, the district lying between Tanganyika and Mweru, and the country round Bangweolo, and to the east of the River Luapula, with the exception of an enclave round the south end of Lake Mweru and east of the Luapula, which is inhabited (at any rate as a dominant race) by the

2. A-lunda. The Alunda are related to the A-rua, farther to the north, and belong to a very important and widespread branch of the Bantu people in the heart of South Central Africa. The Alunda or A-rua race once formed a huge kingdom in the southern part of the Congo Basin—a kingdom which extended from the vicinity of Angola on the west to Lakes Tanganyika and Mweru on the east, but which gradually split up into independent satrapies which became in time kingdoms by themselves.

3. The A-lungu.[4] This group which like the A-lunda is specially notable for having reduced the plural prefix from *aba-* to *a-*, occupies the southern and south-eastern shores of Tanganyika, and a portion of the Nyasa-Tanganyika plateau.

---

[1] In Itawa these people call themselves Aba-emba, and are sometimes spoken of as the Ba-bemba.
[2] In these parts the *b* is already melting into *w* at the beginning of words.
[3] Or We-usi.
[4] Sometimes called the Arungu-Amambwe stock, which again are related to the A-fipa on German territory.

4. The Awa-nkonde[1] stock. This includes amongst other tribes the Awa-wandia, the Awa-nyakiusa, the Awa-ndali, the Awa-kukwe, the Awa-rambia, the Awa-wiwa, the Awa-nyamwanga, and the Awa-wanda and the Awungu[2] (the two last on German territory). The languages of the Awa-nkonde stock are generally remarkable for their archaic character in preserving many old Bantu roots and grammatical forms. Their full form of the plural prefix of the second class (referring to human beings) is almost always *Awa-*, the only races, with the exception of the Awemba, in which this form is met with. They inhabit the northern and north-west coasts of Lake Nyasa and much of the Nyasa-Tanganyika plateau, and extend north-westwards to the shores of Lake Rukwa.

5. The Ba-tumbuka stock. This includes the Wa-tonga, the A-timbuka or Ba-tumbuka, and to some extent the Wa-henga, A-nyika, and A-poka, though these two latter groups are of somewhat obscure affinities. The Wa-henga may possibly be a mongrel race, formed by the mingling of refugees from many tribes. It is possible that this linguistic group may extend to the Upper Luangwa River.

6. The Nyanja stock. This is the largest and most important of all and includes the following tribes :—The A-senga[3] of the north bank of the Zambezi and the river Luangwa; the A-maravi; the A-chipeta; the A-makanga; the Va-dema; the Va-nyungwi of Tete; the A-mañanja,[4] of the Lower Zambezi, the Lower Shire, the Western Shire, the Shire Highlands, the Mlanje district and the Upper Shire; the Ambo, south of the River Ruo; the Ma-chinjiri of the eastern bank of the Lower Shire ;[5] the A-nyanja of Lake Chilwa, of the south coast of Lake Nyasa and of the eastern coast of that lake about as far north as the Portugo-German frontier; and finally the A-chewa of the west coast of Lake Nyasa.[6]

7. The Ba-tonga or Ba-toka stock, which includes amongst other sections the Ba-ramba

A MNYANJA

---

[1] The word "Nkonde" means "banana" in some of the adjacent languages, and was no doubt applied with aptness to the North Nyasa district which is singularly rich in banana groves.

[2] Originally Awa-ungu. [3] Sometimes called Ba-senga : their language is closely related to Ki-bisa.

[4] This is a case of a double plural. The root -*ñanja* is the same as -*nyanja* (meaning a lake, a sea, a big water). *Ma-* which is often used as a tribal prefix would mean, "the people of the lake," but in course of time it became so united to the root -*ñanja* that it is now preceded by an additional plural prefix, *a-* (*aba-*).

[5] This branch of the Nyanja stock reaches to the vicinity of the Quelimane district where it touches the Makua races.

[6] These people are sometimes called the A-nkomanga.

and Ba-lala, and which occupies the country on the banks of the River Kafue and between the Luapula and the Luangwa, and to which are related the Ba-nyai and Ba-toka on the south bank of the Central Zambezi.

8. Along the course of the Zambezi from Zumbo to its mouth are a people, more or less attached to the Portuguese, of very mixed origin, the A-chikunda, who speak a mongrel dialect chiefly based on the Nyanja stock. The A-chikunda have no homogeneity but are compounded of the old slaves of the Portuguese brought from many different parts of Eastern and Central Africa, who are more or less loyal subjects of the Portuguese and who have developed this *lingua franca*, the Chikunda, into which a large number of the Portuguese words are introduced.

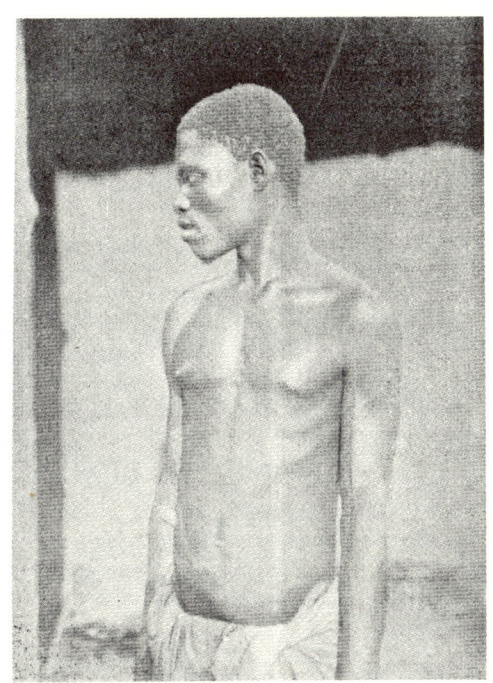

A YAO MAN

9. The A-lolo and Makua group. This section only enters into a very small portion of the territory of the British Protectorate in the Mlanje district. Elsewhere it extends right across to the east coast of Africa in the province of Moçambique and along the Moçambique coast southwards to Quelimane, where a kindred language is spoken: and lastly,

10. The Yao peoples, the "Wa-yao."[1] The Yao are not present in British Central Africa as indigenous inhabitants but rather as invaders whose coming was not earlier than the middle of this century. At the present time they are settled in more or less numerous proportion among the indigenous Anyanja in the east part of the Shire province, on the south-east coast of Lake Nyasa and at one or two places on the south-west shores of the lake. Elsewhere they extend as a native people along the banks of the Lujenda and Ruvuma rivers, and also inhabit the high plateaux between those streams, and march with the Makua on the south-east and the Magwangwara[2] on the north-west.

In addition to the foregoing list of tribes which are really native to British Central Africa, may be cited the Angoni and the Makololo, who are in reality not races but simply a ruling caste dwelling in the midst of British Central African tribes whom their ancestors subdued. The Angoni, and the Magwangwara on the north-east of Nyasa, are relics of former Zulu invasions of the

---

[1] The Yao pronunciation of their tribal name is usually Wa-hiau with a distinct aspirate, which is the more remarkable as in all other words of the language the aspirate "h" is unknown, and where "h" has to be pronounced in a foreign word "s" is substituted. "Yao" however is evidently a modern contraction of Yawa or "hiawa." By the A-nyanja people they are known as A-jawa.

[2] A tribe of Zulu mongrels.

country.[1] The Makololo, as already related, were brought by Livingstone and were mostly Bechuana and Baloi people from the Upper Zambezi. In their case they are scarcely even a ruling caste, having simply furnished some twenty headmen and chiefs to the Mañanja people who dwell on the Central and Lower Shire; but inasmuch as their tribal name of Makololo has been adopted by most of their subjects, and has become famous by the resistance offered in days gone by to the Portuguese, it is better not to leave them out of this catalogue.

In the northern part of the British Central Africa Protectorate there are a few Wa-nyamwezi hunters and adventurers who are mostly in the employ of Arabs, or free lances on their own account. These men sometimes go by the nickname of "Ruga-ruga." A few mongrel Arabs and Swahili Coastmen may still be seen no doubt in the Marimba district of the Protectorate, at the north end of Lake Nyasa, and in the Yao country; but there are numerous Arab settlements south of Tanganyika and near Lake Mweru. Here the Arabs are of a better class, and having managed to keep on good terms with the Europeans they remain there undisturbed. Arabs are also said to have formed trading stations to the west of Lake Bangweolo. Where the Arab is not of African birth (a man of Zanzibar for instance) he is usually a native of Maskat, in South Eastern Arabia.

The following information in regard to the Anthropology[2] and Ethnology of the negroes of British Central Africa may be taken to have a general application to the natives of the eastern portion of this territory, except where any particular tribe is instanced, and where special features, manners and customs are noted in relation to one tribe which may not be shared by another.

ANTHROPOLOGY

All black negroes possess a certain uniformity of type apparent to the European: that is to say, all the negroes inhabiting the coast regions of Western Africa, the basins of the Lower Niger and the Benue, the shores of Lake Chad, the basins of the Shari River and the Congo, of the Upper Nile and the Great Lakes, the East Coast, the Zambezi, and South West and South East Africa. The Nubians, Fulas, Hausas (perhaps) and the Mandingos may be excepted

[1] This is the history of the Angoni (Zulu) invasions of British Central Africa according to various authorities, especially Dr. W. A. Elmslie of the Livingstonia Mission, Upper Nyasa, who has worked for many years among these people: A tribe of Zulus originally conquered by Chaka at the beginning of this century assumed the name of Ngoni (Aba-ngoni). They were only partially conquered however, and retained their old chief under Chaka's suzerainty. But becoming dissatisfied with the central tyranny of the Zulu monarchy they started off in a body with women, children, and cattle for the north. They crossed the Zambezi at Zumbo, marched up between Nyasa and Bangweolo, and entered the Fipa country (which they conquered) south-east of Lake Tanganyika. From Fipa (where they settled for a long time) some stragglers under the name of Watuta reached as far north as the Victoria Nyanza; others struck to the south-east and by dominating the indigenous people of Hehe and Ngindo stock east of Lake Nyasa founded the tribe of mongrel raiders known as the Magwangwara. Then came a disruption of the Zulu kingdom in Fipa. The Ngoni-Zulus quitted that country and turned back to the West Nyasa countries. One section under Mombera settled in the Tumbuka country; another under Mpezeni in the lands between the Nyasa watershed and the River Luangwa; and a third established the small Zulu kingdom in Central Angoniland which is now ruled by Chiwere. Where Chikusi's Angoni came from is not very clear: perhaps they branched off to South-west Nyasa at the time of the original crossing of the Zambezi, which took place in June, 1825 (the date is marked by an eclipse of the sun). Angoni is the Chi-nyanja form of their name in the plural and has become the customary term; but Ngoni or Abangoni is more correct.

[2] Anthropology is the science descriptive of the physical characteristics of man; Ethnology the consideration of his mind and the result of his mental processes, that is to say his arts, his customs, his beliefs. The first treats of man purely as one amongst many mammalian types; the other deals with him in his progress towards the demi-god.

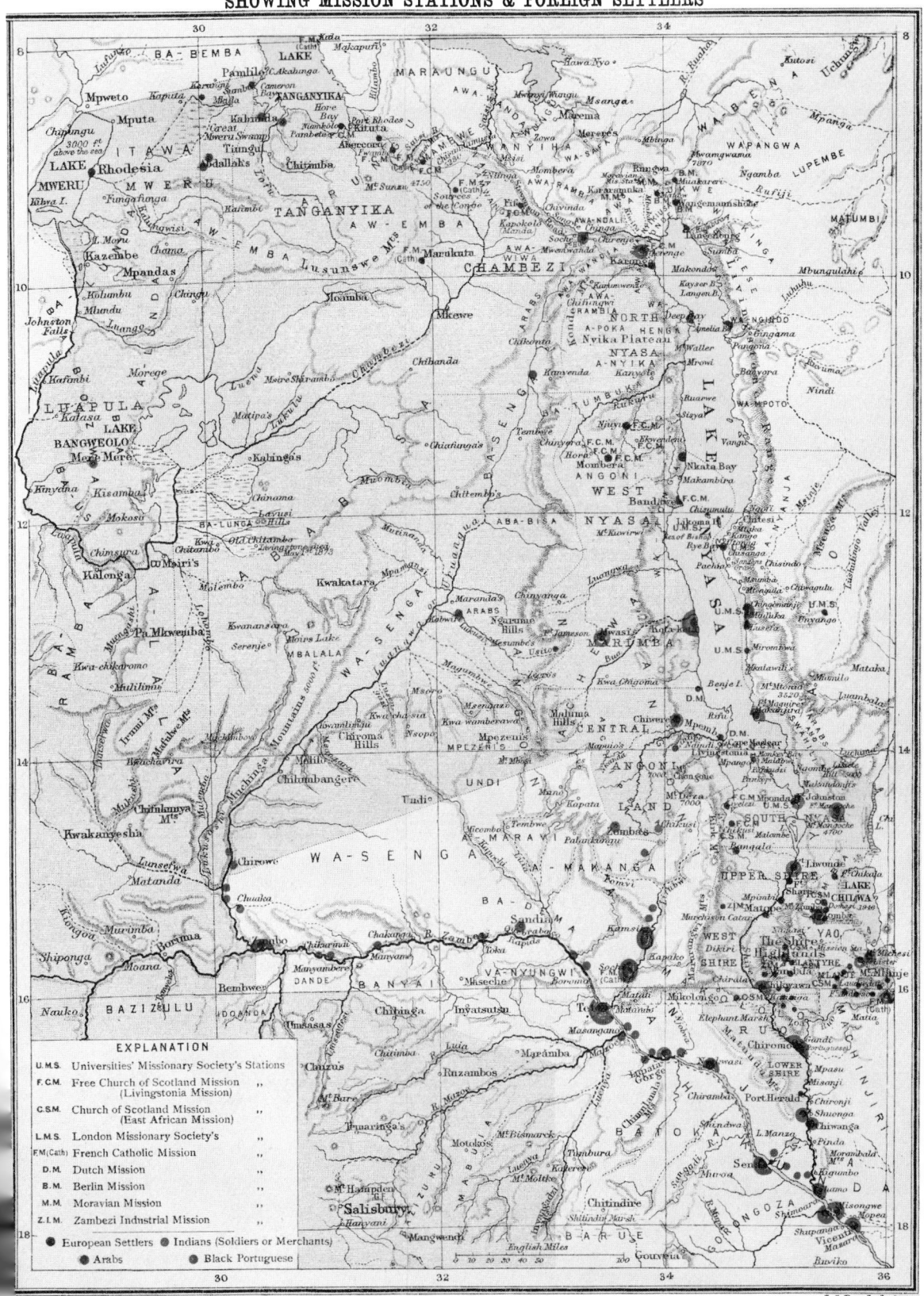

from this sweeping statement as showing an unmistakable mingling with a lighter race and being more Negroid than negro.[1] Nevertheless, within this wide domain of the black negro there is a remarkable general similarity of type; though it is usually possible for the practised eye to distinguish one tribe from another by the physiognomy. Yet if you took a negro from the Gold Coast of West Africa and passed him off amongst a number of Nyasa natives, and if he were not remarkably distinguished from them by dress or tribal marks, it would not be easy to pick him out; but though there is often an indefinable resemblance between the individuals of one tribe which distinguishes them from the average individual of another tribe, still there are so many exceptions to this uniformity of type that the negro from a widely-removed part of Africa might pass muster in almost any people in the British Central Africa Protectorate as merely a slightly aberrant local type. The average individual of one tribe is taller or shorter than another, but all races of black negroes can exhibit very tall individuals and very short ones belonging to the same racial type. In the colour of the skin there is a considerable amount of variation. Here again there are extremes met with in the individual members of a tribe, as well

AN ARAB OF TANGANYIKA (RUMALIZA)

as a general tendency to be detected in one tribe or another towards greater average darkness or lightness of skin. As a rule the negro of British Central Africa is decidedly black, so far as any human skin is really black — the nearest approach to actual black being a deep, dull, slatey-brown. I should say that the average skin tint is represented by No. 3 in Topinard's specimens of the colours of skins,—that is to say it is a dark chocolate. But cases of a yellowish brown are not at all uncommon in individuals. This tint would be represented by No. 4 in Topinard's scale, except that it has a little more of the raw sienna colour than is given in Topinard's example. The negroes of the western parts of the regions under review, in Itawa, on

---

[1] The Galla and Somali are of course emphatically Negroid, and are not included in this statement at all. They are simply darker types of the Hamitic branch midway in type between Semite and the Negro.

the south end of Tanganyika and along the Luapula, might appear to the unobservant traveller a very red brown in tint; but this would be owing to their habit of colouring themselves (like the people of the Congo basin) with powdered redwood or camwood mixed with oil, or red-ochre mixed with fat. Occasionally there are cases of positive "Xanthism," or a state of coloration similar in a much less degree to Albinism—namely that wherein the colour of the skin and the iris of the eye is quite a light yellowish brown. This type is very much admired by the negroes, especially in a woman; for their general tendency is to admire the lighter-coloured skin rather than the darker. The wives of chiefs have often been pointed out to me for special notice who have skins and eyes of this rather disagreeable pale yellow brown. Perhaps it is the iris of the eye being of this light yellow colour like that of a lion's eye, which is so disagreeable. Fine dark eyes with a pale golden skin would certainly appeal to the European's sense of beauty.

Cases of Albinism, where the hair is yellowish white, the iris of the eye pink, and the body-skin an unwholesome-looking reddish white, are not uncommon, though perhaps not quite so common as they are on the West Coast of Africa

I do not think that any of the tribes in British Central Africa can show a difference of colour between the rulers or the ruling caste and the mass of the people. Some of the chiefs are blacker than the majority, others again are relatively light coloured. In regard to average depth of tint amongst the various tribes, I should say that those with the blackest skins[1] were the A-lolo, the Atonga, the Awa-nkonde, the A-mambwe, the A-lungu, perhaps the Aba-bisa and the A-senga. I have seen slaves from the Upper Luapula River, and from the still more distant Lualaba, who were so very black as almost to approximate in tint to the deepest shade given by Topinard, No. 2 (which shade however I believe to be impossibly black and not actually to be found on the skin of any human being existing). Some of the Senga and Ba-tumbuka slaves amongst the northern Angoni are very black in colour.

The lightest-tinted tribe is probably the Yao. A good many of the A-nyanja are light tinted, but it is a dirty yellow, which suggests ancient Bushman-Hottentot intermixture, and is often associated with a low type of face and a squat body. Occasionally a light-coloured Angoni is seen, which is no doubt due to his being of a more or less Zulu origin.

As in all other negroes and dark-skinned races, the skin of the inner part of the hands and the sole of the foot is a pinkish-yellow.[2] The skin of the arm-pits is often much lighter in colour than the rest of the body. Negro children are invariably born with skins of a pinkish yellow, similar in colour to that on the hands and feet of the adult. The colour of their skin darkens rapidly, though in some infants more rapidly than in others. Negroes who are clothed from their youth up, and lead a life which does not much expose the naked body to the air, would appear to have skins slightly paler in tone than those of the average naked negroes.

The texture of the skin is usually coarse and rough unless kept in good condition by constant washing and oiling. Its natural oily secretion does not seem to be abundant, to judge by the dry scaly appearance of the skins of men who from one cause or another have been unable to have recourse to

---

[1] Each tribe however constantly offering individual exceptions with specially light colour.
[2] Apud viros incircumcisos, glans penis colore carnoso est; sed glans circumcisa, ubi exponitur, nigrescit.

rubbing themselves with oil or fat. At the same time they perspire easily and freely, and the pores are certainly larger than in Europeans. The most offensive negro smell would appear to be connected with the glands under the arm-pits, which exude at times a secretion often confounded with sweat, but which would appear to me to be of a different character and more oily

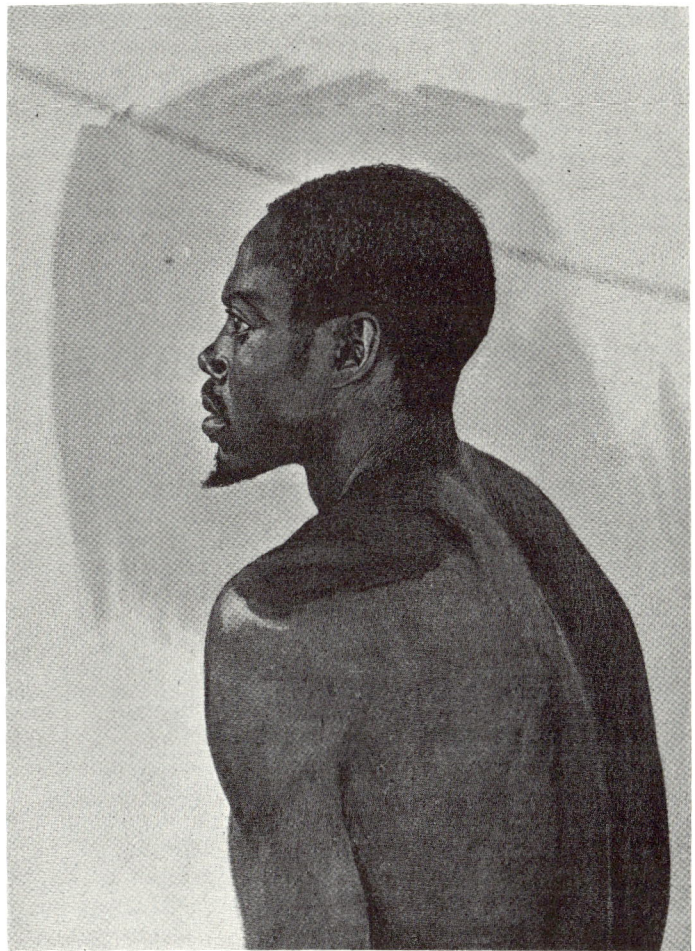

A MTONGA MAN (to show profile)

in composition. I cannot assert that this exudation is specially connected with the sexual functions, or with any particular state of mind or body. Perhaps when the negro is perspiring heavily, he is more odorous than at other times. Yet this trait varies a good deal in individuals, and on the whole (though not altogether) is more or less prominent according to the degree of cleanliness observed by frequent baths. In the clothed negro it is sometimes offensive to an appalling degree, rendering it well nigh impossible to remain in a closed room with him. The odour is certainly stronger in men than in women.

Except in cases of Xanthism the colour of the iris of the eye is black, brown, or very dark hazel. In some individuals the sclerotic, or "white" of the eye, is yellow and clouded; in others again it is very clear and white. The clear sclerotic generally accompanies the more refined type of feature, and the obverse is the case when the "white" is yellow and murky. The eyes are rather deeply set than otherwise. I have not seen any case in which they were prominent or *à fleur de tête*. Both the upper and under eyelids are occasionally thick and prominent, especially in the dull, heavy countenances of slaves, but in smart well-set-up men and women the upper eyelid is often covered by the protuberance of the skin in such a way as gives a clear-cut, sharp, decided look to a face. I will not say I have never seen the eyes with an upward turn on the outer side suggestive of an almond shaped and a Mongoloid look; but such cases are very exceptional and rare —much more so than they are in the Congo region, where I have occasionally noticed negroes with a distinctly Mongoloid cast of countenance. The cheek bones are usually prominent—in some cases they are very prominent, though naturally in a good-looking face their development is less marked. The nose is almost always a negro nose—that is to say with a broad depressed bridge (depressed in the malar region), a snub tip, and broad, expanded nostrils. The average, not by any means the ugliest, type in it may be observed in my accompanying drawing of the head of an Atonga seen in profile. In some of the people of Itawa I have noticed noses with rather arched bridges, somewhat Papuan in type, the arch being rather over the tip than at the beginning of the bridge.

There is never any prominence of the brows equal to what is seen in the Australian man. Still on the whole the brow is fairly prominent. Yet many of the women and some of the men exhibit that peculiar *bombé* forehead with brows depressed over the nose which is rather well illustrated in the portrait of a young Bushman given on p. 53 of Chapter III. The lips are usually everted and very large. In some of the finer types there is, of course, considerable modification in this feature, though the thin lip seen in the European or the Asiatic is never found amongst them. Some of the lips are so much everted that a considerable amount of pink skin shows. In the cases where the mouth is of a finer design and the lip is thinner nothing but the black skin of the outer part of the lip is visible.[1] The teeth are uniformly excellent—rather large-sized, white, and regular. I have never noticed any marked projection or exceptional size of the canines, not even as much as I have often seen in Europeans; certainly not such as can be seen in the remarkable Tasmanian skull at the Anthropological Institute,[2] where the canines, especially of the upper jaw, are prominent, projecting, and slightly pointed.

[1] The thick everted lip of the negro is not, in my opinion, a Simian characteristic. The most ape-like faces in existing humanity are seen amongst the Chinese and Annamites. In these the upper lip is long, broad and rather turned in. The long ape-like upper lip is not infrequently seen amongst Europeans, in certain Celtic types. I imagine that when the negro type began to diverge from the original human ancestor he retained his long Simian lips, and he got into the habit of turning them inside out in order to expose the teeth more readily, and to accommodate the inconveniently long lip to the decreasing size of the jaws and the diminishing prognathism.

[2] Happy Tasmania, to have possessed the most ape-like form of man! Unhappy Tasmania, to have been so ignorant as not to appreciate your privilege, and to have exterminated in your wanton ignorance this priceless survival!

The chin is rather retreating in the women, but occasionally the men will have fine strong chins, though strong and prominent in a peculiar way by a sharp bulge immediately under the lower lip, a bulge which is clearly scooped out in a circular form on either side. As a rule there is a decided falling in of the jaw under the cheek bones while the jaw-bone again bulges out at its angle near the ear. I have never seen a continuously firm line of jaw, and another sign equally rare or non-existent is the cleft chin which is often seen in Europeans. The most prominent points of a negro's face, even of a good type, are the projecting cheek bones, the bulging forehead, the broad flat nose, deep and expanded nostrils, the everted lips, and the sharp, rounded, narrow chin.

Almost all the male negroes of British Central Africa grow some moustache. It is ordinarily of scattered, thick, bristly hair, but sometimes the moustache hairs at the side are rather tightly curled. The beard is generally present but often reduced to a long tuft on the chin. In some cases, however, it crosses from ear to ear (often diminishing or falling off in the depressed portion of the jaw-bone on either side of the chin), and a narrow line of whiskers (little curled hairs) is also present in exceptionally hairy men. The question of face hair is largely one of cultivation, or no cultivation. Some of the men discourage hair on their faces and pluck out the hairs with a tweezer, others allow them to grow unchecked, and never shave, with the result that the face hair is often scattered and weak in growth. The negro men of Central Africa, as of other parts of the continent, who attempt to live like Europeans and begin by shaving their faces regularly (instead of plucking out the hairs as the savages do), can in course of time grow beard, whiskers and moustache not very much less in volume than those of the average European.

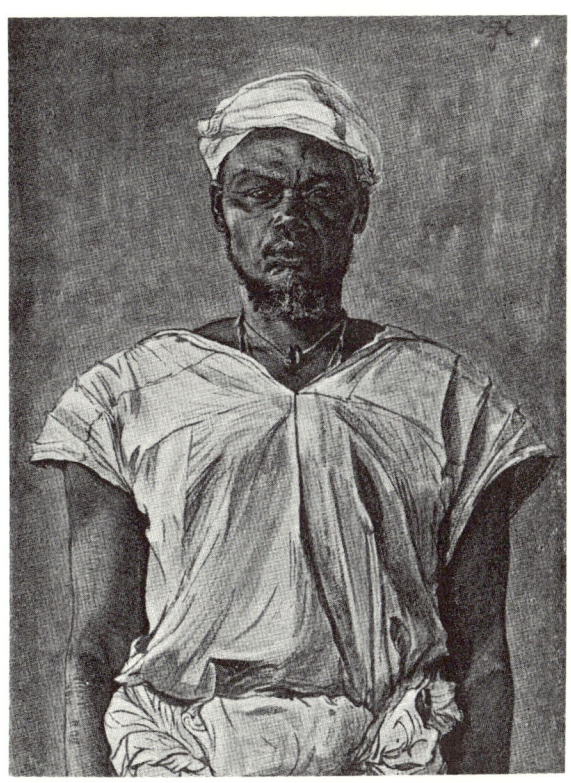

A YAO OF THE UPPER SHIRE

In some of the Yao a beard of considerable length grows from the chin, but this would seem to hint occasionally at some distant intermixture with the Arab. On the other hand, the Atonga, who betray in their history and racial type no trace of intermixture with a foreign race, or with the coastmen, often possess long, pointed beards. The hair of the beard has less tendency to curl than that of the head or body

The colour of the hair on the head and face is invariably black in adults, though in extreme childhood the hair of head and body is distinctly brownish, even to being a light brown. In the children at birth and for a little time after birth the hair on the head and body is nearly straight. The body-hair in children is a faintly discernible pale-coloured fluff, apparently a vestige of the body-hair which at one period of development, antecedent to expulsion from the womb, clothes the human fœtus in all races. It seldom lasts on the negro child for many weeks after birth.

On the adult man body-hair is almost always present when not plucked out. Amongst many of these negroes there is a dislike to any hair on the body. That on the chest, arms and legs is plucked out, and the hair of the arm-pits and pubes is shaved, or also plucked out. But in many tribes and individuals no check is put on the growth of the body-hair. It is then most abundant round the nipples and right across the chest, and down the median line of the stomach. There is considerable growth of hair on the pubes,[1] and in the arm-pits, on the shins of the legs and, in a lesser degree, on the forearms. I do not ever remember to have seen hair growing on a negro's back, as may often be observed on the backs of Europeans and sometimes of the hairier races of Asiatics. The negro's body-hair is usually curled semi-circular in growth, but not as tightly curled as the hair on the head. Among these negroes of Central Africa, as among almost all the true black negroes, the hair grows evenly over the scalp and not in sparse separate tufts as in the Bushman-Hottentots. This style of growth, which the French call *floconné*, is well illustrated in the photograph of a Bushman boy given on p. 53 of this book.

The ear is ordinarily small, rounded, well shaped, and set far back, close to the head, but its original shape is often much modified by the various fashions which are in vogue for the lengthening of the ear-lobe. In some portions of British Central Africa, notably among the Angoni-Zulus, the A-lungu, and A-mambwe (as amongst the Masai and other Eastern African races) a hole is drilled in the lobe of the ear, through which a small quill or reed is passed. By degrees the hole is widened by the introduction of larger substances till at last the lobe hangs down in a hideous loop on to the shoulders.

AN ANGONI FROM MOMBERA'S COUNTRY

As in all true negroes there is a marked development of the breasts in the male. Pictures and photographs of beardless men are often taken for representations of women owing to the marked swelling of the breasts, and their slightly pendulous nature. Sometimes it has occurred even to myself to ask, looking at some youth, "Is it a man or a woman?"—so woman-like would be the well-developed *mammæ* which yet seemed inconsistent with the very straight shoulders and small hips. But with this exception there is nothing dubious about the manly appearance of the

---

[1] In Portuguese Guinea, or that portion of Africa which lies between Sierra Leone and the Gambia, there is a race which possesses such an extraordinary growth of hair on the pubes, both in the male and female, that it hangs down in a thick mat and covers the pudenda.

male negro, whose virile development is as marked as it is in the man of European race.

In the young woman who has not borne children the breasts are plump, but are set rather low down on the thorax and the nipples have a tendency to turn up. As soon as a woman has borne a child the breasts are dragged down and become two ugly leather bags in appearance. This change is much aided by the prevailing fashion which holds such a thing creditable, if not beautiful. Many women flatten their breasts by tying a band tightly round their chests. In some women the length of the pendulous breast is such that it can be turned back over the shoulder, and the child can be suckled when tied to its mother's back. The drawing on the next page shows this condition of the breast clearly. Cases of umbilical hernia are very common and begin in childhood from various causes. Occasionally the protuberance at the navel is considerable, resembling the curved neck of a gourd.

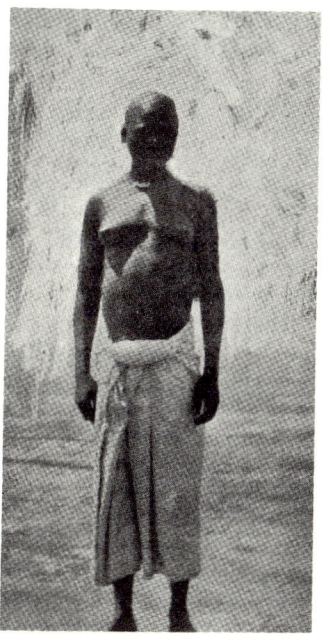

BOY WITH WELL-DEVELOPED BREASTS

In both sexes the development of the external sexual organs is large—larger than in the European (white) race, more considerable still than among the Mongoloid (yellow) races of Asia, America, and the Pacific.[1]

Amongst the men I have never noticed any cases of steatopygy. The women have, as a rule, well-developed buttocks, but nothing approaching the extraordinary appearance so characteristic of the Hottentot. In men the development of the buttocks is less than in the Europeans, and in children it is extremely small, the child being almost straight up and down.[2]

The hands and feet vary a good deal in type.

The thumb is often well developed, but the fingers have a tendency to be stumpy. I have never seen any but short nails. The lines in the palm of the hand are usually few and simple, but are very deeply marked in dark colour. The "line of head" is as might be expected usually short and not unfrequently is missing. Strange to say there is very often a "line of fate" extending right up and down the palm.

[1] Pudenda muliebria augentur simili sed non æqua ratione atque in simiis: nam simiarum et cynocephalorum labra circum vulvam habent multo majora quam mulieres. Præterea apud simias os vulvæ solum a tergo ostenditur: anus alte locatus clunibus non celatur. Hoc modo etiam Æthiopissa ex Africa centrali simiis similis est: nam præter labrorum clitoridisque auctum, os vulvæ magis quam apud mulieres Europæas retro dirigitur. Mares Æthiopes penem eximia magnitudine habent; magis ex ratione cynocephalorum quam simiarum: nam simiae anthropoïdes penem non perbrevem sed tenuem et glande minima atque præamta habent. In hac re inter multas alias indoles prisca in hominibus apparet, neque in simiis quæ aliter evolvuntur. In hac nudorum hominum terra penis parvus rarus est: in Africa Centrali, præsertim apud Nyasæ septentrionalis indigenas (Wankonde), vir mediocri corpore grande membrum virile plerumque habet. Membrum quiescens fere sex uncias longum, excitatum usque ad novem vel decem uncias porrigitur. Præputium natura prælongum est: multae tribus igitur circumcisione utuntur.

[2] One of the chief points in which the anthropoid apes differ from man is in the poor development of the gluteal muscles. Sir Richard Owen styled them "bird-rumped" in consequence of this want of posterior development, a development which is to some extent the result of the upright position, though that the remote ancestors of man had a tendency to fleshy protuberances on either side of the sacrum is shown in the swollen callosities on monkeys' rumps.

The commonest type of foot is one which is well illustrated in the accompanying illustration of Wankonde men, in which the great toe is rather short and much on a level with the other toes. Sometimes the toes are a good deal spread out, and there is certainly a tendency for the foot to assume slightly simian characteristics by the tread being a good deal pressed on the outer side of the foot while the instep inside is somewhat incurved, and the wide-spread

A YOUNG MOTHER (SHOWING PENDENT BREASTS)

toes slant somewhat inwards. The shins are slightly bowed. The development of calf varies a good deal. Amongst the natives inhabiting mountains it is as well developed as in Europeans. Elsewhere in the plains it is sometimes rather sparse.

As regards height: the average height of the men is about 5 ft. 6 in. The tallest male measured was 6 ft. 3 in.; the shortest, 5 ft. Tall men of 5 ft. 10 in. to 6 ft. are very common especially among the Wankonde, Yao, and Angoni. The average height of the women would be about 5 feet.

The average of measurements taken of a number of well-grown males (5 ft. 8 in. in height) gave the following results:—Round the chest, a circumference of $34\frac{5}{8}$ inches; round the waist, $29\frac{7}{8}$ inches; round the buttocks,

WANKONDE MEN

33⅛ inches; thickest part of thigh, 18¾; length of arm from shoulder to tip of second finger, 32½ inches; from chin to pubes, 26¾ inches; pubes to ankle-bone, 31¼ inches; fork of legs to heel, 32⅜ inches; wrist to end of second finger, 8¼ inches; first joint of thumb to tip, 1½ inch; ankle-bone to tip of big toe, 8 inches.

In women of an average height of 5 ft. the measurement round the buttocks ranged from 35½ in. to 37½. The women have thumbs of slightly smaller proportionate length than those of the males.

As regards the quality of the voice in these Central African negroes, although there is never any marked development of "Adam's Apple" in the throat the men have full, deep, virile-sounding voices; much deeper and more manly in tone than is the case with the natives of India. In singing, the commonest kind of men's voices is tenor and after tenor, baritone. A bass voice is rare. When untrained by Europeans their singing is nasal and they are much given to using the falsetto voice.

The women's voices are usually low and melodious, not differing ordinarily very much in tone from those of European women. The laugh of an African man is deep-chested and hearty, and does one good to hear; but the boys and youths and the full-grown girls can develop under European influence what is known as the "mission giggle," as it is peculiarly characteristic

A MUNKONDE
FROM NORTH NYASA
(to show shape of legs)

of the young people attached to the mission schools. I suppose it arises from the constant desire to laugh and a feeling that such merriment is unseemly and should be suppressed.

These negroes, considering their almost absolute nudity in the savage state, bear cold remarkably well up to a certain point. Beyond that point, especially if the cold be accompanied by wet, they collapse with such suddenness as actually to be in danger of dying from cold. But they will reside for weeks on the top of high mountains and plateaux like Mlanje where the temperature may be down to 40° in the daytime, and 29° at night, and yet wear nothing but the usual loin cloth in the daytime, and consider themselves sufficiently shielded by a covering of thin calico at night provided they can light a fire and go to sleep with their feet towards the blaze. In the Zambezi Valley and on the Lower Shire, where the climate is hottest they are apparently more sensitive to night chills. In this region they weave a curious bag or case of matting which is called "mfumba." They creep into this at night and look exactly like so many bales done up in matting.

Exposure to the sun, when not combined with severe fatigue and thirst, does them no harm whatever.

Their skulls are very thick and though the hair is often shaved for cleanliness they require no head-covering to break the force of the sun's rays. Nevertheless here again, in the regions bordering on the Zambezi from copying European habits the natives have become more sensitive to the want of a head covering, and wear large broad-brimmed straw hats of native manufacture. Muhammadanised negroes use the small white skull-cap characteristic of the Arab, round which they often wind a piece of cloth as a turban. After a time these people get used to a head-covering and do not like to dispense with it.

Central African negroes are very thirsty people and scarcely suffer less than Europeans in travelling long distances on foot without frequent drinking. A thirst of several hours under a broiling sun, combined with a long march and a heavy load to carry will soon make them "sun-sick," but I have never known a case of actual sunstroke, or any fatality to arise from exposure to the sun's rays.

Their strength, speed and endurance vary somewhat between tribe and tribe, some peoples being by inherited use and custom able to travel long distances and carry heavy loads, while others are bad walkers or bad climbers and of little use as porters. As a rule, however, the native is a good walker and without a load can travel easily thirty miles a day on foot. With a load of 45 lbs. he can do a steady twenty miles a day when in good condition. The Wanyamwezi carriers of East Central Africa are celebrated for being able to carry loads of 100 lbs. and to keep on the march at a good rate of speed for twenty to twenty-five miles a day. No race that I know of within the limits of British Central Africa can do as much. The Wa-yao are the best carriers we possess. They can manage a load of from 50 to 55 lbs. with ease; but the A-nyanja will scarcely carry any single load that weighs more than 45 lbs. The Wankonde people at the north end of Lake Nyasa only quite recently averred that they could carry no loads at all; and certainly those amongst them who volunteered as carriers for my expedition to Tanganyika in 1889, though they seemingly started with the best intentions, so completely went to pieces after the first few days of porterage that in pity I had to relieve them of their loads. The Atonga are good carriers though not so good as the Yao. They are celebrated, however, for their confidence in the white man and their willingness to accompany him on journeys of very great length. The Makua and Alolo make excellent carriers. They probably rival the Yao in regard to the weight of loads they will cheerfully bear (50 to 60 lbs.) and the speed at which they will travel (twenty miles a day). It is rare to find even a native brought up in the plains who cannot climb mountains better than a white man, but those tribes who dwell in the hills are veritable goats in agility and sureness of foot. In ascending the steep face of a mountain like Mlanje it is marvellous to see native porters with a box of 50 lbs. weight on their heads crawling up the face of a rock like so many cats and not dropping their loads, which they will hold on with one hand while with the other they clutch at any little projection which may assist them, or use a long wand like a small alpenstock. They assist themselves a good deal with their slightly prehensile big toe and the foot gets a better grasp of a rounded surface than it does with the European [1] who is booted.

The women have considerable muscular development owing to the hard work to which they are put from childhood. The average muscular development in the men is good; their figures are well knit and harmonious in outline. As regards pace in running they can outrun most Europeans and almost any native of India that has yet competed with them. They can likewise jump well. Here again the Wa-yao excel most of the other tribes. On the other hand in such experiments as we have made we have found that they could neither hurl a spear nor shoot an arrow as well as an average untrained European. Nor are they, as a rule, good at throwing; yet, when cricket is introduced they soon pick up the idea of bowling.

They are good acrobats. Here, again, the Wa-yao surpass the others. At our military sports or other great gatherings of this description Yao, Atonga, Makua, and Mambwe will turn somersaults, walk on their hands, stand on their

---

[1] At the same time the English seaman can probably climb better than any native.

heads, and perform some very passable clowning. The natives dwelling in the vicinities of lakes or rivers almost invariably swim from childhood. They can swim long distances without becoming unduly exhausted. When swimming at great speed they proceed hand over hand, otherwise they move their arms and legs simultaneously.

Briefly, it must be said in regard to exercises of the body there is almost nothing that the Central African negro will not rapidly learn. In no exercise of skill or speed that we have yet tried (whether it be native or foreign) is the

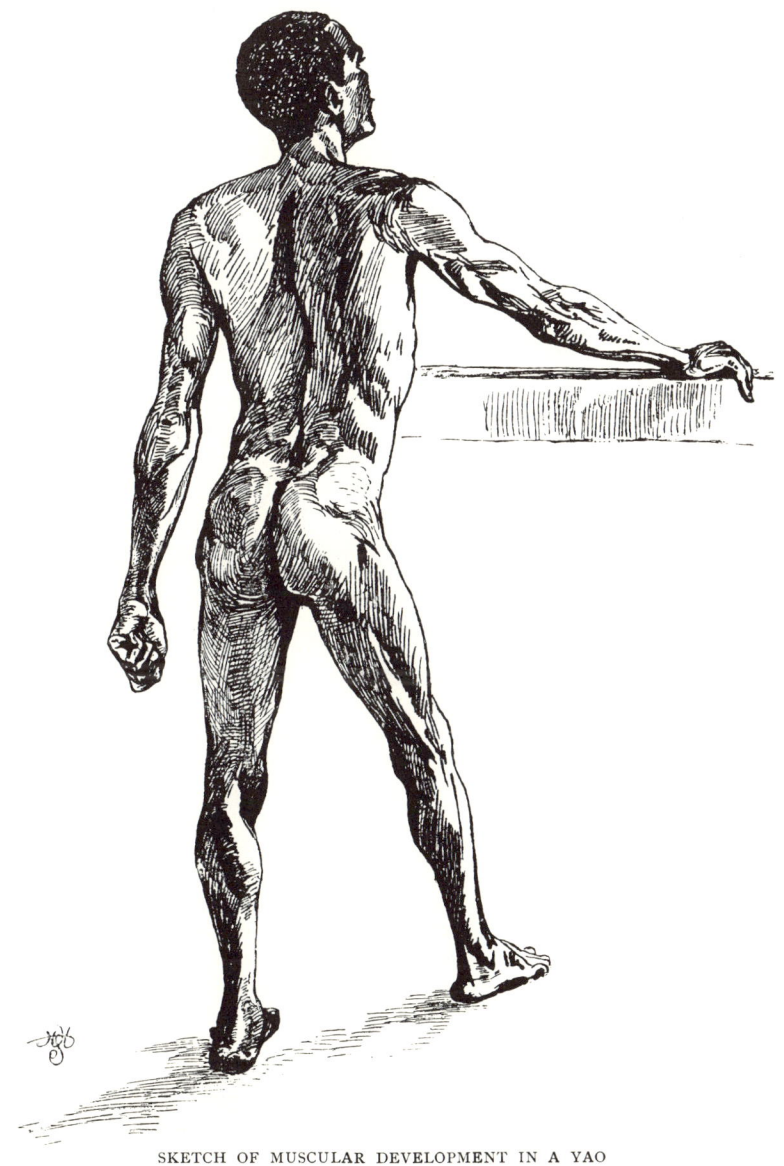

SKETCH OF MUSCULAR DEVELOPMENT IN A YAO

negro able to excel the better type of white man, but it is conceivable that with a few generations of careful physical training he may be able to perform some physical feats better than the European.

Their sight is excellent. In this respect they are much superior to the average European. Cases of myopia are very rare, if indeed they exist at all. Their sense of hearing is probably better than ours, but on the other hand I should think that we had an acuter sense of smell, certainly of taste and probably also of touch.

As regards the postures and movements of the body, the native is able to put himself into positions almost impossible to a European or, at any rate, very uncomfortable. Thus, when he is tired of standing on both legs, he will rest himself by bending one leg and placing the foot against the inside of the knee of the other leg. This is a position often assumed by the natives of all Tropical Africa, and is very well illustrated in Dr. Schweinfurth's celebrated book.[1] Sitting down, the native will squat on his heels and rump, exactly like a baboon. It is almost impossible for a European to do this. They can also sit with crossed legs as is done by Asiatics, but this is not a posture much affected except by the Muhammadanised, or by those who are mixed with Arab blood. The favourite position in sleeping is to lie flat on the stomach with the forehead resting on the folded arms. They will also occasionally lie on the back or on the side, and if they are suffering from cold and endeavouring to cover their bodies with a small piece of cloth they can curl themselves up with the knees almost touching the chin.

In micturition the position is a standing one except where Muhammadanism has introduced a squatting posture, which is of course that assumed by the women. In parturition it is said that the women ordinarily stand upright, often holding on to a beam or supported under the arm-pits by other women.

The body is well balanced and upright in walking, and in fact their carriage is singularly erect and often very graceful. This applies to both sexes and arises to some extent from the custom of balancing loads on the head. It is rare to see a negro in ordinary good health with bowed shoulders and a convex curve to the back. Perhaps, on the whole, the tendency as regards the position of the toes in walking is slightly inwards and in some tribes of a lower physical type the weight of the body is often borne on the outer edge of the foot and heel giving an inward twist to the lines of the toes.

Undoubtedly the favourite mode of carrying things of any weight is on the head where they are kept in position by the left hand. They seem to object to carrying loads on the shoulders or back even if the load itself is fixed to a pole and the other end of the pole is borne by another porter. This dislike, however, is lessening now by the necessity for transporting loads which are beyond one man's endurance, and still more by the increasing use of the " machilla " or hammock, a travelling conveyance slung on a long bamboo pole which pole is borne on the shoulders of two or four men, as the case may be, walking in single file. The use of the machilla, however, is a quite recent institution except in those lands bordering the Zambezi. When Europeans first came to British Central Africa the natives disliked carrying them in this way, though they were willing on occasions to deal with them as they would with their own chiefs, by bearing them for short distances on their shoulders, in the position in which the unfortunate Sindbad had to carry the " Old Man of the Sea." Even now, in the northern part of British Central Africa it is

[1] *Heart of Africa.*

customary for the chief to travel in this fashion, and it is a means of progression I have frequently made use of myself with great advantage when traversing marshes or thick grass jungle.

Various positions and gestures are used in salutation. In the southern part of British Central Africa the natives kneel and clap their hands. In the countries bordering on some of the Portuguese possessions and in Makualand, the natives clap their hands and simultaneously scrape their feet backwards along the ground, one foot at a time. In the northern districts of Lake Nyasa and thence westward, the position in salutation is most extraordinary, especially if it is an inferior saluting a superior. The man who is greeting you will throw himself on his stomach and smack himself violently on the hinder parts. Nearly everywhere the salutation of the women differs from that of the men and is generally confined to kneeling down with the back held erectly whilst the hands are placed over the knees. In exceptional circumstances, however, the women will positively wallow at the man's feet and endeavour to place his foot on their necks. This also is a posture occasionally assumed by suppliants of the other sex or by prisoners abjectly entreating for pardon. From this gesture arises the well-known phrase indicative of absolute submission, "To catch the leg," the idea being that the suppliant endeavours to seize the leg of the great personage so that he may place the foot on his neck. In our various wars, whenever the defeated chief has sought for peace he has always sent in a message that he wishes to "catch the Queen's leg."

A YAO WOMAN

As regards physiognomy, the expression of the negro's face is somewhat stolid and there is not nearly as much play of emotion in his features as there is with the European. I am afraid the preponderant expression is a sulky one though that arises more because the coarse heavy features express sulkiness to our ideas than because the man intends to look sullen. In reality they are almost always of cheerful disposition and even when all the surrounding circumstances are most gloomy it is easy to provoke a laugh; and as already recorded, they laugh well; and laughter lights up their faces to advantage making them quite like a man and a brother. They will somewhat readily shed tears either for pain or for sorrow. As regards psychology there are tribes from the very far interior—those about the Upper Luapula and the Luangwa Valley—who really seem to be of slow and brutish understanding, as a tribal characteristic, and there may also be exceptionally stupid individuals in the cleverest tribes; still, taken as a whole, I think it must be admitted that the average negro of British Central Africa is not a born fool. His mental powers are not much developed by native training, but I am certain that he has in him possibilities in the present generation as great as those of the average Indian; and there is really no saying what he may come to after several generations of education. I think it is truly remarkable the way in which a little savage boy can be put to school and taught to read in a few months and subsequently become a skilful printer or telegraph clerk, or even book-keeper. The little boys are much sharper and shrewder than the grown-up male. When the youth arrives at puberty there is undoubtedly the tendency towards an arrested development of the mind. At this critical period many bright and shining examples fall off into disappointing nullity. As might be imagined, the concentration of their thoughts on sexual intercourse is answerable for this falling away.

This is the negro's great weakness. Nature has probably endowed him with more than the usual genetic faculty. After all, to these people almost without arts and sciences and the refined pleasures of the senses, the only acute enjoyment offered them by nature is sexual intercourse. Yet the negro is very rarely knowingly indecent or addicted to lubricity. In this land of nudity which I have known for seven years, I do not remember once having seen an indecent gesture on the part of either man or woman and only very rarely (and that not amongst unspoilt savages) in the case of that most shameless member of the community—the little boy. An exception must be made to this statement where the native dances are concerned, and yet here, also, the statement is really equally true, for although most tribes have initiation ceremonies or dances which are indecent to our eyes since they consist of very immodest gestures and actions, they can scarcely be called wantonly indecent, because they almost constitute a religious ceremony and are performed by the negroes with a certain amount of seriousness. These dances are never thrust on the notice of the European; it is with the greatest reluctance that they can be brought to perform in his presence. Indeed in many cases tribes will stoutly deny the existence of any such dances amongst them, and as to their initiation ceremonies, I believe I am right in saying that they have never yet been witnessed by a European, that is to say any portion of them that may be indecent or coarse. Our only knowledge is derived from the more or less trustworthy accounts of educated natives. So far as I know, the only dance of a really indecent nature which is indigenous to Central Africa and has not been introduced by low caste Europeans or Arabs, is one which represented originally the act of coition, but it is so altered to a stereotyped formula that its exact purport is not obvious until explained somewhat shyly by the natives.[1]

[1] Nevertheless, it is reported to me that after these dances (especially where a large quantity of native beer has been drunk) orgies of what are conventionally called a "shameful" character ensue. These, however, are seriously entered upon at certain seasons of the year just as they are at fairs in Egypt, a custom which has been handed down from remote antiquity through different forms of religion and under many different practices, but originating undoubtedly in the worship of the *phallus*, as a symbol of creative power. It may safely be asserted that the negro race in Central Africa is much more truly modest, is much more free from real vice than are most European nations. It is absurd to call misuse or irregularity of sexual intercourse "vice." It may be wrong, it may be inexpedient, it may conflict with the best

ETHNOLOGY

In regard to initiation ceremonies. These are more or less connected with sexual matters and with the arrival at or approach to the age of puberty on the part of the boy or girl. In certain characteristics they are common to the greater part of Pagan Tropical Africa. Customs met with on the Gold Coast may be recognised again in Nyasaland or among the Zulus. Yet although agreeing upon certain general principles there is a considerable difference in detail even amongst the tribes of British Central Africa. In some races, however, the tribe being constantly harried by slave raids or civil wars or other disturbing conditions, initiation ceremonies, like other customs, may lapse and almost disappear.[1] It is said that the following customs are observed by the Wa-yao in the initiation of boys:—Like most ceremonies it begins by a dance which takes place in a clearing in the uninhabited woodland at or near the place where the youths, under the direction of their preceptors (one or more elderly men), have run up low shelters made of branches, bamboos and grass thatch. The dance with intervals for eating and sleeping lasts perhaps three days. It is said to be of a slightly obscene character. Usually towards the end of the dance the old man who is to circumcise takes the boys aside one by one; arrangements are then made for their circumcision and they are suddenly told to look at a strange figure in the sky; whilst their gaze is thus diverted the act is smartly performed. "The boys cry a great deal," I was informed, but a few days' rest in the grass hut and the application of certain astringent remedies soon heal the wound. Much good advice is said to be given to the boys by these elderly instructors, but there is also much loose talk and the boys are thoroughly enlightened as to sexual relations. They are given (by their guardian or sponsor,[2] generally, who usually sees them through the ceremonies) a new name and the appellation they have hitherto borne is absolutely discarded. It must never be again used and to call a youth who has been initiated by the name of his childhood is an unpardonable offence. Access to the place where the initiatory ceremonies are taking place is strictly forbidden to all not concerned therewith. The boys are armed (as on the Congo) with long sticks and will mercilessly beat any stranger who invades the precincts. About a month to six weeks usually elapse before the boys issue from their hiding-place and return to their homes. Their mothers prepare food for them during their seclusion and place it usually at the place where the public path divides from the trodden track leading to the "lodge." There is no doubt that much good

interests of the community and require control and restriction; but it is not a "vice." And in this sense the negro is very rarely vicious after he has attained to the age of puberty. He is only more or less uxorious. (Here, again, to give a truthful picture it must be noted that the children are vicious, as they are amongst most races of mankind, the boys outrageously so. A medical missionary who was at work for some time on the west coast of Lake Nyasa gave me information concerning the depravity prevalent among the young boys in the Atonga tribe of a character not even to be expressed in obscure Latin. These statements might be applied with almost equal exactitude to boys and youths in many other parts of Africa as almost any missionary who thoroughly understands the native character would know.)

As regards the little girls over nearly the whole of British Central Africa chastity before puberty is an unknown condition. (Except perhaps among the A-nyanja.) Before a girl is become a woman (that is to say before she is able to conceive) it is a matter of absolute indifference what she does and scarcely any girl remains a virgin after about five years of age. Even where betrothed at birth, as is often the case, or at a few months old, she will go to the family of her future husband when she is four or five years of age and although she will not formally cohabit with him till she has reached the age of puberty, it constantly happens that she is deflowered by him long before that age is attained.

[1] There are said to be no initiation ceremonies for the boys among the A-nyanja or Atonga.
[2] Often an uncle; someone chosen at the birth of the child by the father.

advice is given to the boys during this initiation: they are warned against selfishness specially, are instructed in the way to return polite answers to their elders, in the traditions of the tribes, in their duties towards the community and chief, and often in special subjects such as the augury of favourable conditions of travel, methods of warfare, and religious beliefs connected with the worship and propitiation of ancestral spirits.[1]

As to the initiation ceremonies[2] for the girls among the Wa-yao they are stated to be as follows. When there are a number of girl children in a village or collection of villages who have reached an age of from eight to eleven years they are taken away to the bush by elderly women and are lodged there in shelters of grass and branches much as I have described in regard to the boys. The ceremony usually begins with the new moon and lasts for the lunar month. One old woman presides over the other instructresses, who is called the "cook of the initiation," and who receives a fee of about four yards of cloth for each girl initiated. A huge amount of corn has been pounded and flour (utandi) prepared beforehand ready to feed the girls during their seclusion. The children are instructed in household duties, in their obligations to their future husbands, in the principles of good behaviour (which includes injunctions against loud-tongued quarrelling). The marriage question is thoroughly explained and warning is given that unfaithfulness to the marriage tie may result in death at the hands of the husband. The girls' heads are shaved and they are anointed with various "medicines" and rubbed with oil. Miniature house roofs are made and each girl has to carry one on her head indicating that she is the support of the home. Then follows (it is said) a forcible *vaginæ dilatatio*[3] by mechanical means, an operation which the girls are enjoined to bear bravely. At the same time they are told that it must be followed by cohabitation with a man. This is regarded by the Yao as a necessity to render the girl marriageable before the age of puberty. The girls and their mothers believe that if after these initiation ceremonies nisi cum mare coitus fiet they will die or at any rate will not bear children when eventually married. Pater puellæ virum robustum (sæpe attamen senem) legit atque ei pecuniam dat ut puellæ virginitatem adimat. Hoc ante pubertatem fieri necesse, ne coitum conceptio sequatur.

There are no such proceedings amongst the A-nyanja though Dr. Cross hints that something of the kind may obtain among the Wankonde. The A-nyanja, probably the Atonga and most of the other races west of Lake Nyasa hold but simple initiation ceremonies among the girls—they only take place after puberty is reached, and last for a day or so. The young maidens proceed to a cleared place outside the village where they recline upon dry grass. No man is allowed to approach this college of women and the approaches thereto are carefully guarded by matrons, while other married women proceed to the instruction of the girls not only in sexual matters but in the management of the home and all other matters concerning the woman's life and work.

Following on this initiation is a dance, of course—a dance in which both sexes join. Men dress themselves up in masks and skins and romp with the initiated girls rather roughly but with no immodesty, and after the dance is over the girls are taken back to their homes by the matrons who are careful to see that they behave themselves with propriety.

---

[1] Under this last head but little instruction may be given now, as so many of the Yaos affect Muhammadanism.   [2] *Unyago* in Chi-yao.   [3] Aliquando clitoride simul excisa.

After it is known that a young married woman is with child another ceremony takes place (this is nearly universal). A great feast is got up for which immense quantities of food are prepared. The woman with child sits outside her hut, and her head is anointed with castor oil. The chief woman presiding over the ceremony then directs her assistants to shave the patient's head. Nothing further is done that day except the continued preparation of food for the coming feast. On the morrow the young woman is anointed with oil and red-ochre and sits out again in front of her door while a dance of matrons takes place before her which is said to be of an indelicate character and at which songs of considerable coarseness are sung. One of the women dancing has a large gourd tied under the waist cloth to simulate advanced pregnancy and struts about in this "honourable" condition. These ceremonies finish on the night of the second day by a secret conclave inside the young woman's dwelling at which it is said her husband is present and that much advice—some good, some silly, and some immodest—is given by the assembled matrons to the young couple. The woman who presides over these first-pregnancy customs is paid a fee of a goat or a certain quantity of corn. Among most of the tribes when these ceremonies are complete (part of their object being the ascertainment by the matrons beyond a doubt that the young wife is pregnant) the husband will cease to cohabit with his wife until the child is born and weaned.[1] If he has another wife he will take to her society; if not he will strive to remain chaste in the fear lest if he commit adultery his unborn child will die. Many young husbands choose such a time to make a trading or hunting journey or engage for service with Europeans. Once removed, however, from the vicinity of the wife and village they appear to hold but lightly the restrictions or incontinence and act on the proverb "What the eye does not see the heart does not grieve for."

YOUNG MUNKONDE GIRL
(One of the "Awasungu")

Amongst the Awa-nkonde at the north end of Lake Nyasa similar ceremonies are performed on the young girls at puberty and on the wives after pregnancy. After the first menstruation the girl is kept apart with a few companions of her own sex in a darkened house. The floor is covered with dry banana leaves, but no fire is allowed in the house, which is named "The house of the Awasungu" ("maidens who have hearts").

The following may be regarded as the general principles on which marriage customs are based. (I will subsequently note special customs of several tribes.) Marriage is usually by purchase. Arrangements are often made long beforehand by the youth or man or, on his behalf, by his "godfather," or father, or patron (if he be a slave). It may be desired to contract an alliance with a certain man of near relationship or of influence, and the bargain may be commenced when this man's wife is known to be with child, and before the child is born, that is to say, the individual who wishes to get married or whose matrimonial affairs are being arranged for him, makes an offer for the betrothal of the as yet unborn infant should it prove to be a

---

[1] In many tribes where monogamy among poor people is the common state the husband resumes cohabitation soon after the child is born.

female, which arrangement, if concluded, holds good if the child turns out to be of that sex. Or the betrothal may take place a few months after the female child is born, or when she is a little girl. Of course there are many instances when a young man will take a fancy to a young unmarried woman without any such previous arrangement and will, through his surety or godfather, apply for her hand in marriage. Whenever marriage is by an arrangement in this manner a certain value is paid for the wife. It may be as small as two dressed skins in Angoniland, or as high as several cows and a large quantity of trade goods in the case of a chief's daughter or in wealthy cattle-keeping tribes.

Then there is marriage by capture—one of the chief inducements to indulge in war and slave raiding. When the Administration first began to get into conflict with the slave traders and required an armed force to put them down, from first to last thousands of natives must have offered to volunteer for service on the understanding that they were to be allowed to carry off the enemy's women. Naturally they were not accepted on those terms, but even in the case of our unarmed porters we had the greatest difficulty in restraining them from helping themselves to wives when marching with us into the enemy's country. The women as a rule make no very great resistance on these occasions. It is almost like playing a game. A woman is surprised as she goes to get water at the stream, or when she is on her way to or from the plantation. The man has only got to show her she is cornered and that escape is not easy or pleasant and she submits to be carried off. Of course there are cases where the woman takes the first opportunity of running back to her first husband if her captor treats her badly, and again she may be really attached to her first husband and make every effort to return to him for that reason. But as a general rule they seem to accept very cheerfully these abrupt changes in their matrimonial existence.[1]

Concubinage represents another form of marriage. The man may purchase one or more female slaves and it is always assumed that all the women folk of his household are his wives. In like manner a free woman, especially if she be a chieftainess, or daughter of a chief, may for motives of policy make no regular marriage but take a male slave to live with her. Polygamy is, of course, very general though at the same time poor men often confine themselves to one wife. Adultery is extremely common and in very few parts of British Central Africa is looked upon as a very serious matter, as a wrong which cannot be compensated by a small payment. Yet in a way the natives are jealous of their women; they are not at all anxious to encourage intercourse between their wives and white men, though they seem to be much more jealous about the white man than their brother negro. As a general rule it may be said that illicit intercourse with women on the part of Europeans causes great dissatisfaction in the native mind and invariably gives rise to acts of revenge on their part and even to serious risings. On the other hand if the European tries to obtain a wife in a legitimate manner by negotiation and purchase they are not at all unwilling to treat and no ill humour whatever results from his intermarrying with them. In their eyes it is simply a matter of justice. They regard it with the same amount of emotion as they would the stealing of their

---

[1] The Rev. Duff Macdonald, a competent authority on Yao manners and customs, says in his book *Africana*: "I was told . . . that a native man would not pass a solitary woman and that her refusal of him would be so contrary to custom that he might kill her. Of course this would apply only to females that are not engaged."

fowls or corn in lieu of buying them, even though the price charged for them is very small.

Polyandry, or the possession of more than one husband at once is very uncommon amongst the women. However ready some of them are to dissolve the marriage tie they are generally faithful to one husband at a time. Indeed I should say their tendency was to be chaste and virtuous after marriage and not to willingly depart from the one husband unless he shows indifference or cruelty.

Marriage by purchase or arrangement is conducted as follows amongst the Yao: The suitor if he be of age or the suitor's godfather[1] if he be a boy hears that a girl-child is born to a man with whom a marriage connection is desired. Or a child nearer the marriageable age is being solicited. The young man wishing to marry or the godfather on behalf of a boy not yet betrothed seeks out the guardian or godfather of the girl and proposes the match. The godfather refers him to the girl-child's mother. If he be the first applicant and bring a nice present consent is almost always given. Then the two are betrothed, the boy or man gives another present, and henceforth keeps the girl supplied with cloth to wear until the marriage. The public intimation of the betrothal being complete is the acceptance and wearing of this cloth.

A betrothed girl often cooks food for her future spouse. It is rare for children thus growing up together to fail to marry or to dislike one another. Sometimes however a young girl betrothed while very young to a grown man may refuse to carry out the bargain when she attains marriageable age and if she has taken a dislike to her proposed husband.

Amongst the Atonga on the west coast of Nyasa the following are the customs observed in regard to marriage. A youth or man who wishes to marry pays about eight yards of cloth to the aunt (mother's sister) of the girl he fancies. If this gift is accepted the prospective husband proceeds to build a house close to that of the man who will become his father-in-law. Whilst the house is building he sends a present equivalent to about four yards of cloth to the girl's mother. (It would appear as if amongst the Atonga cases of a girl being betrothed very young are less common than elsewhere, and that the majority of marriages are only arranged when the boy and girl are approaching or have passed puberty.)

When the day for the marriage is come a number of young girls who are friends of the bride take possession of her, put cloth over her face as a veil and deposit her in the bridegroom's house. The husband is awaiting her inside the house. She stops at the threshold and will not cross it until the bridegroom has given her a hoe. She then puts one leg over the lintel of the doorway and the husband hands her two yards of cloth. Then the bride places both her feet within the house and stands near the doorway. Upon doing so she receives a present of beads or some equivalent. She then advances to the middle of the hut and there receives four yards of cloth. All the bridesmaids except one accompany her thus far but remain at her back. One of them goes in front. Then the bride sits on the bed and the bridesmaids leave. The husband, after their departure, places a lot of beads on the mat at the bride's feet. After this he removes her clothing and leaves her naked save for a bead girdle which she may probably wear, but whilst stripping her he gives her a present of eight

---

[1] I can only use this word to express the individual (of the male sex) who after the birth of the child is appointed its guardian by the parents. The father's brother (uncle) is usually chosen for this position, and henceforth transacts all business for his male or female godchild.

yards of cloth which is put aside with the accumulation of the other presents. They then sleep together, but usually not on the bed but on a mat placed before the fire burning in the centre of the hut. The next morning the bridesmaids return. They affect to gaze round about the bed and exclaim upon seeing the mass of beads poured out on the mat, "You have a generous husband." If, however, an ample supply of beads has not been exhibited in this fashion the bridesmaids sneer and utter contemptuous remarks, the more genuine in feeling because these beads thrown on to the mat are supposed to be their perquisites and are taken away by them. Soon after the bridesmaids have gone the father of the newly-wedded wife pays an early visit to the husband's father and invites him to a friendly talk. Much native beer is made and drunk. The "big women" (matrons of the village) then go to the bride's home and remove her head veil of cloth. All the husband's brothers, if he has any, give presents to the bride. The bride's father catches two fowls, male and female, and should give the hen to the bridegroom's father to keep, saying, "You have got my daughter, I have got your son"; but if for any reason the bride's father is dissatisfied with his son-in-law he gives the male bird to the groom's father as a sign that he returns the son and will not have him as a son-in-law. If the

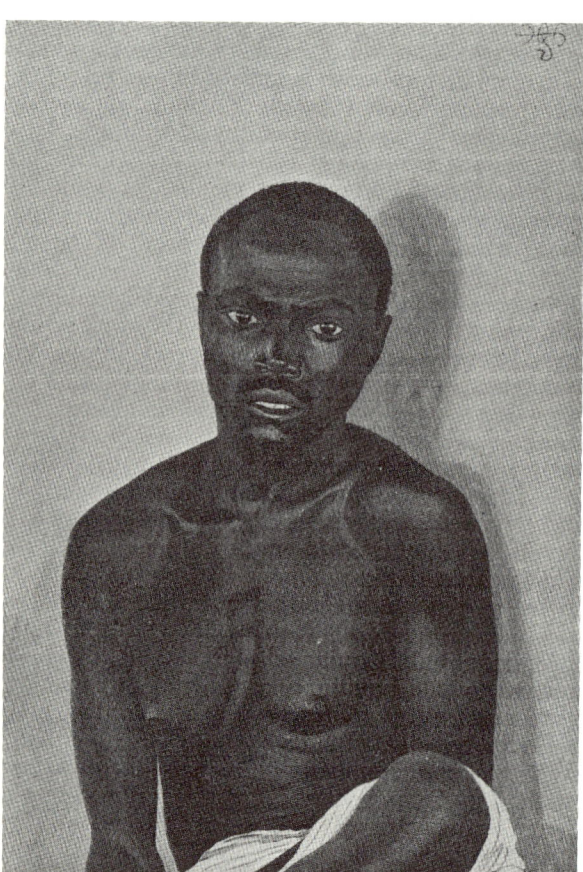

A MTONGA MAN

hen is given, however, the marriage is considered to have been satisfactorily settled and the father calls his daughter to him and lectures her on her duties as a married woman. On the second night of the marriage nupta parvum pannum inter clunes celat, quo post coitum semen a vulva detergit, ut postridie matronis pagi ostendat. Illæ semine inspecto utrum ex mare valido emissus sit pronuntiant. Quodsi aliter decernunt, nupta patrem suam docet, qui quum ad mariti patiem accessit, dicit: "Mi amice, filius tuus non ad generandum idmeus est: lege alium ex filiis tuis filiæ meæ conjugem."

Amongst the Atonga the wife does not leave her husband directly she is *enceinte*, but perhaps at the sixth month. The husband does not resume relations with his wife until five or six months after the birth of the child. If in this interval of some nine months he has connection with any other woman the popular belief is that his wife will certainly die. The Atonga widower seldom remarries until five months after the death of his wife.

Amongst the Wankonde at the north end of Lake Nyasa men seldom marry out of their own tribe but avoid marriage between cousins. Polygamy is prevalent among them. As one amongst many reasons given for polygamy it is stated that as a man cannot cohabit with his wife during the menstrual period or during pregnancy, he must have more than one wife, as once married he cannot exercise self-restraint.

When desirous of marrying a girl the young Munkonde approaches her parents through a comrade or friends. If the parents are willing to treat of marriage, and the girl herself consents, the young man gives the father or guardian a present of one or more cows[1] (some tribes give goats, hides, cloth,[2] &c.). Then the parents on both sides meet and agree to the union. They deny that this is purchase: it is merely a token of good will and good faith. Should the married persons quarrel in after days and the young woman run away to her father's house her husband can demand the return of the goods.

Contrary to the custom that prevails in the greater part of Southern Nyasaland, where the husband invariably goes away to live with the people of his wife, among the Wankonde the husband takes his bride to his own village, though Dr. Cross has heard of cases where this custom has been reversed.

Among the Wankonde a man's widow usually becomes the wife of the next brother. The Wankonde have that curious custom by which a man is practically forbidden to speak to or even look at his mother-in-law. This also obtains amongst the A-nyanja to some extent; yet here the son-in-law has to hoe his mother-in-law's garden and assist her in many other ways. The Rev. D. C. R. Scott states, "The children endeavour to heal the breach between their father and his mother-in-law (their grandmother)."

Apparently the A-nyanja are less "emancipated" than the other tribes of British Central Africa. Among the A-nyanja if a man commit adultery during the pregnancy of his wife and the wife or child should die in the delivery, the wife's people gather together and demand compensation, sometimes asking for the sister of the husband. Amongst the A-nyanja also the custom prevails that if a man be caught in adultery he is obliged to get another man as a substitute to cohabit with his wife before he can return to her, and he must pay his substitute for this service four yards of cloth or an equivalent present, or else the substitute can claim and carry away the wife.

The marriage customs amongst the A-mambwe and A-lungu of Lake Tanganyika and the Tanganyika plateau are very similar to the Wankonde. Those of the Angoni resemble the customs amongst the Zulus of South Africa. Among the Aba-bisa, the A-senga, and the Awemba, and, indeed, most of the tribes between Nyasa and the Luapula River, there are similar customs to the rites which prevail amongst the Atonga; but those of the A-lunda (a people dwelling on the south shore of Lake Mweru and the banks of the Luapula River) present, as might be expected, features more similar to the marriage customs of West Central Africa and Angola, since the A-lunda came from that direction.

---

[1] In the case of a chief's daughter fifteen to twenty head of cattle may be the present given.
[2] Mr. Yule states that in some of the poorer Wankonde tribes the usual gift is three hoes, two brass waist-rings, and a few yards of cloth.

The Wankonde express great horror at the idea of cousins marrying. The Yao on the other hand marry their cousins frequently.

As regards the customs relating to parturition and to the treatment of the newly-born child, there is probably not much difference between the various tribes, and what is reported of one set of people might be found to exist in another upon closer observation. The Rev. Duff Macdonald, in his interesting book on the Yao customs,[1] makes a statement which appears difficult of belief were it not that so many of his remarks are found to be perfectly accurate. He writes that Yao women "when the time of the child's birth draws near do not stay in the house or even in the village. Accompanied by one or two female friends the woman who is about to become a mother goes forth to seek the retirement of the great forest." He goes on to state somewhat ambiguously that she remains in the bush until delivery has taken place and that if any complications ensue a native doctor is applied to who sends medicine to drink. After the birth of the child one of the female friends of the mother carries it back to the village, the latter accompanying it on foot. I confess that I have not been able to find confirmation of this statement in my own notes respecting the Yao. Perhaps I took it too much as a matter of course that the woman was delivered in a hut, but the tenour of the answers I received from Wa-yao as to their customs would certainly show that in most cases the woman awaits the child's birth in the shelter of a house, usually her own hut. It is so certainly amongst the A-nyanja, the Atonga, the Wankonde, and tribes of the Nyasa-Tanganyika plateau.

"A GOOD MOTHER"
(Sketch of a Mnyanja woman)

The Atonga inform me that in their country the child's navel string is not severed for two days after birth, and that the mother during that period carries the child about with the navel string unsevered. On the third day the mother anoints it with the bitter juice of a fruit called "Mutura." This dries up the string and it breaks off without harm to the child. According to the Rev. D. C. Ruffele-Scott in the notes on native customs published in his Mañanja dictionary the parturient woman remains for eight days in her house after the child's birth. It would seem amongst all the tribes that after the birth has taken place the child's head is shaved and the mother's hair is either cut off around the forehead or the whole of her head is shaved likewise.[1] The child also is usually well oiled. Mr. J. B. Yule informs me that amongst the A-mambwe on the Nyasa-Tanganyika plateau the afterbirth is carefully buried under the floor of the mother's hut. He also states that if the firstborn child of a woman be a boy it is rarely allowed to live and, further, that if the girl cuts

[1] *Africana*, vol. i.   [2] Shaving the head accompanies most ceremonies; the hair is always carefully buried.

the first two upper incisors before the lower teeth make their appearance, the child is usually strangled and thrown into a stagnant pool. Amongst the Mambwe, if a child is prematurely born it is cut into five pieces (two legs, two arms and trunk) and is then buried under the floor of the mother's hut. Mr. Yule states that these customs also prevail amongst the nearly allied A-lungu. Amongst the Atonga, when the child's navel string has been removed the mother is thoroughly smartened up and walks round the village to receive congratulations. Usually the husband and father of the child keeps carefully aloof from his wife for some days before and after child-birth. Amongst the A-nyanja the door of the house where the woman stays with her newly-born child is always kept a little ajar. The woman usually remains therein for three days after confinement, her woman friends or the old women of the village staying with her, one at a time. These women generally remain till the child is eight days old.

The Wankonde have these birth customs: The mother is secluded for a lunar month after the birth of the child, and is regarded as unclean. Before being readmitted into society she must go alone into a running stream, wash in the water and anoint with oil. With this same people it is held that if the children in a family die one after another in succession the father must kill himself. "I have known of a case," writes Dr. Cross, "where when three children died in succession this thing happened. I was told that the father in such a case would hang himself, or would put his gun into his mouth and pull the trigger with his toe." "The children of an adulterous intercourse are killed in the Wankonde tribe. The people also practise the adoption of children extensively, especially where couples are childless."

Children that are born deformed or defective are almost invariably killed. Respect for the life of very young children is not great though of course the mother from natural instincts is loth to lose her child. It was related to me once of the head wife of some man that, being extremely angry with one of the junior wives, and seemingly for good reason, she punished her by taking her young baby and throwing it on the fire where it burned to death. This fact was told to me to indicate that the woman in question was a person of determined character but it did not seem to strike my native informant that it was a particularly wicked or cruel thing to do. Yet children on the whole are kindly treated if they are reared at all. They grow up much like children do in all uncivilised countries—treated somewhat heedlessly but seldom harshly. The mother will place a charm round her baby's neck, and in some cases ornaments. As a rule the child that can walk is allowed to run about naked and dirty so that it may not be bewitched; but babies in arms are scrupulously washed and kept clean.

In spite of their desire to honour their husbands with offspring it is not at all a rare thing for women to bring about abortion between the third and fifth month, either to spite their husbands with whom they may have quarrelled, or who have given them cause for jealousy, or because the child is the result of illicit intercourse. Abortion is procured by drinking a decoction of the bark of certain trees, or else by the insertion of a sharply pointed piece of bamboo.

Amongst the A-nyanja and the Wa-yao, the child is usually named by one of the women who attend the mother; amongst the Atonga the father gives the name. If the child is a son he receives the name of either his father or grandfather, if it is a girl the name of the paternal or maternal grandmother.

Native names almost invariably have some meaning; that is to say, with the exception of inherited names which have come down for many generations. The name of nearly every individual is a living word of plain meaning.

The birth of twins is not ordinarily well received and in some tribes one of the two children is killed. I have never heard of any case of triplets or quadruplets; and when I have told natives that such cases occurred in England occasionally, they expressed the greatest horror.[1]

After the mother begins to go about again she usually takes part in a dance which is attended by women only, if she has borne a child for the first time.

Children early enter upon the duties of life. Little girls soon begin to assist their mothers in preparing food and in garden work. The little boys mind the goats or the fowls or scare away the baboons from the crops, and when they are seven or eight years old commence to follow their fathers on short journeys. The little girls amuse themselves by dancing and singing, even playing with monstrous dolls that are hardly to be recognised as imitations of the human baby. Little boys, if they dwell near the river, play with toy canoes, or they throw wooden spears and shoot with tiny bows and arrows. The initiation ceremonies more or less attendant on puberty have been already described, and it has been related how both girls and boys at that time change their childish names for other appellations. In the case of the boys the names are sometimes given by the persons who preside over the ceremonies or by the headman or chief of the village from which the boys come; or the youths themselves may insist on choosing their own names.

The Rev. D. C. R. Scott writes in his dictionary: "A person is supposed to change so radically at puberty that the utterance of his first name is a very great insult. A boy called by this name will probably answer, 'There is no such person here.'" But even after puberty the names are changed with the greatest facility. Persons who are very great friends may interchange names, or a man may go on a journey and prefer to call himself by a new appellation, on his return, which refers to some important event which has occurred in his travels.[2]

The age of puberty amongst the girls is usually eleven years: with the boys, twelve to fourteen; but neither sex attains its full maturity till about sixteen years in the woman and twenty years in the man. The beard and moustache in men make their appearance relatively late, not beginning to show much before twenty-four or twenty-five years of age.

Neither boys nor girls wear clothing (unless they are the children of chiefs) until nearing the age of puberty. Amongst the Wankonde, except in such few of those people as have come under European influence, practically no covering is worn by the men except a ring of brass wire round the stomach. It is the custom now, however, amongst the Wankonde men who frequent trading or mission stations to suspend a piece of cloth from this brass girdle or if there is

---

[1] A curious custom obtains amongst the Wankonde if twins are born. Both parents are put into a grass hut in a secluded part of the village and there they abide for one month. No villager can see the face of the secluded persons. The father hides himself lest his enemies should kill him.

The Atonga consider the birth of twins a most unlucky circumstance, and although they will not admit it I think that one of the twins is very frequently killed. The belief on their part is that if both live then both will suffer double, for the tie between them is so strong that even although separated by distance each will feel the other's pain in addition to his own sicknesses and hurts. On the other hand the Anyanja and the Yao do not seem to care very much one way or the other whether twins are born.

[2] Names are most changeable amongst these negroes. Sometimes for mere caprice they will say, "I intend to call myself so-and-so," and henceforth the new name out of politeness is scrupulously remembered.

no cloth at hand a small leafy branch or a folded banana leaf. The Wankonde women are likewise almost entirely nude, but generally cover the pudenda with a tiny beadwork apron, often a piece of very beautiful workmanship and exactly resembling the same article worn by Kaffir women. A like degree of nudity prevails amongst many of the Awemba, amongst the A-lungu, the Batumbuka and the Angoni. Most of the Angoni men, however, adopt the Zulu fashion of covering the *glans penis* with a small wooden case or the outer shell of a fruit. The Angoni—especially those who are not of Zulu extraction, but merely of the widespread A-nyanja race—usually wear a small piece of leather or a kilt made of animals' tails or of serval-skin, in place of or in addition to any special covering of the male organ. The Wa-yao have a strong sense of decency in matters of this kind, which is the more curious since they are more given to obscenity in their rites, ceremonies and dances than any other tribe. Not only is it extremely rare to see any Yao uncovered but both men and women have the strongest dislike to exposing their persons even to the inspection of a doctor. The Yao men now almost universally wear cloth round their waists extending to the knee—this as an ordinary covering, though in time of war or when they are out hunting they will tuck the cloth up between their legs in a compact way. Before the European introduced cloth, however, or the Yao caravans brought back quantities of it from the coast, these people, like most others in South Central Africa, wore bark cloth,[1] but except amongst the remoter valleys of Yao-land, or amongst the A-nyanja who are far removed from Lake Nyasa, or the still more barbarous people of the Lubisa country or the banks of the Luapula River, cloth—chiefly European calico or a native towel-like manufacture—is now worn. In Angoniland and on the Nyasa-Tanganyika plateau and in parts of West Nyasaland a good deal of weaving is carried on and the native cloth thus made is substantial and somewhat ornamental, though its web is many times coarser than the finely woven cotton cloths of European civilisation. Formerly skins were much worn as cloaks or coverings to keep off the cold, but they too like the bark cloth are fast disappearing.

The Atonga and many of the A-nyanja people, and all the tribes west of Nyasa (with the exception possibly of the A-lunda) have not the Yao regard for decency, and, although they can seldom or ever be accused of a deliberate intention to expose themselves, the men are relatively indifferent as to whether their nakedness is or is not concealed, though the women are modest and careful in this respect. The chiefs and men of any importance amongst the Yao, especially in the vicinity of Lake Nyasa, often adopt an Arab costume, wearing a long *kanzu*, or white shirt nearly down to the heels, a piece of cloth wound round the head for a turban, a shawl over the shoulders, and so on. There is a great desire amongst the A-nyanja to dress like Europeans if they can afford it. The Makololo chiefs, for instance, on the Central and Lower Shire, dress more or less in European style except when in the intimacy of their homes. The Atonga have a great leaning for European clothes. One of the most remarkable specimens of this intelligent race that I have known—Bandawe, *alias* Maferano,[2] who has risen to a high position in our native army, who is able to read and write, and even, I believe, to play the harmonium, had a passion for accumulating suits of European clothes of every description. When serving a planter as interpreter some years ago, he asked, as part payment of his wages, for a disused dress suit and tall silk hat. These garments he used to don on Sundays to our

[1] They strip the bark off the tree, soak it in water and beat it out with wooden hammers.
[2] His original native name, which means "a mortal conflict."

A YAO OF ZOMBA

inextinguishable merriment. Finding himself too much laughed at he made over the clothes, as a very special honour, to his head wife who is quite a heroine in her way. This woman used at one time to accompany him on most of our campaigns, even insisting on going into battle, till one day she was wounded and this procedure was discovered and immediately put a stop to. It was found out in this way. When going into action at Kawinga's one of the officers of the Indian contingent noticed a strange being charging in line with the Sikhs. It was a black person dressed in ludicrous caricature of a "masher" in a very tight-fitting evening suit and tall hat. The masher, however, was knocked down by a spent bullet (fortunately not much hurt) and upon being picked up was found to be Bandawe's wife thus strangely habited.

Amongst the still untamed savages of Angoniland and elsewhere to the north and west of Lake Nyasa many strange additions to their costume are worn by the men upon going to war. The Angoni generally tie a piece of red cloth round the waist and don a huge kilt of animals' tails or of dressed cat skins. On the head they will place either a circlet made of zebra mane or a huge headdress of black cock's feathers. White frills are worn round the ankles, made of the long white hair of the *Colobus* monkey or, failing that, of goat's hair. The fighting men of the Awemba or of other tribes between Nyasa and Tanganyika are fond of wearing as a headdress the head and beak of a large hornbill. The illustration which is given here of a "Ruga-ruga" illustrates this, and it also shows other features of the war dress mainly derived from the Wanyamwezi people to the north. The coils of rope which this drawing represents, are theoretically intended for binding the Ruga-ruga's captives. In the countries west of Lake Nyasa and on Tanganyika (I believe also in the Makua countries to the east) wooden masks are more or less worn either during certain dances or as part of the war dress.

A "RUGA-RUGA"

Most tribes anoint the hair with oil, generally castor oil, but some use the fat of animals. The Awa-bundali, a tribe of the Wankonde group, comb out their wool, plait it, weave into it strips of bark and loop these plaits back over the ears like "bandeaux," tying the plaits at the back of the head. Many tribes not only among the Wankonde but of A-nyanja, A-lolo, Ba-bisa, Awemba stock, endeavour to lengthen their hair by plaiting into it black thread or the hair of animals, or other substances which may appear to lengthen it. The Angoni, where they do not adopt the Zulu fashion among the married men of wearing a head-ring (made round the head with plastered hair), train their hair into long wisps which they tie up with grass or straw. It is the fashion amongst some tribes—especially to the south-east of Nyasaland and on the Nyasa-Tanganyika plateau—to wear wigs made of plaited thread. Into these wigs cowry shells are sometimes threaded.

The tribes on the south of Tanganyika occasionally make a headdress of black goat skin the hair of which hangs down over the forehead, simulating the appearance of a long-haired race. Other people, again, manage to attach false hair or imitation hair to their own wool and give themselves the appearance of a fine mop of long hair. Bracelets, necklets, anklets, and similar ornaments are almost universally worn. Some bracelets are made of elephant's hide; others of ivory—a section of a tusk being pierced with a hole large enough for the passage of the hand; others of plaited grass or of brass wire or iron.

The Angoni men will generally have a string on which a charm is carried, some object supposed to preserve the wearer from harm, or to give him especial good fortune. Or they may be necklaces of the black seeds of the wild banana (*Musa ensete*) or various other and larger seeds, or sections of shells, or animals' teeth, or the glass beads of commerce. The women will frequently wear huge collars which are one mass of beads or long ropes of beads often very tastefully formed. A girdle of beads is usually worn amongst the women who seldom remove it after it has once been put on. Both men and women will wear anklets of much the same material as their bracelets. Women are especially fond of thick brass or copper rings round the ankles. Some of the wives of the Yao chiefs wear heavy silver anklets of Indian manufacture brought from the coast.

The tribes to the west and north of Lake Nyasa sometimes use sandals when on a journey. As a rule, however, the people of these countries go about barefooted always, even though the soles of their feet may be terribly scorched during journeys in hot weather when the sun at times makes the path hot enough to burn the skin. I have sometimes noticed the Yao wearing sandals roughly made of a piece of hide.

As regards adornments of the person which consist in marking or decorating the skin:—Not many of the tribes go in for tatooing on the scale to which it is developed in the Pacific, though most of them have a tribal mark. In some the skin is ornamented with raised weals and lumps made by incisions into which some irritating substance (usually charcoal) is rubbed, which causes the flesh to heal with a raised bluish cicatrice. To the east of the British Central Africa Protectorate amongst the Makua and the Alomwe, hideous scars are thus raised on the forehead. These are sometimes of indigo blue and probably some other colouring matter than mere charcoal has been inserted. The people in the countries between Lake Nyasa and the Luapula—both men and women —cover their bodies with cicatrices arranged in various patterns.

Amongst the Yao tatooing is usually limited to a kind of rosette, or round mark on the temples and three or four longitudinal marks on the forehead, just above the nasal bone.

The A-nyanja tatoo on the forehead and they also, especially to the west of Lake Nyasa, practise cicatrisation. Ordinary tatooing is done by making punctures or cuts in the skin and afterwards rubbing in charcoal. In cicatrisation cuts are repeatedly made in the same place until they heal with a swollen blob of flesh which remains as a raised lump. If charcoal is rubbed into this in the process of healing, these raised lumps are blue in colour.

NATIVES OF BRITISH CENTRAL AFRICA 423

The Wankonde tatoo extensively about the age of puberty. They make small incisions with a pair of pincers and a knife and rub in wood ashes or charcoal. The Wankonde cut marks like those given in the accompanying illustration over the breast, above the mammæ, in both sexes. Some tatoo over the abdomen, others over the hypogastrium, where they make a series of long lines, which are wonderfully straight.

The Awemba make large St. Andrew's crosses on the back, reaching from the top of the blade-bone on either side to the point of the hip on the opposite side. As a rule, both sexes are tatooed, and the tatoo marks certainly serve both among the A-nyanja, the Wa-yao, and the Wankonde to distinguish tribe from tribe.

The Angoni and some of the A-lungu and Awemba puncture the lobe of the ear and insert a quill. The quill is presently changed for a thicker wad of bone until at last the hole has been so far widened as to admit an article the size of an ordinary cotton reel, and the ear often hangs down a considerable distance, though this deformity is not pushed to the extremes I have observed in parts of East Africa.

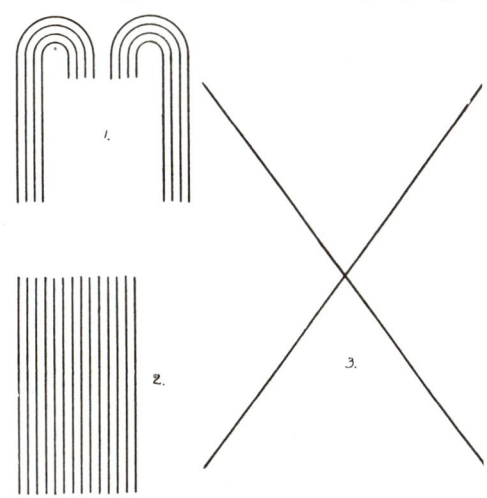

SPECIMENS OF TATOOING
1, 2. Lines drawn on the breast and stomach of the Wankonde.
3. St. Andrew's Cross, drawn across the back by the Awemba.

1. Native comb.
2. Various plugs, for insertion in the lobe of the ear, the lips, or the nostril (half actual size).

Many of the Yao women insert a small piece of bone, or ivory, or metal through the wing of the nose. Probably this custom has been borrowed from the coast. In the wives of big chiefs under Muhammadan influence a little silver ornament replaces the ordinary wad which is thrust through the outside of one nostril. The most hideous deformity of all is the celebrated *pelele*. This is a round, hollow disc of wood, or bone, or metal, which is worn in the upper lip. The upper lip is pierced first of all, and the aperture is gradually widened, first by the insertion of a quill or a long, round acacia thorn (with the point removed) or a grass-stem; then of some article of greater size, such as a ring of bone or stone or wood, and so on until the pelele, a ring one inch to one inch and a half in diameter, can be thrust into this hole in the upper lip. Nothing could be more ugly. The pelele makes the woman's lip project until it looks like a duck's bill. It must incommode her very much in eating and drinking. Yet it is a fashion not only prevalent amongst all the A-nyanja, but to some extent amongst the Yao, though in this case I think it can only be where the Yao woman is really of A-nyanja origin.

EXAMPLE OF PELELE IN UPPER LIP

It is a custom not peculiar to British Central Africa, but may be met with in widely removed parts of the continent.

There are few tribes within the limits of the country under description which deliberately knock out any of the front teeth as is so much the custom with the people dwelling on the Upper Zambezi and within the watershed of the Kafue river; but I learn that this practice prevails in some tribes of North-West Nyasaland where the two middle lower incisors are knocked out at puberty, and that the A-nyika of the same district chip the upper incisors by means of an axe. The A-lolo to the south-east of Nyasaland file their teeth into sharp points. This is also done sometimes amongst the Awemba Babisa, and tribes on the Upper Luapula.

Not even the slave trade devastations and the continual warfare between tribe and tribe for the past two hundred years have succeeded in destroying agriculture amongst the British Central African negroes: though it must be admitted that many tribes have degenerated in the exercise of this industry through their harried existence. Those among whom agricultural skill is best preserved are the Wankonde of North Nyasa (a tribe which until the recent invasion of the Arabs had enjoyed centuries of undisturbed peace) and the A-nyanja of South-West Nyasaland.

ANOTHER EXAMPLE OF THE PELELE

As a rule, native agriculture is conducted on a heedless system, ruinous to the future interests of the country. A negro household wishes to start a new plantation. The husband sallies out and selects a piece of land in the wilderness, generally well forested and therefore offering indications of fertile soil. Having chosen his "estate" he lets other people know it by gathering tufts of grass and tying them round the trees, so that passers-by may know that the land has been "betrothed" (that is often the term used). Then he cuts the trees down (leaving stumps in the ground) over the area intended for cultivation and often in addition pollards those standing round the boundaries of the field. The trunks and branches are left to dry during the rainless season of the year. At the close of the dry season they are burnt and their ashes are dug into the soil which at this time is carefully hoed up and turned over, all weeds being cut down, burnt, and buried. By the beginning of the wet season the land is ready for sowing with a crop of maize or sorghum. When the corn comes up, the plants are carefully thinned and those left are often earthed up and are separated one from the other by a space of (say) three feet. Sometimes pumpkins are planted in the furrows, in between the raised mounds from which the cereals grow.

Beyond the burning of the hewn trees and the weeds no attempt is made to manure the soil which, being virgin, yields a very large crop and is then greatly exhausted. The next year the native cultivator abandons the plantation of the year before and prepares another section of forest-land for corn-growing by felling and burning the trees. The result of this procedure is naturally the gradual disforesting of South Central Africa. Only in small areas near a river or lake, which in the wet season are marshes or at that time of the year are under water and enriched by the deposit of alluvial soil, does the negro plant crops annually in the same locality. With rare exceptions he has no idea of manuring the ground and so continuing to cultivate the same piece of land for ever, as would be the case in Europe and in most parts of Asia. Imagine what would be the result in other continents more populated than Africa if year by year each family required to transfer their cultivation to a different piece of ground. What a contrast to Africa is India, a mere peninsula of Asia with its teeming population three times larger than the total population of Africa, and yet for generations subsisting in the same continually cultivated soil whereon their forefathers dwelt before them! One of the great lessons we have

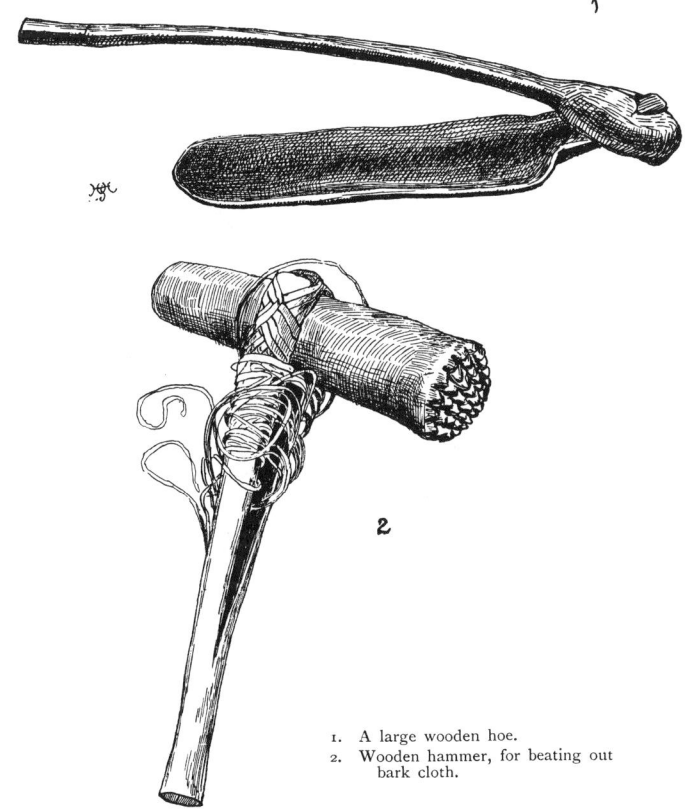

1. A large wooden hoe.
2. Wooden hammer, for beating out bark cloth.

to teach the Central African negro is fixity of tenure, the need of settling permanently on one piece of land, and, by careful manuring, the constant raising of crops from within a certain definite area. The keeping of cattle, pigs, goats, and sheep will assist in manuring the soil.

The Wankonde are somewhat more careful in their cultivation than the other negroes of this territory. They carefully return all weeds, wood-ashes, and village refuse into the soil, while the grass and weeds growing on the fallow land are cut down and burnt in heaps; or else they are laid out on the surface of the soil in long rows, the soil on either side of these layers of cut herbage is dug into trenches or furrow, and what is taken out is thrown on the top of the weeds. These then decay underneath and enrich the soil of these raised beds.

The principal, almost the only, agricultural implement known is the hoe. A sickle may be used for cutting grass, and a wooden rake may possibly be employed in very tidy and prosperous communities for smoothing the seed beds; but the hoe fulfils nearly all the purposes of plough (the plough is quite unknown), harrow, spade, pick, fork, and drill. Nowadays the hoes are chiefly made of iron, but in some of the wilder, remoter, more mountainous tracts long hoes are made of hard wood. In Tropical Africa one is inclined to believe that an age of wood was either antecedent to or parallel with an age of stone, and certainly preceded the age of copper and iron. Not a few native weapons and implements of iron at the present day still have their wooden prototypes lingering alongside. Some ceremony is always observed by the natives at the commencement of the hoeing season, and often at or after harvest. The household fire is extinguished and relit by making fire afresh; dances of various kinds are indulged in.

The order of crops is usually this:—As soon as the first rains have fallen and the ground is moist, pumpkins and maize are sown; then gourds and cucumbers, millet (Mchewere), sorghum (Mapira) and *Eleusine* (Maere); French beans, large beans, small beans, peas, Dhōl,[1] ground nuts, cassava, sweet potatoes and rice. The pumpkins ripen first; then the maize, the cucumbers and gourds. The millet, sorghum, *Eleusine*, and rice are not harvested till June or July. Then follows much beer making (with the grain) and consequent drunkenness. The maize is eaten green—raw, boiled or roasted—but the bulk of it is saved till it ripens and it is then consumed in the form of "pop corn" or flour. In certain favoured localities maize is grown in rotation all the year round. In the dry season it is planted in damp hollows, on river islands, and on land by the river banks, which is thoroughly moist. Many other crops can in this way be raised during the dry season and but for inherent laziness the negro of British Central Africa need never be in want of perpetual supplies of food.

The following are the cereals and plants grown for food or for other purposes by the natives of this part of Africa. (In industrious or specially favoured districts all these things may be grown; but among a lazy people or where the soil is poor and the water supply defective the list may be much reduced.):—

CEREALS.

Sorghum.[2] (Latin: *Sorghum vulgare*. Common native name "Mapira.")

Maize. Introduced by the Portuguese into Zambezia *circa* 1570.

Rice. Introduced by Portuguese and Arabs. The inferior red rice comes from the Zambezi; the good white rice is of Arab introduction.

Millet. (Latin: *Pennisetum typhoideum* Native name in Chinyanja: "Mchewere,") probably introduced by the Portuguese.

Eleusine. (Latin: *Eleusine coracana*.) Native name: "Maere."

Wheat. Introduced by the Portuguese into the Zambezi Valley; and by the Europeans into Nyasaland and the Arabs to Tanganyika. Except in the Zambezi Valley scarcely grown at all by the natives.

Of *beans* there are no less than nine kinds cultivated. One kind is the Indian "Dhōl" (*Cajanus indicus*), another is almost spherical, slightly flattened, a dark brown with a white streak round the rim; a third is very large—

---

[1] Dhōl is a small pease much grown in India.
[2] The *Durrha* of the Sudan. There are nearly nine varieties grown in British Central Africa.

somewhat like the "broad bean," a fourth and fifth are small and white, a sixth and seventh are kinds of peas, an eighth is long and flat, and the ninth is excellent eating, rather small but oblong and dark chocolate-brown. Probably none of these beans is indigenous: they are all no doubt importations of ancient or modern date from the Mediterranean or Asiatic countries. Some of the smaller beans are eaten in the pod like "French beans."

There are two kinds of ground nut: the ordinary *Arachis hypogæa* and the large *Voandzeia subterranea*. The Cassava or Manioc of two or more kinds is abundantly cultivated and is often made into flour. One form of Cassava has a root which is without any of the poisonous qualities so associated with this Euphorbiaceous plant and can be eaten raw without ill effects even by Europeans. It has a pleasant nutty flavour and a creamy sap. The ordinary Cassava is made into flour, but the Missionaries manufacture from it excellent tapioca.

Sweet potatoes are cultivated nearly everywhere. They are palatable and nutritious food. As is no doubt known to my readers the sweet potato is the tuber of a Convolvulus. The *common potato (Solanum tuberosum)* has been introduced by the Missionaries and thrives in the higher districts of the Protectorate. The natives grow it for trade with the European and do not much care to eat it themselves. The *Tomato*, a degenerate kind, grows semi-wild round most of the villages. *Tobacco* is cultivated everywhere and so is *Hemp*. The latter is smoked, the former usually taken in the form of snuff. The *Sugar-cane* is cultivated in the low-lying regions near water: so is the *Saccharine Sorghum*, which like the sugar-cane secretes a sweet juice. As regards cultivated *Cucurbitaceæ* there are about five or six kinds of what we should call "pumpkins" or "vegetable marrows." One of these is like the American Squash with orange-red pulp, another is as delicious as any custard marrow grown at home. Of *cucumbers* there are two or three kinds, all very short and thick and one with large prickles on the rind. There is a *water-melon* (Dzembe or Liembe) and there are *gourds*, more grown for their bottle- or gazogene- or retort-shaped rinds (which make admirable receptacles, pipes, drinking vessels and

NORTH NYASA NATIVE
SMOKING HEMP FROM A PIPE MADE OUT OF A
"GAZOGENE-SHAPED GOURD"

bottles) than for their edible pulp. A kind of spinach is made from the leaves and flowers of certain pumpkins. The *Plantain* or large *banana* is universally cultivated. Small sweet bananas or red bananas are not common and are of recent introduction, Arab or Portuguese. The *papaw* tree[1] is fairly abundant of course as a cultivated tree: it is not indigenous. The *Lime* is met with in many villages but only those under English, Portuguese, or Arab influence. The *Orange* is very rarely met with and such trees as there are (except those on Mount Mlanje) are of young growth. The *Castor oil* plant is (seemingly) indigenous, though one scarcely meets with it far from a native settlement. It is grown for the oil, which is not used medicinally but chiefly

[1] *Carica papaya.*

for anointing the body and occasionally for cooking. Oil derived from the *Sesamum* plant is much used in cooking. The oil palm (*Elæis guineënsis*) is semi-cultivated and grows wild in North-West Nyasaland, on the south coast of Tanganyika and on the Luapula river. The husks of its nuts express the rich "palm oil" of commerce which the natives of those few parts of British Central Africa where the oil palm grows, use in their food and cooking similarly to the West African negroes.

The roots of the *Borassus palm* are sometimes eaten in seasons of scarcity. The seeds of the Itch bean (*Mucuna*) are also roasted and eaten when food crops are lacking, and the grains of certain wild grasses allied to the millet are gathered and made into a poor flour when other resources fail. Several wild herbs furnish a kind of spinach, which mixed with oil and condiments is a favourite relish to be eaten with the porridge made of flour that forms the staple of their existence. *Red peppers* (*capsicums*) are one of the condiments referred to. Though of relatively recent introduction, these "chillies," both red and green, are found growing in nearly every native village.

Some fifteen species of edible and nutritious *fungi* grow in British Central Africa in the rainy season and are much appreciated by the natives. Many roots, which I cannot identify, are devoured; the "heart" is cut out of certain palms (*i.e.*, that soft portion containing the undeveloped fronds) and is stewed and eaten. The roots of *Trapa natans*, a water weed, the flowers and roots

BANANA GROVE (MLANJE)

of the blue water-lily, the leaves of the *Protea* shrub, the gums of certain acacias and of papilionaceous trees, the stalks and leaves of a bean (*Crotalaria*), the seeds of certain Hibiscuses are also consumed by the natives in times of scarcity. For fruits they have the "plums" of the *Parinarium* and of several *Diospyros* trees and shrubs, the sweet "Masuku" (*Uapaca kirkiana*—a fruit something like a medlar with orange-coloured honey-tasting pulp), sycomore figs, wild dates, "bush oranges" (the fruit of several species of *Strychnos*), custard apple (*Anona*) and the bright crimson seed-vessels of the Amomums.

Many more seeds, roots, leaves and fruits than those I have enumerated are cooked and eaten, and not always because of scarcity, but because they are palatable. It is, however, truly remarkable—and here is a trait characteristic of the entire negro race—that throughout the ages during which the black man has inhabited Tropical Africa he has not, with one or two doubtful exceptions, cultivated a single indigenous food plant or domesticated any wild beast or bird of his own portion of the continent.[1]

Of his cultivated plants: maize, manioc (cassava), sweet potato, common potato, tobacco, tomato, "chilli" (red and green) pepper, pineapple, papaw, yams, reached him from America. Although these things are now spread right across Africa in their cultivation they are natives of America and were introduced from two to three centuries ago by the Portuguese.[2] The sorghum (Holcus, Durrha) grain, the millet, the eleusine, the *colocasia* (arum) yam, and the banana, the oldest of his cultivated plants, are natives of the Mediterranean basin, the Nile valley, or Tropical Asia, were first cultivated (on African soil) by the Ancient Egyptians, and reached the negro by slow descent from Egypt. Sugar-cane, rice, wheat, oranges, limes, cucumbers, melons, pumpkins, gourds, onions, not improbably the castor oil plant, the *Datura*, hemp (from India) and most peas and beans were first introduced by Arabs and were re-introduced by the Portuguese. The coffee shrub, though indigenous to Africa only, was not cultivated till the Arabs, Abyssinians, Portuguese and English took it in hand. The cocoanut was introduced from Asia, the edible date palm from the Mediterranean basin.[3] The oil palm of West Africa and Nyasaland is not cultivated —no trouble has been taken to improve it. The only doubtful exceptions to this rule are the ground nuts (*Arachis and Voandzeia*) which *may* be indigenous to Africa,[4] and certain semi-cultivated beans of the genera *Tephrosia* and *Crotalaria*, which the native tolerates in his plantations rather than deliberately cultivates. The *Sesamum* plant, the seeds of which produce such a fine oil, is probably in its cultivated form an introduction from Egypt or India. Indigo and possibly cotton are indigenous but what has the native done to improve them by cultivation?

I am not of course referring to the negroes of British South Africa or Portuguese East and West Africa or those under French tutelage or Arab or Abyssinian or Berber rule, or to the mixed races between negro and Arab, Egyptian, Abyssinian, Libyan or Berber. I am dealing with the pure negro uninfluenced and unmixed as you find him throughout Tropical Africa between the Sahara and Cape Colony.

The *Domestic animals* of the Central African negro are the following: the ox, sheep, goat, dog, cat, fowl, muscovy duck and pigeon. It is hardly correct to include the pig, because pigs are only kept where they have been introduced by Portuguese or British and are not popular as domestic animals. The cattle are almost always of the Indian Zebu type, with the tendency to develop a hump, a dewlap, and short thick horns. But the Angoni-Zulus on the plateaux, west of Lake Nyasa, have a few cattle of the southern type which are recent introductions from across the Zambezi. Though dwarfed in size they are like Cape cattle, with long horns and straight backs and without dewlaps. Another difference between these two breeds of cattle lies in the coloration. As a rule, the long-horned variety is unicoloured, dun, chestnut, greyish-white, "strawberry," or bluish-grey. The humped or short-horned kind is most commonly black, or black and white, or grey, dun, chestnut and white; nearly

---

[1] I am referring of course to the pure-blooded negro, uninfluenced by the Semite or European.
[2] With the exception of the common potato which has been quite recently brought in by the English.
[3] Though several wild species of date grow abundantly in Tropical Africa no one of them has ever been cultivated by the natives.
[4] Some think that these ground nuts came from America. Their cultivation in Tropical Africa is very partial.

always parti-coloured, with white as one of the ingredients. Of course on the borderland the two breeds occasionally intermix, forming types of mingled characteristics. As a rule, the long-horned kind is large and the short-horned small; though through lack of attention in breeding and other causes of degeneration the long-horned breed may become dwarfed while the short-horned humped cattle under favourable circumstances may increase in average size. Sir John Kirk found a very small breed of (I think) humped cattle in the Batoka Highlands (Central Zambezi): the Angoni long-horned cattle west of Lake Nyasa are small; the humped cattle of North Nyasa and the Yao country are large and handsome.

The same interruption in the distribution of the long-horned breed of domestic cattle occurs in South-Central Africa which is characteristic of the range of so many wild animals.

In much of the Egyptian Sudan, Abyssinia, Galla-land, the Central Sudan, Nigeria, and Senegambia the long-horned cattle predominate. They reappear again in South-West Africa and in Africa south of the Zambezi, where they are either the exclusive or the predominating race. On the other hand in East Africa, Moçambique, British Central Africa, the Congo Basin, Angola, the West Coast of Africa, and Lower Niger the humped short-horned cattle are the only kind seen with rare exceptions.

The humped cattle found in British Central Africa originally entered that country from the north and are the direct descendants of the domestic cattle of the Ancient Egyptians which appear to have been derived from Asia. They resemble very strongly the domestic cattle of India. Until our administration of the country commenced, cattle were not widely kept by the natives of the eastern part of British Central Africa, partly owing to the tsetse-fly and the dread of attracting raiders. The following tribes and districts in 1891 possessed domestic cattle: there were a few in the countries round Lake Bangweolo and in the Lunda Kingdom near the south end of Lake Mweru, but very few, owing to the tsetse-fly. The Awemba on the Nyasa-Tanganyika plateau kept large herds. Cattle to a less extent were present in the villages to the east of the Tanganyika plateau and thence onwards to the Uhehe country. The Wankonde people of North Nyasa were and are great cattle keepers and evidently had been for untold generations. The Angoni and Achewa on the high plateaux west of Lake Nyasa, and thence right away down to within the Zambezi Basin were abundantly supplied with cattle. There were a few kept by the Arabs at Kotakota and one herd by Mponda, the Yao chief in South Nyasa. In the Shire Highlands a few head of cattle were to be seen at the villages of the more important Yao chiefs, and in Yaoland proper (east of Lake Nyasa) and on the whole eastern shore of the lake (among the Wayao, Anyanja and Wangindo), wherever Yao or Zulu raiders permitted.

Nowadays, the Awemba of the Tanganyika plateau have lost most of their cattle from the rinderpest, a disease which also decimated the Wankonde herds but fortunately spared the rest of the Protectorate.[1] On the other hand cattle-keeping in Angoniland, on the Upper Shire and in the Shire Highlands has greatly increased owing to the prevention of raids and the spread of prosperity. Of course the Europeans now settled in the Shire province keep cattle to a large extent.

With most of the tribes in British Central Africa the keeping of cattle

[1] When it made its appearance in the north we put a rigid cordon on the entry of infected cattle till the disease was over.

is an accident, an appanage of chieftainship; but with the Wankonde at the north end of Lake Nyasa it is a matter of national existence. Their cattle are supreme in the place they occupy in the life and habits of the people. Elsewhere in Central Africa though cattle may be kept and occasionally eaten, they are not milked any more than are the goats. To most of these Central African negroes it is disgusting to drink milk. But with the Wankonde milk is an important article of diet. Milking is only performed by men: women are not allowed to have anything to do with the cattle. Milk is not drunk fresh but curdled. They wait till they can separate whey from curd; the former is drunk, the latter eaten by means of spoons made of leaves. The

WANKONDE CATTLE

urine of the cows is not thought unclean. Occasionally it is mixed with the milk and drunk; milk-pots are washed in it; and the cowherds often wash themselves in the cow's urine. After the birth of a calf it is said that the herd wishing to ingratiate himself with the cow, wraps the *placenta* round him. The cow will then follow him anywhere. Cattle certainly become extraordinarily attached to their Wankonde herdsmen and these people are in much request as cattle-tenders in the Shire province. Cow-dung is preserved, chiefly for washing out and purifying the interiors of huts (mixed with water) as an insectifuge; also to bind plaster and mud on the walls and floors. It is burnt to drive away mosquitoes, but is not used for manure except that tobacco may be planted on a dung-heap.

The ears of Nkonde cattle are cropped and notched according to the owner's private mark. Many of the cows have wooden bells on the necks, and it is delightful in the beautiful Nkonde and Bundale mountains to hear the tinkle-tinkle which reminds one so of Switzerland. Cattle in this country (Nkonde) are killed by pole-axeing, ordinarily; sometimes by running a spear into the heart. Elsewhere in Nyasaland they are usually thrown and their throats are cut, or they are shot and speared. Amongst the Wayao cattle are extremely wild.

The Wankonde house their cattle in long rectangular buildings, well and strongly built of stout poles. The Yao and Angoni usually drive their cattle at night into unroofed kraals—enclosures with a very high, strong fence of young trees placed closely together two or three deep. The approach to the fence is also defended by thorn branches.

Amongst most of the tribes which possess guns, long powder-horns are used made of the horns of oxen. These very long horns are said to come either from the countries south of the Zambezi or from Madagascar (where the cattle are of the long-horned breed), whence they are exported to the East Coast of Africa.

The domestic sheep of South-Central Africa is of the hairy kind: like the sheep of Syria, Persia and India it develops no wool. Originally this hairy type of domestic sheep was the fat-tailed variety found in Asia, North-East and East Africa and South Africa. In Western and West-Central Africa the fat-tailed sheep lost its fat tail which became a very thin appendage, and developed instead of a dewlap in the male a long mane extending from the throat to the chest. In British Central Africa the two breeds of fat-tailed and maned sheep have mixed. Few or no examples are found with either a pronounced mane or a very fat tail. A variety is occasionally met with which is of considerable size and is tall on the legs. Many sheep are black and white (with black heads—like Persian sheep); others are almost the colour of the mouflon or are grey, white or yellow. The development of horns in the male is seldom large; in the female horns are often wanting. The mutton they provide for the table is *excellent*, much superior to that of the Indian sheep.

But the little African goat is a universal favourite. In this country it and not the dog is "the friend of man," plump, sleek, tame, friendly, intelligent, cheerful. The goat is found in all the villages even where no other domestic animals are kept, and is much petted by the natives. Intellectually it differs from the sheep as a cheery London boy from a heavy-minded rustic. The goat in Africa is an optimist; the sheep a melancholy baaing pessimist. The goat will make himself comfortable under all circumstances, and quite identify himself with the fortunes of his human companions; the sheep will hasten its death by loud lamentations, by bolting into the bush and being devoured by a leopard, or by incontinently falling sick when worn out with lamentations on its sad lot in life. The young and the female goats are good to eat—the flesh of a young kid being excellent; but it is as milk-producers that the female goats are so valuable and admirable. Their yield is not heavy but the quality is very rich. Goats will accompany a caravan on the march and give no trouble; stopping when the men stop; going on when the journey is resumed; feeding and chewing the cud in the intervals of rest and always ready and willing to be milked. In 1889-90 a couple of goats travelled the whole way with me from Moçambique to Tanganyika and back. To one who like myself cannot get on without tea and coffee, cannot drink them without milk, yet loathes tinned milk with all his soul, think what a comfort it must be to have a perambulating supply of rich milk walking along with you, giving no trouble and feeding itself as it goes. So great is the debt which all European explorers, pioneers, missionaries, planters, and settlers in Africa owe to the cheery little African goat that I have often thought a gold medal should be subscribed for and at some public festival be hung round the neck of a representative clear-eyed, spruce, clean, plump and friendly nanny-goat in token of all we owe to her kind for solace in sickness and comfort in health.

The African goat is usually small, short on the legs, very plump, with erect ears, short horns, and (as a rule) short hair. The beard in the males is not long. In the females it is often absent or is replaced by two small pendulous wattles. Some of the old "billies" develop a great growth of hair about the throat and neck, looking almost like the Thar goat of India.[1]

THE DOMESTIC GOAT OF SOUTH AND CENTRAL AFRICA

The wild species of goat, to which the domestic animal of Tropical Africa bears the most resemblance, is the Cretan Ibex.

The dog of Central Africa is the usual small fox-coloured pariah with erect ears and jackal-like head. The tail which is generally long and smooth is sometimes carried over the back. Sometimes the colour is mottled—brown and white, or black and tan, or black and white. Still, where these piebald tints are found there is reason to suspect intermixture with foreign breeds, the usual African type of the pariah dog being a uniform fox-colour. I have sometimes fancied I saw native hunters using a smaller breed of dogs with short legs for terriers' work, but I have never actually ascertained that there *is* such a breed. Dogs are used a good deal for hunting small game. I have never heard of their being employed as in South Africa to tackle big animals and bring them to

[1] Which is not a true goat, but a different genus—*Hemitragus*. Of course the resemblance is accidental.

bay. This African pariah dog has a certain attachment to its native master, but it is always suspicious, furtive and cringing. Europeans they dread strangely, but though they growl angrily they are much too cowardly to bite. They have one good negative quality: they cannot bark.

The domestic cat is (unless in or near European settlements) of that lanky, thin-tailed, small-headed Indian type. It is evidently closely related to the wild native cat (*Felis Caffra*) with which it freely interbreeds. The cat is by no means universally met with as a domestic animal in Central Africa. There is always a suspicion about its being a foreign introduction from Europe, India, or North-East Africa.

The domestic fowl is a most useful bird. It is small—not much larger than a bantam—short-legged,[1] inclining to the game-cock breed but for its full comb. This bird can be excellent eating if a little attention is paid to its fattening. It is not a good layer from our point of view, the hens laying about every two or three days for some eight months in the year. They sit well and are good mothers, especially in rearing foster-children such as young turkeys, geese, or ducks.

There is no such thing as a domestic goose throughout all Africa (except in European settlements) from the borders of Egypt to the Cape. The Portuguese have in their East and West African possessions done much to try and domesticate the spur-winged goose and the *Vulpanser*,[2] but the idea has not caught on among the natives. The Muscovy duck, introduced by the Portuguese from Brazil, has, however, come into favour among the negroes of Nyasaland, Moçambique, East Africa, West Africa, and the Congo Basin as a domestic bird.

The common blue pigeon (with white, mottled, dark-slate-coloured and fawn varieties) is kept as a domestic bird in the Shire Highlands, on the east and west coasts of Nyasa, and on part of the Nyasa Tanganyika plateau and the south coast of Tanganyika; also in all the Arab settlements. But it is not found far away from villages which are in touch with European or Arab civilisation.

From the foregoing list (which with the addition of the horse, donkey, camel, pig, and turkey may be made in varying degree to apply to all Tropical Africa) it will be seen that as in plants so in animals nothing indigenous has been tamed, adapted, cultivated by the negro.

With the exception of the donkey all the beasts and birds above enumerated are Asiatic, European, or American in their origin. Cattle, goats, sheep, came down through Egypt in very ancient time. Earlier still from Arabia and India came the pariah dog.

The pig was introduced by the Portuguese.

The cat was brought here (probably from India) by the Arabs and Portuguese. Farther north in Tropical Africa the cat may have found its way southwards and westwards from Egypt. From Egypt also came the domestic fowl.[3] The Muscovy duck and turkey were introduced by the Portuguese; and the same people, together with the Arabs, brought the pigeon.

The very guinea fowl, though domesticated after a fashion by the Berbers, Libyans, Egyptians and Arabs in the early part of the Christian era, and by

[1] Except where infected by that awful long-legged Indian variety introduced by the Arabs and Portuguese.
[2] "Egyptian goose," "Zambezi duck"—a bird which is a connecting-link between the ducks and geese.
[3] Which the Egyptians received from Persia and the Persians from India.

them passed on to the Roman world, remains undomesticated to this day in Negro Africa.

The donkey, though derived from the wild ass of Abyssinia, Nubia, and Galaland, is really only tamed by people of Hamitic or Semitic stock or intermixture, and by these is passed on in a domesticated state to East Africa. The negroes, who may have herds of these tame asses, cannot domesticate the zebra. They may be devoted to cattle-keeping, yet it never enters their heads to utilise the buffalo or eland of their own land. The wild dogs and cats of Tropical Africa, the gazelles, antelopes, wild swine, giraffe, elephant; the guinea fowl, francolin, turtle doves, cranes, hawks, duck, geese, and ostrich are all capable of domestication, but the negro makes no effort, expresses no desire to undertake this task, though by subduing and utilising these beasts and birds he might add enormously to his material wealth and comfort.

Hunting in this part of Africa is not carried on with quite the same vigour as in the countries to the south of the Zambezi or west of the River Kafue: no doubt because it is more densely wooded. Before guns were introduced in the last century the natives usually dug large pits along the elephant tracks which they skilfully covered with branches and grass. The elephants were then driven in that direction by shouts or bush fires, and one or more of the huge beasts would fall into the pit and remain at the mercy of its captors who killed it with spears. Or bolder hunters might steal up to a drowsy elephant in the noonday and ham-string him by cutting the tendons of the heel. Then he would be done to death with spears and arrows. Others again might be killed by poisoned arrows: but with all these ways (similar no doubt to those which primeval man employed with the mammoth and mastodon) no large number of elephants were killed until guns were introduced, and then the steady diminution of the elephants commenced.

Lions and leopards would not (in those days before guns) be tackled except under great provocation. The buffalo and rhinoceros were let alone (the rhinoceros was and is much dreaded), the larger antelopes and zebras were driven by huge numbers of men ("Bua," the hunt, as it was called) towards converging hedges of stout wattles often built for miles, and when massed together in a cul-de-sac (which sometimes ended in a huge pit) were speared or clubbed. The smaller antelope and rodents were and are pursued by dogs and are also netted. [Nets are put up like a converging fence and the bushbuck or other small antelopes are driven into them and become entangled.] Birds were shot with arrows or were limed. [Bird-lime is made from sticky sap and is used not only for catching birds but large insects.] But as a rule the natives cared and care still little for the flesh of birds.

The hippopotamus is harpooned by some tribes.[1] They pursue him in canoes with a long heavy spear, the base of the blade being prolonged into spikes on either side of the haft so that it enters the body easily but cannot be drawn out. This harpoon is of course attached to a stout rope. But the sport is a dangerous one. The hippopotamus is also killed in traps. A sharp, heavy spear is poised (weighted with a big beam) over the path along which he goes to feed, and is held up in such a way by ropes that when the hippopotamus moves a rope the spear falls and usually severs the spine or penetrates

---

[1] There are certain castes of Zambezi people who make hippopotamus hunting a profession and travel far and wide for the purpose. They are a very civil folk, always careful to ask permission from the "lord of the manor," from the chief of the waterside, to whom they scrupulously hand over a proportion of the flesh and the ivory.

some vital part. These hippopotamus traps are common sights in the natives' plantations by the river side or on the lake shore.

Birds and small mammals are caught in a running noose, or clever little traps are made for the same purpose.

"The old order changeth," however, and most forms of native sport are being brought to the dead level of gunnery. This induces more selfishness than formerly, when successful hunting was a matter which depended on the friendly co-operation of large numbers of men. Formerly a rigid etiquette was observed in the killing of game. No stranger would attempt to hunt in a country which was not his without first obtaining the chief's permission; and when successful a portion of the meat was sent to the chief or the proprietor of the land as a present or tribute. The "ground tusk" of elephants was always given to the chief, also the skins of lions or leopards, both by strangers and by his own subjects. In many of these tribes it is a treasonable offence for any one but a chief to sit on a lion or leopard skin.

Fishing is carried on by the rod and line (possibly learnt from Europeans), by netting, and by erecting fish weirs and basket traps; also by poisoning the water and stupefying the fish in certain still or stagnant river pools. The fish baskets are often cleverly constructed with long recurved strips of bamboo arranged in the neck of a funnel. The fish forces its way in after the bait and cannot return. The netting is usually done with large seines, though I have seen hand nets used.

The preceding remarks on cultivated and wild fruits, grains, and vegetables, on domestic animals and the beast of the chase will have given a fairly comprehensive description of the natives' dietary. To complete it I have only to add that in some tribes (especially among the women) and in some districts there is a craving for argillaceous clay, which they eat with (I imagine) results that are eventually fatal; and further that they consume with gusto certain insects: these are the flying white ants, the "Kungu" fly of Lake Nyasa, large beetle grubs, caterpillars, and locusts. The white ants are roasted wings and all, dried in the sun, pounded in a mortar and made into cakes, which are eaten as a relish. The minute "Kungu" fly (which rises from the water of Lake Nyasa in the dry season in dense clouds) is treated in the same way. It flies against mats which are hung up, is swept off, packed into oily cakes, roasted, and eaten. I believe in some districts the grubs of bees are eaten, taken from the honey-comb. Most of these insects are served up as a relish to be eaten with the porridge. In the same way small fish are dried, mixed with salt and pounded into a paste. Honey is much appreciated. In some districts hives are made of bark and placed in the trees near a village for the wild bees to build in. The quality of the honey depends on the prevailing flowers from which the bees draw their supplies. Occasionally it is white, firm, and exquisitely flavoured. The natives of the West Shire district (where much honey and wax are collected) make a kind of mead from the honey, which is diluted with water and fermented.

Farinaceous food is the mainstay of the Central African negro and is chiefly eaten in the form of porridge—the *Ugali* of the Yao and Swahili; the *Nsima* of the A-nyanja, A-mambwe, A-lungu, A-senga, and Aba-bisa; the *Ikindi* of the Wankonde. This is made ordinarily of the flour of Sorghum,[1] maize, cassava, or banana; nearly always of Sorghum, however. The grain is

---

[1] To give my readers some idea of what Sorghum grain is like I might say it is similar to a huge millet seed, nearly round, about the size of swan shot.

softened with water, pounded in a large wooden mortar, winnowed in long flat baskets, then ground to flour by a smooth stone working on the flat smooth surface of a much larger block of stone. The flour thus made is whitish-grey—sometimes pure white—and feels more granular to the touch than would be the case with mill-ground wheat flour. It is said that the trituration between the stone surfaces causes minute particles of stone to mix with the flour (as must be the case since the nether stone is soon worn into a hollow by the process), and that this slight admixture of grit has a very bad effect on the digestive organs of Europeans and Indians. Certainly neither can eat "ufa"[1] (as the native flour is called) long without getting diarrhœa or dysentery.

The flour made from various farinaceous substances is mixed with water and boiled in a pot, being constantly stirred with a stick to prevent lumps forming. When it is cool it is rolled into balls with the fingers and eaten usually with a relish[2]—fish, fowl, meat of any kind, spinach made from various leaves or flowers, white ants, etc.

Rice is boiled in a measured quantity of water in a covered pot until the water is all absorbed by the swelled grain, which is thus "steamed." Those natives to whom rice is known cook it admirably. Indian corn if it be not made into porridge or boiled or roasted on the cob,[3] is (when the grain is old) held over the fire on a tin plate or dish cover until it is parched into "pop corn," when it is eaten with much gusto. This is usually the way of feeding during a hurried march.

Millet and eleusine[4] grains are usually reserved for making beer. For this purpose, too, large quantities of sorghum and maize are used. The grain is soaked till it sprouts. Then it is pounded and thrown into a large pot of boiling water, to which is also added a thickening of flour to give body to the beer. After boiling and straining the beer is poured out into pots or huge jars of basket work so tightly knit as to hold liquids. The beer must stand for a day and then it is fit for drinking, but after about four days it is sour and unwholesome. Sometimes bran, gruel of flour and water, half pounded corn, and the malt made from the germinating grain are all mixed together, and form a sweet thick beer full of nutriment. Sick or convalescent people are fed on this. Some chiefs at the south end of Tanganyika scarcely take any other food than this beer-gruel and grow fat on it.

The sap of most of the palms is tapped and drunk as a sweet heady drink, which when quite fresh from the tree (palm wine) is not intoxicating but becomes very alcoholic after fermentation. Milk is the favourite food in North-West Nyasaland. It is also drunk in the Awemba country, and round Lake Bangweolo. On the other hand it is ignored or disliked by the Yao and the A-nyanja peoples. No tribe within the confines of this territory makes any form of butter or ghi out of the milk except the Arabs and their followers. Wherever Arabs are settled a supply of milk may almost always be counted on. Eggs are seldom eaten and then usually when they have been sat on for

---

[1] *Ufa* of many Nyasa tribes, *Usu* of South Tanganyika, *Utandi* of the Wa-yao, *Uwufu* of the Wankonde, *Unga* of the Swahili.

[2] Swahili, *Kitoweo*; Chi-nyanja, *Ndiwo*; Yao, *Mboga*; Iki-nkonde, *Iliseke*; *Kifwa* of South Tanganyika.

[3] Sometimes the soft grain of the young sorghum and maize is mashed on a stone, tied up in leaves, and boiled.

[4] A small grain which grows at the end of a short stalk on three broad racemes like three split capsules. In Swahili, *Ulezi*; Chinyanja, *Maere*; Ki-mambwe, *Malesi*.

some time and are deserted by the hen. Like the Kruboys of West Africa, the negro of Central Africa likes his egg "full of meat." Fish is usually split open and roasted. It is often dried first in the sun and may be eaten in this way without further cooking. Sometimes it is made into a stew with peppers and vegetables and is then used as a relish to be eaten with the porridge; or, more rarely, it is fried in fat or oil.[1]

The meat of poultry or beasts is roasted (spitted on sticks stuck in the ground against a fire) or stewed in a pot with vegetables and condiments (peppers, turmeric, salt, etc.). When men are very hungry flesh is but slightly cooked before it is devoured.

The native likes a little meat as a relish with his doughy porridge or rice: but he can quite well do without it and can get on much better without meat than if deprived of all vegetable food. Still when meat comes in his way (after successful hunting or at big feasts) he can devour an enormous quantity and gorges himself till the pains of indigestion are intense. In some districts a meat diet is partaken of by the young men for several days before going to war. I have nowhere met with any among whom obtained the practice of drinking blood or eating it cooked, as is characteristic of so many East and North-East African peoples.

Salt is much liked. It is an absolute necessity of existence in the negro's opinion. Salt is put into porridge and above all into the relish eaten with the porridge or rice.

The cooking is done in small and large clay pots. Where tins have not been introduced by the Europeans, large potsherds are used as frying-pans. Women do most of the preparing and cooking of the food; but any man or boy can at a pinch cook for himself or his comrades.

Certain fancies and peculiar customs prevail regarding articles of diet. Eccentric things are eaten by persons of both sexes for special purposes, while on the other hand wholesome and ordinary forms of food may be excluded for more or less fanciful reasons. Thus among the Wankonde the women never eat fowls. The Angoni, Yao and A-nyanja men sometimes eschew fowls as an article of diet for various reasons. Some men never eat goat, affirming that it makes them unwell.[2] Other tribes refuse to eat fish or a particular kind of fish. Men will eat the flesh of lions to make them brave; libidinous persons consume the *testes* of goats as an aphrodisiac; the heart of a brave enemy is cooked and devoured by those who wish to share his courage. Many people have a particular liking for the half-digested grass found in the stomach of antelopes or oxen.

Fire is made by twirling a short cane or stick in a notch or hole cut in a flat piece of wood. The stick is continually pressed down and is twirled backwards and forwards between the palms of the hands till the tinder (usually dry bark-cloth) is ignited. Then the smouldering tinder is placed in a handful of dry grass leaves and blown gently into a flame. Fire, however, is not often made in this special way. In the village there is always sure to be a burning brand in one or other of the house fires from which a new fire can be lit; and men going on a journey will take smouldering sticks along with them and endeavour to transport fire in this way rather than go to the trouble of creating it by friction.

[1] Frying is not a common method of cooking among those natives who are not under the influence of Europeans or Arabs.
[2] And, according to Dr. Cross, goat's flesh does occasionally have this effect on individuals.

In some tribes fire is carefully extinguished on the hearth and made anew by friction when a death or a birth takes place; at the beginning of the hoeing season and at harvest.

It is an interesting consideration whether fire was known to the earth before man first made it accidentally, and then of set purpose. I think it was, in Central Africa at any rate; and this through the action of lightning. Again and again in the great thunderstorms at the end of the dry season cases have occurred, under the observation of Europeans, of lightning striking a living tree or dead tree-stump, setting it on fire and communicating the flames to the surrounding herbage, thus starting a bush-fire. This action of the lightning is of almost yearly occurrence, even so far as our limited records go. Therefore it is quite possible that in the drier parts of East Africa bush-fires may have occurred year after year from natural causes alone without man's intervention: and that even from this cause man may have become acquainted with fire and the effects of fire before he had evolved the art of fire-making. Fire may even have been preserved from one of these annual conflagrations for days, weeks, months afterwards until it became such a necessity to man that the human mind sought eagerly for a means of creating this force without waiting for the hazardous accident of a thunderstorm.[1] So the sparks from the chipped flints and the kindling tinder made in boring into hard wood would suggest the means of accomplishing the first miracle.

Most of the natives in this part of Africa ascribe the causes of disease and death in the first place to witchcraft and secondly to the direct action of God. They draw a marked distinction between death from disease—which usually means death from witchcraft—and death from accident or in warfare. These are more or less the acts of God and not to be helped, though sometimes an accident may be ascribed to a person having been bewitched, especially if it is a man out hunting and death has been due to wild beasts. In this respect the belief in "were" animals, that is to say in human beings who have changed themselves into lions or leopards or some such harmful beasts, is nearly universal. Moreover there are individuals who imagine they possess this power of assuming the form of an animal and killing human beings in that shape.

I remember a case which occurred at Chiromo soon after we commenced the administration of the Protectorate. A series of murders and mutilations took place in the vicinity of the native village. At last they were traced to an old man who, it was found, concealed himself in long grass near the route to the river side and when solitary passers-by came near him he would leap at them unawares and stab them. He then mutilated their bodies. He was caught almost red-handed and abundant evidence was given as to his being the author of every one of these crimes: but the old man himself talked very freely about the whole matter and admitted having committed the murders. He could not help it (he said) as he had a strong feeling at times that he was changed into a lion and was impelled, as a lion, to kill and mutilate.[2]

Nevertheless though the natives ascribe death in so many cases to the extraneous action of other persons as well as to an evil spirit they have much

[1] Bush-fires of this kind may even have taught early man the advantages of cooking. Following in their track he would come upon roasted rats, small antelopes, and birds which he would find singularly toothsome.
[2] As according to our view of the law he was not a sane person he was sentenced to be detained "during the chief's pleasure" and this "were-lion" has been most usefully employed for years in perfect contentment keeping the roads of Chiromo in good repair.

practical good sense about applying remedies and have a considerable knowledge of therapeutics. They make infusions from the leaves, flowers, bark, wood, or roots of certain plants to be used as medicine for various diseases. There is naturally a good deal of empiricism in their remedies as they will add the blood of a white or red cock to the infusion of herbs, which is given to a sick man.[1] Sometimes a piece of the bark from which the infusion is made is worn round the neck. For some maladies they scarify the skin extensively and are very successful in dry-cupping.

Mr. J. O. Bowhill, the collector for the West Shire District, states that the Mañanja in that district use many indigenous drugs, such as *Bobwana*, an anodyne; *Jigagaru*, a sedative; *Sabu*, a carminative; *Nsonga*, a medicine for the ears; *Petere*, "good for asthma"; *Chisungwa* (red seeds and bark pounded), used as an emetic; *Mpiu*, a medicine used in child-birth; *Kanyanja*, a drug for curing headaches; *Pichiru Maungu*, another medicine for dulling pain; *Mobi*, for burns, and *Mlaza*, a sedative for mad people.

Charcoal is used for painting wounds and ulcers. Some drugs are employed as emetics, others to induce premature labour and abortion. "Charcoal is used" (states the Rev. D. C. R. Scott) "for painting wounds and ulcers with a thick black paste. This is guarded by a piece of gourd-shell neatly cut, pierced with holes by which strings fasten it over the sore place. Clean leaves also are used as dressing. . . . Severe caustic medicines are employed in some instances for painting ulcers. . . . In cases of neuralgia or rheumatism blood-letting is frequently resorted to with a cup made for the purpose. Boils are opened and are carefully treated; small-pox pustules are let out with a thorn and the body is protected with banana leaves. Affections of the chest and throat are treated by inhaling a steam which can be made from various boiled barks; the body is similarly steamed."

The natives throughout this country and elsewhere in Tropical Africa have a great belief in curing sickness, especially if it be a fever or a chill, by the Turkish bath system. They will shut themselves up in a hut before a blazing fire and sweat profusely. Limbs afflicted with rheumatic pains are often "massed." Massage is very commonly met with among the people round Tanganyika and on the west coast of Lake Nyasa, but has probably been introduced by the Arabs who are great believers in it.[2]

But there is another side to medicine, in which the belief of the natives is equally strong. It can be used empirically. Love potions are made which sometimes appear to have this amount of reality in them that they are aphrodisiacs to some extent.

Thieves believe that a medicine or charm can be concocted (called in Chinyanja "Chikululu," by the Wa-nyamwezi of East Central Africa, "Mionga"[3]) which if worn round the thief's neck will cause any persons with whom he comes into contact to fall asleep or else will make him come and go invisible to other men. (Sometimes this medicine appears to be compounded of the very strong drug *Strophanthus,* locally known as *Kombe,* a medicine which is also

---

[1] Not only are there infusions, but roots or fruits are ground to powder and taken in that form.

[2] The very word "Massage" comes from the Arabic *Mās*. This word is adopted also into Hindustani, where *Mās krna* means "To Mass or Shampoo." The Arabic word apparently comes from *Masa*—he touched, handled.

[3] The late Colonel J. A. Grant says that this "medicine" is a branch of the *Steganotænia* tree. "With a branch of it in the hand or by placing the branch over the doorway a man may rob a house without detection; or if he places the branch alongside a goat's body which has been sacrificed at the crossroads all persons will go to sleep where he intends to plunder."

used to stupefy fish and to poison arrows.) The thief or person wishing to escape consumes some himself, believing that it renders him invisible. It is possible that this belief might arise from the action of the drug which taken in quantities not large enough to cause death merely brings about a temporary insensibility. A case illustrating this occurred once at Fort Johnston, and is referred to in my review of the History in Chapter IV.[1]

While on the one hand medicines are supposed to give thieves good luck in stealing, on the other, counter-charms buried in the house or garden will protect property against thieves. Very often these charms are hung up on sticks at the entrance to plantations. Again, other medicines will bring good luck in the shooting of wild animals, or when fixed in some way to the stock of the gun will enable the possessor to shoot straight in time of war; while there are innumerable recipes for rendering one's person safe from risks in warfare. The natives have a firm belief in this last. White men exhibiting bravery in battle, or gaining victory after victory, are simply said to possess "war medicine" which renders them both invulnerable and bound to succeed. These negroes can sometimes be made recklessly brave by their firm belief in the medicine of some particular chief. Not until many of them have fallen on the field of battle will they lose faith in the potency of the chief's charms. These medicines are sometimes heterogeneous substances reduced to powder and enclosed in the horns of small antelopes. Drugs which are supposed to act by occult means are thrown at the person whom they are intended to influence, or they may simply be buried, and, as it were, dedicated to him, sometimes in the vicinity of his habitation.

The poison ordeal is universal as a custom and prevails over the greater part of pagan Negro Africa, the same substance being used throughout for the ordeal. This is known in British Central Africa as Muavi, or Mwai, and is made of the triturated bark of the *Erythrophlæum guineënse*. Certain individuals undertake as a kind of trade the special business of pounding the Muavi bark. It is usually prepared in a small wooden mortar, with a wooden pestle. The water is gradually mixed with the bark as it is being pounded and this is generally done just when the stuff is wanted so that it may be drunk fresh.

Natives are despondent patients in sickness in their own communities, as illness is so often ascribed to witchcraft, and they believe themselves to be in the power of some evil-disposed witch or wizard, who has doomed them to death and whose spells are stronger than those of the friendly medicine man. But they have an almost sublime faith in the European doctor and in his hands they are usually confident of recovery while their remarkable insensibility to pain makes them admirable subjects for operations. Many things may be done to a Central African negro without anæsthetics which in the case of a European or Indian would not only require the application of chloroform or ether, but might even then prove to be too severe a shock to the system for subsequent recovery. It has been remarkable sometimes, after one of our

[1] Msamara, a chief, had been imprisoned in Fort Johnston. His friends were allowed to have access to him and brought him one day a horn of medicine which was probably powdered *Strophanthus*. The next night he took a dose and stripped off his clothes (the idea being that the clothes could not be rendered invisible) and attempted, stark naked, to walk out of his prison. On the Sikh sentries, who were not asleep, presenting their bayonets, Msamara had to retire to the cell once more and explain away the matter next morning by saying that he had been walking in his sleep. The following night, however, he apparently took an extra strong dose of *Strophanthus* and was found lying dead with the empty horn of medicine in his hand and all his clothes removed.

battles, to see the wounded on both sides being dealt with by our surgeons. Operations of the most terribly painful character are being carried on and the patients are smiling, with an occasional wince or grimace, but meantime plaiting grass with their fingers or watching the application of the surgical implements with positive interest.

There are amongst them two classes of medicine man, or woman—the acknowledged or suspected wizard or witch, who by his or her own confession aims at influence over the human frame with the aid of spirits or charms; and the genuine doctor or doctress, a person who by no means discards the use of empirical methods or the action on the patient's imagination secured by mystic rites and substances supposed to have magical value, but who nevertheless has a considerable knowledge of drugs, and frequently effects remarkable cures by honest therapeutics. When a man, woman, or child falls ill the relatives (for there is much mutual help and sympathy amongst these people) go to the nearest and best doctor of repute. He is told the symptoms and asked to prescribe for the patient. If it be the opinion of the sufferer himself, or of his relatives, that his malady is solely due to witchcraft, the person appealed to may be a witch-finder—often a woman. In such a case the patient is visited, various incantations and absurd rites are gone through, usually ending in a little clumsy *léger de main*. The magician, having previously secreted some substance, will pretend to have drawn it from the person's body and with it the sickness, or will have previously buried it at the base of a tree or at the lintel of the hut, and will then in the presence of the gullible bystanders dig it up, accompanying most of these actions by frantic leaping and gesticulation and even by involuntary self-induced convulsions. If the patient does not recover then the magician owns that the opposing witch or wizard has stronger spells and nothing can be done. If suspicion falls on any individual he or she is sometimes propitiated by presents and if recovery then follows all is well; if not then there is strong presumptive evidence that the death is due to this obstinate wizard, who to prove his or her innocence must submit to the Muavi ordeal.

But it may be that the patient or his friends are convinced in the first instance that he is suffering from some well-known malady which can be easily cured by native drugs, or this is the opinion entertained by the doctor they have called in. This individual then proceeds to the woods and prepares from bark, leaves, flowers, seeds, or roots, such medicine as he may consider meets the case. It is noteworthy how efficacious these medicines are. In an obstinate case of seemingly incurable sickness, where a native soldier or policeman is apparently going to pieces, he will ask permission to return to his own people and go through a native cure. After a lapse of about three months, having completed his cure—whatever it may be—he returns sound and well.

The whole subject of native drugs is a most important one, which is being carefully investigated by certain Europeans in the country. Already, it must be remembered, the valuable *Strophanthus* drug, now much used in the British Pharmacopœia, was originally sent home to this country by the late Mr. Buchanan, who had noticed that it was largely used in native medicine, and also for the purpose of stupefying fish and poisoning arrows. It is now one of our regular articles of export.[1]

---

[1] Dr. Kerr Cross states:—"The Wankonde have a wonderful knowledge of herbs and medicinal plants. Of these they make infusions from the leaves, flower, bark, wood or roots. Often the blood of a white or red cock is added to the infusion which the sick man must drink. When he has done this a piece of the healing bark is worn round the neck. They also scarify the wound extensively to counteract

The patient, however, fails to recover, we will suppose, either by faith cure in the belief that the evil influence of the witch is averted, or by good nursing and suitable drugs. He dies. If he has been a chief or a rich man and has lived in a district where European influence does not prevail, a sudden capture is made of a number of his slaves who are put in slave sticks to be subsequently slaughtered at their master's grave, so that they may go with him to the spirit world.

Amongst the Wankonde at the north end of Lake Nyasa the female relatives wash and anoint the dead body with oil ; and this custom of washing, anointing and subsequently swathing the corpse after death is almost universal in this part of Africa.

But the Wankonde have a peculiar custom (as I am informed by Dr. Cross) of making a *post mortem* examination immediately after death, in order that the cause from which the person has died may be fully ascertained. The body is laid out in the shade of a tree, and one of the elders of the village takes a sharp bamboo and makes an incision in the median line of the stomach from the end of the breast bone to the navel. He then carefully examines the mesentery, and according to what he sees in the distribution of the blood-vessels confirms or denies the supposition that death has been due to witchcraft. This is done to the corpse of every person not dying in warfare.[1]

Among all tribes the persons who have handled, washed, anointed and laid out the corpse are considered to be unclean for several days afterwards. They eat amongst themselves and if they have to approach the village remain outside calling for what they want. Ordinarily the people who perform these services for the deceased are his relations—the brothers or sisters. If the dead person be a woman she is attended to in the first instance by women. The body is swathed in cloth among those tribes who are in contact with supplies of European goods; but this would appear to be rather a custom imported from the Muhammadan. In the wilder parts of the country corpses are usually tied up with strips of bark in a sitting position. When these services are completed and the deceased is ready for burial those who have prepared the body perform various ablutions and get rid of their " uncleanliness."

---

one pain by another; they dry-cup freely and seem to be very successful in this. We have a lot to learn from the Wankonde doctors."

In regard to dry-cupping it is usually performed in this way :—First of all the place on the skin where the cupping is to take place is moistened, then a cup-shaped instrument made of antelope horn with a small hole bored at the end is firmly pressed on to the moistened skin. The hole at the stem of the cup is filled up with wax. Through this is thrust a tube of grass—similar to the straws with which people absorb cooling drinks. The doctor then sucks hard at the grass tube, the blood comes to the surface of the skin and the drawn-up flesh rises into the cup. The grass tube is withdrawn and the hole closed with wax after the air is exhausted. When the horn is removed the blood has formed large weals or lumps under the skin.

[1] The Anyanja divide the causes of death into three. One is the direct act of God, namely some sudden accident or the outcome of some widespread epidemic ; occasionally also the result of well-known diseases obviously incurred in a natural manner. Secondly, death in warfare or by open assassination, for the murderer may or may not be held responsible according to native law ; these deaths at any rate demand no further enquiry. Thirdly, death by witchcraft, where the malady is of an obscure kind, or where an individual has been killed by some wild beast, either in hunting or as an act of unprovoked aggression on the part of the animal. On these occasions the wild beast is supposed to be either inspired by the spirit of the witch or to be actually a " were," or human being disguised as a wild animal. The Wa-yao hold much the same ideas. When during a truce the Yao chief Makanjira was considering the terms of peace proposed by Major Edwards one of his councillors rose and advised war with the British to the bitter end. The discussion was taking place in the bush, and by a curious coincidence at that moment an enraged bull buffalo charged the whole party, singling out (and so wounding that eventually he died) the aforesaid councillor. The Yao at once declared that this buffalo was none other than Major Edwards and war was resumed with greater bitterness on this account.

In the case of the A-nyanja the body is usually stretched at full length when prepared for burial; amongst the Wa-yao the legs are bent; with the Wankonde the body is tied up in a sitting position, the knees drawn up against the chin with the hands clasped round the legs. This appears to be the position adopted by almost all the other tribes of British Central Africa.

Muhammadans are, of course, swathed in cloth and buried at full length.

Wailing begins as soon as the death is officially announced: it is generally commenced by the wives of the deceased (if a male) or by the mother or sister of the dead woman. Mourning consists of plaintive songs, much drumming, and mystic dancing. Where the people have been in contact with the coast Muhammadans, guns are fired if a great man has died. This firing of guns is kept up at intervals until the burial is finished. The Wa-yao and some other tribes throw flour over their heads and shoulders when in mourning; the A-nyanja and the people of the west coast of Lake Nyasa tie strips of bark cloth, or plaited straw, or blue calico round their arms and waists. Amongst the Wa-yao and A-nyanja the corpse, whether swathed or not, is usually rolled up in the mat which belonged to his bed, or in cases where the mourning on account of a chief or big man is to last a long time the body is enclosed in a cylinder of bark. It is then placed over a hole dug in the floor of the hut so that the inconvenience caused by decomposition may be thus got rid of. The smell attending decomposition is neutralised by hemp and other aromatic weeds being burned. It often happens, however, that the deceased person who is to be mourned such a long period has his body poised over what is to be subsequently his grave; for men are often buried in their own houses.

If, however, the dead person is to be buried away from the village a long pole is passed through the mat or cylinder enclosing the body and the corpse is then carried along on the shoulders of undertakers who go out accompanied by a number of men and women marching with drums and chants. The grave is dug, the body buried, the earth heaped over it and fences are erected to which there may be subsequently added a grass roof.

The Rev. Duff Macdonald states that amongst the Yao no one very closely related to the deceased accompanies the body to the grave if it can possibly be helped—that is to say, if there are enough people in the village not thus related to carry out the ceremony. Mothers are allowed to go to the funerals of their children if they have died in infancy, not otherwise; a father will not go to the funeral of his children nor the husband to that of his wife. Mr. Macdonald also states that the chief relative of the deceased—what we should call the first mourner—does not come to the grave, as that would unfit him for the task of prosecuting the witch that caused the death.

The grave is not dug, nor is the site of it actually indicated until the funeral party arrives, after which grave-digging commences. The diggers are supported from time to time by rations of food brought by the women and the grave is dug with hoes and according to the measurement of the body. When the grave is finished two forked stakes are driven into the ground at each end of it. The body is then lowered and the forked sticks receive the projecting parts of the bamboo that carried the corpse to the grave. It is thus suspended between these two sticks without touching the bottom of the grave. The top of the grave is roofed in by logs of wood. Articles which are to be buried with the deceased are then put in and earth is finally sifted over the hole.

According to Mr. Macdonald this strong wooden fence round the grave is supposed to keep out the witch who has caused the death and who now wishes to eat the flesh of her victim and may come there in the shape of a hyena to dig up the body.

As to the articles buried with the body:—Amongst the Wa-yao if the deceased is a rich man a small portion of his ivory is ground to powder and handfuls of beads are smashed up before they are put into the grave. This appears to be done with the double object of preventing thieves from robbing the graves and also of "killing" the articles put in so that they may accompany the deceased to the spirit world. In like manner his pots and drinking vessels have holes drilled through them or are broken, and likewise added to the stock of utensils in the grave.

Where the custom is carried out of killing slaves to accompany the deceased on his journey the grave is of course a very much larger one, and the slaves are either buried alive or have their throats cut and their bodies are laid at the bottom of the grave. On them the body of the deceased reposes.

Amongst many of the tribes of the Nyasa-Tanganyika plateau, of Tanganyika and elsewhere to the west, the corpse is usually left in the grave (which is a round hole about five feet deep) for ten lunar months, after which time it is taken up at midnight and the bones (for by this time it is practically reduced to a skeleton) are carried to one of the sacred clumps of forest on the high hills in the neighbourhood, a forest to which only the sorcerers and medicine men go. Forests all over the country are used for burial, either for the bestowal of bones or for the interment of the undisturbed corpse. Consequently natives often oppose one's exploration of the thick jungle just where it is most attractive to the botanist—more I think because they do not wish you to come to any harm by offending the spirits than because they are shocked at your profanity. Sometimes when I have explained to them I merely wished to go there to gather flowers they have raised no objections, although I remember in one case a strong protest being uttered against my taking away some gorgeous yellow blossoms from a shrub which grew in one of these native cemeteries.

Among the Awa-wamdia of North-West Nyasa the bones after they are disinterred are burned; they are not thrown into the forest. A great festival takes place when the bones are burnt, at which a quantity of native beer is drunk.

Amongst the Awa-ndali of North-West Nyasa the corpse is interred outside the hut in which the person has died, at one side of the door. A grass covering is put over the mound. Should, however, any member of the deceased's family become ill within a year, the misfortune is attributed to the deceased, and to obviate any further harm the nearest relative of the person there buried digs up the bones at midnight and carries them to the dense bush where they are deposited. Dr. Cross writes:—"I have gone into several of the thick clumps of trees in this country and have found the ground covered with human bones."

All the Wankonde peoples are particular about their mourning customs. The banana trees which may have belonged to the deceased during his life are cut down. His or her pots and baskets are broken or destroyed and the home is often left to decay. But the dead are not forgotten. The grave is usually marked by a small grass covering (this also applies to the Wa-yao and the A-nyanja), and from time to time the relatives place on this mound little baskets of meal or pots of native beer. I remember after the capture of Zarafi's stronghold (which was a very large rambling Yao village up in the mountains) there was quite a large native cemetery, outside the town, each grave being marked by a neat little house made of bamboo stakes with a grass roof and with a mound over the grave. Each grave was well supplied with little offerings of food which had evidently been freshly placed there just before the town was captured. Nothing, I was subsequently told, operated more in our favour, or induced the natives more readily to sue for peace, than the fact that these graves were respected and left undisturbed. On the other hand Makanjira, in the course of our warfare, was infuriated by the destruction of his "father's" tomb.[1] At the time we destroyed it we did not realise it was a tomb. We took it for an unusually stylish house. The roof of this large mausoleum was entirely covered with white calico intended to imitate the white tombs in Muhammadan countries, erected over the grave of some saint. At Mponda's town to the south end of Lake Nyasa there was likewise a huge circular tomb with its thatched roof covered with white calico. This was partially destroyed during the bombardment. It was the place where the former Mponda had been buried. On entering the tomb, the roof of which only had been destroyed, we found the grave was a huge sarcophagus of hardened clay, very similar in shape to the great stone tombs of the middle ages, with earthenware plates embedded in the mud, so that at a distance it had rather a fine, coruscating effect from this enamel of coarse pottery (which of course was derived from the coast in the course of trade). Finding that the building was the burial place of the Mponda who had been good to Livingstone, we restored the roof and re-covered it with white calico of our own will, and that went so far to conciliate Mponda's people that although their present chief again fell out with us some years later on his people did not join him in the rising.

Amongst all those Nyanja tribes where the custom does not prevail of taking up the bones and scattering them in the forest after a certain lapse of time, the grave is held sacred. To swear by the grave is a solemn oath. Sentiment regarding the place of interment is very prevalent even as regards the burial of Europeans. Such explorers as have visited the place where Livingstone's heart lies buried, or the graves of Bishop Mackenzie or other missionaries who have died in British Central Africa, have been struck with the great care taken of the graves by the natives.

Reference has been made to the belief that deaths can be caused by occult influence, by witchcraft. Except in the vicinity of mission stations or such districts as are entirely under the control of European officials this belief is widespread, and probably no tribe or section of people is exempted from it.

The witch, or wizard, *Mfiti*—as opposed to *Siñanga*, the doctor, the medicine man—is the terror of the Central African negro community. And in most parts of British Central Africa—especially among the A-nyanja—there is a real excuse for this terror in the fact that *Mfiti*—or *Zimfiti*, as the plural is sometimes—are depraved persons with a craving for putrefying human flesh. This is no fancy; it is a fact. It is probable that not more than one or two centuries have elapsed since the bulk of South Central Africans were cannibals, in the cheerful, daylight manner of the Upper Congo, where people are killed and eaten for gastronomic pleasure and the act is normal and unconcealed. Gradually, however, with the vague influence of the Portuguese to the south and the Arabs to the north, the natives became

---

[1] Not really his father but the chief who preceded him, as amongst the Yao son does not succeed father.

ashamed of eating human flesh, and they grew to regard such a practice as most abhorrent.[1]

But while cannibalism in the main disappeared as an avowed custom it has lingered as a horrible practice amongst depraved people, who now do not care for healthy human flesh—namely the bodies of people killed in battle—but crave for dead bodies which have been in the grave a few days or weeks, and which they exhume and devour. No doubt this custom prevailed among many other races of man in the savage stage and was the grain of truth at the bottom of the Eastern myth of the Ghūl.

I had not been long in Nyasaland before I heard that cannibalism of a more or less secret kind still lingered amongst the timid mountaineers of Nyanja race on Cholo Mountain midway between Chiromo and Blantyre; and in 1891 a French priest who had been stationed for a year as a missionary at Mponda's town at the south end of Lake Nyasa, described to me how frequently people of Nyanja race dug up corpses and devoured them. He described the horror with which the Muhammadanised Yao regarded this practice, and went on to relate how a certain woman was accused of being a witch and of eating human flesh from the graves; that she stoutly denied the accusation and they then forced her to drink *mwavi*; she found she could not vomit and that death was certain. She therefore shrieked out "It is true: go to my house and you will find the remains of a man's leg hidden in such and such a place." People rushed to the house and the priest followed them, and to his horror he saw them bringing out from the interior what seemed to be the bones of a leg with fragments of putrefying flesh still remaining attached to the bones. The woman was killed and burnt by the populace.

The idea amongst the natives is that these *Mfiti* will the death of a certain person which they compass by occult means—namely, by secret spells and charms, by the burying of medicine "against" a person (that is, they take some stuff which is supposed to possess mysterious properties and bury it, dedicating it as they do so to the individual whose death they wish to bring about). Their main object in causing a person's death is to be able afterwards to eat his body. Of course with this substratum of fact that these acts of nauseous cannibalism do occur, there is an enormous amount of superstition mingled. Supernatural powers are ascribed to these *Mfiti*, with whom the eagle-owl, the jackal, the leopard or the hyena are specially associated, those creatures being supposed to be the servants of the witches or to be the forms which the sorcerers assume when they visit the graves or dig up the bodies. The wizard is believed to be able to make himself invisible, to transport himself as a spirit rapidly from place to place, and to fly through the air with fantastic gyrations. He may still be invisible to ordinary eyes while he is taking up and mutilating the corpse. "When the jackal barks,[2] 'there,' says the listener in the night, 'is the messenger calling these midnight wretches to their awful orgies'; when

---

[1] Yet one constantly meets with cases of it occurring, especially if the act of cannibalism be associated with rage and the desire to utterly consume the enemy or for the wish to secure his qualities of bravery by eating his heart. The old Makanjira met his death through cannibalism. He was jealous of a headman who had acquired power and influence after Makanjira's first defeat at the hands of the British. He had this man secretly killed, and his body cooked and served up with an enormous mess of native porridge. A number of chiefs and persons of importance were invited to the feast. After it was over they were told that the meat they had consumed was the body of So-and-so. One young fellow, a nephew of Makanjira, was so enraged at having been made to commit this act unconsciously, that he killed Makanjira then and there, and thus avenged the deaths of Captain Maguire, Dr. Boyce, and Mr. McEwan. He was however slain himself by the chief's adherents.

[2] I quote from the Rev. D. C. R. Scott, in his Mañanga Dictionary.

a fire is seen on a distant hill where no fire should be, 'there is the light of their cooking fire.'"

The grave is supposed to be alight, to shine with a phosphorescent light where the *Mfiti* gather. It is said that the wizards summon the dead man by the name of his childhood which he laid aside on his initiation. Such a summons he cannot resist. He emerges from the grave even if it be through a small hole, then the wizards torture him and knock him down, divide him limb from limb, cook the flesh and eat it.

Naturally with beliefs like this it is the constant object of the more wholesome-minded natives to discover and destroy the abominable sorcerers, and some people are supposed to possess great powers as witch-finders.

These may be male or female; more often than not they are elderly women. The witch-finder is sent for after the death has occurred and stays for some time in the village cross-questioning everyone she can get hold of. She pretends to have much the same power as the witches, and by means of medicines and charms to be able to track the witches at night-time in their transformed shapes. Having thus professed to attend the witches' sabbath she discovers the names by which they are addressed among themselves, and then by her own occult powers identifies these assumed names with the appellations they are known by in the village.

Negroes are gulled most easily and by the rudest sleight-of-hand. They will believe almost any stories they are told. Probably what the witch-finder really does is to listen to all the gossip of the village and by observation to ascertain (1) if any particular person had a grudge against the deceased and (2) if there is anyone in the place who probably has a leaning to the horrible practice of rifling the grave and eating decayed human flesh. If she believes herself to have alighted on such a person then she affects to have arrived at the knowledge through supernatural means, and clothes her denunciation with the sanction of the occult. When she has made up her mind she summons the people together. All the inhabitants of the village must attend. The witch-finder then commences a fantastic dance in which she works herself up to the condition of seeming epilepsy. She tears round the informal circle of spectators, dashes first at one then at another, affects to smell them to see if she can discover the odour of putrefying meat; at last she pronounces the name of the person, the name which she is supposed to have heard at the witches' sabbath. No one replies. Then the witch-finder says "that is the name by which the *Mfiti* is known to the other sorcerers: his or her real name is such and such." Persons thus accused have to submit to the *Muavi* ordeal to prove their innocence. The most remarkable thing about the whole procedure is that the witch-finder's allegations are sometimes supported by the supposed culprit who, either from a desire to enjoy renown as a wizard (with the hope of vomiting the *Muavi* and thus escaping the consequences), or because he or she may really believe through disordered dreams that they have the power to do such things, submits unhesitatingly to the ordeal and does not attempt to escape.

No doubt it rests a good deal with the individual who prepares the *Muavi*, to make the dose strong enough to prove fatal or weak enough to act merely as an emetic.

A considerable amount of bribery is sometimes resorted to by the accused or accused's friends. If, however, the *muavi* remains in the stomach, and the wretched creature is unable to vomit, a murderous madness seizes the surrounding crowd and the now-convicted sorcerer is lynched, the body being subsequently burnt.

The negro, it will be seen, believes that life does not finish when the body dies. He has been led to this vague hope of immortality insensibly. It has seemed impossible that the father of the household, the headman of the village, or the chief of the tribe could abruptly vanish when he has exercised such an important influence during his lifetime. It would appear as if the Bantu negro had built up God by degrees out of ancestor worship. Dr. Bleek pointed out years ago that the common word for God over the eastern half of Bantu Africa —Mulungu—could be traced to the Zulu word "Munkulunkulu"—the great, great one, or, the old, old one. There is some truth in this, but I think that a second belief has come to meet ancestor worship, a belief in the personification of the heavens, of the sun, moon, and stars, the rain, thunder, lightning: some mighty Being or Agency who exercises ruling powers over the Universe, the Being which may by tribe after tribe have been identified with some great dead chief. Still their idea of God—and they all believe in a supreme God—is somewhat dissociated from their firm belief in life beyond the grave: in the existence after death of their ancestors, though this existence is not held to be necessarily perpetual. The ghost or its influence fades away after a time. Yet they believe that some spirits live interminably especially if the deceased has been a chief of great influence. Originally, no doubt, they were in the habit of thrusting their dead into caves or the hollows of mountains.[1] Then at other times and places dense forests were specially used for the secretion of the dead body; so in time it came to be thought that most mountains and thick black forests were haunted by spirits of deceased persons. They have the firmest belief possible in ghosts, and will tell long circumstantial stories about the "spooks" they have seen—prosaic stories usually connected with daylight, as where a woman declares that while winnowing or pounding corn in the noontide, she looked out in the courtyard and saw the spirit of So-and-so passing along looking exactly as though he were alive. It is thought that these ghosts have considerable power for good or evil, and they are often propitiated, though if they become troublesome (that is to say, if vexatious incidents occur or their descendants fall sick or meet with misfortunes) revenge may be taken on the bones of the dead persons to whose spirits the annoyance is attributed. They are dug up from their graves and thrown away, or removed to a far place to be buried under some tree which is supposed to have a restraining influence over the spirit. Occasionally one of these departed ancestors is believed to have taken an affection for some eccentric looking rock, or waterfall or rapid, but I have never met with any belief in this part of Africa in spirits which were like the demigods of the Greeks—the soul of the river, the lake, the tree, the mountain.[2]

Yet in some tribes there is a distinct belief in an evil deity either as the

[1] There is a large native sepulchre in a ravine at Zomba mountain with precipitous sides. Into this hole many dead persons have been thrown, and their whitened bones can be seen there. There are numerous legends about all the great mountains of the Shire Highlands. In the caves of this mountain such and such a chief was buried; on that hill another, and so on, these mountains now being more or less the home of the chiefs' spirits.

[2] Dr. Cross differs from me in this respect. He asserts that a belief of this kind in earth and water-spirits is held by the Wankonde. I am inclined to think that it would be found that these lesser divinities are really the spirits of departed ancestors who may be associated with some remarkable object or scenery. Still the Wankonde are a people somewhat apart and peculiar who have evidently been isolated for centuries at the north end of Lake Nyasa, and have maintained many old beliefs elsewhere worn away just as they have retained a singularly archaic form of Bantu language.

rival ruler of the universe or as an alternative to the good God, in short some tribes believe—without outside influence—in a devil. This is the case with the Wankonde at the north end of Lake Nyasa, who, according to Dr. Cross, believe that Mbase (the spirit of evil) lives in a remarkable cave in the side of the mountain called Ikombwe. This cave has stalactites and stalagmites in abundance. As Mbase is considered to be the source of many troubles people worship him and propitiate him constantly. When Dr. Cross visited the cave it was nearly filled up with old broken pots and rotten cloth. These pots had been deposited full of meal for hundreds of years in the cave so that it is now almost blocked up. Two years ago a harum-scarum son of chief Mwankenja determined to set Mbase at defiance and robbed his cave of large quantities of cloth and offerings of brass-wire and beads. As no harm happened to him subsequently the belief in an evil spirit is said to have received a severe shock, and this, with the growing influence of the missionaries, is bringing about a cessation of the worship.

With all this implicit belief in the lingering life or the immortality of the soul after death, the natives of Central Africa do not believe in any form of resurrection. All these peoples have numerous sayings and proverbs expressive of the fact that the dead never return. If they analysed their own beliefs they would probably admit that in most cases spirit life had a definite duration, after which it faded away into the central God, "Mulungu," or into nothingness. Certain great men might linger on for centuries.

At the north end of Lake Nyasa the natives constantly offer sacrifices to the spirits of the dead. Secret places for worship are known as *Ilisieta* (plur. *Amasieta*). They are usually thick clumps of forest or groves of trees in which people have been buried for generations. The offering is generally a bullock. The animal is killed by striking it on the back of the neck with a sharp axe of a special kind kept for the purpose. The blood is carefully collected and poured over the ground in one of the *Amasieta*. Prayers are then offered to the spirits of the forefathers. The head of the ox is laid on the ground as a further offering while the rest of the body is consumed by the worshippers.

Divination and the drawing of lots are constantly practised. In Southern Nyasaland it is a common practice to ascertain whether a certain journey will be favourable by sticking a knife in the grass and leaning against the blade two small sticks, or else by laying two tiny sticks on the ground and placing a third one athwart the two. The person making the experiment then turns aside for a minute or two and if on looking at the sticks again one or other is found to have fallen to the ground from against the blade of the knife, or if the stick laid athwart the other two is disturbed in its position (from any passing breeze) then the omen is a bad one. Among the more superstitious A-nyanja, *muavi* or other medicines are given to fowls or to goats. (There is evidence to show that originally the medicine would have been given to a slave.) If the creature thus doctored dies it is an ill omen, if the reverse a good omen. This is used constantly to try the good faith of strangers. Colonel Edwards, Mr. Sharpe and myself have often sat anxiously waiting for the result of some such ordeal in visiting a suspicious tribe, and have been delighted to see the fowl eject the noxious dose from its crop, or the goat refuse the bolus, knowing then that our cause was gained. Besides the great Muavi ordeal there are other methods of testing guilt or innocence. People will plunge their hands into boiling water. If not scalded they are innocent. A remarkable instance of divining occurs amongst the Wankonde. They use a divining stick—apparently a long flexible wand which has been partly bent or snapped below the portion seized by the hand, so that it is provided with a kind of hinge and is susceptible to the least tremor. When a person is accused of stealing they commence by burning certain roots in a fire. The rod is then shaken over the fire while simultaneously they call upon the spirits of the departed to use it as a means of enabling the diviner to discover the thief. The thief-finder then starts off on his quest much as a thought-reader might do. Whichever way the rod waggles the diviner follows and at last he affects to have been led to a certain house, the owner of which is taken to be the thief.

Another widespread belief lies in the power of certain wizards to make lions or other wild beasts or to inspire such as are naturally created with a mission to destroy. Dr. Cross informs me that there is a man in the Bundale country at the north end of Lake Nyasa who is believed to make lions. He is very old and lives in great seclusion, and is said to have several lions lying in the long grass surrounding his house. He can make these lions do his will, and if properly paid will undertake the commission of sending the lions to a specified neighbourhood to devour or harass the people. Should one man have a dispute with another he can enforce his case powerfully by these means. "I have frequently been astonished," writes Dr. Cross, "to see how tenaciously even the most intelligent cling to this belief. They are firmly convinced that lions do not roam aimlessly but are sent to a neighbourhood with a definite object in view."

When we were preparing our expedition to fight the great slave-raiding chief, Matipwiri (to the east of Mount Mlanje in South Nyasaland), he sent to another Yao chief, Zarafi, for assistance. Zarafi could not aid him in men or guns but sent his son, who was reputed to be a wizard, to make spells which should raise up all the lions, leopards, and hyenas in Matipwiri's country against the invading force. These animals were to meet us half way in the wilderness and utterly destroy us. The absurd thing was that Matipwiri and his brother chief Mtiramanja, although they were intelligent men (Matipwiri had once obtained, probably from a trader, the full uniform of a Portuguese colonel, and used to style himself a colonel in the Portuguese Army!), who had constant intercourse with the coast, they nevertheless believed in the supernatural powers of Kadewere, the wizard referred to; and were so convinced that the wild animals would stop us from coming that they remained in their villages until our troops entered the suburbs. Even then on the first day of our invasion they made but a faint resistance, so astounded were they that the lions and leopards had not obeyed the orders of their master to harass our expedition.

Amongst other beliefs is a certain dread of women who are menstruating. It is thought that if a woman in this condition puts salt into the food her husband or child eating the food will then become ill and hot and feverish, with a bad cough. Also it is believed that if a husband or wife has been guilty of adultery and while under the shadow of the fault puts salt into the food the children eating thereof will fall sick.

A belief that certain persons have power over the atmosphere so that they can make rain fall or wind rise or drop is universal, though it is not perhaps such a prominent subject of consideration as in Africa south of the Zambezi where the gradual desiccation of the country makes the fall of a shower a crying necessity.

At the north end of Lake Nyasa there was an old rain-maker named

Mwaka Sungula, much revered for his powers of bringing down rain or of changing the wind. He was often resorted to when the weather required amendment. Some six or seven years ago the African Lakes Company's steamer *Domira* was stranded in the shallows a little distance to the north of Karonga. Hundreds of natives were employed for days tugging and hauling and pushing at the steamer without any result; she still remained hopelessly stuck in the sand. At last they called Mwaka Sungula to their assistance. Having been "squared" by a small present he went through several incantations in the evening of the day and wound up by sprinkling the blood of a white cock on the natives around the steamer. Next morning the steamer was afloat. The wind had changed in the night, had blown up the water of the lake and raised the vessel from off the sandbank. Naturally ever since all failures of Mwaka Sungula have been forgotten in the face of this one crowning success.

Among other superstitions in Northern Nyasaland no woman will state the name of her husband or even use a word that may be synonymous with his name.[1] If she were to call him by his proper name she considers it would be unlucky and affect her powers of conception. In the same way the women do not, for superstitious reasons, use the common names of articles of food but special terms peculiar to the women's use.

The life of an African is rigidly ruled by custom. He is more of a slave to custom than the average European. I have noticed most of the ceremonies connected with birth, marriage, death and burial; but all the important phases and functions of their lives are attended with special customs, almost invariably expressed by much dancing, and brewing, drinking, and libations of native beer. At the beginning of the hoeing season (say October) feasts are held. In some cases there is a "hoe" dance, wherein the dancers carry hoes which they strike together with a musical clang, in rhythm with the beating of the drums. Beer is brewed from various grains in great quantities and not only drunk by the dancers but poured out on the soil in libations. Much the same is done at harvest time. No important journey is undertaken without small sacrifices to ancestors and consulting the oracle by means of the small "divination" sticks already described, which according to whether they shift their position or not determine a man whether he shall stay or go. A snake or a hare crossing his path at starting will turn him back; the sight of the stinking *Ponera* ant will encourage him; still more the song of certain birds.

These negroes delight in fables and in beast stories. They may be truly said to "speak in parables," parabolic metaphor entering largely into their speech. In the beast stories—which are usually somewhat inane and without a very clear point—the Hyena, the Leopard, the Jackal, the Tortoise, the Owl, and the Hare figure principally, the Hare being usually the leading character and taking the place of the Fox in European folk-lore for cunning and independence of action, while the Hyena is nearly always the butt, the greedy fool who is the victim of practical jokes. It is difficult to see how this view of the Hare's character arose, as the African species of this animal do not strike a European as being particularly astute or wily. These stories are very similar to such as are found in Zululand and elsewhere in Bantu Africa.

Riddles, proverbs, and "hard sayings" are most numerous in all the

[1] There is a remarkable degree of demonstrative affection between the Wankonde husband and wife, a phase of character very rare amongst Central African negroes. This has been noticed by many travellers—Thomson, Giraud, Nicoll, Fotheringham, Dr. Kerr Cross and myself.

languages, and are favourite exercises of ingenuity and wit. Here are some samples culled from the Rev. D. C. R. Scott's Mañanja Dictionary:

"I built my house without a door."
Answer: "An egg."

"My hen laid eggs in the thorns."
Answer: "The tongue between the teeth."

"The sick man does not wish to run, but when he sees this he must; the chief who comes to this must run whether he will or no."
Answer: "A steep descent."

"When either a man or a seed dies there grows up another." (There are as many good fish in the sea as ever came out of it.)

In regard to their habitations: the original form of house throughout all British Central Africa was what the majority of the houses still are—circular and somewhat like a beehive in shape with round walls of wattle and daub and thatched roof. This style of house is characteristic of (*a*) all Africa south of the Zambezi; (*b*) all British Central Africa; as much of the Portuguese Provinces of Zambezia and Moçambique as are not under direct Portuguese or Muhammadan influence which may have introduced the rectangular dwelling; (*c*) all East Africa[1] up to and including the Egyptian Sudan, where Arab influence has not introduced the oblong rectangular building; (*d*) the Central Nigerian Sudan, much of Senegambia, and perhaps the West Coast of Africa as far east and south as the Gold Coast, subject of course to the same limitations as to foreign influence.

A TYPICAL NATIVE HOUSE IN SOUTH NYASALAND

But over the greater part of the Congo Basin (with a few marked exceptions in the north-east and east of that region) and the western part of Africa down as far south as Mossamedes, the house is rectangular in shape but sometimes a very long building indeed or a great many houses united to form the side of a street.[2]

This rectangular house in Western Africa is so universal and is found in such remote districts as are only being entered for the first time by white men at the present day, that it is improbable it could owe its origin to the Portuguese, and there has been no other extraneous influence over those regions within the historical period. Nevertheless, Portuguese influence never spread very far beyond the coast in West Africa and there is evidence in all books of travel

---

[1] In parts of East Africa, the normal type of house differs from the ordinary round house of Central Africa by being more exactly beehive-like in shape, with the thatch of the roof touching the ground. See for this the illustrations in my book on Kilimanjaro.

[2] Samples of these different kinds of houses are illustrated in my book on the River Congo.

to show that the rectangular house was found there when the first Portuguese explorers arrived in West Africa.

The native house of the White Nile, of Nyasaland and of Zululand is so similar in structure that in photographs taken in these different countries it is difficult to say to what part of East, Central or South Africa the building belongs. But although for an ordinary dwelling this round house is universal (except where a different style of architecture has been introduced by coast men or Europeans), rectangular buildings are made, especially for housing cattle or occasionally for providing a large dormitory for the unmarried men, or a kind of shelter under which the elders of the village may gather.

A NKONDE HOUSE

The houses are usually constructed of these materials:— A wooden framework is made in a circle marking the size of the hut; it is composed of strong poles. Around these, split bamboos are bound transversely which are tied together tightly by wetted bark-rope on either side of the pole they clasp. The bamboo ribs are close together, and the structure resembles roughly the commencement of a huge hamper. In between the split bamboos mud is squeezed. This mud is usually made by women carefully puddling it with their feet, and the mudding of the houses is nearly always done by women. In most of the houses of Nyasaland after roughly filling in the interval between the wattles by this thick mud a further coating of mud is plastered on both sides. This mudding is done right up to the top of the round wall. After the first coating the mud dries and cracks. The cracks are then filled up with more mud until the surface is fairly smooth. Sometimes cow-dung or a little lime is mixed with the outer coating of mud, and the floor may likewise be prepared with hard mud mixed with cow-dung. The level of the house is usually slightly raised above the surrounding ground. There is an outer circle of posts going partly round the house which eventually constitutes a verandah, and the floor of the verandah is also of hard mud raised about six inches to a foot above the ground. The Wankonde build rather a special type of house. The walls are not straight, but slope outwards from the bottom. The interstices between the neatly-bound wattles of bamboo are filled not with an indiscriminate mass of mud, but with round bricks of white clay, giving a much neater appearance to the houses. The style in which these Wankonde houses are built will be better understood by the accompanying illustration than by any further verbal description.

When the walls of the house are complete the roof is made. Usually this is done by constructing apart from the house a huge framework of thin poles and bamboo, shaped like a funnel and coming to a sharp apex at the top. When the walls of the hut are dry this skeleton roof is hoisted and poised over them. Men then ascend and begin to cover the framework with thatch. They commence at the bottom, usually with separate bundles of grass which are tied on to the bamboo withes. Sometimes the thatching is very neatly executed; at other times a large quantity of grass seems to have been carelessly thrown on to it; but the disorder is more apparent than real, the outer surface of the grass having been blown about by the winds. The well-thatched roof of a native house is singularly rain-proof.

In larger round houses there are naturally modifications of this style of building. There may be one or more poles of considerable height rising up from the central part of the hut and assisting to support the roof, the rafters of which will be the long, light, but strong midribs of the *Raphia* palm. Attached to the house there is almost always a yard enclosed by a reed fence of nearly six feet in height and communicating with the verandah. In this yard the women do almost all their cooking. The interior of the hut is usually divided into two sides, one called "the side for sleep," the other "the side for the fire." The interior of the huts is very dark, because there are no windows, and the low door admits but little light owing the overhanging eaves of the roof round the verandah.

A wood fire is constantly burning inside the hut which gives the rafters a black and shiny appearance and causes disagreeable cobwebs of soot to hang from the interior of the roof.

Rectangular houses of course are built in a different style; the structure of the roof of the house forms part of the original framework and grows as the house grows in building. There is a little skill in joinery shown in putting up these rectangular houses, but it must be regarded as due to the teaching of the white man or the Arab. All fastening of poles, however, except where foreign influence prevails, is done by lashing with bark-rope. I think the case of native building is one of arrested development. It is wonderful how smart they are in running up temporary houses. The forest provides them with all they want—poles being obtained by cutting down saplings and severing the spreading branches; bark-rope is made by soaking the bark in water—when it dries it contracts and therefore binds very tightly, moreover the bark lasts undecayed for years. Bamboos which can be split or used whole as the case may require are very useful wattles; grass to thatch the roof and reeds with which to make fences or gates are all at hand; while the nearest ant-hill will supply material for mudding the walls and making raised seats for benches or beds.

It was reported by earlier travellers that on the east coast of Lake Nyasa villages had been built on piles by the timid A-nyanja people who preferred to live out in the lake to avoid the attacks of slave-raiders. I have never succeeded in seeing any of these pile dwellings though I am told they are also built on Lake Chiuta. When I first saw Lake Nyasa they had all disappeared, and I found the inhabitants who dreaded the raiding of Magwangwara or Wa-yao lived on small islands or islets where their little beehive houses were perched amid the stones.

As a rule each grown-up individual has a house to him or her self, though amongst very poor folk husband and wife may share the same dwelling. But a man who has several wives will probably have a house to himself and each of his wives will occupy her own dwelling. There is often a large house built to be used in common by the unmarried men and boys of the village. Where this is not the case the mother will cause a small hut to be built near to her own to be occupied by her boy children when they are too old to share the hut with her. Girls will probably continue to use the mother's dwelling till they are married.

There is little or no order in which the village is built. A chief suddenly determines to found a new settlement. He starts with most of his people, selects a site, and houses are quickly run up with little or no relation to each other, but all tolerably close together. There is usually reserved, however, a large space of open ground more or less in the middle of the village. This is called in Chi-nyanja the *Bwalo*, and the place selected usually has a large and shady tree. If there is not, however (or if there is, in addition to the tree), a rough building may be run up with open sides and grass roof, under which shelter can be obtained from the sun during the daytime. In this open piece of common land all the public meetings and dances take place; and here the "Milandu," or judicial cases are tried by the chief or headman and his assistants.

The vicinity of native houses is usually kept fairly clean. Much of the refuse is eaten up by village dogs, fowls, and goats, but apparently the natives from time to time carry it away into the bush. I do not mean to state that the lanes between the houses and their precincts are always clean, but they are seldom encumbered by such filth as one would see in any squalid Eastern town or village.

Interspersed amongst the houses of the village are the *Mikokwe* or granaries. These are huge circular erections of basket-work plastered with mud outside and built on a raised platform, standing on short legs made of forked branches stuck into the ground. The platform is built in such a way as to make it difficult for rats to ascend to the granary. The roof is funnel-shaped and thatched. Henhouses of wicker-work are often built and are usually placed on a raised platform. Rough dove-cots are put up for the pigeons where these birds are kept. But the goats are either housed in a small house or hut. In any of the places where leopards are dangerous the goats and sheep are sheltered at night in pens made from stout planks placed side by side, with a roof of heavy logs. The goats are let in or out by removing one or more stakes.

The planks of the goathouse are hewn, not sawn. The native, until taught by the European, had absolutely no idea of sawing wood, nor has he much notion of splitting by means of wedges. He quite ignores joinery in his furniture and all articles are hewn out of the solid block. This is the case with his wooden spoons and ladles, his pillows or head-rests, his wooden mortars, pestles, benches—all his simple implements and articles of furniture. Likewise when he wishes to obtain planks for any purpose they have to be adzed from logs of wood and are consequently very thick.

Canoes are mere dug-outs. Certain trees of the forest, such as the Parinariums, are used for canoe making. A large party of men go to the forest not far from the river bank and there cut down one of these trees in such a way as to allow it to fall on a slope towards the water. Then they commence to hollow it out, partly by burning and partly by incessant chipping with their small adzes. The canoe is at last hewn into shape. If there are any cracks in it they are covered by patches of wood which may be fastened on by drilling holes through which leather thongs or bark strings are passed and tightly tied. All small holes and apertures are stopped up with india-rubber derived from the rubber vines or some other source. Smooth, lopped branches of trees are placed on the ground as rollers and an enormous crowd of people push the canoe down to the water and launch it. The canoes are worked by punting poles and by paddles.[1] Though the natives seem to have little idea of using the mast and sail they rapidly pick up the notion when taught by Arab or European.

NATIVES MAKING A PRONE TREE TRUNK INTO A CANOE

The people of Nyasaland and of most parts of British Central Africa near the great lakes or rivers become singularly adept in the management of boats and ships. All the seamen on the lake gunboats are now natives of the country, whereas formerly we imported sailors from Zanzibar, or even employed bluejackets from the British Navy.[2] The natives can be taught to row well, and are very smart in managing sails. Not infrequently the launching of a canoe is accompanied by feasts and dances and by prayers to the ancestral spirits with their accompanying libations or sacrifices.

The large importation of European cloth has almost killed the native weaving industry. Before the advent of Europeans they wove—and in outlying districts they still weave—very coarse-textured cotton cloth. As is probably well known to my readers the cotton plant grows wild or semi-wild over large portions of this country and the cotton produced is excellent. It is spun by the natives and woven by them in the following manner:—A frame is made of two heavy smooth bars of wood supported at either end by a couple of short posts which bifurcate. The beams are steadied and fastened to the ground by pegs. The cotton threads are then stretched across the frame lengthwise, from end to end. The alternate threads are "locked" on a smooth stick (ordinarily a bamboo). When these alternate threads are raised a long bamboo shuttle with the cotton thread wound round the end is passed between the upper and lower threads and the cross-thread is tapped up tightly by another smooth bamboo. The cloth is usually finished with a fringe.

A RIVER PILOT
(Mnyanja, of the Lower Shire)

[1] Outriggers are ignored. All canoes are of rough construction, simple dug-outs, and have no seats, no elaboration, no ornament. Punting poles (*mapondo*) are usually of bamboo and are much used in shallow rivers.

[2] We only employ naval seamen now as petty officers.

Baskets of many kinds and shapes are made. There is the *mtanga*, a basket made by weaving flat strips of cane or wood over a framework of more rigid circles of wood which are sometimes the midribs of palm fronds, sometimes split and pared bamboos. This style of basket usually has a solid wooden rim of some flexible white wood. Then there are large flat baskets of tightly-plaited straw with a firm rim of wood, which are used for winnowing meal. Small baskets are made for holding all manner of food, grain, eggs, etc. Some

WEAVING IN ANGONILAND

of these baskets, especially in cattle-keeping countries, are so admirably and tightly plaited that they will hold milk. Enormously large baskets, shaped somewhat like a demijohn, are closely woven and in addition are smeared with sticky, rubber-like juice derived from the roots of a shrub, and are then impervious to water. These baskets are used for holding beer. Some baskets of plaited straw are made to fit into one another so that one acts as a cover to the other. A somewhat flattened form, known amongst the A-nyanja and Wa-yao as *mtungwi*, is made out of a soft, flexible wood in two pieces, one of which is slightly scooped out to form the bottom of the basket, and the other, a broad strip of wood, is bent round and attached to the sides of this flat piece so that one half of the basket is thus formed. The sides are often beautifully decorated by staining the white wood black and then cutting away portions, leaving a raised pattern of black on white. Occasionally these bands of thin wood are attached to baskets which have bottoms of plaited straw. Sometimes sandals are made of basket-work.

Pottery, like many other arts in Central Africa, has retrogressed from a once higher standard to a low one. The old earthenware we dig up from time to time is superior in design, shape, and finish to the native pottery of the present day. The women are the potters. The best pottery is made at the north end of Lake Nyasa, on German territory, by the Ba-kese people. The kind of pottery ordinarily made is :—(*a*) cooking pots—wide mouth, no neck, sides nearly perpendicular; (*b*) porridge pots — shaped very similarly ; (*c*) large ovoid beer pots—shaped like an egg with the pointed end cut off ; (*d*) water jars—with a "neck" broadening into an everted rim ; (*e*) round pots with a hole at the top: some of these have a short narrow neck ; (*f*) many kinds of *small* pots resembling the preceding somewhat in shape—used for storing medicines, condiments, fat and salt ; (*g*) saucers and pans ; (*h*) the bowls of pipes. Some of the smaller ware is coloured with red oxide or a black glaze. The inscribed patterns are not of any elaborate design and much of the pottery is without any ornamentation. Such decoration as there is, is either made by cutting marks into the soft clay with a sharp pointed stick or else painting a design in black or red. After the pot is finished it is put in the sun to dry for a day or so and is then burnt in a wood fire.

WEAVING ON THE NYASA-TANGANYIKA PLATEAU

String is fabricated by the natives from the fibre of a *Hibiscus* shrub, from plaiting palm leaves, from the skins of animals, from bark and above all from the leaves of the Hyphæne fan palms.[1]

The strands of the fibre of such shrubs and plants as are made into string are rolled by the hand on the thigh. String is sometimes made in this way from cotton, especially for stringing beads or ornaments.

Bowstrings are usually formed of thin strips of skin, softened, pulled out, and tightly twisted. Gut is sometimes used for this purpose also. Fishing nets are made of string, usually string of Hibiscus fibre. They are sometimes of fine mesh and are very strong.

The Rev. D. C. R. Scott states in his Dictionary, that the Wambo tribe of A-nyanja, living to the south-east of the Protectorate, are able to construct wooden locks and keys. The keys have teeth of two or three inches ; when they turn they move a wooden bolt into its place. It is probable that these locks and keys are not of indigenous invention but are derived from the teaching of the Portuguese.

Skins are dressed in an elementary manner. They are pegged out to dry ; most of the thicker part of the hide and the tendons are removed by scraping

---

[1] This palm is singularly useful. From its leaves are made mats, baskets and head coverings, besides many kinds of string and stout rope for tying fences.

with a knife, and the skin is then well rubbed with earth and water and made thoroughly soft. Although the country abounds with acacia trees which would provide bark for tanning purposes, I have never heard of it or any other form of tan being used by the natives for curing skins; except on the Lower Shire where they have been taught by the Portuguese, and where some native leather workers make excellent boots and shoes. Leather is not used for as many purposes as might be imagined. Skins are dressed in order to be worn on the body and are occasionally used as mats.

Drums are covered with skins from which all the hair has been removed. Sometimes the outside of the drum is very neatly covered with ox-hide which retains the hair, and has been stretched over the body of the drum whilst still moist.

For the smaller drums, skin of the monitor lizards (*Varanus*), or of snakes,

WOMAN MAKING POTS

is used. Often a piece of india-rubber is worked into the leather covering of the drum as it is supposed to give greater resonance.

Dyes are obtained from certain roots and leaves but are not much used In adorning the person a red ointment is often made from clay impregnated with red oxide of iron, which is found in the river valleys. This red oxide is often mixed with the clay of their pottery and gives it a beautiful Indian red tint.

Copper and iron are almost the only metals worked in British Central Africa, though lead is said to be used by the Yao for making small plugs to go through the wing of the nose in women. This they probably obtain from leaden bullets or from lead bought at the European stores. I have not yet heard that lead is found and smelted in British Central Africa. I doubt whether copper is actually obtained by the natives from the soil in British territory though it is certainly worked in great quantities in the region of Katanga to the north, and possibly in some of the Zambezi countries to the west. If copper is worked at all within the territory under description it would be in the mountains to the west of Lake Nyasa. There are evidences of its presence in the rocks. But the copper of Katanga finds its way down in large quantities to the tribes of British Central Africa and many of them are very

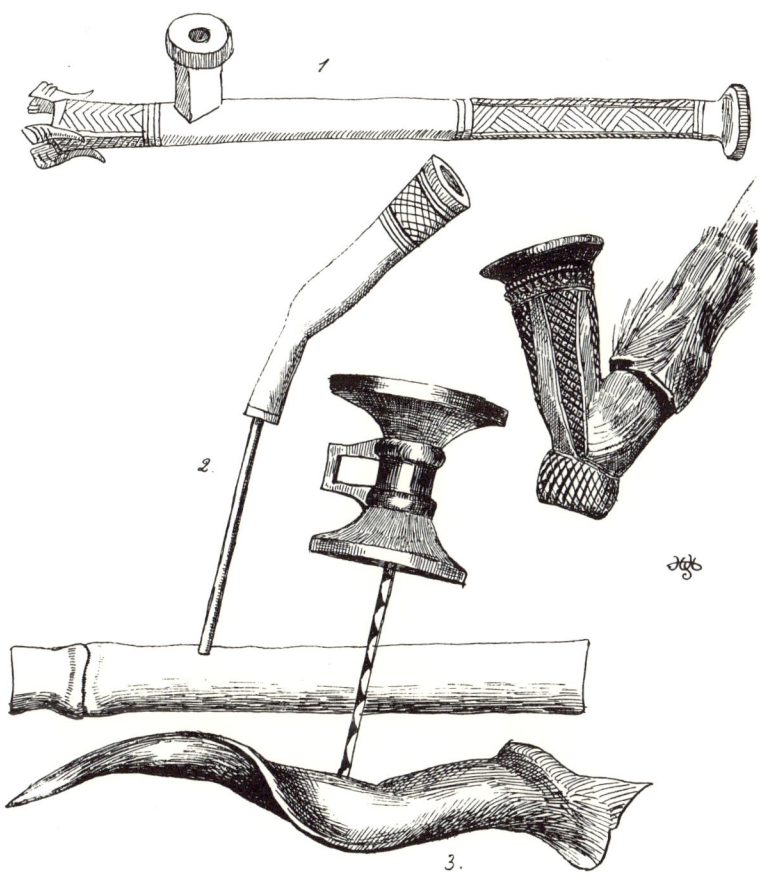

PIPES FOR HEMP AND TOBACCO.

1. Wooden pipe for tobacco, and clay, skin-covered bowl of another tobacco pipe.
2. Pipe for smoking hemp, with wooden mouthpiece and bamboo receptacle.
3. Hemp pipe with ebony mouthpiece and handle; receptacle of eland's horn.

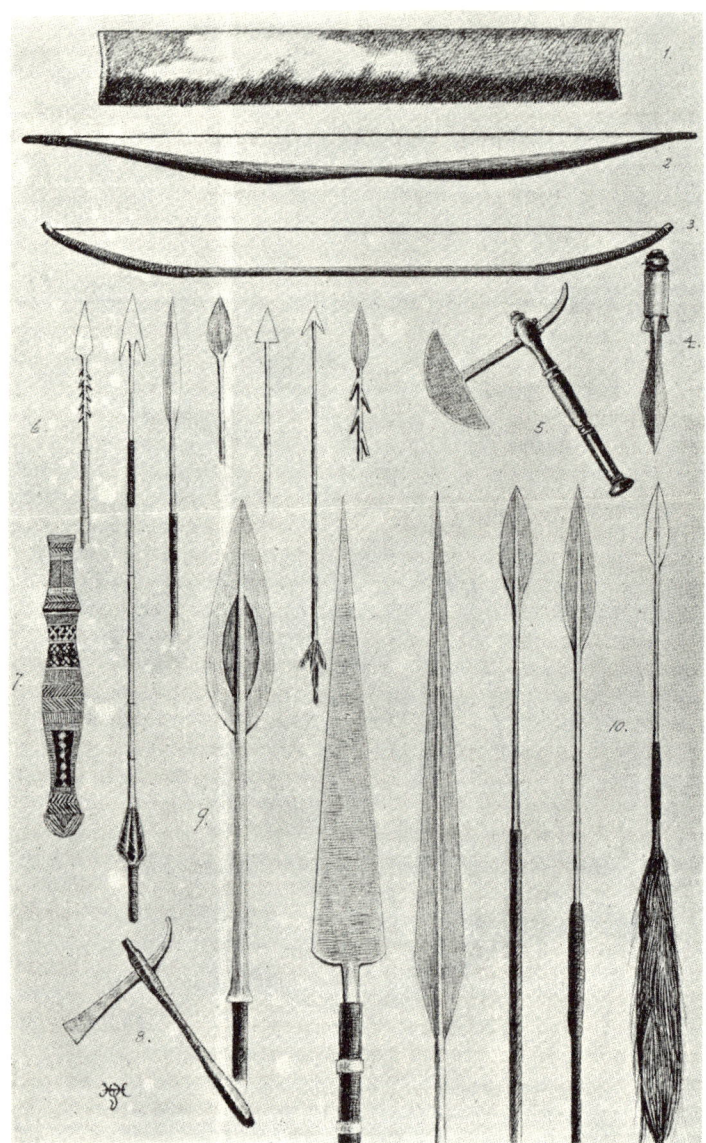

CENTRAL AFRICAN WEAPONS, ETC.

1. A Nkonde shield.
2. A bow from the Marimba district.
3. An ordinary Central African bow.
4. A Yao knife.
5. An Achewa axe.
6. Various arrows and arrow-heads.
7. A Yao knife and scabbard (haft of knife and scabbard made of wood).
8. A common axe for felling timber.
9. Various spears.
10. A stabbing spear (assegai).

skilful in using it for ornamental purposes on the handles of their spears and axes.

Over the greater part of Nyasaland, however, brass is of more common use for decorative purposes than copper. All the brass in Central Africa must, of course, be procured from the outer world, from the Europeans or Indians trading on the coast, as there is no race in Africa which combines zinc and copper to make brass. Nevertheless, this amalgam may be found in use among African tribes that have never seen a white man, possibly never even heard of a white race. It is like tobacco and Indian corn: articles which have defied all obstacles and have swept across Africa and into its darkest recesses in two or three centuries. But if the native of British Central Africa cannot make brass he can work it into all manner of things from the rough form in which it is introduced in the course of trade. Brass wire of various thicknesses is made in the following manner:—After cutting the brass (which may have arrived in thick coils a quarter of an inch in diameter, or in rods or buttons or in other forms) into convenient sized bits the metal is put into the forge and smelted. When it is thoroughty fused in a mass and has cooled down, the metal-worker beats it out until it is in very long thin strips. One end of a strip is then seized with pliers and is forcibly drawn through a plate of iron which is pierced with a number of holes of graduated sizes. The strip of brass is first dragged through the largest hole. Then the end is beaten and pointed and dragged through the second hole. The iron plate in which the holes are pierced is generally fixed in the fork of a tree so that it may be pulled against from the other side with great force without being dislodged. As the wire is pulled it is being wound round a neighbouring branch or sapling. From time to time the brass is dipped into oil and passed through smaller and smaller holes until the wire is of the necessary fineness. Molten brass is also hammered out and shaped into bracelets and necklets, or is made into rings for the ears or fingers. On the Lower Shire and Zambezi the brass work is extraordinarily good; the handles of spears or walking-sticks will be beautifully worked with a filigree of brass wire.

Though gold may be present in the rocks of British Central Africa, or even found alluvial here and there, it is not known to the natives except as an introduced article. But within the watershed of the Zambezi the negroes have for untold centuries collected the alluvial gold, and, under Portuguese tuition, they have learned to do goldsmiths' work with extraordinary skill and delicacy. This art even extends to British territory on the Lower Shire. Here the natives will make exquisitely fine gold chains, scarcely thicker than a stout thread, besides finger rings in which an elephant's hair is often enclosed.

Iron ore is dug and smelted in a furnace, which is made of clay and is let down into a hole in the ground. Above this cavity they build up a clay wall all round the edges till it appears to form a huge chimney. A tunnel is dug from the surface of the ground down to the bottom of the bed where the charcoal is laid and ignited. The iron ore is put into the clay furnace. A goat-skin bellows[1] with a stone nozzle is then plied vigorously till the charcoal is in a white heat. The clay chimney conserves the heat and the iron is smelted. Then it is taken out and hammered. After that it is removed to the forge and worked in a somewhat similar manner with a charcoal fire blown by bellows of goat-skin. The ore is hammered by rude iron hammers

---

[1] I have seen bellows in West Africa made of banana leaves, and no doubt other substances are used besides skin.

on an iron or stone anvil and is laid hold of by iron pincers. In spite of the inefficient implements with which the native works his iron he achieves extraordinary results. When these people are instructed by a European smith, and have a proper forge to work at, their skill is quite remarkable. The chief things made of iron are spears, knives, axes, arrow-heads, musical instruments known as "Sansi," hoes, tools for working metal, and various articles used as ornaments.

The musical instruments are the drum; the horn; a viol-like instrument called the "Pango";[1] a "limba"; a "kalirangwe," a one-stringed banjo; a kind of wooden piano; a flute; and an instrument called in Nyasaland a "sansi,"[2] which I here illustrate.

Drums are of nine or ten kinds. One is often as much as five feet long. It may be supported on a rest made of a forked stick, or a man may straddle across the lower end of it with a leather band going round his waist, so that he holds up the drum while it is beaten by his hands. Other smaller drums are held under the arm, or slung round the chest. In some cases the drums are beaten with drum-sticks, but more often they are struck with the fingers. Sometimes they are constructed in rather a graceful shape like a huge cup or calyx of a flower standing upright. A drum of this description will be probably encased in hide with the hair remaining on it, and ornamented by strings and strips and loops of twisted skin. Although ordinarily standing on its smaller end this drum is generally supported on a man's stomach, with the skin loops round his neck while it is being played. Some of the little drums that are held under the arm are not more than eighteen inches long. They are often covered with *Varanus* lizard skin. The parchment of the larger drums is made of the skin of various mammals, oxhide being used for the largest. The skin is, of course, entirely free of hair, and is very tightly stretched over the mouth of the hollow wooden tube. Frequently they put dabs of india-rubber in the centre, as I have already stated.

ANGONI DANCER AND DRUM PLAYERS

Natives have a regular "Morse" system of communication by drum taps, so that they can send messages to one another at distances of a mile or under.

Trumpets are made of elephant tusks in the countries to the north and west. I give here an illustration of a Mu-lungu of South Tanganyika blowing an

---

[1] These names are the Chi-nyanja forms, common however to many of the other tongues of British Central Africa.   [2] In Chi-yao, *lulimba*; the "Marimba" of the Congo and Angola.

A MU-LUNGU OF SOUTH TANGANYIKA BLOWING IVORY TRUMPET MADE OF AN ELEPHANT'S TUSK

NATIVES OF BRITISH CENTRAL AFRICA

ivory horn. But with the increasing value and scarceness of ivory these trumpets have passed out of use in Nyasaland, where they chiefly use the horns of the kudu, eland, or reed-buck.

The *pango* is made thus:—A long broad slip of wood is passed through a large hollow gourd which is carefully cut in half. A bridge is fixed transversely across this flat piece of wood, and four or five strings are then strung over the bridge and fastened at either end with a piece of wood which traverses the gourd or sounding-board. This instrument, which in a rude way answers to a fiddle, is played with a bow, and that is generally a piece of split and smoothed bamboo or stout reed. The bow is smeared with wax.

The *limba* slightly resembles the guitar. It usually has six strings, and is strung somewhat like a violin in appearance. The strings are struck with the thumb-nails.

The *kalirangwe* is a one-stringed instrument stretched over a gourd-resonator. The string is twisted fibre dipped into melted wax. It is either played by twanging it with the fingers or with a reed-bow.

The "wooden-piano," as I call it for want of a better word, is rather a large instrument and is generally placed on the ground, the person who wishes to play squatting down before it. It consists of long slabs like huge "keys," made of the wood of the *Mbwabwa* tree. These slabs are laid athwart two long pieces of wood, and are kept in their places by wooden pegs on either side. When struck with a baton, being very resonant, they give out musical sounds, and as they are of different sizes and degrees of thickness appear to almost constitute a gamut. They are usually five or six in number, but may be more numerous. The instrument which I have illustrated, and which is known in Nyasaland as the *Sansi*, has a sounding-board of some hard wood, presumably ebony. Slips of smooth welded iron with a slight upward turn and flattened out at the musical end, are fastened to the top of the instrument and are raised up over the bridge. In some of the elaborate Sansis (only to be found now in the more remote interior, where native arts are carefully preserved) there are a great many of these iron keys —perhaps over forty—placed in separate rows; but ordinarily the instrument is as I have drawn it, with one row of keys graduated in size and length. The Sansi is played by the thumbs pressing down and releasing the flattened ends of the iron keys, the fingers being employed to hold the sounding-board. There are many melodies in the minor key

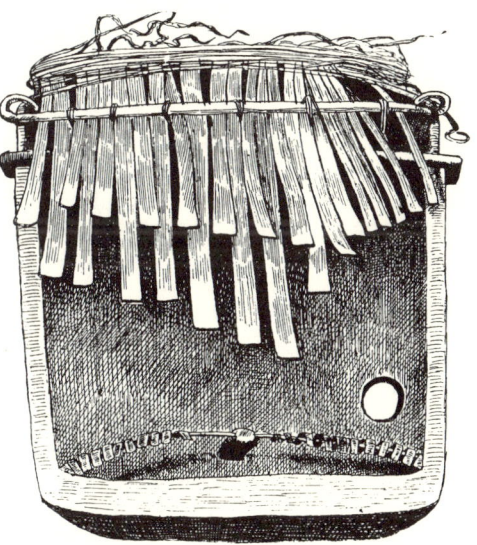

A "SANSI"

(sounding somewhat like a Jews' harp) obtained from the Sansi, which is one of the most pleasing of all African musical instruments. The Sansi is sometimes made with keys of bamboo instead of iron. Slips of bamboo are pared down and fastened to the sounding-board much in the same way as the iron keys.

The flute is made of a hollow reed. This is an instrument which is very rarely seen nowadays in the better known parts of the country, but it is still met with in Yao-land, in the countries to the west of Lake Nyasa, and in all the regions where the cheap penny whistles of the white trader have not penetrated. The Rev. D. C. R. Scott states that in former days the big chiefs of Nyasaland used to have bands of performers on the flute which accompanied the armies to the battle-field much as the fifes in a fife and drum band.

In addition to these regular musical instruments the native delights in the use of rattles which are made of hard seeds and pieces of wood and are hung round the ankles, the armpits, or the waist; or are shaken by the hands; or a small gourd may be filled with pellets or seeds and rattled.

Music is one of the many arts in which the negro has degenerated. There is evidence that before the coming of white men to these countries bringing the abominable concertina, panpipes, penny whistle, and harmonium, the natives played more musical instruments of their own than they do now, and thought much more of native music.

The administration of justice has already been touched upon to some extent in the reference to the trials by ordeal. The headman of the village in council, the petty chief of the district and his headman, and the supreme chief of the country (if there be one) try cases according to their importance, give decisions and enforce them. In the case of powerful chiefs like Mpezeni, Chikusi,[1] Chiwere, Mombera[1] of the Angoni, the Kazembe of Lunda, Ketiamkulu[1] of the Awemba, the power would be more or less autocratic, and the chief would probably give decisions and execute sentences without consulting his sub-chiefs; but smaller chiefs do not rule so despotically and seldom arrive at any important decision without being in accord with their advisers.

In every important village there is usually an open space with a shady tree in the middle or some other shelter from the sun, and here the cases are tried by the Village Council or the Chief alone. In a civil case the plaintiff and defendant set forth their case, each in his turn, and do not interrupt one another more than they would do in a civilised Court. Then various Elders, or men of mark,[2] give their views on the subject, arguing on one side or the other, and the chief pronounces his decision. Sometimes the defeated party appeals to the bigger chief or, if it is a serious case, secedes from the community sooner than abide by the decision, and runs away to the court of another potentate. Ordinarily, however, the decision given at these trials is accepted. Where it is a criminal case it is often referred to the poison ordeal, from which the prisoner emerges with declared innocence after vomiting the dose, or either dies from the poisonous draught which his stomach cannot reject, or is done to death by the onlookers when his guilt is made manifest by the inability to vomit This form of trial is often resorted to in serious cases involving capital punishment, as the chief usually shrinks from pronouncing a death sentence unless he is a blood-thirsty despot of considerable power who delights in cruelty; in which case he will kill or mutilate for his own good pleasure, not necessarily for the execution of the judicial sentence.[3]

Minor ordeals may be undergone, such as plunging the hand into boiling

---

[1] Now dead.
[2] In the case of a woman, she generally chooses a male advocate to plead her cause: usually a relation.
[3] In the Alunda and Awemba countries a great deal of mutilation goes on—hands are lopped off, ears or noses removed for trivial offences.

water, to prove innocence from charges of stealing, adultery, and so on. The native, as I have said, shrinks from the responsibility of pronouncing a death sentence, but once such a decision is given the thirst for bloodshed is aroused and the execution is usually a cruel one. Persons who have been unsuccessful in the Muavi ordeal, or who are otherwise sentenced to death, are often killed by a general assault of the surrounding crowd who stab, hack, stamp on, kick, and smother the wretched victim, usually ending by cutting off the head, and, in the case of sorcerers, burning the body. In executions conducted more soberly by persons whom the chief deputes to inflict the death sentence, the convict has his throat cut or is stabbed with a spear. I do not remember to have heard in this part of Africa of any cases of hanging or strangling. It is said that in some of these countries criminals are crucified. I fancy this is a custom more of the Zambezi Valley or of the extreme west of British Central Africa than attributable to the eastern part of the territory which I am describing.[1]

Small cases are generally dealt with summarily by the chiefs or elders, who usually give wise decisions. The regular judicial trials take a longer time and there is a great deal of forensic eloquence displayed, not only by the parties to the case but by the bench of magistrates, who, with the exception of the chief, are mostly partizans. Some of the speaking is remarkably good—the argument being subtle, well sustained and copiously illustrated by analogies and references to other cases. A speaker will at times lash himself into a simulated fury, but the proceedings as a rule are orderly.

These trials are called in Chi-nyanja *Milandu ;* in Chi-yao, *Magambo ;* and in Iki-nkonde, *Amasyo*. These words are soon only too familiar to the European travelling through the country. Any subject of dispute is called a " Mlandu "; and amongst a litigious people not standing in awe of the European the traveller will constantly be harassed by threats to bring him up before the chief or magistrate to cause him to be mulcted for some imaginary grievance.

War may be suddenly waged without warning and without reason. Petty warfare may be constantly carried on between the border villages of two chiefs who are on unfriendly terms, without the main forces of the countries becoming involved. In such cases men from one or other village will hide in the bush outside the place they wish to annoy, and attack unarmed persons, killing them if they are men, and carrying them off if they are women.

If one chief resolves to proceed to war with another he usually sends a messenger stating his cause of complaint and offering the offending chief a bullet (or where guns are not used, a spear) or a hoe. The chief thus addressed will retain the bullet and send back the hoe, if he takes up the challenge and is prepared for war; if not he returns the bullet and thus implies that he intends to yield to the demands made of him. Or a defiant potentate may simply send to another ruler bullets or spear-heads as an insolent provocation. When we were having our difficulties with the slave-raiding chiefs on the borders of the Protectorate they were always sending me iron bullets, generally by persons whom they had kidnapped for the purpose of carrying back this challenge.

When war is inevitable preparations are made for it by drumming, dancing, beer drinking, high feeding and the making of war medicine which is usually hung about the person in amulets of horn. The forces then advance to the attack.

[1] In the Niger Delta I have several times noticed cases of men or women who were sentenced to death, being tied by stout ropes round the trunk of a tree and left there to die of hunger and thirst.

If it be warfare with the Angoni or the Awemba against some weaker tribe it means that a relatively large force will sally out to attack a small village. They will creep up to it during the night and deliver the attack at earliest dawn, endeavouring to surmount the defences of the place and enter it before the inhabitants are fully awake; for even in times of warfare all Africans are singularly negligent about keeping watch. Having entered the town they slay and pursue as hard as they can to keep the people whom they are attacking in a demoralised state, unable to concentrate and make a stand. As quickly as possible, to add to the panic, they set fire to the buildings. Then they commence to loot and capture the women and children whom, together with the cattle and ivory and other valuable goods, they carry off.

ANGONI WARRIORS

The Wa-yao do not much care for attacking a well-defended place; they prefer bush fighting, as they possess guns nowadays almost universally, whereas the Angoni and Awemba are chiefly armed with spears, clubs and assegais. The Yao are rather cunning in tactics, and have a great idea of surrounding the enemy. When attacking they crawl on their stomachs or run with the body bent, taking advantage of cover as much as possible. Having dropped on one knee, and fired their guns, they hastily retreat and reload whilst another rank takes their place in firing. Behind cover such as boulders or trees the Yao will fight obstinately; in the open he is a coward, as he feels himself justly to be at a disadvantage. The Angoni and Awemba, on the contrary, like a clear open space in which to fight, and the former adopt to some extent Zulu tactics. They put several or many thousand men in the field. Their "impi" has a central attacking force, and two wings or horns to endeavour to envelop the enemy. As they are practically without guns this is a policy they can pursue more easily than people like the Yao who fight with firearms, and who might be shooting at each other and wounding their own men if they fought in a circle.

It is doubtful whether in this part of Africa great loss of life occurs in any of the wars amongst the natives. The party that has least stomach for the fight is so good at running away and can so soon get out of range of the guns, spears, assegais or arrows of the attacking party that not many dead bodies are usually left on the field of battle. As a rule, the lives of women are spared, as they are valuable captures;[1] but whilst the battle fury rages I am afraid little heed is paid to the sex of the flying enemy, the conquerors being only too anxious to signalise their victory by killing. The bodies of the slain are invariably mutilated. Heads are cut off to be hung on poles round the stockade of the chief's town, or otherwise displayed as relics in the vicinity of his dwelling. Bodies of men are further mutilated, and the parts cut off are also hung up for display. All loot is, theoretically, given up to the chief, who reserves a proportion for himself and distributes the rest amongst his soldiers.

If it is a drawn battle, or the defeat of the retreating party has not been conclusive, and prisoners of importance have been taken on both sides their lives are generally spared and they are reserved for exchange and for use as hostages. A defeated chief who seeks peace from his

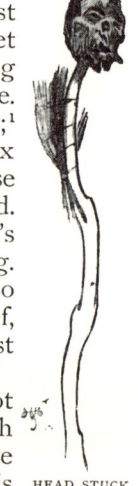

HEAD STUCK ON A POLE AFTER A NATIVE WAR

---

[1] Either as wives for the captor, as slaves, or as hostages for peace negotiations.

conqueror and desires to tender his submission sends word that he wishes "to catch his leg," and, if the conqueror consents, this ceremonial act of homage is performed and peace is declared. Sometimes tribes that have been savagely fighting with all the horrors and barbarities of such warfare a few days prior to the conclusion of peace, will become quite sentimental, patch up a friendship, and chiefs and headmen will exchange daughters or sisters as wives, and their peoples mingle with joyous expressions of goodwill, while the decaying heads and other relics of the mutilated dead still remain on exhibition.

These negroes have clear ideas of property. The waste land is usually considered to belong to the chief, but plantations and enclosures belong personally to the individual who originally made them, or who has inhabited them. Private property also includes all movables in the possession of the individual who originally acquired them. Sometimes land is held to belong to the tribe or to a certain family rather than to the supreme chief. The natives have a clear idea of the boundaries of large or small estates, or of their kingdoms; and in the case of the former they are marked by the planting of certain trees of quick growth, while of course streams and mountain ranges are recognised as boundaries and natural limits of territories.

The laws of inheritance are by no means uniform. Amongst the tribes in North Nyasa property descends from a man who has died to the brother next to him in age. If there are no more brothers the eldest nephew follows the uncle.

Amongst the Anyanja the sons usually divide the father's or mother's property. In the case of the Yao a woman usually leaves her property amongst her sons and daughters. In the case of a man the right to his chieftainship or personal property usually passes to his eldest sister's son or to any other descendants of his other sisters (in order of seniority) who may be living. In fact amongst the Wa-yao succession is almost always on the female side. The women may not, theoretically, govern (though they often do so practically) but at the same time the right to govern can only pass through the sister and mother; thus when Makanjira I. died the successor was not one of his sons, but his nephew—son of one of his sisters. This man again left the chieftainship to his sister's son, and so on.

This custom also obtains amongst some of the North-West Nyasa people.

All Africans are fond of trade. Commerce has a great attraction for them and it is thought to be a bad policy on the part of a chief to drive away trade by deeds of injustice or rapine. The men and women both make long journeys to sell their goods, the men always travelling farther. Salt is hawked about the country—also tobacco, smoke-dried fish, the material for various medicines, and charms (such as crocodile's liver), fowls, goats and sheep, cloth, beads and other trade goods. Nothing, probably, except ivory or gunpowder is sold by weight—and the sale of these articles is usually in foreign hands (Arabs, Europeans, or half-castes)—natives usually sell by measures of length and capacity. Salt will be sold by the bag—generally of regular bulk and weight—grain or flour by measure of capacity which can be gauged by the hand; cloth is measured by the arm—the commonest measure being the ell, from the point of the elbow to the end of the second finger, or from the end of the second finger to the wrist, or along the outstretched arms from finger tip to finger tip across the chest. Beads would be sold by the bunch; other articles that could not be sold by measure would be valued by number and in some cases by divisions or subdivisions.

Such is the Negro of South Central Africa. I have endeavoured to place before the reader an accurate summing up of his physical and mental characteristics. He is a fine animal, but in his wild state exhibits a stunted mind and a dull content with his surroundings which induces mental stagnation, cessation of all upward progress, and even of retrogression towards the brute. In some respects I think the tendency of the negro for several centuries past has been an actually retrograde one. As we come to read the unwritten history of Africa by researches into languages, manners, customs, traditions, we seem to see a backward rather than a forward movement going on for some thousand years past—a return towards the savage and even the brute. I can believe it possible that had Africa been more isolated from contact with the rest of the world, and cut off from the immigration of the Arab and the European, the purely negroid races, left to themselves, so far from advancing towards a higher type of humanity, might have actually reverted by degrees to a type no longer human, just as those great apes lingering in the dense forests of Western Africa, into which they are, relatively speaking, quite recent immigrants from Asia and Europe, have become in many respects degraded types that have known better days of larger brains and smaller tusks and stouter legs. Fortunately for the black man, in all his varieties but two or three of the most retrograde, he is not too far gone for recovery and for an upward turn upon the evolutionary path— a turn which, if resolutely followed, may with steady strides bring him upon a level at some future day with the white and yellow species of man.

"YOUNG AFRICA"

APPENDIX

DISEASES OF THE NATIVES OF BRITISH CENTRAL AFRICA

By DR. D. KERR CROSS, M.B.[1]

DISEASES OF THE SKIN.

These are very prevalent, owing to the want of cleanliness, etc.

I. ECZEMA.—Mostly brought on by excessive scratching.

II. URTICARIA.—Very common amongst the natives. It is like a nettle rash. Characterized by great itchiness and evanescence. Due to errors in diet. Some people cannot eat certain seeds.

III. BOILS AND CARBUNCLES.—Caused by micro-organisms. Very common amongst the natives. Boils appear in the arm-pit and groin. They say if they have boils they have no fever.

IV. TROPICAL SLOUGHING PHAGEDÆNA.—Caused by micro-organisms. The same as Moçambique Ulcer, etc., etc.—a sloughing ulcer, due to bad food, etc.

V. PEMPHIGUS CONTAGIOSUS.—Caused by micro-organisms. Seen in damp tropical countries. Begins as a bulla, or even a papule, then becomes a contagious sore.

DISEASES OF THE SKIN DUE TO ANIMAL PARASITES.

Lice (1) on the body, (2) head, (3) pubis.

Jigger or sand flea.

House-bug (Acanthia lectularia).

Ifwingire.—Not mentioned in any book. It is from the word "Ingira," to enter. It is due to maggots in the tissues. Native children suffer greatly. I have seen the whole side of a child riddled with holes. These maggots are common in dogs and antelopes.

The Itch.—Native name, Pere. Most common. Due to the female *Acarus Scabiei* burrowing in the skin, and laying her eggs.

Mosquitoes.—There are very many varieties. They are so bad during the wet season that the Awanyakyusa work all night and sleep all day. Their tissues afford the second stage in the life history of the three low forms of life found in the blood of man—the *Filaria sanguinis homininis diurnus; Do. do. nocturnus,* and *Do. do. perstans.* This leads to

(1) *Elephantiasis* of Scrotum and leg and breast. One year I removed at the north end of Lake Nyasa eleven tumours of this disease weighing from 52 lbs. to 7 lbs. This disease is very common amongst the Wanyakyusa. These filarial worms have a remarkable periodicity.

(2) *Orchitis.*—This is also very common. Almost every man has abnormally large testicles due to this. I have removed two weighing 3 lbs. and $2\frac{1}{2}$ lbs. respectively.

(3) *Chyluria.*—It is a white urine.

(4) Varicose groin glands.—The glands in the groin are like walnuts or small crab-apples.

(5) *Lymph scrotum.*

Ticks are troublesome before the rains.

Leeches.—In marshes.

[1] For ten years a medical missionary in North Nyasaland.

Diseases of the Skin due to Vegetable Parasites.

Very prevalent. Due to heat, moisture, habits of people, racial proclivities, etc.

(1) *Tropical Ringworm.*—Due to a fungus. Found on the body. It may, in the case of a native, extend over the whole body. Seen on the body, on the head, and on the hands. I have never seen a case of Guinea-worm.

KELOID.—Is very common. The tissues of the negro seem to have a tendency to take on a keloid (or, as some call it, a false keloid) growth. That is to say, cicatricial tissue grows large. If a native gets a cut, it becomes like a tumour or a new growth. If he has been vaccinated, the mark rises up like a two-shilling piece. If he tatoos himself, the surface becomes a series of little growths protruding above the general level of the skin.

LEUCODERMA is an extremely interesting form of disease that is found at the north. It consists of the hands being white, or covered with great patches of white. The lips may be white also, so too may the feet, and there may be white patches on the breast. The natives say it is due to their eating a certain kind of fish. They say many people can eat the fish with impunity, but that if others eat they are seized with this disease.

CANCER is not very common. Shortly before I left for home a woman came into my dispensary with cancer of the left breast. She had come from beyond Lake Mweru —450 miles.

GENERAL DISEASES.

RHEUMATIC FEVER.—Is very common. Many of their joints are affected by this disease.

CHRONIC ARTICULAR RHEUMATISM.

GONORRHŒAL ARTHRITIS.—This is a form of Synovitis which occurs as a sequel to Gonorrhœa. I have seen it several times in Mlozi's Village.

SUNSTROKE.—Have seen it in certain forms amongst natives. Have also seen it once in its worst form in one European, when the subject was unconscious for nine days.

SPECIFIC DISEASES.

SMALL POX.—A specific, contagious, eruptive fever. Is endemic in some localities.

WHOOPING COUGH.—This is not very prevalent, but I have sometimes had children with cases at my dispensary.

MALARIAL FEVERS.—Most prevalent. All natives suffer. I divide them thus :—

I. *Forms of Malarial Fever without marked fever or Apyrexial Forms.*

(1) Malarial Diarrhœa.

(2) Malarial Dysentery. Not responsive to Ipecacuanha, but to Quinine and Perchloride of Iron.

(3) Malarial Ulcers may be in crops of pimples, or one sore the size of a shilling, or a large sore like the palm of the hand.

When the sufferer has a sore he has no fever, and *vice versâ*.

(4) Malarial paleness or cachexia.

(5) Malarial Headaches, Neuralgias, and other nervous disorders.

II. *Intermittent Forms.* Forms which relax at intervals.

(1) Intermittent, with Delirium.
(2) ,, ,, Convulsions.
(3) ,, ,, Complete Insensibility.
(4) ,, ,, Excessive Shivering.
(5) ,, ,, Biliousness.
(6) ,, ,, Dysentery.

III. *Remittent Forms.* These only relax a little, but the temperature never goes down to the normal.

        (1) Mild Remittent. Only feverish for days.
        (2) Bilious „
        (3) Gastric „
        (4) Cerebral „
        (5) Algic „
        (6) Typhoid „
        (7) Black Water, or Bilious Hæmoglobinuric.

DYSENTERY.—A specific, febrile disease, characterized by inflammation of the mucous coat and glands of the lower bowel.

LEPROSY is very common all over Africa in both forms, tubercular and nerve. As long as the natives disregard all forms of segregation this disease will continue to abound.

SYPHILIS.—In all its stages very prevalent. I have often treated from ten to twenty cases a day. Natives call it the Disease of the Arabs.

Where Malaria abounds there seems to be a remarkable immunity from the other fevers.

DISEASES OF THE DIGESTIVE ORGANS.

The TEETH seem to be affected by some chemicals in the water in Africa.

PARASITIC STOMATITIS.—Very common in unhealthy children.

GASTRITIS is very common amongst Europeans and natives.

DYSPEPSIA is very common. When we consider the food of the natives, the manner of its being cooked, and the way they masticate it, we cannot wonder at there being Dyspepsia.

PYROSIS.

INFLAMMATION OF THE BOWELS.

DIARRHŒA.

CONSTIPATION.—Not very common in natives.

ASCITES.—Dropsy of the Peritoneal Cavity.

PERITONITIS.—Inflammation of the Peritoneum.

ABDOMINAL TUMOURS.—Carcinoma of the Bowel is known. The spleen is often enormously enlarged.

The UTERUS and OVARIES are affected somewhat.

DISEASES OF THE LIVER.

CONGESTION is common.

HEPATIC ABSCESS.—Often in conjunction with Dysentery. Common amongst Europeans and natives.

HYDATIDS OF THE LIVER.—This organ is more frequently infested with Hydatids than any other organ of the body. The cyst may be the size of a cherry, or that of a boy's head.

JAUNDICE.—A symptom more than a disease.

INTESTINAL WORMS.

TAPE WORMS are very common. At least three different varieties are found.

ROUND WORMS.—There are a number of varieties. At least one Liver Parasite is common—the *Bilhartzia Hæmatrobia*, which is the cause of what is known as the Bilhartzia disease. Endemic hæmaturia is somewhat common amongst the north end people, and due to the presence of this worm.

FILARIA SANGUINIS HOMINIS is a nematode worm, and is the cause of much trouble, as is indicated under "Mosquito."

DISEASES OF THE RESPIRATORY SYSTEM.

ACUTE LARYNGITIS.

BRONCHITIS is not very common either in its acute or chronic forms. The people live too much in the open air for this disease to find a *nidus*.

ACUTE PNEUMONIA is common during the cold season, or at the beginning of the rains. I had a few cases every year.

PULMONARY TUBERCULAR PHTHISIS.—In all my experience I have only had one genuine case. Malarial fever seems to immunise the country from the tubercular bacillus.

ACUTE PLEURISY.

CHRONIC PLEURISY.

HYDRO- AND PNEUMO-THORAX.

DISEASES OF THE VASCULAR SYSTEM.

VALVULAR DISEASES are not very common.

DILATATION.

DEGENERATION OF THE MUSCULAR WALLS.

ANEURISM.

EXOPHTHALMIC GOITRE.

ANÆMIA, or deficiency of blood, is rather common.

CHLOROSIS is common in many girls.

DISEASES OF THE SPLEEN.

HYPERTROPHY OF THE SPLEEN is very common.

GOITRE or enlargement of the thyroid gland. I have seen this very often in Mlozi's village. I never saw any of the north end natives suffering from it.

DISEASES OF THE KIDNEYS.

ACUTE TUBAL NEPHRITIS.

CHRONIC TUBAL NEPHRITIS.

RENAL CALCULUS.

URÆMIA.—Nervous symptoms supervening on suppression of the Urine.

HÆMATURIA.—Blood in the Urine.

PAROXYSMAL HÆMOGLOBINURIA.

CHYLURIA.—I have seen some cases of this disease among the natives. It is white urine, and is due to chyle or lymph being present. It is caused by obstruction and rupture of the lymphatics; also by the presence of the nematoid worm, *Filaria sanguinis hominis*. To me this is a most wonderful worm. The embryo is sucked from the blood of man by a female mosquito, and enters the stomach of the same. There it develops an alimentary canal, and an instrument for boring. By-and-bye the mosquito dies, and falls on water, but the parasite is not dead. It sleeps till it reaches a human stomach by the medium of drinking water. From there it travels through the tissues to the lymph vessels of the human being, where it becomes sexually mature, and breeds. It lies in one of the lymph vessels, and may measure from 3 inches to 6 inches long. The embryos of this worm are only seen active in the blood at night, and may be present in the human being to the extent of millions. There is another form of embryo that is only seen active by day, and a third is seen active at all hours of the day or night.

DISEASES OF THE NERVOUS SYSTEM.

SIMPLE MENINGITIS may be seen.

APOPLEXY is not very common.

EPILEPSY.—Falling sickness is very common, strange to say. Very often it is seen in children and young people.

LESIONS OF ANY OF THE CRANIAL NERVES may be seen.

SPINAL PARALYSIS is sometimes met with.

LOCOMOTOR ATAXIA is seen.

LATERAL SCLEROSIS.

NEURALGIA.

SCIATICA.

HEADACHE.

MEGRIM.

CONVULSIONS.

TETANUS.—I have seen this in three different surgical cases.

INSANITY.—I have seen several varieties. One form has come frequently under my observation in which a native during the course of a disease, such as small pox, or after some exposure to the sun, will suddenly become mad and rush to the woods where he behaves like a madman—shouting, rushing about, eating leaves. His comrades follow him in numbers without the slightest fear, saying he has "*kifunte*." I have seen such men brought back to the village, limbs tied, rolling on the ground and eating the dust. In a few days the fit of insanity disappears. The cases are peculiarly amenable to drugs of the nature of Bromide of Potassium.

I have more than once been struck by the wisdom the natives manifested in dealing with fractures of the bones. They dealt with them in a most rational manner, by putting on rude splints and setting the bones in a natural position. Very often, however, the bones rode over one another; but still, they had grasped the principle. Then, again, in their treatment of a deep-set inflammation they show a great deal of wisdom. They may scarify the surface which in principle we know to be good. They do it in a rude way, but they really draw the blood from the deeper organ to the surface. They do the same in their dry-cupping. They dry-cup by means of a horn, first scarifying the surface, and then putting a piece of flaming moss inside and suddenly applying the cup. This is in principle what we do in dry-cupping. The north end natives, too, have, it seems to me, a wonderful knowledge of roots and leaves and medicinal plants. This I feel sure would reward anyone who had time to devote himself to the subject.

CHAPTER XI.

LANGUAGES

THE native languages of British Central Africa belong exclusively to the great Bantu group of Negro tongues. Arabic[1] used to be spoken by the Arabs and coastmen temporarily settled in the South Tanganyika, North Nyasa, and Marimba districts, but is probably now replaced by Ki-swahili—the language of Zanzibar and the "Hindustani," or *lingua Franca* of East-Central Africa between the White Nile and the Zambezi. Portuguese is slightly known by the people on the Lower Shire; English is rapidly becoming familiar to all the tribes of Nyasaland, South Tanganyika, and Mweru. In time it will be the common language spoken by all sorts and conditions of men in South-Central Africa for purposes of intercommunication in matters of Government, Religion, Commerce, Mechanics, Arts and Sciences. But in some respects it will be run hard for supremacy by Ki-swahili,[2] the language of Zanzibar.

This remarkable tongue offers a parallel to English, with its absorption of Latin; and Hindustani, with its Hindi basis and heterogeneous additions of Arabic, Turkish, and Persian words. Its main stock of words and its grammar are purely Bantu; but about twenty-five per cent. of its vocabulary is corrupt Arabic. Arab influence, however, has simplified the grammar and the numerals, and has provided Ki-swahili with a copious, apt diction capable of expressing almost any ideas with exactitude and precision. When new words for new concepts are wanted they have only to be looked out in the Arabic dictionary and pronounced in an easier African manner to at once become incorporated in "the Queen's Swahili." Say that you want a word to express "Witness; witnesses in a court of law"—you look out the word in an Arabic dictionary—*Shahid*, turn it into Swahili pronunciation—*Shahidi*, add on the *Ma-* prefix and pluralise it as *Mashahidi*—"witnesses." "Call your witnesses—*Ita mashahidi yako*."

The pronunciation of Arabic words is facilitated—"Swahili-ised"—thus: *Sanduq* (box, chest) becomes *Sanduku*, the difficult pronunciation of the Ṣ (ص) and the q (ق) being ignored.[3] *'Ilm* (science) becomes *Elimu*; *'Aql* (intelligence) changes in the soft African pronunciation into *Akili*. The following sentence will give some fair idea of the proportion of Arabic words in Ki-swahili, and the kind of concepts for which they are used (I place the words derived from Arabic in italics):—Si-nge-*thubutu* kuja kuku-ōna, *Bwana*;[4] lakini ni-me-pata

---

[1] The Arabic spoken was the corrupt jargon of the Hadhramaut and 'Oman.
[2] *Ki-* is the prefix denoting "kind of, sort of"—and is frequently, but not always, applied to languages. *Swahili* is derived from the Arabic *Sawahel*—"the coastlands"—the people of the coast.
[3] Though in writing Swahili in the Arabic character the original Arab spelling of the transmuted words is retained.
[4] A corruption of the Arabic *Abuna*, "our father."

jeraha kwa ku-pigwa *risasi* na *Askari* yako: natafuta *hakki* yako. (I should not *dare* to come and see you, *Master*, were it not that (*but*) I have got a *wound* through being struck with a *bullet* (shot) by your *soldier*: I seek your *justice*.)

But the basis of Ki-swahili is thoroughly "Bantu," and Bantu of a fairly old and uncorrupted type. Consequently it is singularly well adapted for a universal language in East-Central Africa, as so much of its vocabulary can be understood by the Yao, the A-nyanja, the Makua, the Ba-bisa, the Awemba, the Wa-nyamwezi, the Ba-ganda, and the tribes of all the coast regions of East Africa. It is impossible for the traveller to learn all the many different dialects of British Central Africa; equally impossible to expect that all the natives for a hundred years to come shall learn to speak English. Therefore Ki-swahili—like Hindustani in India—presents itself as a solvent of the difficulty. Anyone speaking the language of Zanzibar well and fluently[1] cannot fail to make himself understood wherever he may go from the Zambezi to the White Nile.

The languages of the country I am describing are allied to Kiswahili as Bengali, Hindi, Panjabi, Sindi, Mahratti, Gujrati, are allied to Hindustani: that is to say, they are pure Bantu (with, it may be, some deep-disguised infusion from the older stock of languages? Bushman? Hottentot which they displaced one to two thousand years ago), just as the Indian dialects above named are pure Aryan (save for some prehistoric absorption of Dravidian elements). Before proceeding to describe the principal languages here illustrated I may be allowed, perhaps, to say a few words on the Bantu family of African tongues.

Some three thousand years ago we may imagine the southern half of Africa[2] but sparsely peopled. In the great Congo forests a few pigmies wandered; Eastern, South-Central, and Southern Africa were given up to Hottentot and Bushman races; the Nilotic negroes, perhaps, extended in their range to the latitude of Zanzibar, and the West African negro crept down the west coast as far as Angola. Then somewhere in the very heart of Africa—north of the Congo Basin, west of the Nile Valley, south of the Shari River, and east of the Benue—a small tribe of negroes arose speaking a language remarkable for its development of governing prefixes, and for the concord system by which the pronominal prefix which begins the noun prefaces or is inserted into all the adjectives, pronouns, and verbs in the sentence which refer to that noun. The "Bantu"[3] mother-tongue spoken by this tribe was a sister language to other Central and West African forms of speech—related to the stock from which the Sierra Leone, Gold Coast, Dahome, Lower Niger, Benue, Niger Delta[4] languages sprang. In a more distant way the archaic Bantu tongue must have had relationships with the Fūl or "Fulfulde" language (of the so-called "Fulahs"), with the Tumale speech of Northern Darfur; even with the Hausa.[5]

---

[1] Any diligent person can master Ki-swahili in three months' study. Too often, however, this harmonious, apt, and concise language is misrepresented in Central Africa by a vile jargon picked up in the bazaars of Zanzibar—the "Mimi kwenda huku, wewe kuja hapa" style.

[2] South of the northern parts of the Congo Basin, the Victoria Nyanza and Zanzibar.

[3] *Bantu* is a representative name applied to this great group of languages by Dr. Bleek, the first philologist to study them. It means literally "people"—*Ba-ntu* (*Mu-ntu* = a person) and is illustrative of the prefix system.

[4] With the exception of the Bonny and Benin languages. These are quite isolated and highly-peculiar.

[5] The most remarkable Hausa speech is a connecting link between the Hamitic and the Negro language groups. Even at the present day there are many links existing which show the original connection—both physical and linguistic—between the Arab and the Negro.

The tribe speaking this elaborately constructed prefix-language—the Bantu mother-tongue—must have waxed very numerous and powerful, have enjoyed a certain amount of culture remotely derived from Egypt, and have possessed already such domestic animals as the ox, goat, dog, and fowl. Then—and not longer ago than two thousand years[1]—the original Bantu people overflowed

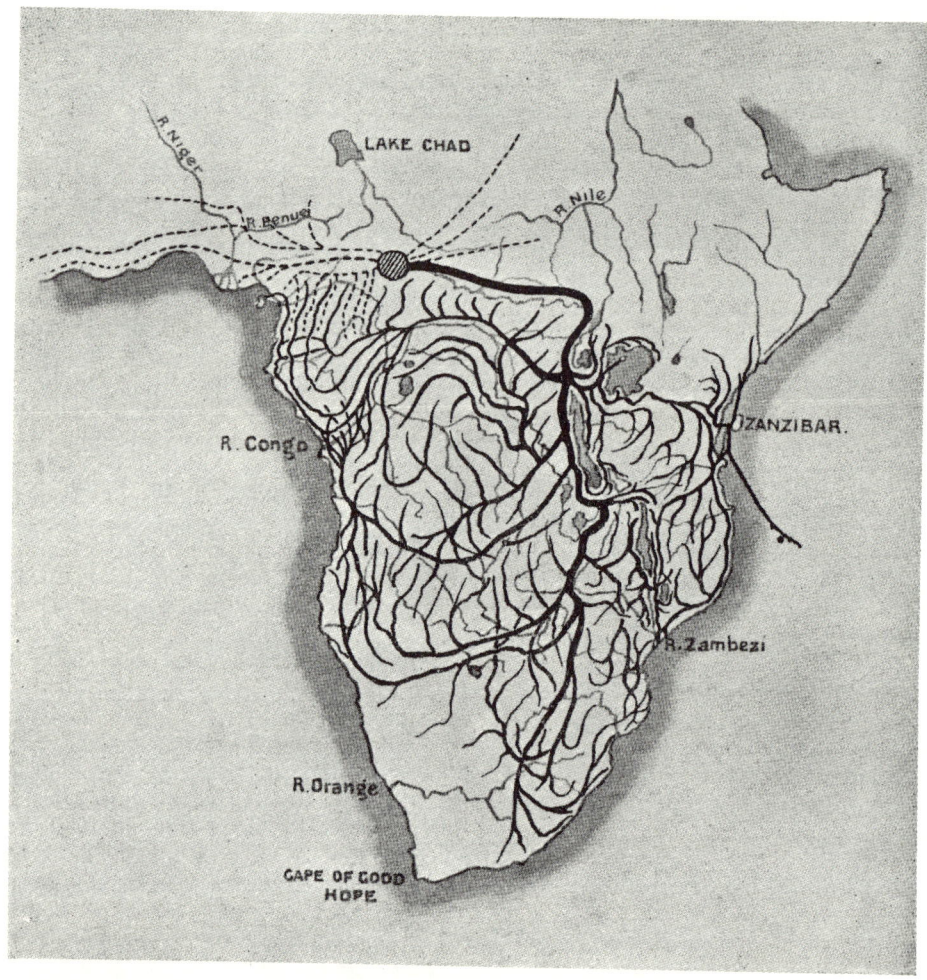

MAP SHOWING THE LINES OF MIGRATION OF THE BANTU TRIBES IN THEIR INVASION OF SOUTHERN AFRICA : the dotted lines show migration-routes of Semi-Bantu tribes ; the shaded circle indicates site where Bantu languages were first developed.

[1] I calculate this date as follows :—Almost all the Bantu peoples have a common word root expressing the domestic fowl: *Kuku*. (Nkuku, Ngoko, Nchuchu, Nsusu, Nguku, Nkū.) Now the domestic fowl reached Africa first through Egypt at the time of the Persian occupation—not before 400 B.C. To possess a name for this bird common to Zululand, the extreme Upper Congo, the Cameroons, and the Victoria Nyanza, it is clear that the Bantu knew the fowl prior to their dispersal. As they could not have received it from Egypt much more than two thousand years ago, this limits the period which has elapsed since they started from their first home to occupy half Africa. I have been working for a good many years at a "Comparative Grammar of the Bantu languages," which I hope to publish before long. In this I adduce many other reasons for fixing the date of the Bantu exodus.

the country to the south of their first area of development, and rapidly spread over all the southern half of Africa except the extreme south-western corner (Cape Colony and Namakwaland). The antecedent populations they absorbed or exterminated.

Henceforth, with the exception of the Hottentot-Bushman, there has been but one linguistic family over this huge area of Africa which lies to the south of a line cutting the West Coast of Africa between the Cameroons and the Cross River, skirting the northern limits of the Congo Basin, traversing the Albert Nyanza, passing round to the north of Bu-nyoro, Bu-ganda, and Bu-soga, reaching the Victoria Nyanza at its north-eastern extremity, leaving out its east coast, striking eastwards again from its south-easternmost gulf, and eventually attaining the Indian Ocean at Lamu, following a very irregular course, and including Mount Kilimanjaro within its limits, but leaving several detached islands of Bantu-speaking areas as *enclaves* in the Masai and Galla countries to the north-east.

The lines of dispersal of the Bantu negroes appear to have been something like the routes given in the accompanying diagram.

Of course the original home of the Bantu is now occupied by other tribes of negroes, not Bantu though, perhaps, speaking languages distantly akin to the original Bantu mother-tongue. Probably the original cause of the Bantu dispersal was the driving away of the tribe from their first home by alien invaders. Checked for a time by the dense Congo forests on the south, the movement of the Bantu was at first in an easterly direction. Then reaching the Albert Nyanza the main body took a southward direction, and persisted in this while sending off important branches to the west and east.

To some extent the most archaic Bantu tongues existing are still found along this main line of route—Ki-rega, Ki-guha, Ki-emba,[1] Ci-bisa, Zulu (Isi-zulu)—though a primitive type of Bantu may be found stranded here and there off the main route—such as Ki-makonde on the east coast, near the mouth of the Ruvuma River, the Nkonde dialects of the north end of Lake Nyasa, and Oci-herero of Damaraland.

The following propositions may be laid down to define the peculiar features of the Bantu languages :—

1. *They are agglutinative in their construction, their syntax being formed by adding prefixes and suffixes to the root, but no infixes* (that is to say, no syllable incorporated into the root word).
2. *The root is unchanging to all intents and purposes, though its first or last letter* (vowel or penultimate consonant) *may be modified in pronunciation by the preceding letter of the prefix or succeeding letter of the suffix. With one exception there is no inflection: that exception* (scarcely in origin a true one) *is in the case of the preterite tense of the verb in certain languages where the root changes in its termination probably by the absorption of a suffix.*
3. *No two consonants come together without an intervening vowel* (except where one of them is a nasal, a labial, or a semi-vowel): *no consonant is doubled* (except by the accidental juxtaposition of two m's or n's, one of which represents an abbreviated particle): *no word ever ends in a consonant except in rare instances where the termination through contraction and the dropping of a vowel becomes a nasal sound.*

[1] Probably the most primitive of all, as spoken in South-West Tanganyika.

4. *Substantives are divided into many classes or genders indicated by the pronominal particle prefixed to the root. Some of these prefixes are used in a plural sense, others in the singular. No singular prefix can be used as a plural, nor can a plural prefix be employed in the singular number. There is a certain degree of correspondence between the singular and plural prefixes, thus, No. 2 prefix invariably serves as plural to No. 1; No. 8 (plural) corresponds to No. 7 (singular), but this cannot be depended on as a rule. The full number of the prefixes is sixteen.[1] The pronominal particle or prefix of the noun is attached to the adjectives, pronouns, and verbs in the sentence which are connected with that noun, and though in course of time these particles may differ in form from the noun-prefix, they were formerly identical in origin.* (This system is the "Concord" of Dr. Bleek). *The pronominal particles whether in the nominative or accusative case must always precede the verbal root, though they often follow the auxiliary particles used in conjugating the verbs.* (An apparent but not a real exception to this rule is in the second person plural of the imperative mood where an abreviated form of the pronoun is affixed to the verb[2] and other phases of the verb are occasionally emphasised by the repetition of the governing pronoun at the end.)
5. *The verbal-root may modify its termination by a change of the last vowel or by suffixing certain particles; or it may even change its radical vowel either to form a tense or to alter the original meaning of the simple stem.*
6. *The root of the verb is the second person singular of the imperative.*
7. *No sexual gender is recognised.*

The sixteen original prefixes of the Bantu languages are given below. I state them in the most archaic forms to be found in living languages; but there are evidences to show that some of these prefixes are not now found in their oldest types, and these latter, obtained by deduction from the other forms of the particle used in the syntax, are given in brackets.

BANTU PREFIXES.

Singular.		Plural.	
Class 1	Mu-(Ngu-)	Class 2	Ba-
" 3	Mu-(Ngu-)	" 4	Mi-(Ngi-)
" 5	Di-(Ndi-)	" 6	Ma-(Nga-)
" 7	Ki-(Nki-?)	" 8	Bi-
" 9	N or Ni	" 10	Ti-, Ti-n-, or ƅi-,[3] ƅi-n-, or Zi-, Zi-n-
" 11	Lu-(Ndu?)	" 12	Tu (often diminutive in sense).
" 13	Ka (usually a diminutive).		
" 14	Bu- (sometimes used in a plural sense; generally employed to indicate abstract nouns).[4]		
" 15	Ku- (identical with preposition "to," used as an infinitive with verbs but also with certain old nouns indicating functions of the body primarily).		
" 16	Pa- (locative: applied to nouns and other forms of speech to indicate "place" or position. Identical with adverb "here," as ku- is with "there.")		

---

[1] Possibly seventeen.
[2] *Ita*=call! *Ita*ni=call ye! *ni*=ye.
[3] English Th- in "think."
[4] As Mu-ntu=a man; Bu-ntu=humanity.

To these sixteen prefixes should perhaps be added the preposition mu- "in," "into," which in some languages is used as a prefix or pronominal particle, as in the Swahili phrase "M'nyumba-ni mw-ace" = In his house—where the preposition M' (abbreviation for Mu-) has the particle Mw (Mu) agreeing with it and placed before the pronoun -ace.
_{In house in it (in) his}

Also the prefix in the singular number having a diminutive sense, which is found in some of the North-Western[1] Bantu tongues—Fi- or Vi-. This is possibly an additional prefix which has come into independent being in that rather divergent group. It cannot be traced to derivation from any of the other prefixes among the sixteen. It is always used in the singular, and its corresponding plural prefix is the twelfth (Tu-).

The concord may be explained thus:—

Let us for a moment reconstruct the original Bantu mother-tongue (as attempts are sometimes made to deduce the ancient Aryan from the most archaic of its daughters) and propound sentences to illustrate the repetition of pronominal particles known as the "concord."

OLD BANTU:

A*ba*o   *Ba*ntu   *ba*bi   *baba*ota;   tu*ba*oga.
They   they person   they bad   they they-who kill;   we them fear.

("They are bad men who kill; we fear them.")

Now let us render this into a modern dialect, Luganda of Buganda:

Bo   *Ba*ntu   *ba*bi   *babo*ta;   tu*ba*tia.
They   they person   they bad   they they-who kill;   we them fear.

Or, again—

OLD BANTU:

Ngu-ti   *ngungu*o   *ngu*gwa;   ku*ngu*mbona?
This tree   this this-one   this falls;   thou this seest?

("The tree falls; doest thou see it?")

Rendered into Kiguha of Tanganyika, this would be:

*Mu*ti   *gu*no   *gu*gwa;   u*gu*mona?
It tree   this (one)   it falls;   thou it seest?

The prefixes and their once identical particles have varied greatly in form from the aboriginal syllables as the various Bantu dialects became more and more corrupt. The eighth prefix, Bi-, becomes Vi-, Pi-, Fi-, Fy-, Si-,[2] I-, By-, Bz-, Py-, Ps-, Zi-. Further confusion is caused by the retention and fusion in the prefix of the preceding vowel which marked the full definite form when the prefix was used as a definite article or demonstrative pronoun. The definite forms of the prefixes were these:—1. Umu (Uñgu, Uñu), 2. Aba, 3. Umu (Uñgu, Uñu), 4. Imi (Iñgi, Iñi), 5. Idi (Indi), 6. Ama (Añga, Aña), 7. Iki, 8. Ibi, 9. In-, 10. Ibin- or Izin, 11. Ulu, 12. Utu, 13. Aka, 14. Ubu, 15. Uku, 16. Apa. Umu contracts into Um', M', U'; Aba into Awa, A'; Idi into Edi, Ei, E', I', and so on.

The Bantu dialects illustrated in this volume by vocabularies fall into groups more or less coincident with the tribal or racial congeries of peoples enumerated at the beginning of the chapter on Anthropology; but in drawing

---

[1] Perhaps also in the Eastern Congo basin. In the form of I- it is seemingly present in Manyema.
[2] Shi-, the F palatalised.

up vocabularies I have passed beyond the political limits of British Central Africa and have, for the sake of comparison, included tongues spoken in other and adjoining spheres.

The Manyema language which comes first on my list is illustrated by a vocabulary supplied to me by Manyema slaves in the Arab settlements on the south coast of Tanganyika. Manyema is a remarkable tongue. Its *locale* is the country west of Tanganyika, on the Congo versant, and its nearest allies are the languages spoken on the Upper Congo below (*i.e.*, north of) the Stanley Falls, on the Aruwimi River, and south of the Central Congo (Bololo). Manyema is an extremely corrupted and worn-down language as will be seen by my vocabulary. Some of the sixteen Bantu prefixes are apparently dropped. The few that remain are abbreviated almost beyond recognition.

Ki-guha is a most interesting form of Bantu speech. It is spoken on the west and north-west coast of Tanganyika and is allied to Ki-rega (a language spoken in the countries on the Congo Watershed, somewhere to the south of the Albert Nyanza), and to Lu-nyoro and Lu-ganda.

Ki-wemba or Ki-emba is a tongue of very archaic features, especially that dialect which is spoken in Itawa, on the south-west coast of Tanganyika. The Ki-wemba of the Awemba country further south does not retain so many interesting primitive features. Ki-wemba offers points of resemblance to the remarkable Nkonde dialects on the north and north-west of Lake Nyasa and on a portion of the Nyasa-Tanganyika plateau. Their influence extends as far to the N.E. as the south shore of Lake Rukwa, where the Wungu language obviously belongs to the Nkonde group. Perhaps Ki-bisa and other languages further to the west are also allied. All these tongues are remarkable for retaining the full form of the prefixes when the latter are used as definite articles—*Umuntu*, a man; *Abantu* or *Awantu*, men, and so on. The Ki-lungu and Ki-mambwe (with the allied Ki-fipa) languages of South and South-East Tanganyika and the Nyasa-Tanganyika plateau are disappointing in that they present few, if any, archaic features; though Ki-lungu is less altered than Ki-mambwe and may be connected with the Ki-emba stock.

The Ki-kese of North-East Nyasa is interesting as offering points of resemblance to the Yao as well as to the Nkonde dialects.

The Bisa language while belonging to the same stem as the Ki-wemba evidently represents somewhat closely the original stock from which the Tumbuka group (Ci-tumbuka, Ci-henga, Ci-tonga, etc.) and the Ci-senga and Ci-nyanja dialects were derived. The Tumbuka and Tonga tongues exhibit a phonetic feature almost unheard of elsewhere within the Bantu Family— the approximation of two consonants (s and k) neither of which is a nasal or semi-vowel. This however really arises from the gutturalising of a "y" sound—what should be pronounced *sya* becomes *sχa* and *ska*.

Ci-nyanja is the dominant language of Nyasaland. It is represented by the Ci-nyanja, Ci-cewa, Ci-cipeta, Ci-maravi, Ci-makanga, Ci-mañanja, and Ci-mbo dialects, but the Senga, Nyungwi (Tete), Sena, and Mazaro languages of the Luangwa Valley and the Lower Zambezi are closely allied. In true Ci-nyanja the second prefix shrinks to *a-*, though in some of the north-western dialects it is *wa-*, and in the Machinjiri country south of the River Ruo, especially in the hills, there is a suspicion of an aboriginal *ba-* (in the language of Tete it is *va-*). The Ci-nyanja language is further remarkable for the curious changes of the eighth prefix (*bi-*). In one or two dialects this becomes *vi-*, here and there in remote corners it is *byi-* or *pyi-*, but in the south-western forms of Chinyanja this changes to *bzi-* or *psi-* and in Central Ci-mañanja to *zi-*; a parallel to Zulu. The Ci-pozo language represented in my vocabularies is a very interesting tongue. It is spoken in the Zambezi Delta and retains many old roots extinct in adjoining dialects. The form of the eighth prefix, *pi-*, is a rare one shared with the Sena dialect. On the whole Ci-pozo offers strongest affinities with the Ci-nyanja group though it has evidently influenced and been influenced by I-cuambo, the language of Quelimane. This last-named tongue is the most southern representative of the Makua group.

The Makua language and its allied dialects (I-lomwe and others) is a very remarkable form of Bantu speech, which has evidently been long isolated in this projection of South-East Africa, the Moçambique province, shut in between Lake Nyasa, the Ruvuma River, the Indian Ocean, and the Zambezi Delta. While preserving many primitive roots, the prefixes have altered strangely; and a dislike to certain consonants or combinations of consonants has changed the appearance of many familiar words, so much that, until the genius of the language has become understood, the Makua dialects are apt to appear more peculiar than they really are. Nasal sounds are disliked in combination with labials: thus instead of *nyumba, ñombe, mbuzi*, they say *enupa, iñope, epuri*. R is constantly substituted for t and z, k for f, and h for s: thus *makura*, "oil," instead of *mafuta; uhiu* instead of *usiku*. H, also, is constantly substituted for k. On the whole, Makua—or I-makua[1] as it is called—is nearest in its affinities to the tongues of the east coast on its northern borders, and has some distant resemblance to Yao. It may also have been influenced by the proximity of the Ci-nyanja group; but it represents an old type of Bantu long isolated. Some of its prefixes are well nigh inexplicable. Two curious classes it shares with Yao—words beginning in the singular with *Mwa-* which in the plural are prefixed by *Asi-* (Yao-*Mwa-*; plural, *aci* or *aca*). *Mwa-* may be short for Mwana—"child" (of); *asi-* appears to have been derived from a Yao honorific prefix, used both in singular and plural—*aca* or *aci*, and often reduced in conversation to *Ce* (*che*), as *Ce Mataka*—Mr. Mataka.

The Yao language and its relative Ci-ngindo of N.E. Nyasaland are connected with the languages of the Swahili coast. Ci-yao is a very difficult language to learn, on account of the complicated changes that take place in the verb (of which there are some nineteen tenses duplicated by an almost equal number of negative tenses) and the clumsy method of dealing with adjectives. As regards the changes of the actual root of the verb, these only take place in the preterite tense (though there is the usual change of the terminal vowel in the subjunctive mood). There is the customary change of the terminal vowel in the preterite from *a* into *-ile*, which is so widespread in slightly varying forms among the Bantu languages (as *Menya*, beat! past tense—*menyile*); but in addition there are some seven irregular forms, which can be studied in the Handbook to the Yao language, by the Rev. A. Hetherwick.

In regard to the adjectives: instead of the simple system in vogue in the more primitive Bantu tongues by which the adjectival root is merely preceded by the particle in agreement with the noun-class to which the substantive belongs—as *Mu*ntu *Mu*kulu = a great man—we have first the noun's particle
  man   great
applied to the adjectival root and then the conjunctival particle of the noun's

---

[1] For Ki-makua. K is disliked at the beginning of a word. The Ki- prefix becomes I- and the Ku- prefix, U-.

class superadded. Thus: not *Mundu m*kulungwa, but *Mundu jua*[1]*-m-kulungwa*
             man   great   man this of this greatness
= Man of greatness, "great man."

Ci-yao from its many difficulties will never become a useful language in British Central Africa. The Yao themselves seem to feel this from the assiduity with which they employ Ki-swahili and Ci-nyanja in their trade transactions. From a philological point of view, however, it is a most interesting language, the construction of which throws considerable light on the genesis of the Bantu speech.

Among the languages spoken in British Central Africa should be enumerated Zulu. The use of Zulu still lingers among the older men and the "aristocracy" of the Angoni kingdoms in South-West, North-West, and Eastern Nyasaland, though it is rapidly disappearing. In some districts it is spoken without the clicks: in others the seventh prefix has been changed back to *Ici-* from *Isi-* and the eighth prefix has been restored to *Ivi-* from the Zulu corruption *Izi-*. This no doubt is borrowed from the Wa-tonga, Wa-chewa, and Ba-tumbuka, who are the indigenous inhabitants and subject peoples of Angoniland. Just possibly it may be that the ancestors of the Angoni who left Zululand about 1820 retained the older forms of these prefixes. Zulu will probably leave traces of its intrusion into these lands by grafting on to the speech of the Nyasa peoples many words of South African origin, but as a spoken language it is destined to a speedy disappearance north of the Zambezi.

Although the various Bantu dialects of British Central Africa have reached this country by many different routes and are derived from many different subsidiary stocks—their common origin in some cases going back to a distance of time and space both remote—they are already reacting on one another in a manner to produce a certain surface resemblance often deceiving to the casual traveller who requires to examine closely into their structure and vocabularies to realise that although outwardly alike in some respects, there are in reality well-marked differences between the minor groups; and still more between the languages to the west of Lake Nyasa and those to the east of that Lake (Ci-yao and I-makua).

The vocabularies which now follow have all with four exceptions been collected by myself from natives who spoke one or other of the languages as their mother-tongue. The four exceptions are Ci-mañanja, Ci-mbo, Ci-cuambo, and Ci-mazaro, which were kindly collected for me by the Rev. D. C. Ruffele-Scott of Blantyre. Some of the words in the Ci-cipeta vocabulary are supplied by Mr. Scott also.

The system of orthography which I have deemed it wise to adopt is practically that of Lepsius, with slight modifications which make it easier for printing purposes. The consonants are pronounced as in English with the exception of *c*, which always stands for *ch* in "church." Ñ represents the ringing nasal sound in the word "ringing" (as contrasted with "ng" in stro*ng*er"): thus Mañanja is pronounced Mang'anja but without any pause. ɖ stands for *dh* (*th* in "this"), ƀ stands for *th* (*th* in think); ṣ is the equivalent of *sh*; ẓ the equivalent of *zh*; γ (Greek *gamma*) represents the guttural sound of *gh* (Arabic ع *γain*—like the German pronunciation of *r*); χ (Greek

---

[1] Although it will not at first seem apparent to the reader, *jua* and *m-* are really of the same origin. They both go back to the oldest form of the first prefix—*ngu-*. This became in time *ñu-* and *mu-* as a *prefix*, but as a *particle* it has in many languages an older type—*gu-, ju-, yu-, wu-, w'-*. The *m-* in *m'*kulungwa stands, of course, for *mu-*.

chi) is *kh* (*ch* in "loch"); and *q* stands for the Arabic guttural *k*, "kof," ق. Whenever *h* is seen it is to be pronounced as an English aspirate. Thus: *Katha* would be pronounced kat-ha, not *katha* as in "Katharine"; *bakha* would be *bak-ha*, not *baχa;* and so on.

Vowels are pronounced as in Italian, with *ü, ö* as in German. *O* is like "o" in "not"; *ō* like "o" in "store." The Greek ω stands for the diphthongal sound of "o" in "bone." The diphthong *ei* must be carefully and logically pronounced like *ey* in "grey"; *not* like *ey* in "eye,"[1] as it is a conjunction of *e* (ay) and *i* (ee).

The *numbers* placed against words in the vocabularies indicate the original classes of the Bantu mother-language to which the nouns belong and correspond with the numbers attached to my foregoing table of the classes. Thus "9 and 10" attached to a word mean that it belongs in that form to both the ninth and tenth classes, the prefixial distinction being lost but the class of the noun being still preserved in the other syntaxial particles.[2] Often after a noun the word "two" or "many" will be placed as the explanation of an accompanying native word. This is to show the form of the plural adjectival particle or prefix. Of course your negro informant would simply gape if you asked, "Now tell me the plural adjectival prefix of the fourth class"; but if you put it this way, "How do you say 'Two Trees'?" he will at once reply: "Miti gibili" = "Trees two," and you at once put down delightedly "gi" as the adjectival particle belonging to nouns of the fourth class or "*Mi-*" prefix. In like manner the sentences at the end are not the senseless rubbish they seem, but are intended to disclose the structure of the language.

[1] English people with their dull hearing and want of knowledge *will* pronounce the name of the Portuguese town of Beira, "Byra," instead of *Bayra*.
[2] For instance: in Ki-swahili, *nyumba* (class 9) is "a house"; *nyumba* (class 10) is "houses." But *Nyumba* hi*i* is "this house," and *Nyumba* hi*zi* is "these houses": showing that the prefix *zi-* has been lost in the noun.

VOCABULARY OF ENGLISH WORDS AND SENTENCES TRANSLATED INTO

English.	Manyema.	Ki-guha.	Ki-wemba of Itawa.	Ki-emba of Luemba.	Ki-lungu.	Ki-mambwe.
Ant	I-fumba limo, *plur.* a-Mswa (*termite*)	Mbasi Njoroa (*termite*)	Impasi (siwiri = *two*)	Nyelele, impasi	Kalandu Wonyi (*termite*)	Impasi
Antelope (eland, pallah)	Kai(*eland?*), *plur.* nkai Yoruku	Nsefu = *eland* Nzunu = *pallah* (kibili = *two*)	Nsefu (*eland*) Impala (*pallah*)	Nsefu Impala, 9 & 10 (ziwiri = *two*)	Insefu (*eland*) Kakole, *plur.* akakole (airi = *two*), *pallah*	
Ape (or baboon)	Soko (*chimpanzee*) Mbwabwa (*baboon*)	Tolue (9 & 10).	Koroe	Kolowe, *plur.* wa-	Koloe, *plur.* yakoloe yairi = *two*	
Arm	Loanya (*same sing. and plur.*)	Kuboko (kumo = *one*, maboko gawele = *two*)	Ku-woko, ma-	Ku-woko, ma- (yawiri = *two*)	Ikasa, *plur.* makasa	Ikasa, *plur.* makasa
Arrow	Likura (*plur.* = akura) (6). Akura ape = *two arrows*	Nketo (gumo), miketo (giwili)	Mu-fwi, mi-	Lifumo	Umūvwi. Mivwi iidi = *two*; indyi = *many*)	Muvwi
Axe	Kenge, *plur.* tokenge (12). Tupe = *two*	Katemo (kamo), *plur.* tutemo	I-sembe, ma-	I-sembe *or* Li-	Impasa	Impasa
Back	Okongo, *plur.* ekongo (3 & 4). Epe = *two*	Ngoño (kiali = *shoulder*, biali = *shoulders*)	Musana Inuma (*shoulders*)	Musana	Musana (*small of the back*), itundu (*all the back*)	Musisi
Banana	Dinkondo, *plur.* akondo (5 & 6). Ape = *two*	Toka (limo = *one*), *plur.* matoka	Nkonde	Nkonde	Konde	Nkonde
Beard	Ndedu	Kalesi, tulesi	Mwefu	Mwevu	Kilezu, vilezu	
Bee	Nzui	Nyuki (gingi = *many*)	Ulusimu	Uluzimu Buci = *honey*	Inzimu Indilwa	Nzimo Ndilwa (?)
Belly	Kunju, *plur.* a-Esopo (*bowels*).	Gumo Mila (*bowels*)	Difumo Mala (*bowels*)	I-fumo Mala = *bowels*	Mala ya liminda (*bowels*)	
Bowels						
Bird	Ifuro (imo = *one*), tufuro tupe = *two*	Unoni (gumo = *one*), *plur.* minoni (gingi = *many*)	Kioni, ifoni	Cipele, *plur.* vi-	Kiunyi (kimwi = *one*), biunyi	Kiuni
Blood	Ikira	Miloa	Mulopa	Milopa	Uwazi	Uwazi
Body	Yungi	Mbili	Muwiri	Muwiri	Mwidi	Mwili
Bow	Wuta (*same in plur.*)	Buta, *plur.* mata (gengi = *many*)	Wuta	Wuta	Ulapwa, amalapwa (yindyi = *many*)	Ulapwa
Bone	Ufwa, *plur.* ifwa (3 & 4)	Kuja, makuja	I-fupa, ma-	Lifupa	I-fupa, ma-	Fupa
Brains	Wongo	Bōngo	Itōmpwe	Itompwe	Tōmpwe	Uwongo

VOCABULARIES

English						
Breast	Tωlo (*male*), *sing.* diefe, *plur.* aele (*female*)	Kiali kia mele (*male*), bele (limo = *one*), *plur.* mabele (*female*)	Kifuba	Cifuba	Kifia = *male*; iede, maede = *female*	
Brother	Onango, *plur.* wanango (1 & 2)	Mwan' etu, bana wetu	Umīnyina, *plur.* banyina	Ndume (yanji = *my*)	Ulupwa, *plur.* ndupwa, (luane = *my*), mwina	Mwina (?)
Buffalo	Mbōō	Mogω (9 & 10)	Imbōō	Imbōō	Imbωω	Imbωω
Buttocks	Akoma	Matako	Imputi	Matako	Matako	
Canoe	Watu, *plur.* yato	Buatω, mato	Bwato, amato	Bwato. (Tu tira = *we say*)	Uato, mato	Uwato
Cat		Nyavu	Sumbwe, basumbwe	Icona	Nyau	Nyau
Chief	Kango umo = *one*	Kolo, ma-	Imfumu, 9 and 10; si- *is the plur. particle*	Imfumu	Mwene, aene-	Mfumu, *plur.* afumo
Child	Akanga ape = *two* Ωna, wana	Mwana, bana	Mwana. Kana (*dim.*), utwana *plur. of diminutive*	Mwana, awana Cireziee = *baby*	Mwana, ana	Mwana, *plur.* ana-
Cloth	Esinda	Mwenda	Insalu	Insalu	Insalu	Insavu, mwenda
Borassus palm	Tωku, atωku	Belewili, ma-	Mt-koma, mi- (ingi = *many*)		Mukoma	
Country	Luanza (luam = *my*)	Inzi	Impanga	Mumpanga	Panga	Insi
Cow	Ñombe (*possibly a borrowed word. There are none in Manyema*)	Ñome	Ñombe (inkota = *female*)	Ñombe	Iñombe	Ñombe
Crocodile	Ñgwena	Ñwena	Ñwena	Ñwena	Ingwena	Ingwena
Day	Lusu (lomo = *one*), *plur.* isu epe = *two* (10 & 11)	Busigi (bumo = *one*), *plur.* masigi	Uwusiku (bumo = *one*, insiku isingi = *many*)	Wusiku; wumo = *one* ,, sinji = *many*	Wanda, manda	Mwanda
Dog	Mfwa	Kambwa, tumbwa	Mbwa *or* imbwa	Mbwa	Simbwa	Simbwa
Devil	Ωloki, a-	Nzimu, mizimu	Kinkala, kiwa	Mipasi	Kiwa, biwa	
Door	Lokuke-, *plur.* kuke	Njiaño, mijiaño (gingi = *many*)	Mwinsi	Ciwi, viwi	Kisasa	
Dream	Ndota	Kilω, bilω	Ki-roto, ifi	Ciroto, *plur.* vi-Ñoma	Kiloto	
Drum	Ngoma	Ñoma	Ñoma	Ñoma	Ifigoma	Ñgoma
Ear	Tui, atui	Kutū, matū	Kutwi, matwi	Utui, matui	Kutwi, matwi	Kutui, matui
Egg	Okire, ekire	Udzi (limo = *one*), maudzi	Dini. Amani aengi = *many*	Lini, mani	Dienza, maenza	Liensa, mensa
Elephant	Com'	Nyωgi	Insofti	Insofti	Inzωvu	Nzωvu
Excrement	Tūi (12)	Tuwi	Amafi	Amafi	Amavi	
Eye	Diso, *plur.* wasiu	Liso, meso	Dinso, amenso	Dinso, maso	Dinso, maso	Linso, manso
Face	I-luñgi	Kukiene (konze = *all*)	Kumenso	Kumenso	Kumaso (konse = *all*)	Kumanso
Fat	I-diswa	Makita	Amafuta	Amafuta	Amafuta	Mafuta, manona
Finger	Pita	Nwe (gumo = *one*), minwe (giwili = *two*)	Munue, mi-	Cala; *plur.* ifala, viala	Umūnūe, minue	Munwe, minwe
Fear	Ioñgi	Bwenyo	Mwenso	Mwenso	Intete	Ntete
Fire	Iω	Kaia	Muriro	Mulilo	Mōtω	Moto
Fish	Lusē, *plur.* nse (ape = *two*)	Nyama	I-sabi, ama-	Lisawi	Insui	Nswi

VOCABULARY OF ENGLISH WORDS AND SENTENCES TRANSLATED INTO

English.	Manyema.	Ki-guha.	Ki-wemba of Itawa.	Ki-emba of Luemba.	Ki-lungu.	Ki-mambwe.
Foot	Lukuru, *plur.* ikuru (epe = *two*)	Ki-kasa, bi-	Lukasa, inkasa (sibidi = *two*)	Lukasa, ma-	Inyazo	Luazo
Forest	Ɔkunda	Mwitu	Musitu	Musitu	Musitu	Latala
Fowl	Koko	Ngoko	Inkoko	Nkoko	Inkoko	Nokoko
Ghost	Dieledi	Nkisi (gumo = *one*), mikisi	Mupasi	Mupasi	Muzimu, mi-	Mupasi, mipasi
Goat	Mbodi	Muji (gimo = *one*), *plur.* mabuzi	Imbuzi	Mbuzi	Imbuzi	Mbuzi
God	Lɔula (?)	Kabejea	Ilesa	Lilesa	Ileza	Mulungu; leza
Grass	Sɔno	Yasi *or* kiasi; *plur.* biasi	Kiani, ifiani	Cani, viani	Isote	Isote
Ground	Nkeci	Mabue	Musidi	Musidi	Ivu	Musili
Ground nut	Cuku	Kajugua, tu-	Inṣiama	Inkalanga	Mbalala	Mbalala
Guinea-fowl	Ɔkorongo	Kaña, ma-	Di-kanga, ama-	Nkanga	Ikanga	Kanga
Gun	Kiwonge (same in *plur.*)	Bunduki	Imfuti	Mfuti	Mputtu	Mputtu
Hair	Lifu *or* difu (*plur. and sing.*)	Nyuwele	Muṣiṣi	Musisi	Inyele	Nyele
Hand	Loo (same in *plur.*)	Mwiswe, maswe	Lupi, amapi	Lupi, mapi	Ikufi	Ikasa
Head	Otoe, *plur.* etoe	Tue	Mu-tue, mi- (ibidi = *two*)	Mutue	Mutue	Mutwe
Heart	Édiko	Ntima	Mutima	Mutima	Mwenzo	Kintunta
Heel	Iporo	Kasindagolo	Ka-tende, utu-	Ka-tende, tu-	Kitunta	Kivuu
Hippopotamus	Ngio	Nyigi	Cɔfwe, ba-	Imvuwu	Inkambwe	Uki
Honey	Uki	Buki	Buci	Buci	Ugyi	Pembe
Horn	Seṅgwa	Meega, *plur.* (luega lumo = *one*)	Insengo	Mu-sengo, *plur.* mi-	Impembe	
Horse (donkey, zebra)		Ngenga, *plur.* ban-genga (benyi = *many*) Ndamwe = *zebra*	Indɔkwe (*donkey*) Kibyɔbyɔ (*zebra*)	Mpelembe Mkoloto = *zebra*	Ndokoi (*donkey*) Kingalika (*zebra*)	Ndogowe (*donkey*) Sinka (*zebra*)
House	Lɔm', Lɔmu ipe (*plur.* = *two*)	Ndzese, mazesi	Ñanda	Ñanda	Ñanda	Nganda
Hunger	Njala	Nyala	Insala	Nzala	Inzala	Nzala
Hyena	Lulu	Ki-mbwi, bi-	Kimbwi	Cimbwi	Kimbwi	Kimbwi; asugutu (?)
Iron	Ziwa	Ki-geala, bi-	Kieala, ifi-	Ulungu	Ikieala, bieala	Kiera
Island	Uwanga a Cōm	Kilela	Kirira, ifi-	Cisiwa	Kidila	Kilila
Ivory		Meno ga nyɔgi	Dino *or* idino nsɔfu lia	Lino lia nzɔfu	Dino la inzɔvu	Pembe zia nzovu
Knee	Dinue	Si (*plur.* masi)	Dikufi	Likɔfi	Kɔkɔla	Ikokɔla

VOCABULARIES

English		Kele, twele	Mwele	Mwele	Mwele	Mwere
Knife	Lukula		Mwele (miele ili inji = those many knives)	Mwele		
Leg	I-lemba, *plur.* bi-	Kugulu	Mukonso (umo = *one*)	Kulu, mukulu, kukulu	Kulu; impamba = *thigh*	Kuulu, maulu
Leopard	Ngoi	Nge	Imbwiri	Mbwiri or umbwiri, *plur.* wambwiri	Nangu	Inanga
Lips	Olomo-, e-	Miromo (*plur.*)	Muromo	Mulomo	Milomo	Mu-romo, mi-
Magic	Usunga	Buganga	Bwanga	Wulozi	Uwanga	Uwanga
Maize	I-popo *or* di-	Kisaka	Inyange	Nyanje	Kisaka	Kisaka
Man	Oto *or* untu; wato yeēē = *many men*	Ndu, bandu	Muntu (umo = *one*), Bantu (babidi = *two*)	Muntu, wantu Mumana = *male*	Muntu, antu	Muntu, antu
Meat	Nyama	Nyama	Inama	Inama	Inyama	Nyama
Monkey	Kima	Ngema	Insokǫ (?)	Mu-penje, wa-	Sāngye	Nkima
Moon	Uedi, eedi	Mwejé	Mwezi	Mwezi	Mwezi	Mwezi
Mountain	Ekundze (emo = *one*) (9 & 10?)	Ntando	Lupiri, impiri	Lu-piri, ama-	Mwamba	Mwamba
Nail (of finger or toe)	Nkala	Luala, mala	Wala *or* luala *or* duala, *plur.* ngala	Luala	Inyala	
Name	Yima	Zina (liane = *my*)	Isina (liangi = *my*)	Lizina (lianji = *my*)	Izina (liane = *my*)	Kera, tuera (13 & 12)
Neck	Kingo	Ngiño	Mukosi	Mukosi	Insingo	Zina
Night	Ucu	Busigi	Busiku, Kwafita = *darkness*	Wusiku	Usiku	Nsingo
						Usiku
Oil palm	Mba	Kigadzi	Kuimbu (?)	Takwawa (?)	Kiazi	Ngazi
Ox		Ñome (yanalume = *male*)	Ñombe (mulume = *male*)	Ñombe	Yonsi	Ñgombe
Palm wine	Wanua	Ngusu	Kibale (?)	Mutondo	Nzamba	
Parrot	U-kungu, e-	Bolo	Kirongo (?)	Mucence	Kusu	
Penis	Usuka	Nguluwe	Bukala		Imbolo	Mbolo
Pig	Sumbu		Kapoli, ba-	Kapoli, wa-, Njiri = *wart hog*	Kapoli	Kapori Mungili = *wart hog*
Pigeon	Luefiga	Ngunda	Nkunda	Cipele, nkunda	Kunda	Kipele, nkunda
Place	Luanza (lolo = *good*); a- is the locative particle, asi is "down"	Anzi (asoga = *good*)	Apasuma (apawama = *good*, showing that apa- is the form of the 16th particle)	Icalo, *plur.* vialo, pasuma (pa = *prefix*)	Palia	Pa-
Rain	Mfula	Mila	Imfula	Mvula	Imvula	Mvula
Rat	Ikoso *or* li-	Linde, ma-nde	Impuku	Mimpuku (*plur.*)	Kusulu	Kuza
River	Okedi, e-	Nkone, mikone	Mumana	Mumana	Luzi, nguzi	Luzi
Road	Onkulu, e-	Nyila	Insila	Inzila	Nzila	Nzila
Sheep	Okoko, e-	Nkoko	Impanga	Impanga	Mfuele	Fwere
Sister	Amuntu	Ngozi (yane = *my*)	Mwinyinane	Muviala	Kazi ya mwine	Kati (wane = *my*)
Skin	Ekoa	Kilinga	Inkanda	Inkanda	Impapa	Mpapa; nkwa
Sky	Lola *or* loa	Gulu	Inkuba *and* ilesa	Likumbi = *clouds*, ileza	Iyulu	Yulu
(cloud)		Lezi			Ikumbi	Fwimbi; kumbi = *cloud*
Sleep	Tolo, Mbitama = *I sleep*	Tulo	Tulo	Tulo	Utulo	Tulo

VOCABULARY OF ENGLISH WORDS AND SENTENCES TRANSLATED INTO

English.	Manyema.	Ki-guha.	Ki-wemba of Itawa.	Ki-emba of Luemba.	Ki-lungu.	Ki-mambwe.
Smoke	Udiifiga	Lingi, mingi	Cunsi	Cusi	Cunsi	Kiunsi
Snake	Nzoa	Nyoka	Insoka	Nzoka	Nzoka	Nzoka
Son	Onape, wa-	Mwana (lume = male)	Mwana (mwaume = male)	Mwana	Monsi, akanya = small child, plur. utunya	Mwana
Song	Luimbo, plur. nyimbo	Luimo, ngimo (gini = many)	Luimbo, inyimbo	Cila	Uluimbo	Luimbo
Spear	Ulumbo	Simo	I-fumo, ama-	Ifumo	Isumo	Isumo
Spirit (or shadow)	Dikoi, a-	Naya, binyaya	Kinsingwa	Cinsingwa	Muzā	Kinziñgwa; mupozi
Star	Ekui-kui, plur. tukui-kui	Kambalambala	Intanda	Intanda	Intanda	Lutanda
Stick	Ute, e-	Kabuli	Inkota	Inkonto	Ntuwa	Kalinda
Stone	Difwe	Bue (limo = one), mabue	Dilwe or ibwe, amabwe	Livwe	Iwe, amawe	Iwe, mawe
Sun	Diani	Juba	Kasuba	Kasuwa	Akasanya	Iransi
Tear	Epombo	Lisozi, mesozi	Idinsosi, amansosi	Munsozi	Linsozi	Munsori
Testicles	Apole (plur.)	Mauli	Mawolo		Matulu	Matulu
Thief	Ambo-iba = lit.: he is stealing. Mbiba (?)	Mwibi, bebi	Muñø	Pompwe, wa-	Mupupu	Mwivi
Thing	Ntu (mo = one) (same in plur.)	Kindu, bindu	Kintu, ifintu	Cintu, vintu	Kintu, bintu	Kintu, vintu
Thorn	Efwa (same in plur.)	Mwiba	Munga	Muñga	Munga	Munga
Tobacco	Fwanka	Njungø	Mfwaka	Fwaka	Fwaka	Fwaka
To-day	Elo	Bulegulu	Lelo	Lelo	Ilelo	Lelo
(to-morrow)	Lumu = to-morrow	Dzo = to-morrow	Mairo = to-morrow	Mairo = yesterday	Mutondo (to-morrow)	Katondo
(yesterday)		Bulabusigi = yesterday	Mairo adia = yesterday		Mutondolia (yesterday)	Mutondo
Toe	Pita.	Kiala	Ckumo	Ckumo	Kikando	Kando, makando
Tongue	Ulim, ndim, ipe = two	Lulimi, nimi	Lulimi, indimi	Lulimi	Lulimi, indimi	Lulimi
Tooth	Dinyo dimo = one, wanyo ye = many	Lino, meno	Dino, ameno	Lino	Dino, mino	Lino, mino
Town	Luanza lumo = one, lumwa = two	Ngutu	Musi	Musi	Umuzi	Muzi
Tree	Ute (omo = one), ete (epe = two)	Nti, miti	Muti	Citi	Muti	Muti
Twins	Waasa	Maasa	Bampundu	Wampundu	Mapasa	Yampundu
Urine	Wayi	Masø	Masu		Tunzi	Matunzi
War	Vita	Biluba	Fita	Vita	Musika	Nkondo; vita
Water	Asi	Maji	Amensi	Menzi	Manzi	Mansi
White man	Mzungu (Kiswahili), azungu	Ndzungu, badzungu	Musungu, aba-	Muzungu	Muzungu, azungu	Muzungu, azungu

VOCABULARIES

Wife	Wadi, -am = *my*, -e = *thy*, -andi = *his*	Lupelele, Olωki	Nkasigω	Mukasi (wangi = *my*)	Mukazi (awenji = *many*)	Wane	Umuki
Wind			Nyaγa	Impepo	Impepo	Muzā	Umuza
Witch			Nωgi (gumo = *one*), banωgi	Mulosi, siñanga (*doctor*)	Mulosi, Siñanga = *doctor*	Mulozi	Mulozi
Woman	Omuntu, wamantu (*plur.*), je = *many*		Mbakadzi	Mukasi	Mukasi	Mwānakyi	Mwanaki
Wood	Idya, *plur.* tωdya, dye = *many*		Nguni	Inkuni	Nkuni	Inkwi	Nkwi
Yam	Kirunga, *plur.* either virunga *or* runga		Kigaci	Ki-rungwa, ifi	Cirungwa	Kirungu	Ulungu
Year	Ωwa, ewa		Ki-mula, bi-	Mwaka	Mwaka	Mwaka (umo = *one*)	Mwaka
One	Omo		Kamo	Kamo	Kamo	Umwi (-mwi)	-onga, -enga
Two	Epe		Tuwiri	Tubidi	Tuwiri	Ziidi (-idi)	-iri
Three	Esatu		Tutatu	Tutatu	Tutatu	Zitatu	-tatu
Four	Enem		Tuna	Finne	Vinne	Zini	-ni
Five	Tanu		Tutano	Fisano	Visano	Zisano	-sanu
Six	Samaro		Ntanda	Mutanda	Vilimo-tanda	Mutanda	Mutanda
Seven	Sambele		Kilωwa	Apainye-apaitatu	Visana na viwiri	Kineruwari	Kinimbali
Eight	Enanem		Mwanda	Kine konse-konse		Kinani	Kanani
Nine	Diowa		Habula	Fundi lubali		Fundi	Fundi mbali
Ten	Vum		Kumi	Ikumi	Likumi	Ikumi	Ikumi
Eleven	Vum la mω		Kumi na kamo ,, na tupere = 12	Ikumi na umo		Kumi na imwi	Ikumi na longa
Twenty	Gumu ape		Makumi gawere	Makumi-abidi		Makumi airi	Makumi yairi
Thirty	Ωm *or* gumu asatu		Makumi gatatu	Amakumi atatu		Makumi atatu	Makumi yatatu
Forty	Ωmu anei		Makumi gana	Amakumi anne		Makumi anni	Makumi yanni
Fifty	Ωmu atanu		Makumi gatano	Amakumi asano		Makumi asano	Makumi yasanu
Hundred	Lukama		Zana	Mwanda		Mwanda	Mwanda
Thousand				Empoșωmω			
I, me	Nim		Nene	Nebo	Ninō, newω, neka (*alone, myself*)	Nene	Nene
Thou	We		Gūe	Webo	Wewo	Wewe	Wewe
He	Yandi		Gujω	Uyn		Widia (?)	We
We	Ishu		Betwe	Fwebo	Fwewo, fwe	Afwefwe	Sweswe
You			Benyi	Mwebo	Mwewo	Mwemwe	Mwemwe
They			Babo	Babo	Wawo	Ao	O
All	-amwa *or* -mwa (wamwa, 2; yamwa, 4, 6, 8, 10; tomwa, 12)		-onze (bonze 2; gionze 4; gonze 6, bionze 8, gionze 10, tonze 12, bonze 14, konze 15, onze 16)	-onse (abantu bonse = *all men*)		-onsi (onsi, yonsi, onsi, vionsi, zionsi, *etc.*)	-onsi
This man	-ne (untu one = *this man*), *pl.* watu wane		Ndu gūju, bandu baba	Muntu uyu, abantu aba		Muntu wi, antu aa	Muntu wiwi

VOCABULARY OF ENGLISH WORDS AND SENTENCES TRANSLATED INTO

English	Mauyema.	Ki-guha.	Ki-wemba of Itawa.	Ki-emba of Luemba.	Ki-lungu.	Ki-mambwe.
That man	-ńko (untu unko = *that man*), *pl.* watu anko	Ndu gulia, bandu balia	Muntu udia, abantu badia		Muntu widia, antu adia	Muntu wilia; antu yalia
This tree	Ute onę, *plur.* ete ene	Nti guju, miti giji.	Muti uyu, imiti iyo		Muti ū, imiti ii	Muti uu, miti ii
That tree	Ute unko, *pl.* ete enko	Nti gulia, miti gilia.	Muti uyọ, miti iyi		Muti udia, miti idia	Muti ulia
My house	Lum luam	Ndese giane	Ñanda anji		Ñanda ane	Nganda yane
Thy house	Lum lue .	Ndese gịọwe	Ñanda yọwe		Ñand' ako	Nganda yako
His house	Lum luandi	Ndese giege	Ñanda yakwe		Ñand' akwe	Nganda yakwe
Our town	Luanza luasa	Ngutu gia *or* ya betwe	Musi wesu		Muzi witu	Muzi witọ
Your children	Ltanza luanu	Nsi gia *or* ya benue	Impanga yenu		Panga inọ	Mpanga inu
Their children	Wana ao .	Bana ba bebo	Bana babo		An' ao	Ana ao *or* yao
Bad	-be .	-bi .	-bi		-wi	-ki
Female	Wadi	-bakadzi	Mwanakasi		-nki, nci *or* mwanaci	
Good	polo, -olo, -lọ	-soga (ndu usoga = *good man*)	-suma		-zipa	-zipa
Great	-nene	-kulu (*applied to men*), -la (*applied to things*), nti (*tree*), gula (*a big tree*), *plur.* miti gila	-kulu		-kalamba, kulu .	-kulu; -kalamba
Little	-alonga	-anike	-nini		-nonọ	-nini
Male	-pe .	-balume	Mwaume .	Mulume .	-onsi (monsi, aonsi)	Monsi; kalume
White	-tọ .	-münge	Yawuta (busafu buawuta = *white cloth*)		-tiswe	-tiswe
Here	Ane	Haha	Apa.		Apa.	Apa; pano
Black	-pi .	-gasuke .	Yafita		-tifi	
Plenty	Yē *or* dyeē	-iñi *or* -inyi	-ingi (abengi, șingi, *etc.*)		-ingi	
There	Enkọ	Kulia	Kulia, palia		Kuku	
No, not	Alańgi	Naleña!	Lika		Awe	
I am	-le. Nimkalem = *I am here*	Nali (maliho = *I am here*), (*is* = ni, *all tenses*)	Ndi. (Epondi = *I am here*)		Ndi (ndipo = *I am here*)	
I bring	lambuela	-sia (*come*), nakio (*with it*), *imp.*	Naleta		Naleta	
I come	lakaye	Nasia	Naya		Niza	
I come not	Halayi	Ndisia (-ko) .	Șileako (?)		Takwiza *or* takwiza -ko (enclitic)	
I dance	lakanue	Nakēeña .	Ndecinda .		Nakina	
I die	lakafwe. Nim palafu = *I do not die*	Nakia .	Nafwa (silefwa (*neg.*) = *I do not die*)		Nafwa	
I drink	la-mbo-nywa *or* nua	Nkūnūa			Nkufiwa	
I drank	la-ọ-nua	Nantine .			Nafiwire	
I drank not	pa-nyue *or* pa-la-nyue	Nzinuine .			Ntafiwire = *I did drink*	

VOCABULARIES

I eat	la-mbo-dia	Nkulia	Nalia
I eat not	palali	Nzilia	Ntakulia
I give	la-mbo-pa	Naha (-ha or- wa = give)	Nakupa (?), -pa (give)
I give you	la-ka-*ku*-pe	Nakuwa gŭe	Nakupa-wi
I gave him	lakupe	Namuhele	Namūpile
I go	La-ka-cŭi	Nagia	Napita
I went	La-cui or lakacui	Nagŭile	Napişile
I kill them	La-mbo-wa-saka	Nabaniga	Nayakωma
I know	La-mbo-ewa	Namanya	Namanya
I know not	Palewi	Nzi-manya or nzidzi	Tamanya
Thou lovest	Wa-mpenda or wa-mbo-mpenda	Ωlωgelelwa	Watemwa
We make	Ishiu tωkia intu (we make a thing)	Tuloñe	Tuōmbe
We say	To-mbo-alonda	Tujωgωme	Tuvwange
We sold not	patusombi	Tusigulile	Tutakasidi
He stinks	a-mbo-ponda	Waninga	Wanūnka
He steals	a-mbo-iba	Wagiba	Wiiya
They laugh	Wa-mbōla. (*I did not laugh* = pa-mbo-le; *they did not laugh* = wanko ha-wōle)	Baseka	Yaseka
You weep	-lela = *weep*	Mwalela- (muliñku- or mwa-)	Mulila *or* musulila
Where did he go ?	Akacui endi ?	Wayakwe ?	Walaide kwi ?
What do you say ?	Wambolondena ?	Ωdzωga make ?	Wino kuvwanga kyi ? or ci
What shall we drink ?	Tōlōñŭana ?	Tulekanwa ke ?	Tulañwa ci ?
When art thou coming ?	Wa-kaye lusuma ?	Ωzia mageñoke ?	Wiza lilaki ?
Give me food	Umpa dyemanda	Mbe cakulia	Mpe cakudia
Cut me a small stick	Untenene ote alonga	Ongale kabuli kakekake	
I want a little stone	Lakala difwe dalonga	Natωke libue likelike	Nkωme intuwa inono
Which (fowl) will you give me ?	Ulumpa koko ape ?	Ωlemba koko ke ?	Nkulonda iwe linono Ulampa nkokω idikwi ?
He is inside the house	Ale nu lum	Gujω gule ndzese	Awidia ali muñanda
The birds flew away	Tufuru tuamo tuaka fumbwe	Minωni gibukile	Viunyi vialamvire
The parrot screams	Ukuñgu ambolela	Ngusu yalela	Nkusu yalila
The rotten tree falls	Otewakilampode wambo-kwa or wa-kakwe (*fell*)	Nti wabola wagwila hanji	Muti wawola wawa
Can you see me ?	Wakameni = *did you you see me ?*	Ωlimona (*do you see me ?*)	U wiza mwandola ?
No, I cannot	Palewe. *I cannot*; *I know not*	Njikuwa !	Nakana !

495

VOCABULARY OF ENGLISH WORDS AND SENTENCES TRANSLATED INTO

English.	Ki-fipa.	Ici-wuŋgu.	Ki-sukuma.	Isi-nyixa.	Ici-wandia.	Iki-nyikitsa.
Ant	Kalandu	Insuṅgwa. Ruswa (*termite*)	Pisu, swa (*termite*)	Indóndomi. Ruswa = *white ant*. Amaswa	Ic-ndundu, *plur.* ivi-Uruswa, *plur.* ama-ruswa	Ngēsa. Unswa gumo = 1 (*white ant*), *plur.* miswa
Antelope (eland, pallah)	Mbesi (*eland*). Nswala (*pallah*)	Ndongoro (*eland*). Imbala (*pallah*)	Mpoku (*eland*). Mhala (*pallah*)	Intóngoro (*eland*). Bondoro (*pallah*)	Insefu, 9 & 10 (*eland*). Impara (*pallah*)	Isesema, *plur.* misesema (*eland*). Akasia, tusia (*pallah*). Kaki, bakaki. Bakaki babiiri = 2
Ape (or baboon)	Isike	Indumbi	Kukū (inkuku iwiri = *two*)	Imbwadyi	Ukórœe, awa-	Lukongi, ingōngi; luete, lumoluene
Arm	Ikasa, ma-	M-kono, mi-	Kono, mi-	Ixœno, amaxœno	Icianza (7)	Iki-boko, *plur.* ifi-
Arrow	Incetu (dziiri = *two*)	Umwambi	I-songa, ma-	Liēre, amēre	Umūvwi, imi-	Untipuru
Axe	Impasa	Indemo	Mpasa	Themo	Inthemo	Induwanga (9 & 10). Siosa = *all*
Back	Inthindi	Mgongo	Gongo	Umtenzi, mitenzi	Umongo roro, *plur.* imiongo. Insizi (*small of*)	Lugongo; romia. Msana = *small of back*
Banana	Insambala	Ngombwe	I-toki, ma-	Nkōmbwe	Nkōmbwe, amakombwe. Ikiyindya	Itoki, *plur.* ma-. Ngēgo. Ikijinja
Beard	Ikirezu	Ndevu	Ntesu	Ndefu (*plur.*), rurefu (*sing.*)	Ikirefu	Ndefu (*plur.*) Lulefu lumo = *one* (*beard*)
Bee	Inzimu	Inzuci	Nsuki	Nduzusi, nzusi	Uruzimu, *plur.* inzimu	Ndzuki
Belly	Inda	Inda	Nta. Mula (*bowels*)	Ruanda, *plur.* inyanda. Uwura (*bowels*)	Akati. Mukasi (*inside*); amara (*intestines*)	Ruanda. Munda (*inside*), wura (*intestines*)
Bowels	Amala (*bowels*)	Uwula (*bowels*)				
Bird	(*For the rest, very much like Ki-luŋgu.*)	Inœni, icœni, ivi-	Nœni (9 & 10)	Isiyunyi, biyunyi	Ikiyuni, ivi-	Injuni
Blood		Ulanda	Mininga	Mnanda	Uwuryazi (ubwiza = *good*), *plur.* amabuyazi	Irœpa or lirœpa
Body		Umwiri	Medi, *plur.* miwedi	Muwiri	Umuwiri, imi-	Umbiri, *plur.* imibiri
Bow		Uwuta	Buta (*same in plur.*)	Wudabi	Uwuta, *plur.* amawuta	Wu-pindo, *plur.* mi- or imi-
Bone	Ifupa	Ifupa	Ikuha	Ifupa	Ifupa, amafupa-	Rufupa or uru-, *plur.* ifupa- or amafupa
Brains		Uwongo	Bōngo	Uwōngo	Uwōngo	Bōngo
Breast		Ikifua(*male*), amawere (*female*)	Kikuwa	Isifua, ivifua; iwere (*female*)	Ikifua; iwere, ama-	Kipambaya (*male*), Iwere, mawere (*female*)
Brother		Mwan 'itu	Muzuna (wane = *my*)	Umu-ninu, awa-	Umu-zuna, awa-	Unūguna
Buffalo		Imbœo	Bokœ	Imbogo	Imbogo	Imbogo, injati
Buttocks		Amatako	Matako	Isiduru, ividuru	Urutungu, intungu	I-tanga, ma-
Canoe		Uwato, amato	Wato, mato	Ujwato	Ubwato, amabyato	Bwato, mi-

VOCABULARIES

	Inyao	Caungu	Unyawu, awanyawu	Aka-nyawa, utu-	
Cat					Niaru. Wanyaru awengi = *many*. Akanyaru = *dim*.
Chief	Umwene, amwene	Mufumu, bafumu	Umwene, awamwene	Imfumu	Marafiari; warafiari
Child	Umwana, awana	Mwana, bana; kana, twana	Umwana	Umwana, awana	Umwana; awana, Akana = *dim*.
Cloth	Mwenda	Mwenda	Umwenda, imenda	Umwenda	Mwenda (3)
Borassus palm	Mkoma	Muhama (*borassus*)	Iχoma, ama-	Umukoma (*borassus*)	Nkoma, mi- (*borassus*)
Country	Insi	Calo (kimo = *one*, şialo şiwiri = *two*, şiswe = *our*)	Insi	Insi	Ikisu, ifi-
Cow	Ñombe	Ñombe (ñhima = *female*)	Ñombe ntigano	Ñombe indama	Ñombe indama
Crocodile	Indo; ōlo	Ñwena	Ndlowor̄o	Ifiwina	Ingwina
Day	Uwusiku, *plur.* isiku	Luziku (lumo), *plur.* siku	Uwanda	Ubuanda, ubyanda	Uwusiku. Pamosi pakiru (*darkness*)
Dog	Imbwa	Mfwa	Imbwa. Imbwa nthende = *bitch*	Imbωa	Imbwa
Devil	Umzimu, azimu (wawiri = *two*)	Kuwe	Işiwa	Umuzimu umuwi (*bad spirit*)	Mbasi
Door	Uluigi, ingiyi *or* iniyi	Muliango	Işiriango	Umuriango; urutanga	Uruigi (11), *plur.* nyigi
Dream	Kirōto	Ki-roto, *plur.* şi-	Işiroto	Ikiroto	Injosi
Drum	Ifioma	Noma	Nthaya	Ifioma	Ifioma
Ear	Ikutwe, ama-	Kutu, matu	Ikutwi	Ikutu (5), ama-	Imburi kutu (9 & 10)
Egg	Iyi, amayi	Iki, magi	Idyi, amadyi	Irienza	Ilifumbi (5)
Elephant	Izovu	Mhuli (9 & 10)	Inzofu	Inzofu	Isofu (9)
Excrement	Amavi	Mafwi	Ivi, amavi	Imvi, amanvi	Amafi
Eye	Irinso, amanso	Diso	Idiinso, aminso	Irinso, aminso	Idiso, amaso. Kisigi = *eyelid*
Face	Kuminso (konse = *all*)	Uşu	Kuminso	Kuminso (konse = *all*)	Kumaso
Fat	Amafuta	Makuta	Impama	Amafuta	Amafuta
Finger	Ulowe, *plur.* inowe (3 & 4)	Luala, *plur.* nzwala	Rusanzo	Urōwe	Urōbe (11)
Fear	Uwowa	Bōwa	Uwoga	Uwω; wa	Wōga
Fire	Umōto	Moto	Umu-riro, ama-	Umōto	Mōto
Fish	Inswi	Şi	Inswi	Inswi	Iswi
Foot	Ikinama	Lupambala	Uruaiyo, nyaiyo	Ikinama, ivi-	Lujaijo, njajo
Forest	Msitu	Mōngo	Isitu	Umusitu	Ulusiñgi
Fowl	Ifiguku	Kokω	Iñkuku	Inkuku	Inguku
Ghost	Umuzimu	Muzimu	Umuzimu Işinziunguri	Umu-zimu, awa- Ikinsiunguri (*shadow*)	Unsinka. I- *or* in- siunguru (*shadow*)
Goat	Imbuzi	Puri *or* pudi	Imbuzi	Imbuzi	Imbeni
God	Murungu *or* uzuwa	Ikulu	Umurungu	Umurungu	Mbamba; kiara
Grass	Isote	Isωa, masωa	Isωre	Isote (5)	Iriso
Ground	Irongo	Masalu	Itope	Iriongo	Umftu

VOCABULARY OF ENGLISH WORDS AND SENTENCES TRANSLATED INTO

English.	Ki-fipa.	Ici-wungu.	Ki-sukuma.	Isi-nyixa.	Ici-wandia.	Iki-nyikusa.
Ground nut		Imbalala	Mhande	Imbarara (plur.), urubarara (sing.)	Insiawa	Isiawara or iri-siawara, plur. ama-
Guinea-fowl		Ikhanga	Nhanga	Ikanga	Ikanga	Ilikanga
Gun		Bundusi	Munducω	Imbundusi	Inyundusi	Nduso, plur. manduso
Hair		Inyere	Nzwiri	Insisi, sing. urusisi	Isisi	Inyuwiri. Urusioja (of animals)
Hand		Iyaza, amayaza	Ki-kanza, ʃi-	Iʃianza	Ikasa	Ikianja
Head		Umtwe	Mutue	Itue	Umutu	Untu, plur. mitu
Heart		Umoyo	Moyo	Umwaya, am-	Umoyo	Ndumbura
Heel		Indiñginya	Iʃigina	Iʃihankari	Icitende	Ikitende
Hippopotamus		Iviũ	Ñguwu	Imvuwu	Imvuwu	Ifiuwu
Honey		Uwuci	Bωki	Ubũũʃi	Uwuci	Ruki
Horn		Impembe	Mhembe	Urupembe	Urupembe	Urupembe
Horse		Insami (zebra)	Nzωwe (zebra)	I-dogωwi, ma- (ass)	Imbunda (donkey)	Imbanda (donkey)
		Indωgwe (ass)	Mhunda (donkey)	Ujiga (zebra)	U-corwa, awa- (zebra)	Isendzewere (zebra)
House		Nyumba	Numba	Inyumba	Iny.umba	Nyumba
Hunger		Inzala	Inzala	Inzara	Inzara	Indzara
Hyena		Imbisi	Piti	Nzumbi	Ucimbui	Kindingo
Iron		Icera	Kisuiza (?)	Iʃijera	Icera	Ikiera
Island		Intipa	Icinga		Icintenʃerezia	Lusungo
Ivory		Rupembe	Mino ga mhuli	Urupembe ruanzωfu	Rupembe rua nsωfu	Rupembe rua isωfu
Knee		Ikokōla	Icwi	Iʃizwi, iviʃwi	I-kωkora, ama-	Lifindo
Knife		Rukamanga	Luʃu	Umu-fiu, imi-	Umu-fiu, imi-	Mmage, plur. mimage
Leg		Umnūndi	Kukulu	Iʃinama	Ik-nama, ivi-. Insango nyama = thigh	Kirundi. Ndapatapa (thigh)
Leopard		Ngωi	Suwi	Inzωwe	Unziera	Liwole
Lips		Milωmo, umlωmo (sing.)	Nomo, minomo	Umurωmo, amarωmo	Umurωmo, imi-	Ndomo, mirωmo
Magic		Undωzi	Bukanga	Uwurωzi	Uwurωzi	Ndωsi, plur. amarωsi
Maize		Masaka	Dimbutkiri	Isaχa, masaχa	Ikirombe	Kirombe
Man		Umtu, awantu	Munhu, banhu	Muntu, awantu	Umuntu, awantu	Mundu or umundu, awa or aba-
Meat		Inyama	Nyama	Inyama	Inyama	Inyama
Monkey		Imbwadzi	Ntumbiri	In-tumbi, ama-	I-tumbiri, ama-	Kabukabu, plur. ba-
Moon		Unwezi	Mweci	Unwezi	Unwezi	Mwezi
Mountain		Umwamba, imiamba	Lukulu, nkulu	I-gamba, ama-	Icipiri	Kiamba
Nail (of finger or toe)		Iniñgwa	Inonga	Urūzura, inzura	Urωwe, inyōwe	Kiara
Name		Irina	Dina (liane = nyr)	Izina	Izina., amazina (gawiri = two)	Ingamu

VOCABULARIES

English					
Neck	Isingo	Nhingo	Insingo	Insingo	Ikosi, ama-
Night	Wusiku (icisi = dark)	Buciku	Uwusiku. Iṣisi = darkness. Pa wusiku = at night	Uwusiku. Amasiku (days), ikisi (darkness)	Pakiru (darkness). Busiku, plur. ama-
Oil palm					
Ox	Iñombe (indume = male)	Kombitale Ñombe (ñoṣa = male)	Ñombe nkambaku (male)	Iñombe (nkambaku = male)	Iñombe
Palm wine					
Parrot	Iriia	Nzanza			
Penis	Ukapōdi, akapōdi	Ikusu	Wu-χara, ama-		Mboro
Pig	Indziwa	Bolo	I-guruwe, ama-	Imboro	Nguruwe
Pigeon	Wōno	Kapodi, ba-	Ngugu	Inguruwe	Ngunguwidza
Place	Ivula *and* insemba	Nkunda	Pawugono	Intωzi	Bugono, *plur. same*
Rain	Mbiringa	Hanhu (ha, *particle*)	Imvura	Uwuraru, amawuraru	Ifura
Rat		Pula	Ukuza	Imvura	Imbewa
		Kosω	Ukuza, awakuza, awindzi	Ukuza	
River	Umbana, imimbana	Mōngo	Idzendze, usumbi, ama- (?)	Uruizi, usumbi, ama- (?)	Uruisi. Sumbi (*lake*)
Road	Izira	Dzira	Inzira	Inzira	Indzira
Sheep	Iñozi	Nholω	Ifionzi, amagonzi	Ifionzi	Iñosi
Sister	Runbu *or* irumbu	Irumbu		Umuyenba, awayemba	Irumbu, amarumbu *or* uru-rumbu, ama-
Skin	Incimba	Nkωlω	Ingora	Ikikωwa	Kikanda
Sky	Kululu	Ikulu	Kunwanya, iwingo	Kunwanya. Iwingu (*cloud*)	Kuwanya. Iwingu (*cloud*)
Sleep	Uturo	Tulo. (Kulala = *to sleep*)	Uturo	Uturo (12)	Turu (12)
Smoke	Idiōsi	Yoci	Iriosi, amōsi	Icusi, ivyusi	Iliōṣi
Snake	Inzoka	Tsωka	Injωχa	Inzωka	Njωka
Son	Umwana, awana	Mwana mkoṣa	Umwana, awana	Umwana	Umwana, awana
Song	Uruimbo	Luimbo	Uruimbo	Uruimbo, inyimbo	Luimbo
Spear	Lupalala	Icimu	Imparara	Imparara	Ingwego
Spirit (or shadow)	Umzimu	Mwengeji	Umuzimu	Umuzimu	Nsinka
Star	Ntongwa	Sōnda	Uruzōta	Urutondwa, intondwa	Urutōndwa, intondwa
Stick	Ntiwa	Nanga	Ndisa	Inkomo	Ingiri
Stone	Ifinga	Iwe	Iwe	Ibye *or* ibwe, amabye	Idibwe
Sun	Msanya, idiuwa	Dimi	Izua	Izuwa	Idisuwa
Tear	Umsωzi	Disoji, misoji	Insωzi	Irinsωzi (5)	Irisosi, ama-
Testicles	Ituru	Mabolo	I-turu, ama-	I-turu; ama-	Urutungu
Thief	Umwivi	Mwibi, bibi	Unwiwa, awiwa	Unuño, awaño	Nheji; baheji
Thing	Ikindu, ivindu	Kinhu, ṣinhu	Iṣintu, ivintu	Ikintu, ivintu	Ikindu, ifindu
Thorn	Irifwa, *plur.* amifwa.	Diihwa	Idiimviva	Uminga	Mwifwa
Tobacco	Itumba	Itumbate	Itumba	Itumba	Ngambo
To-day	Lero	Lelo	Ilero	Lero	Dirinu; umwisingu
to-morrow	Mlao (*to-morrow*)	Ikolo (*to-morrow*)		Indawi (*to-morrow*)	
yesterday	Yōlo (*yesterday*)	Mazuli (*yesterday*)		Mabyira (*yesterday*)	
Toe	Iminue (*plur.*), umnue (*sing.*)	Luala	Insanzu (*plur.*), uru-sanzu (*sing.*)	Urusarara, insarara	Urōwe, inyōwe

VOCABULARY OF ENGLISH WORDS AND SENTENCES TRANSLATED INTO

English.	Ki-fipa.	Ici-wungu.	Ki-sukuma.	Isi-nyixa.	Ici-wandia.	Iki-nyikusa.
Tongue		Lulimi	Lulimi	Ururimi, imiri	Ururimi, amarurimi	Ururimi
Tooth		Ilino, amino	Dino, mino	Idino, amino	Irino ; amino	Irino, amino
Town		Kaya, makaya	Kaya	Inkaya (9 & 10)	Akaya, utwaya	Kaija or kaya, tuaija
Tree		Umti	Muti	Ikwi, amakwe	I-komo, ama-	Mpiki
Twins		Imbasa, mambaza	Mawasa	Ipasa	Ipasa	Ipasa, mapasa
Urine		Matuzi	Mine	Amantunzi	Amatunzi	Matusi
War		Uluwu (14)	Buluku	Uwurugu, awa-	Uwurugu	Buite
Water		Amazi	Minzi	Aminzi	Amenzi	Misi or mesi
White man		Umziunfigu, aziunfigu	Mzungu, bazungu	Umuzungu (tumozi = one)	Umuzungu	Mu-sungu, ba-
Wife		Umcimane	Mkima (wane = mŋy)	Umisi (wane = mŋy)	Mukazi (wane = mŋy)	Kikuru, bakikuru
Wind		Imbepo	Impeho	Impepo	Impepo	Um-bero, imi-
Witch		Mlozi	Mu-loki, ba-	Umurozi	Umurozi	Ndwosi, barwosi
Woman		Mwanace	M-kima, ba- (wingi = many)	Mwan' tanda	Mwana kazi or umukazi	Nkazi, bakazi
Wood		Ingwi	Mhwi	Urukwi	Urukwi, inkwi	Du- or ru-babu
Yam			Itukii	Ifugo	Ikituwo	Ki-tugu or iki-
Year		Umwaka, miaka	Mwaka	Umwaxa, amaxa	Icaka	Ikienja
One		Kamwi	Solo	Woka, yoka	Yoka	Jumo or kumo
Two		Tuwiri	Biri	Ziwiri	Ziwiri	Iwiri
Three		Tutatu (tuntu = little things)	Tatu	Zitatu	Zitatu	Itatu
Four		Tuni	Inne	Zinne	Zinne	Ina
Five		Tusano	Tano	Zifundisire	Zisano	Ihano
Six		Tulintanda	Tandatu	,, na puru woko	Zisano na purwe iweka	Ihano na rumo
Seven		Mpungate	Pungate	,, na puru wawiri	,, na wapurwi wawiri	Ihano na iwiri
Eight		Mnane	Inane	,, na puru watatu	,, na wapurwewatatu	Ihano na itatu
Nine		Icenda	Kenda	,, na puru wanne	,, na wapurwe wanne	Ihano na ina
Ten		Ikumi	Ikumi	Ikumi	Ikumi	Murongo
Eleven		Ikumi na kamwe	Ikumi na lumo	Ikumi na puru woka	Ikumi na purwi iweka	Murongo na rumo
Twenty		Makumi yawiri	Makumi awiri	Amakumi gawiri	Amakumi gawiri	Marongo mawiri
Thirty			Makumi atatu	Amakumi gatatu	Amakumi gatatu	Marongo matatu
Forty			Makumi anne	Amakumi ganne	Amakumi ganne	Marongo mana
Fifty			Makumi atano	Amakumi gafundisire	Amakumi gasano	Marongo mahano
Hundred		Igana	Ikana		Amakumi geka ikumi	Marongo murongo
Thousand			Kihumbi			

VOCABULARIES

I, me	Nene	Nene	Ine (-ane = *my*)	Une (ane = *my*)	Une
Thou	Wewe	Bebe *or* wewe	Iwe (-ax' = *thy*)	Uwe (ako = *thy*)	Ugwe
He	Wiyω	Uyu	Uyω (-akwe = *his*)	Yuyω (ace = *his*)	Dyudyo
We	Isweswe	Iswe	Sweswe (-itu = *our*)	Sweswe (-itu = *our*)	Uswe, etu = *our*
You	Mwemwe.	Iñwe	Mwemwe (-inyu = *your*)	Mwemwe (-inu = *your*)	Umwe, -enu
They	Wawo	Babo	Wuwo (-awo = *their*)	Wawo (-awo = *their*)	Awa, -abo = *their*
All	-onse, pie	-ose (wose 2, yose 4, kōse 6, şiose 8, cose 10, hose 16)	-onti (wonti (*No. 4 missing*), gonti, vionti, zionti, tuonti, wonti, ponti, konti)	-onse (wonse, yonse, gonse, vyonse, zionse, tonse, wonse, ponse, konse)	-ōsa (bōsa, giōsa, gōsa, fiōsa, siōsa, tōsa, bōsa, pōsa, kwōsa
This man		Munhu uyu, banhu babo	Umunt' unu, awant' awa	Umuntu' we	Mundu uju
That man		Banhu nyω, banhu babooo	Umunt' ura, awantu waro	Umuntu yura	Mundu jura
This tree		Muti guyu, miti iyω	Ikwi iri	Ikomo lio (5)	Umpiki ugu
That tree			Ikwi rira	Ikomo rira	Umpiki gura
My house		Numba yane	Inyumba yane, *plur.* inyumba ziane	Nyumba yane	Nyumba jangu *or* yangu
Thy house		Numba yako	Inyumba yaχo Inyumba ziaχo	Nyumba yako	Nyumba jako
His house		Numba yakwe	Inyumba yakwe	Nyumba yace	Nyumba jake
Our town		Mpuri iswe	Inkaya yitu	Akaya kitu	Akaidza kitu
Your country		Calo ciñwe	Insi yinyu	Insi yinu	Ikisu kiako
Their children		Bana babo	Awana wawo	Awana wawo	Awana wawo
Bad		-wi	-wiwi, umuntu muwiwi -anthanda (*animals*) -rindu (*human*)	-wi -anakazi	-biwi -ndinduana; -bwakasi, gikuru
Female			-inza	-iza	-nunu
Good			-mpiti	-kuru	-kurumba
Great			-indu, -ndω. Umuntu mundω = *little man*	-nandi	-nandi
Little			-anávuri		
Male				-anarumi (-rumendo = *human beings*)	-ndumiana; -mbongo (*goats*), -ngámbako (*ox*), -nyambara (*other animals*) -wero
White			-zeru = *white*. Hanyawa hazeru = *awhite cat*	-swepu	
Here			Ipa	Apa	Apa
Black			-hiru, -iru	-tifi	Ntitu
Plenty			-inji	-enji	-ingi
There			Kura	Para	Para
No, not			Ndari	Awe	Mma
I am			Ndi. Name = *I was*	Indi Nari = *I was*	Indi
I bring			Nkusenda	Nkuseñda, -senda	Nduere

VOCABULARY OF ENGLISH WORDS AND SENTENCES TRANSLATED INTO

English.	Ki-hpa.	Ici-wungu.	Ki-sukuma.	Isi-nyixa.	Ici-wandia.	Iki-nyikiusa.
I come				Nkwinza; zaga = *inf.*	Nkwiza; -iza = *inf.* Ntizite = *I came not (pret.)*	Nkuisa
I come not				Takwinza, taminzire.	Takwiza. Ntizite = *I came not (pret.)*	Ndikwisa
I dance				Nkwānga	Nkucina	Nkufina
I die				Nkufwa	Nkufwa or nkufγa	Nkufwa
I drink				Nkufwera	Nkuñwa	Nkunwa
I drank				Nañwereye	Nañwire	Nanuiri
I drank not				Ntañwereye	Ntañwire	Ndanuiri
I eat				Nkuria, nariye	Nkudia or kuria. Narire = *I ate*	Ndire (*I ate*), nikudia (*I eat*)
I eat not				Takuria	Ntakudia	Ndikudia
I give				Kupa	Kupa	Nikupa
I give you				Kukupa	Kukupa	Nikukupa
I gave him				Nampiye	Na-mupire. Nta-= *neg.*	Nampere juje Mayoro (*yesterday*)
I go				Kuwuh'a	Kuwuka	Nikuwuka
I went				Nawusire	Nawukire	Nawukire
I kill them				Kuwagωga	Kuwakoma	Nikuwagωga
I know				Manyire. Namanyire = *I knew*	Menye. Namenye = *I knew*	Nikumanya
I know not				Ntamanyire	Ntamenye	Ndamenye
Thou lovest				Ukwanza	Ukurōnda	Ukuronda. (Pa-ku-ronda = *to love*)
We make				Tukupera.	Tukupera = *we make*	Tuku pera. (Pa-ku-pera = *to make*)
We say				Tukuyanga	Tukunena	Tukuyωwa. (Pa-ku-yωwa = *to say*)
We sold not				Tutakazire; kara = *imp.*	Tutawurite; wura = *imp.*	Tutadinlire. (Pa-ku-ura = *to sell.* Na-rinlire = *I sold*)
He stinks				Akununka; amanunsire	Akunuka. Anuncite = *he stank*	Ikununga. (Itiku-nunga = *he does not smell*)
He steals				Akwiwa, amwire	Akwiba. Iwite = *he stole*	Ikwiba. (Ariwire = *he stole*)
They laugh				Bakuseγa	Wakuseka	Witiku-seka = *neg.*
You weep				Mukurira.	Mukurira.	Mukurira. Mutikurira = *neg.*

VOCABULARIES

Where did he go?	Amawusire kwi?	Awucitį kwi?	Awukire kungu?
What do you say?	Ukuyanga 'ṣi?	Ukunena ci?	Ukujɷwa fiki?
What shall we drink?	Tukwinza tuñwere'ṣi?	Tukwiza tuñwe ci?	Twisakunwa fiki?
When art thou coming?	Ukwinza 'ri?	Ukwiza ri?	Ukwisa ndiri?
Give me food	Mpanene viakuria	Mpanene, iviakuria	Mbapo kudia
Cut me a small stick	Temera nene ndisa inyindo	Temera une inkɷmo i- nandi	Mbutira une ingiri inandi
I want a little stone	Kwanza ah'awe ah'ando	Kuronda akabγe akanandi	Nikuronda iribwe irinandi
Which (fowl) will you give me?	Inkuku yirikwi yiyɷ yukwanza pakumpa?	Inkuku jirikwi jijo ukurönda pakumpa?	Inguku jiriku ukumba une?
He is inside the house	Alimkazi munyumba.	Ari mukasi munyumba	Ali nyumba nkati
The birds flew away	Iviɷnyi viapururusire	Iviuni vyapururucite (pururuka = to fly)	Injuni siapururuike
The parrot screams	Iṣiɷni ṣikukuta	Iciuni cikurira	Injuni yikujɷega (this bird)
The rotten tree falls	Ikwi iwōzo liagwa	Ikɷmo iwose diawa	Umpigi umbɷfu gu ku gwa (or gu gwire = fell)
Can you see me?	Umanyire pa kun- dorera ine?	Umenya pakundora nene?	Umenya pakungeta une?
No, I cannot	Ndari, ntamenyire	Awe, ntamenye	M'ma, nda-ku-manya- (to see; also kuōna, past = wene)

VOCABULARY OF ENGLISH WORDS AND SENTENCES TRANSLATED INTO

English.	Ki-kese.	Ci-henga.	Ci-tonga.	Ki-senga or Ci-senga.	Ki-bisa.	Ci-cewa (Ci-nyanja).
Ant	Digongoro, ma-	Ki-ndundu, vi-	Nyerere (small) Sungunungu (biting) Muswa (termites)	Mpasi. Cusi (termite)	Mpasi. Huweñse or weñsi (termite)	Lintumbwi, plur. same (ziwiri = two)
Antelope	Imbatu (eland). Suera (pallah)	Sefu (eland) Impara	Mparapara (sable antelope) Nchefu (eland) Ngoma (kudu) Nkhozi (hartebeest) Cuzu (waterbuck) Mphoyo (reedbuck) Mbawa (bushbuck) Nyiska (small buck)	Sefu (eland)	Nsefu (eland)	Ncefu
Ape (or baboon)	Dijani	Mbwengo	Munkweri, plur. wamunkweri	Koloe	Koloe	Mχweri, pl. wamχweri
Arm	Kiwōko, fiwōko	Kawoko, plur. mawoko	Janja, plur. manja	Kwanja, plur. manja	Okoboko, kuwoko (?)	Zanja plur. Manja awiri = two
Arrow	Rucinji, njinji	Mu-vwe, mi-	Muvwi. Mivi yiwe = two arrows	Mumvwi	Mufue, plur. mifui	Muvi. Mivi iwiri = two
Axe	Iri- or diwago, plur. mawago (mawere = two)	Mbavi	Mbavi	Katemo; tutemo	I-sembe, plur. masembe	χwangwa (9 & 10)
Back	Ngongo; kiwunu (small of)	Muγongo, muciwunu (small)	Msana	Msana	Musana	Msana
Banana	Dikombwe, ma-	Dikombere	Doci rumosa = one; matoci χatatu = three	Cikonde, vikonde; mumbu	Likonde, plur. makonde	Ntoice (9 & 10)
Beard	Rurefu, ndefu	Mwembe	Mwembi	Ndevu	Miefu	Ndevu
Bee	Lu-, du-, or ru- juki, plur. njuki	Ruzimu, zimu	Njuci	Nzimo	Insimũ	Njuci
Belly	Dideme, mareme Matumbo (bowels)	Ntumbo Matumbo (bowels)	Ntumbu	Mara	Mala	Mimba (9 & 10)
Bird	Kidege, vi- or fi-	Ki-yuni, fi- or vi-	Ciyuni, viyuni	Koni, tuni	Niñuni. (Niñuni ninji = many birds)	Mbarame
Blood	Mwazi	Ndωpa	Ndopa	Murωpa	Molωpa	Mwazi
Body	Umbere	Mtupi	Ruvavu. (Rōse = all)	Muwiri	Muwiri	Tupi, plur. matupi
Bow	Upende, ma-	Wuta	Wuta, mawuta	Utu; manta	Owuta, plur. mata	Wuta, mawuta
Bone	Kifupa, fi-	Ci-wangwa, vi-	Ciwanga	Mfupa	Lifupa, plur ma-	Fupa
Brains	Wōngo	Wōngo	Wongo	Tōmpwe, wōngo	Tōmpwe	Uwōngo
Breast	Kifua (male), di-were, ma- (female)	Kifua (male) diwere, ma- (female)	Maweē	Kifua, maziwa	Kifua (male), mawere (female)	Mawere Cifua. (female)

VOCABULARIES

Brother	Mbenawi, ba-	M-nuñúna, wa-	Mukuwangu. Muzi-chewangu=*sister*	Karangosi, vikaran-gosi	Mwina wanji, weina wanji	Mbare. Mlongo(*sister*)
Buffalo	Njati	Njati	Njati	Mbωω	Mbωω	Nyati *or* njati
Buttocks	Madako (di-dako = *one buttock*)	Di-tako, ma-	Viskunku, chiskunku	Matako	Matako	Matako
Canoe	Bwato, mawato	Watu	Watu	Wato, mawato.	Buato, mato	Bwato, mabwato; mankhana = *many*
Cat	Kanamanga (kamo = *one*), twanamanga (tuwiri = *two*)	Kanamanga (kamosi = *one*), twanamanga (tuwiri = *two*)	Mbuyao	Cωna, wacona	Tyωna (9 & 10)	Cωna, *plur.* wacona
Chief	Mutua, abatua	Fumu	Fumu; akweni; ab-wana	Mfumu	Mfumo (*plur.* mfumo siwiri=*two chiefs*)	Mfumo
Child	Mwana, abana	Mwana (yamo = *one*), *plur.* wana	Mwana	Kasaza, tusaza	Kana, twana	Mwana
Cloth	Ngωω	Nguwo	Saru	Salu	Insalu (insalu sinji = *plenty*)	Saru
Borassus	Mkoma (*borassus*)	Mkoma (*borassus*)	Mivumu, makama, (*borassus palm*); hyphœne, mgwarangu			
Country	Ndema	Caru	Caru	Cialu	Cialu	Ziko (5), maziko
Cow	Ñombe ndara (ndara =*female*)	Nombe yanakazi	Nombe. Ñombe yinti-kazi=*cow*	Nombe, ñombe ana kazi	Nombe; ñombe awenji = *plenty cows*	Nombe eikazi
Crocodile	Ngwina	Mfiwina *or* ñgwina	Muñona	Mwena, ñwena	Ifiwena	Mñõna, *pl.* wamñona
Day	Digõno (dimo = *one*), ma-	Wusiku (wumo = *one*), *plur.* masiku	Msana. Umoza=*one day*. Kasuwa (*day-light*=sun)	Siku. Kasuwa (*day-light*=sun)	Lusiku (lumo = *one day*). Kásova = *daylight*	Siku (5) Msana = *daylight*
Dog	Iribwa *and* nyakawa.	Ncewe	Garu	Imbwa, zimbwa (zin-yinji=*plenty*)	Nimbwa	Garu (5)
Devil	Dirongo, ma-	Ciwanda (kihene = *bad spirit*)		Maashawi (*plur.*)	Kiwanda *or* ciwanda, *plur.* viwanda	Ci-wanda, vi-
Door	Ndiango	Muriango	Komo, ma-	Muliango	Mwinsi (3)	Kωmω
Dream	Dirōto	Cirōto	Kurota	Cozi	Nalota *or* ncωsi (isinji = *plenty*)	Wazimu (? spirits) Narota = *I dream*
Drum	Ñoma	Ñoma	Ñoma	Ñoma	Ñoma	Ñoma
Ear	Ri-kutu, ma-	Kutu, ma-	Kutu *or* gutu, ma-	Litwe (5)	Kutwe, *plur.* amatwe awiri = *two ears*	Kutu (5)
Egg	Difumbi	Sumbi, ma-	Zia, ma-	Isumbi (5)	Idini, *plur.* amani	Dzira (5). Mazira yañkhana = *many*
Elephant	Ndembo	Zωvu	Njovu	Nzovu	Nyisofu	Njωvu
Excrement	Dif, mafi	Mavi (ivi = *sing.*)	Mavi	Tuvi	Tufi.	Tuvi
Eye	Idiho, amiho	Diso, maso	Jisu, masu	Riso, *plur.* meso	Idinsi, dimo = *one eye*, *plur.* amensi	Liso (5)
Face	Kumaso. (Kose=*all*)	Kumaso	Cisu	Kumanso	Kumenso	Kumaso (15)
Fat	Mafuta	Mafuta	Mafuta	Mafuta	Mafuta	Mafuta
Finger	Dukonji, ngonji	Munue, minue	Mu-nue, mi-Cukumba=*thumb*	Munue, minue	Munue	Cara (7), vyara

VOCABULARY OF ENGLISH WORDS AND SENTENCES TRANSLATED INTO

English.	Ki-kese.	Ci-henga.	Ci-tonga.	Ki-senga or Ci-senga.	Ki-bisa.	Ci-cewa (Ci-nyanja).
Fear	Bwōga	Bōñ or wōñ	Wenimanta. Ku opa = to fear	Kuopa	Mwenso	Mantha
Fire	Mōto	Mōto	Moto	Moto	Mulilo	Moto
Fish	Somba	Somba	Somba	Sawi (5), plur. ma-	Inswi	Somba
Foot	Luayo, njayo	Cayo, vy-ayo	Pazi, ma-	Kwendo, plur. miendo	Lukasa, plur. makasa	Mwendo, pl. minyendo
Forest	Mabehe	Makuni	Musitu	Msangu	Iconde, plur. ifionde fiwiri = two	Thengo
Fowl	Nguku	Kuku	Nyŵli. Zinandi = plenty	Kuku	Nkŵkŵ	Kuku
Ghost	Murongu, mi-	Ciwanda	Ci-wanda, vi-	Cinzingwa	Ikinsiñgwa. Ifnsing-wa vinji = many	Mtunzi, mitunzi
Goat	Mene (9 & 10), ziwiri = two	Mbuzi	Mbuzi	Mbuzi, plur. zimbusi	Mbuzi	Mbuzi
God	Murungu (same as ghost)	Murungu	Murungu	Reza	Lēsa mkulu	Cuüta
Grass	Dinyasi	Uteka	Uteka	Uşwa, plur. ma-; ucani	Masani	Udzu (14)
Ground	Didopi	Dongo	Pasi	Pasi. Mrota (earth)	Pansi	Pansi, pa (16)
Ground nut	Dirawi, marawi	Syawa (plur.), rusiawa (sing.)	Mbarara	Nziama	Mbalala	Kamburundzi, same in plur.
Guinea-fowl	Dicundu	Nkanga	Nkanga	Nkanga, zinkanga	Likanga, amakanga	Mkanga
Gun	Ndusu	Funti	Futi	Futi, zifuti	Temfuti	Fufi
Hair	Djunju	Sisi	Sisi	Sisi	Isisi	Sitsi
Hand	Kikŵfi	Cimanja	Cikufi	Ciparam' pantiro (palm)	Kisanza, plur. ifisanza	Zanja
Head	Mutu	Mutu	Mutu	Mutwe	Mutwe	Mutu
Heart	Ndumbura	Moyo	Mutima	Mutima	Mutima	Mtima
Heel	Kisekeseke	Cigunu	Ka-ngolingoli, tu-	Katende, plur. vi-	Ikitende	Citende
Hippopotamus	Domondo, plur. man-	Cigwere	Cigweri	Mvu	Mvuu or mvubu	Mvuu
Honey	Wuci	Wuci	Uci	Uci wa nzimu	Uwuci	Uici
Horn	Di-nyero, ma-	Rusengwe, ma-	Sengwe, lisengwe (sing.)	Nyanga	Masengo (plur.)	Nyanga
Horse	Mbonda (donkey and zebra)	Punda (donkey) Bori (zebra)	Kavalo Bori (donkey) Capinda (zebra)	Cimpwete (zebra)		Mbizi = zebra
House	Nyumba	Nyumba	Nyumba	Ñanda, ziñanda	Ñanda	Nyumba
Hunger	Njara	Njara	Njā	Njara	Nsala	Njara
Hyena	Bōndēra	Cimbwe	Pundu, a-	Cimbwe	Cimbwi, plur. vimbwi	Fisi
Iron	Kiuma	Cuma	Nthali. Mporokoto = welded iron	Cisengo	Cela, plur. vyela	Citsuru

VOCABULARIES

English					
Island	Kirwa	Cirumba	Cirwa, virwa	Pa kandindi, *plur.* vindindi	Kirumba	Ciphole, *plur.* vi-
Ivory	Rupembe	Munyanga	Munyanga (*plur.*)	Minyañgu njovu	Nyinanzovu	Minyanga (*plur.*)
Knee	Dipefu	Kongono	Gongono	Koñko	Likoñko	Kungono
Knife	Mpamba	Cimaye	Cimayi	Ruezi *or* duwezi, *plur.* maruezi	Mwere	Cipula
Leg	Kirundi	Rundi, ma-	Ciga, viga	Citewero (*thigh*) Mukonzo (*shin*)	Mukonzo	Msoro (*shin*), ncafu (*thigh*)
Leopard	Ntorome	Vingo	Nyarubwi	Kaingo, *plur.* vikaingo Ingo, vingo	Niñgo	Nyarubwi
Lips	Ndomo, miromo	Muromo	Miromo (*plur.*)	Miromo	Miromo	Miromo
Magic	Wuhawi (nthende = *medicine*)	Wuhawi, munkhwara	Fwiti	Lozi	Nindoci	Fiti ; msiñanga
Maize	Dirombe	Ñgōma	Cingoma	Vitoñga. Masaka = *millet*	Vitoñga	Cimanga
Man	Mundu, aba-ndu *or* awa-nyama	Muntu, wantu	Muntu, *plur.* wāntu	Muntu, wantu	Muntu, wantu	Muntu, *plur.* wantu
Meat	Nyama	Nyama	Nyama Liwise	Nama	Ninama	Nyama
Milk	Mbwengo	Mbuyi	Pusi	Mancanca	Nisanje	Pusi
Monkey	Mwezi	Nyanga	Mwezi	Mwezi	Mwezi	Mwezi
Moon	Kidonda	Rupiri	Piri	Lupiri, malupiri	Lupiri *or* ulupiri ; *plur.* ma-	Phiri (5)
Mountain						
Nail (of finger or toe)	Kiogo	Njowe	Cara, vyara	Cala ; vyala	Iciala, *plur.* ifala Diala ; mala	Cikamba, vikamba
Name	Dihina, mahina	Zina	Zina	Zina	Isina (dianji = *my*)	Dzina
Neck	Siñgo	Mukosi ; singo	Kosi	Mukosi	Munkosi	Khosi
Night	Pakiro	Usiku *or* wu-. *darkness*	Usiku. Usiku wa pakati = *midnight* Msikisi. (*Is present in Tongaland*)	Usiku. Finzi (*darkness*) Mpani	Busiku (nimfinsi = *darkness*) or ubusiku Musikisi	U-siku, *plur.* ma-
Oil palm				Cisi = *darkness*		
Ox	Ñombe ; likambako, *plur.* makambako	Ñombe yanalume (*male*)	Ñombe. Yinti kazi = *cow* Makama	Nombe, *plur.* viñombe	Ñombe *or* iñombe	Ñombe
Palm wine					Manyemo *or* amanyemo Cusu	
Parrot	Mboro	Mboro	Uka. Tongo = *glans*	Kope kope Mboro	Wukala, *plur.* Amakala ; Mbolo	Mboro
Penis						
Pig	Nguruwe	Ki-henehene, vi-	Ngurui. Munjiri = *wart hog*	Nguluwe	Nguluwe	Nguruwe
Pigeon	Njewa	Njiwa	Khunda	Ciwa, viwa	Kiwa, *plur.* fiwa. Iciwa ; viwa	Njiwa
Place	Pangono	Paciraru, pakugōna (pa = *prefix*)	Caru	Conde	Paconde. (*Apawemi = good*)	Paja
Rain	Ifura	Vura	Vua	Mvula	Nimfula *or* mvula	Mvura
Rat	Dikenje	Mbewa	Majanca	Marindie (*plur.*)	Mbewa ; koswe, bakoswe	Koswe

VOCABULARY OF ENGLISH WORDS AND SENTENCES TRANSLATED INTO

English.	Ki-kese.	Ci-hengа.	Ci-tonga.	Ki-senga or Ci-senga.	Ki-bisa.	Ci-cewa (Ci-nyanja).
River	Rusɷko	Muronga	Musinji	Mana or kamana	Akanika, *plur.* tunika; Mumana, mimana = *lake*	Msinje Nyanja = *lake*
Road	Njera *or* ndera	Ntɷhwa	Ntowa	Nzira	Ninsila	Njira
Sheep	Diñosi, *plur.* miñosi	Berere	Mberere	Mbelele, vi-	Inipanga	Bira
Sister	Ndumbu, *plur.* barumbu	Dumbu, wa-	Msici wangu	Mukwaso	Nkasianji (?) or imi-kasanji	Mlongo, *pl.* warongo
Skin	Kikɷwa	Cicimba	Ruwavu, ma-Cukumba = *hide*	Kanda, vinkanda	Kanda or nkanda, *plur.* nyinkanda	Khunga
Sky	Kukianya; difundi (*cloud*)	Kucanya	Mitambu	Mukumbi	Ikumbi	Mtambu
Sleep	Rugōno	Turo (12). Tueme = *good*	Kurā = *to sleep.* Usiwa = *sleep*	Tulu (-lala = *sleep, verb*)	Utulo (12)	Turu
Smoke	Diɷsi	Jɷsi	Jɷsi	Cusi	Uwusi, *plur.* amosi	Uci
Snake	Idijɷka, mayɷka	Njɷka	Njoka	Nzoka, *plur.* vinzoka	Nisɷka	Njoka
Son	Mwana; nsoñgoro	Mwana (mwanalume = *male*). Kana = *dim., plur.* twana	Mwana	Mwana, wāna	Mwana lume, *plur.* awana	Mwana, wamwamuna
Song	Uruembo	Luimbo	Rusumu. Sumu = *songs*	Nyimbo	Pluimbo, *plur.* nyimbo isindzi = *many*	Nyimbo
Spear	Ngɷha	Mukondo	Mukondo	Fumo, mafumo	Ifumo (dimo = *one*), *plur.* amafumo	Mkondo
Spirit	Mahɷka; *sing.* dihɷka	Ciwanda	Viwanda (*plur.*)	Ciwanda	Ifumo ya mpasi	Mzimu
Star	Ndondo; *sing.* rutondo	Nyenyezi	Nyenyezi. Tondo = *planet*	Lutanda (lumose = *one*), *plur.* vintanda	Ntandala	Nthanda
Stick	Nsagı	Nthonga	Ntonga	Kɷta, vinkɷta	Iciti (cimo = *one*), *plur.* iviti	Ndɷdɷ
Stone	Liganga	Ribwe *or* dibwe, *plur.* mawe	Mwā, miā	Dziwe, mawe	Ibwe	Mwara
Sun	Dijuwa	Dazi	Dazi	Kazuwa	Kasowa (Kamo = *one*), *and daylight*	Dzuwa
Tear	Lihɷsi	Di-ssɷzi, ma-	Misozo (*plur.*)	Munsɷzi, mi-	Munsosi (*plur.* minsosi)	Msɷzi
Testicles	Ditongo	Di-tongo, ma-	Matongo	Makandi	Makandi	Macende
Thief	Muheji, ba- *or* awaheji	Muñkhungu	Munkungu	Pɷmpwe, vipɷmpwe	Pompwe, *plur.* wapompwe (Awenji = *many*)	Mkungu, *plur.* wankungu
Thing	Kindu, findu	Cintu, vintu	Cintu, vintu	Kintu (ico = *that*)	Icintu, *plur.* ivintu	Cintu, *plur.* vintu
Thorn	Mwifwa	Munga	Munga	Munga	Munga	Munga

VOCABULARIES

English					
Tobacco				Fwaka, *plur.* vifwaka	Fódia
To-day	Ngambo *or* dihōna Lero *or* irero Kirawo = *to-morrow* Soro = *yesterday*	Hōōna. Lero. Musanya wa lero = *daylight* Machero = *to-morrow* Mayiro = *yesterday* Munue	Fɔja Lɛ̄	Fwaga Lero	Lelo
Toe	Lukonji *or* du, *plur.* ngonji	Rurimi	(*Same as finger and thumb*)	Cikumo	Icikumo, *pl.* ivikumo	Cara, vyara
Tongue	Irino, amino	Dino, mino	Lilimi	Lulimi	Irimi; amarimi	Lirimi
Tooth	Akaya (13); kōsaka = *all the*	Muzi	Jinu, *plur.* minyo	Lino	Irino; ameno	Dzinu
Town	Dibehe	Kuni	Muzi	Caro, vyaro	Musi	Muji
Tree	Dipasa	Pasia, ma-	Cimuti (*large*) Muti (*small*)		Muti (muti umo = *one*, muti iwiri = *two*)	Mtengo
Twins	Makōjo	Matuzi	Wana wa nwōli		Wampundo	Mapasa
Urine	Ngōndo	Nkhondo	Makozo		Miso	Mkojo
War	Amaji	Maji	Nkhondo	Nkondo	Vita (8)	Kōndo
Water	Musuṅgu	Muzungu	Maji		Mezi	Maji
White man	Mgori (wangu = *my*), *plur.* bagori	Mukazi. Wane = *my*	Mu-zungu, a- *or* wa- Mtikazi		Musungu Mukasi, *plur.* awakasi	Mzungu Mkazi
Wife						
Wind	Mbepu	Mwera	Mphepo		Mwera	Phepo
Witch	Muhawi, bahawi	Mu-hawi, wa-	Fwiti		Fwiti *or* mfwiti *or* ifwiti (9 & 10)	Fiti
Woman	Undara, badara *or* awa-	Mwanakazi	Mtikazi, *plur.* antikazi		Mukasi	Mkazi
Wood	Imbawu	Nkuni	Nkhuni		Inkuni (*firewood*), imbau = *plank*	Kuni
Yam	Kituū	Ciawo	Ciyao, *plur.* viao		Di-peta dimo = *one*, *plur.* ama-	Cinkumba
Year	Mw-aka, mi-	Mwaka, mi-	Cilimika		Mwaka	Cirimika
One	Kamo	Kamo	Cimoza		Kamo	Cimozi
Two	Tuwere	Tuwiri	Viwi		Viwiri *or* tuwiri	Viwiri
Three	Tudatu	Tutatu	Vitatu		Tutatu	Vitatu
Four	Ncece	Tunaye	Vinai		Tunne	Vinai
Five	Tuhano	Tusano, tuṅkonde	Vinkhonde		Tusano	Visano
Six	Tulintanda	Sano na kamo	Konde di cimoza		Tusano na kamo	Visano ni cimozi

VOCABULARY OF ENGLISH WORDS AND SENTENCES TRANSLATED INTO

English.	Ki-kese.	Ci-henga.	Ci-tonga.	Ki-senga or Ci-senga.	Ki-bisa.	Ci-cewa (Ci-nyanja).
Seven	Tulimhano na tuwiri	Sano na tuwiri	Konde di viwi		Tusano na tuwiri	Visano ni viwiri
Eight	Mhano na tutatu	Sano na tutatu	Konde di vitatu		Tusano na tutatu	Visano ni vitatu
Nine	Mhano na ncece	Sano na tunaye	Konde di vinai		Tusano na tunne	Visano ni vinai
Ten	Cɷmi	Kumi	Cumi		Dikumi	Kumi
Eleven	Cɷmi na kamo	Kumi na kamo	Mkati ci moza		Dikumi la dimo	Kumi mkate cimɷzi
Twenty	Makɷmi gawere	Makumi gawiri	Macumi ɣavi		Makumi awiri	Makumi awiri
Thirty	Makɷmi gadatu	Makumi gatatu	Macumi ɣatutu		Makumi atatu	Makumi atatu
Forty	Makɷmi mcece	Makumi ganaye	Macumi ɣanai		Makumi anne	Makumi yanai
Fifty	Makɷmi mhano	Makumi gasano	Macumi ɣankonde		Makumi asano	Makumi asano
Hundred	Makɷmi galikɷmi	Makumi kumi	Macumi ɣankonde mikumuku		Mwanda	
Thousand					Kirowa or kiroba	
I, me	Nenga	Ine	Yini		Nine	Ine
Thou	Wenga	Iwe	Yiwe		Wewo	Ife
He	Yɷra	Yuyu	Uyu		Uli	Iwe
We	Twenga	Ise	Yifwe		Nifwe or fwe	Ife (?). -atu = *our*
You	Mwenga	Imwe	Yimwe		Mwevo	Inu, -anu = *your*
They	Bara	Awo	Yiwɷ		Bawo	Yawa (woyiba = *they are bad*)

VOCABULARIES

All	-ωha (bōha, yoha, goha, fioha, sioha, toha, woha, koha, poha, classes 2, 4, 6, 8, 10, 12, 14, 15, & 16	-ōse (wōse, yōse, γōse, fiōse, zōse, tōse, wōse, kose, pōse)	-ōse	Wonse	-onse
This man	Mundu uyu; plur. bandu aba or awa	Muntu uyu; awantu awa	Muntu uyu	Muntu uyu	Muntu amene
That man	Mundu yura; bandu bara	Muntu yura; awantu wara	Muntu yūwa	Muntu ngudia	Muntu uyu
This tree	Dibehe eri	Mu-kondo uwu (spear), plur. mi-iyi	Muti wuwu	Muti uyu	Mtengo ūū
That tree	Dibehe rera	Mu-kondowura (spear) plur. mikondo yira	Muti wuwa	Muti ūdia	Mtengo uja
My house	Nyumba yangu	Nyumba yane; plur. nyumba ziane	Nyumba yangu	Iñanda yanji	Nyumba yanga
Thy house	Nyumba yako	Nyumba yako	Nyumba yako	Iñanda iyωwe	Nyumba yako
His house	Nyumba yake	Nyumba yake	Nyumba yake	Iñanda yakwe	Nyumba yake
Our town	Akaya kaitu or kitu	Muzi witu	Muzi widu	Musi wesu	Muji watu
Your country	Ndema winu	Ciaru cinu	Caru cinu	Icialu icenu	Dziko lanu
Their children	Bana bawo	Wana wawo	Wano wawo	Awano wawo	Wana wao
Bad	-befu	-hene	-heni	Waωipa; muntu wa wipa = bad man	-yipa
Female	-ndara	-anakazi	-ntikazi	-ana kasi	
Good	-nωfu	-eme	-a mampa	wa wama	
Great	-baha (men); -gorongo (things)	-kuru; -rara	-kuru. (1, ukuru) (2, wakuru)	-kulu	
Little	-cωko	-dōno; -ntini (men)	-manavi, -mana	-ike. (Akana kaike = little son, plur. otuana tuike)	
Male	Ngambako	-anarume	-rumi (yintu rume) (9)	-lume	
White	-futo	-tuwa	(Nsaru) yitūwa (ituwa = white)	-wuta. (Omukopo owa wuta = a white hide or skin	
Here	Apa	Apa	Pano	Mpano (?)	
Black	-titu	-fipa	Yifipa. (Mufipa = one)	-fita	
Plenty	-ingi	-ingi	-nandi	-inji, iñgi, or indyi	

VOCABULARY OF ENGLISH WORDS AND SENTENCES TRANSLATED INTO

English.	Ki-kese.	Ci-henga.	Ci-tonga.	Ki-senga or Ci-senga.	Ki-bisa.	Ci-cewa (Ci-nyanja).
There	Para	Para	Kūwa	.	Mparia	.
No, not	Dietu!	A', a', cara!	Cā!	.	Tapari, iyo	.
I am	Ne	Ndiri	nde	.	Ndi	.
I bring	Nitora	Nkupe*r*a Ndanguwa = *I was*	Ndituzanaco	.	Naleta	.
I come	Niyica	Nkwiza, ndañguiza	Ndituza	.	Naisa	.
I come not	Niyica-ri; nikana (*no!*)	Nditikwiza. Ndañgwizako = *I came not*	Kuza cā!	.	Sikuisa	.
I dance	Njumba	Nkuvina	Nditumba	.	Nakinda icira	.
I die	Nifwa	Nkufwa. Ndañgufwa = *I died*	Nafwa, nditufwa	.	Nafwa	.
I drink	Ninywa	Nkuñwa	Nditumwa, namwa	.	Nkonywa	.
I drank	Nanyuise (soro = *yesterday*)	Ndañguñwa	Ningumwa (*past*), namwa (*imperfect*)	.	Dinyuene	.
I drank not	Nanyuise-ri = *neg. suffix*	Ntanguñwako	Kutinungumwa cā!	.	Sinyuene	.
I eat	Nidakura	Nkuria	Ndarya, nditurya	.	Nkodia	.
I eat not	Nidakura-ri	Nditikuria, ntakuria	Kutindarya cā (sono = *now*)	.	Sikodia	.
I give	Nipa; (nipari = *neg.*)	Kupa	Ndaninka	.	Nákupa	.
I give you	Nikupa	Kukupa	Ndakuninka	.	Nákupa webo	.
I gave him	Nampere	Ndañgumupa	Ningumuninka = *I gave him.* Mairo = *yesterday*	.	Nalimpere (mairo = *yesterday*)	.
I go	Niwoka	Nkuwuka	Ndiruta. Ruta = *go*	.	Nkoya	.
I went	Nuwokire	Ndañguwuka	Nunguruta	.	Naire	.
I kill them	Niwakoma	Kuwakoma	Ndawabaya	.	Nawepaya	.

VOCABULARIES 513

English			
I know	Nimanye	Kumanya; ndamanya. Wa-ndi-manya = You know me	Ndiziwa	Naisiwa
I know not	Nimanye-ri	Nditikumanya ndirivie kumanya	Ndilivi ku ziwa	Sisiwile (*pret.*)
Thou lovest	Urōnda *or* wirōnda	Ukupenja	Ulembe	Walintemwa
We make	Tipere; taperite=*pret.*	Tikucita	Ticita	Tukωcita
We say	Tijωwa	Tikuyowoiya	Tikamba	Tukósωsa
We sold not	Tagoriteri gura humera = *also* Anuñga	Titagūūra	Kutitisaska ca!	Tatwasitire
He stinks	Ahēdya	Akunuñka. Atakunuñka (*neg.*)	Wanunka (uanunka)	Ukωnuñka (?)
He steals	Baheka	Akwiba	Wabba	Waiba
They laugh	Mwirera	Wakuseka	Waseka	Wakωseka
You weep	Awokire ku?	Mkurira	Mulia. (Vimwe=*you*)	Mkolila (?)
Where did he go?	Ujωwa kiki?	Anguwuk' anku?	Waya pani?	Kwilakwi uko waile
What do you say?	Tiza kuñwa kiki?	Ukuyowo' aci?	Utitinji? (*thou*)	Findu ukωsωsa?
What shall we drink?	Upwiza ndiri?	Tizakuñwa cici?	Tika kumwa cinē?	Findu tukωnywa?
When art thou coming?	Mbera nenga	Ukwiza ndiri?	Unguza zuwanji?	Wakwiza lini?
Give me food	Ndemera nenga (*me*) msimbati mnandi	Ndipa ine (*me*) viakuria	Ndininke kurya	Nimpa cakulia
Cut me a small stick	Ngurōnda diganga dinandi	Ndi temere ntonga idōno	Ndidumuwe ntonga yimana (*or* kantonga, *plur.* tuntonga)	Nipinikire kiti
I want a little stone	Ukumbera yireku ngωkω?	Kurōnda ribwe ridōnō	Ntirembe *or* ntikumba kamwa kamana	
Which (fowl) will you give me?	Ali nyumba mukati	Kundipanji nkuku?	Ninc' nyōli ya-kuninka ine?	
He is inside the house	Madege gagoruike Didege (*bird*) diyemba Iribehe riboriite dikugwa (digwire=*fell*)	Ali munyumba mkati	We mnyumba	
The birds flew away		Viuni viaduka	Viyuni vyáuruka	
The parrot screams		Kiuni (*bird*) cikwimba	Nkulekwe waturya	
The rotten tree falls		Kuni dia kuvunda dikūwa	Cimuti cikuω cawa	
Can you see me?	Umanyi ku ni rora?	Umenye pa ku ndi wona?	Ungakumba kunduona?	
No, I cannot	Nikumanya; diebu!		Cá; ndilivi kukumba	

VOCABULARY OF ENGLISH WORDS AND SENTENCES TRANSLATED INTO

English.	Ci-nyanja (Ci-cipeta).	Ci-mañanja (Eastern Ci-nyanja).	Ci-sena (or Ci-nyungwi).	Ci-mbo.	Ci-mazaro.	Ci-podzo.
Ant	Nyerere ; Nswa (termite) ; lintumbɔ	Nyerere, ciswe, lintumbu	Nyerere, ucenje, magugu	Ntuta, kalanzi, ncirafu	Nyerere, ucenje, magugu	Nyerere Uyece (?) (white)
Antelope	Mbawara, gwape, ncefu	Mbawala, gwape, ncefu	Mbawala, lunzwa, ntuka	Kadumla, kasenye, pofu	Mbawala, nyasa, ntuka	Mbaya Mulimba Sefu (eland) Ngoma (kudu)
Ape	Nkwere	Nyani	Bongwe, abongwe	Bongwe	Bongwe	Bongwi
Arm	Mkono	Mkono	Mkono	Ncafu	Mkono	Nkono, plur. mi-
Arrow	Mulvi	Mulvi	Mulvi	Mpamba	Mulvi	Mphina (dziwiri = two)
Axe	Mkwangwa	Nkwangwa	Mbadzo	Liwago (Yao)	Mbadzo	Mbadzo (9 & 10)
Back	Msana ; mbuyo	Msana	Msana	Gongo (Yao)	Ntana	Wakorokoro; perepere
Banana	Ntoci	Ntoci	Mafigu (plur.)	Magombwa Mpalukwa (bears one)	Mafigu	Figu ; mfigu ; mfigu (libodzi = one)
Beard	Ndebvu	Ndebvu	Ndebvu	Ndebvu	Ndebvu	Ndebvu
Bee	Njuci	Njuci	Nyuci	Kaluna	Njuci	Nyui, nuzi
Belly	Cipfu Matumbo (bowels) Mimba (womb)	Mimba (belly) Cipfu (stomach) Matumbo (bowels)	Cifu, matumbo, mimba	Cintumbo	Cifu, marumbo, mimba	Mimba
Bird	Mbalame	Mbalame	Mbalame	Mbalame	Mbalame	Mu-bvi, mi-
Blood	Mwazi	Mwazi	Mulopa	Magasi	Mulopa	Miropa
Body	Tupi	Tupi	Manungo	Tupi	Manungu	Manungo
Bow	Uta or buta	Uta	Uta	Cimanganze	Uta	Uta, ma-
Bone	Pfupa, fupa or li-fupa	Pfupa	Kugodo	Ligodo	Kugodo	Gogodo
Brains	Bongo	Uwongo	Wongo	Tompwe	Wongo	Wongo
Breast	Cipfua ; bere (female)	Cipfua, bere	Pa mtima ; bere (female)	Pantimanzi; lizamwe	Cikua ; bere	Bere, plur. ma-
Brother	Mbali	Mbali	Mbali	Mbali	Mbali	Mbali
Buffalo	Njati	Njati	Nyati	Nyati	Nyari	Nzati
Buttocks	Matako	Matako	Matako	Matako	Marako	Matako
Canoe	Bwato	Ngalawa	Mwadia	Bwato	Mwadia	Mwadia
Cat	Mpaka	Mpaka	Mpaka	Mlamu ; mwenye (large)	Mbhaka	Mphaka (9 & 10)
Chief	Mfumu, wa-	Mfumu	Mambo ; fumu	Mfumu	Mfumu	Mfumu, a-
Child	Mwana, wana	Mwana, ana	Mwana, ana	Mwana	Mwana, ana	Mwana, ana Mwaina (young boy)
Cloth	Nsaru	Nsaru	Nguo	Lifuka	Nguo	Nguo
Cocoanut palm		Mngoli (Yao, mngole)	Nnazi	Wisawisa	Nnazi	Nadzi, mi-
Country	Dziko, maiko	Dziko	Dziko, maiko	Ntaka	Idziko	Tigu

VOCABULARIES

Cow	Ñombe	Ñombe	Ñombe, ziñombe	Ñombe	Ñombe	Ñombe. Ñombe isigana (*male*), ñombe mombwana (*female*)
Crocodile						
Day	Nona / Tsiku	Nona / Tsiku	Nona / Siku	Nonantondo / Tsiku	Nona / Tsiku	Nona Masikati, Manru = *evening*
Dog	Garu	Garu	Mwanambwa	Imbwa (Ma) foka (*male*) Gogo (*female*)	Mwanambwa	Mwanambwa
Devil	Mzimu, wazimu	Mzimu (*evil spirit*)	Ndzimu		Nzimu	Afiti (?)
Door	Citseko; pa komo	Citseko. Pa komo = *doorway*	Ciseko pa nsuo	Citseko, nkowa	Citseko, pa nsuo	Nsuo. M-suo, mi-
Dream	Ku lota; ndota	Ndota; *verb* ku lota	Ku lota, ndota	Ndota	Matulo, ku lota	Kurota
Drum	Ñoma, ziñoma	Ñoma	Ñoma	Ñoma	Iñoma	Ñoma. (Kubvina = *dance*)
Ear	Kutu	Kutu, *plur.* makutu	Kutu	Lipilikanilo (*Yao*)	Baru	Kutu
Egg	Dzira	Dzira, mazira	Zai	Lindanda (*Yao*)	Zai	Zai, li. Mazai
Elephant	Njobvu	Njobvu	Nzou	Ndembo; matsutame	Dou	Nzw
Excrement	Tubzi (12)	Tubzi	Matubsi	Mangwenu (?)	Malubvi	Matubvi
Eye	Diso, maso	Diso, *plur.* maso	Diso, *plur.* maso	Dziso, *plur.* maso	Liso, meso	Diso, maso
Face	Cidzo, *plur.* psi-	Nkope	Kope *and* nkope		Kope	Nkhope Mangungu = *cheek*
Fat	Mafuta	Mafuta	Mafuta	Mafuta	Makura	Mafuta
Finger	Cara, *plur.* bzara	Cala, zala	Cibunu; cara, *plur.* piara	Kapfunya	Cibunu	Cibune. Vi-bunu = *finger-nails*
Fear	Manta, opa	Manta; *verb* ku opa	Manta, gopa	Manta	Manta, gopa	Gopa
Fire	Moto	Moto	Moto	Moto; nansali	Moto	Moto
Fish	Nsomba	Nsomba	Nsomba	Nsomba	Nsomba	Nsomba
Foot	Padzi, pazi mwendo	Pasi (*sole*), mwendo (*leg*)	Nyalo, mwendo	Mwendo	Nyalo, mwendo	Nyala (libodzi = *one*), ma-
Forest	Nkalango	Nkalango (*thicket*) Tengo (*wood, thicket*) Msitu	Msitu	Udzu (*lit. grass*); nsitu	Musitu	Msitu
Fowl	Nkuku	Nkuku	Mwanankuku	Nkuku; dzoye	Mwanamkuku	Nkuku
Ghost	Cidzodogwa, *plur.* pfidzodogwa	Mdzukwa	Muzukwa, azukwa		Mdzukwa.	Dzimu, a- (adzimu)
Goat	Mbuzi, zimbuzi	Mbuzi	Mbuzi	Mpema (*he goat*)	Mbuzi	Mbuzi. Saboko (*male*)
God	Mulungu, cintu	Mulungu, cinta	Mulungu (*also rain*)	Mpambe	Mulungu	Mulungu
Grass	Maudzu	Maudzu	Udzu *or* maudzu	Manyazi	Manyazi	Manyasi
Ground	Ntaka	Ntaka	Taka	Ntaka	Maraga	Mataka
Ground nut	Nteza	Ntedza	Manduwi	Ciwirinkate	Manduwi	Mandui
Giraffe						
Guinea-fowl	Nkanga, zinkanga	Nkanga	Kanga	Njopilo	Kanga	Kanga Kwai = *francolin*
Gun	Mfuti	Mfuti	Mfuti	Mfuti	Mfuti	Futi
Hair	Tsitsi	Tsitsi	Ititi	Tsitsi. Kobwe (*curls*)	Sisi	Sisi
Hand	Dzanja, manja	Dzanja	Dzanja, manja	Dzanja; kafunya	Ðanba	Dzanja

VOCABULARY OF ENGLISH WORDS AND SENTENCES TRANSLATED INTO

English.	Ci-nyanja (Ci-cipeta).	Ci-manyanja (Eastern Ci-nyanja).	Ci-sena (or Ci-nyungwi).	Ci-mbo.	Ci-mazaro.	Ci-podzo.
Head	Mutu, mitu	Mutu	Msoro	Nsolo	Muru	Msoro
Heart	Mtima, mitima	Mtima	Mtima	Mtima	Ndrima	Nrima (r' very trilled)
Heel	Citende, psitende	Citende, dzitende	Citiri; citende	Cinzongoniko	Itiri	Ji-sondo, bi-
Hippopotamus	Mvu	Mvu	Mvu	Domondo	Tomondo	Mvu
Honey	Uci or buci	Uci	Uci	Njuci; bwa njuci bo	Uwi	Mata. Sera = wax
Horn	Nyanga	Nyanga	Nyanga	Nandadalala; nyanga	Nyanka	Nyanga
Horse	Kavalo; mbidzi (zebra)	Kavalo	Kavalo		Kavalo	Kavaru. Mbizi (zebra)
House	Nyumba, zinyumba	Nyumba	Nyumba	Nyumba	Nunpa	Nyumba Pazulu (roof)
Hunger	Njala	Njala	Njala	Calema	Ntaia	Ndaya or nda
Hyena	Fisi, wafisi	Fisi	Tika	Pesi; lubvu	Nankunu	Tika, ma-
Iron	Cisulo	Citsulo	Utale	Dzifuzo	Utale	Mpara, ferro
Island	Cirumba, psirumba; cilwa	Cisi, dzisi	Nsua	Cigunda; cisenjerere; kalungu	Nsua	Pansua
Ivory	Nyanga	Njobvu (elephant) Nyanga (horn)	Nyanga	Ndembo	Nyanga	Nyanga
Knee	Kongono	Bondo	Bondo	Bondo	Bonto	Bondo
Knife	Mpeni	Mpeni	Mpeni	Mpeni; mkalo; mpopo (large)	Mbeni	Mpeni
Leg	Mwendo, plur. nyendo	Mwendo		Mwendo	Mwendo	Mwendo
Leopard	Nyaribwe	Nyalugwe	Nyalugwe	Kambuku	Nyalugwe	Nyarugwe
Lips	Milomo	Milomo	Miromo	Milomo	Miomo, sing. mwiomo, plur. myiomo	Muromo
Magic	Maere; ufiti	Tsenga, maere	Male	Tsenga		Ufiti
Maize	Pamanga	Cimanga	Mpira manga	Pamangwe	Piamanga	Mapiramanga
Man	Muntu, wantu	Mwamuna. Muntu (person), plur. antu	Mwamuna. Muntu (person), plur. antu	Mwamna. Mutu (person), plur. ziantu	Mumbwana. Mutu (person), plur. atu	Muntu, antu
Meat	Nyama	Nyama	Nyama	Nyama	Nama	Nyama
Monkey	Pusi	Pusi	Kolo; pusi; nṣima	Njanjama	Kolo	Koro
Moon	Mwezi	Mwezi	Mwezi	Ndendekezuwe	Mweri	Mwedzi
Mountain	Piri, plur. ma-	Piri	Piri	Piri	Piri	Piri
Nail (of finger or toe)	Nyara	Cikabado	Nyala	Cikanambira	Ngole	Kyara
Name	Dzina, maina	Dzina	Zima	Dzina	Dzina	Dzina
Neck	Kosi	Kosi	Kozi	Cikota	Kosi	Kosi
Night	Usiku	Usiku	Usiku	Usiku (bwa)	Matiku	Masiku
Nose	Mpuno	Mpuno				Mpunu
Ox	Mfule	Ñombe ya mfule	Ñombe ya kapado	Ntonga	Ñombe ya kapale	Ñombe
Palm wine	Ucema	Ucema	Ucema	Nsomo	Wiema	Ucema
						Mdikwa (borassus)

VOCABULARIES

English					
Parrot				Papagai (Portuguese)	Tangwi
Penis	Cinkwe, psinkwe	Cinkwe, dzinkwe	Papagaya (Portuguese)	Cinkwe	Mboro
	Mboro	Mbolo	Sondo	Mbolo	Majende = *testicles*
Pig	Nguluwe; nkumba, mdudu (*domestic*)	Nkumba	Nkumba	Gudani	Nkumba Njiri = *wart hog*
Pigeon	Nkunda	Nkunda, njiwa (*wild*)	Kangaiwa	Mbalame (*bird*)	Jiwa
Place	Mbuto; maro	Mbuto	Mburo	Mbuto	Mbuto
Rain	Mbvula	Mbvula	Mvula	Mbvula	Mulungu
				Mtsecero (*heavy, sends indoors*)	Anavumba = *rains*
Rat	Koswe; mbwea	Koswe	Ciru	Koswe, gudani (?)	Nciru, ma-
River	Nyanja	Nyanja	Nyanja	Nyanja	Nyanza
Road	Njira	Njira	Njira	Njira, kwalala, nkwasa	Nsia. Pambseno = *cross-roads*
Sheep	Mbira; nkosa	Nkosa	Bira	Nkosa	Bia
Sister	Mlongo, walongo	Mlongo, alongo	Mwanankazi	Mlongo	Nronkorio; mwanansikana Mbananga, mwana sigana
Skin	Kungu, cikopa	Kungu (*human*) Cikopa (*animal*)	Kanda, ntembe	Kungu	Kunku; tembe Kungu
Sky	Mtambo	Nnenere, tambo kumwamba (*above*)	Ntambo	Ku dzulu	Tambo Tambo
Sleep	Tulo	Tulo	Tulo	Tulo	Gona; jiruo; tulo Jiruo
Smoke	Utsi	Utsi	Uci	Ntunzi	Uci Uci
Snake	Njoka	Njoka	Nyoka	Njoka	Noka Noa
Son	Mwana wa mwamuna	Mwana wa mwamuna	Mwana mwamuna	Mwana wa mlumbwana	Mwana, mombwana Mwana, nombwana
Song	Nyimbo	Nyimbo	Nyimbo	Nyimbo	Nyimbo Nyimbo
Spear	Ntungo	Ntungo	Dupa	Nkondo	Dipa Mwarango
Spirit	Mzimu	Mzimu	Muzimu, nzimu	Soka	Mdzimu
Star	Nyenyezi	Nyenyezi	Ntondowa	Nyenyezi. Pulupulu (*morning star*)	Neneri, meri Tondwa
Stick	Ndodo, zindodo	Ndodo, ngolomondo, etc.	Ngolomondo (*large*) Msimbo (*small*)	Ndodo	Golomondo (*large*) Fimbo (*small*) Ndonga
Stone	Mwala, miala	Mwala	Mwala	Tsangalabwe	Mwala Ibwe, mabwe
Sun	Dzuwa	Dzuwa	Zuwa, dzuwa	Dzuwa	Dzuwa Zua
Tear	Masozi (*plur.*)	Msozi	Msozi, nsodzi	Msozi	Msori Msori
Testicles	Matodzo	Mpulumo, wa ku ba	Mpumba		Mpumba Majende
Thief	Mkungu; mbara	Mkungu; mbala	Bava	Mbala	Mbava; jio Mbava, ma-pi-ntu
Thing	Cintu, psintu *or* bzintu	Cintu, dzintu	Cintu, pintu	Cintu	Vinto (*plur.*) Cintu, vi- *or* bi- *or* pi-ntu
Thorn	Munga, minga	Munga	Munga	Mnga	Munka Munga
Tobacco	Fodia	Fodia	Fodia	Fodia. Faikala (*snuff*) Kambuya (*plant*)	Foria, foiya Fodia
To-day	Lero	Lero	Lero	Lero	Lero Dambuno
Toe	Cara, psara	Cala, zala	Cibuno	Kafunya	Dambwino Piara, *plur.* Ciara = *one toe* Cibuno, jibuno

VOCABULARY OF ENGLISH WORDS AND SENTENCES TRANSLATED INTO

English.	Ci-nyanja (Ci-cipeta).	Ci-mahanja (Eastern Ci-nyanja).	Ci-sena (or Ci-nyungwi).	Ci-mbo.	Ci-mazaro.	Ci-podzo.
Tongue	Lilime	Lilaka	Lingwa (*Portuguese*).	Lulime	Iyumi	Lirumi
Tooth	Dzino, mano	Dzino, *plur.* mano	Zino	Dzino, mano. Msingo (*back*), Apaululu (*front*)	Dzino	Dzino ibodzi = *one* Mano onsene = *all*
Town	Mudzi	Mzinda	Mzinda, mudzi	Mzinda	Mudi (*village*), dula (*small*), mzinda (*large*)	Mudzi
Tree	Mtengo, mitengo	Mtengo	Muti	Mtengo	Muri	Muti
Twins	Mpasa	Mpasa	Anampasa	Mpasa	Anapata	Mapata
Urine	Mkodzo	Mkodzo	Mitundo	Mkodzo	Mirundo	Mitundo
War	Nkondo	Nkondo	Nkondo	Mpamba	Ikondo	Nkondo
Water	Madzi	Madzi	Mazi	Madzi	Masinje	Masinje
White man	Mzungu, wazungu	Mzungu, azungu	Mzungu, azungu	Mzungu	Mtsunku, mdzunku	Nzungo
Wife	Mkaz'ace (*his wife*)	Nkazi. Nkaz'ace (*his wife*)	Mkaz'ace (*his wife*)	Nkazi	Mtsigana	Nkazanga, a-
Wind	Mpepo	Mpepo	Mpepo	Mpepo	Pevwo	Pewo
Witch	Mfiti, zimfiti	Mfiti	Mfiti	Msawi	Mkwiri	Mkwiri
Woman	Mkazi, wakazi	Nkazi	Mkazi		Mtsikana	Mwavi
Wood	Mtengo Ci-dziki, *plur.* psi- (*log*)	(*See tree.*) Mtengo; Nkuni (*firewood*) Matsatsa (*twigs*)	Muti	Mtengo	Kuni (*firewood*)	Msigana, a- Kuni, nkuni
Yam	Cirazi, bzilazi	Citsiga (*log*) Cilazi, dzilazi	Mpama	Cicece	Mpama	Za kunjipa = *much, many*
Year	Caka, *plur.* bzaka	Caka. (*Also period, season, time,* plur. zaka	Caka, pyaka	Nyaka	Jaka	Ji-aka ; *plur.* pi-
One	Cimodzi	Modzi	Posi	Modzi	Posi	Posi
Two	Ziwiri	Wiri	Piri	Wiri	Piri; mbiyi	Piri
Three	Zitatu	Tatu	Tatu	Tatu	Raru (*of persons*), tatu (*things*)	Tatu
Four	Zinai	Nai	Cina	Nai	Cina	Jina
Five	Zisanu	Sanu	Shanu	Sanu	Shanu	Sano
Six	Zisanu ndi cimodzi	Sanu ndi modzi	Tantatu	Ntanda	Tantatu ; tānabŏde	Tandatu
Seven	Zizanu ndi ziwiri	Sanu ndi wiri	Cinomwe		Cinomwe ; tanambiyi	Anomwe
Eight	Zisanu ndi zitatu	Sanu ndi tatu	Seri	Tanataru	Sere ; tana taru	Asere

VOCABULARIES

Nine	.	Zisanu ndi zinai	Sanu ndi nai			Femba; tananai	Femba
Ten	.	Kumi	Kumi	Kumi		Kumi	Kumi
Eleven	.	Kumi ndi cimodzi	Kumi ndi cimodzi	Mpambu		Posi; kumi na bode.	Kumi na bozi
Twenty	.	Makumi yawiri	Makumi awiri			Mayumei	Makumi awiri
Thirty	.	Makumi yatatu	Makumi atatu			Mayumararo	
Forty	.	Makumi yanai	Makumi anai			Mayumanai	
Fifty	.	Makumi yasanu	Makumi asanu			Mayummabanu	
Hundred	.	Dzana	Dzana (*and* mwanda, *yao*)	Dzana		Dzana	
Thousand	.		Cikwi (*Cikunda*)	Cikwi		Cikwi; jigwi	
I, me	.	Ine, ndi	Ine -ndi	Ine; ndi		Imi; ndi	Imi, wano
Thou	.	Iwe	Iwe	Iwe		Iwe	Iwe
He	.	Iye	Iye	Iye		Iyene	Iye
We	.	Ife	Ife	Ife		Isu	Ife
You	.	Inu	Inu	Inu		Inyu	Imwe
They	.	Iwo; awo	Iwo, awo	Iwo		Awene	Awo
All	.	Onse	-onse, *etc.*	Onse		Otene	Onsene
							Pintu pionsene=*all things*
This man	.	Muntu uyu	Muntu uyu	Mtu u		Mutu wene u, mumbwana (*man*) uyu	Muntu uyu, antu ao
That man	.	Muntu uja	Muntu ule			,, wene uye	
This tree	.	Mtengo u	Muti u	Mtengo u		Muri wene uno (muri wumbu)	Muntu uyu
That tree	.	Mtengo uo	Muti ule			Muri wene uye (muri umbwiye)	
My house	.	Nyumba yanga	Nyumba yanga	Nyumba yanga		Numbanka	
Thy house	.	Nyumba yako	Nyumba yako	Nyumba yako		Numbako	
His house	.	Nyumba yace	Nyumbache			Numbashe (dzh)	
Our town	.	Mudzi watu	Mzinda watu	Muzinda watu		Mzindesu. Mudiesu (*village*)	
			Mudzi (*village*) Mpala (*capital*)				
Your country	.	Dziko latu	Dziko lanu	Dziko latu		Wudziko yago, dziko yenyu	
Their children	.	Wana wao	Ana ao	Wana wao		Anao	
Bad	.	-ipa; bi	Ipa	Wo-sakala		U-ibaya	-ibaya
Female	.	-kazi	-kazi	Nkazi		Mtsikana; seva	-sigana
Good	.	-bwino	-bwino, -koma	Bwino		Cadredu (*Portuguese*); cadidi	-didi
Great	.	-nkuru	-kulu, -tatao, -tunta	Wa-ukulu		Caci ndumuka	-ndimuga
Little	.	-ñono	-ñono	Wa-uñono		Caci-ñono	-ñono
Male	.	Mwamuna, mpongo	Mwamuna; pongo	Mpongo		Mumbwana	

VOCABULARY OF ENGLISH WORDS AND SENTENCES TRANSLATED INTO

English.	Ci-nyanja (Ci-cipeta).	Ci-mañanja (Eastern Ci-nyanja).	Ci-sena (or Ci-nyungwi).	Ci-mbo.	Ci-mazaro.	Ci-podzo.
White	Ku-yera	-yera, mbe, mbu	-cĕna	Ku yera	Ku cena ; jena	-cena
Here	Kuno ; apa	Kuno, pano, muno, etc.	Kuno	Kuno	I'uno	Apa
Black	Kuda	-da, bi	Ku-swipa	Da	Ku rimba	-rimba
Plenty	-mbiri	-mbiri, etc. (much)	-zinji	Wa maere	Vyavi-zinji	Guya ule. Njipa = plenty (food)
There	Apo ; uko	Apo, uko, umo	Apo ; uko ; pale	Apo	Apai, awo, avo	
No, not	Iai, si	Iai, -i, si	Tayu, si	Iai, si	Tayu, se	
I am	Ndiri	Ndi-ri	Ndiri	Ine ndi-ri	Ndimi	
I bring	Ndi tenga ; ndidza	Ndi tenga, ndi dza naco, etc.	Ndi tukula, ndi dza naco	Ndi tenga	Nada kwata duca (lift up)	
I come	Ndi dza	Ndi dza	Ndi dza	Ndi dza	Nada najo (bring it). Nada	
I come out	Sindi dza	Si ndi dza	Si ndi dza	Si-dza	Si na da	
I dance	Ndi bvina	Ndi bvina	Ndi bvina	Ndi bwina	Na jina (naceta)	
I die		Ndi fa, ndi mwalira	Ndi fa	Ndi fa	Na kwa	
I drink		Ndi mwa	Ndi mwa	Ndi mwa	Na mwa	
I drank		Ndi na mwa	Ndi namwa	Nda mwa	Na mwa	
I drank not		Si ndi na mwa	Si nda mwa	Si-nda mwa	Si na mwa	
I eat		Ndi dia	Na dia	Ndi dia	Na ya	
I eat not		Si ndi dia	Si na dia	Nda sa diai	Si na ya	
I give		Ndi patsa	Na patsa	Ndi patsa	Na vasa	
I give you		Ndi ku patsa, ndi ku patsani	Ndi kupatsa	Ndi-kupatsa	Na-u-vasa	
I gave him		Ndi m'patsa	Ndi-na-m-petse	Ndampete	Na m'vaseda	
I go		Ndi nka	Ndinenda	Ndi nka	Nnenda	
I went		Nd 'enda, ndi nka	Ndi denda		Ndi denda	
I kill them		Ndi a pa	Ndi pa awene ; ndiapa	Ndi pa iwo	Na pa awene	
I know		Ndi dziwa	Na ziwa	Ndi dzive	Na dziwa	
I know not		Si ndi dziwa	Si ndi ziwa	Si ndi dzive	Ka na dziwa, si na dziwa	
Thou lovest		U-konda		U-konde	U konda	
We make		Ti panga		Ti-pange	Isu wano ina panga	
We say		Ti nena		Ti-nene	Isu wano ida onka	
We sold not		Si ti na gula		Si-ti-na-gule	Si daguye	
He stinks		A-nunkiza		A-nunkie	A na nuka	
He steals		A-ba		A-ba	A de ba	
They laugh		A-seka		A-seka	A na teka	
You weep		Mu lira		A-lira	Inyu mnaiya	
Where did he go ?		A-na-nka kuti ?		A-na-nka-kuti ?	A denda ?uvi ?	

VOCABULARIES

What do you say?	Unena ciani?	Nunkani; nonkajini?
What shall we drink?	Ti-dza-mwa-ciani?	Isuwano na mwa jini?
When art thou coming?	U-dza liti?	U nada ini?
Give me food	Ndi patse kudia,	Ndi vase imi-wano ɣuya gagade
Cut me a small stick	Ndi dulire katsatsa	Ndi duye cifimbo ca ciñono
I want a little stone	Ndi funa kamwala	Na funa mwala woñono
Which (fowl) will you give me?	Njiti u dza ndi patsa?	Ikugu waje ivi, ina fume we wasa imi fáno?
He is inside the house	A li m'nyumba-mo	Iyene ayi m'gari mwa numba
The birds flew away	Mbalame zina-uluka (*flew*) coka (*flew away*)	Mbame da puka
The parrot screams	Cinkwe ci lira	Papagau adaiya
The rotten tree falls	Mtengo wo-bunda u-gwa	Muri wobvunda uda gwa
Can you see me?	Kodi u-nga-ndi-ona ine?	Kodi iwe nona imi pano?
No, I cannot	Ine i ndi ngate	Tayu si na ku ona

	Walakanena hani?	
	Ti-mwe hani?	
	U-dzadza lini?	
	Undi patse cacudia	
	Undi dulire tsatsa	
	Ndi funa namweli	
	A-li-m'keti	
	Mbalame zatava	
	Cinkwe ci kulira	

521

VOCABULARY OF ENGLISH WORDS AND SENTENCES TRANSLATED INTO

English.	Ci-cuambo.	I-lomwe.	I-makua.	Ci-yao.	Ci-ngrindo.	Other Bantu Languages.
Ant	Nyerere, wiece, ma-gugu	Talako; namarakolo (termite)	Etui, plur. tui. Enenele (9 & 10) Overa (3 & 4)	Salaŭ. Siasijinji salau = many ants. Njece = white ant	Harahu, ipamba, mpamba; mkeke, mi-, ma- (termite)	Isi-pompolo (Zulu); termite, umuhlwa (Zulu)
Antelope	Mbaala	Pala (bushbuck) Nahe (duyker) Ndoda (eland) Namgoma (kudu) Ŋkondo (hartebeest)	Ebala (bushbuck) Etove (duyker) Etata (eland) Enari (kudu) Namdoro (hartebeest)	Mbawala (bushbuck). Ngolombwe (duyker) Mbunju (eland) Ndandala (kudu) Ngose (hartebeest)	Mbawara. Ndopi; tambalamba Mbunju (eland) Ndandala (kudu) Mbarapi (hartebeest)	Imbabala (Zulu)
Ape (or baboon)	Bongwe	Mnyani	Kole (baboon)	Li-jani, ma-.	Liyani, ma-.	Imfene (Zulu)
Arm	Mono	M-nono, mi-.	Mono, miono	M-kono, ma-. Mkono wa-umo = one	Ci-woko, ma-. (Wa-wiri = two; nkwapa = armpit)	Umkono "
Arrow	Muvi	N-tere, ma-. Matere mancici = many	Ntere (5). Matere (6)	Mpamba. Mipamba yiwiri = two	M-pamba, mi-. (Yiwiri = two)	Mwambi (Luganda)
Axe	Badu	Epaso. Epaso sincici = many	Epazo (9 & 10)	Li-wago, ma-.	Liwago, ma-, ga-.	Imbazo (Zulu)
Back	Mtana	Mtana Nturi = shoulders Muyunuui = loins	Mtana-, mi-. Eyuno = loins, wanturi = shoulder-blades, makata = shoulders	Ngongo. Kunyuma = shoulders Liuli = loins	Ngongo. Liwega = shoulders; ciwenda = loins	
Banana	Mafigwi	Muopɷ	Enika = tree, nika = fruit	Li-gombo, ma-.	Litoki = fruit and tree	Toki (Luganda)
Beard	Ndevu	Ereru	Erori	Ndeu	Cinjuemba. Ndefu = chin	Kilevu "
Bee	Nui	Enũ	Ezui	Nyuci	Njuci	Njuki "
Belly	Cifu, masubo, erugulu	Erukulu Marupo = bowels	Erugulu = stomach Marubo = bowels	Ki-tumbo, plur. i-.	Lu-tumbo, ma- = bowels, uru-, ama-	
Bird	Balame	Epalame	Mwanuni, plur. enuni	Ci-juni, plur. i-.	Iyuni (plur.), ciyuni (sing.)	
Blood	Mlowa; mañ-mlopa	Likame	Epome	Miazi or miasi	Mwahi, mwasi	Igazi (Zulu)
Body	Manugu	Kakada	Erutu	Ciwiru	Mbiri	Mu-bili (Luganda)
Bow	Ura	Mutira	Mu-ũra-, mi-.	Ukunji	Wuta; upindi	
Bone	Nikuva	Likuwa	Nikuva, ma-.	Liupa, ma-.	Lihupa, lifupa	
Brains	Wongo	Marohi	Ogogo (mwinjeni = many)	Ututu	Wongo	Bwongo "
Breast	Wa mrimāni; nibère	Meèle; sing. liwele (limoha = one)	Mabele = female, ebeto = male	Liwere	Li-were, ma-.	Isi-fuba (Zulu) Ibele
Brother	Mbale	Qhande (1), ahande (2)	M-rokoraga, a-.	Mpwanga, plur. aci-apwanga. Mlongo	Ndongo, plur. ma-longo	Mu-ganda (Luganda) Ndugu (Swahili)

VOCABULARIES

English					
Buffalo	Nari	Enari	Njati		Inyati (Zulu)
Buttocks	Marao	Marɔ	Li-tako, ma-	Matako	
Canoe	Mwadia	Mwatea	Watu, mawatu	Watu, uwatu	Lyato (Luganda)
Cat	Paka	Mohae	Ciome, plur. iyome	Mbuyari, kimlamo, ma-, fi-Mfumo	
Chief	Fumu	Amwene	Mbewe, a. Eli=two. Enjeni=many	Mcimwene (jumo= one), plur. wa-i-mwene	
Child	Mwana, ana	Mwana	Mwana, plur. anaga.	Mw-ana, wa-; akana, plur. utwana	Umntwana (Zulu)
Cloth	Guo	Ekuo	Guo, eguo	Mwana, plur. wa-mwanace	Ingubo (Zulu)
Cocoanut palm	Mnasi		Mgɔle	Nguwo	
Country	Nzio	Elapo	Elabo, yotene=all	N-gore or mgore, mi-Musi, plur. misi Cirambo	Insi (Luganda)
Cow	Ñombe	Ñombe; amtiana=female	Ñombe. Ja ñkolo=female, ja ji lume=male	Mdina or ndina Ñombe. Ya nkoro=female, likambako=male	Inkomo (Zulu)
Crocodile	Nyakoko	Ekɔnya	Ngwena	Mwina, iñwina (9 & 10)	Ingwenya (Zulu)
Day	Labo, siku	Ɔtana. Mahiu=night	Liuwa, plur. mɔwa Muūhi=daylight	Liuwa, plur. macuwa	Ulu-suku ,,
Dog	Mwanabwa	Mwanapwa, anapwa.	Mwalabwa, plur. elabwa	Nakawa, plur. waka-nakawa. Umwe=one	Mbwa (Luganda)
Devil	Mzimu	Anepa	Jini (Arabic)	Lihoka	
Door	Iseko; mlagu; msuo	Amlakoni	M-kora, mi-	Ndiango	
Dream	Matulo; verb urɔea	Ɔroha	Olohá	Mahoka (plur.)	Kiloto ,,
Drum	Ñoma	Ekɔma	Egoma	Mahambo	Ñoma ,,
		Wina=dance	Wina=dance	Kuihina=dance	
Ear	Niaru, mayaru	Li-naru; plur. maru	Niaru, maru	Likutu	Kutu ,,
Egg	Nzai, mazai	Lɔci, mɔci	Niyɔce, plur. mɔce	Lihumbi	
Elephant	Dou.	Etepo	Telbo or etebo	Ndembo	Indhlovu (Zulu)
Excrement	Mãri	Mapi	Mavi	Mahi	Ulu-tuvi ,,
Eye	Ninto, plur. meto	Litu, metu	Nito, meto	Lihu, mihu	Iliso ,,
Face	Kope	Witoni	Owito	Ciwingi	Ubuso ,,
		Marama=cheek	Marama=cheek	Litukwa=cheek	
Fat	Makura	Makura and ekura	Makura	Maüta	Amafuta ,,
Finger	Ibuno, vibuno (yala, nail)	Epunu Ekáruka=finger-nail	Cala, iyala Cikalawesa=finger-nail	Ngonji (finger-nail); plur. hiuwu, sing. ciuwu	Umunwe ,,
Fear	Mãta; verb wɔva	Ɔva	Wɔva.	Wɔga. u-kulungwa=great	
Fire	Moto	Mulu	Moro	Moto	Umlilo
Fish	Oba	Ehomba	Ehoba	Somba	
				Lihomba (sing.), ohomba (plur.)	
Foot	Nnyalo, mwẽdo	Nyalu	Nyao, plur. enyao	Lu-sayo, ma-	Unyawo
				Luayo, maluayo	

VOCABULARY OF ENGLISH WORDS AND SENTENCES TRANSLATED INTO

English.	Ci-cuambo.	I-lomwe.	I-makua.	Ci-yao.	Ci-ngindo.	Other Bantu Languages.
Forest	Mwiru, kokola (*Anguru*)	Tsambene	Etapa. Etakwele ektulu pale = *that forest is very big*	M-sezo, mi-	Mikongo	
Fowl	Mwanaku	Mwanakū	Mwalaku, elaku	Nguku	Nguku	Inkuku (*Zulu*)
Ghost	Muzimo, azimo	Mnepa	M-nepa, mi-	Ausiri (?)	Ciwanda	
Goat	Mbuzi	Epuri	Eburi, Elobwana = *male*	Mbuzi. Tōnde = *male*	Mbuhi. Mene (yimo = *one*) Mene (ziwiri = *two*)	Imbuzi ,,
God	Mulugo	Mhale	Mluku	Mlungu	Mbamba	
Grass	Maani	Manasi	Malashi	Linyasi, *plur.* mayasi	Manyahi, linyasi	
Ground	Taka	Etaya	Otope, matope	Litaka	Litaka, lidupi	Umdaka ,,
Ground nut	Manduwi	Elo, mandawi	Manduwi	Njama; ntesa	Njugu, marawi	
Giraffe					Cunju; ndwika	Ntuga (*Luganda*)
Guinea-fowl	Kaga	Ekaga Ekwali = *francolin*	Ekaga, ekaga. Ekwali = *francolin*	Nganga Ngwale = *francolin*	Licundu Ngwari = *francolin*	
Gun	Futi	Kaputi (9 & 10)	Kabuti, ekabuti	Uti, maiiti	Huti Huti yimwe = *one* Huti nyingi = *many* Ihuti zidatu = *three*	
Hair	Nititi	Mehe	Ekarali	Umbo, ma-	Lijunju	Unwele (*Zulu*)
Hand	Nnada	Ntata, mantata	Wasanja, esanja	Ligaza	Ciganja	
Head	Muru	Muru, likuva	Muro Nikuru kuja = *skull*	Ntwi, *plur.* mitwi Cikalakasa = *skull*	Nduturu Cihuhu = *skull*	
Heart	Mrima	Murima	Mrma	Ntima, mitima	Mtima	
Heel	Itilini	Enyingala	Egogwino	Cindende	Cisukururo	
Hippopotamus	Tomodo	Napetu	Tomondo	Ndomondo	Ndomondo	Imvubu ,,
Honey	Uci *and* ui	Makalapa Ekita = *wax*	Oravo Ekita = *wax*	Masega Mbotole = *wax*	Wuci Mahiu = *wax*	
Horn	Nyaka	Nyaka, ma-	Enyaka	M-sengo, mi-	Mara, li-mara	
Horse	Kavalo	Kavala Mupisi = *zebra*	Ekavalu Etugo = *zebra*	Kawalo Mbunda = *zebra*	Mbunda	
House	Nuba	Mpa Lipalapago = *roof* Ncisi = *wall*	Enupa Nipato = *roof* Ekisisi = *wall*	Nyumba Msakasa = *roof* Lipupa = *wall*	Nyumba, ma-	
Hunger	Dala	Etala	Edala	Sala	Njara	
Hyena	Namgudu	Kuzupa	Kuzupa	Li-tunu, ma-	Lipundu	Impisi ,,
Iron	Utale	Mkoko	Eyuma	Cipala	Livumbu	

VOCABULARIES

	Suwa	Ωcilwa	Ekisira. Bili = *two*	Cilwa, *plur.* filwa	
Island				Cilwa (*rocky*), *plur.* ilwa; ki-rumba (*low, sandy*), i-	
Ivory	Nyaka	Muyaka	Minyaga	Ndembo	
Knee	Nibodo	Likuta	Nikuta	Ciyuwa, *plur.* hiyuwa	
Knife	Mbêni	Mpadi	Mw-ălo, mi-	Cipura, *plur.* ipura	
Leg	Mwĕdo	Mwetu	Mweto, *plur.* meto-	Lukôngolo, ma-	Mugulu (*Luganda*)
Leopard	Nyarugwe	Severe	Havara, a-, *plur.*	Li-huwi *and* ci-Kisuwi, isuwi	Ingwe (*Zulu*)
Lips	Miromo	Ulomo	Ndere	Miromo	Udebe ,,
Magic	Senga, *male*	Ukwiri	Okwiri	Uhawi	
Maize	Nambedi	Nahepwe	Nakuo, a-	Cirombe	
Man	Miŭlobwanna. Mutu (*person*), *plur.* atu	Mutu, atu	Mtu, atu	Mu-ndu (umo = *one*), wa-	Umuntu; abantu (*Zulu*)
Meat	Nama	Enama	Enama	Nyama	
Monkey	Kolo	Nakarama	Koto, a- Niyove = *colobus*	Litumbiri	
Moon	Mweri	Mweri	Mweri	Mwehi	Mwezi (*Luganda*)
				Mwezi, *plur.* miezi (giwiri = *two*)	
Mouth		Wayanuni = *mouth*	Mwano = *mouth* Mwako, mi-		
Mountain	Mwango	Mwagu		Citumbi	
Nail (of finger or toe)	Yala		E-kata, ma-	Ciuhu	
Name	Nzina	Nsina	Nzina	Lihina	
Neck	Nikoti	Likohi	Siko	Hingu	
Night	Matiu	Mahiu	Ohiu	Kiru	
Nose		Epuna	Epula	Mbuno	
Ox	Ñombe ya kapado	Eñombe	Eñope	Ñombe	Ciro ,,
Palm wine	Wiema	Mgwarangwa	Mvumo	Nkomangoma = *borassus*	
		Liale = *raphia*	Mwale = *raphia*	Liwigi = *raphia*	
		Kanjesa = *date*	Erende = *date*	Uliri = *date*	
		Uwema = *palm wine*	Sura = *palm wine*	Majenga *and* ucema = *palm wine* Ndahi = *palm wine*	
Parrot	Papagaya (*Portuguese*)	Namame	Ekwia	Namame, *plur.* akina-mame	
Penis	Sondo	Mpolo	Mbolo	Mboro	
				Liolo Lugomo = *glans* Mapende = *foreskin*	
Pig	Guluwe	Guluwe	Eguluwe	Liuluwe	Ingulube (*Zulu*)
		Muciri = *wart hog*	Pago, a-	Liguluwe Mbango, *plur.* ma- = *wart hog*	Lipango = *wart hog*
Pigeon	Kangaiwa	Nbia	Ekunda	Njuwa	Njiwa
Place	Mbuto	Elapo	Niburo	Kirambo; pa-	Ijuba ,,
Rain	Mzogwe	Msonkwe	Ebula	Ula, ma-	Ndima
	Mcilu	Nsilu, masilu	Nikule	Likoswe	Ihura ,,
Rat		Mtoro = *field rat*	Atoro = *mice*	Libuku = *field rat*	Mcenje
River	Nyanja	Muhici	Muro	Lusulo	[*Luganda*] Nyanja; mugga (*Luganda*) Mkuka

VOCABULARY OF ENGLISH WORDS AND SENTENCES TRANSLATED INTO

English.	Ci-cuambo.	I-tonwe.	I-makua.	Ci-yao.	Ci-ngindo.	Other Bantu Languages.
Road	Dila	Etila	Epiro	Litala	Ndira	Indhlela (*Zulu*)
Sheep	Bira..	Epila	Ebuti-buti	Ngoza	Berere	Imvu ,,
Sister	Mlogoriye (*his sister*)	Murukω. Raka = *my*	Nrubo	Lumbu, *plur.* a-c'-a-, aca lumbu	Mgoli	
Skin	Nikada, tebe	Likwiniba	Ekataka	Lipende	Hiega	
Sky	Ndrabu	Mirapo	Wirimu	Kwi unde	Kumani	Izulu ,,
Sleep	Tulo	Erulu	Oruba, ekove	Lugono	Lugono	
Smoke	Mwici	Mwisi	Mwişi	Liosi	Liohi	Umusi ,,
Snake	Noa	Enωa	Enωa	Lijoka	Lioka	Inyoka ,,
Son	Mwana ; mlobwana	Mwana, mlopwana. Likanda = *baby*	Mwana, mlobwana	(*See Child*)	Mwana, *dim.* kana, *plur.* twana	Unyana ,,
Song	Nyimbo	Livaka	Ezibo	Nyimbo	Nyimbo	Luimbo (*Luganda*)
Spear	Mwalagu		Nivaga	Lipanga	Mkoha	Fumo ,,
Spirit	Mşimu *or* muzimo			(*See Ghost and Devil*)		
Star	Neneri	Teneri	Etωdwa	Ndondwa	Lutondo	
Stick	Ndodo	Emwiri	Ekωpo	Ngongo ; bokola	Mbihu	
Stone	Mwala	Lugu	N-lugu, ma-	Liganga	Iriwe, *plur.* mawe	
Sun	Nzua	Nsua	Nzua	Liuwa	Liuwa	
Tear	Mtori	Msodi, mi-	Wunla	Msozi, mi-	Mholi, miholi	
Testicles	Puru	Epulu	Ekete	Matongo	Matongo	Amasende (*Zulu*)
Thief	Mbava	Nimiya	Mwiyi, eyi	Juawi,*plur.* wawi(*adj.*)	Mkungu	
Thing	Ilobo, vilobo	Etu (9 & 10)	Etu (9 & 10)	Cindu, kindu ; *plur.* indu	Cindu, hindu	Into ,,
Thorn	Munga	Mwuva	Mwiwa, miwa	Mwiwa	Mwiha	
Tobacco	Fodia	Sωla	Sωne	Sωna	Lihona	
To-day	Dabuno	Elelo	Elelo	Lelo	Larinu	
Toe	Ibuno	Ekωkω = *big*	Pito	Ciala. Cikongo = *big toe*		
Tongue	Mlumi	Lumi	Nlimi	Lirumi	Lulimi	Ulu-limi (*Zulu*)
Tooth	Lino	Linu	Ninno, menno	Lino	Lino (limonga = *one*)	
Town	Mzinda	Wawani. Waka = *my*	Elabo	Muzi	Muzi	
Tree	Muri	Mtapikω	Muri	Mtera	Mtengo	Umuti ,,
Twins	Magwira	Anasa ambili (?)	Masa	Mawira	Mapaha	
Urine	Miridu	Unωsω	Minyωza	Makwezo	Makojo	
War	Kodo	Ekωto	Ekoto	Ngondo	Ngondo	
Water	Mainje	Mainji	Mari	Mezi	Maji	Amanzi ,,
White man	Mzugu	M-zungu, a-	M-gunya, a-	Mzungu, wazungu	M-sungu, wa-	Umlungu ,,
Wife	Mwadie	Mwar'aka (*my*)	Mtiana, a-	Asωnu, Wangu = *my*, *plur.* ac'asono	Mbumba	Umka ,,

526 BRITISH CENTRAL AFRICA

VOCABULARIES

English						
Wind	Pevo	Lipevo	Epeu	Mbepo	Mbepo	
Witch	Mkûri	Mkwiri Mukē=ordeal water	Mkwiri Mwavi=ordeal water	Msairi Mwai=ordeal water	Mhawi Mwai=ordeal water	Umtakati (Zulu)
Woman	Muiana	Mtiana	Mtiana Mwāraga=wife	Jua nkongwe, aca-kongwe	Muhano, wa-	Umfazi ,,
Wood	Muri	Ekuni	Ekuni	Ngwi	Hanju	
Yam	Mzama	Etelu Mpwani=cassava	Ekirazi	Lipeta Cinangwa=cassava	Ciparu Mayao=cassava	Inkuni ,,
Year	Gole	Mnyaka	Eyaka	Caka, *plur.* yaka	Caka	Ummyaka ,,
One	Moda	Mosa, moha	Mozā	Cimo	Cimwe	
Two	Biri	Pili	Bili	Iwiri	Iwiri	
Three	Taru	Taru	Taru	Itatu	Itatu	
Four	Nai	Nai	Jeṣe	Ncece	Ncece	
Five	Tânu	Tanu	Tanu	Isano	Muhano	
Six	Tanu na mŏda	Tanu na moha		Isano na kimo	Muhano cimwe	
Seven	Tanu na biri	Tanu na pili		Isano ni iwiri		
Eight	Tanu na taru	Tanu na raru		Isano ni itatu		
Nine	Tanu na nai	Tanu na nai		Isano ni icece		
Ten	Kumi	Likumi	Mlogo	Likumi	Kumi	
Eleven	Kumi na moda	Likumi na moha		Likumi ni kimo	Kumi na cimwe	
Twenty	Makummedi	Makumi meeli	Milogo miili	Makumi gawiri	Makumi gawiri	
Thirty	Makumi mararo	Makumi mararu	Milogo miraru	Makumi gatatu	Makumi gatatu	
Forty	Makumi manai	Makumi mannai	Milogo mijeṣe	Makumi ncece	Makumi ncece	
Fifty	Makumi matanu	Makumi matanu	Milogo mitanu	Makumi isano		
Hundred	Zana	Mloko	Mlogo zene mlogo	Mwanda		
Thousand	Cikwi				Kumi licira limwe	

VOCABULARY OF ENGLISH WORDS AND SENTENCES TRANSLATED INTO

English.	Ci-cuambo.	I-lomwe.	I-makua.	Ci-yao.	Ci-ngindo.
I, me	Mio; di	Mia, Miano	Mio	Une, Unejo	Nenga
Thou	Weyo	Iwe, iweano	Wē	Ugwe (?)	Wenga
He	Iyene	Eyω	Ωle	Ajo, ajojo	Nono (?) nonoyo (?)
We	Iyo	Hiyano	Hiyano	Uwe, uweji (?)	Twenga
You	Nyuo	Nyuano	Nyenyu	Mwe, mwejo	Mwenga
They	Awene	Ayo	Ahowa	Ao	Wawere (?)
All	Obene	Atene, -tene	Ωtene	-ose-pe	-oha
This man	Mutu udu	Mutu uyω; atu ayo	Mtu ula	Mundu ajω, *plur.* wandu awa	Mundu uyu, awandu awa
That man	Mutu udule	Mtu ωle; atu ala	Mtu ule	Mundu ajula, *plur.* awala	Mundu jola, awandu wara
This tree	Muri ubu	Mtapik' uyu	Muri ula	Mtera au	Libihi iri
That tree	Muri ubule	Mtapik' ωle	Muli ule; ori vale = *that is there*	Mtera ula	Libihi lera; mabihi mingi = *many trees*. Mabihi gara = *those*
My house	Numba aga	Mpa' ka	Enupa aga	Nyumba jangu	Nyumba yangu
Thy house	Numba ao	Mpa' yao (?)	Enupa ao	Nyumba jako	Nyumba yako
His house	Numba ai	Mpa' we	Enup' awe	Nyumba jakwe	Nyumba yake
Our town	Mzinda eu	Elapo yihu	Elabω' ehu	Muzi wetu	Likaia litu
Your country	Nzio lenyu	Elapω enyu	Elabω' enyu	Muzi wenu	Muzi winu
Their children	Ana awa	An'ae	Ana aya	Aciwana wao, *sing.* mwana gwao	Awana wao
Bad	U-tākāla	Otakala	Wolowa, kanifai, otākāla	Ngalumbala, (?) lumbana	-himu

VOCABULARIES

Female	Muiana; seva	Orera	Tiana	-dara
Good	Ya dretu	Orera	-orera	-nofu
Great	Indimua	-ulupale	-kulungwa	-kurungu (libihi likurungu)
Little	Iñono	-ñono-ñono	-nondi. Nkalo o nondi = *little knife*	-cokope. Akabihi aka-cokope = *a little tree*
Male	Mlobwăna; pogo	-lopwana	-lume	-pongo
White	U-cĕna	Yowela	-otela	-barafu
Here	Okuno	Ava, vā	Vava; vale = *there*, vati = *below*	Apa
Black	Oriba	Oripa. Orumala = *red*	Piriu. Mlangali, nceyeu = *re.t*	-piri. -ngere = *red*
Plenty	Vyinji (8)	Ɖincici, ancici, *etc.*	-jinji	-ingi
There	Apale	Uwω!	Vale; nω-; wω-	Kora
No, not	Seye, ke	Akipale!	Iii	Lietu!
I am			Ki- (?)	
I bring	No ica, no ɖana	Kimakusa	Kinawiha, *pret.* kωwika	Niletite (ikindu iki = *this thing*) Nalileta = *brought*
I come	No ɖa	Kimarwa	Kinawa	Nicite (*pret.*)
I come not	Ka ndi ɖa	Aki narwao	Aginiwa	Niici lietu
I dance	No ceta	Kinimihina	Kinarugunea	Nihina
I die	No kwa	Kωωpwa	Kinakwa, *pret.* kωhωkwa	Nawire (*pret.*)
I drink	No mwa	Kωωwiria	Kinavuria	Mwereji
I drank	Ɖa u mwa	Kawiria (?)	Kωhωvuria	Namweri
I drank not	Ka ɖi mwile	Akiwiriale	Akivuriale	Nganimwa
I eat	No ja	Kωωca	Kinaja, kihωja	Ndile. Nirire = *I ate*

VOCABULARY OF ENGLISH WORDS AND SENTENCES TRANSLATED INTO

English.	Ci-cuambo.	I-lomwe.	I-makua.	Ci-yao.	Ci-ngindo.
I eat not	Ka di nja	Akicile	Haginja; aginale nzana = I ate not yesterday	Nganindia	Nirire lietu
I give	No vaa	Kohuñya = I give thee	Kinavaha, pret. kihuvaha	Nimpere	Nipire (pret.)
I give you	No-u-va-a		Kihuvaha wē Kinamaha ωla = I give him	Nimpere umwe	Nikupire (pret.)
I gave him	Ndi-u-vaa	Kuhumwinya	Kahomaha	Nampere aju	Nimpire. Mundu yura = that man
I go	No doa	Kinimarwa	Kinaroa	Ndenda . Kwaula = walking	Ngenda
I went	Da u doa	Karoa	Kahorwa	Nayawiri. Juzi = yesterday	Nigendite, nakupite
I kill them	Noapa, no apa awene	Kiniwaipa	Kinawiva	Tinaulaje. Osepe = all	Nawakomite (pret.)
I know	No zewa	Kosuwela	Kinizuela	Nimanyi	Nimanyi
I know not	Ka di ziwa	Akisuela	Aginzuela	Nganinimanya	Kimanya
Thou lovest	Weyu no a daña	Oniatuna	Onaatuna. Unaamtuna = thou lovest him	Ukusaka	Ulondē
We make	No panga	Nimapanga	Nawira. Kaniirali etu = we made nothing	Tutupanganyi	Ti henga
We say	No loga	Nirimpa	Naïluma	Tukuti	Ti jowa
We sold not	Kaningula	Kantumali	Kantumihali. Natūmiha = we sell, ωtumiha = he sold	Nganitu suma. Suma = sell	Ti kugura lietu. Ti gurite = we sell. Ligoro = yesterday
He stinks	Ununka	Uni manka	Onaünuka	Atenda ku nunga	Anunga
He steals	Unoiba	Uni miya	Onaüia. Ohiya = he stole	Ajiwireje	Ajiwa. Akujiba lietu = he does not steal
They laugh	A-no-bea	Animatea	Anäatea Ahωtēa = they laughed	Atenda ku seka	Waheka
You weep	Mu no unla	Munimanla	Mnaünla	Ntenda ku lila	Mulira. Kiani = why?
Where did he go?	U dowe leuvi?	Akele uvi?	Ωrvale vahi?	Ajirekwapi?	Abite ku?

VOCABULARIES

What do you say?	U nlo-gani?	Mnakati?	Mnihimia zahi?	Nkuti uri?	Mujowa kiki?
What shall we drink?	Mngwani?	Nawiri'eti?	Nintunaωwuria şeni?	Tutumwe cici?	Tinywa kiki?
When art thou coming?	Undalini?	Unarwe lini?	ωmwa lini?	Waice liuwa ci?	Ucite ri? Ririno = to-day
Give me food	Ndi va ene yoja	Kiwahe kice	Kivahe yωya	Mbani cakudia	Mbera kiakulia
Cut me a small stick	Ndi gwadile simbo	Kakate mtapiko ñoñoño	Kitigile ekobwaga yamkane	Tingate simbo	Nidumura msagi njoko = little. Msagi = stick
I want a little stone	Di funa mwala wañona	Kinavia nluko liñoñoño	Kinatuna nlugunaga nikane	Ngusosa liganga lianoñdi	Nifuna libwe lijoko
Which (fowl) will you give me?	U ndi va auvi?.	Kiwahe eku 'yamkolo?	ωntuna ωtanla yωgivaha?	Nguku ci timumbe?.	
He is inside the house	U li m'numba	Ulimpámwe	Urinebani mwanuba	Cenyōno a li nyumba jumo = Mr. So-and-so is, etc.	(Mu- is the 'in' prefix)
The birds flew away	Balame ahi uvava	Epalame ɗovava	Enuni zotene zωωwawa	Ijuni iguluice	
The parrot screams	Papagaza unounla	Epalame ni manda	Ekwia enaūnla	Namame atenda mañgwembe	
The rotten tree falls	Muri uti u-no-ubwa	Mtapiko owuta, nimatongwa	Mtale wωwunda ωnavulua	Mtera wowole ugwile (fell)	
Can you see me?	U no dŏna nodi?	Unimasowela okona?	ωniwẽrea ωgona?	Mwejo (yot) mwambweni?	
No, I cannot	Seye ka ndi nu ona		Iii, kahiki kanakinahatuna	Gwamba; nganiniwona = I do not see you	

INDEX

NOTE.—All African names of countries, languages, or peoples, which are not found under their initial letter in this Index, should be looked for under the initial of the root-word. Thus for Ci-Yao see Yao, Ci-, or Yao language; for Wunyamwezi see Nyamwezi, Wu-; Anyanja, Nyanja, A-. In all cases, however, where the reader might be supposed not to be acquainted with the root-word, the commonest compounds are also given—Awemba, as well as Emba, Aw-.

The lists of scientific names given in the Appendices are not always referred to in the Index.

Aard-wolf, 285
Abu Bakr, 116
Abyssinia, 286, 295, 303
Acacia trees, 3, 29, 209, 220
Accountants, B.C.A. Administration, 151
Addax antelope, 314
Aden, 63
Aden Arabs, 102
Administration of B.C.A., 107; Appendix to Chap. IV. (Attitude of —— towards slavery), 158
Advantages of B.C.A., 178
Africa, Central, 181-2, 211
"Africa Orders in Council," 114, 154
African Lakes Company, 67, 71, 74, 77, 78, 82, 97, 98, 116, 121, 137, 143, 147-8, 149 (Bank), 150; 160-1, 165, 176, 181
"Africana" (by Rev. A. Duff Macdonald), 68, 416
Afzelia, 224
Agriculture, Native, 37, 424, *et seq.*
Albert Nyanza, 480
Albizzia trees, 2, 4, 220
Alcohol (in Africa), 180-1
Algæ in Lake Nyasa, 283
Alluvial soil, 48; —— gold, 49
Aloes, 4, 222-223
Alston, Lieut., 134, 136, 138, *et seq.*, 140, 141, 144, 146
Ambo, Wambo Tribe, 459
America and the Slave Trade, 156, 157
Amomums (Malaguetta pepper), 225, 226
Amphibia, 362
Anoa, 303
Ancestor-worship, 449
Anderson, Sir Percy, 119, 129
Anderson Fort (see Fort Anderson),
Anemone, 211, 234
Angas's Tragelaph, *vide* Inyala,
Anglo-German Convention, 94, 96
Anglo-Indian, 147
Anglo-Portuguese Convention, 96, 98
Angoche, 56, 99, 156
Angola, 59, 286, 334, 479
Angoni, the, 28, 32, 62-3, 70, 106, 144, 157, 162, 392, 419, 421, 423, 432, 470
Angoniland, 49, 421

Angræcum orchids, 210
Anguru (people and country), 58, 130
Anona (Custard apple), 220, 226, 428
Ansellia orchid, 210
Anseres, 337
Ant-eater, Scaly (see Manis)
Antelopes, 10, 309
 ,, Sable, 4, 317 (see Sable)
Anthropology, 392, *et seq.*
Ants, 375
Apes, Anthropoid, 285
Arab, Arabs, 23, 24, 30, 31, 32, 54, 56, 62, 64, 71, *et seq.*, 82, 92, 94, 102, 124, 135, *et seq.*, 156, *et seq.*, 392, 429, 434, 437, 440, 478
Arab town, word picture of an, 22, *et seq.*
Arabia (Southern), 54, 71
Arabic, 478-9; —— (Coast), 55, 478
Aristea (iris), 212
Armed Forces of B.C.A., 152-3
Arnot, F. S. (Plymouth Brethren Mission), 190
Artillery (used against Arabs), 75, 139, 140
Artiodactyla, 291
Arums, 216
Atonga, 70, 72, 104, 116, 118, 130, 131, 168, 404
 ,, Marriage customs, 413, 414, 417, 419
Aulacodus swinderenianus, 291
Australians in B.C.A., 147
Austro-Hungarian settlers in B.C.A., 147
Author (commencement of interest in affairs of Nyasaland), 80; Kilimanjaro Expedition, 82 (and see Kilimanjaro); work in Niger Coast Protectorate, 80; conversation with Lord Salisbury, 80; made Consul in Portuguese East Africa, 81; proceeds to Lisbon, 81; article in the *Times*, 81; ——'s interview with Serpa Pinto 83; with Mlauri, the Makololo Chief, 84; makes treaties with Makololo, 85; ——'s ride to Blantyre; arranges for British Protectorate and leaves for Upper Shire, 86; reception at hands of Lieut. Coutinho, 88; reaches Mponda's, journeys to Island of Likoma, Bandawe, and Kotakota on Lake Nyasa, 90; secures first portion of B.C.A. by arrangement with Jumbe, 92; makes peace with North Nyasa Arabs, 94; starts for Tanganyika, 95; explores Lake Rukwa, 95; leaves

INDEX

Tanganyika for Moçambique, 96; returns to England, 96; made a C.B., 96; appointed Commissioner for B.C.A. and Administrator of the B.S.A. Co.'s territories North of Zambezi, 97; returns to B.C.A., 97; arrives at Zomba and starts for Mponda's, 100; leaves for Lake Nyasa on Christmas Day, 1891, after Captain Maguire's death, 105; makes war on Zarafi, 105-6; troubles with European settlers, 108; "Job" experiences, 108; imposes Hut Tax, 110; commences Land settlement, 112; spends Christmas of 1892 at Blantyre, 115; goes on expedition against slave-traders on Upper Shire, 116; goes to South Africa to confer with Mr. Rhodes, 117; divides B.C.A. into administrative districts (1893), 119; restores order at Fort Lister after attempted assassination of Captain Johnson; proceeds on 2nd Makanjira expedition, 121; founds Fort Maguire, 126; returns to England (1894), 126; organises Civil Service of Protectorate, 129; establishes postal service, 129; proceeds to India, 129; returns to B.C.A., 129; proceeds against Matipwiri, Zarafi, and Mponda, 133, *et seq.*; accepts Mponda's surrender, 134; continues campaign against Arabs, 136; lands at Karonga and starts for Arab stockades, 138; interview with Mlozi during truce; offers Arabs terms, 140; resumes bombardment, 140; enters stockade, 142; tries Mlozi and sanctions his execution, 143; falls ill with black-water fever, 143; returns to England on leave of absence (1896), 146; introduces cash currency (English coinage) into B.C.A., 149; experiences in regard to Black-water fever, 179; botanical collections of, 233; views regarding elephants, 291-2; classification of zebras, 292, *et seq.*; of antelopes, 309, birds, 333, *et seq.*; feeling towards the African goat, 432; receives "war" messages from Yao chiefs, 469
Awemba, 135, 145, 157, 389, 421, 423, 430, 468, 470

Babisa (see Bisa)
Baboon, 286-7
Bain, Rev. Mr., 73
Baker, Sir Samuel, 292
Baloi or Balui, 77
Bamboos, 4, 7, 8
Bananas, 427, 429; —— wild, 217
Bandawe (place), 70, 90
—— Sergeant-Major, 130, 131, 142
Bangweolo, Lake, 39, 45, 61, 64, 65
Bank (A. L. Co.'s), 150
Bantu languages, 54, 478, *et seq.*; origin of the, 54, 479, 480; prefixes of, 482, *et seq.*; propositions defining, 481, 482
Bantu negroes, 55, 389, 479
Baobab tree, 20, 221, 223, 229
Baptist Mission, 189
Barbets, 332, 350
Barutse, 65, 66, 69, 77, 156, 190
Baskets, native, 458
Basuto,—land, 65, 156; —— ponies, 164
Batoka or Batonga, 58, 77, 233
Batrachians, 359
Bats, 288
Beads, 422, 471
Beans (native, cultivated), 426, 427, 429
Bechuana, —land, 65, 66, 77

Bedford, Admiral, 121
Bees, 374, 381
Bee-eaters, 335, 351
Beetles, 196, 368, 385
Beira, 55, 56, 487
Belcher, Mr. Ralph, 97
Belgians, 71
Bell, Mr. F. Jeffrey, 365
Berndt, Captain, 137
Bicycles in B.C.A., 164, 187
Birds, 11, 329, *et seq.*
—— and crocodiles, 355
—— singing, of Africa, 195, 332
Birth customs (see Customs, Ethnology)
Bisa, Ba-, 62, 71, 389, 479; —— Ci-, 480, 484, and Vocabularies; —— Lu-, 71, 156
Blacksmiths, native, 51
Black-water Fever, 19, *et seq.*, 172, 178-9, *et seq.*, 184-5
Blantyre, 27, 28, 66, 86, 130, 149, 154, 161, 166, *et seq.*, 189
—— "atrocities" (Commission thereon), 68
Bleek, Dr., 449
Bocarro, Jaspar, 57, 58
Boma (a stockade), 130, 175
Bombax, 210
Boö; see *Tragelaphus angasi*
Books in Central Africa, 188
Borassus palms, 1, 213, 214, 231
Boroma, 234
Botanists, 211
Botany, 207, 211
Botanical gardens at Zomba, 151, 174
Bovidæ, Bovinæ, 309, *et seq.*
Bowhill, J. O., 440
Boyce, Dr., 104, 125, 144
Brachystegia, 229
Bradshaw, Lieut.-Colonel, 136, *et seq.*, 141
Brass, 463
Brass wire drawing, 463
Brickmaking, 173
British Central Africa: name first given, 96; first European to enter, 58; general situation in, in 1889, 76; inaccessibility of, in 1889, 77; declared a Protectorate, 86; first portion secured, 92; declared a British Sphere of Influence, 95; eastern boundaries of, 146; devastated by slave trade, 156; a field for coffee planting, 164; steamers of, 147; trade of, 147; a clearly-marked Zoographical sub-region, 285
British Central Africa Administration, 107, (Appendix to Chapter IV.) 153-4, 158; attitude of, towards slave trade, 156, *et seq.*
British Central Africa Gazette, 154
British Concession, Chinde, 164
British Government discouraged in Zambezia, 63; unable to assist settlers against Arabs in 1889, 78; considers financial position in B.C.A., 126, 129
British South Africa Company, 36, 50, 81, 89, (agreement for support of B.C.A. Administration) 97, (subsidies of) 117, 126, 129, (assumes direct administration of its northern territory, 1895) 129; 146, 148, 158
British subjects in B.C.A., 146-7
Bua river, 49
Bubalis, 321
Buchanan, Mr. John, 66, 68, 74, 76, 77, 85, 86, 96, 103, 160, 161, 233

Budorcas, 321
Buffalo, 10, 303, *et seq.*, 329; Indian, 64, 303, 305
Bugs, 369, 381
Bulbul, 195, 332, 349
Buntings, 331, 348
Burchell's zebra, 292, 295-6
Burial customs; see Customs, Ethnology
Burkill, Mr. J. H., 233
Burton, Sir Richard Francis, 63, 64
Bushbuck, 305-6, 329
Bush fires, 37, 42
Bushmen, 52, 53, 389, 479-80; stones, 52
Bush pig (*Potamochærus*), 296-7, 329
Bustards, 329, 341, 351
Butterflies, 196, 367-8, 381, *et seq.*

Cameron, Mr. K. C., 233
Cameron, Capt. V. L., 66
Canaries, wild, 331
Candido de Costa Cardoso, 60
Cannibalism, 446, *et seq.*
Canoes, native, 456-7
Cant among Missionaries, 190, *et seq.*
Cape Colony, 429
Cape-oak (*Ilex*), 10
Cape of Good Hope, 59
"Cape to Cairo," 81, 96
Cape Town, 28, 59, 60
Capital needed in B.C.A. for coffee planting, 160, 163, 164
"Capitao," 168, 204
Capricorns, 309, 327
Capsicums, 428
Carr, Lieut.-Commander, 117
Carson, Mr., 234
Cash (introduction of), 149, 178
Cassava, 427, 429
Castor Oil, 223, 427, 428; —— plant, 223, 224, 429
Castration of slaves, 158-9
Cat, domestic, 289, 434
 ,, wild, of B.C.A., 289
Cattle (of European planters), 160, 177
 ,, of natives, 429, *et seq.*; domestic breeds of Africa, 430
Cavendish, Captain Hon. W. E., 133-4, 136
Ceará rubber, 160
Cedar (Mlanje), 12, 13, 150, 224, 232
Celibacy among missionaries, 198-9
Centipedes, 364-5
Central Africa (see Africa, Central)
Central Angoniland, 144, 154
Central Zambezi, 89, 190
Cephalophus, 309; Cephalophines, 309, *et seq.*
Cercopithecus, 287
Cervicapra, 311
Chambezi (District), 119; (River), 65
Chameleons, 356, 362
Champagne in fever, 180
Chapman's Zebra, 295-6
Charles Janson, Mr., 69
Charles Janson, s.s., 55, 69, 76, 90, 93
Cheetah, 286, 289
Chewa, A, 144-5, 430; Ci- (Ci-cewa), 484, and Vocabularies
"Chicote" (Hippo-hide whip), 169
Chiefs, native, 114, 468-9

Chifisi, 106, 132
Chikala, Mount, 115, 131, 132
Chikumbu, Chief, 91-2
Chikunda, A., 391
Chikusi, 100, 132, 146
Chikwawa, 154
Chilwa, Lake, 46, 47, 51, 60, 130, 174, 296, 318
Chinde, 98, 148, 149, 164, 165
 ,, River, 63, 79, 82, 165
Chipatula, 69; sons of, 84, 85, 87
Chipeta, A-, 145
Chiperone, Mount, 319
Chipoka, Chief, 99, 107, 108, 330
Chiradzulu, Mount, 38, 69, 84, 87, 88, 98, 132, 149, 154, 164, 166
Chiromo, 303, 335, 439
Chiuta, Lake, 46, 455
Chiwaura, 121, 122-4
Cholo, Mount, 447
Chongone, Mount, 45
Church at Blantyre, 28, 175
Church of Scotland Mission (*vide* Missionary Societies)
Churchill, Mr. W. A., 82, 96
Cinchona, 160
Cinnabar, 50
Civet, 289
Civil Service, B.C.A., 152, 153
Civilisation (at Blantyre), 27, 28
"Claims, Certificates of," 113
Clematis, 7
Climate of B.C.A., 39, 40
Cnestis, 210
Coal, 49, 51, 151
Coape-Smith, Lieut. H., 133-4, 135, 136, *et seq.*, 141, 143-4
Cobras, 356, 359
Cobus antelopes: *C. ellipsiprymnus*, 312; *C. lechwe*, 286, 312; *C. vardoni*, 286, 312; *C. senganus*, 312; *C. crawshayi*, 312-3; *C. penricei*, 313; *C. maria*, 314
The *Cobus* group generally, 309
Cockroaches, 367, 371-2
Cocoanut-palm, 23, 212, 214
Coffee (introduction of, 66), 160, 429; (—— planting), 77, 160, 161, 163; Export and prices of, 147, 162; Kinds of, 161; Manures for, 162; Methods of planting, 162, 170; yield of, per acre, 162; "topping," 163; treatment of ripe berries, 170
Coinage (see English Coinage)
Colobus monkey, 285, 287
Colocasia, 429
Cold temperature, 41, 186
Coleoptera, 385, *et seq.*
Colies, 332-3, 350
Collectors and Assistant Collectors, 152-3
Commelina, 210
Commissioner of B.C.A., 97, 114, 152
 ,, ,, ,, Deputy, 152
Comoro Islands, 64
Concession, British (see British Concession)
Congo Basin, 54, 303, 479
 ,, Free State, 89, 148, 285, 334
 ,, River, 60, 66, 80, 303
 ,, Treaty of 1884, 80
"Conquistadores," 56
Consul for Nyasa, 68

INDEX

Cooking, native methods of, 436, *et seq.*
Coots, 27
Copaifera, 210, 220, 224, 229
Copper, 51, 460, 463
Coreopsis flowers, 7, 212
Cormorants, 27, 342, 353
Cost of living in B.C.A., 178
Cotterill, Mr. H. B., 67
Cotton, 160
Courts of Justice, foundation of, 114
Coutinho, Lieut., 87, *et seq.*
Crabs, land, 363
Cranes, 338, 352
  ,,   Crowned, 27, 338, 340-1
Crawshay, Mr. Richard, 74, 94, 97, 116, 135, 295, 298, 312-3, 322, 325, 326
Crickets, 374
Crinum lilies, 209
Crocodiles, 73, 343, 355-6, 361
Cross, Dr. D. Kerr, 73, 74, 95, 135, 137, 180, 184, 442, 449, 451, 473, *et seq.*
Crotalaria, 210, 428-9
Croton, 224
Crow, 11, 330 (South African, 330), 349
Crown land, 113
Crystals, Quartz, 51
Cuambo (Chuambo) I- (I-cuambo), 485-6 and Vocabularies
Cuckoos, 332, 350
Cucumbers, 426, *et seq.*
Cullen, Commander Percy, 49, 51, 138, *et seq.*, 140, 141
Cultivated plants, 426, *et seq.*, 144
Cumming (see Gordon Cumming)
Cunningham, Mr. J. F., 115
Customs, Native: Birth, 416
  ,,   ,,   Burial, 444, *et seq.*
  ,,   ,,   Death, 443
  ,,   ,,   Initiation, 409, *et seq.*
  ,,   ,,   Marriage, 411, *et seq.*
Customs (fiscal), Organization of B.C.A., 110
Cycads, 7, 214
Cynoglossum, 212
Cypresses (at Blantyre), 29, 175
  ,,   Mlanje (see Cedars)

Daily Telegraph, 66
Damaliscus (Tsessébe antelope), 286, 309, 326, 329
Dances, native, 409, 411, 452
Darter (*Plotus*), 3, 343
Date palms, wild, 2, 7
Dau (Arab sailing vessel), 102, 103, 125, 148, 153
Decency, sense of, among natives, 419
Décle, M. Lionel, 115
Dedza or Deza, Mount, 45
Deep Bay, 94
Depth of water on Chinde bar, 79; —— Kongone bar, 78
Devil (Natives' idea of a), 449
Devoy, Sergt.-Major, 136, 138, 140
"Dhōl," 426
Dhow (see Dau)
Diamonds, 51
Disa, ground-orchis, 211
Diseases of Natives, 439, 473, *et seq.*
Dissotis, 7
Districts of B.C.A. Protectorate, 118-9, 154
Divination rod, 451

Dog (Native), 433
Domasi, 130
Domestic animals, 429, *et seq.*
Domira, S.S., 102, 103-4, 116, 121, 136, 143
Donkeys, 379, 434-5
Dorcatherium, 285, 310
Doves, 11
Drugs, 222, 440
Drums, 460
Dry season, 42
Duala language of West Africa, 61
Ducks, 26, 338, 353, 434; tree ducks, 26, 338
Duckweed, Giant (*Pistia stratiotes*), 17
Duff Macdonald, Rev. Alex., 68, 412, 416, 444
Duncan, Mr. Jonathan, 160, 161
Durban, 164, 179
Durrha grain, 429
Dutch in B.C.A., 147
Duyker antelope, 309, 310, 329
Dyes, 460

Eagle, Bateleur, 345, 352; Warlike, crested, 345, 352; Fish, 27, 345, 352
Earthworms, 365
Ebony, 220, 224, 228
Edentates, 321
Edinburgh Botanical Gardens, 161
Edwards, Lieut.-Colonel (Lieut., Major), 117, 120, 122, *et seq.*, 126, 132, 133, 134, *et seq.*, 141, 143, 146, 152, 443, 450
Eggs as food, 437
Egrets, 1, 27, 342
Egypt, 480
Eland, 305, 329
Elæis palm, 35
Electric Fish (*Malapterurus*),
Elephants, 29, 30, 291-2, 435
Eleusine (Maere, etc., small grain), 426, 429, 437
Elmslie, Dr., 392
Elton, Capt. Fred, 66, 67
Eltz, Herr von, 117
Emba, Aw- (see Awemba); Emba, Ki-, 480, 484 and Vocabularies
Emba, Lu-, 189
English (in B.C.A.), 147
  ,,   perverse inaccuracy of the —— in spelling foreign names, 62, 487
English coinage, 149
Equus, 295-6
Eriosema, 210
Erythrina, 209, 227
Erythrophlœum, 224, 441
Ethnology, 392, 409; Ethnological characteristics of the natives of B.C.A.; initiation ceremonies, 409, *et seq.*; marriage customs, 411, *et seq.*; customs relating to birth; procuring abortion, 417; naming of children, 417, 418; change of names, 418; clothing, 418, 419, *et seq.*; sense of decency, 419; hairdressing, 421, *et seq.*; ornaments, tatooing, 422-3; ear, nose, and lip appendages, 423-4; deformation of teeth, 424; agriculture, 424, *et seq.*; cultivated plants, 426, *et seq.*; domestic animals, 429, *et seq.*; hunting, 435-6; fishing, 436; food and cooking, 436, *et seq.*; fire making, 438; ideas about death and disease, 439, 443; therapeutics, 444, *et seq.*; ordeals by poison and otherwise, 441, 468; death and

burial customs, 433, *et seq.*; witchcraft, sorcery, and cannibalism, 446, *et seq.*; ideas of God, ancestor-worship, belief in an evil spirit, 449, *et seq.*; divination, magic, rain wizards, superstitions, 450, *et seq.*; fables, 452; houses, 453, *et seq.*; villages, 456; canoes, 456; weaving, 457; pottery, string, leather work, 459-60; dyes, metal work, 460, 463; musical instruments, 464-7; justice, 468, *et seq.*; war, 470; property, 471; trade, 471; diseases, 473, *et seq.*
Euan-Smith, Sir Charles, 76
Eucalyptus, 29, 175
Euphorbia, 174, 220, 222, 224
Eurafricans, 66
Eurasians, 147
European (First to enter B.C.A.), 58
Europeans, 28, 113, 146, 149
European officials, 24
,, settlers, 146, 149 (relations with natives), 182, *et seq.*
Executions for murder in B.C.A., 154

Falcons, 352
Faulkner, Mr., 66; ——'s son, 66
Felis, 289
Fenwick, George, 68, 69
,, Mrs., 69
Ferns, 14, 215
Ferns, Tree, 7, 215
Fever, 167, 179, 198, 474-5
Fever, Black-water, 19, *et seq.*, 172-3, 178-9, *et seq.*, 184-5, 475
Fibre, fibre plants, 223
Ficus, 162, 220, 226, 228
Fig trees, sycomore, 3, 4, 162, 226, 228
Finfoot, 337, 352
Fipa, A, 389, 392; ——Ki-, 484 and Vocabularies
Fire (originated sometimes by lightning), 439; how made by natives, 438; customs as to, 439
Fish, 359, 360, 361-2
Fish-eagle, 27, 345
Fishing-owl, 337
Flamingoes, 26, 341-2, 352
Flannel, 185
Fleas, 368; Burrowing —— (see Jigger)
Fletcher, Corporal W., 130
,, Mr. S. Hewitt-, 130
Flies, 350, 375, *et seq.*
Flogging of Natives, 169
Flora of B.C.A., 207, *et seq.*, 233, *et seq.*
,, mountain, 14
Flowers (beauty of), 7, 11, 172, 177, 208, 211
,, (wild), 11, 14, 177, 208
Fly-catchers, 350
Foa, M. (French traveller), 290, 323
Fogs on the rivers, 42
Foliage, spring, 4
Folk-lore, 452
Food, native, items of, 436; preparation of, 436
Foot, Consul, 68, 79
Foreign Office (action in regard to Blantyre atrocities), 68; (modus vivendi with Portugal), 81; written to by missionaries, 108; 150
Forests, 35, 208, 216
Forsyth-Major, Dr., 52, 297
Fort Anderson, 119, 149, 154
,, Hill, 145

Fort Johnston, 61, 100, 105, 106, 109, 132, 135, 143, 154, 189
Fort Lister, 119, 120, 133
,, Maguire, 103, 126
,, Mangoche, 134, 146
,, Sharpe, 117
Fotheringham, L. Monteith, 72-3, *et seq.*, 96, 97, 105
Fowl, domestic, 434, 480
Foxes, 285
Francolin, 11, 347, 351
Free Church Mission (Livingstonia), 66, 70, 135
French, the, 146, 147
,, Mr. (P.M.G., Cape Colony), 126
,, Evangelical Mission, 77
Fruits, 226
Fruit-bats, 288
Fungi, 428
Fūl language, 479
Fwambo, 95

Galago, 287-8
Gallinules, 27
Gambia, River, 288
Game, Big, regulations dealing with, 150, 296, 303, 326, *et seq.*
Games, native children's
Gamitto, Captain, 60
Ganda, Ba-, Bu-, Lu-, 479, 480, 483, and Vocabularies
Gardenia tree, 209
Gardens at Zomba, 150-1
Garnets, 51
Garrod, Professor A. H., 309, 333
Gazelles, 285
Gazette, B.C.A., 154
Geese, 353, 434
Geese, Egyptian, 26, 338, 434
,, Spur-winged, 26, 337, 434
,, Knob-nosed, 338
Genet, 289
Geographical Society, Royal, 63
,, ,, ,, Scottish, 79
Geology of B.C.A., 47
German Government, 94, 148
,, Steamer, 137, 143
Germans in B.C.A., 147
Germany, 85
Giraffe, 150, 286, 298, 328
Giraud, Monsieur, 39
Gladioli, 212
Glave, Mr., 122, 124
Gnu, 320, 321, 328; Nyasaland Gnu, 318, 321, *et seq.*
Goanese, 59
Goat, the African, 432, *et seq.*, 456
Goats, 309
Goat-suckers, 335, 350
God, Bantu Negroes' idea of, 449
Gold, 21, 49, 50, 56, 57, 463
Gomphia trees, 4
Gordon Cumming, Mr. Walter, 136, 138, 141, 143-4
Gori or Goli Stick (see Slave Sticks)
Granite, 4, 17 (*footnote*), 48
Grant, Mr. J. A., 90, 118
Graphite, 51
Grass, 193, 214, 218

INDEX

Graves, native, 444
Gray, Dr., 292, 295; Mrs. Gray's Waterbuck, 317
Grebes, 353
Grewia, 224
Ground-nuts, 223, 424, 429
Guano, 162
Guha, Ki-, 480, 483, 484, and Vocabularies
Guinea-fowl, 329, 346-7, 351, 434; Crested ——, 329, 346
Gulls, 26, 344, 354
Guns (in outfit), 164, 186
Gunboats (Lake Nyasa), 109, 121, 138, 153
,, (Zambezi-Shire), 98, 130, 146-7
Günther, Dr., 360-1
Gypohierax, 285, 345-6
Gyps, 285

Haliælus (Fish Eagle)
Hæmoglobinuria, Hæmoglobinuric Fever, 184-5
Hajji Askar, 125
Hamilton, Lieut., 131, 132
Hamitic races or tongues, 54, 179
Hare, 290, 452
Harrhy, Mr. E., 126
Harrison, Mr. James, 318, 326
Hartebeest, 320, 321, 329
Hausa language, 479
Hawes, Consul, 74, 76, 119
Hawks, 346, 352
Heat (great heat of portions of B.C.A.), 40, 41
Heath, heather, 11
Helichrysum, 212
Hemipode (*Turnix*), 337, 347, 351
Hemiptera, 381
Hemp, 223, 427, 429, 461
Henderson, Mr. Henry, 68, 161
Henga, Wa-, 94, 390
,, Ci-, 484 and Vocabularies
Herald, H.M.S., 98
,, Port (see Port Herald)
Herons, 27, 342, 353; Goliath —— 27, 342
Hetherwick, Rev. Alex., 68, 84, 205, 224, 485
Hibiscus, 210, 223, 459
Hides, 182
Hill, Sir Clement, 145
Hill, Fort, 145
Hillier, Mr. H. A., 110
Hindustani, 479
Hine, Dr. (Bishop of Likoma), 189
Hippopotamus, 56, 108, 182, 296, 435
Hippotraginæ, 314, 316, 318
Hoare, Mr. George, 116
Hoes, 425, 464; —— for trade, 182
Holub, Dr. Emil, 77, 233
Honey, 436
Honey-guide (*Indicator*), 332, 350
Hoopoes, 335, 351; Tree Hoopoes, 335, 351
Hornbills, 335, *et seq.*, 351; Ground ——, 336
Hornets, 375
Horse, 377, 379
Hoste, Captain, 67
Hottentots, 52, 53, 394, 399, 479, 480
Houses (European, in B.C.A.), 173
Hunting, native methods of, 435
Hunting Dog (*Lycaon*), 290
Hut-tax, 110, 111
Huts, native, 453, *et seq.*
Hyena, 289, 452

Hynde, Mr., 131
Hypericum, 212
Hymenocardias, 220
Hymenoptera, 380
Hyphœne palm (see Palm) —— Forest, word-picture of, 29
Hyrax, 291

Ibis (Hagedash), 27, 342; (Sacred), 27, 342
Ichneumon, 290
Ilala, the, 66, 67, 90, 92-3, 121
Impala antelope (see Pallah)
Indecency, natives unconscious of, 200, 408, 419
India, 129; India, the place of man's origin, 53
Indian government, 97, 129
,, immigrants, traders, 147, 177
,, surveyors, 152
,, troops, soldiers, contingent, 98, 100, 129, 152
Indicator (Honey-guide), 332, 350
Induna, s.s., 164
Inge, Mr. H., 106
Inheritance, laws of, 471
Initiation ceremonies,
Insectivora, 288
Insects, 196, 366, *et seq.*
Inyala (*Tragelaphus angasi*), 305-6, 329
Irish in B.C.A., 147
Iron, 51, 460, 463-4
Italians in B.C.A., 147
Itawa, 145
Itch-bean (*Mucuna*), 221
Ivory, 177, 182, 464, 467, 471

Jackal, 290
Jack-in-the-Beanstalk's Country, 9, 10
Jamaica Coffee, 161
James Stevenson, Mr., 47
James Stevenson, s.s., 38, 78, 82-3
Janson, Charles (see Charles Janson), 69
Jāt Sikhs, 118
Jerboas, 285
Jesuit missionaries, 57, 189, 190
Jigger (burrowing flea), 367-9
Johnson, Capt. C. E., 108, 116, 118, 119, 120, 122, 123, *et seq.*, 126
Johnson, Rev. W. P., 69, 76
Johnston, Sir Harry H. (see Author)
,, Fort (see Fort Johnston)
Johnston's pallah, 318, 326
José, Amaro, and Baptista, 59
Jumbe of Kotakota, 50, 71, 76, 90, *et seq.*, 107, 121, 122, 124
Justice, administration of, 154; 468-9
,, courts of, 114, 154; (native), 468

Kada, 120
Kafue R., 45, 78, 190
Kahn and Co., 181
Kalahari Desert, 65
Kalungwizi R., 234
Kambwe Lagoon, 94
Kapemba, Mt., 25
Karonga, 72, 94, 135, 137, 154
Katanga, 50, 65, 114, 190, 460
Katunga, 85, 166
,, Road, 114, 149
Katuri, 146

Kawinga, 103, 115, 129, 131, 175
Kazembe (of Lunda), 59, 468
,, (of Rifu), 102, 124
Keane, Commander J. H., 98, 105, 106, 108
Keiller, Mr., 103
Kese, Ba-, Ki-, 484 and Vocabularies
Kew Gardens, 151, 211, 233
Khaya tree, 220, 223, 228
Kigelia, 223
Kilimanjaro, Mt., 63, 289, 480; Author's book on, 154, 318, 330, 365, 453
Kilwa, 56, 100
King, Mr. J. G., 105, 106
Kingfishers, 2, 27, 335, 336, 351
Kiongwe, Ali, 82, 90, 96
Kirk, Sir John, 58, 60, 61, 233
Klipspringer, 309, 310, 311, 329
Kniphophia, 222
Koelle, Rev. Mr., 156
Kongone, mouth of Zambezi, 78, 79
Kopakopa, 137, 138, 140, 141
Kotakota, 71, 76, 90, 124, 154, 177, 189, 214
Kudu, 305, 317, 329
Kuluunda, 124-5
Kumtiramanja, 133-4
Kunene R., 53
Kungu fly, the, of Lake Nyasa, 436
Kwakwa R., 78
Kwango R., 59

Labour, native, 168
Lacerda, Dr. F. J. M. de ———e Almeida, 59
Lady Nyasa, the, 68, 78, 84
Lake (word picture of), 17, 18
Lakes, fluctuations in Lake levels, 38, 47
Land, price of, 154, 166-7; Land under cultivation, 149
Land Claims, 113
Land Claims, settlement of, 107, 112-3
Landolphia, 223, 226
Langenburg, 94
Languages of B.C.A., 478, *et seq.*
,, Bantu (see Bantu)
Larks, 329, 348
Last, Mr. J. T., 233
Laws, Dr. Robert, 66, 70
Leather, 460
Lechwe Antelope, 286, 314, 329
Lemurs, 287
Leopard, 288
Leopard Bay (Rifu), 124
Lepidoptera, 381, *et seq.*
Lianas, 223
Liberian Coffee, 161
Likoma, Bishop of, 70, 189; Id. of, 70, 90, 189
Likubula R., 177
Lilies, carmine, 4, 177
,, crimson,
,, (*Gloriosa superba*), 221
,, tree, 11
,, water, 3
Lily-trotter (*Parra africana*), 27, 343
Limestone, 48
Lion, 288
Lip ornaments, 423, 424
Lissochilus ground orchids, 210, 312
Lister, Sir Villiers, 119; ———, Fort (see Fort Lister)

Livingstone, Dr., 24, 27, 37, 38, 60, 61, 63; (third expedition), 64; (death of), 65; 71, 145, 156, 157, 446
Livingstonia, 70
Livingstonia Free Church Mission, 66, 70, 189
Liwonde, 115, 116, 117
Liwonde, Fort, 117, 143, 149, 154
Lizards, 356, 361
Lobelia, 9
Locks, native made, 459
Locustids, 373
Locusts, 369, 370, 373
Lofu R., 27
Lolo, A-, 119, 134, 391, 421, 424
Lomwe, A-; I-, 391, 485 and Vocabularies
Lonchocarpus, 208
London Missionary Society (see Missionary Societies)
Lovebird of the Upper Shire, 333
Lower Shire District, 98, 110, 154, 463
Lualaba R., 64, 156, 303
Luangwa R., 40, 45, 46, 61, 62, 64, 72, 77, 82, 89, 156, 158, 286, 298, 320, 390-1
Luapula (District), 119; River, 47, 60, 61, 64, 65, 212, 213, 389
Lubisa, 71
Luemba (*vide* Emba, Lu-)
Lugard, Major, 74
Lujenda R., 47, 58, 391
Lunda, 59; Lunda, A-, 76, 212, 389, 419, 468
Lungu, A-; ——— Ki-, 389, 417, 464-5, 484, and Vocabularies
Lusewa, 64
Lu-wemba (*vide* Lu-emba)
Lycaon, 286, 290
Lydekker, Mr., 303
Lynx, Caracal; lynxes, 285, 289

Macdonald, Rev. Duff, 68, 412, 416, 444
Machilla (hammock or chair), 91, 149
Mackenzie, Bishop, 61, 69
Mackinnon, Sir Wm., 67
Maclear, Cape, 70, 134
Madness in natives, 477
Madagascar, 156, 179, 184, 364
Magistrates, 114
Maguire, Captain C. M., 98, 99, *et seq.*, (death of) 103-4; 105, 109, 121, 125
Maguire, Fort, 103, 126
Magwangwara, 70, 391-2, 455
Maize, 182, 426, 429, 436, *et seq.*
Makandanji, 100, 101
Makanga country, 290
Makanjira, 76, 102, 103-4, 107, 121, 124-5, 126, 135, 443, 446, 447, 471
Makanjira Fund, 97, 121
Makololo, the, 66, 69, 77, 83, 84, 156, 391-2
,, Livingstone's, 65, 66, 69
Makua, the, 391
Makua (porters, soldiers), 83, 91, 116, 117, 118, 123, 331
Makua language, 134, 485 and Vocabularies
Malachite, 51
Malay archipelago, 211
Malemia, chief, 129, 131
Malindi, 55, 57, 58
Mallows, 7
Malo Island, 69

INDEX 539

Malombe, Lake, 46, 60
Mambwe, A-, 72, 95, 389, 417
,, Ki-, 484 and Vocabularies
Mandala, 67, 176
Mangoche Mt., 134, 146, 189
Manioc (see Cassava)
Manis, 321, 371
Manning, Captain W. H., 118, 121, 131, 146
Mantis, 196, 371-3
Manyema language, 484 and Vocabularies
Mañanja, A- and Ci-, 66, 176, 390, 440, 485 and Vocabularies
Mañanja Hills, 233
Maples, Bishop Chauncy, 70, 94
Marabu storks, 27
Maravi, 57, 62
Marimba, District of, 154, 177
Marriage Customs (see Customs)
Marsh, Elephant, 47, 84, 303, 320, 328
,, Morambala,
,, papyrus, 17
,, Pinda,
Marshes, 47
Mashonaland, ruined cities of, 53
Maskat, 62, 155
Massage amongst the natives, 440
Matabele, 62, 146
Matipwiri, 107, 119, 120, 130, 132, 133-4, 189, 451
Matope, 107, 117
Mauni Hill, 134
Mazaro dialect, 484 and Vocabularies
Mazbi Sikhs, 98, 118
Mbewe (Makololo town), 84
Mbo, Ci-, 484 and Vocabularies (see Ambo)
McClounie, Mr. J., 233
McDonald, Mr. H. C., 318, 326
McEwan, Mr., 104, 124, 144, 154
McMaster, Mr. J. E., 126
Medicines, native, 440, *et seq.*
Meller, Mr. J. C., 233
Menyharth, Rev. L., 234
Merere of Usango, 72
Mfiti, 446-7
Michesi Mt., 119, 295
Military Forces of Protectorate, 118
Milk, 203, 432, 437
Millet, 426, 429, 437
Millipede, 364-5
Mimosas, 216
Miners, gold, word-picture of, 19, *et seq.*
Misale, 49, 57
Mission doctor, 19, 21; pupils, 28, 197, 198, 202
,, Station, word-picture of, 193, *et seq.*
,, Work, disappointments of, 203, 204; results of, 204; successes of, 204-5; industrial teaching of, 205
Missions, Christian, 189, *et seq.*
Missionaries, 108, 130, 190, *et seq.* (too great asceticism of), 201
Missionary hospitality, 201
Missionary Societies: Church of Scotland, 66, 67, 130, 160, 189; Dutch Reformed Church, 189; Free Church of Scotland (Livingstonia), 66, 70, 135, 189; French Catholic (Algerian), 189; French Evangelical, 77, 190; Jesuit Mission, 189; London, 70, 71, 95, 189; Nyasa Baptist Industrial, 189; Universities', 61, 63, 69, 70, 77, 189, 198; (*vide* Universities), 201; Zambezi Industrial, 189
Missionary's wife, A, 195, *et seq.*
Misuko trees, 29, 220, 222, 224, 226
Mkanda, 120
Mlanje cedar, 12, *et seq.*, 150, 232
,, district, 154, 189
,, mountain, 12, *et seq.*, 17, 39, 42-3, 48, 51, 107, 119, 150, 295, 332
Mlauri, 69, 84, *et seq.*
Mlozi, 72, 74, 135, 137, *et seq.*; (wounded), 141; (captured), 142; (tried and executed), 143, 145
Moçambique, 55, 58, 82, 88; (Governor of), 88, 118, 150, 285, 391, 485
Mocha coffee, 161
Moir, Lake, 46
,, Mr. Fred M., 67, 74, 75, 161
,, Mr. John, 67, 69, 74, 85, 86, 161
Moma R., 156
Money introduced into B.C.A., 149
Monitor lizard, 356, 460, 464
Monkey, *Colobus*, 287
Monkeys, 287
Monkey Bay, 124
Monomotapa, 56
Monteiro and Gamitto, 60
"Montisi," 72
Molluscs, 363
Moore, Mr. J., 363
Morambala Mt., 82, 165
,, marsh, 47, 165
Mosques, 56
Mosquito, H.M.S., 98, 117
Mosquitoes, 375-6
Mosses, 281
Mother-in-law, superstitions concerning, 415
Moths, 368, 384
Mountain (birds), 11; (climbing a ——), 4, —— (flora), 10, 11. 14; (plateaux), 10
Mountains of B.C.A., altitudes of, 45; aspects of, 9; geology of, 48; —— of Portuguese East Africa, 134;
Mpata (Mlozi's town), 74
Mpatamanga (see Botanical Appendix, Chapter viii.)
Mpatsa, *footnote*, p. 86
Mpemba, 144
Mpezeni, 49, 158, 468
Mpimbi, 116
Mponda, 65, 83, 90, 96, 100, *et seq.*, 105, *et seq.*, 107, 134-5, 446
Msalemu, 137, *et seq.*
Msamara, 90, 105, 441
Msiri, 89
"Muanza" (name given to Lower Congo and Cameroons), 61
"Muavi" (poison ordeal), 224, 441, 442, 448, 450, 469
Mucuna bean, 321, 428
Mudi R., 176
Muhammadan Sepoys, Indians, 64, 104, 105, 117
,, Yao, 61, 76
Murchison Falls, 38, 65
Music, native, 468
Musical instruments, 464, *et seq.*
Mwasi Kazungu, 144
Mwera (south-east wind), 17

Mweru (District), 119, 306, 312, 321; (Lake), 39, 46, 48, 59, 60, 61 (discovery of), 64; 148, 234, 290
Mweru Salt Swamp, 46, 51

Namasi R., 171
Names, absurd—given to Mission children, 203
Nandinia, 285, 290
Natives of B.C.A., 182, 389, *et seq.*; see Negroes, Central African (Bantu)
Native contingent, 134, 152
Naval service, B.C.A., 153
Ndirande Mt., 107
Negritic group, 54
Negro culture retrograde, 55, 183, 472
Negroes, future of the, 182, 472; proper attitude towards, 183–4; West Indian, 203; tendency of —— to relapse into savagery, 202, 203; distribution of true ——, 3000 years ago, 54; uniformity of type of, 392–3; carelessness and indifference in cultivating plants and domesticating animals, 429
Negroes, Central African (Bantu), physical description of, 392, *et seq.*; uniformity of type, 393; colour of skin, 393–4; albinism, 394; exudations of skin, 395; eyes, 396; physiognomy, 396; lips, 396; chin, 397; hair on face, 397, on body, 398, on head, 398; ear, 398; breasts, 398–9; sexual organs, 399; buttocks, 399; hands and feet, 399; height and other body measurements, 400, 403; voice, 403; power of withstanding cold and heat, 403; strength, speed, and endurance, 404; muscular development, 404–5; physical feats, 405–6; postures and movements of body, 406; methods of carrying loads, 406–7; salutations, 407; expression of face and disposition, 407; intelligence, 408; relative "uxoriousness," indecent dances, 408; lack of chastity, 408, 409; Ethnology of, 409, *et seq.*; see Ethnology, and also Customs, Religion, Domestic animals, Cultivated plants
Negroes, past and future of the, 472
,, diseases of the, 473, *et seq.*
Negroid Races, 393
New York Herald, 65
Ngindo, Ci-, 485 and Vocabularies
Nicholson, Admiral, 108, 109
Nicoll, John L., 72, 82, 90, 95, 97, 109
Nigerian Sudan, Niger, 453, 469
Nightingale, 332
Nile, 65, 182, 479
Nilgai, 309
Nilotic negroes, 479
Nkata Bay, 154
Nkonde (country), 72, 390
,, (languages), 390, 480
,, Awa-, Wa- (people), 72, 73, 139, 141, 143, 390, 399, 415, 417–9, 423–4, 430–1, 443–4, 445, 451, 452, 454
North Nyasa, 94, 154, 471
Nsese R. (Botanical Appendix, pp. 233–283)
Nunes, Vice-Consul, 68
Nutt, Mr., 234
Nuxia, 228
Nyamwezi, Ki- (language: also *vide* Sukuma, Ki-), Vocabularies
,, Wa-, 392, 404
,, Wa- (country), 67, 157

Nyanja (the true name of Laka Nyasa), 61
,, A-, 62, 99, 119, 145, 390, 417, 419, 422, 424, 443, 444, 446–7, 471
Nyanja, Ci-, 484–5 and Vocabularies
Nyanza, 61 (*vide* Victoria Nyanza, Albert Nyanza),
Nyasa, Lake, 17, 18, 38, 45, 48, 52, 60; (first discovery of), 61, 71, 94, 102, 148, 153, 360
Nyasa steamers, gunboats, 17, 109, 138, 153
Nyasa-Tanganyika Plateau, 72, 95, 135, 145, 149, 189, 234
Nyasaland, 55, 62, 65, 68, 71, 80, 88, 286, 288, 317, 318
Nyaserera, 119, 120
Nyih'a (Nyiχa or Nyika), language, Vocabularies
Nyika Plateau, 45
,, A-, 390

Oceana Co., 181
Octodont rodent, an, 291
Odete, 146
Oil palm, 35, 212, 222, 428
Oil seeds, 182, 222, 428
"Old man's beard" lichen, 10
Oldfield Thomas, Mr., 288, 311, 322, 324, 325
'Oman, 62, 71
O'Neill, Consul, 74
Opisthocomus, 333
Orange, 427, 429
Orchids, 210, 211
,, Ground, 7, 210, 211
Orchilla lichen, 10
Ordeal for witchcraft, etc., 441, 468
Oribi, 311
Orioles, 330–1, 348
Orthography, 486
Orthoptera, 371, 380
Orycteropus, 285, 321, 371
Oryx, 285, 314, 317
Osmunda fern, 220
Osprey, 346, 352
Ostrich, 285, 286, 329, 347
Oswell, Mr. (the explorer), 60
Otogale, 287
Otter, 290
Ourebia, 311, 329
Outfit needed for B.C.A., 164 and Appendix II., chap. vi., pp. 186-188
Owls, 337, 351; the eagle owl, 337, 447
Ox, oxen, 309 (see Cattle)
Ox-pecker (*Buphaga*), 330

Pallah or Impala, 318, 329; Johnston's —— 318, 326
Palm wine, 437
Palms, Borassus, 1, 213, 214, 231, 428
,, Cocoanut, 23, 213, 217
,, Wild Date, 2, 174, 213, 217, 230
,, Hyphæne, 29, 213, 214, 231, 292, 459
,, Oil, 35, 213, 428–9; Raphia, 174, 212
Papaw tree, 427, 429
Papio pruinosus, 286–7
Papyrus, 17, 26, 219
,, Marsh, 17
Paradoxure (*Nandinia*), 290
Parinarium trees, 4, 220, 224, 226, 230, 428, 456
Parkia, 231
Parra, 343
Parrots, 333–4, 351; (grey parrot, 334)

INDEX

Pay of native labourers, 168
Pelele ring, 423-4
Pelicans, 343, 353
Peppers, red and green, 428-9
Pereiras, the, 59
Perissodactyla, 291
Persia, Persians, 155-6, 159
Petre, Sir George, 81
Petrodromus, 288
Pettitt, Messrs.: Mr. Harry —— 84, 292
Phacochœrus, 296, 298, 329
Phillips, Lieutenant-Commander, 138
Phragmites reed, 217, 291
Physiological description of the Negro (see Negro)
Pigs, 296, 429 (see Bush pig and Wart hog)
Pigeons, 344, 354, 434
Pinda Marsh, 38
Pineapple, 429
Pioneer, H.M.S., 124
Pipes, 459, 461
Pipits, 331
Pistia stratiotes, 17
Planters, European, 160, 163, *et seq.*
Plantation (clearing of), 169
Plovers, 27, 343, 354
Pocock, Mr. R. I., 365
Pœcilogale, 290
Pœocephalus, 334
Poles (Austrian), 146-7
Polyboroides typicus (naked-cheeked Hawk), 346, 352
Polyglotta Africana, 156
Poole, Dr. Wordsworth, 136, 138, 143, 179
Population of B.C.A. Protectorate, 146-7
Porcupine, 291
Porphyrio, 337
Porridge, native,
Port Herald, 117, 125, 154, 165
Portal, Sir Gerald, 91, 118
Portuguese, 52, 56, 59, 63, 82, 88, 147, 155, 157, 201 (hospitality of), 201; 391, 426, 429, 434
Portuguese Foreign Office, 81
    ,, Government, 88
    ,, half-castes ("Black Portuguese"), 59, 69, 156, 391
Portuguese East Africa; Zambezia, 59, 78, 81, 134, 156-7, 292, 318, 377
Postage stamps of B.C.A., 129, 149
Postal service of B.C.A., 148, 171
Potatoes, 427, 429; Sweet ——, 427, 429
Potamochœrus, 296-7, 329
Pottery, native, 459
    ,,   ,, old, dug up near Lake Nyasa, 55, 459
Poultry, 182
Pozo, Ci-, 485 and Vocabularies
Pratincoles, 27
Prefixes, Bantu (see Bantu)
Printing at Zomba, 205
Procavia, 291
Protea, 11, 223, 428
Proteles, 285
Protectorate (proclamation of British), 86, 96, 147
Protopterus, 359
Pseudogyps, 285
Pterocarpus, 209, 220
Pterocles, 344, 352

Puff-adder, 359
Puku antelope, 286, 312-3; Senga Puku, 312, 329
Pumpkins, 329, 426, 427
Python, 359

Quagga, 285, 295-6
Quail, 351
Quartz, 48, 50, 51
Quebrabaço rapids, 60
Queen, H.M. the, 25, 91
"Queen's Regulations," 154
Quelimane, 55, 60, 78, 82, 148, 156, 391, 485

Rails, 27, 337
Rain, 42; "rain-makers," 451-2
Rainfall of B.C.A., 36, 42
Rainy season, 39, 42, 170
Ramakukane, 69
Rankin, Mr. D., 69, 79, 81
Raphia (see Palms)
Raphicerus sharpei, 309, 310, 329
Raptorial birds, 337, 344, 352
Rat, 291
Ratel, 290
Raven, great billed, 11, 330; —— black and white, 330
Reed buck, 311, 312, 329
Reeds, 3, 209, 217
Religion of the Natives, 449, *et seq.*
Rendall, Dr. Percy, 287, 288, 322-4
Revenue of B.C.A., 150
Rhinoceros, 292, 328
    ,, horns, 182, 292
Rhoades, Lieutenant-Commander, 138, 360
Rhodes, Right Hon. Cecil J., 81, 117, 121, 129
    ,, Herbert, 67
Rhynchocyon, 286, 288
Rice, 426, 429, 437
Rifu, 124
River, word-picture of a, 1
Roads made by Administration, 114, 149
Road-making, 114, 153
Roan Antelope, 317-8, 329
Robberies, Highway, 107, 108, 132, 149
Robertson, Commr. Hope, 109, 122
Rodents of B.C.A., 290
Rollers, 336, 351
Roman Catholic Missionaries, 200, 201
Roscher, Dr. Ernest, 64
Ross, Mr. A. Carnegie, 97
Rubber, 160, 182, 226, 464
Rufiji R., 285, 286, 329
Rugaruga, 158, 392
Rukuru, R., 137, *et seq.*
Rukwa, Lake, 45, 95, 390, 484
Ruo District, 154
    ,, River, 58, 83, 87, 292, 390; Falls of, 40; Upper Ruo, 43
Ruvuma R., 58, 62, 324, 391, 480, 485
S——, Mr., 85
Sabæans, 54
Sable Antelope, 4, 286, 317, 329
Sacred Ibis, 27, 342
Sahara desert, 286
Saidi Mwazungu, 102, 104, 144, 154
Salisbury, Lord, 80, 88, 96, 109
Salt, 51, 438, 471

Salt, manufacture of, 51
Sand-grouse, 329, 344
Sandpipers, 27
Sandstone, 48
Sansevieria, 182, 223
Sarcidiornis (knob-nosed duck or goose), 26, 338
Scenery of B.C.A., 35
Schizorhis, 333
Sclater, Capt. B. L., 97, 106, 107, 108, 112, 114, 117
Sclater, Mr. P. L., 292
Scotus umbretta, 342
Scorpions, 364-5
Scotch, the, 147
,, Missions, 66
,, Settlers, 147
Scotland, Church of, Mission, 66, 67, 130
Scott, Rev. D. C. Ruffele, 68, 85, 415-6, 440, 447, 453, 459, 468, 486
Scott, Mr. L., 233
Scott-Elliot, Mr., 233
Seamen, excellence of native, 457
Seasons, Rainy and Dry, 39, 40, 211
Secretary to the Administration, 152
Secretary Vulture, 285, 329, 337, 346
Selous, Mr., 77, 292
Semitic (races), 54
,, (tongues), 54
Sena, 83; Ci-, 484-5 and Vocabularies
Senegambia, 286, 329, 346
Senga country, 72, 141, 156
,, *puku* (antelope), 329
Senga, Ba-, A-, Ci-, 390, 484 and Vocabularies
Serpa Pinto, Colonel, 53, 81, *et seq.*, 86, 88, 233
Serpents (see Snakes)
Serpentarius (see Secretary vulture)
Serval cat, 288, 289
Sesamum plant and oil, 223, 428-9
Settlers, European, 113
Seven-pounder gun, 102, 105, 106, 122, 134
Sharpe, Mr. Alfred, 45, 74, 89, 97, 107-8, 112, 116, 119, 122, 124, 126, 130, 132, 146, 212, 291, 296, 310, 326, 450
Sharrer, Mr., 77, 147, 161
Sharrer's Traffic Co., 176, 181
Sheep, 182
Shells, 363
Shikulombwe, Ba-, 77
Shire Highlands, 27, 45, 48, 61, 62, 66, 77, 88, 130, 170, 234
Shire Highlands Shooting Club, 170
,, Province,
,, River, 3, 38, 58, 60, 149, 165, 390 (*vide* West Shire, Lower Shire, Upper Shire)
Shrews, 286, 288; Elephant, 288
Shrikes, 349
Siege of Mlozi's stockade, 138-140
Sikhs, the, 28, 30, 98, 102, 103-4, 105, 117, 118, 120, 123, 124, 129, 130, 141, 152
Silva Porto, 60
Silver, 57
Simpson, Mr. A. C., 66, 84
Situtunga (Speke's Tragelaph), 286, 305, *et seq.*, 329
Slavery, 149, 155, 156
Slave States in W. India, 155
Slaves, 31, 155
Slave-sticks, 31, 158

Slave-trade 149; (worst horrors of), 155-6
Slave-traders, 115, 119; (of ancient times), 155; (American), 156
Slugs, 363
Smilax yam, 221
Smith, Lieut. G. de Herries, 136, *et seq.*, 141
,, Mr. Edgar A., 363
Smythies, Bishop, 70, 90
Snails, 363
Snakes, 356, 359, 362
Snipe, 343, 354
Soapstone, 48
Somaliland, Somalis, 54, 56, 62, 63, 285, 295, 298
Songwe River, 94, 303
Sorcery, 441-2, 446, *et seq.*
Sorghum, 426, 429, 436
South Africa Chartered Company (see British, etc.)
South Africans in B.C.A., 147
South Nyasa District, 109, 149
Spathodea, 210
Speke, Captain, 63
Speke's Tragelaph (see *Tragelaphus spekei*)
Spiders, 364-5
Sport (big game shooting), 171
Spring foliage, tints of, 4
Stairs, Captain, 89, 114, 115
Stanley, Mr. H. M., 65, 66
Starke, Mr., 131
Starlings (Glossy), 330, 348
Steamers (on Lake Nyasa), 66, 70, 109
,, (on Rivers Shire and Zambezi), 98, 109, 147
,, (on Lake Tanganyika), 70, 75
Steere, Bishop, 70
Stevenson, Mr. Gilbert, 105, 116
,, Mr. James, 71
,, ,, the (Steamer) (see *James Stevenson*)
Stevenson Road, 71
Stewart, Mr. James, 67
Stewart, Captain F. T., 136, 144, 146
Stick-insects, 373
Stilt-plover, 343, 354
Stipa grass, 213
Stockade, Mlozi's, 137, *et seq.*
Storks, black (*Anastomus*), 27, 342
,, saddle-billed (*Mycteria*), 17, 342
,, marabu, 27, 342
,, (generally), 353
Stork, H.M.S., 82
Strawberries at Zomba, 174
String, native, 459
Strophanthus drug, 182, 224-5, 440-1
Strychnos, 226, 428
Sudan, 329, 346, 379, 453
Sudanese, 117
Sugar, sugar-cane, 182, 427, 429
Sultan, Arab, 23, 24, 31
,, of Zanzibar, 76, 90, 118
Sunbirds, 347
Sus genus, 297
Swahili (people), 64, 91, 104
,, (language), 478, 479, 486
Swallows, 332, 350
Swann, Mr. A. J., 95, 96, 97, 144
Swifts, 334, 350

INDEX

Swine (vide *Sus*, Wart hog, Bush pig, *Phacochœrus*, and *Potamochœrus*),
Syndactyla, the, 335

Tabernæmontana, 226
Tamarind, 226
Tambala, 144. 154
Tanganyika, Lake, 25, 39, 45, 48. 52, 60; (discovery of) 63; (South end of) 64, 70, 71, 95, 96; (North end of) 96; 148, 189, 234, 285, 360, 484
Tanganyika, Lake, Birds on, 26, 27, 342
  ,,   ,, Marine Fauna of, 363
  ,, District, 119
Tasmanians, 396
Tax, Gun, 111
Tax, Hut, 111, 150
Taxation, 111, 150
Taylor, Mr. G. A., 145, 318
Tea. 160
Teak, African, 223
Teal, 26
Temperance in Tropical Africa, 180-1
Temperature, high, 40, 41; low, 41
Tephrosia, 210, 429
Termites, 174, 370, 371
Terns, 26, 344
Tete, 57, 60, 62, 484
Therapeutics, native, 477 (see Ethnology)
Thomson, Mr. Joseph, 46, 70, 90, 118, 233
Thrushes, 331-2, 349
Ticks, 364-5
Tiger-cat (*Felis serval*), 288, 289
Timber, 182
Times newspaper, 79, 81
Tiputipu (Tippoo-tib), 76
Tits, Titmice, 348
Tobacco, 160, 182, 427, 429
Tomatoes, 427, 429
Tonga, Ci-, 484 and Vocabularies
  ,, Wa-, A-, 390, 486; Ba- (Batoka), 390, 391; see Atonga
Tortoises, 356, 361
Trachylobium, 220, 226
Trade (among natives), 177, 182
  ,, goods, 182
Traders, 177, 181
Tragelaphs, the (*Tragelaphinæ*), 303, 305-6
Tragelaphus angasi, 305, *et seq.*, 329
  ,, *scriptus*, 305, *et seq.*, 329
  ,, *spekei*, 286, 305, *et seq.*, 314, 329
Traps, 435
Treaties with native chiefs, 81, 86, 94, 113
Treatment of Black-water fever, 180
Trees, Forest, 216
  ,, Useful trees of B.C.A., 224, *et seq.*
Tree-ducks, 26
Tree-ferns, 7
Tree-lilies, 11, 211
Trogon, 335, 350
Trollope, Major Frank, 136, *et seq.*, 141, 318
Tropical vegetation, 2
Tsessébe antelope, 286, 309, 326, 329
Tsetse Fly, 56, 64, 367, 377, *et seq.*
Tumbuka, Ba-, 390, 484
Tundu Hill, 133
Turaco, 7, 8, 333, 350
Tusks, Elephants', 291-2

Uapaca kirkiana, 220, 224, 226, 227, 428
Uganda, 295
Ujiji, 64, 71
Umbre, Tufted (*Scopus*),
Universities Mission to Central Africa, 61, 63, 69, 70, 77, 159, 189, 198, 201
Unyanyembe, 64
Unyamwezi (see Nyamwezi, Wu-)
Upper Congo, 65
Upper Shire, 115, 149; (District), 154
Upper Zambezi, 77, 234, 285
Urquhart, Mr., 103-4
Usnea lichen, 10

Varanus lizards, 356, 460, 464
Vasco da Gama, 55
Vegetable earth, 48
Vegetation, tropical, 2, 35; (graceful), 213; (malicious), 220
Vellozia splendens, 211
Vesperugo, 288
Vicenti, 78
Victoria Nyanza, 63
Victoria Falls, 233
Village, native, 456
  ,, word-picture of, 19, 20
Villiers, Lieutenant, R.N., 124
Vitex, 223, 224, 227
Vitis, 221
Vocabularies of B.C.A. languages, 488, *et seq.*
Volcanoes, 48
Volcanic lavas, 48
  ,, tuffs, 48
Vultures, 285, 329, 344, 352
  ,, relative scarcity of in B.C.A., 344

Wages, native, 168
Wagtails, 331, 348
Waller, Rev. Horace, 48
Wankonde (see Nkonde, Wa-),
War (word-picture of a), 30, 31; native methods of, 469, 470, 471
Warblers, African, 332, 349
Wart Hog, 296, 298, 329
Wasps, 374; Mason wasps, 374
Water lilies, 3
Waterbuck (*Cobus*), 312, 313, 329
Watson, Dr. A. B., 105, 106, 122
Wax, 182
Waxbills, 331, 348
Weapons, native, 462
Weasels, 290
Weatherley, Mr. Poulett, 39, 46, 326
Weaver-birds, 331, 348
Weaving, 457
Wells, Mr. H. G., 366
Welsh in B.C.A., 147
Wemba, A- (see Awemba, Emba)
West Africa, 35, 42, 55
  ,, Indians, Indies, 203
  ,, Nyasa District, 49, 112, 154
  ,, Shire District, 49, 51, 154
Wheat, 182, 426
Wheeler, Mr. Wm., 107
Whicker, Mr. F. J., 117
Whisky, 19, 21, 168, 171
White men in a native village (word-picture of), 19
White-ants (see Termites)

Whyte, Mr. Alexander, 97, 119, 150-1, 212, 330
Widdringtonia Whytei, 12, 13, 150-1, 224
Widow-birds, 331
Wildebeest (see Gnu)
Winds, prevailing, 42
Winton, Mr. W. E. de, 295, 297, 298, 319
Wissmann, s.s. *Hermann von*, 137
Wissmann, Major von, 110
Witch, witchcraft, wizards, 441, 446, *et seq.*, 451
Women, European, in Africa, 177, 199, 200
  ,, as missionaries, 198, *et seq.*
  ,, native, 20, 470 (succession through the), 471
Woodcock, 343, 354
Woodpeckers, 332, 350
Worms, 365, 473, 476

Xantharpyia, 288
Xanthism, 394, 396

Yao, Wa-, 61, 62, 77, 99, 119, 131, 157, 391, 394, 397, 404, 416, 444-5, 470, 471
Yao, Muhammadan, 61, 447
  ,, land, 62
  ,, language, 485-6
Young, Lieut., 65
Yule, Mr., 145, 289, 415-6

Zambezi, 55, 56, 59, 60, 63 (Chinde, mouth of), 63 (Delta of), 63, 65, 78, 79, 89 (slave trade of), 156, 165, 182, 189, 190, 234, 285, 329, 390-1
Zambezia, 63, 182, 303
  ,, Portuguese, 59, 78, 81, 156, 292
Zambezi expedition (Livingstone's), 60, 63
  ,, (Upper), 77, 234, 285, 286
  ,, Industrial Mission (*vide* Missionaries)
Zanzibar, 62, 67, 71, 78, 91, 148, 478
  ,, Sultan of, 76, 90-1, 118
  ,, Arabs, 118
Zanzibaris, 100, 117, 118
Zarafi, 101, 105, 106, 130, 132, 134, 146, 451
Zebra, 285, 292, *et seq.*, 329
Zebras, classification of, 292, 295-6
Zoa, 114
Zomba, 39, 41, 130, 149, 154, 370
  ,, Mountain, 45, 330
  ,, Residency, 130
Zoography of Africa (distribution of animals), 285-6
Zoological Society, Gardens, 288, 298, 310, 318, 336
Zulu (language), 480, 486 and Vocabularies
  ,, (people), 62, 156
  ,, (soldiers), 83
Zululand, 62, 156
Zumbo, 57, 58, 391
Zygodactyle development of fruit-pigeon, 344